# The Handsewn Wardrobe

# The Handsewn Wardrobe

## A COMPLETE GUIDE TO MAKING YOUR OWN CLOTHES
from Patternmaking to the Finishing Stitches

LOUISA OWEN SONSTROEM

*For all who know,*
*deep down,*
*that they are capable of*
*incredible things.*

The mission of Storey Publishing is to serve our customers by publishing practical information that encourages personal independence in harmony with the environment.

EDITED BY Deborah Balmuth, Diana Rupp, and Carleen Madigan
ART DIRECTION AND BOOK DESIGN BY Alethea Morrison
TEXT PRODUCTION BY Erin Dawson and Jennifer Jepson Smith

COVER PHOTOGRAPHY BY © Melinda DiMauro, except back b., © 2025 Louisa Zhao
INTERIOR PHOTOGRAPHY BY © Melinda DiMauro, with makeup and hair styling by Liz Washer
ADDITIONAL PHOTOGRAPHY BY Courtesy of Alexis Bailey, 207; Courtesy of Cal Patch, 223; 2022 © kzstevens, 255; © 2025 Louisa Zhao, 221; Courtesy of M. Gnagy Design/The Modern Maker, 135; Mars Vilaubi © Storey Publishing, 1, 3–5, 9, 12–14, 16, 18–19, 29, 40–42, 45, 49, 90 and throughout (background), 108, 145, 183, 344; RaasLeela Textile, 157; © Robert Rausch for The School of Making™, 329; © Sarah Woodyard, 295; Courtesy of Sofia Alba Mateo, 187; © Tama2u/Shutterstock.com, 22 and throughout (background); © Tiffany Downs, 113
ILLUSTRATIONS AND DIAGRAMS BY © Louisa Zhao



Storey Publishing
210 MASS MoCA Way
North Adams, MA 01247
storey.com

Storey Publishing is an imprint of Workman Publishing, a division of Hachette Book Group, Inc., 1290 Avenue of the Americas, New York, NY 10104. The Storey Publishing name and logo are registered trademarks of Hachette Book Group, Inc.

ISBNs: 978-1-63586-626-1 (hardcover); 978-1-63586-627-8 (ebook)

Printed in China by R. R. Donnelley on paper from responsible sources
10 9 8 7 6 5 4 3 2

APS

Library of Congress Cataloging-in-Publication Data on file

# Contents

# THE JOY OF SEWING BY HAND

When you close your eyes, you can see it already: a garment that you would love. You can see its clean lines, its beautiful details, its silhouette over your body. The perfect proportion, the perfect shape—it's all right there in your mind.

That picture strengthens, clarifies, as the days pass. Finally one day, you feel ready. You scrounge up your tape measure, a pencil, a ruler or two. Standing in front of the mirror, you hold the pencil between your lips and the tape measure around your body. You squint, assessing the perfect dimensions for each element of your vision. Intermittently you scribble measurements on the back of a scavenged envelope. Mostly, though, you just stand there, pondering.

Eventually the envelope is filled with scrawled numbers. Scanning it, you realize you're ready to draft. So off you go, off to the kitchen table or the living room floor or the basement ping-pong table. You unroll a couple yards of some junky old wrapping paper, flipping it so you can draft onto the clean white side. You sharpen your pencil and find a soft old eraser, a ruler or two, a squaring tool.

It's hard to know exactly where to begin, but you know that the best way to start is to simply draw a line. So you place the ruler and slide your pencil along it. A tick mark here, another there. You square out, measure along, plot a tick mark, connect. Measure, plot; measure, plot. Sketch a curve, refine it, squint, refine. The measurements are essential, but your eye is everything. Breathless, you're gorgeously lost in pursuit of that perfect shape. You're getting there. Measure, plot. Points and lines and space and thought.

Often the lines seem to draft themselves. At other times, you're unsure how to proceed. In those moments you dig a shirt out of your laundry hamper to check its collar shape, or you strip off your pants to measure their rise lengths. Maybe these extra bits of information bring clarity, or maybe you realize you'll just need to try something—anything—and see how it goes. There is a freedom in the shrug-and-draft method. Your shoulders soften.

Eventually the draft is complete. You trace off your pattern pieces, label them, cut them all out. You step back and see a mess of beautiful shapes arrayed on the table before you.

Do you cut and baste a fit sample? Perhaps. After all, it's the only way to know if your draft—your educated guess—is a good match for that vision in your head. Then again, perhaps you skip the fit sample. I'll never tell.

Life gets busy. It's a month before you're ready to cut the pieces out of your "real fabric." Cutting time necessitates good tunes, so you press play on an album you loved in your early twenties. You spread out the fabric, arrange the patterns, and secure them with a water bottle, a couple of soup cans, and some nice rocks you once gathered at the beach. Your fabric shears glint as they work through the material. Straight lines are easy enough; sharp curves take focus. After the perimeter, you snip the little notches. Just as the album finishes, your pieces are cut. Tomorrow morning you'll begin to sew.

Hand sewing is quiet, both literally and figuratively. You can stitch late at night or early in the morning without disturbing sleeping housemates. Breathe and listen: The only sounds are the soft tug of thread through fabric, the dull tap of needle touching thimble, an occasional snip of scissors as you prepare another length of thread. Perhaps, too, a warm puff from a nearby steam iron. The creak of a chair beneath you, or the rustle of blankets as you shift on your bed. Breathe, stitch, and notice your thoughts focusing, coalescing, dissolving—hand-sewing time offers a rare spaciousness. Watch as a line of stitches accumulates beneath your fingertips: a visual map of your inner progress through this moment in your life.

The sun rises higher in the sky, and you pack your hand sewing into a bag. You go about your morning routine, go off to work or errands or whatever else today brings. But you carry something with you: your hand sewing. In spare moments of time, you place a few more stitches. During phone calls, in waiting rooms, on a lunch break, on a train commute, at school pickup—the day is full of these moments. By nightfall, you've made unhurried but significant progress on your project.

As modern humans, we live our lives in clothes. But as hand sewists, we have the privileged option to also live our lives in stitching practice. Our handsewn projects absorb the memories of where we've been, the people who've surrounded us, and the feelings we've held along the way.

Someday, when your garment project is done, you'll slip into it. The cloth will fall gently around your body. Wrapped in handsewn softness, you'll feel a quiet, steady strength in the garment's seams, along its hem, around the neck.

*Now pause.*
*If you listen, you'll hear them:*
*the whispered stories of a life—*
*yours—lived in the making.*

## A Bit of Context before You Start

As I wrote this book, I found myself assembling a list of philosophical "disclaimers." They're bits of context to help you interpret the following pages. Reference materials and project instructions are great in their own way, but more than anything, I hope to share the spirit in which I make things, including this book, and the spirit in which I hope you'll receive what I'm offering.

### OWN YOUR SKILLS

First, and most importantly, I hope you'll take these skills and ideas and run off in your own direction with them. You don't need to make a single project from this book or follow a single piece of advice I give. The skill-building information I share is meant to provide tools for you, but you can choose to leave those tools in your toolbox and reach for others instead. The "rules" of patternmaking and hand sewing are just utensils, really. They don't know what you want, they can't think for you, and they certainly can't make clothes for you.

If you take away nothing else from this book, I hope you'll hear me when I say: You already know more than enough to start figuring out how to make yourself amazing clothes.

Truly.

This book represents what I currently consider to be really good, helpful ways of approaching clothes-making. And it's skewed toward techniques that I believe can be effectively communicated in book form. But there are a million ways to do everything. Please believe in your own understanding.

At its core, this is a project book and provides visual proof that hand-sewing techniques can be applied to creating modern clothing. The bulk of the book is filled with projects—modern, basic garments—that offer specific, applied instances of patternmaking and hand sewing. They are meant to be examples, though. Take what you find here and then make whatever you'd like to wear. That's the best way to learn.

### HAND SEWING IN OUR MODERN WORLD

Humans have been hand-sewing for tens of thousands of years. The sewing machine only came into widespread use beginning in the mid-nineteenth century. Before that time, absolutely everything was stitched by hand. There's no need to prove that clothing can be sewn by hand—people have already been doing that for a dizzyingly long time. What is new is the idea of applying these ancient techniques to the types of clothes we wear today. For that, there is little precedent. How should we stitch a T-shirt by hand? There is no "should"—there is no tradition to follow—so we get to make it up ourselves. And isn't that exciting?

I work in the garment industry as a technical designer, which means I deal with the "engineering" behind the clothes. I'm coming from a very modern, industrial perspective, and the instructions in this book are grounded in my modern, industrial experience. There are many people who know a great deal about historical traditions and techniques in clothes-making. I'm not one of them. I'd encourage you, if you're interested, to learn more about historical sewing methods. There is so much to be learned from those tens of thousands of years of sewing tradition, even if you plan to stitch only modern clothes. At the same time, I think it's kind of exciting to stitch up clothing without knowing all of the old, "right" ways to do things. How should it be done? Any way you like! There is no right way, so do it any way that works or that you suspect will work. (And if it doesn't work, that's great, too—you get to learn from that, build what you know, and adventure on.)

## WHAT'S (NOT) IN THIS BOOK

This book is really two books in one: It includes distinct patternmaking and hand-sewing sections for each garment project. You can use either section or both—whatever suits your needs and goals.

Why does this book give patternmaking instructions rather than include a pattern envelope glued in back? Personally, I feel strongly that predrafted patterns, just like ready-to-wear clothes, can be helpful but are often limiting. They work well for a lot of people but not for everyone. Whether because of shape, size, style, or whatever else, some of us are not able to find what we really need in the world of preexisting patterns. If that resonates with you, hooray! I hope you'll enjoy making patterns to fit your body and your preferences. And, oh my goodness, patternmaking is magical.

For some people, though, this book's lack of printed patterns may feel frustrating. Not everyone has the time or inclination to make their own patterns. If you'd rather buy a predrafted pattern for a similar garment, that is a great option, too. There are so many lovely indie pattern companies these days—see if you can find a pattern you like that's similar to whatever project you'd like to make from this book. Then you can skip straight to the hand-sewing instructions.

Conversely, if you're very excited about making your own patterns (me too!) but don't want to hand-sew your clothes, you can follow the patternmaking instructions, then head over to your machine and construct your garment that way.

You can construct a garment using both hand and machine sewing—you don't have to be a purist. A lot of people love to construct seams by machine, then do finishing by hand. That's wonderful. Or you can be less methodical than that—just sew in whatever way is easiest or most satisfying for you in the moment. Are you near your machine and in the mood to use it? Great. Are you heading out for a long afternoon of meetings? Pack your hand sewing. It's all great.

## THE WORK OF OUR HANDS

"Handsewn" is a tricky term when used in contrast with clothes that are "machine-sewn." This is a problematic distinction because machine-sewn clothes, too, are made by real people and their real hands, even in large industrial production settings. Let's honor the work of all of our hands, everywhere, in all of its forms.

By now, you can probably guess how I feel about perfectionism. Your stitches don't need to be perfectly even, perfectly spaced, or perfectly tidy. They don't need to be super tiny. The insides of your clothes don't need to be pretty unless you want them to be. Heck, the outsides don't have to be pretty, either!

You are choosing to make clothes in a slow, unusual way. This experience can be whatever you want it to be. For me, that means I don't often mark my stitch lines, and if they waver a bit, I feel completely fine with that. (If you look inside historical handsewn clothes, you'll probably find that their stitches aren't perfect, either.) But I also recognize that for some people, handwork is an opportunity to escape into beauty, order, and care. You can be as meticulous or as sloppy as you like. It's all valid. (Just be gentle with other makers if they do things differently.)

Lots of disclaimers! But really, it boils down to this: Patterning and hand-sewing your own clothes is a radical act of reclaiming. You and your hands and your amazing mind can make the things you dream of. Own this truth.

# THE BASICS

In the pages that follow, we'll explore some of the concepts, tools, and techniques that will empower you to create the clothes of your dreams. If you're new to these skills, you may wish to linger here, practicing and experimenting with what you're learning. Or if you're a more experienced sewist, feel free to skim and then head off to Part 2: The Clothes, in which the actual garment-making magic happens. Either way, welcome! It's a joy to celebrate these exciting skills with you.

# PATTERN-MAKING

Learning how to make patterns is one of the coolest, most transformative experiences. You can make anything! Patternmaking may have a bit of a reputation as an intimidating, difficult discipline, but it needn't be that way. There are so many more possibilities than limitations in this craft. And, by the way, no one knows everything about patternmaking—no one!—so just relax and enjoy yourself. Make note of the principles shared in this book and elsewhere, but lean into the gray areas and creative opportunities, too. You'll learn just as much by messing around with patterns as by following anyone's instructions. The more you try, the more you'll learn.

# Why Build Your Own Pattern?

Before you can begin stitching up the clothes of your dreams, you'll need a pattern. Simply put, a pattern is a template for the two-dimensional shapes you'll cut from fabric in order to form three-dimensional clothes. Some garments can be made using very simple pattern shapes—a couple of rectangles, perhaps—while others require a large set of complex, carefully contoured shapes. Either way, the pattern determines the size and silhouette of the final garment.

## Store-Bought vs. Handmade Patterns

You can buy a pattern or make one yourself. Regardless of origin, all patterns can be altered and refined until they are exactly the size, fit, and style of the sewist's dreams.

When you buy a pattern, just as when you buy an off-the-rack garment, it's drafted based on the pattern company's best guess as to the shape of their average customer. Even if the pattern includes a broad size range, all of those sizes are still developed with a specific body proportion in mind. This means that the pattern might fit you really well if your body happens to match the intended shape that the patternmaker was drafting for. On the other hand, the pattern might not fit you very well at all, even if your body's dimensions technically fall within the pattern's size range. We all have different body shapes with different proportions, postures, and distributed volume. None of this is to discourage you from using purchased patterns—I highly recommend giving them a try. And if needed, you can certainly adjust purchased patterns to fit you better. But there are compelling benefits to making your own.

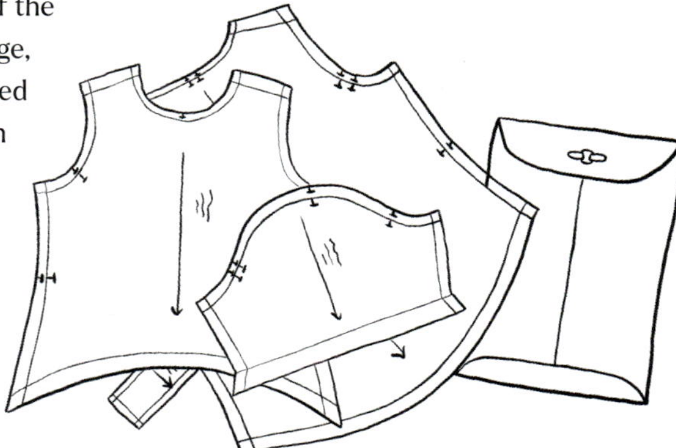

## Achieving a Perfect Fit

By building your own patterns, you won't need to try to place your body within an externally imposed structure of sizes or body "standards." There's no such thing as sizes when you make the pattern yourself! You will still want to test and refine your patterns by stitching up test garments, but you'll no longer need to anticipate or analyze how your body deviates from someone else's concept of what a typical body looks like.

Instead, you'll be on a quest to learn and celebrate your own body's particulars. You will also get to study and define for yourself what "well-fitting" means. And the more patternmaking experience you gain, the more you'll be able to design and create patterns to suit your exact style and preferences. If you can make the pattern, truly *any* design is possible.

Patternmaking skills enable creative clothing design, and I'd also argue that patternmaking itself is a creative endeavor. Patternmaking is both a science and an art. There are guiding principles that, once internalized, will help you to reason your way through a lot of your work. But this analytical approach will only take you so far—there will be inevitable moments when you'll need or want to do some creative problem-solving and decision-making. Whether you're an analytical or free-spirited type (or both!), there will be moments of both delight and frustration. And it's incredibly energizing to dance between two-dimensional and three-dimensional thinking.

Ultimately, the patternmaking process is entirely yours. Make it your own.

# Getting Started

We've established that making your own patterns offers you control, creativity, and individual empowerment. But how do you go about actually making a pattern?

There are three main ways to create a pattern:

- ***Patterndrafting.*** To draft, you develop a set of measurements, plot them onto paper, and connect the dots using straight and curved lines. Sometimes people call this process "flat patternmaking," because the patterns are developed as flat, two-dimensional shapes on paper. Almost all of the projects in this book will be drafted, because drafting gives you all of the power to devise clothes that will suit you perfectly.

- ***Draping.*** In this method, the shapes are developed three-dimensionally by sculpting fabric onto a form or body and then marking the resulting outlines. None of this book's projects will feature draping, but it can be a very creative, intuitive option if you have a mannequin.

- ***Rub-offs.*** You can develop a pattern by tracing a preexisting garment's panels. It's an efficient way to capture elements of good fit that already exist in your wardrobe. Once traced, these patterns can be modified into new styles and fits, all building on the "good bones" of your old clothes. This is the method we'll use to create the jeans project pattern on page 297.

You can use more than one method to create a single pattern. For example, you might take a rub-off of a preexisting garment's bodice but draft a different style of collar and then drape the skirt. Each method offers its own strengths, and you may find yourself especially drawn to one over another.

This book will use mainly the third method of patternmaking—taking a rub-off—because it gives you all of the power to draft clothes that will fit your individual body and your individual taste. You'll measure key points on your body, connect the dots on paper, and begin to engineer custom-fit clothing that way. You might also measure some preexisting clothes to inform your decisions about how you like your clothes to fit, but you'll essentially be drafting your pattern shapes from scratch.

If you're eager to skip straight to the sewing, you're also welcome to opt out of the patternmaking, and instead acquire premade patterns similar to the styles I'll be showing you how to sew.

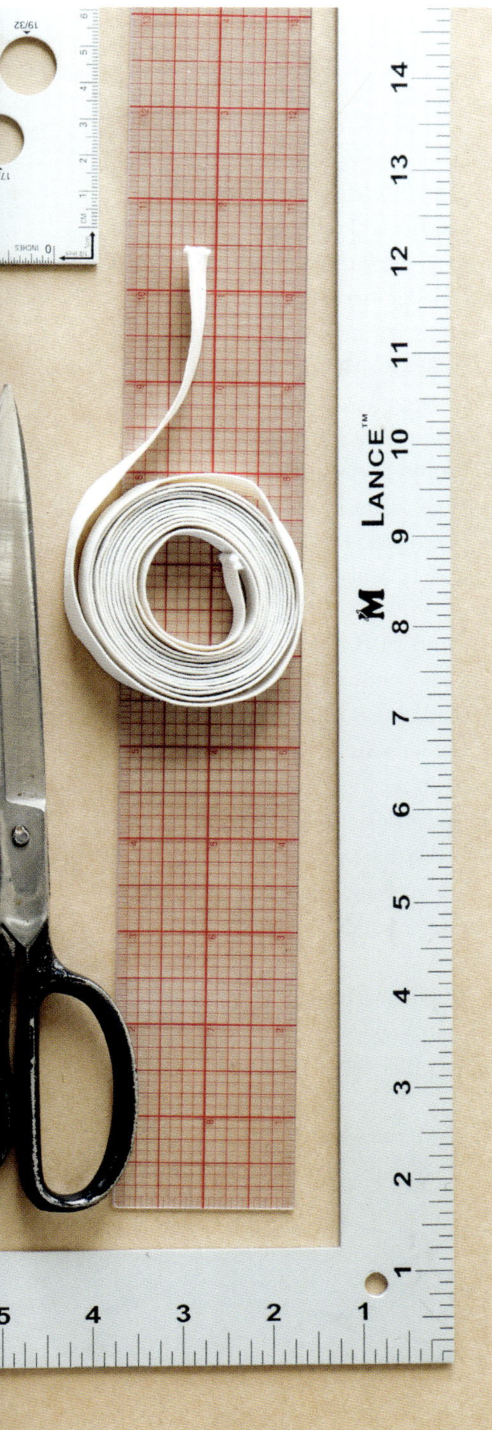

## Tools and Materials

One of the cool things about patternmaking is that it requires almost no specialized tools. If you've been sewing for any length of time, you probably already have nearly everything that's needed. Even if you've never sewn, you likely already have some common household tools that will work perfectly.

The main items are wonderfully basic:

- ***Sharp pencil.*** I like to use a mechanical pencil because it stays sharp throughout the drafting process, but any pencil will do as long as you sharpen it regularly.
- ***Eraser.*** Patternmaking often involves drafting multiple versions of a line before you land on the final version. Keep a good-quality eraser nearby so you can easily remove any markings that are no longer useful.
- ***Gridded ruler.*** This is the most important patternmaking tool. My favorite kind is a clear 18" by 2" gridded ruler (something like a 60 cm by 6 cm ruler, for metric folks), because you can see through the ruler as you align it with your work. Its grid (in ⅛" increments for imperial and 0.5 cm for metric) also works as a mini squaring tool for finding right angles quickly. And these plastic rulers are usually somewhat flexible, so you can stand them on edge to bend and measure along curved lines. Another nice thing about clear gridded rulers: They're usually pretty cheap—less than $10.
- ***Tape measure.*** This soft measurement tool is perfect for measuring around your body. My absolute favorite tape measures have both imperial and metric measurements. Another thing to note, especially if you're making clothes for larger bodies: Most tape measures in the United States are 60 inches in length, but much longer ones (such as 120-inch options) are also available. For metric users, you may often encounter 150-cm lengths, but 300-cm tape measures can also be found.
- ***Paper scissors.*** Any reasonably sharp household scissors will work. They should be sharp enough to cut paper easily. Please don't use your fabric shears, since paper will dull their sharp edges.
- ***Straight pins.*** These allow you to hold layers of paper together while cutting, and sometimes while marking, too. In addition, a sturdy straight

pin works well for transferring lines when taking a rub-off from a preexisting garment or when copying a pattern's shape onto a new piece of paper.

- ***Tracing wheel.*** My favorite type has blunted points and makes quick work of transferring lines from one layer of paper to another. Roll the tool along a line you'd like to trace, and the wheel's points will create indentations in the layer of paper beneath the original. You can do this with or without transfer paper—the indentations are usually visible enough until you're able to darken with a pencil. (However, if faint indentations are harder for your eyes to see, or if you do a lot of pattern work in the evening or in other situations with dim lighting, then you might like to purchase some waxy transfer paper, too.)

- ***Patternmaking paper.*** You'll need lots of paper for patternmaking, but the type of paper doesn't matter. You can buy large rolls of "official" patternmaking paper at specialty suppliers. Dotted patternmaking paper has a grid of letters and numbers printed on it to help you make squared lines. My personal preference is for blank white patternmaking paper, but you can do just as well with pretty much anything else—the backside of old wrapping paper, pads of newsprint, kraft paper rolls, sheets of old printed newspaper, or plain printer paper taped together into larger sheets.

- ***Tape.*** You'll want to have plenty of tape on hand for patternmaking. Frosted translucent tape is great—you can see through it while working, and the frosted texture allows you to draw on top. Masking tape also works well because it tends to be somewhat translucent and comes in large, cost-efficient rolls.

- ***Pattern weights.*** These hold layers of paper in place while you transfer lines from one sheet of paper to another. You can buy formal pattern weights, but lots of people use soup cans, mason jars, washers, or other weighty household objects. (Paperweights, dumbbells, kettlebells, and dense books also come to mind.) Personally, I use smooth, flat rocks I've collected on hikes and at the beach.

- ***A flat, pinprickable work surface.*** Sometimes you may want to pinprick through your paper to transfer markings, and at these times, it's important to have a relatively soft, nonprecious surface to work on. You can spread a couple of layers of bath towel over your table for this purpose. Other options: a large collapsed corrugated cardboard box, a bulletin board, firm wall-to-wall carpeting, plywood.

- ***Yarn and/or elastic.*** When taking body measurements or auditioning seam placements, you may find it useful to have a few longish strands of yarn, elastic, or string, or long strips of fabric. These can be tied around your bust, waist, hips, ankle, or anywhere else that needs measuring or considering.

In addition to the main tools mentioned above, you may wish to acquire some other "nice-to-haves":

- ***Colored pencils.*** A few colors will help you differentiate between drafted lines.

- ***Waxy transfer paper.*** Slip between layers of paper when tracing, with waxy side oriented down toward the new sheet, to make traced markings more visible. For pattern work, I recommend red transfer paper. You can also use waxy (or chalky) transfer paper to mark garment fabric when cutting, but for fabric use I'd recommend lighter colors such as white or yellow.

- ***L-square.*** This makes quick work of drafting right angles. If you don't have one, though, the corner of a book or folder will generally work just as well.

- ***Notcher.*** This tool is designed to mark notch placements by punching tiny U-shaped snips out of pattern edges.

- ***Awl.*** This tool will allow you to create drill holes through your paper so they can be marked easily onto your fabric.

- ***Curves.*** There are all sorts of curved template tools designed specifically to guide you in drafting smooth curves for patternmaking.

- ***Sampling fabrics.*** You'll likely want to test your patterns before cutting into nice fabric. If you're testing a garment that will be made from a midweight woven fabric, then muslin (plain, unbleached woven cotton fabric) is a good option. If not, use a cheap fabric with similar properties to your final fabric. For example, if you're planning to sew stretch jersey leggings, then find inexpensive, four-way stretch jersey fabric that has a similar stretch percentage to your final fabric.

- ***Oaktag.*** In the garment industry, tried-and-true patterns are often transferred onto oaktag, a thick and sturdy type of cardstock that can be used many times before beginning to deteriorate. You can buy rolls of oaktag, but I've also used cheap sheets of presentation board from the drugstore. Depending on the size of your pattern pieces, you may need to tape a couple of sheets together.

- ***Calculator.*** Although the math involved in patternmaking is usually relatively simple, you may find it helpful to have a calculator nearby.

## Taking Body Measurements

You can take a full set of measurements now and record them somewhere safe to refer back to for each project. (If your body changes, though, you'll want to take an updated set.) Alternatively, you can take measurements each time you make a new pattern. This way you'll be sure to get all the measurements you need, and you'll be sure they are as accurate as possible for your current body.

Here are most of the body measurements you may need to take for the projects in this book. Generally it's a good idea to measure your body while wearing very slim-fitting clothes, or while wearing just your underwear.

*By making your own pattern, you'll no longer need to anticipate how your body deviates from someone else's concept of what a typical body looks like.*

# Body's Basic Measurements

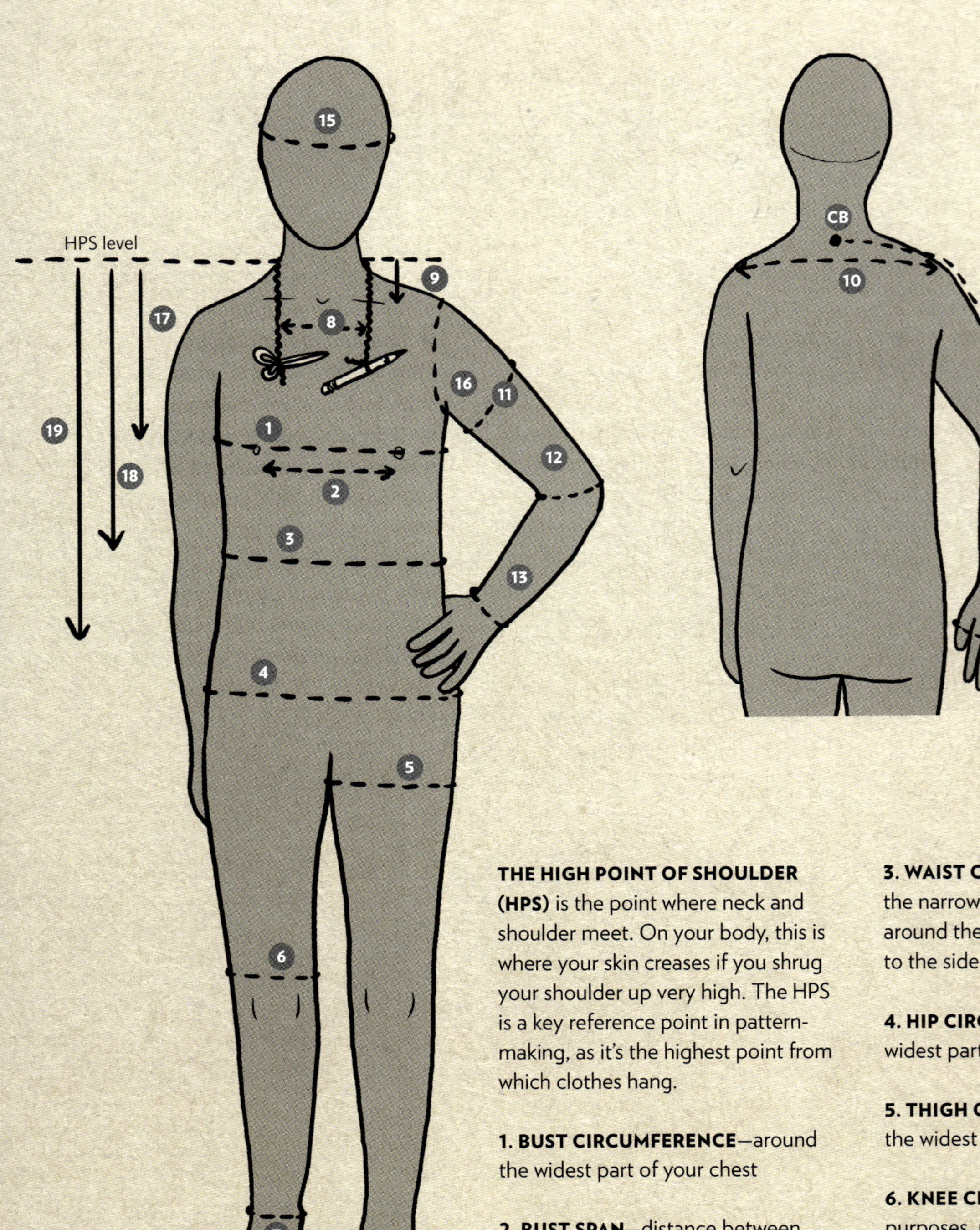


**THE HIGH POINT OF SHOULDER (HPS)** is the point where neck and shoulder meet. On your body, this is where your skin creases if you shrug your shoulder up very high. The HPS is a key reference point in patternmaking, as it's the highest point from which clothes hang.

**1. BUST CIRCUMFERENCE**—around the widest part of your chest

**2. BUST SPAN**—distance between nipples or between outermost points of projection

**3. WAIST CIRCUMFERENCE**—around the narrowest part of your torso, or around the part that creases if you tip to the side

**4. HIP CIRCUMFERENCE**—around the widest part of your buttocks

**5. THIGH CIRCUMFERENCE**—around the widest part of your upper thigh

**6. KNEE CIRCUMFERENCE**—for our purposes, measure this right above the kneecap

**7. ANKLE CIRCUMFERENCE**—around the anklebone

**8. NECK WIDTH**—distance between HPS and HPS; this is easiest to measure by hanging a strand of yarn around your neck and tying weighted objects to each end, then measuring the distance between them

**9. FRONT NECK DROP**—for our purposes, measure vertical distance between HPS and the manubrium (the bony dip between clavicles, or collarbones, at the base of your throat)

**10. SHOULDER WIDTH**—the distance between shoulder tips; find each shoulder tip by lifting your arm above your head and feeling for a crease, then measure between those points from shoulder to shoulder

**11. BICEP CIRCUMFERENCE**—around widest part of upper arm

**12. ELBOW CIRCUMFERENCE**—around elbow with arm slightly bent

**13. WRIST CIRCUMFERENCE**—around wrist bone

**14. HAND CIRCUMFERENCE**—around hand with all five fingers smooshed together tightly but flat

**15. HEAD CIRCUMFERENCE**—around your head just above eyebrow level

**16. ARMHOLE DEPTH**—distance from shoulder tip (find by lifting arm and feeling for a crease) to center of underarm, with tape measure pulled snug along your skin

**17. BUST LEVEL FROM HPS**—vertical distance from HPS to widest level of your chest

**18. WAIST LEVEL FROM HPS**—vertical distance from HPS to narrowest part of your torso or to where your torso creases if you tip to the side

**19. DESIRED BODY LENGTH FROM HPS**—vertical distance from HPS to where you'd like garment's bottom hem to fall

**20. DESIRED SLEEVE LENGTH FROM CENTER BACK (CB)**—three-point measurement from CB to shoulder tip to desired sleeve hem level; measure with arm gently bent if you're planning a sleeve below elbow level

## Avoiding Number Shame

Many of us feel a certain amount of societal pressure about our bodies' shapes and sizes, so taking numerical measurements can produce some anxiety. If you'd like to forgo numerical measurements but still pull accurate dimensions from your body, you can also take a long strip of thin paper or a piece of nonstretchy cord (such as twine) and pull your body's measurements that way. In this case, you can either record the markings on your strip of paper for later reference, or you can just pull the dimensions as you need them while patternmaking.

Another tip for those who'd prefer to avoid the pressure of measurements: If you usually take measurements using the imperial system, try using metric increments instead, and vice versa. Many tape measures include both measurement systems, so you can toggle between them with relative ease. Using less-familiar numbers may feel less loaded and allow you to focus, objectively and calmly, on setting up garment dimensions that meet your true needs and wants—not the arbitrary demands of an image-obsessed society.

## How to Measure Preexisting Clothes

In addition to measuring your own body, it can be helpful to measure well-fitting clothes you already own or have access to. These measurements can help inform your decisions as you plot out patterns for new clothes. If you're drafting a V-neck T-shirt, for example, you can measure a garment you already own that has the perfect V-neck depth. Or if you're drafting a jacket, measure your sister's jean jacket that you've always coveted, and figure out exactly which dimensions you'd like to replicate. Feel free to measure multiple pieces of clothing and compare measurements until you've settled on some solid theories as to what you prefer.

To measure, lay the garment flat on a table. Arrange it so that it is centered and symmetrical, with minimal rippling. If it's a shirt, for example, pinch at both underarm–side seam intersections and pull gently to smooth the area between your hands. Then smooth the rest of the torso by patting any wrinkles toward the edges until they are gone. The sleeves will not lie flat at this point, but that's fine—focus on the torso measurements first. Mark these down. Then readjust the garment so that the sleeve is flat, and proceed with the dimensions of the sleeve- and armhole-related areas. Continue in this way, readjusting your particular garment for the particular measurements you want to take.

## Understanding Ease

When you're wearing a piece of clothing, your body takes up a certain amount of room within that garment's available space. Usually, though, and especially if the garment is made from woven fabric, there's at least a little bit of extra space built in so that you have room to breathe and move. This extra is called *wearing ease,* and it allows you to function comfortably in your clothes. Additional volume is also often added to garments for stylistic reasons.

For woven fabrics, there are certain standards for baseline wearing ease. Basic woven garments (not including overgarments such as jackets and coats) usually include at least these amounts of minimum ease:

- Bust circumference: 2 to 3" (5 to 7.6 cm)
- Waist circumference: 1 to 1½" (2.5 to 3.8 cm)
- Hip circumference: 2 to 3" (5 to 7.6 cm)
- Bicep circumference: 2" (5 cm)
- Elbow circumference: 1" (2.5 cm)
- Wrist circumference: ¼" (6 mm)
- Knee circumference: 1" (2.5 cm)
- Ankle circumference: ¼" (6 mm)

More minimum wearing ease is needed for overgarments, because the clothing you're wearing underneath will also take up space inside the outer garment.

Really, wearing ease is best determined individually, because we each have our own preferences for how something should fit. Curious what your own wearing ease preferences are? Try comparing your body's anatomical measurements with the dimensions of clothes you like. For each drafting project in this book, I'll share the wearing ease amounts I like to add, but please feel free to use your own preferred ease amounts instead.

In a close-fitting garment made from stretchy fabric, there may be no wearing ease, because the fabric's stretching capacity provides enough give. In fact, a very slim-fitting garment made from stretchy knit fabric may even have what is called negative ease, which means that your garment is actually smaller than you are. Leotards and many bathing suits, for example, are usually drafted with negative ease, and many body-conforming tank tops and dresses are also cut this way.

### Patternmaking without Numbers

Did you know that you can make great patterns without using any numerical measurements at all? When you think about it, the real function of a numerical measurement system is to communicate dimensions to people who aren't physically nearby and to enable them to replicate those dimensions with accuracy and ease. If you're working on patterns for yourself, you can certainly try patternmaking without using numbers. For example, you can pull dimensions from your body by pinching along a length of twine or other nonstretchy cord. Then you can transfer these dimensions directly to your paper as you draft. If you pull a circumference dimension using the twine but need to transfer only half or one quarter of that length onto your actual pattern piece, just fold the pinched part into halves or quarters, and transfer the resulting length onto the paper. Pretty neat!

# Drafting Your Pattern

Before you start making your own patterns, it will be helpful to know your way around the parts of a pattern.

- ***Armscye/armhole.*** The line, usually curved, that connects the shoulder seam to the side seam. This line creates the saddle-shaped opening in which your arm will sit.
- ***Stitch line.*** The line you'll actually sew along. This line, also called the seam line, does not include seam allowances. When you're drafting a pattern, you'll start by drafting just these stitch lines. Later, once your shapes are finalized, you'll add seam and hem allowances to create the cut lines.
- ***Cut line.*** The line you use to cut out your fabric pieces. This is the outermost outline of your pattern, and it includes built-in seam and hem allowances.
- ***High point of shoulder (HPS).*** The intersection of a neckline and shoulder. (Often when the garment is laid flat, this point falls a little bit behind where the actual shoulder seam is located.) Because of gravity, this is the point from which the entire garment hangs.
- ***Shoulder slope.*** The amount that a shoulder seam slopes down from the neck toward the shoulder tip.
- ***Low point of shoulder (LPS).*** The shoulder tip, or intersection of the shoulder and armhole. (Often when the garment is laid flat, this point falls a little bit behind where the actual shoulder seam is located.) The vertical difference between HPS and LPS is a garment's shoulder slope amount.
- ***Grainline.*** A straight line marked somewhere in the middle of the pattern piece. This line, which includes an arrowhead at one or both ends, shows you how to align the pattern piece with your fabric's weave or knit structure. By aligning carefully, you'll be able to achieve the intended drape and stretch in your stitched garment.
- ***Notch.*** A little cross-cut along a pattern's edge that indicates how that piece should be aligned when joining to another. Notches make sewing much easier and more accurate. They are often marked on purchased patterns as triangle shapes, but I like to mark mine with simple slit or "T" notations.
- ***Center lines.*** Center front (CF) and center back (CB) lines indicate the anatomical center of the torso. Patterns are often drafted (and sold) as half pieces, to be cut with the CF or CB line aligned with a folded fabric edge. Alternatively, you can make a mirrored version of a pattern piece while it is still in paper form so that you have a full front or back piece. This is the typical process in industrial sewing, and home sewists can enjoy its benefits, too—full pieces facilitate tighter (more fabric-efficient) cutting layouts, and they help with stripe- and plaid-matching, too.
- ***Seam allowance (SA).*** The extra margin added to your pattern's seam edges, beyond the stitch lines, to allow for sewing pieces together.

- ***Hem.*** A folded edge along an opening of your garment. Hems are typically along the bottoms of garment areas—the bottom edges of pants, skirts, shirts—but hemming techniques can sometimes be applied to other nonseamed edges, such as button plackets.
- ***Hem allowance (HA).*** The margin added to the edges of openings. This extra fabric allows for the raw cut edge to be folded under, creating a clean look on the completed garment.
- ***Sweep.*** The bottom edge of a garment (a fashion industry term).

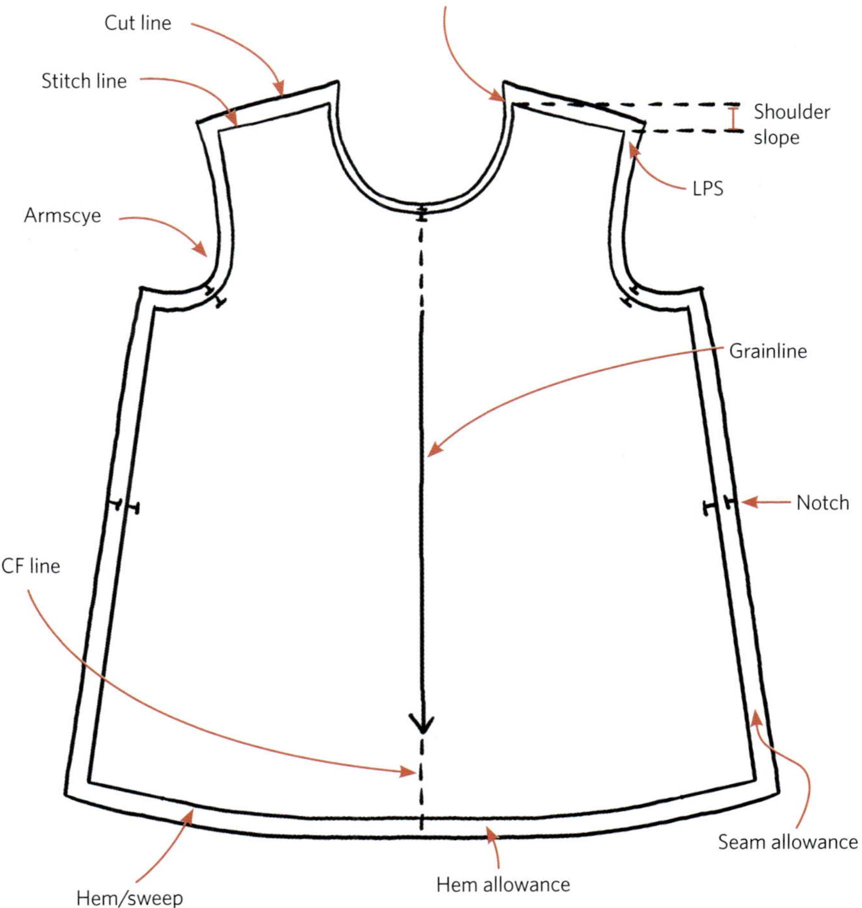

- ***Neck drop.*** The depth of the front or back neck.
- ***Drill hole.*** A drill hole is a precise point on a pattern piece that indicates an element's placement. For example, drill holes may indicate dart points or pocket placements. In industrial sewing, these placements are often marked by actually drilling tiny holes through many layers of fabric, but in home sewing, drill holes can be marked onto fabric using water-soluble pencil, thread tacks, or any other method of your choice.
- ***Sleeve cap.*** The section of a sleeve above the underarm level; usually somewhat bell shaped. The length along the curved edge of the cap is drafted to fit into the specific garment's armhole opening. The height of the cap (how tall the bell-shaped area is) plays a major part in determining how the sleeve will hang and move on the body.
- ***Pattern labeling information.*** Pattern pieces should also include some text that indicates the name of the design, the name of the pattern piece, what type of fabric or other material is needed (main fabric, ribbing, interfacing, etc.), how many to cut, and perhaps the size. If nothing else, I'd recommend writing the date you made the pattern. This way, if pieces get separated later, it will be easier to reunite them.

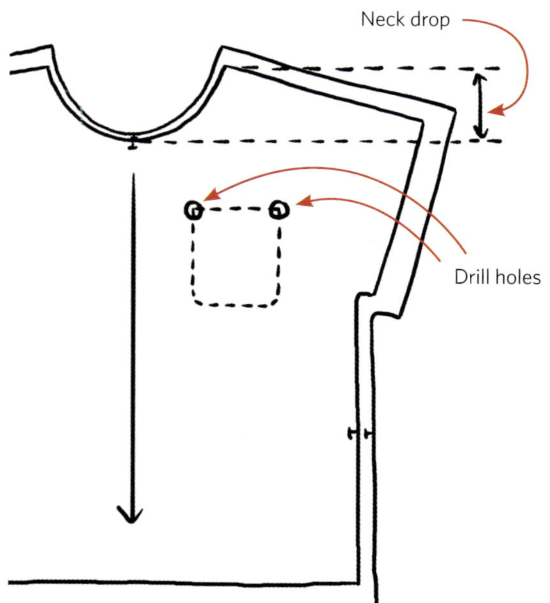


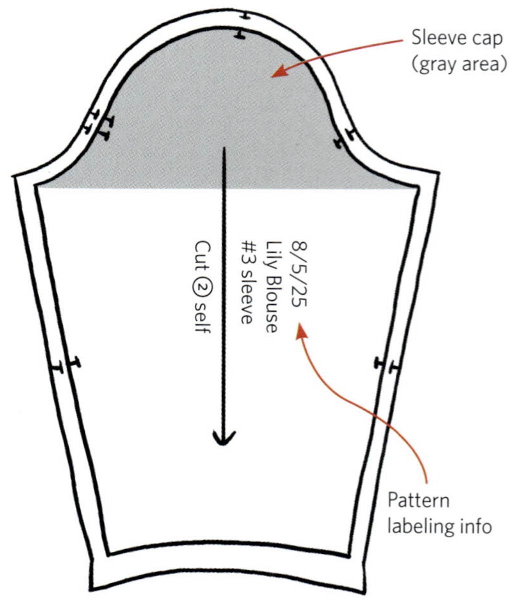

A few more pattern concepts to know:

- ***Draft versus pattern.*** For most projects, you'll begin by creating a draft of your pattern shapes, with front and back layered on top of each other or otherwise connected. You'll be drafting only half of the garment because it is symmetrical (so you can save time and paper for now). Afterward, you can trace off the individual, full pattern pieces, then add seam allowance. If your body is significantly asymmetrical, you can draft full panels instead to differentiate as needed, but you'll probably still need to trace finished copies to use as final pattern pieces.

- ***Wearer's right (WR) and wearer's left (WL).*** When drafting a pattern you'll typically be drafting one half of the body, and then you'll mirror the draft later when you create final pattern pieces. Wearer's right (WR), for example, is the half of the garment that will be on the right-hand side of the person wearing the garment.

- ***Tick mark or cross-mark.*** A short line intersecting a longer line to indicate a precise point on a pattern. For example, a tick mark placed at a right angle along a side seam may be used to indicate a notch point.

- ***Trueing a pattern.*** Testing seam lines against each other to ensure they are well aligned and do not meet with jagged intersections. The goal is usually to form smooth, continuous lines when panels are joined.

## How to Use a Ruler

Though it may seem basic, knowing how to use a ruler is an essential skill for drafting patterns. For those without much ruler practice, here are a few helpful tips:

- To draw a straight line, hold the ruler firmly against paper with nondominant hand. Then slide your sharpened pencil's tip along the edge.
- If you're using a clear gridded ruler meant for drafting, it may have a bevel-cut edge so that you can tilt your pencil's tip just beneath the ruler's edge. This lets you draw a line that is true to the edge of the ruler, instead of drawing a line that is actually a pencil tip's width away from the ruler.

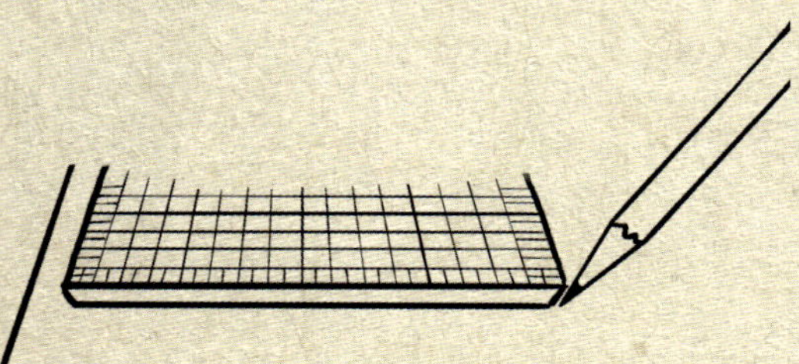

- To draw a line that is longer than your ruler, you'll need to patchwork two or more ruler lengths. Begin by tracing a line along your ruler's length, then slide the ruler so that about half of it extends beyond the line you've just drawn. Align the ruler carefully with the existing line, then hold it in place as you pencil in the extended line. Repeat as needed until your line is the desired length.

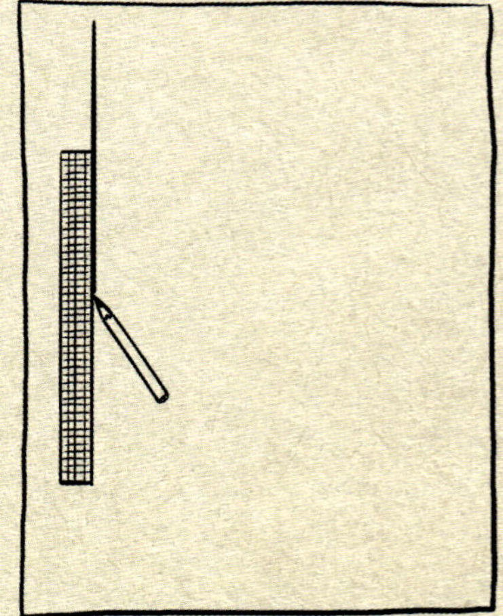

- To square a line using a clear gridded ruler, make a tick mark along the original line at the point from which you'd like to create a perpendicular. Then make one of the ruler's long edges level with this tick mark, and align one of the short lines printed across the ruler with the original line. Proceed to draw your new line.

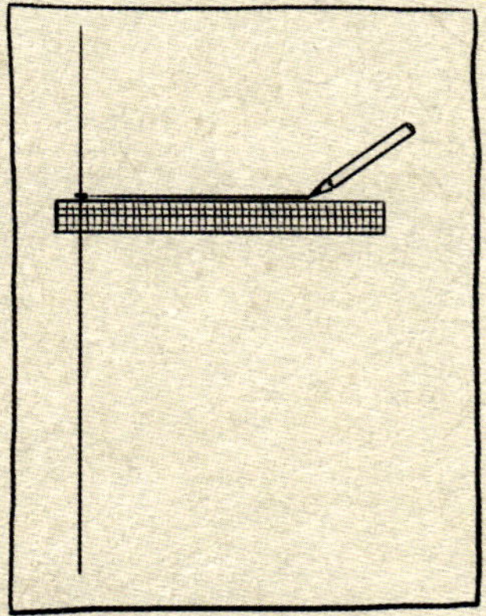

- To draw a parallel line, such as when adding seam allowance, first determine the distance your new line should be from the original. Find the line on your clear gridded ruler that represents that distance from one of the long edges, and align it with the original line. Slide your pencil along the edge.

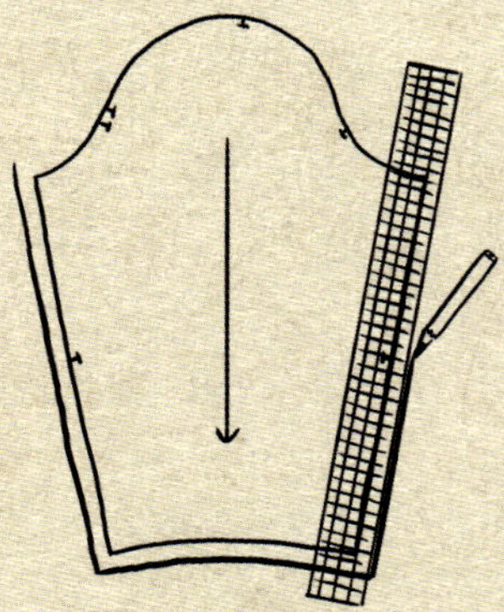

- If you're drawing a parallel curve, use the previous instructions, but draw small sections of the line, pivoting your ruler between each one to reflect the changing contours of the original curve.

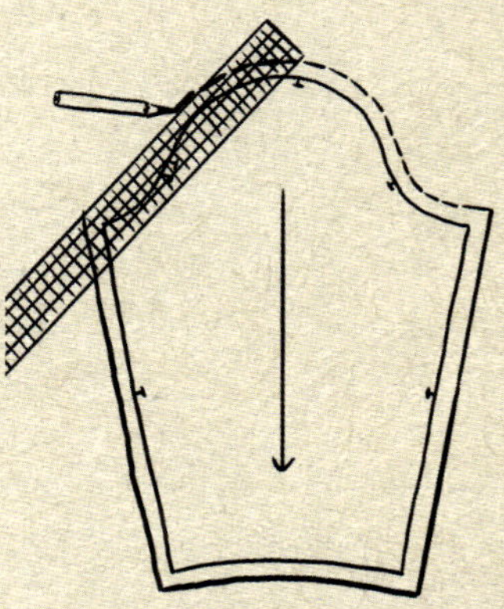

- To measure along a curve, set your flexible clear gridded ruler on its long edge and bend it along the line.

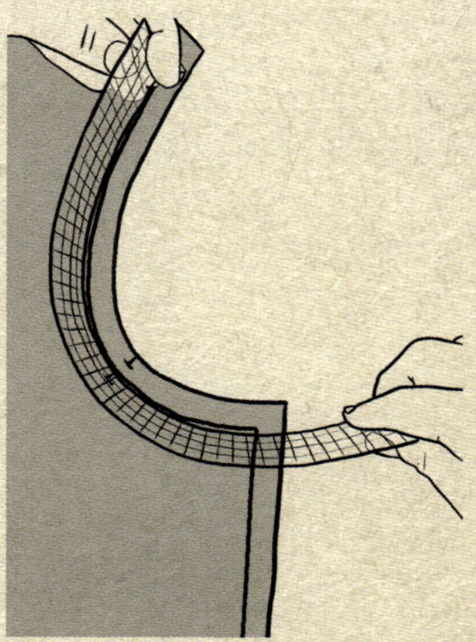

## Tracing Patterns

You'll often need to trace parts of patterns onto fresh paper. There are lots of ways to trace, depending on what you have on hand.

My favorite method requires a tracing wheel or pin and a nonprecious work surface. Lay down a fresh sheet of paper, then place the original draft on top. Weight down to secure. Use a tracing wheel to trace along all needed lines and markings, or use a pin to prick holes. Then remove the original and connect all indentations or markings with a pencil.

If you're having trouble seeing the traced indentations, you can place a large sheet of waxy or chalky transfer paper between the layers, with the pigmented side facing down toward the fresh paper.

### How to Snip a Notch

Notches should be drafted at right angles to their seam lines. Then you can extend these little perpendicular notch lines out to meet the cut lines.

With notches marked at cut edges, you can snip them using either a notching tool or a basic pair of scissors. If using scissors, cut a skinny V shape into the edge. The V width should be no more than ⅛ inch (3 mm) or so, and it needn't extend much more deeply than 3⁄16 inch (5 mm) into the paper.

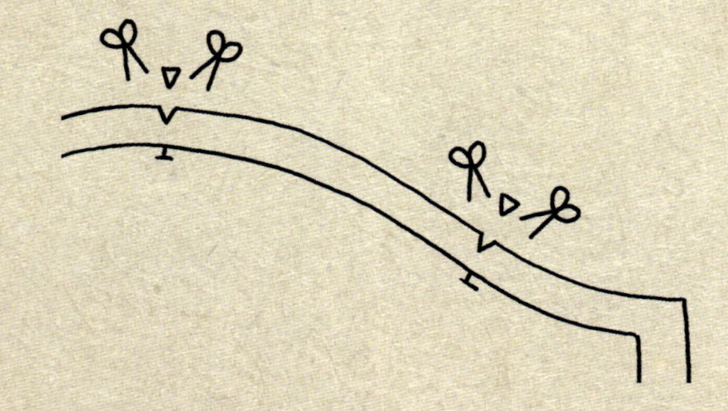

## Adding Style Lines

As patternmaker, you can choose to place extra seams in your garment for stylistic reasons. This simple tweak adds visual interest and enables you to experiment with a lot of stylistic details.

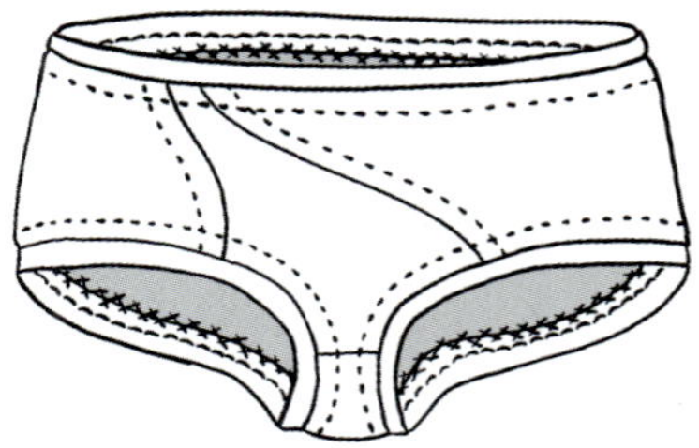

**1.** On your draft, draw one or more style lines. They can be any shape you'd like: straight, curved, or both.

**2.** Add perpendicular cross-marks along your style lines. These will become matching notches to facilitate sewing. Be sure to add extra cross-marks along curves.

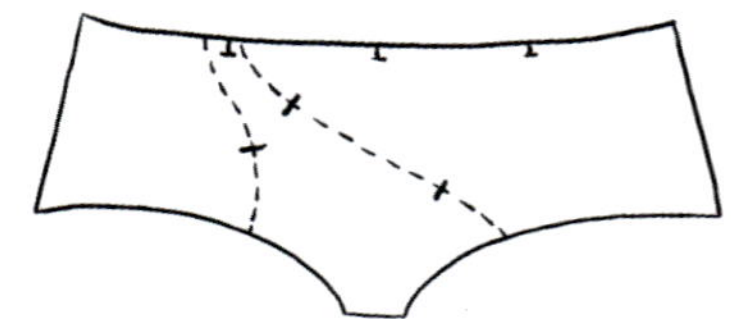

**3.** Trace off each panel as a separate pattern piece.

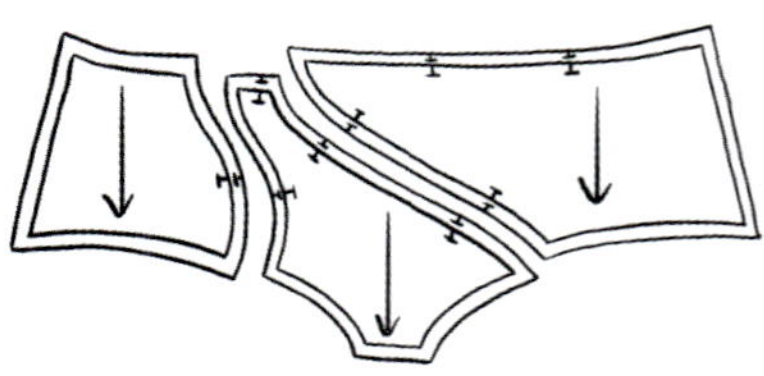

## Adding Volume with “Slash-and-Spread”

One of the most useful pattern manipulation techniques is the “slash-and-spread” method. This allows you to add extra volume for gathers, flares, pleats, tucks, and so on, but it also can be used for fit adjustments to a pattern if you decide you need to add more length or girth. You can also “slash and close” if you feel length or girth needs to be reduced.

### HOW TO SPREAD

1. Determine where you'd like to add fullness. You can add it throughout a panel, or only to certain areas. Draw one or more slash lines (lines that you will cut open) along this section.

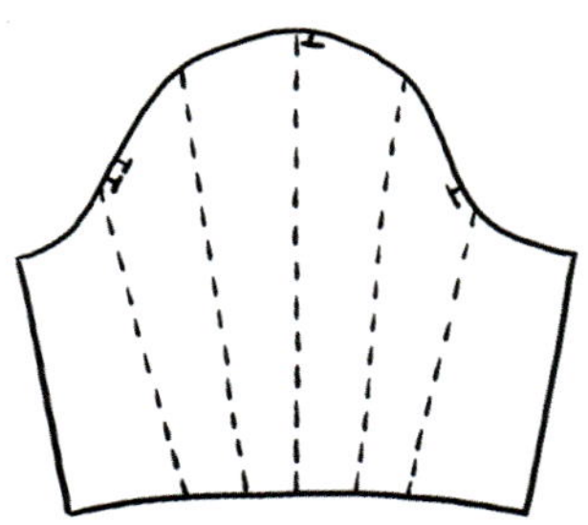

2. Slip a separate large piece of paper underneath your pattern, then cut along each slash line and spread the pieces apart, creating gaps between each section. The gaps can be however wide you'd like. These gaps create the fullness that you're trying to add. You can make the gaps evenly wide at top and bottom, or you can taper them to zero at one end, or anything in between.

3. Tape the sections down to secure them.

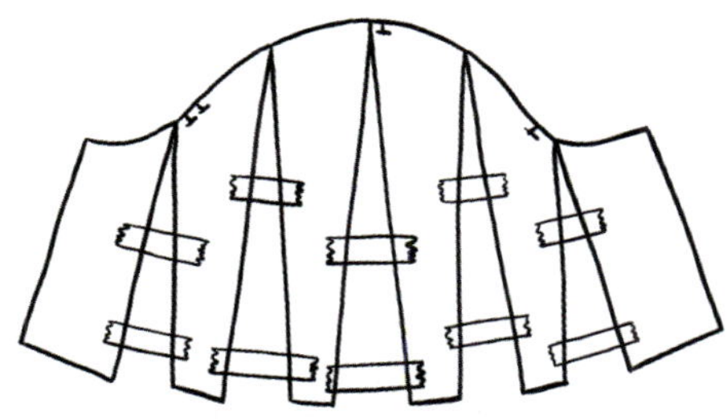

4. Connect the outer pattern lines across the gaps, redrawing as needed to create smooth, gradual outlines. If any notches are present along an edge, make sure they are clearly marked, and allow them to remain in whatever locations they have fallen.

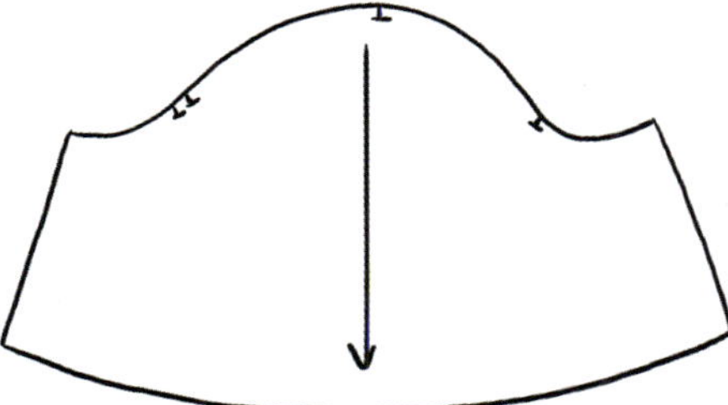

### HOW TO CLOSE

**1.** Determine where you'd like to reduce fabric. Draw one or more slash lines in this area.

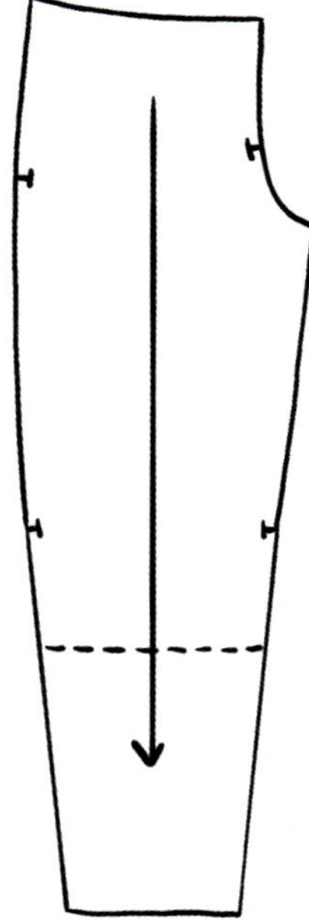

**2.** Cut along each slash line and overlap the paper's cut edges by the desired amount.

**3.** Tape to secure.

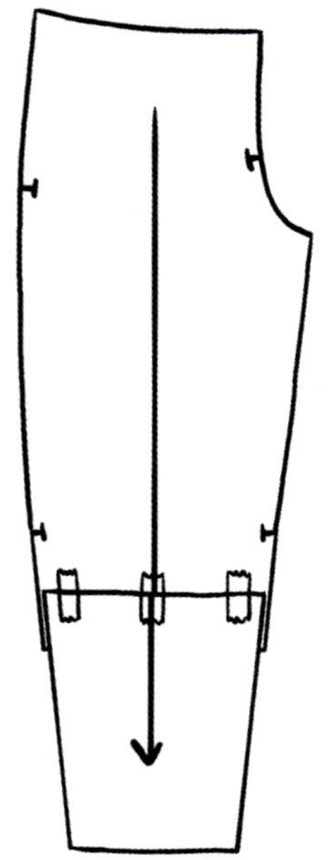

**4.** Smooth the outer pattern lines as needed.

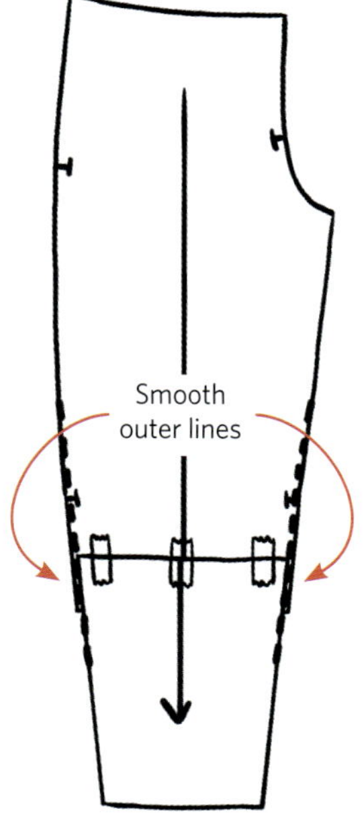


## Understanding Darts

You may be familiar with darts, which are pinched wedges of fabric that help shape a garment as it navigates around projections such as busts, buttocks, elbows, knees, and shoulder blades.

Most of the featured garments are boxy or stretchy enough that they don't necessarily require darts. However, as you're fitting and refining your patterns, if you feel that your design would benefit from a dart, feel free to pinch and pin it closed on your test garment, then mark the dart onto your pattern and include it in your final garment.

Here are a few dart terms to understand:

***Dart takeup.*** The amount pinched out by a dart to shape a projection such as the bust, hip, elbow, or shoulder blade. The more dramatic the projection, the larger the dart takeup. (A bust dart that accommodates a larger cup size will have a larger dart takeup, for example.)

***Apex.*** The outermost point of a projection. On the bust, for example, the true apex is typically located at the nipple point.

***Dart point.*** This is the tip of a dart's triangle or diamond shape. It may be located at the true apex point, but is more often placed slightly away from that apex—1" (2.5 cm) or more—to accommodate the roundness of a body's projecting areas. Typically, the larger the bust, the farther the dart point is placed from the apex.

***Dart legs.*** The two long, symmetrical lines along a dart's sides that are stitched together to construct a dart. On triangle-shaped darts, these lines connect the dart point to a fabric panel's cut edges. On diamond-shaped darts, the dart legs connect the top and bottom dart points to each other.

Once you have a well-fitting dart built into your pattern, you can absorb that shaping into a style line or other seam, or you can rotate it to all sorts of other locations.

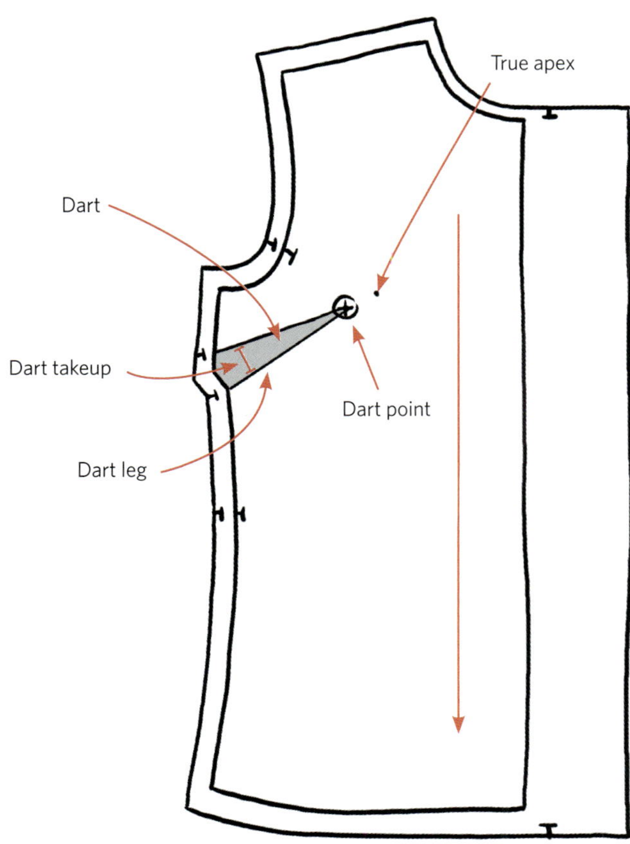


## ABSORBING A DART INTO A SEAM

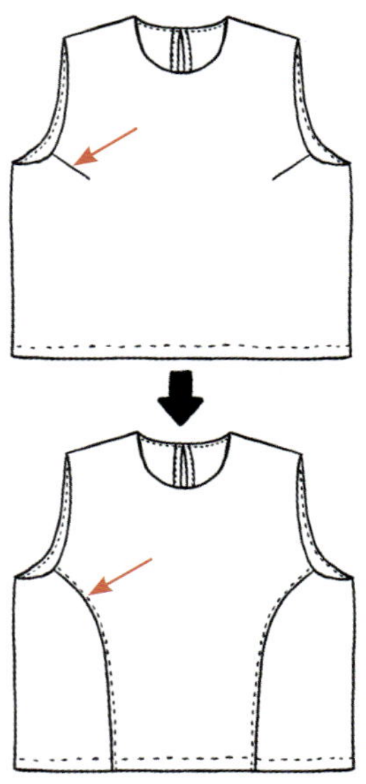

1. Draft a seam line that connects a dart point to a garment edge (or to another dart's point).

2. Draw a perpendicular cross-mark at the dart point, and perhaps at one or more additional points along the newly drafted seam line. These will become matching notches.

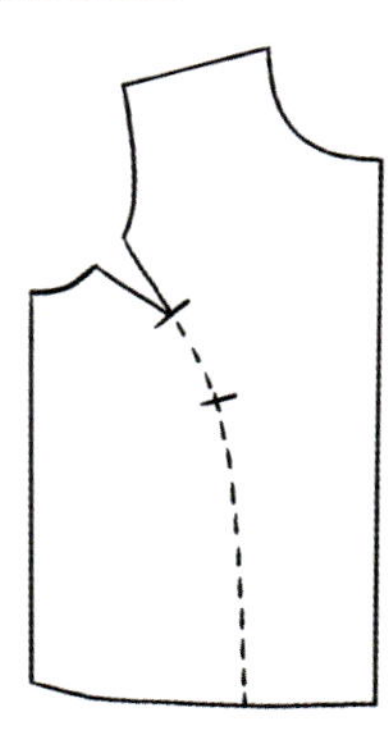

## ABSORBING A DART INTO A SEAM, continued

**3.** Cut the garment panel apart along the newly drafted seam line. In the dart area(s), cut along both dart legs to remove the paper representing dart takeup.

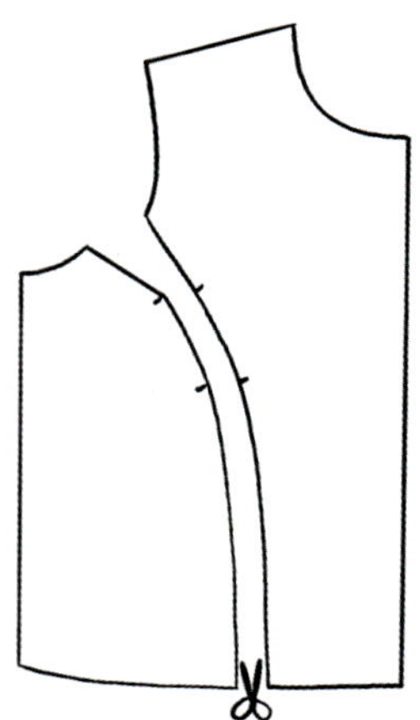

**4.** Smooth lines as needed in the dart point areas.

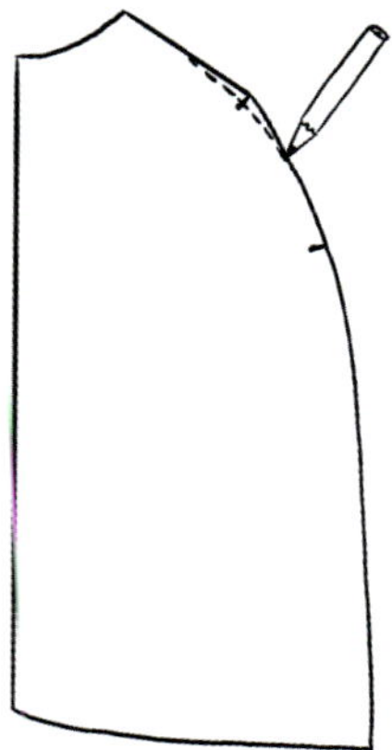

## ROTATING A DART

One of the more mind-bending concepts in patternmaking is that a dart can be rotated anywhere around the area of projection it's accommodating, and the garment will still maintain its basic fit and shape.

In traditional patternmaking textbooks, this concept is usually demonstrated in the context of bust darts, but please know it's relevant for any type of dart (including darts that shape elbows, knees, shoulder blades, buttocks, and more).

**1.** Identify the true apex projection point (which might be at the dart point or a short distance away). The apex is easiest to find if you've stitched up a muslin, but you can also approximate its location by simply holding up paper pattern pieces against your body. Mark the apex point onto the pattern.

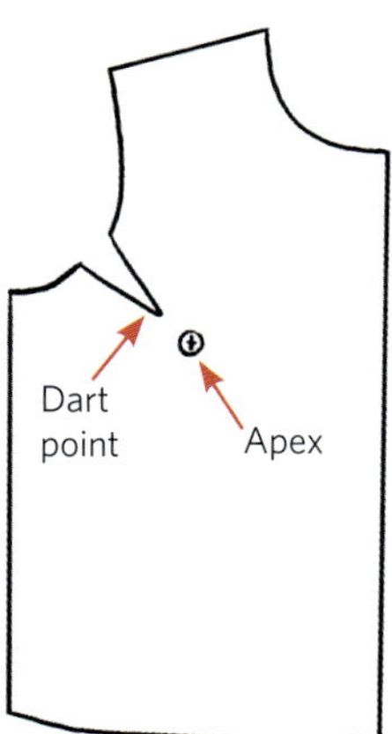


**2.** Locate the dart legs' bases along your pattern's edge and draw straight lines connecting them to the apex point.

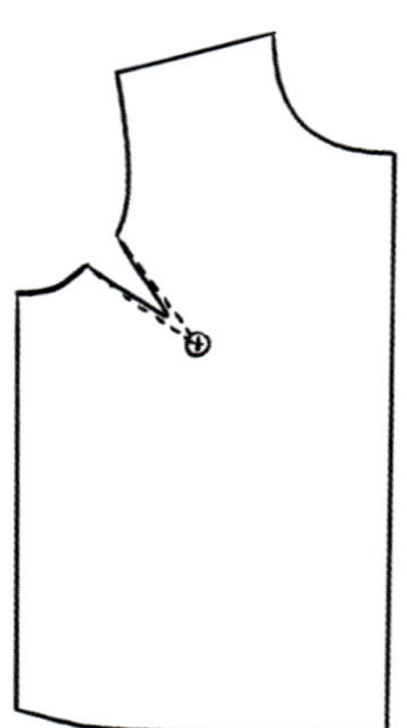

**3.** Determine where you'd like the new dart to be. It will always need to point toward the true apex, but its legs can extend to any pattern edge that is near that projection. Make a mark at the new location.

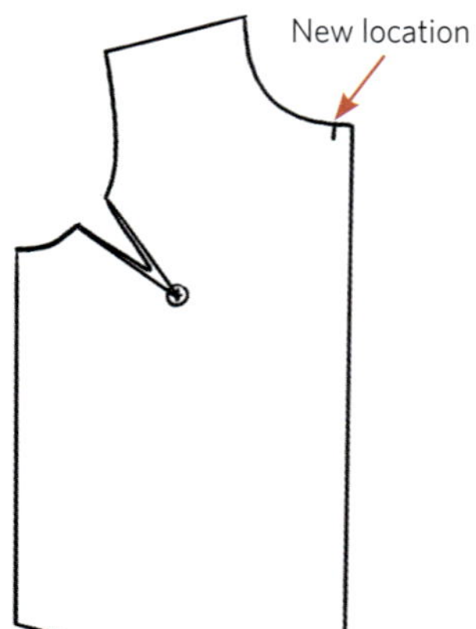

**4.** Connect the apex point to the new location with a straight line.

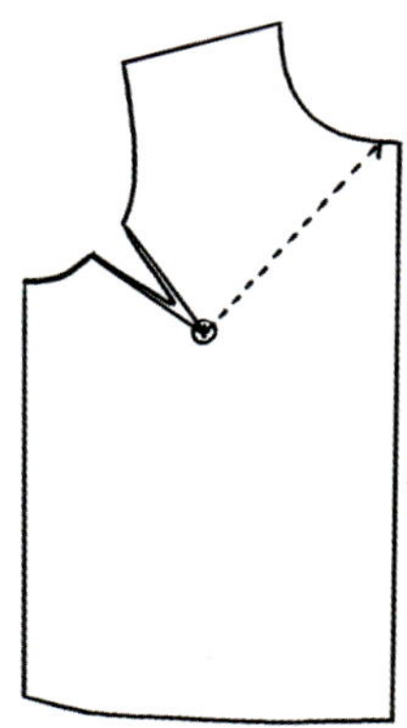

**5.** Cut along one of the original dart legs until you're almost (but not quite) at the apex.

**6.** Cut along the new dart line until you're almost (but not quite) at the apex.

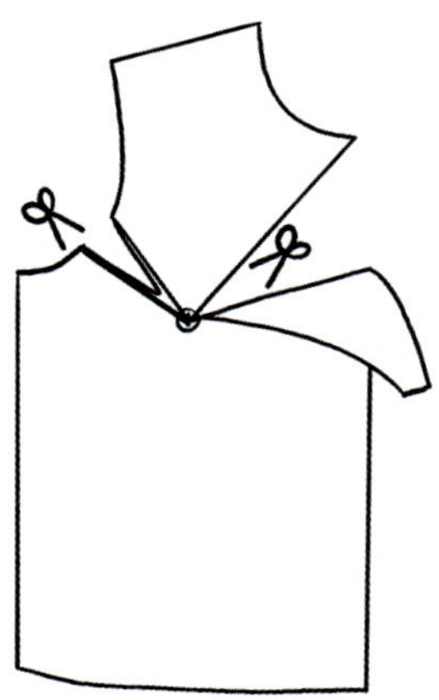

**7.** Swing the pattern to close the old dart, and tape to hold. If needed, add extra paper underneath and redraw the pattern edge in that area so that it creates a smooth line.

**8.** Slip extra paper underneath the new dart and tape it.

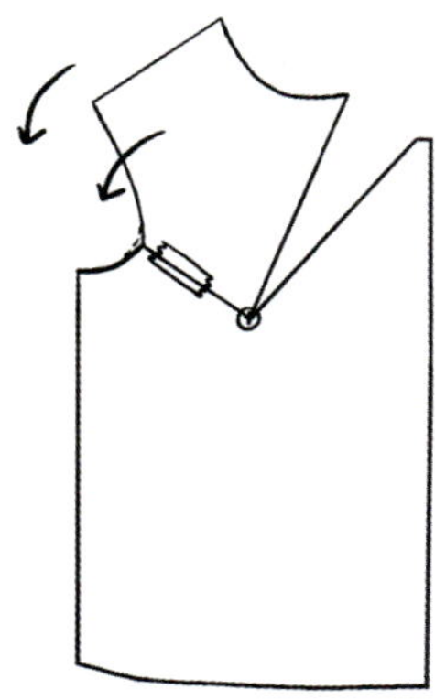

**9.** Determine where you'd like the dart point to be located. This could be at the true projection point, but you can also place the dart point a short distance in (toward the dart legs' base) from the projection point to create a softer shaping effect. For example, a bust dart's point is often located about 1" (2.5 cm) in from the bust's true outermost projection point to accommodate the roundness of the bust mound.

**10.** If your desired dart point is moved slightly away from the projection point, then redraw the dart legs connecting to the new dart point.

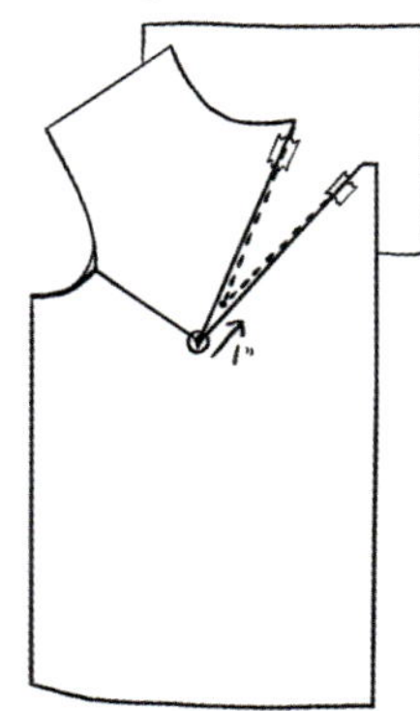

**11.** In order to ensure your dart takeup will stitch neatly into the seam line, there's one more step to take on your paper pattern. Fold the dart closed, making sure that you're pushing the dart takeup toward whichever side you'll want it sewn in real life. Now use a tracing wheel or pin to create a perforated line along the pattern's edge over the dart takeup area. Open the dart again and trace along the perforations to mark the dart takeup.

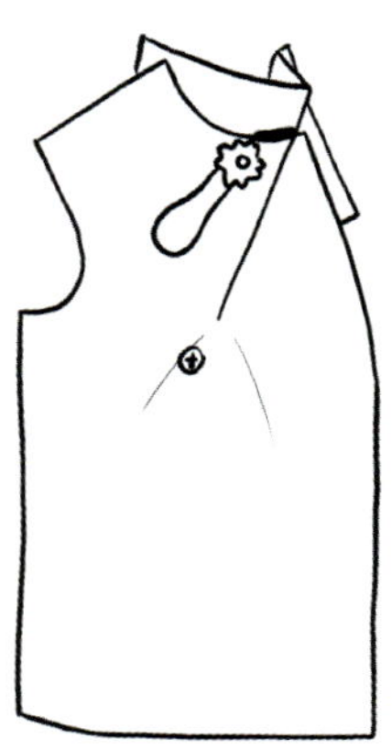

## Assessing Pattern Fit and Balance

Fitting is its own discipline, and quite a few good books have been written on the topic. (See page 330 for recommendations.) In the meantime, I'll try to share a few guiding principles. Please bear in mind that "good fit" is a highly subjective, personal matter, so let your own preferences guide your process.

I'd recommend stitching together at least one test garment while refining the fit of a pattern before you cut into your good fabric. Your test garment should be sewn from fabric that is cheap but quite similar to your intended final fabric in terms of weight, drape, and stretch. Using a light color can help you to see everything more clearly. Feel free to skip stylistic details and just mock up the main panels (unless you're also hoping to assess those details ahead of time).

This test is meant to be a fitting tool, not a final product, and you may need to cut and mark it up during fitting, so try not to get too attached to the idea of preserving a "wearable muslin."

I like to fit in front of a full-length mirror with a notepad, pencil, tape measure, and safety pins nearby. Fabric shears and a marker are also handy. It's incredibly helpful to use a self-timed camera to take clean photos of the front, back, side, and close-up views, because photographs have a useful way of flattening images to highlight fit issues you might not otherwise have noticed.

Here are a few general standards of good fit that may be helpful to consider:

- Fabric should fall smoothly down your body, without unwanted wrinkles, puckers, gaping, pulls, folds, buckling, or "drag lines" (diagonal or horizontal lines created when fabric is pulled toward an edge).
- Side seams should fall straight down toward the floor.
- The garment's volume should be distributed evenly between front and back.
- Hems should hang parallel to the floor, without hiking up in front or back.
- The garment should be comfortable to wear, and you should have enough range of motion to move, sit, and stretch while wearing it.

### Advice on Using a Purchased Pattern

This chapter has focused on preparing you to make your own patterns. But if you opt instead to use a purchased pattern for a hand-sewing project, you may want to make a few tweaks.

In this case, I'd recommend spreading out all of the pattern pieces on the floor next to you and sitting down to thoroughly review the pattern's instructions. Take notes, paying particular attention to the following: seam and hem allowances, gathered/pleated/eased areas, recommended order of operations, recommended machine stitches, and other construction techniques.

You don't actually need to follow any of the pattern's instructions, but by getting clear about the pattern company's suggestions, you'll be able to analyze and decide for yourself how you'd like to construct your handsewn version. Once you've developed your hand-stitching plan, make any needed adjustments to seam and hem allowances or other areas.

If you notice elements of the garment's fit that you'd like to change, mark them all down, but try to correct only two or three significant fit areas per fit test, then test and correct again. Oftentimes tweaking one area of a pattern will significantly change several other areas, so it's usually best not to change the entire thing at once. To prioritize, it often makes sense to start with the fit changes that are closest to the top of the garment (closest to your head) because the entire garment hangs down from there.

If you're aware of a fit problem but don't know how to correct the pattern for it, try turning to the internet. A quick search can yield lots of helpful videos, blog posts, and other tutorials on most fit adjustments. Review them carefully to determine which ones make the most sense for your situation. If you're having trouble finding relevant search results, try tweaking your search terms. Often there's more than one way to refer to a fit problem. And if you're still struggling, consider reaching out to your local sewing community or to fellow sewists on social media. You'll doubtless be met with generosity, ingenuity, and lots of collective wisdom.

Fitting can be a challenge, but it's rewarding and well worth the trouble. Stick with it, keep a sense of humor, and try to enjoy the process, as there's much to be learned through these fit tweak experiments. I think you'll be glad you spent the time getting your pattern just right.

## Hand-Sewing Games

Sometimes life gets far too serious. Why not round up a friend and have some good old hand-sewing fun?

### THIMBLE DUELS

Early in the pandemic, after weeks of being stuck inside with nowhere to go and not much to do, my now-husband and I devised a couple of thimble-related games. The first is "Thimble Duels." It's a two-player game.

Each player wears a thimble on their finger. Ideally, the thimbles should fit well—not too tight, not too loose. To play, use your thimbled finger to try to knock the other person's thimble off. You can only use your thimbled finger. Those are the only rules. It's a very silly, strangely exciting game.

### THIMBLE FOOTBALL

This is the other thimble game we invented during quarantine. It's also meant for two players, but I suppose you could get fancy and figure out a way to include more.

One person rests their hands on a table and arranges their fingers into a goalpost configuration. The other person sets a thimble on the table in front of the goal, then tries to flick the thimble through. If you have a variety of thimbles, bring 'em out and try each one. See what's silliest or most challenging. Thimbles were definitely not intended to be used in this way. But, ha! Look at you, making something out of nearly nothing.

## TUG-OF-WAR WITH A HANDSEWN SEAM

This is great fun, but it's also a legitimately good way to study how strong hand stitches can be, even under significant stress. This is another two-person game.

Cut two longish strips of fabric—maybe 6 inches (15 cm) wide by 12 inches (30 cm) long each—and sew them together. For a proper challenge, use smallish even backstitches, then fell the seam allowances with whipstitch, hemstitch, or another stitch of your choosing. If you'd like to test another seam finish, though, try whatever you're interested in.

Now each person grasps an end and pulls. If you've sewn a sturdy seam, it will probably be very, very hard to break. We tried this a few years ago and, after seven minutes of determined, full-bodied tugging, finally ripped the fabric, not the stitches. *Hand sewing is strong.*

## THE THIMBLE GAME

An internet search turns up "The Thimble Game," which is a great option for a group of people. It's best played with at least three.

You'll need a cup of water, a piece of paper, a pencil, and a thimble. (For this game, choose a closed-top thimble made of a nonporous material.)

One player chooses a category (*fruit*, for example, or *sports*, or *letters of the alphabet*). They announce the category to everyone else and privately write down a particular word from that category (such as *pomegranate*, or *water skiing*, or *Q*). Then the other players have to take turns guessing what's written on the paper. Whoever guesses correctly gets a thimbleful of water thrown at them. (How exciting!) That person becomes the next word-chooser.

# HAND SEWING

It's a radical, simple act to make your own clothes by hand. The tools are few, and most are relatively inexpensive. The techniques needn't be complicated, either—with a handful of good stitches at your command, you'll be able to construct all manner of beautiful, sturdy garments. And if you approach your projects with a willingness to experiment, you'll never stop learning. Empowerment, accessibility, mental stimulation, endless opportunities for growth, and a set of amazing clothes—what's not to love? Let's get started.

# Why Sew by Hand?

These days, it's far from the norm to stitch clothing entirely by hand. There are faster, often easier ways to make or acquire clothes. But if you picked up this book, you probably already believe that hand sewing clothing is worth doing.

People come to hand sewing clothing for different reasons. What are yours? For me it began as an experiment. I was concerned with the unsustainability of my enthusiastic sewing practice on a planet that already has far too much clothing. Hand sewing was the most effective way I could think of to slow down my sewing output. Once I began making and wearing these garments, though, I realized how many other lovely benefits the practice offers.

Here are a few of the many reasons hand sewing clothing is wonderful. It is:

- Slow, so it dials down your output and calms your mind
- Far, far, far more portable than machine sewing
- Much more productive than you might think, because you can work on it everywhere, anytime—slow and steady really can win the race
- Much less expensive than machine sewing
- Amazingly strong and sturdy, as long as you use good thread and appropriate stitches
- Deliberate and controlled—your speed will always match your attention, and the results will reflect your intention
- Precise
- Quiet, which means you can stitch beside a napping baby, or late at night in an apartment with thin walls
- Different from anything you can find in a store or in anyone else's closet
- Simple in process yet sophisticated in the result
- Soft to touch—the seams are less stiff than machine-sewn ones
- Personal
- Yours—your hands will be directly responsible for the beautiful things you make, and that's an empowering feeling

# Tools and Materials

One of the lovely benefits of hand sewing is that the tools tend to be simple, portable, and relatively inexpensive. You won't need to save up for a machine that will set you back $300 or more. Instead, a little basket of tools is all you need. You may already have nearly everything here.

***Needles.*** The most basic but essential hand-sewing tool is the needle. Needles are sold in packages and come in a range of sizes, styles, and price points. Some are good for all-purpose sewing, while others are meant for darning, leather work, quilting, embroidery, millinery, and more. I'd recommend picking up an assorted pack from your local craft store and experimenting to see what you like to use. This will vary with the project, the fabric, the thread, and your mood. You'll probably find yourself reaching for sharps a lot—these are medium-length, pointy-tipped needles that come in lots of thicknesses and glide easily through most woven fabrics. Some people like to use quilter's between needles, too, which are short and fine. For knits, use ballpoint needles. They have blunted tips that push between knit fabrics' yarns instead of puncturing them. (Avoiding punctures is important because punctured yarns in a knit fabric become holes after a wash or two.) For knit sewing, I also like slim "tapestry" needles, which have large eyes for easy threading and blunted tips for gentleness on knits.

***Thread.*** There are lots of thread options available, and I'd recommend experimenting to see what you like. Feel free to use those poly-cotton all-purpose threads used for machine sewing, for example. Just make sure you're using nice fresh thread that's strong enough to hold your handsewn garment together for many years. Those sweet vintage thread spools are tempting, but old thread tends to break more easily, which means your slow, carefully placed stitches could deteriorate and snap before their time. If you want to get a bit more deliberate about your materials, consider the fiber content of your fabric and match your thread fiber to it. If I'm hand-stitching a cotton jersey T-shirt, I reach for a spool of cotton thread. A linen dress might do well with a linen

## The Time Factor

Hand sewing is slow, certainly, but it's not endless. The exact amount of time depends on many factors particular to your situation. How fast are you stitching? How dense is your fabric, and what tools are you using? What techniques are you using? Are you batching tasks for efficiency or moving through in a different order (which is totally legitimate, by the way)? Are you making revisions and adjustments along the way? Of course, many of the same factors affect how long a machine-sewn project takes, and there are other machine-specific obstacles, too: switching needles and presser feet, snafus with the feed dogs, troubles with tension, speed-produced mistakes that require seam ripping.

It's true that a machine-sewn project is generally faster, if you're counting minutes. (If you count days, you might actually finish a handsewn garment first, because you can bring it everywhere and work on it in tiny, casual pockets of time.) A few years ago, I ran a little experiment and tallied how long it took me to sew pairs of garments, one by machine and a nearly identical version by hand. For woven garments, hand sewing tended to take roughly three times as long, and for knit garments it took about two times as long.

The gap is wider when you strictly consider stitching time—my machine speed was about 18 times faster than my handsewn backstitching at a comparable stitches-per-inch ratio. But so much of sewing involves things besides actually stitching—pressing, pinning, seam ripping, checking instructions or notes, etc.—that the speed gap narrowed dramatically.

thread. There's one notable exception to the strong thread rule: basting thread. This is a special type of loosely spun cotton thread that's specifically designed to break easily under strain. It's perfect for temporarily holding layers together, creating tailor's tacks, and placing other stitches you'll want to remove later. Don't have access to official basting thread but curious to try out the concept? Here's where I would recommend busting out those weakened vintage threads, which, like basting thread, will break more easily under strain when you're ready to remove your temporary stitches.

***Thimble.*** While not mandatory, a thimble can be a game changer for the hand sewist. It is quite possible to stitch lots of beautiful stitches without a thimble, but once you've mastered using one, you can stitch with more speed, precision, comfort, strength, and endurance. Thimbling is an acquired skill—no one is born feeling comfortable with a cap at the end of their finger—so it will take some diligent, consistent practice (over a few days or weeks, usually) before you're likely to feel confident stitching with a thimble. If you can persevere through the thimble-bonding phase, you'll be glad you did.

Thimbles come in many styles and materials. I'd encourage you to experiment with a variety of thimbles and use what suits you best. Each style has evolved to meet a specific need and cultural context—some thimbles may be better suited for embroidery, or quilting, or sashiko, or leather work. For more on using a thimble, see page 55.

***Pins.*** You'll need a good set of sharp, smooth pins to do your best work. These little tools hold fabric layers in place so that your hands can focus on stitching. Pins are your friends—use them liberally. The type of pins you use will depend on your preferences and fabric. A basic pack of metal straight pins will almost always work perfectly.

Some pins are thicker, which will be good on thick, dense fabrics like denims and canvases. Other pins are very fine, making them well suited to delicate, thin fabrics such as silks and voiles. If you're sewing with lots of knits, you might want to try ballpoint pins. They have rounded points that slide between knit fabrics' yarns to avoid damaging the cloth. (With my knits, though, I usually just use superfine pins.) You can also use sewing clips in lieu of pins—they're a great option for many projects, and they won't create holes because they never puncture the fabric.

## Pins versus Basting

Sometimes you may find pins frustrating to navigate around as you're stitching. (They do have a tendency to catch the thread as you try to pull it through fabric.) Or perhaps you're prepping a project for travel and you don't want to juggle a million pins while you're out and about. In these cases, you can use basting stitches. Get your work arranged using pins or clips, then replace them with a quick line of basting stitches.

***Scissors.*** You'll need 8-inch dressmaker shears with nice sharp blades to make clean cuts into your fabric. (There are left-handed versions available for the southpaws among us.) Never use these shears for anything except cutting fabric. Compared with other hand-sewing tools, this is a pricier purchase. My current pair cost $40 a decade ago, and while they're by no means top-of-the-line in price point, they certainly felt like an investment. I've never regretted that purchase, though, as they've held up well over the years. You'll also do well to have the blades sharpened from time to time—you'll know it's time when you're having trouble making clean, easy cuts. Oftentimes local hardware stores, knife stores, and scissors manufacturers offer sharpening services. You may wish to acquire additional scissors for more specialized purposes over time—for instance, smaller scissors for sewing on the go, thread snips for clipping threads, pinking shears to reduce fraying on raw edges, or a rotary cutter and self-healing mat.

## Finger-Pressing

Some fabrics are responsive to "finger-pressing," which is when you create a crease using your finger's nail or pad. I like to finger-press with my work laid on a table, hardcover book, or other hard surface.

***Iron.*** An iron's pressure, heat, and steam will help you do your best work by keeping your sewing crisp and tidy. Invest in a decent iron and use it as much as possible. When sewing on the go, though, you may not always have access to one. What then? Prepare several tasks ahead of time using an iron. If you run out of iron-prepped work to do, you can finger-press and place basting stitches to hold things crisply, then iron when you're home again. There are also portable seam roller tools that can help crease cloth by applying pressure along folded areas.

***Thread wax.*** A traditional cake of beeswax or other thread conditioner is a helpful item to have in your hand-sewing toolkit. By melting wax into the thread before stitching (see Waxing, page 52), you add strength and longevity to your sewing. Wax helps prevent curling and kinking in your thread and reduces tangles. It makes your thread behave a bit more like wire (in a good way) while you're stitching with it. The thread is still soft and malleable, but it's snarl-resistant and it glides nicely through the fabric as you sew. I've also experimented with candelilla wax to good effect, and I had one student mention that they used skateboard wax with great success!

***Seam ripper.*** This sharp-clawed little tool enables you to remove stitches with precision. Pulling out stitches can be a bit demoralizing. The good news is that in hand sewing, you're unlikely to have much seam ripping to do compared with machine sewing, because your stitching will be slower and more intentional.

***Gridded ruler.*** I can't overstate the usefulness of a clear gridded ruler. It's invaluable for pattern work but also for stitching—a ruler is great for orienting grain lines when cutting fabric and for measuring and marking stitch lines. It will also help you confirm size, spacing, and placement of elements you're constructing. I'd recommend the same ruler that I like for patternmaking: It's clear, gridded, and 18 inches by 2 inches (50 cm by 6 cm)—long enough for drawing useful lines but small enough to be wielded easily. You might also like to have a short ruler in your to-go sewing kit.

## Marking Stitch Lines

When machine sewing you can maintain accurate seam allowances by aligning the raw edges with the marks on your presser foot or the lines on the needle plate. When sewing by hand you have a few options. You can mark the stitch lines on your fabric using a gridded ruler and fabric-marking tool.

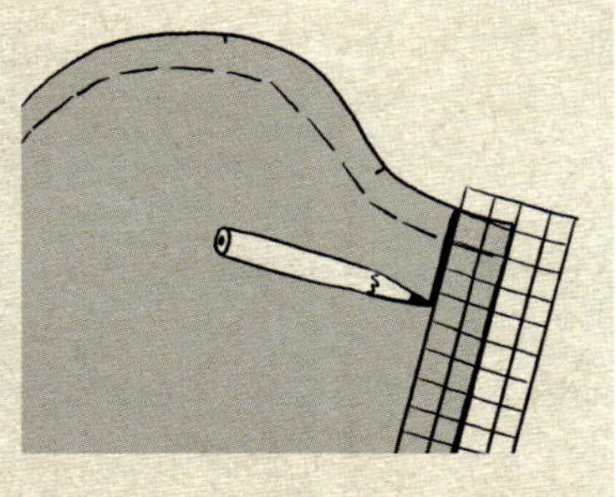

Another option, and the one I employ the most, is simply eyeballing the seam allowance. This is a good option especially on easy-fitting or stretchy garments, in which precision isn't quite as important.

***Fabric-marking tools.*** You'll want a few fabric-marking tools in a variety of colors. These are used to mark stitch lines, placements, and other important elements on your fabric while ensuring that the markings will be removable or invisible on your final project. There are lots of types to choose from. Having more than one type (and maybe in more than one color) will enable you to use whichever works best on the particular fabric you're working with at the moment. Popular options include water-soluble markers and pencils, chalk (either as cakes or wheel-applied powder), pigmented wax, transfer paper, a Hera marker, or a sliver of soap. Although not technically a tool, you can also use thread to mark. I find myself using water-soluble pencils or a Hera marker the most often. Try out a few options and see what you like best.

## Nice-to-Have Tools

Eventually, you might also appreciate having a few other tools, such as:

- Yardstick—for drafting longer lines
- Buttonhole spacer—for evenly spacing elements
- Buttonhole chisel—for slicing slits
- Awl—for creating eyelets, unpicking stitches, and more
- Tailor's ham—for pressing certain areas
- Sewing bird or other "third hand"—for assisting with long straight seams

### What's a Sewing Bird?

You may be able to find an antique "sewing bird," which is a bird-shaped clamp. It affixes to the edge of a table and holds the far end of your seam in its beak, thus helping to hold tension on your sewing. If you'd like help holding tension but don't have a sewing bird, that's fine—you can use any basic clamp from the hardware store instead. You can also just pin the far end of your work onto a weighted cushion, a couch, the leg of the jeans you're wearing (shown here), a backpack, or a strip of twill tape tied onto something.

Using a "third hand" helper is best suited for work on straight lengths of sturdy, stable woven fabric. If you're working with knits or with bias-cut areas, I wouldn't recommend using a "third hand" setup, because all of that tension can distort the fabric and your stitching.

# Suitable Fabrics

As a general statement, I'd argue that all fabrics are appropriate for hand sewing. Each has its own properties, and you'll doubtless enjoy working with some more than others. But I've never met a fabric that was truly impossible to stitch up by hand. Where there's a will, there's a way. Here are the fabrics that I find most suitable for hand sewing:

- ***Light- and midweight wovens.*** These tend to be especially easy to stitch through, and because they generally don't have stretch, you can select stitches without worrying about stretch potential. You can hand-sew lots of clothes using this category of fabrics—dresses, blouses, shirts, tunics, skirts, pants, light jackets, and more.
- ***Heavy wovens.*** You can also hand-sew thick, sturdy, dense fabrics such as denim, canvas, and other heavy wovens. For these you'll want to use a thimble and take plenty of breaks because stitching through thick fabric can be tiring. However, with the right tools, the right techniques, and a good dollop of motivation, you can absolutely hand-sew thick clothes such as jeans, jackets, overalls, and anything else you can dream up.
- ***Knits.*** Many people feel intimidated about sewing with knit fabrics, probably because in the machine-sewing world, it can be a fussy process to get a machine to play nicely with stretchy fabric and avoid problems with tension, puckering, stretching, channeling, and so on. In the hand-sewing world, though, nearly all frustrations are eliminated because your hands and mind intuitively know how to create nice smooth stitches on stretchy fabrics. Using nothing but hand stitches, you can sew up all of the T-shirts, leggings, sweatshirts, underwear,

## My Favorite Stitches for Knit Fabrics

For knit fabrics, use stretchy stitches. Experiment on little swatches of your garment fabric and see what you like best. Here are some of my favorites:

**Super stretchy**

- Even backstitch
- Whipstitch
- Herringbone stitch
- Catchstitch
- Overcasting

**Somewhat stretchy**

- Spaced backstitch
- Combination stitch
- Fell stitch
- Hemstitch

bras, swimsuits, dresses, tops, skirts, and more that your heart desires. Knit fabrics tend to be forgiving in fit, too—a bonus benefit! You'll want to use a ball point needle to avoid puncturing the fabrics' yarns, and I recommend employing the stitches listed on the preceding page that have good stretch potential.

## Less Suitable Fabric

The only category of fabrics that gives me pause, as a hand sewist, is very loosely constructed fabrics. These might include chunky knit yardage, some handwoven fabrics, and other cloth that is very prone to unraveling. Still, it can be done. As you cut out these panels of fabric, I'd recommend reinforcing the raw edges immediately with a serger (if you have one and don't mind including these machine stitches in your otherwise handsewn project). Alternatively, you could use a regular machine's zigzag stitch somewhere within the seam allowances (again, if you don't mind involving a sewing machine). You might even try applying some plasticky paint to seal the yarns along the edges of your pattern panels before cutting out each piece. (I encountered this idea through the work of prominent zero-waste designer Holly McQuillan, who has proposed acrylic house paint as an edge finish option.) Or if you're determined to handle things entirely through hand stitching, you can sew a snug bias binding along each edge as you cut it out. This task would be quite labor intensive, but for a very special project, it might be worth the time.

### What About Fiber Content?

In addition to a fabric's structure—the way its yarns are arranged to form cloth—another consideration is the fiber content: What is the raw material that was spun up to form the fabric's yarns?

Fibers can be broken into two main camps—synthetic and natural—and fabrics can include one or more fibers. The fiber content is very important for reasons far beyond whether it's suitable for hand sewing. Truly, you can hand-sew with pretty much any fiber(s) you like. The question of fiber is really one of personal preference. Which fibers do you like to feel against your skin? Which ones align with your ethics or with your goals for the project? Which ones do you have access to? Which ones can you afford?

# Preparing to Sew

Before you begin placing stitches into cloth, you'll need to get some thread ready.

## Cutting

While it can be tempting to cut a nice long strand of thread, I'd recommend cutting shorter strands. From your fingertip to your underarm is typically a good, manageable length. I'd recommend no longer than 24" (61 cm). Yes, you'll need to cut and attach new thread a bit more frequently, but these shorter lengths tend to be less tangle prone, which saves you time and headaches.

Another counterintuitive tip: Keep track of which end you cut because when the time comes, you should thread the other end into your needle's eye. Thread is directionally spun—its fibers are all pulled in a certain direction in order to form the strand. Imagine a fish's scales: Your fingers could glide smoothly down them in one direction, whereas the other direction would offer a lot of resistance. Try gently pinching a strand of thread between your thumb and forefinger and gliding them toward your spool (pretty smooth, right?) and then away from it (much more friction). The goal is to have your thread gliding through the cloth so that you're working with, not against, the direction of the thread's fibers.

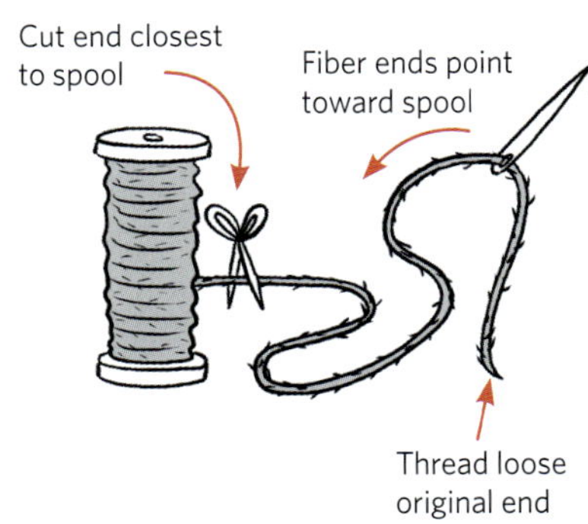


## Waxing

You can use unwaxed thread, straight off the spool, for sewing. But there are significant benefits to working with thread that you've coated in a bit of wax or other conditioner. By working a conditioner into your thread's fibers, you'll add strength and smoothness to that strand. This will help your thread glide more smoothly through the cloth, and it will help your seams stay strong and sturdy over time.

To add wax to a strand of thread, grasp the thread at its original end (the one that was loose before you cut the strand from the spool). Hold a cake of wax with your other hand, and lay the strand over the cake. Pull the thread across the top of the wax until you've covered its full length. Repeat by laying the strand across the wax and pulling it across again. Two or three times total should suffice.

Now there is a coat of wax on the outer surface of your thread strand. If you are near an iron, you'll want to melt the wax into your thread's fibers before you start sewing. Still pinching that original end (the one that was loose before you cut the thread), lay the strand between two layers of thin scrap fabric. Place a heated iron on top of the cloth and pull the thread through and out. Notice how your strand seems stiffer and straighter. This wiry quality will assist your sewing.

I like to prewax a set of threads all at once so I don't need to return to the ironing board every few minutes. I usually prepare a bundle of approximately 10 strands, which will last me through a couple of hours of sewing.

A coil of prewaxed threads stays tidy inside a notebook.

If you're not near an iron, you can sew with thread that has been waxed but not yet iron-set. However, because the wax is sitting loose on the surface, some of it will collect on your fabric when you pull it through during sewing. That's all right, although if you're using dark fabric you may see some wax residue near your stitching. It should melt away later with an iron, but it's still a bit of a waste of wax that ideally would be strengthening the thread over the long term.

## Needling

We usually say "thread your needle," but some people find it more accurate to describe the process as "needling your thread." Regardless of semantics, I find the following steps helpful:

**1.** Hold the thread strand's original end (the one that was loose before you cut the strand from the spool) in your nondominant hand, with only the tiniest bit of thread peeking out from between your fingers. The less that is showing, the better.

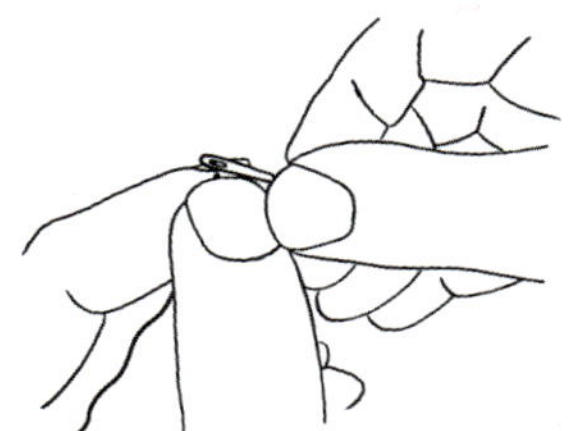

**2.** Use your dominant hand to lower the needle's eye onto the thread end. This is why you're "needling your thread"—because you're applying the eye to the thread rather than the other way around.

**3.** Pull the threaded end partway down, leaving a loose tail. You're ready to secure your thread to the fabric and begin stitching.

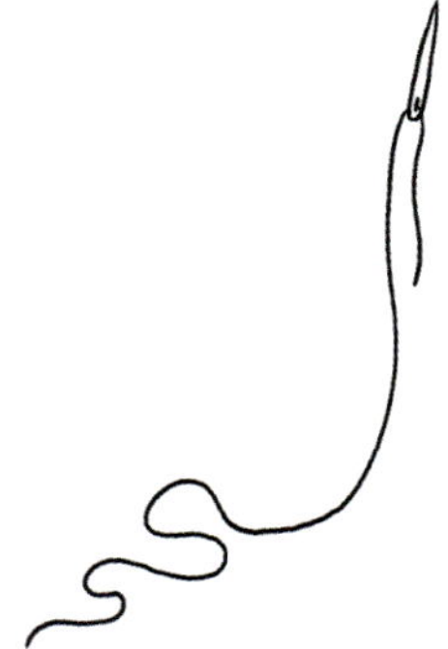

### Single- vs. Double-Stranded Thread

I recommend stitching with a single strand of thread rather than doubling the thread over. While a doubled thread might seem stronger, the true strength of your stitches depends on using fresh, strong thread and on using appropriate stitch techniques for the item you're sewing. Meanwhile, a single strand lends itself to tidier stitches. Bonus: Single-stranded sewing makes it very easy to pull out and redo a few stitches while you're sewing, because you can simply pull the needle off, unpick whatever needs undoing, rethread, and continue on your way.

## Anchoring Your Thread

Most people are taught to create little knots to secure the start and end of their stitching. And for many people, this is a good system. If you already have a confident, successful knotting practice, please continue with it and disregard what I'm about to say.

I always found knotting to be a fiddly experience, and I rarely felt that my knots were very secure. So I was delighted to learn a quick, low-stress, very strong, minimally bulky alternative to knots. It's also ergonomically comfortable and consistent with the general motions of sewing. I call this process "anchoring your thread," and I do it almost exclusively. The process is the same to begin and end your stitching. To secure your thread onto the cloth, you'll make a little pile of stitches. Here's how:

### ANCHORING ON

**1.** Take a single small stitch into your fabric wherever you'd like to place your anchor. You can do this on the right side or the wrong side of your work. The smaller the stitch, the more secure your anchor will be. Pull the thread through, leaving a tail that is at least ⅝" (1.6 cm) in length.

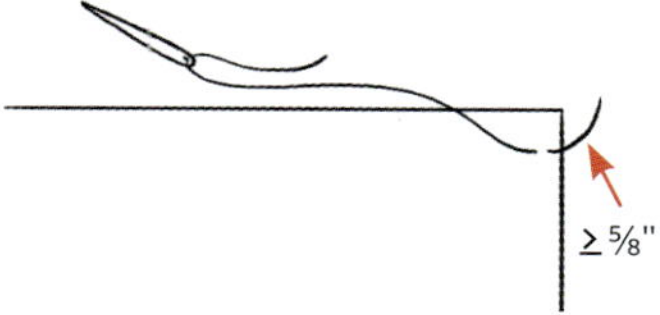


**2.** Repeat, placing another single, equally small stitch exactly on top of your first. As you pull the thread through, be careful not to lose the original tail from step 1. Pinch it with your fingers if needed.

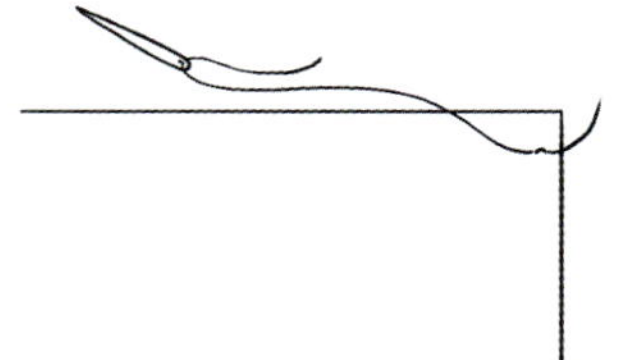

**3.** Repeat again, placing a third single, equally small stitch onto your "pile" of stitches. Give a little tug and determine whether you think the anchoring pile is secure. If desired, add another stitch. Now your thread is anchored on and you're ready to begin sewing.

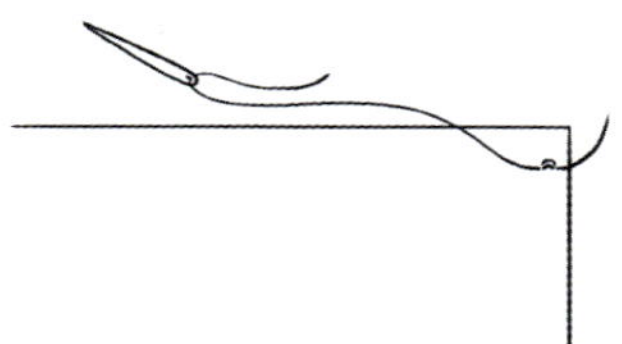

### Burrowing the Tails

When anchoring on and off, you're leaving tails that discourage the anchoring piles from coming undone. When you're working on an actual garment, there's nearly always somewhere to hide away the tails so that they're not visible from either side of the garment. I like to burrow my tails away by slipping the needle between layers of fabric—into a hem, for example, or between seam allowances—where they'll never show.

Alternatively, instead of sliding your thread between layers, you can stitch ⅝" (1.6 cm) of running stitches into your seam allowance before you anchor on or after you anchor off. This line of running stitches will keep the tail orderly, even if there isn't a convenient place to burrow it completely out of sight.

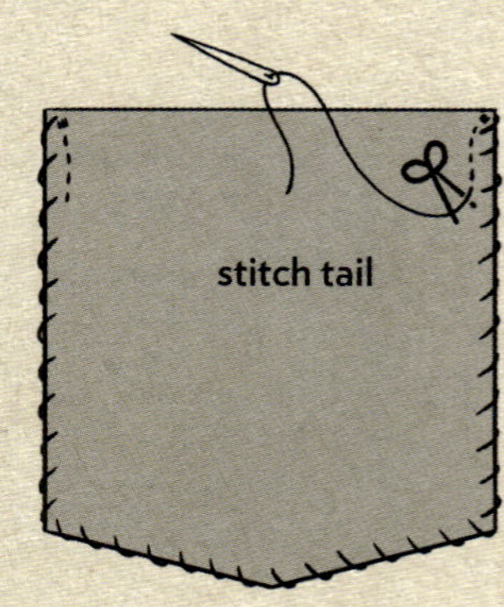

#### ANCHORING OFF

At the end of your line of stitching, or when you have only about a hand's width of thread left on your needle, it's time to anchor off. The process is the same as anchoring on, but in reverse order. You'll make a pile of three-ish tiny stitches, then trim, leaving a ⅝" (1.6 cm) tail.

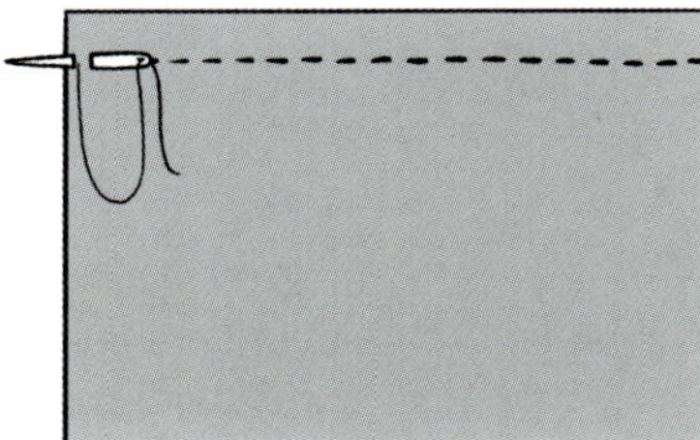

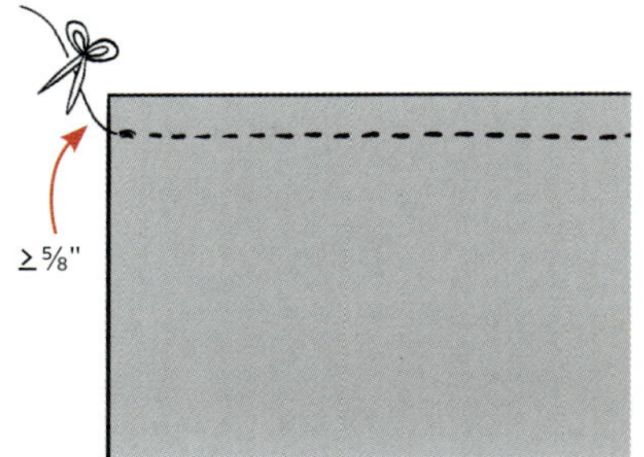


## Using a Thimble

It is possible to hand-sew plenty of beautiful garments without ever touching a thimble. However, the benefits of using a thimble are many, so I'd recommend befriending one as soon as possible. With practice you'll be able to stitch more quickly and precisely, for longer periods of time and through thicker fabrics, with greater comfort and confidence.

There are lots of thimble styles available today and lots of ways to use them. Depending on the thimble you decide to use, you may want to seek online videos for technical guidance instead of my directions below.

My favorite thimbles are open-topped metal tailor's thimbles. They're worn on the middle finger and generally feature dimples along the side and a ridge at the base. They have an opening at the fingertip so that a little bit of the middle finger's tip extends out. This allows for greater sensitivity when handling the fabric, and it also provides breathability during long sewing sessions.

### Thimble Size

Not all thimbles fit all fingers. Try on a few before determining which one is right for you. If you live near a large city with a good garment district, or if you happen to have a really great local sewing shop, you may be able to find a store that carries a range of thimble sizes you can try on. Alternatively, order several sizes from an online retailer and then return the poor-fitting options. There are also some sizing charts available online for certain thimble brands, and you might develop an educated guess by consulting these charts. Or try to find a local antique shop with thimbles and try them on for size.

### THIMBLING 101

If you're using a caplike thimble, whether closed- or open-topped, I'd recommend wearing it on your middle finger. For these thimbles, you'll know it's a good fit if the thimble is unrestrictive but stays on your finger when you dangle and wave your hand upside down. For open-topped thimbles, a tiny bit of your fingertip should extend beyond the opening when viewed from the side. Assuming your caplike thimble has dimples on the sides (which is a feature I specifically seek out), here's the technique I like to use:

1. Hold the needle between your dominant hand's thumb and forefinger. You can tension the thread between the same hand's ring and pinky fingers. Curl your thimbled middle finger down so that the eye of the needle is making contact with one of the thimble's dimples. This will probably fall roughly on the area of the thimble that is protecting the side of your fingernail. Now your needle is being controlled by three fingers: thumb, forefinger, and thimbled middle finger.

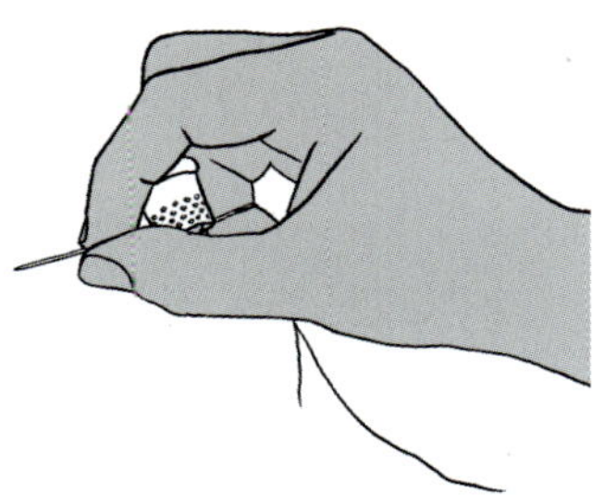

2. Hold the fabric in your nondominant hand. Use your dominant hand to take a stitch into the fabric. Typically you'll take a complete stitch, meaning the needle's tip can be inserted both down and up again, rather than just down to the fabric's backside. The nondominant hand can help bend the fabric to achieve this.

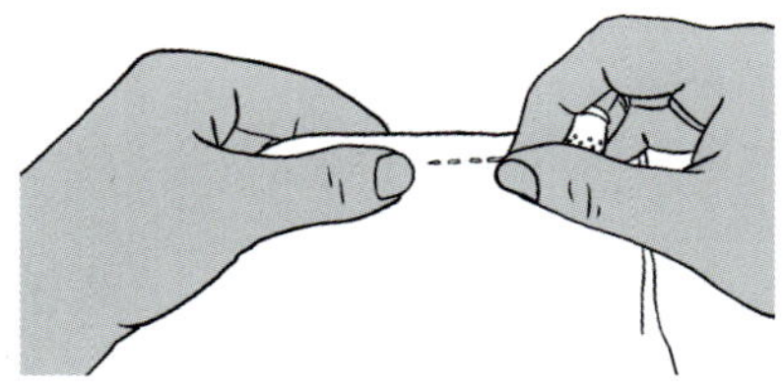

3. Release the needle with thumb and forefinger while continuing to make contact with your thimbled middle finger. Release the thread from your ring and pinky fingers, too. Use the thimble to push the base of the needle through the fabric.

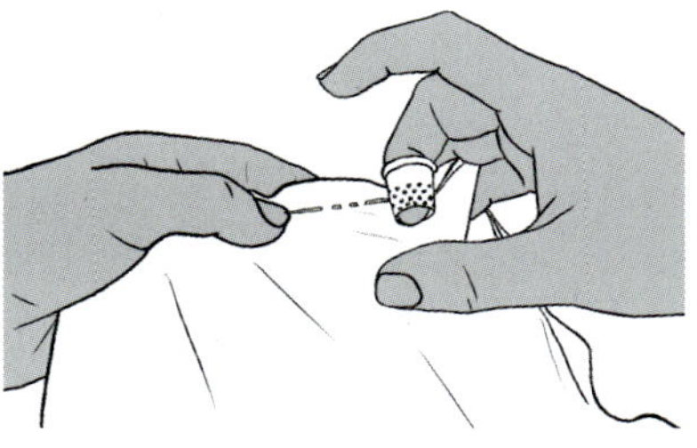

4. Catch the needle with thumb and forefinger and use them to pull the needle all the way out of the fabric. Meanwhile, you may like to catch and tension the thread again between your ring and pinky fingers.

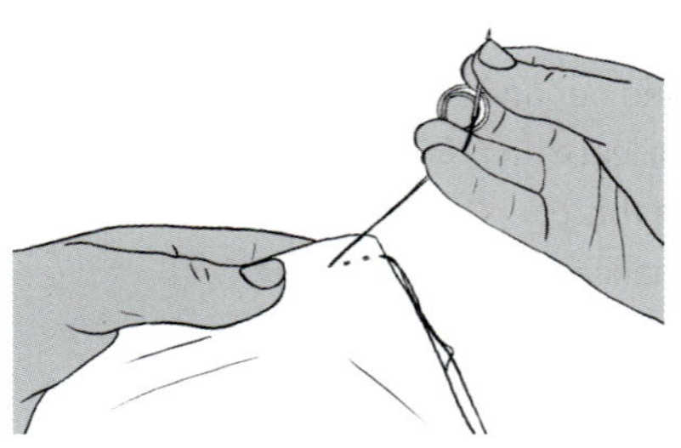

5. Pull the thread until your stitch lies smooth and flat against the fabric.

6. Repeat.

# The Stitches

Over the past few tens of thousands of years, humans have devised many different hand stitches. You only need to know a few, though, in order to construct strong, attractive garments. At the start of each project in this book, I've listed my stitch suggestions. However, you're welcome to trade stitches in and out and to invent new ones of your own. Experimentation is such a great way to learn and discover new things. And you don't need to learn all of the stitches in this chapter, or even all of the stitches I recommend for each project. You can make lots of gorgeous clothes using only one or two stitches. It's all up to you.

## A Stitch by Any Other Name

In this section I'll share some of my favorite stitches, the ones I reach for most often when sewing clothes. Please know that there is very little standardization of stitch names in the sewing world, so you may know these stitches by other names. Call them whatever you'd like—the important thing is to know the mechanics of the ones that you intend to use and to be intentional about choosing. My goal is to help you develop an intuitive, deep knowledge of each stitch so that eventually you feel confident choosing your own stitches. There's lots of creativity to be enjoyed in selecting the stitches you'll use in each area of your garment.

## Stitch Size and Spacing

How long should your stitches be? How far apart? The answers to these questions depend entirely on your circumstances, goals, and preferences. If you're working with thicker fabric, you'll naturally find that your stitches need to be somewhat longer. Thin fabrics enable and benefit from tinier stitches. If you're aiming for an extra-strong line of stitching, you'll want to use smaller stitches, as they are stronger than long ones. However, if you're placing basting stitches that will be removed later, you can probably get away with huge stitches. (Curved lines of basting may require slightly smaller stitches than long, straight areas so that you can hold things precisely.)

Aesthetics also matter—how do you want your line of stitching to look?

Stitch size and spacing should and will vary. But if you're seeking a bit of guidance, most of my stitches are roughly ⅛" or 3⁄16" (3 mm or 5 mm) long. In an area that needs to be especially strong, I might make stitches that are closer to 1⁄16" (about 2 mm) in length. In curved areas of basting, I often make stitches that are about ¼" (6 mm) long. And along straight areas of basting, my stitches might be 1" (2.5 cm) or longer.

## Do a Swatch Test

When planning the stitches you'll use for a project, I highly recommend making little test swatches of those stitches in your intended garment fabric, using the particular thread and needle you plan to use. This will allow you to test-drive your thread and needle before diving into the project. Swatching also allows you to play around with stitch choices, finishing techniques, stitch size and spacing, and so on, without spending much time or fabric. You can see how stitches will look, but you can also test more functional properties: how much stretch your stitching might allow, how soft or stiff your seam technique might be, how durable your hem will be, and more.

A bonus of creating these test swatches: If you pin them into a notebook or collect them in a tin or box, you can build a technique library over time. This library will be an invaluable resource the next time you're seeking ideas or insight about how to handle an upcoming project.

## Running Stitch

This is the first stitch most of us learn, and it's a good one. Featuring the simple "over, under, over, under" maneuver, running stitch allows you to cover a lot of ground quickly, because you can load up your needle with multiple stitches before pulling through. It looks basically identical on front and back, and it's easily removable. It also *looks* like hand sewing, which is worth celebrating—machines can't quite replicate this stitch, so it's a sure sign of handwork.

However, running stitch has basically no stretch potential, which means it's usually not a great option for stretchy fabrics. Running stitch also snaps easily under strain, so even on woven fabrics, it isn't necessarily the best choice for a seam that will be subjected to significant tension.

Running stitch is great for basting because it's quick to perform and easy to pull out later. You can use it to prepare gathers. It's perfect for staystitching (temporary stitching meant to prevent stretching and distortion of a raw edge until permanent edge finishes are complete). Running stitch is also good for long seams that won't come under much strain. For example, you might use running stitch for the side seams of a loose-fitting long skirt.

FRONT VIEW

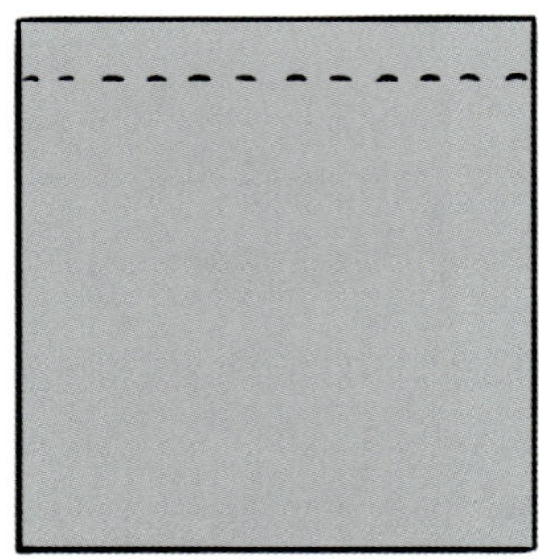

BACK VIEW

Here is a cross-section view, in which you can see why the stitch doesn't have much stretch potential. It's basically a slightly wavy line of thread, so if you were to pinch that thread at both ends and pull apart, you'd quickly run out of thread, and it would snap.

### HOW TO DO IT

1. To take a single running stitch, dip the needle's tip down and then up through the fabric, taking a single "bite." Pull through until the thread lies smooth against the fabric.

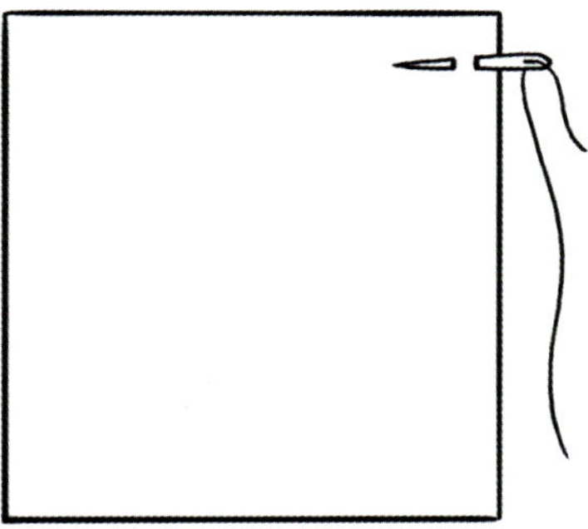

2. To take several running stitches, dip the needle's tip down, then up, then down, then up, and so on, until you've loaded your needle with as many stitches as you can fit. Pull through until the thread lies smooth against the fabric. You may need to smooth the fabric to eliminate any puckers.

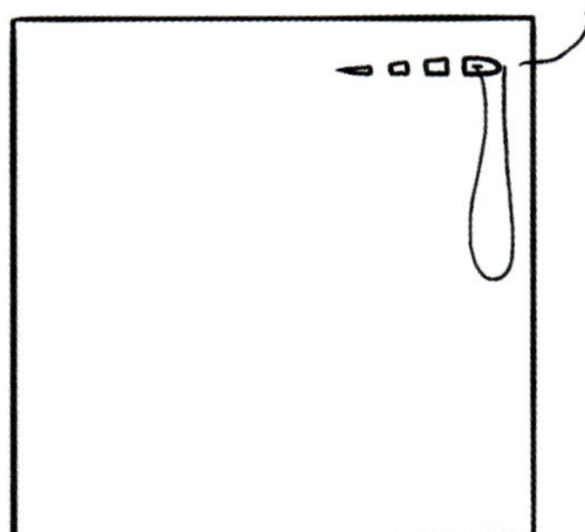

3. Repeat across the fabric.

## What Is Basting?

Basting is temporary stitching used to hold elements together. You might use basting so that you don't have a million pins getting in your way, or you might use it to hold things in alignment (like holding a pocket in place until it's secured with permanent stitches, or testing a hem before committing to a final garment length). Lines of basting can also help you set up gathers or staystitch a raw edge that is vulnerable to distortion. Thread is a gentle way of holding elements together, as it is unlikely to damage delicate fabrics. Unlike pins, basting also enables you to squish your project into a travel bag without worrying about pins falling out or pricking you during transport.

There's no single "basting stitch." Most of my basting consists of long running stitches, which vary in length and spacing based on my goals for that area. But you can just as easily use whipstitch or any other stitch that seems well suited to your purpose. Just remember that you may need to remove these stitches later, so you'll want to choose stitches that are quick to unpick. Usually basting stitches are removed by the end of the project, but some can be left hidden inside the garment if you'd like. Sometimes I leave these lines of basting in my seam allowances—they can be fun secret reminders of the garment's construction history.

## Even Backstitch

Even backstitch is one of the most useful, important stitches for hand-sewing clothing. It is very strong and sturdy, and it has great stretch potential. This stitch looks a lot like a machine's straight stitch from the outside, and that's no accident—the sewing machine's straight stitch was developed to imitate backstitch. On the underside, backstitch tends to look a bit gangly, so I usually use back-stitch in areas where the underside won't show.

Unlike running stitch, backstitch must be performed one stitch at a time, so it's a slower technique. It's also slower to unpick if you need to remove stitches later. That's usually a benefit, because it means that if your thread breaks someday, the seam will resist coming fully undone, buying you a bit more time to mend it.

Even backstitch is a great choice on nearly any seam. Because of its strength and stretch, it's perfect for hardworking areas such as shoulder seams or slim-fitting side seams, as well as for stretchy garments such as leggings and bathing suits. When in doubt, give it a try. In fact, if you're working with a sewing pattern and its instructions are meant for machine sewists, you can easily substitute even backstitch for pretty much all of the steps in which straight stitch was recommended.

In the cross-section view below, you can see why the stitch has so much strength and stretch potential. Each stitch creates a loop, so the strand of thread travels across your fabric as if on a wild roller-coaster ride. If you imagine pinching the thread at both ends and pulling it apart, you can understand that there's a lot of extra thread built into the stitch line through all of those loops. There is a lot of thread to give before the thread will snap. This is nearly always enough to accommodate even the stretchiest fabrics and even the most strained garment areas.

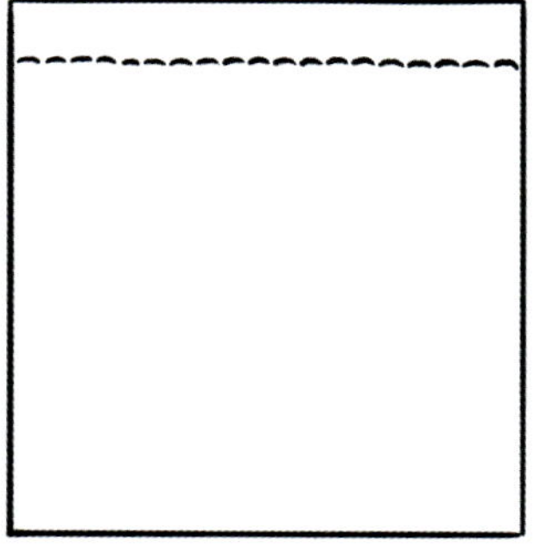

FRONT VIEW

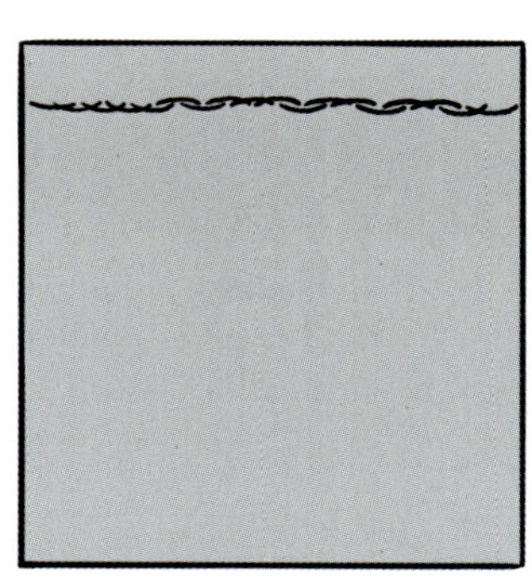

BACK VIEW

CROSS-SECTION VIEW

#### HOW TO DO IT

**1.** Anchor your thread where you intend to sew. Notice where your thread has just emerged from the cloth—let's call this point A. Now insert the needle tip one stitch length before point A, and push the needle tip out one stitch length after point A.

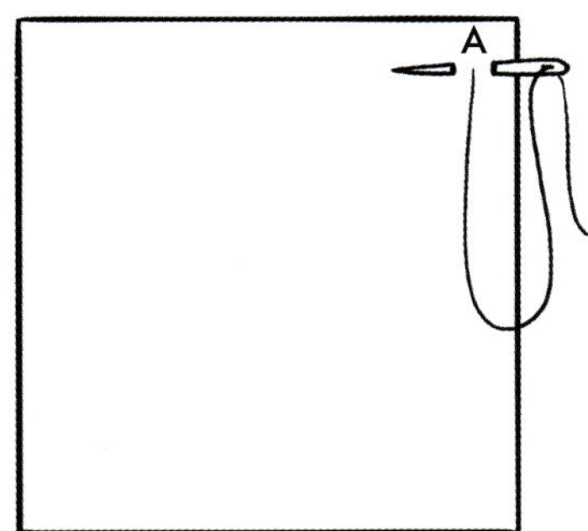


**2.** Pull through. You've just completed a single stitch.

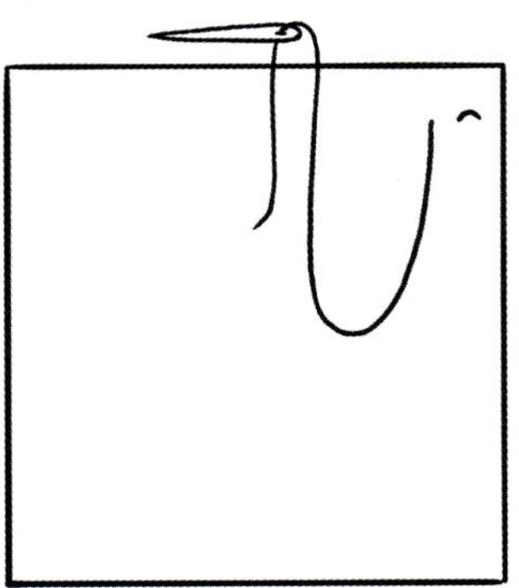

**3.** Repeat steps 1 and 2 for each backstitch. Each time you take a "bite" with the needle, you'll be taking one step backward and then jumping two forward. Notice that these "bites" are therefore double the length of your finished stitches, meaning that you can achieve smaller stitches on thicker fabrics.

## A Note for Lefties

If you are left-handed, you are doubtless already an expert at navigating the right-handed world. I myself am a lefty, but I transposed the diagrams in this book so that they look right-handed, since righties are the majority and they are less accustomed to flipping visuals for their own handedness.

As a lefty, sewing should be no harder for you. Just make sure you have a great pair of left-handed sewing shears, as it will be much harder and less comfortable for you to use righty scissors.

Perhaps you already automatically transpose diagrams to lefty orientation. In case you need some tips, you can:

- Hold a visual up to a mirror and follow that flipped visual
- Take a photo with a phone or camera and flip the image horizontally

The most "handed" area of this book is the section on stitch instructions from this chapter. Once you move into the project chapters, the diagrams indicate how to manipulate garment panels more than how to wield your hands.

For more tips on sewing as a lefty, you can check out Sally Cowan's *Left-Handed Sewing*. Published in 1984, it's still a great little reference, totally tailored to the southpaws among us.

## Spaced Backstitch

Spaced backstitch is a visually subtle stitch, making it a perfect choice for topstitching (stitching meant to be seen on the outside of the garment) and other areas where you might like to apply stitches more "quietly." It looks like a quiet line of little dots. Spaced backstitch is formed the same way as even backstitch, except that you'll take smaller stitches and space them farther apart. The exact size and spacing is up to you.

Spaced backstitch is somewhat strong and stretchy (though not nearly as strong or stretchy as even backstitch). It looks gangly on the backside, so it's another stitch I'd apply to areas that won't be visible on both sides.

I like to use this stitch to topstitch along necklines and cuffs, and to topstitch seam allowances down without creating too much visual noise. Some people also like to create lapped seams (seams made with overlapping pieces of fabric) that use spaced backstitch to hold everything together, which can be another nice application of this stitch. If you're constructing a basic seam in which the stitches won't be visible from the outside, you'll probably want to opt for even backstitch. But if the aesthetics of the stitch line will show on the exterior, you might want to consider spaced backstitch for the job.

Here is a cross-section view, in which you can see the thread's trajectory through the fabric. Each stitch forms a loop, but these loops have calm spaces between them, so there's somewhat less stretch potential built into the stitch line than with even backstitch. If you imagine pinching the thread at both ends and pulling it apart, you can understand that there is some thread built into the stitch line because of the loops, but you'd eventually run out of stretch potential on very stretchy fabrics. Therefore, it's best suited for nonstretchy or somewhat stretchy—rather than extremely stretchy—contexts.

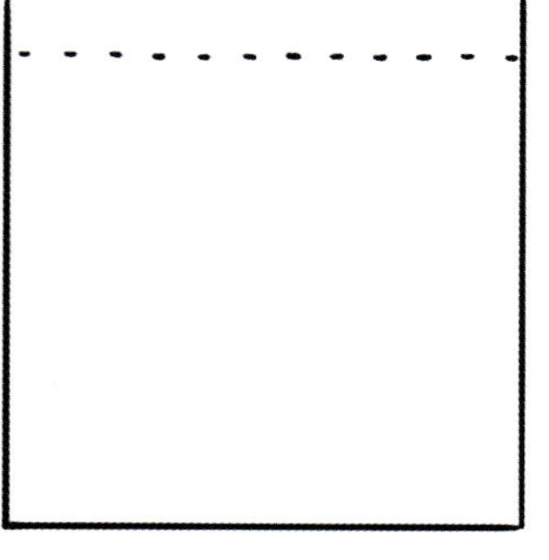

FRONT VIEW

BACK VIEW

CROSS-SECTION VIEW

**HOW TO DO IT**

**1.** Anchor your thread where you intend to sew. Notice where your thread has just emerged from the cloth—let's call this point A. Now insert the needle tip a tiny distance before point A, and push the needle tip out a longer distance after point A.

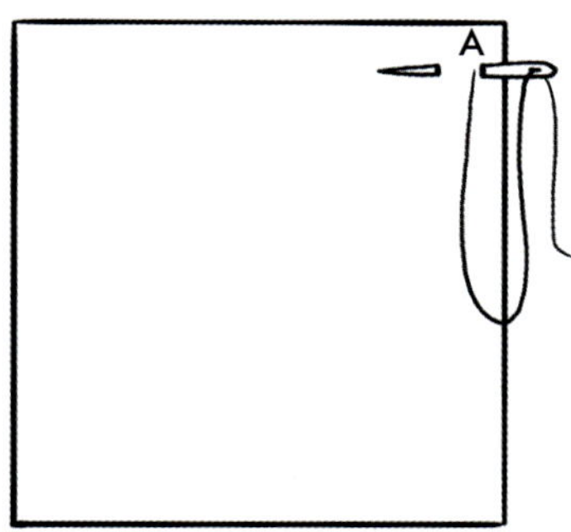


**2.** Pull through. You've just completed a single stitch.

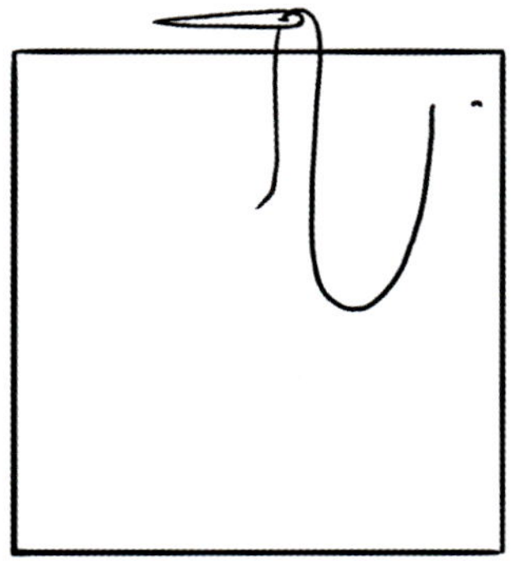

**3.** Repeat steps 1 and 2 for each backstitch. Each time you take a "bite" with the needle, you'll be taking one tiny step backward (determining the visible stitch length) and then shooting forward (determining the spacing between stitches).

## Combination Stitch

Combination stitch borrows its qualities from running stitch and even backstitch—it's somewhat fast to produce, but it's also somewhat strong and a little bit stretchy. To make it, you'll insert your needle a stitch length before the thread, and then load up your needle with several running stitches. In this way, you'll create a line of running stitches punctuated by the occasional backstitch.

From above combination stitch looks sort of syncopated, and from beneath it looks a lot like running stitch. It's unlikely that you'd choose this stitch for its looks, so it's best employed on internal seams where you'd like to achieve some strength and some speed. I wouldn't try it on seams that will come under lots of strain, but the long vertical seams of easy-fitting woven garments, for example, might be appropriate. Side seams and sleeve inseams are good candidates, as long as the torsos and sleeves in question are easy-fitting.

Here is a cross-section view, in which you can see the thread's trajectory through the fabric. The backstitches appear as little loops in the thread, while the running stitches create subtle waves. The loops build a bit of extra thread into the stitch line so that if the thread were tugged at both ends, there would be some give. However, stretchy fabrics would quickly overstrain the thread—even with those occasional loops—so combination stitch is probably best suited to areas where it won't come under too much stretch or strain.

**FRONT VIEW,** showing the stitch with two running stitches for every backstitch

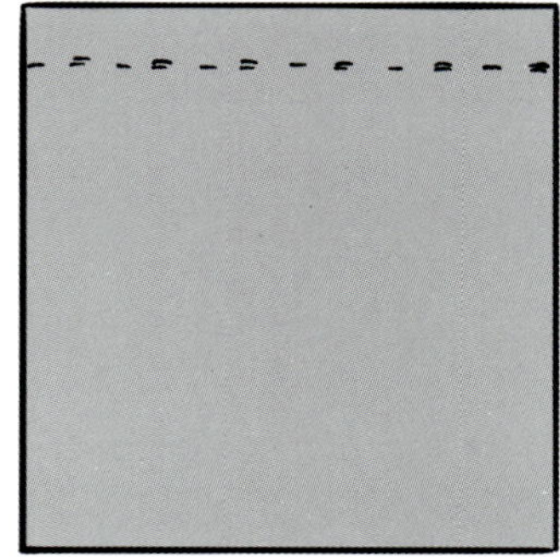

**BACK VIEW**

**CROSS-SECTION VIEW**

## Combination Stitch, continued

### HOW TO DO IT

**1.** Anchor your thread where you intend to sew. Notice where your thread has just emerged from the cloth—let's call this point A. Now insert the needle tip one stitch length before point A, and push the needle tip out at point A. Do not pull thread through.

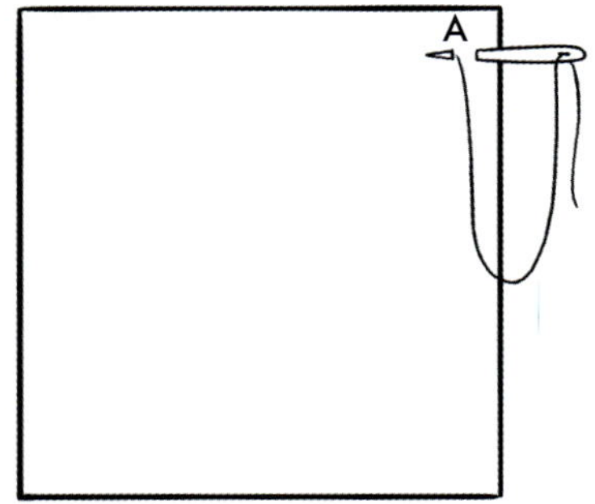


**2.** Take several running stitches (over, under, over, under, etc.) on your needle, accumulating "bites" in addition to the one you already created in step 1.

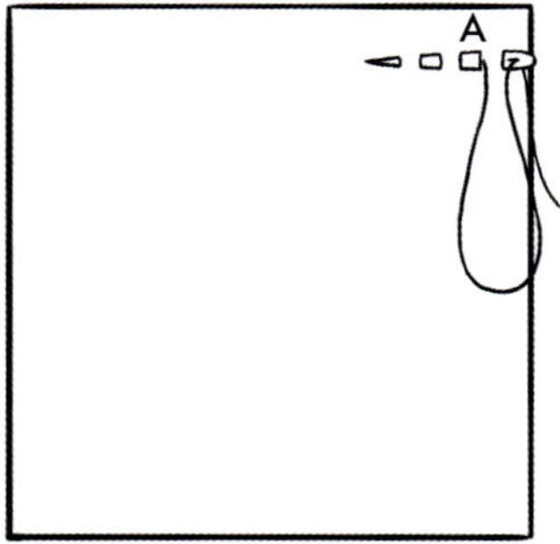


**3.** Pull through. You've just completed a backstitch and several running stitches.

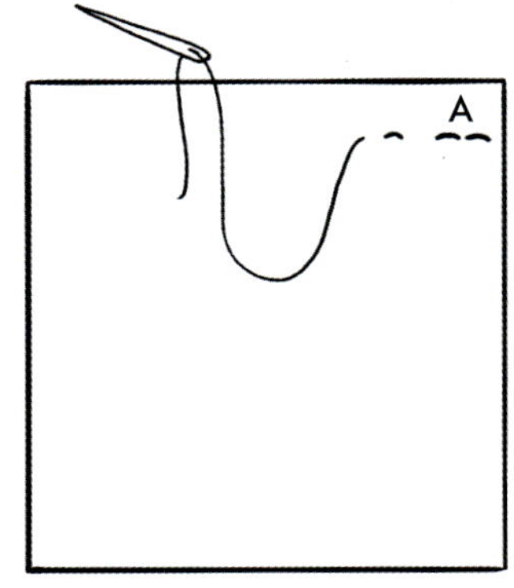


**4.** Repeat steps 1 through 3 as you travel across the fabric. You can experiment with the exact number of running stitches you take in step 2. This will affect the ratio of backstitch-like properties vs. running stitch-like properties that you achieve. In other words, the more running stitches you take after each backstitch, the more your stitch line will behave like running stitch. The fewer running stitches you take after each backstitch, the more your stitch line will behave like backstitch.

## Whipstitch

This is a stitch I use all the time. Whipstitch creates a line of diagonal stitches that travel across your fabric. It's especially useful for affixing layers to each other, as for a patch, hem, felled seam, and so on. Whipstitch makes a zigzag trajectory, offering lots of stretch potential. I find it to be a simple, comfortable stitch to produce.

When in doubt, I consider whipstitch for the job. The only reason I might shy away is if I'm aiming for something a little subtler in appearance (in which case I might opt instead for hemstitch or fell stitch). The working side of whipstitch creates a strong set of diagonals, while the other side looks like a set of vertical bars. You can play around with spacing and sizing of the stitches, but whipstitch will always have some visual element. And if you try to reduce the visual impact of whipstitch by making the stitches too shallow, for instance, you'll be reducing some of the stretch potential, which might be a concern, depending on the fabric and context of your stitch line.

FRONT (WORKING SIDE) VIEW

BACK VIEW

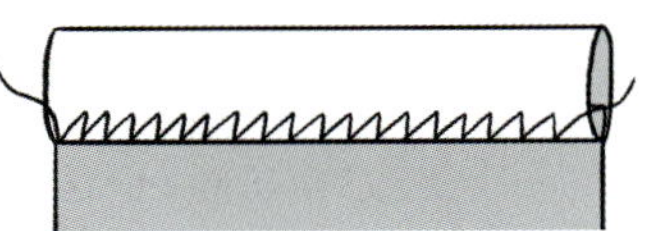

Here is an X-ray view from the working side, in which you can see the thread's zigzag trajectory through the fabric. This zigzagging builds in lots of stretch potential, especially if you make relatively tall, closely spaced stitches so that the zigzags are pronounced and frequent.

## HOW TO DO IT

These steps assume that you're joining an edge to another layer (as when joining hem allowance to the body of a garment, or when joining a patch pocket to a garment). However, know that the stitch can be produced the same way on a single layer of fabric.

**1.** Anchor your thread along the edge you're joining.

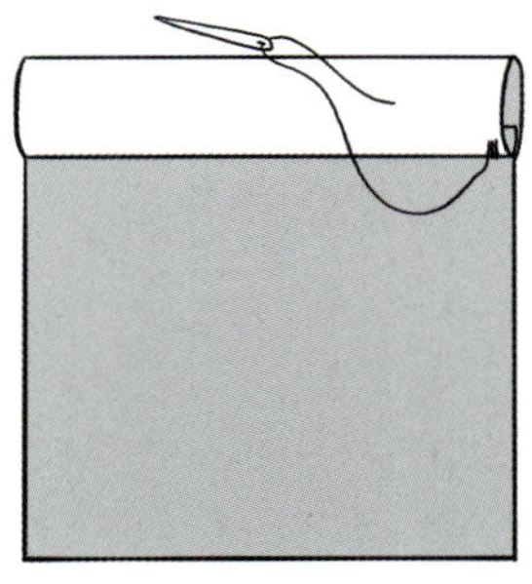

**2.** Insert the needle into the underlayer only, very close to the folded edge. Then, holding the needle perpendicular to the edge, push the needle tip through all layers so that it emerges up on the edge, directly above where the needle entered the fabric.

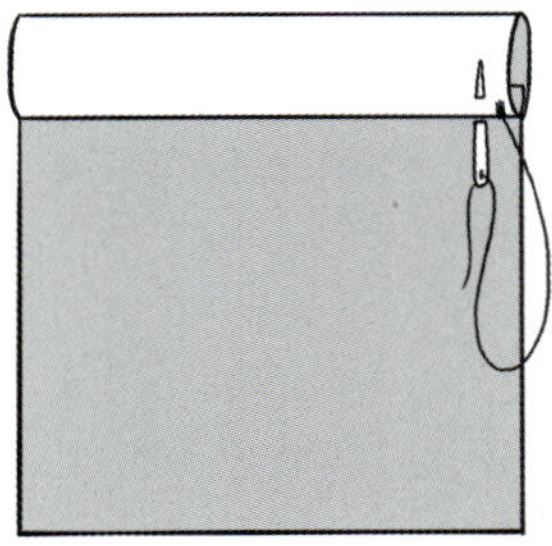

**3.** Pull through until the thread lies smooth against the fabric.

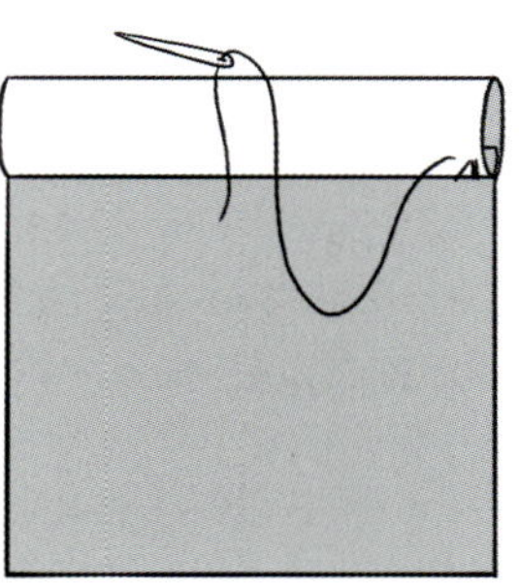

**4.** Advance along the edge (you can experiment with what spacing you prefer to determine the distance between stitches). Repeat steps 2 and 3 to produce more whipstitches, advancing along the edge between each one.

## Hemstitch

Hemstitch is a very close cousin to the whipstitch. It, too, produces a line of diagonal stitches that travel across your fabric, and it can be used in similar contexts: affixing layers to each other as for a patch, hem, or felled seam. The real difference between hemstitch and whipstitch is that hemstitches are created with the needle held at an angle, so that the row of diagonals produces a narrower band of zigzagging thread. These hemstitches still have some zigzag, so they offer some amount of stretch potential, but they're less useful on very stretchy fabrics. On the other hand, they're more visually subtle, making them a great choice for areas where you want the stitching to be less noticeable.

I use hemstitch mainly on woven fabrics, as they usually require less stretchiness. As the name suggests, this stitch is perfect for hems, but it is also a good choice for patches, felled seams, and other areas where you're joining an edge to a layer below. Both sides of hemstitch—top and bottom—look like a subtle line of diagonals. You can play around with the size and spacing of your stitches. Know that the shallower your diagonals, and the farther apart your stitches are spaced, the less stretch potential the thread will have.

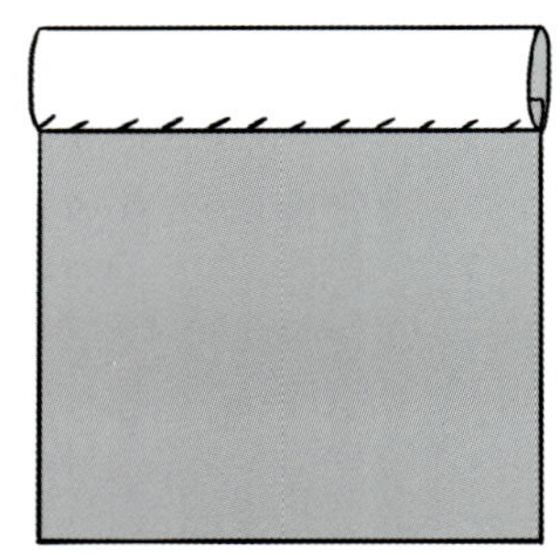

FRONT (WORKING SIDE) VIEW

BACK VIEW

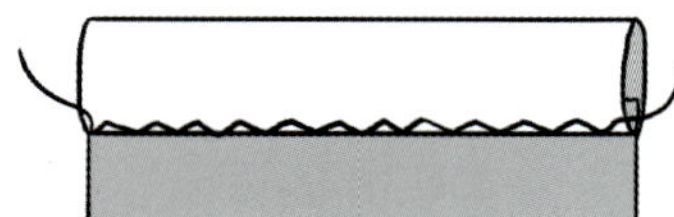

Here is an X-ray view from the working side, in which you can see the thread's shallow zigzag trajectory through the fabric. This zigzagging builds in some stretch potential.

### HOW TO DO IT

These steps assume that you're joining an edge to another layer (as when joining hem allowance to the body of a garment, or when joining a patch pocket to a garment). However, know that the stitch can be produced the same way on a single layer of fabric.

1. Anchor your thread along the edge you're joining.

2. Advance a short distance along the edge and insert your needle into the underlayer only, very close to the folded edge. Then hold the needle at an angle to the edge so that it points toward where you're advancing, and push the needle tip through all layers so that it emerges up on the edge.

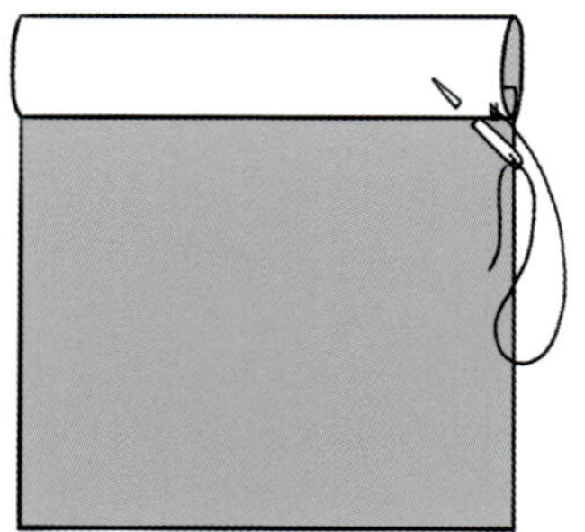

3. Pull through until the thread lies smooth against the fabric.

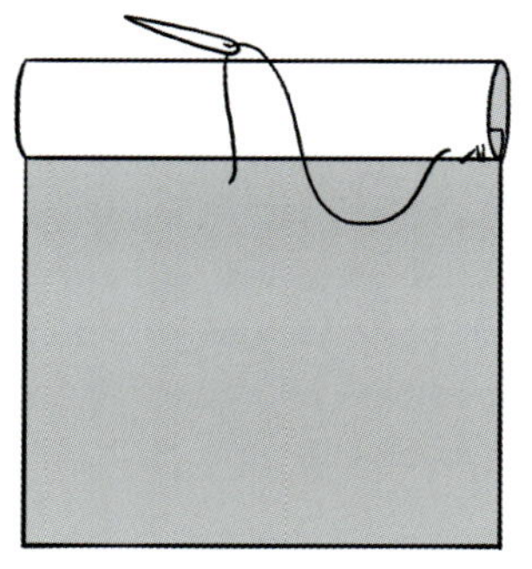

4. Repeat steps 2 and 3 to produce more hemstitches.

## Fell Stitch

Fell stitch is another close cousin to whipstitch and hemstitch. In fact, to me, fell stitch is really the same stitch as whipstitch, except that the vertical bars show on your working side, and the diagonal threads show on the backside of your work. If you make small stitches, this can be a very subtle stitch—nearly invisible in some cases—making it a great option for areas where you'd like to join pieces of fabric from the outside without calling attention to your stitches. Alternatively, if you make taller stitches, so that the zigzag trajectory is more pronounced, you'll create a line of thread with lots of stretch potential. I find fell stitch to be a very useful option, and I suspect that you will, too.

Like whipstitch, fell stitch is a great choice for affixing layers to each other, as for a patch, hem, or felled seam. The working side looks like a set of short or medium-height vertical bars passing along the fabric. The other side shows a line of diagonal threads.

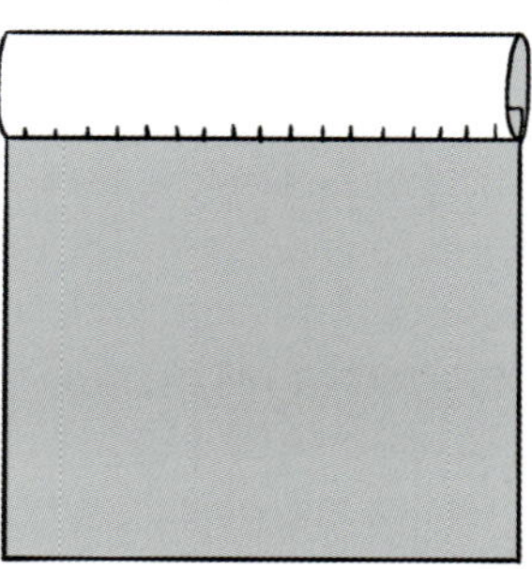

FRONT (WORKING SIDE) VIEW

BACK VIEW

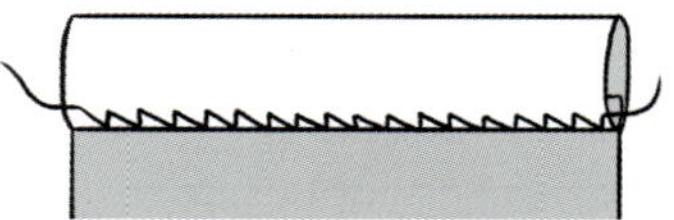

Here is an X-ray view from the working side, in which you can see the thread's zigzag trajectory through the fabric. This zigzagging can build in lots of stretch potential, especially if you make relatively tall, closely spaced stitches so that the zigzags are pronounced and frequent.

### HOW TO DO IT

These steps assume that you're joining an edge to another layer (as when joining one panel to another from the outside of the garment). However, know that the stitch can be produced the same way on a single layer of fabric.

1. Anchor your thread along the edge you're joining.

## Fell Stitch, continued

**2.** Insert your needle into the underlayer only, directly below where your thread emerged.

**3.** Angle the needle along the edge so that the tip points toward the direction in which you're advancing. Push the needle tip through all layers so that it emerges up onto the edge, advancing somewhat ahead along the edge. (The distance between the spot where the thread emerges and the edge is what will determine how invisible vs. how stretchy your fell stitch will be.)

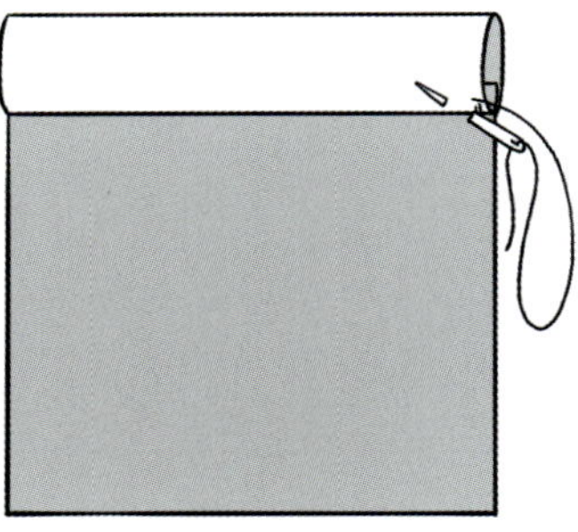

**4.** Pull through until the thread lies smooth against the fabric.

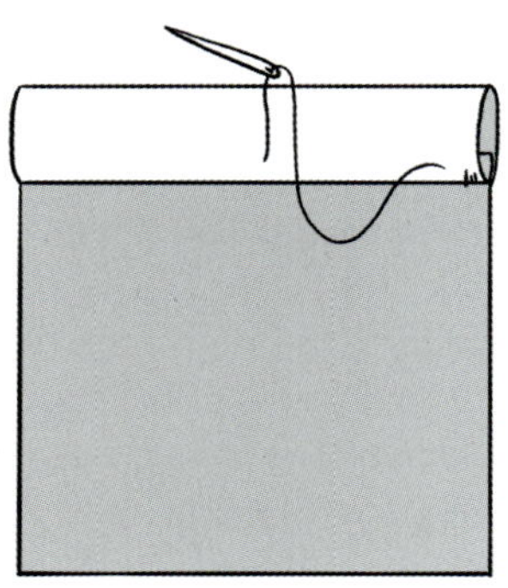

**5.** Repeat steps 2 through 4 to produce more fell stitches.

## Diagonal Backstitch

This is a stitch I devised to solve a problem. Specifically, when sewing stretchy knit garments, I often like to include a few mantua-maker's seams, which use one line of stitching to completely self-enclose the seam allowances. (See page 180 for more about mantua-maker's seams.) I'd been stitching these mantua-maker's seams using hemstitch, but I became dissatisfied with the lack of stretch that resulted, and I found that there was sometimes more "grin-through" (visible thread bars along the seamline when a garment is worn) than I liked. So I came up with diagonal backstitch as a way to build lots of stretch into the stitch line while keeping the stitches nice and shallow against the seamline. (I'm sure other humans have used this stitch before—but it was a new discovery for me.)

To date, the only context in which I've used diagonal backstitch is when constructing mantua-maker's seams, but in theory you could use it for other applications. Like whipstitch, hemstitch, and fell stitch, diagonal backstitch is good at joining a folded edge to a layer beneath it. So depending on the desired appearance, one might consider using it to apply a patch or sew a seam from the outside, or in some other context.

Visually, diagonal backstitch looks like a tidy line of diagonal threads on the working side. In fact, on the working side it looks pretty similar to whipstitch, except that these diagonals tend to be smaller and shorter. On the other side diagonal backstitch looks like a gangly set of long, diagonal threads. So the backside of the work is probably best used only on the interiors of garments, but the working side could be visible if desired.

FRONT VIEW

BACK VIEW

Here is a cross-section view, in which you can see why the stitch has good stretch potential. From this angle it resembles even backstitch, in which each stitch creates a loop so that the strand of thread travels across your fabric as if on a wild roller-coaster ride. If you imagine pinching the thread at both ends and pulling it apart, you can understand that there's a lot of extra thread built into the stitch line through all of those loops.

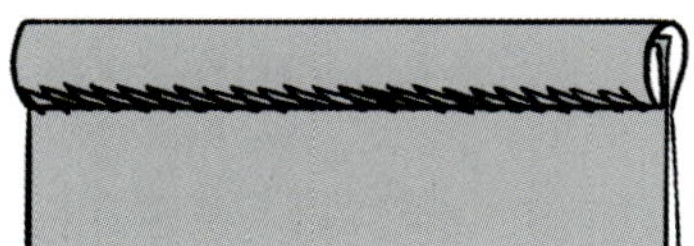

Here is an X-ray view from the working side, in which you can see the thread's strongly slanted zigzag trajectory through the fabric. Like the looping motion described above, this zigzagging contributes stretch potential. Because the stitches are so shallow (slanty), though, they create a seam with reduced grin-through.

### HOW TO DO IT

**1.** Anchor your thread along the edge you're joining.

**2.** Notice where your thread has just emerged from the cloth—let's call this point A. Now insert the needle tip into the underlayer only (exactly next to the edge), one stitch length *before* point A.

**3.** Angle the needle along the edge so that the tip points toward the direction in which you're advancing. Push the needle tip up through all layers onto the edge, emerging one stitch length *after* point A. For minimal grin-through, the needle should emerge very close to the edge.

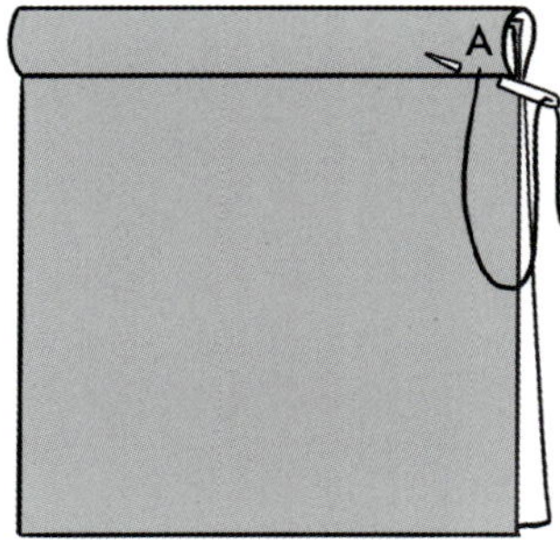


**4.** Pull through. You've just completed a single stitch.

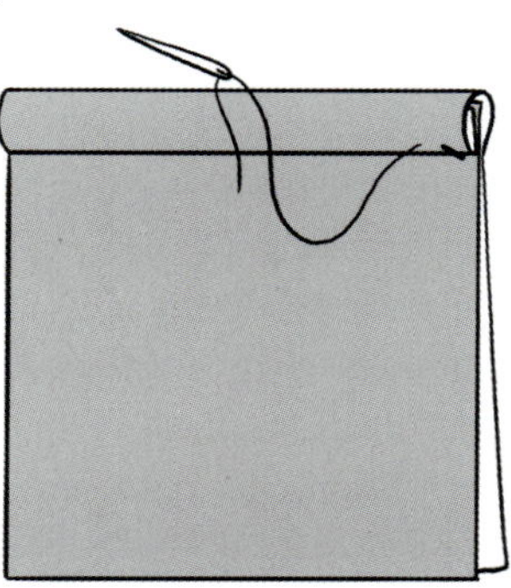

**5.** Repeat steps 2 through 4 for each diagonal backstitch. Each time you take a "bite" with the needle, you'll be taking one step backward and then jumping two forward—the same as with regular even backstitch. However, unlike even backstitch, you're also building a slight slant into your stitches so they can straddle the edge that you're joining.

## Overcasting

When machine-sewing a garment, there are a couple of popular ways to secure raw seam allowance edges using thread. A sewist can use zigzag stitch to "thread-bind" these raw edges so they will not unravel over time. Alternatively, one can use a serger/overlock machine, which produces a similar lattice of threads along a trimmed edge. Unlike fabric bindings, French seam finishes, and other cloth-based methods of finishing a seam, these thread-binding options allow seam allowances to remain malleable and minimally bulky—they're only as thick as the fabric panels being joined, plus a bit of thread.

In hand sewing, we have a great thread-binding option, too: overcasting. In this stitch, the thread spirals around the fabric edge(s), containing the raw edges with a tidy line of diagonals. Overcasting produces an even softer, more malleable, less bulky finish than machine-sewn equivalents. Another plus: Similar to running stitch, overcasting lets you load up your needle with several stitches at once, making it a speedy stitch to produce—it won't slow down your progress much as you're working through a garment project.

Overcasting is perfectly suited to finishing raw seam allowances inside a garment, so that is the context in which I use it. One might also experiment with overcasting as a decorative edge stitch that would be visible on the outside—perhaps you could overcast a collar edge in which the seam allowances were already self-enclosed, for example. If you overcast in both directions, you might even achieve a cross-stitch-like appearance. Or if you kept the thread snug, you could produce a scalloped look.

Overcasting creates a spiraling, zigzagging trajectory of thread, offering a good amount of stretch potential. If stretch is a priority for your project, try to take stitches deeper into the fabric so that the zigzagging trajectory is enhanced.

Notice that the stitch looks the same on front and back.

Overcasting is used along a fabric edge that can contain one or more layers held together. In the illustrated example below, both seam allowance layers are held together with overcasting. However, it can be used separately along each seam allowance edge if desired, so that the allowances can be pressed in opposite directions later.

FRONT VIEW

BACK VIEW

Here is an X-ray view, in which you can see the thread's zigzag trajectory through the fabric. This zigzagging builds in lots of stretch potential, especially if you make relatively tall, closely spaced stitches.

## HOW TO DO IT

**1.** Anchor your thread near the edge you're thread-binding.

**2.** Insert the needle from front to back, close to the edge. The distance from the edge is up to you and may depend on the density and stretch of the fabric—looser or stretchier fabrics will require deeper stitches. I usually try something like ⅛" (3 mm) from the edge as a starting point.

**3.** Do not push the needle through—instead, spiral the needle's tip around the top of your raw edge so that it is on top of your work again.

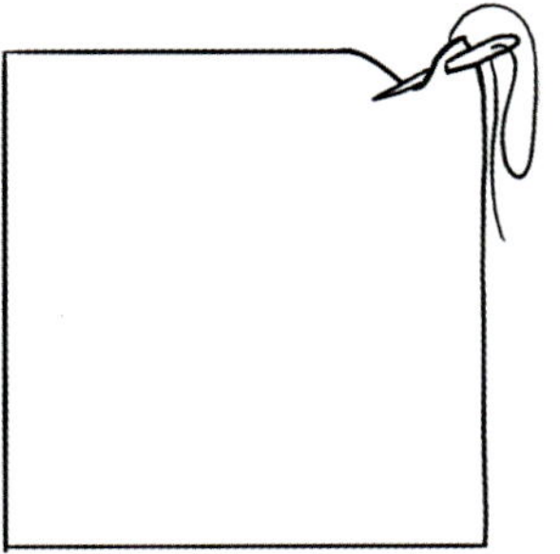

**4.** Advancing slightly along the raw edge, insert the needle again from front to back, close to the edge, as in step 2.

**5.** Repeat steps 3 and 4 until you've loaded your needle with several stitches.

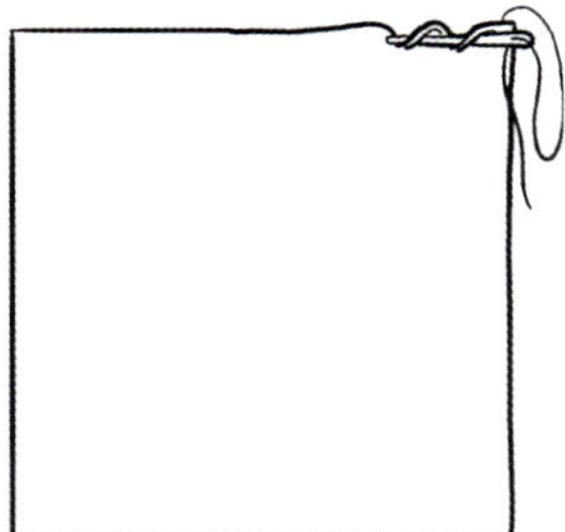

**6.** Pull through, and then massage the fabric briefly so that the fabric and thread lie flat and smooth.

**7.** Repeat steps 2 through 6 to advance across the entire raw edge.

## Herringbone Stitch

Herringbone is a great hemming or felling stitch. It joins an edge to one or more underlayers. Unlike some other hemming stitches, herringbone allows the edge and underlayers to continue shifting slightly against each other. This can be a benefit when working along a strongly curved hem or when securing an outer fabric's hem to a lining, for example.

Herringbone has an unmistakable crisscrossing, graphic appearance on the working side. It looks much more visually subtle on the other side. The crisscrosses build in lots of stretch potential, making herringbone stitch a good choice for stretchy garments' hems. The crisscrossing also serves as a sort of thread-binding stitch for the edge that is being joined, so I often use this stitch to create minimally bulky single-fold hems of knit garments such as T-shirts.

Some people find herringbone stitch to be tedious because, like backstitch, it involves doubling back over fabric that has already been stitched. This also uses more thread than some other hemming stitches. However, I enjoy watching the line of stitching grow, and I appreciate herringbone's stretchy, thread-binding, externally visually subtle attributes. So give it a try—depending on your goals, herringbone may be just the thing.

FRONT (WORKING SIDE) VIEW

BACK VIEW

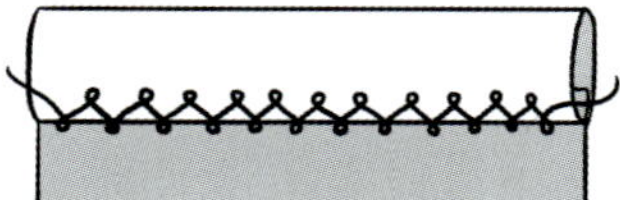

Here is an X-ray view, in which you can see the thread's classic looping and zigzagging trajectory through the fabric. This path builds in lots of stretch potential.

### HOW TO DO IT

As shown here herringbone is performed along a hem edge. However, one can use it in other contexts.

1. When performing herringbone stitch, your needle will be pointed in the usual direction (toward the left if you're right-handed; toward the right if you're left-handed). However, your stitches will accumulate backward along the edge you're sewing (advancing toward the right if you're right-handed; toward the left if you're left-handed). Anchor the thread along the edge to be attached, starting at the opposite end of the work from what is normal (on the left side if you're right-handed, and on the right side if you're left-handed).

2. Advance backward along the edge (toward the right if you're right-handed; toward the left if you're left-handed) and take a small "bite" of fabric exactly next to the edge but only through the underlayer. This small stitch's size will determine how visible it will be from the outside. Pull the thread through until it lies flat.

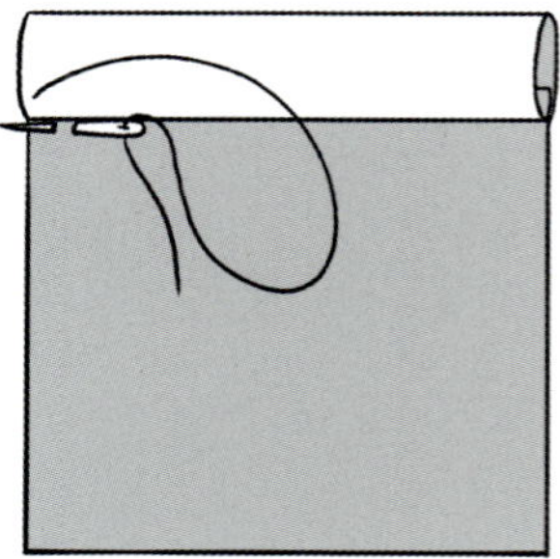

**3.** Advance backward again along the edge and take a small "bite" of fabric only through the hem allowance (up on the edge). This stitch should not catch any of the outer fabric and therefore should not show on the garment's exterior. The deeper into the hem your stitch is, and the closer it is to your previous stitch, the more stretchiness you'll build into your stitch line.

**4.** Repeat steps 2 and 3, taking little stitches that alternate between the hem edge and the underlayer.

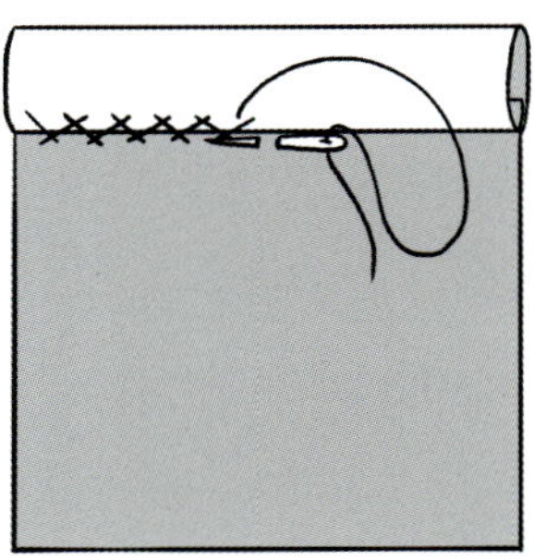

## Catchstitch

Catchstitch is a close cousin to herringbone stitch. Like herringbone, catchstitch is suitable for hemming or felling, as it serves to join an edge to one or more underlayers. Visually, the stitches on the working side of the fabric look less graphic and more functional: a series of diagonal lines, alternating slant between left and right. From the other side of the work, catchstitch looks visually subtle and identical to herringbone's underside.

Catchstitch tends to be slightly less stretchy than herringbone because catchstitch does not loop back on itself. However, it has a strong zigzag trajectory, so it is still a great choice for most stretchy contexts. And like herringbone, catchstitch thread-binds the edge that is being joined, so it is another good option for producing minimally bulky single-fold hems of knit garments such as T-shirts.

Stitch size and spacing are up to you—experiment on a scrap of your project fabric to determine what will work best for your context.

FRONT (WORKING SIDE) VIEW

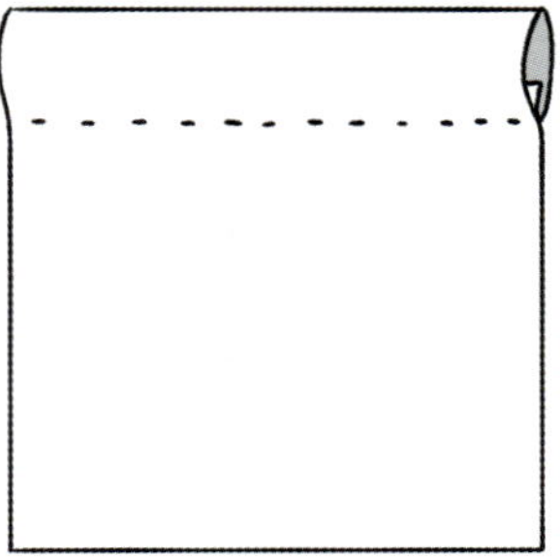

BACK VIEW

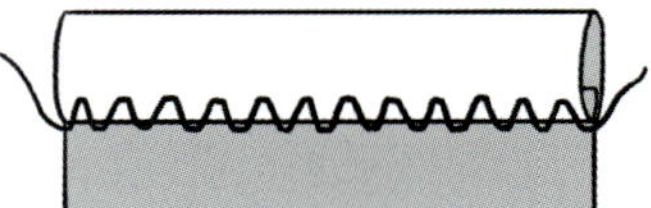

Here is an X-ray view from the working side, in which you can see the thread's zigzagging, plateau-forming trajectory through the fabric. This path builds in plenty of stretch potential.

# Catchstitch, continued

### HOW TO DO IT

As shown here, catchstitch is performed along a hem edge. However, one can use it in other contexts. Also, please note that unlike herringbone, catchstitch is performed in the usual direction, so anchor the thread on the side that you ordinarily would (on the right side if you're right-handed; on the left side if you're left-handed).

1. Anchor your thread along the edge you're attaching.

2. Advance forward along the edge (toward the left if you're right-handed; toward the right if you're left-handed) and take a small "bite" of fabric exactly next to the edge but only through the underlayer. This small stitch's size will determine how visible it will be from the outside. Pull the thread through until it lies flat.

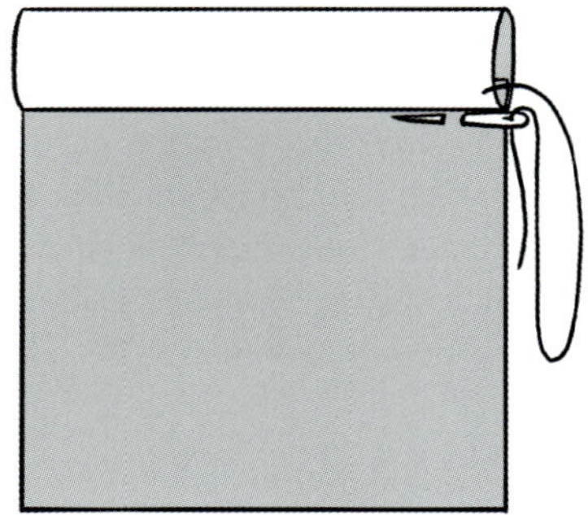

3. Advance forward again along the edge and take a small "bite" of fabric only through the hem allowance (up on the edge). This stitch should not catch any of the outer fabric and therefore will not show on the garment's exterior. The deeper into the hem your stitch is, and the closer it is to your previous stitch, the more stretchiness you'll build into your stitch line.

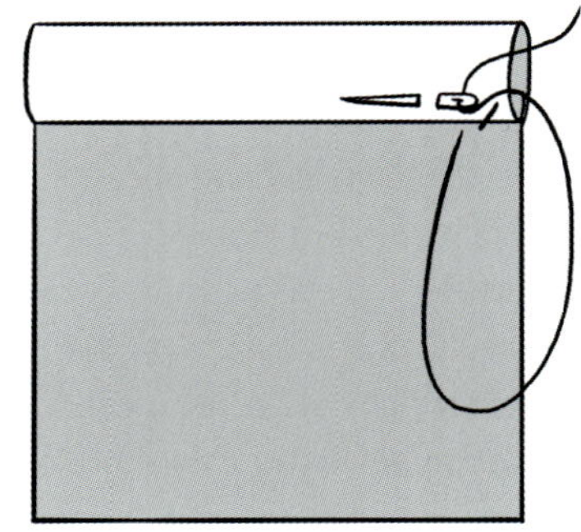

4. Repeat steps 2 and 3, taking little stitches that alternate between the hem edge and the underlayer.

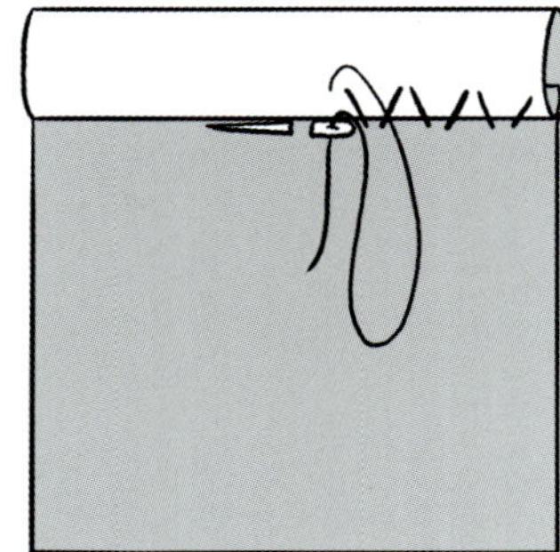

## Blanket Stitch

Blanket stitch makes a lovely decorative edging along necklines, cuffs, hems, pocket edges, and so on. It can also be used as a functional stitch to attach patches or secure hems. In a pinch, you might even use it to finish a buttonhole.

Blanket stitch is somewhat stretchy, so if you're feeling brave and experimental, you might be able to use it in some knit garment contexts. I've never tried this, but based on a few swatch experiments I've tested, I suspect it would provide enough stretch for at least a few areas on knit garments.

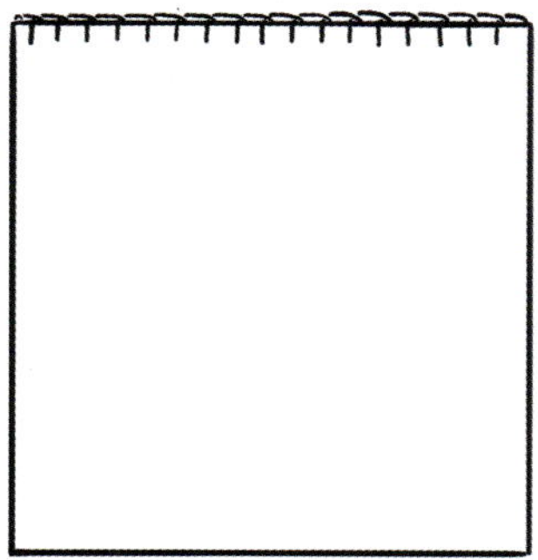

FRONT VIEW

BACK VIEW

### HOW TO DO IT

**1.** Anchor on and push your needle through so the thread emerges along the edge to be finished.

**2.** Arrange the thread in a C shape as pictured (or a backward C for lefties).

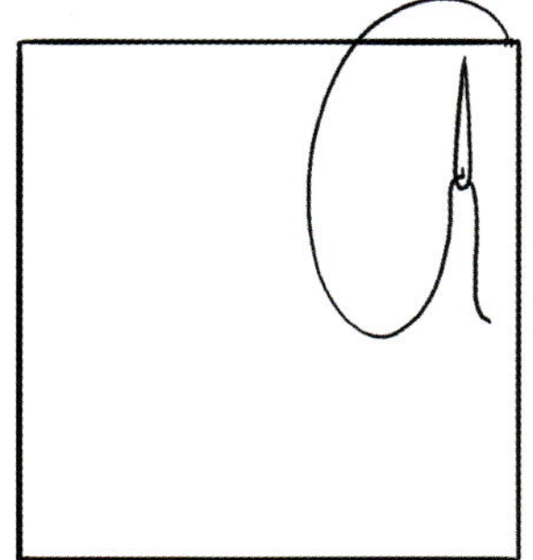

**3.** Advance along the edge (spacing at your discretion) and insert the needle from front to back of the work, with the needle's tip positioned above the top of the thread's C shape (or backward C for lefties).

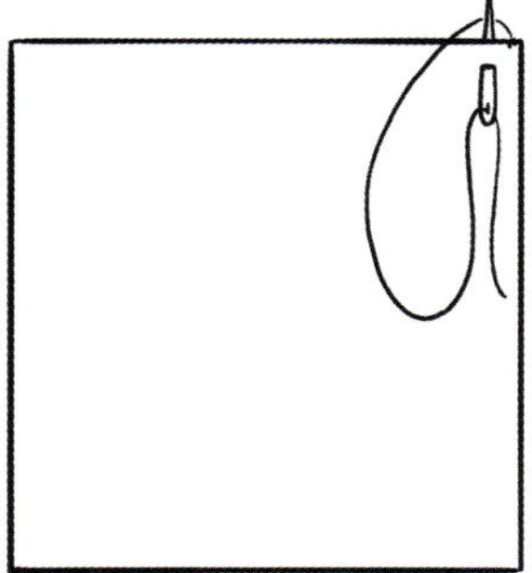

**4.** Pull the thread through until it lies flat against the fabric, with no puckering.

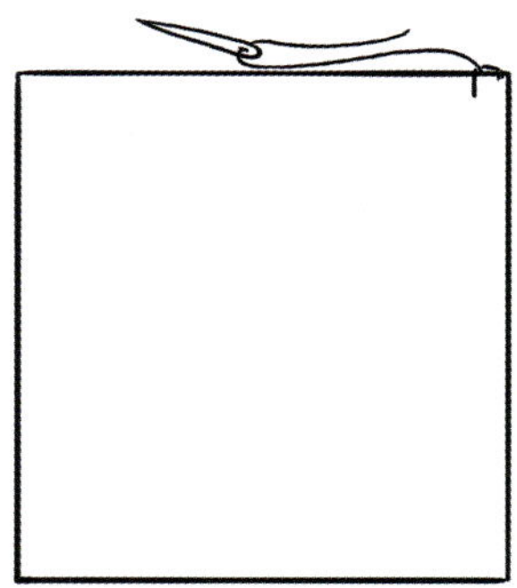

**5.** Repeat steps 2 through 4 to advance across the edge.

## Buttonhole Stitch

There's nothing quite as sweet as a carefully handsewn buttonhole. It takes practice and experimentation to get comfortable with buttonhole stitch, but once you've gotten the hang of it, you can stitch up the cutest buttonholes and the classiest bartacks.

Buttonhole stitch is similar to blanket stitch, but it includes a spiraling of the thread around the needle so that a little thread purl is formed at the cut edge each time you pull the thread flat. These purls make the buttonhole edge clean and strong.

Buttonhole stitch can be used to create several buttonhole shapes, which are featured in various projects in this book (see pages 251, 293, and 324). Here, we'll focus only on the creation of the stitch itself.

### HOW TO DO IT

**1.** Anchor on and push your needle through so the thread emerges along the cut edge to be finished.

**2.** Arrange the thread in a counterclockwise spiral as pictured. (To me, it looks like a lowercase letter *e*.)

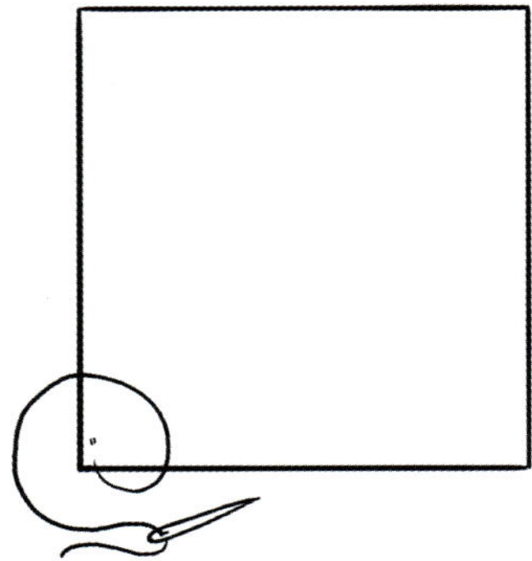

**3.** Bring the needle over the lowest looped thread, then tuck the needle tip under the cut edge. Push the tip out about ⅛" (3 mm) away from the cut edge, with the tip arranged above the upper looped thread.

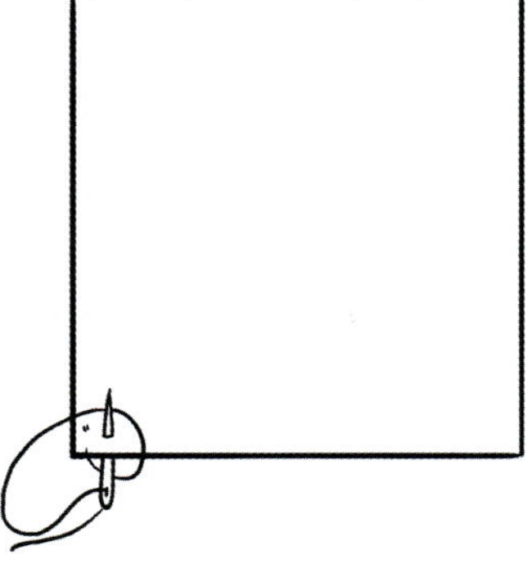

**4.** Pull the thread flat, making sure that the little purl lands exactly along the cut edge.

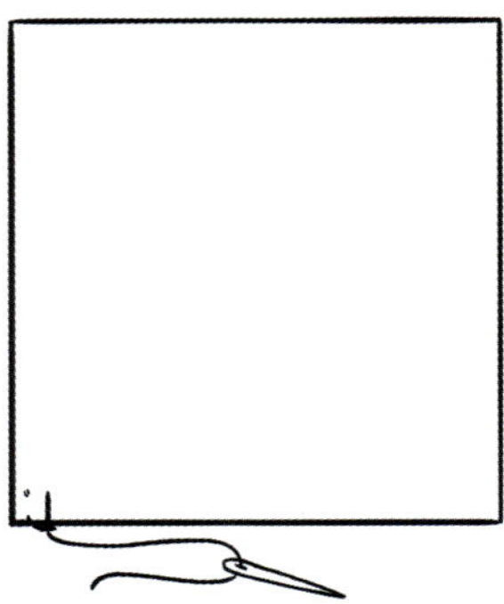

**5.** Repeat steps 2 through 4, placing each stitch very close to the one before it. (The exact spacing will depend on your fabric, thread, and goals. Experiment on a little scrap of project fabric before committing to a spacing for your real garment.)

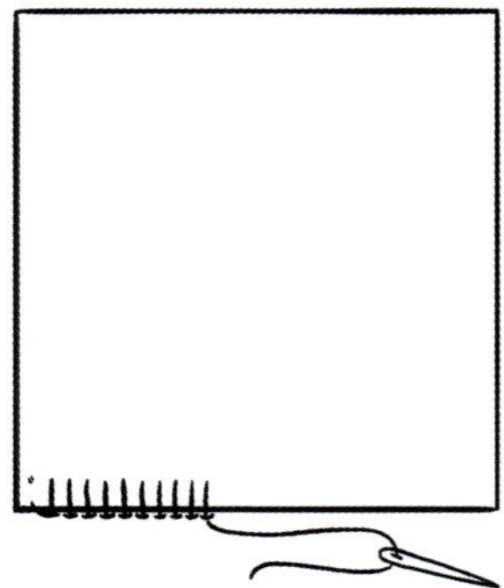

## Chainstitch

Chainstitch is one of my favorite stitches to use when embroidering labels and creating other decorative lines of thread. Chainstitch forms a set of interlocking loops along the top of your work, with a simpler straight-stitch look beneath. Your embroidery will pop thanks to chainstitch's bold lines, and it's gratifying to see how quickly you can travel across a design this way.

You'll want to decide on your design ahead of time (letters? words? a simple line drawing of your neighborhood deli or pet or favorite herb?) and write your text or mark the lines of your design onto your fabric. Then you'll trace those lines with chainstitches.

### HOW TO DO IT

**1.** Using embroidery floss or other thick thread, anchor on where you'd like to begin a line of stitching.

**2.** Pointing your needle along your drawn line, insert your needle at the site of the anchoring pile and take a small stitch. Tuck the thread under the needle's point before pulling through.

**3.** Pull the thread through until it lies flat against the fabric. Notice the teardrop-shaped chain link that has appeared.

**4.** Insert the needle tip right next to where the thread just emerged (inside that chain link), and push the needle tip out farther along the drawn line. Tuck the thread under the needle's point, then pull through until the thread lies flat.

**5.** Repeat step 4 to create a line of chainstitches along the entire design.

**6.** To finish chainstitching, secure the end by positioning the needle tip just outside of the final chain loop, then sinking the needle to the underside. Anchor off on the underside.

## Bartack

A bartack is a dense line of stitching that helps to redistribute strain away from a single line of stitching or a single point in the cloth. Bartacks are often found at pocket corners, the tops of side slits, and other areas that may be vulnerable to strain at a single point.

There are fancy triangle-shaped bartacks that you might see used in fine tailoring contexts. The technique shown here is simpler but produces good, sturdy results for most clothing.

In this illustrated example, a bartack is added to the edge of a chest pocket opening. However, one can apply bartacks in many other contexts. (See the jeans project on page 323.)

**HOW TO DO IT**

**1.** Determine where your bartack should be applied. In this example of a pocket opening, we will apply bartacks horizontally to the corners so they will bear some of the burden of strain when objects are taken in and out of the pocket. Decide, too, how long you would like the bartack to measure. If desired, mark placement with a pencil or other marking tool.

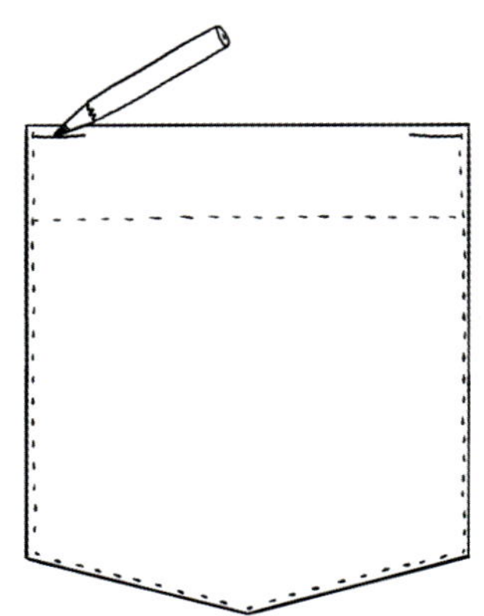

**2.** Anchor your thread to the underside of the work or somewhere within the area where the bartack will be located. (The bartack stitches will cover this anchoring pile.) Then push your needle out, emerging at one of the bartack's intended corners.

**3.** Jump across the bartack's length and take a small stitch at the bartack's opposite end, through all layers of fabric.

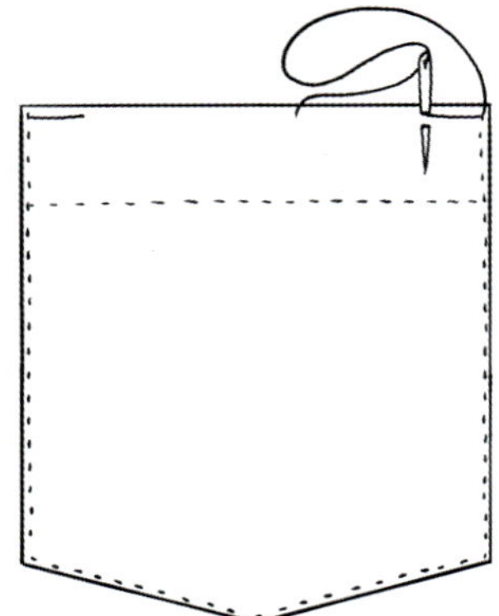

**4.** Jump back across to the bartack's first end and take another small stitch through all layers of fabric.

**5.** Repeat steps 3 and 4 until you've created a set of thread strands that span the bartack's length. The exact number of strands is up to you—I'd recommend at least four strands.

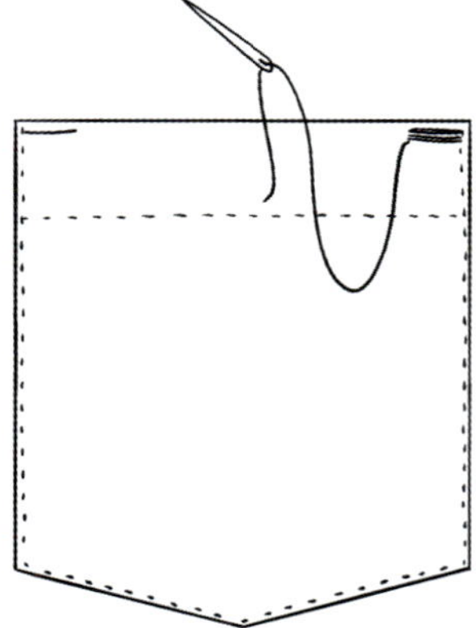

6. Cover this bundle of strands with a line of dense whipstitches, blanket stitches, or buttonhole stitches. For maximum strength, try to catch as many layers of fabric as possible with each stitch.

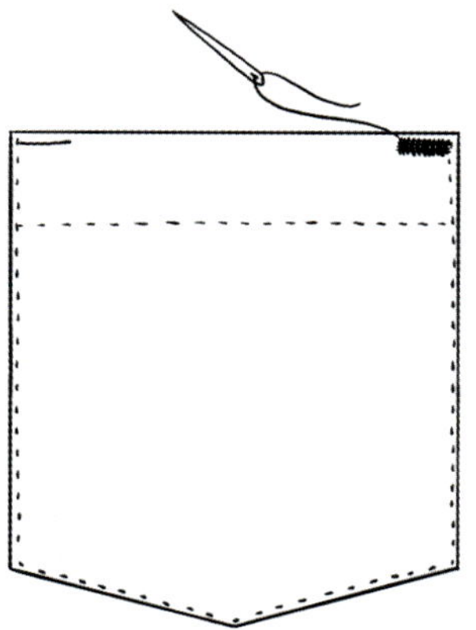

7. When the entire bartack's length is covered with whipstitches, blanket stitches, or buttonhole stitches, push the needle through to the inside of the garment and anchor off. Burrow the tail through the bartack's dense stitches and snip.

## Thread Tacks

Sometimes called "tailor's tacks," these little thready bits are used to mark specific points on your unfinished garment. For example, you can use thread tacks to transfer drill holes from pattern to fabric, so that when you're ready to stitch a pocket onto the shirt's front panel, you know exactly where to put it. Thread tacks stay in pretty well if you're not too rough with them, and they're easy to remove later when they're no longer needed.

### HOW TO DO IT

1. With doubled thread, take a tiny stitch at the point you'd like to mark. Don't anchor the thread, and don't bother making a knot. Leave ¾" (2 cm) tails.

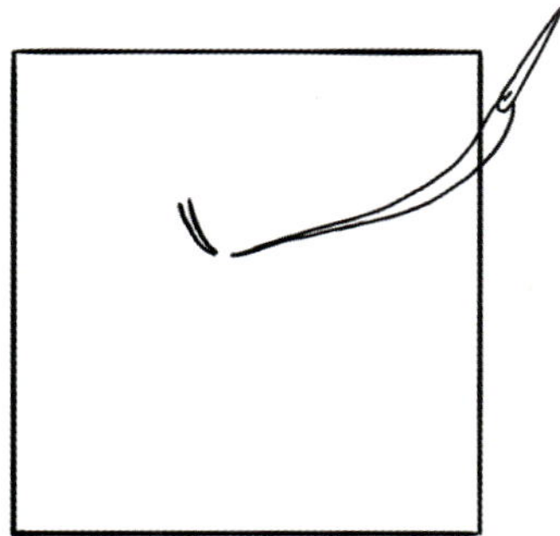

2. Take another tiny stitch on top of the first, then pull the thread most of the way through, but leave a looped bit.

3. Optionally, take one more tiny stitch on top, again leaving loops.

4. Trim the thread, leaving ¾" (2 cm) tails again.

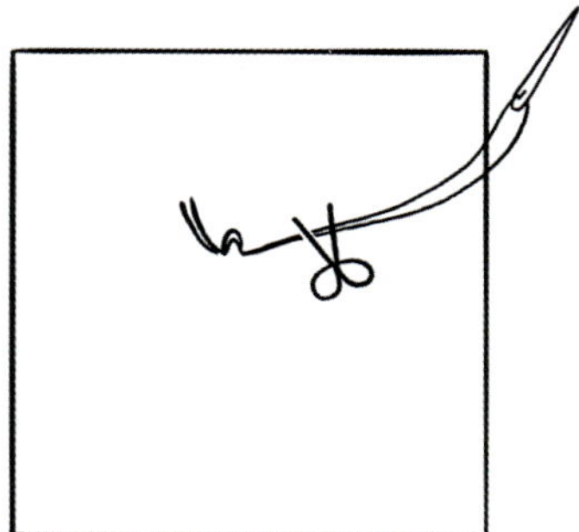

When you're done with this mark, you can easily snip through the loops and pull out those short bits of thread.

# Understanding Fabric (and Cutting It)

If you're new to sewing, you may have some questions about how fabric works. Here's a mini crash course in all things cloth, as well as what you'll need to know to cut it up for sewing.

## How It's Made

Fibers are the basic material of fabric. These fibers are wispy little strands of plant matter, like cotton, hemp, linen, and ramie; animal matter, like wool and silk; or manufactured matter, like polyester and acrylic. The fibers are bundled and spun together into twisted strands of yarn. These yarns are then woven or knit to create fabric.

As a patternmaker and sewist, you'll want to be aware of the particular properties of whatever fabric you're planning to use. Is it stretchy? Is it drapey? Is it thick, thin, soft, dense, loose, spongy? Prone to fraying? What else?

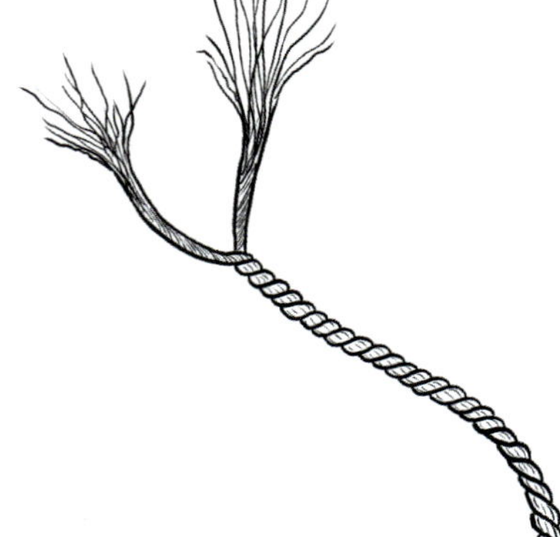

### WOVEN FABRIC

Woven fabric is formed by two sets of yarns—the vertical warp and the horizontal weft. Did you ever make one of those loopy potholders as a child? That's weaving. First, a set of parallel warp strands are set up and held under tension in a loom. Then the weft is brought back and forth through the warp, winding over and under the warp strands in a deliberate pattern. Depending on this pattern, the resulting fabric might be plain weave (the simplest, most basic weave structure), twill, satin weave, or one of many other weave structures. Regardless, woven fabric depends on a basic grid of yarns intersecting with each other.

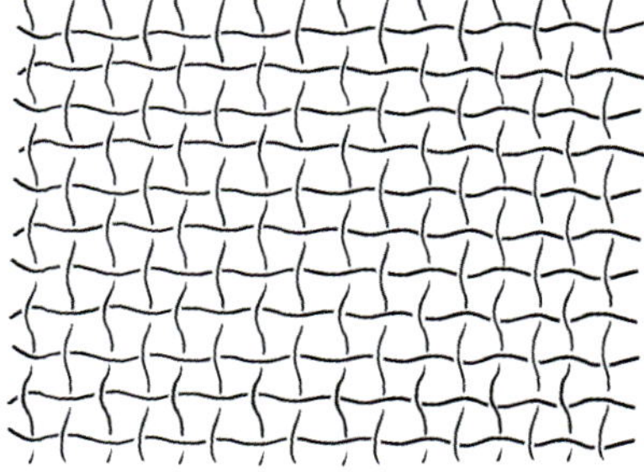

### KNIT FABRIC

Knit fabric is formed by a continuous strand of yarn that is arranged into rows and columns of interlocking loops. Like woven fabrics, knit fabrics can feature a variety of knit structures, based on how the loops are pulled through each other as the fabric builds. Some hand knitting is performed by doubling the yarn back and forth, back and forth, to make fabric, while other hand knitting is performed "in the round." This second method is basically how industrially knit yardage is created: The yarn spirals around and around to form a large tube, which is then cut open flat to produce swaths of fabric. If you're a knitter, this is the

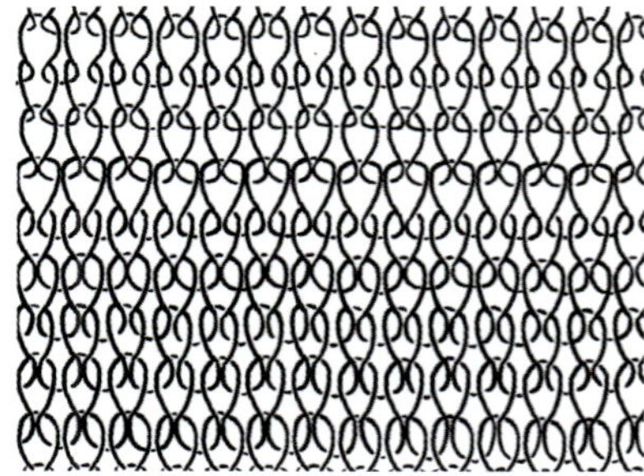

same concept as knitting a cardigan in the round and then steeking it open.

Fabric often undergoes additional procedures to become the product you buy in the store. It might be brushed. It might be fulled (cleaned and shrunk) to create a feltlike appearance. It might be treated with chemicals to achieve or enhance certain attributes, such as stiffness, drapiness, softness, water resistance, or wrinkle resistance.

HAND KNITTING IN THE ROUND

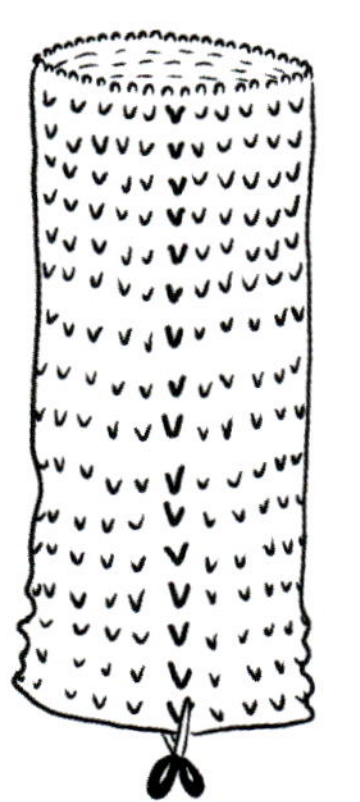

FABRIC KNIT IN THE ROUND, THEN CUT OPEN

## Grainline

You'll also need to be keenly aware of something called the grainline. Just as wood has a grain, and just as that grain is important to a woodworker, so the fabric's grain is important to a clothes-maker. The grainline (or straight grain, as it's often called) is the basic direction in which the fabric is oriented, and it determines a lot about how the fabric will behave. Most pattern pieces are arranged so that the grainline will run down the body (in the direction of gravity's pull) when the garment is worn. This tends to create the best drape, stretch, and silhouette. Of course it's always up to you how you arrange and cut your pieces, but if you do choose to break that rule, it's best to do so with a full understanding of what you're doing so you can be deliberate about the choice.

### IN WOVEN FABRICS

How do you find the grainline, then? In woven fabrics, the grainline runs along the warp threads, and it's parallel to the selvages (the densely woven edges of the yardage). So if you're working with woven fabric, finding the grainline's direction is usually pretty easy—you just locate the selvage.

### IN KNIT FABRICS

For knit fabrics, the selvages are often less reliable because of how the round tubes of fabric are cut open. First, these large industrial machines spiral yarn around, building fabric by pulling loops through loops through loops. The fabric's grainline is established by the columns of interlocking loops. When the yardage is removed from the knitting machine, though, the tube

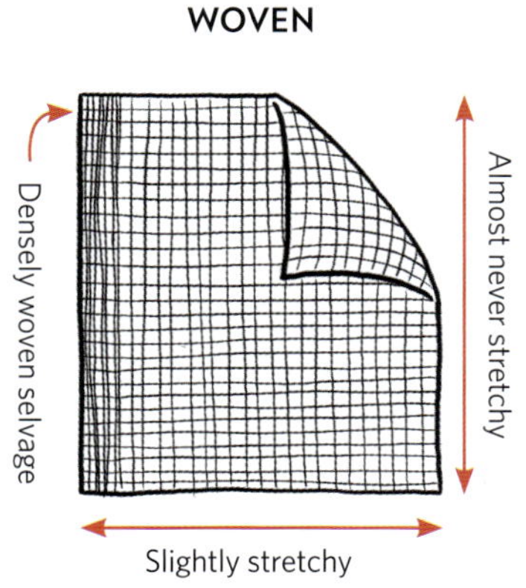


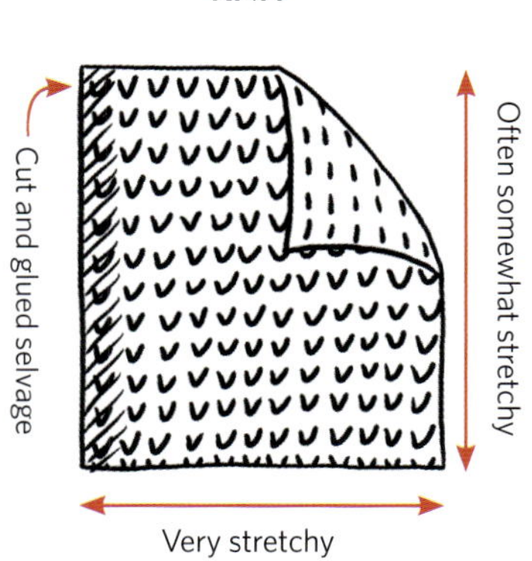

is cut open, often along a strip of glue for sturdiness. Ideally this cut would be made exactly along a column of interlocking loops, with the cut edge parallel to the straight grain. However, in reality the cut is often made less carefully, so that the cut is not a reliable grainline guide. Furthermore, knit fabric's proclivity for curling makes the edge even less reliable.

So how can you find your knit fabric's grainline when laying out pieces to cut? Pull out a magnifying glass or squint. If you look closely at the front of knit fabric such as jersey, you'll see a grid of little V's that are organized into rows and columns. On the back of jersey, you'll see bumpy horizontal lines arranged in the same grid.

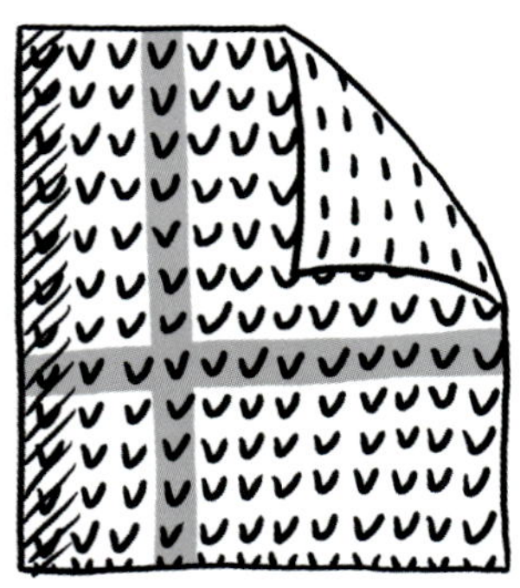

Your fabric may have been cut at an angle, but you can still find the grainline by locating a single little V stitch, placing a pin, and then gazing down that single column of loops for about 10" (25 cm) before placing another pin. The line between your pins is the grain.

## CROSS-GRAIN

There's also a cross-grain, which runs perpendicular to the straight grain. If you can find the grainline, you can be certain that the cross-grain runs at a right angle to it. Sometimes pieces such as collars, yokes, and other garment pieces are cut on the cross-grain. Knit bands such as neckbands, ankle bands, and hoodie cuffs are also typically cut on the cross-grain. In knit fabrics, and even in woven fabrics to a much lesser extent, this is typically the direction of greatest stretch.

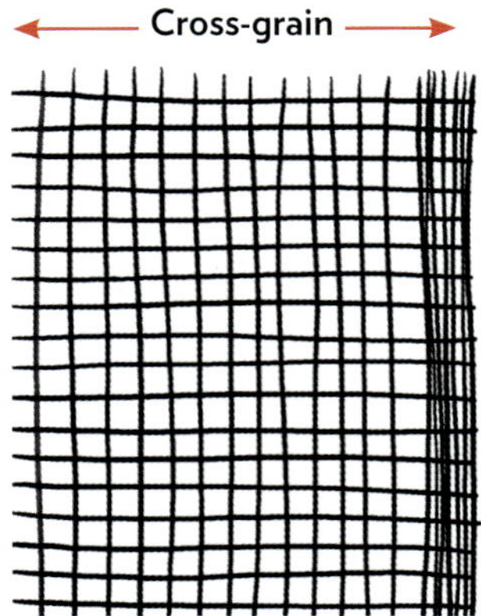


## THE BIAS

The diagonal direction along your gridded yarns is known as the bias. This can be at a true 45-degree angle to the fabric's basic grid (and if so, it's called the true bias).

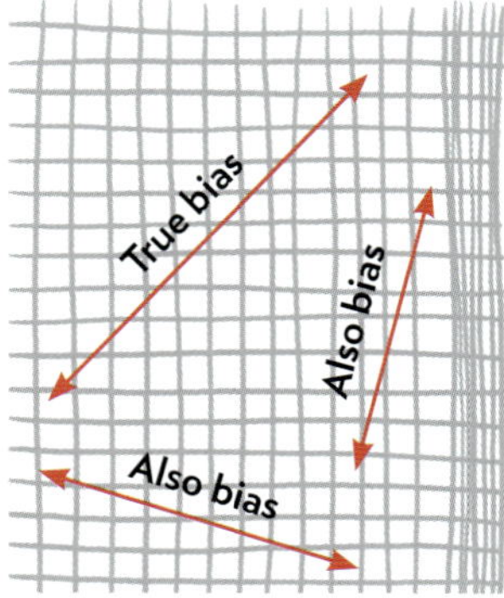

But the bias can also be any sort of diagonal cut such as you typically find on a curved neckline or armhole. These bias cuts are stretchier and more prone to distortion, even in woven fabrics. So staystitching (see page 104) is often a good idea on bias-cut areas such as curved necklines and armholes. In the garment projects ahead, I've sometimes suggested important edges to staystitch. Feel free to add staystitching wherever you see fit, though, or skip it if you think it won't be necessary.

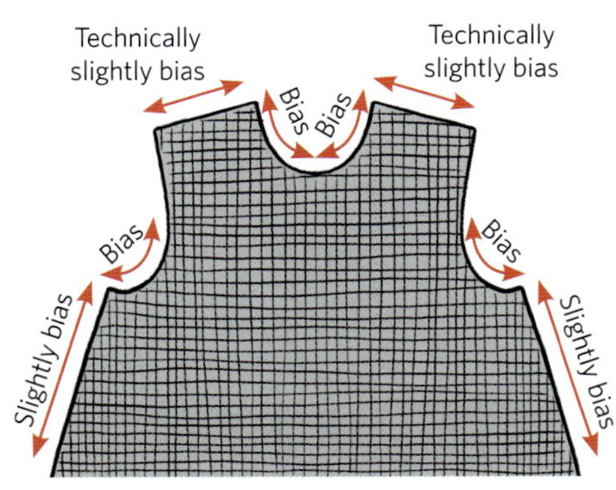


## Fabric and Patternmaking

As a patternmaker, you'll need to be thinking about the fabric as you draft and finalize your pattern pieces.

You'll need to keep the fabric's properties in mind as you're devising measurements and drafting your shapes. You might need to consider how stretchy your fabric is, as you'll see in the leggings project. You might need to think about the fabric's thickness and how it will respond to pleating or gathers. You'll want to imagine how it might drape and whether you'll want lots of volume or just a smidge.

Once you're labeling your finished pattern pieces, you'll need to mark how many pieces to cut, and out of what fabric. There are a few industrial patternmaking terms that I use in my own practice:

- ***Self.*** The "self" fabric is the main garment fabric you're using. It's different from linings, contrast fabrics, rib trims, and so on. You can call it whatever you'd like, but I'll be calling it "self" throughout the following projects.
- ***Combo.*** This is a contrast fabric. If you're using colorblocking, for example, you might call the secondary fabric "combo."
- ***Rib.*** This is what it sounds like: It's the ribbed trim fabric you might use along a neckline or cuff. If I were making an entire garment out of ribbed fabric, though, I'd probably label it "self" instead.
- ***Lining.*** Also what it sounds like, lining is the fabric you'll use if you're including an interior layer.
- ***Interfacing.*** This is a stiffening, structure-building material that you can use to reinforce certain areas of certain garments. It comes in many weights and forms, and you can buy fusible interfacing (which you glue onto your fabric by melting it with a hot iron) or sew-in interfacing (which you stitch on).

## Mirrored Cutting

When marking how many to cut for each pattern piece, be aware that you'll be cutting mirrored pieces for any assymmetrical piece that is a multiple of two. What does this mean? Because we typically draft only one half of the body, you'll need to create the other half somehow. In the case of pattern pieces that will be a single panel across the body, I recommend mirroring those out when you're making final pattern pieces so that won't be a problem. But if you've drafted a single sleeve and need to cut two, you'll need to flip the pattern piece over to cut the second sleeve (or you can cut through two layers of fabric folded over on itself to achieve the same thing). Otherwise, if you cut two sleeves on the same layer of fabric without flipping the pattern, you'll end up with two right sleeves, or two left sleeves. Oops! So when your pattern says to "cut two" or "cut four," know that you'll probably need to mirror those pairs in your cutting layout.

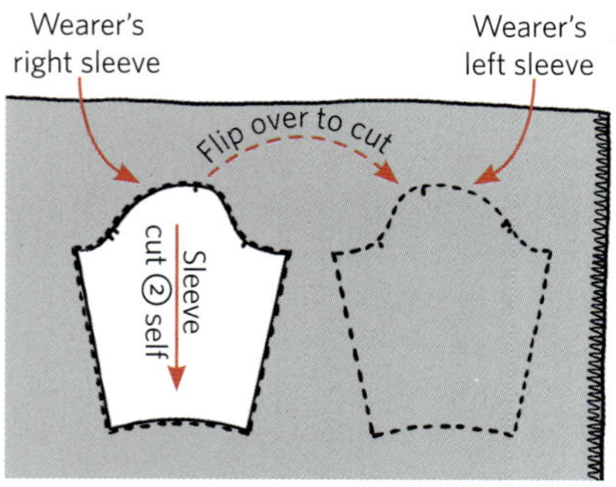

## Calculating Yardage

Calculating the yardage you'll need can be a tricky task when you're the patternmaker. You'll need to know the width of your particular fabric's usable area. To figure out the exact amount required, you can use artist or painter's tape on the floor to mock up the width and arrange your pattern pieces carefully, puzzle-style, to see how much length you need. To be safe, I'd recommend adding at least another ½ or 1 yard (meter) beyond this amount, especially because the fabric you buy will likely shrink when you prewash and dry it. Having extra fabric on hand also makes the occasional cutting error much less stressful.

Truth be told, I never calculate my yardage ahead of time. Instead, I estimate how much I'll need and then round up a bit. This will depend a lot on your fabric's cuttable width and on the size and shape of your pieces. In my experience, for the fabrics I typically buy and the sizes and shapes I typically cut, I generally estimate the following amounts for this book's projects:

- Woven boxy top: 2 yards (2 meters)
- Leggings: 2 yards (2 meters)
- Gathered skirt: 3–4 yards (3–4 meters)
- Short-sleeved T-shirt: 2 yards (2 meters)
- Hoodie: 4 yards (4 meters) self; ½ yard (0.5 meter) rib
- Undies: 1 yard (1 meter)
- Button-up shirt: 4 yards (4 meters)
- Jean jacket: 4 yards (4 meters)
- Jeans: 2½ yards (2.5 meters)

### How to Store Your Pattern Pieces

I like to roll together the paper patterns and cut fabric panels, all in one big roll, then tie with a scrap of fabric until sewing time. Once I've begun stitching, I often hang my paper pattern pieces on the wall near my work space for quick visual reference (to double-check seam allowance amounts and so on). And after the garment is constructed, I put the pattern pieces into permanent storage in a large manila envelope, labeled with style name, date drafted, number of pieces, and (if I have time) a quick sketch and/or key measurements.

Remember, the yardage you'll need may be quite different from these numbers depending on factors such as fabric width, the size of pattern pieces, and fabric shrinkage.

## Cutting Fabric

Prewash and dry yardage to remove chemicals and fast-track any shrinkage. I'm a big believer in machine washing (and sometimes machine drying) hand-sewn clothes. So as long as your fabric can handle it (check the care instructions on the fabric bolt or website when buying), I'd recommend prewashing and drying on your machines' hotter settings. If you have the patience, repeat a couple of times. If your fabric should be hand-washed, you can prewash by hand instead, or if it's dry clean-only, feel free to skip prewashing altogether.

Then press lightly with an iron to smooth any wrinkles.

Lay the fabric smooth and flat in a single layer on a large table or the floor. If you're using a knit fabric, don't stretch the fabric to smooth it—stretching it could distort the cloth. Instead, lay it flat and then pat lightly to chase the ripples to the edges.

Once the fabric is smooth and flat, arrange your pattern pieces with the grainlines parallel to the selvages or your established knit grainline. For fabric efficiency, try to minimize gaps between pattern pieces. Remember to mirror any paired cutting quantities by folding over part of the fabric to form two mirrored layers, or by flipping the pattern piece(s) manually.

Use pins or weights to secure the pattern pieces onto the fabric, then cut them out. Snip a ⅛" (3 mm) cut into the seam allowance at each notch point. Mark any drill holes onto your pieces. Then remove the pins or weights. Store your fabric pieces safely until you're ready to sew.

### Oh, the Places You'll Sew

There are so many great places to hand-sew. Notice that all of these would be impossible—or at least quite impractical—locations for using a sewing machine.

- On a train
- On a bus
- On a boat
- On an airplane*
- On a mountaintop
- In a camping tent
- In a meeting
- In a lecture hall
- In a waiting room
- On your couch
- In your bed
- On the floor
- In a hotel room
- At the beach
- In a park
- At a family gathering
- On a picnic
- At the kitchen counter
- In front of a fireplace
- At a café
- In a hospital
- At a library
- On a road trip
- At the DMV
- Truly anywhere

* It varies by the airline and by the country, of course. But typically, hand-sewing is totally fine on airplanes. In my country (the United States), scissors are generally allowed, as long as their blades measure no longer than 4 inches from pivot point to tips. You can bring needles and pins, too. And nail clippers make good thread snips. When in doubt, only bring tools that you're prepared to surrender—don't bring your favorite scissors. And if you're concerned about pins, you can baste things ahead of time and just bring a needle or two.

# THE CLOTHES

Now that you've familiarized yourself with some of the fundamental techniques of patternmaking and hand sewing, it's time to start applying them to real clothes you'd like to wear. In the pages to come, you'll encounter nine different garment projects, arranged roughly in order of difficulty. For each, I'll detail how to create the pattern. Then I'll share how to hand-sew the garment, stitch by stitch.

If you already have a comparable pattern you'd like to use, feel free to forgo the patternmaking section and skip straight to the sewing instructions. Or if you're drawn to the idea of making one of these designs but would prefer to machine-sew, that's great, too—you can focus on the patternmaking section and opt out of the sewing directions. This book is meant to be useful to you—so use it in whatever way works best.

And with anything I share, feel free to interrogate and challenge it and to innovate however you'd like. There are a million ways to do all of this. What follow are the methods I currently prefer, that make sense to me and that seem useful to convey in book form. But there are many, many more ways to think about everything, to do everything. Ultimately, it's up to you. It's up to your mind and your own two beautiful, capable hands.

Woven Boxy Top,
page 91

Leggings,
page 115

Gathered Skirt,
page 137

T-shirt,
page 159

Hoodie,
page 189

Undies,
page 209

Woven Button-Up Shirt,
page 225

Jean Jacket,
page 257

Jeans,
page 297

# WOVEN BOXY TOP

This simple top is a wonderful start to your patternmaking and hand-sewing journey. It's clean and elegant, with just two main pattern pieces and minimal seaming. It's also an awesome blank canvas for your own creativity—experiment with different stitches, try some embroidery, or add style lines or extra panels. Once your garment is complete, start wearing it as much as you can. It's fun to wear handsewn clothes, of course, but it's also educational—you'll learn a ton from studying how your hand stitches hold up to the rigors of life and laundering.

# Patternmaking

For this project, you'll measure your own body and perhaps a few favorite garments. Then you'll settle on your desired garment dimensions and plot them onto paper. Trace the shapes, add notations, cut, and you'll be ready to start stitching.

## MEASURING YOUR BODY

Before you can draft shapes on paper, you'll need to figure out the dimensions. The best way to make informed choices for a well-fitting garment is to know your own body's measurements. These are the base numbers—eventually you'll add some volume for comfort and style. Meanwhile, mark down your true anatomical dimensions (except where noted).

- Body length (HPS to desired garment length)
- Bust circumference
- Hip circumference
- Neck width
- Front neck drop
- Across shoulder (LPS to LPS)
- Sleeve length (center back to LPS to desired sleeve hem level)
- Sleeve opening circumference (measured at desired sleeve length)
- Head circumference
- Bust level

## MEASURING OTHER GARMENTS

Measuring your own body helps you to understand the baseline dimensions your clothes will need to fit around. But as discussed on page 25, most clothing also needs some wearing ease. (The exact amount of ease is a matter of personal preference.) It can be incredibly informative to measure clothes you already own and love so you can begin to understand the dimensions that you actually like to wear.

Peek in your closet and try to find a few woven garments that have some elements similar to the woven boxy top you're planning to make. You may not have a garment exactly like it, and that's fine. You can measure tops, tunics, dresses—whatever you have.

See if you can find:

- Something that fits you nicely in the bust (whatever "nicely" means to you)
- Something that fits you nicely through the hips
- Something with a neckline that you like—not too high or low, not too wide or narrow
- Something with a sleeve length you feel good in
- Any other garments with additional elements you'd like to incorporate

Try to find clothes to help inform your preferences for each of the measurements you took on your body. (You can skip finding a reference for the across-shoulder measurement, though, because the woven boxy top won't actually have armhole seams.)

If you don't have any garments that seem helpful for this exercise, you might still measure a few of your clothes. Assess critically: How much do you estimate you'd want to increase or decrease their measurements so that you'd like them better? There's lots to be learned by analyzing what you don't like.

Or if you really want to analyze well-fitting clothes but don't own any that seem suitable, pack a measuring tape and go visit a similar-bodied friend's closet or a thrift shop. You can try on a few garments and take some measurements right in the fitting room—no purchase necessary.

## DECIDING THE DIMENSIONS

Once you've measured your body and your favorite comparable clothes, it's time to make some decisions. I hope you're feeling empowered to make these choices now. In case you're still unsure what numbers to use, though, I'm including a few guidelines that reflect my own fit preferences. Feel free to disregard these if you've already determined what you prefer.

- Body length: For a basic top, I like to use the length from HPS to hip level.
- Bust circumference: I like to add 6 inches (15.2 cm) to the anatomical bust circumference.
- Sweep circumference: I like to add 6 inches (15.2 cm) to the anatomical hip circumference.
- Neck width: I like to add 2 inches (5 cm) to the anatomical neck width.
- Front neck drop: I like to add 1 inch (2.5 cm) to the anatomical front neck drop.
- Bicep circumference: I like to add 3 inches (7.6 cm) to the anatomical bicep circumference.
- Sleeve length (measured from center back to sleeve hem): I like to use 8 inches (20.3 cm) beyond LPS. For the construction techniques I'll be sharing, I'd recommend that the sleeve length from center back be at least a few inches longer than one-quarter of your top's bust circumference.
- Sleeve opening: I like to add 2 or 3 inches (5 or 7.6 cm) to the anatomical bicep circumference, but it depends a lot on sleeve length.

## MARKING LEVELS

First you'll create a draft of your pattern shapes, with front and back layered on top of each other. You'll be drafting only half of the torso because it is symmetrical (so you can save time and paper for now). Afterward you can trace off the full individual pattern pieces.

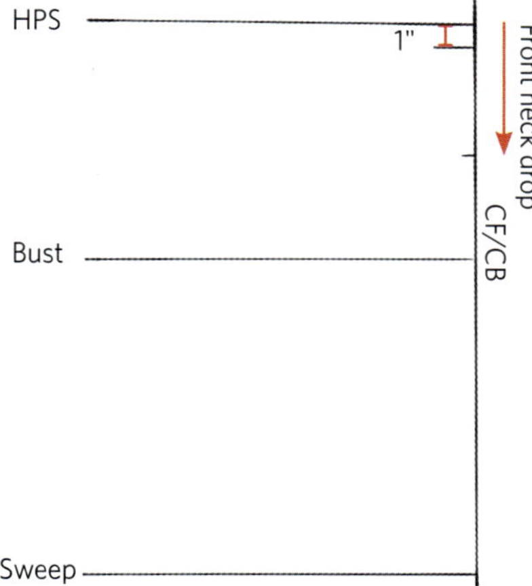


1. With a ruler, draft a long vertical line down the right-hand side of a large sheet of paper. This line will represent your top's center front/center back, and it should be at least as long as your desired body length.

2. Near the top of the CF/CB line, square out a line that is as least as long as your desired sleeve length from CB. This line represents your HPS level.

3. Along the CF/CB line, measure your desired body length down from HPS level, and square out a long line. This line represents your sweep.

4. Along the CF/CB line, measure your chosen front neck drop down from HPS level, and square out a line that is at least ½ inch (1.3 cm) long. This line represents your front neck drop level.

5. Along the CF/CB line, measure 1 inch (2.5 cm) down from HPS level, and square out a line that is at least 2 inches (5 cm) long. This line represents your back neck drop level. (You may need to adjust this level in a later step, but 1 inch (2.5 cm) from HPS level is a good starting point.)

6. Along the CF/CB line, measure your bust level amount down from HPS, and square out a long line. This line represents your bust level.

## MARKING WIDTHS

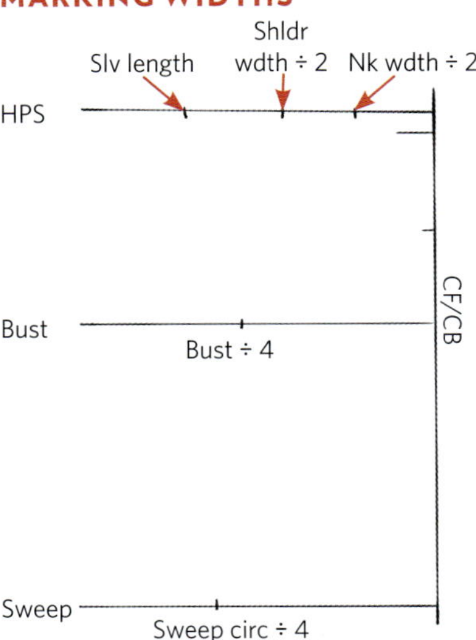


**1.** Along the HPS line, measure half of your desired neck width out from CF/CB line, and make a tick mark. This represents the HPS point, which is the intersection of neck and shoulder.

**2.** Along the HPS line, measure half of your anatomical shoulder width out from CF/CB line, and make a tick mark. You will use this point as a reference for shoulder slope in a later step.

**3.** Along the HPS line, measure your desired sleeve length out from CF/CB line, and make a tick mark. You will use this point as a reference later.

**4.** Along the bust line, measure one-quarter of your desired bust width out from CF/CB line, and make a tick mark. This represents the garment's dimension at bust level.

**5.** Along the sweep line, measure one-quarter of your desired sweep circumference out from CF/CB line, and make a tick mark. This represents the garment's dimension at sweep level.

## CONNECTING THE DOTS

**1.** Now you'll draft the back neck curve. Feel free to experiment with using curve tools, but I prefer free-handing in order to train my hand and eye to work together. Sketch a smooth curved line to connect the back neck drop level to the HPS, as shown. Make sure you're leaving at least 1½" (3.8 cm) of the original straight line you marked before beginning to curve the line up toward HPS.

**2.** Do the same for the front neck: Sketch a smooth curved line connecting the front neck drop level to the HPS. Leave at least ½" (1.3 cm) of the original straight line before curving up toward HPS. (Or you can draft a V-neck or other shape—use a ruler, curves, or freehanding to draw whatever neckline you desire.)

**3.** Holding your flexible drafting ruler on its side, bend it or walk it along the front and back necklines you've just drawn, measuring each one. Mark down their current lengths and add together to get half of the neck circumference. Then double that number to see what the total neck circumference would be. Compare with your head circumference. Is the neck circumference at least as large as your actual head's circumference (or ideally somewhat larger)? If not, then your head won't be able to push through the neck opening, so you'll need to adjust your plans in some way:

- You can enlarge the neck circumference by widening the neck, deepening the front and/or back neckline, or both. Remember that if you widen the neck, you'll need to redraw both front and back necklines. Once you've made your adjustments, remeasure and recalculate to ensure that the neckline is large enough now to accommodate your head. If it's not, keep adjusting.
- If you'd prefer to maintain your current measurements, you'll need to devise an alternative method to get your head through. You could add a keyhole opening to the front or back neckline, add a button placket along center front or center back, or even add snaps at the shoulder seam. In these cases, you'll need to adjust the pattern according to your plans.

**4.** Find the tick mark along the HPS level that represents half of your anatomical shoulder width. Square down ¾" (2 cm) from that point to create some shoulder slope. Now draw a straight line that connects from HPS through the shoulder slope point you've just drawn, and extend the line straight out until it reaches past the width of your sleeve length tick mark. Square down from the sleeve length tick mark to find the intersection with your new shoulder seam line. This intersection point represents the top of your sleeve hem.

**5.** Draw a straight line connecting the bust and sweep tick marks, as shown. This line represents your side seam.

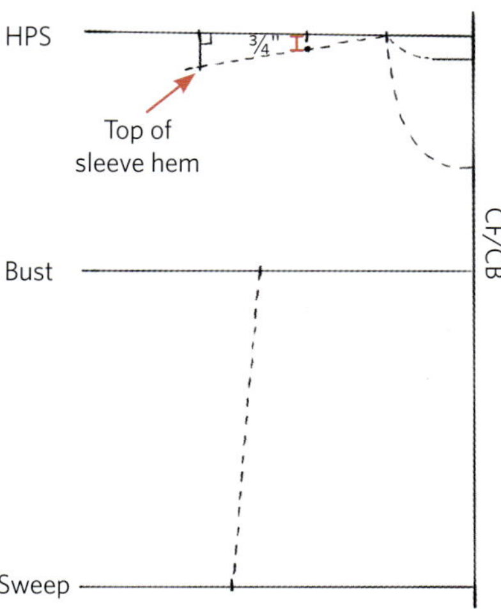


## FINALIZING LINES

**1.** Find the tick mark along your shoulder seam that represents the top of your sleeve hem. Square down for half the amount of your desired sleeve opening circumference and make another tick mark. This point represents the bottom of your sleeve hem.

**2.** Now you'll draw a line to connect the bottom of your sleeve hem with the side seam.

**A.** If the sleeve hem's bottom point falls to the left of the side seam, great! Beginning at the bottom point, square a line for at least ½" (1.3 cm), then continue the line in a smooth, gentle curve that blends into the side seam.

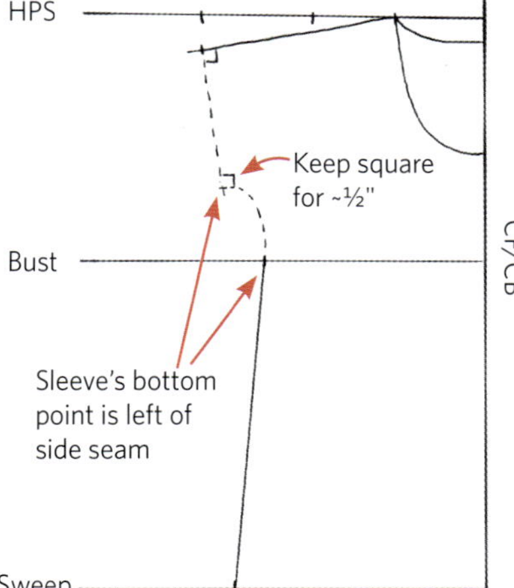


**B.** If the sleeve hem's bottom point falls even with the side seam (neither to the left nor the right), draw a notch at this underarm point, then draw a straight line to connect the sleeve hem to the side seam. The underarm notch point will be important later when you're sewing.

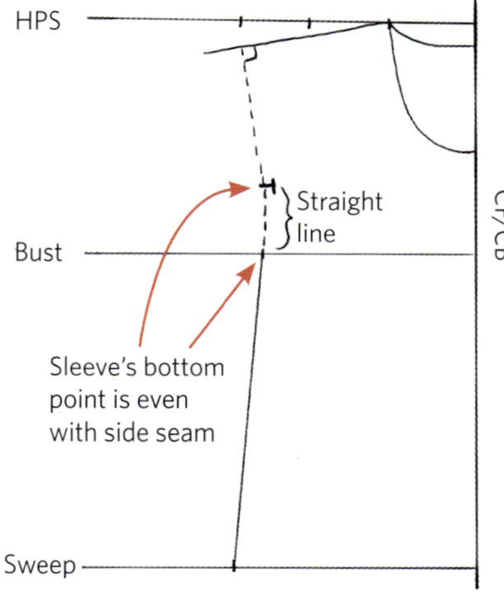

**C.** If the sleeve hem's bottom point falls to the right of the side seam, you'll probably want to lengthen your sleeve. For the construction and styling I'm sharing here, it will be easiest to have a sleeve that extends a few inches beyond your side seam. At minimum, try to achieve a sleeve shape where the bottom point is even with the side seam (not to the right of it). Then draw a line to connect the sleeve hem to the side seam.

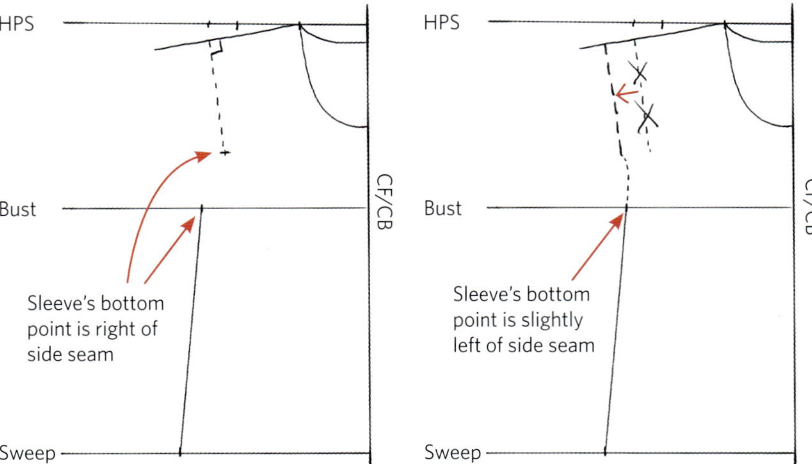


**3.** To ensure clean sewing, you'll need a right angle between the bottom of the side seam and your sweep. Unless you used the same measurement for bust and sweep widths (so that the side seam is exactly parallel to the CF/CB line), you'll need to adjust the sweep line accordingly. Slide your gridded ruler or a square tool along the side seam until its lower edge intersects with the sweep level at approximately one-third of the distance toward the CF/CB line. Draw this line. Then soften where it joins the sweep level by drawing a smooth, gentle curve.

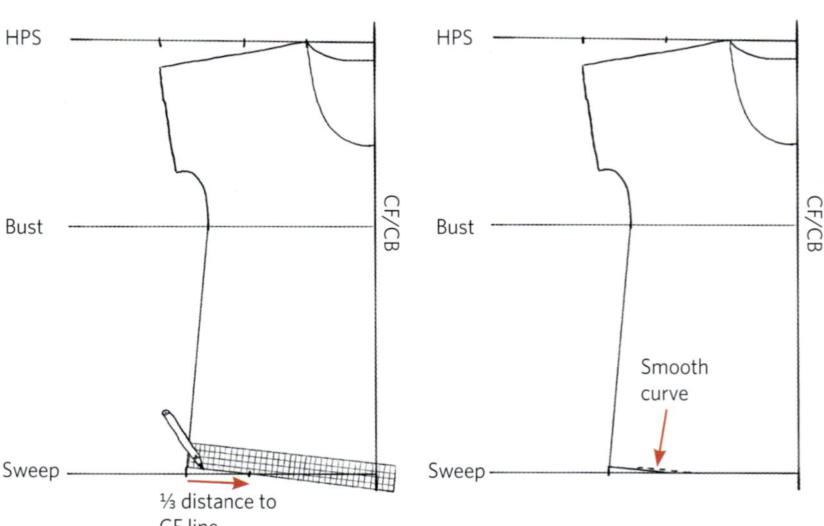

**4.** Garments typically sit on the body better when the shoulder seam is slightly forward of the HPS fold, so draw a new shoulder seam that is parallel to the original but about ½" or ⅝" (1.3 cm or 1.6 cm) lower than the original. The original line will become the line along which the back panel folds toward the front.

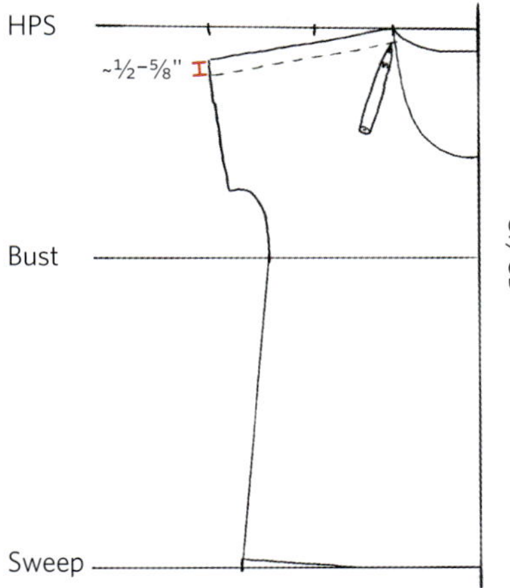


**5.** In order to accommodate the forward shoulder seam you just drew, you'll need to extend the back panel's upper area to include that folded section.

**A.** Fold the paper backward along the original shoulder (the new fold line).

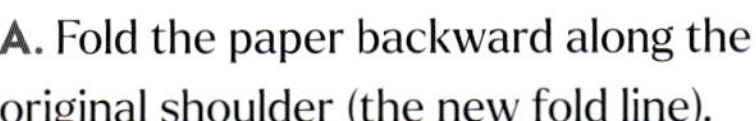

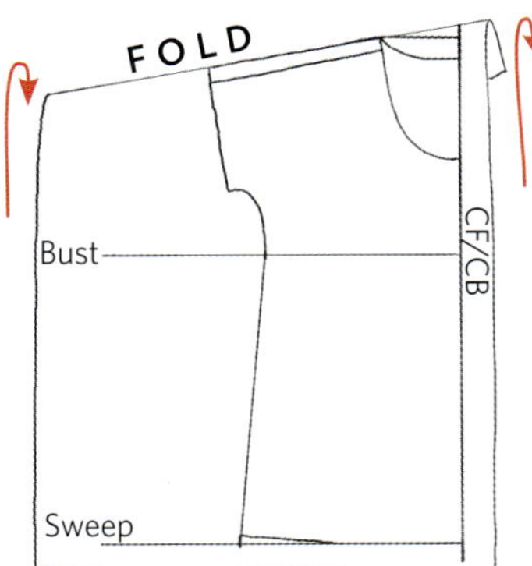


**B.** Use a tracing wheel or pin to trace the new shoulder seam line and the neck and sleeve lines above it.

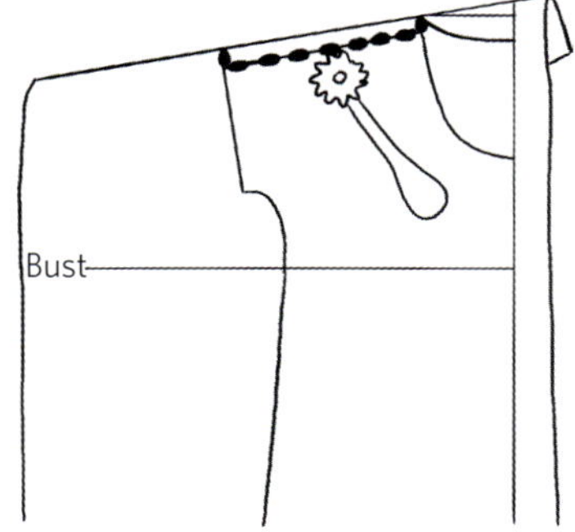


**C.** Unfold the paper and draw over your tracings with pencil to make them clear.

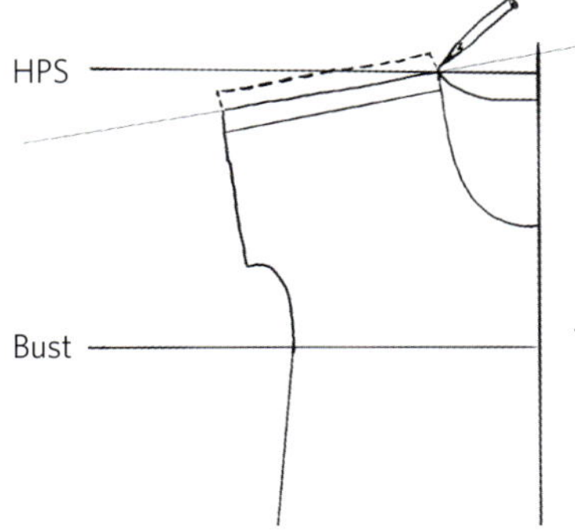


**6.** The neckline will be finished with a facing. To draft the facing shape, use a clear gridded ruler to draw lines onto the garment draft that are parallel to the front and back necklines. The distance away from the neckline will determine the facing's depth. This measurement is up to you. I often like to use facings that are 1¼" (3.2 cm) wide, but that's a design decision, and it is completely your choice. Just be sure to draft facings that are the same width for front and back necklines so they can be sewn together neatly.

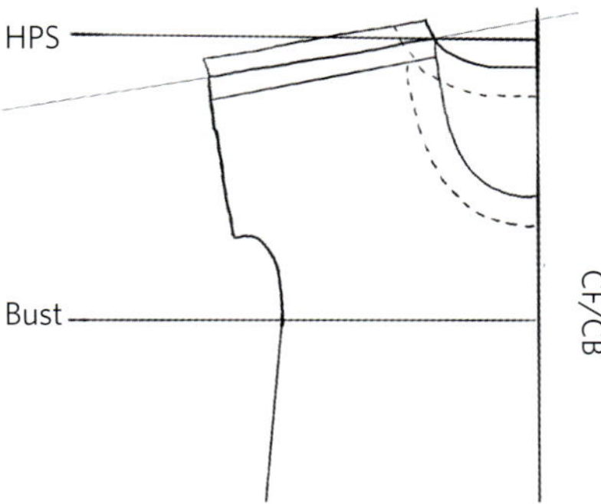


**7.** Add a notch somewhere along the side seam to facilitate accurate sewing.

### TRACING THE FRONT BODY PATTERN

**1.** Get a large piece of paper that is more than twice as wide as current pattern draft. Fold in half and place on table with fold on right-hand side. Lay draft on top of folded paper, aligning CF/CB line with the fold beneath. Use weights to hold in place.

**2.** Use tracing wheel or pin to trace along the front panel's lines: front neckline, forward shoulder seam line, sleeve hem, sleeve inseam/side seam line, and sweep. Trace the side seam's matching notch, too. (See bolded lines in diagram for tracing guide.)

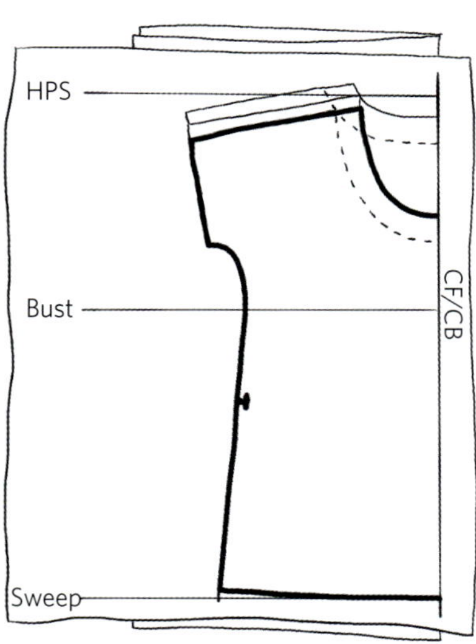


**3.** Lift away draft. With front pattern sheet still folded, draw in traced lines with a pencil and ruler. Then add seam and hem allowances using clear gridded ruler to draw parallel lines. To follow my sewing instructions, I'd recommend:

- ¼" (6 mm) on neckline
- ½" (1.3 cm) on shoulder seam and inseam/side seam
- ¾" (2 cm) on sleeve hem
- 1¾" (4.4 cm) on sweep

If your sleeve shape doesn't extend beyond the side seam—if it instead meets the side seam with a straight line—then you'll have a "stepped" SA along the side, where the ½" (1.3 cm) side seam SA abruptly switches to ¾" (2 cm) sleeve HA. See diagram as guide.

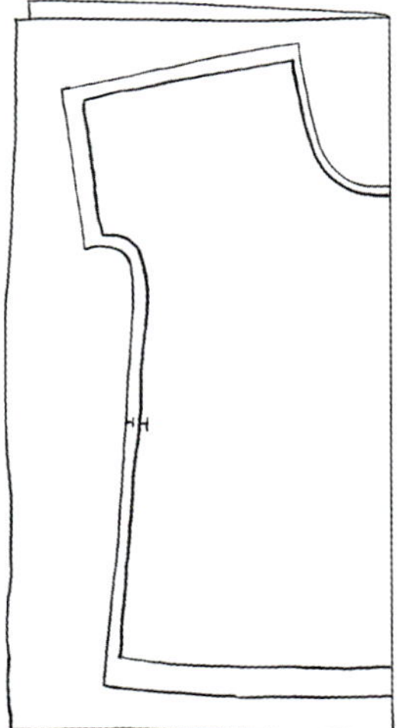

**4.** Pin folded layers together to prevent shifting. Cut out along seam/hem allowance lines. Snip a small V into side seam at notch point, being sure to cut through both layers of paper. Remove pins and unfold.

**5.** Snip another notch at CF point along neckline. Add grainline arrow along CF. Add note: "CUT 1 SELF." (For this pattern and all others, you can also mark any other notations you'd like, including date, name of design, name of pattern piece, etc.)

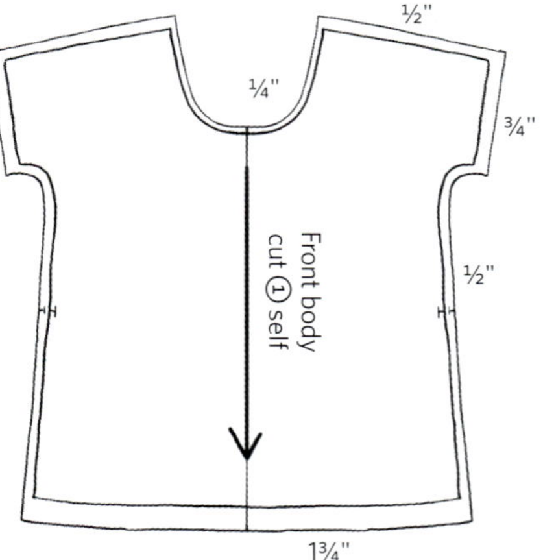

## TRACING THE BACK BODY PATTERN

**1.** Get a large piece of paper that is more than twice as wide as current pattern draft. Fold in half and place on table with fold on right-hand side. Lay draft on top of folded paper, aligning CF/CB line with the fold beneath. Use weights to hold in place.

**2.** Use tracing wheel or pin to trace along the back panel's lines: back neckline, extended shoulder seam line, sleeve hem, sleeve inseam/side seam line, and sweep. Trace the side seam's matching notch, too. (See bolded lines in diagram for tracing guide.)

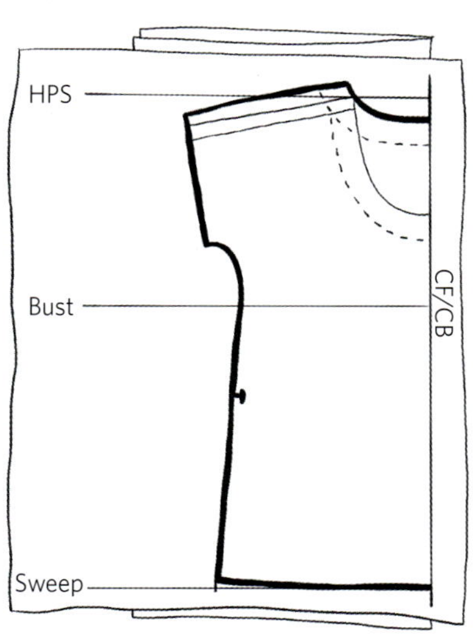


**3.** Lift away draft. With back pattern sheet still folded, draw in traced lines with a pencil and ruler. Then add seam and hem allowances, using clear gridded ruler to draw parallel lines. To follow my sewing instructions, I'd recommend:

- ¼" (6 mm) on neckline
- ½" (1.3 cm) on shoulder seam and inseam/side seam
- ¾" (2 cm) on sleeve hem
- 1¾" (4.4 cm) on sweep

**4.** Pin folded layers together to prevent shifting. Cut out along seam/hem allowance lines. Snip a small V into side seam at notch point, being sure to cut through both layers of paper. Snip another notch along neckline, approximately ¼" (6 mm) from CB fold. Remove pins and unfold.

**5.** Add grainline arrow along CB. Add note: "CUT 1 SELF."

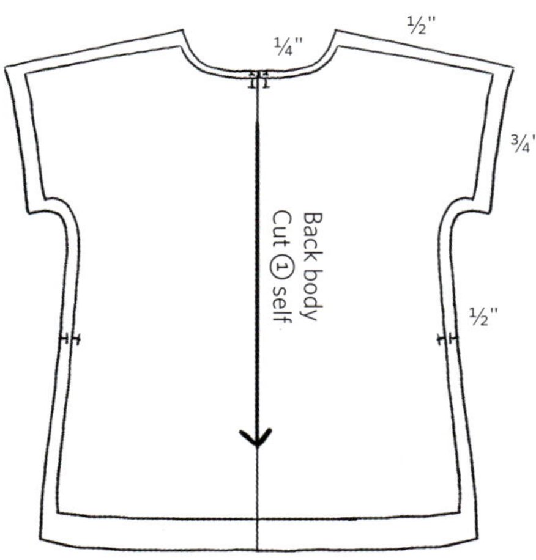

### TRACING THE FRONT NECK FACING PATTERN

**1.** On a new wide sheet of paper, draw a vertical line down the middle of the page. This will represent your CF line. Fold paper in half along this line. Place on table with folded CF line on right-hand side.

**2.** Place draft's neck facing area on top, aligning draft's CF/CB line with the CF fold beneath. Weight down.

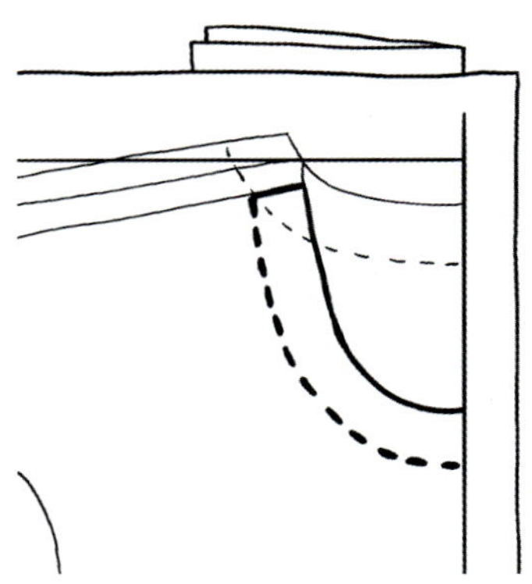

**3.** Using tracing wheel, trace along front neckline, forward shoulder seam, and front facing's outer edge. Remove draft paper and pencil in lines clearly.

**4.** Next, add SAs. I'd recommend:

- ¼" (6 mm) on neckline and outer edge
- ½" (1.3 cm) on shoulder seams

**5.** Pin the two paper layers together and cut out. Remove pins and unfold.

**6.** Snip notch along neckline at CF. Place grainline parallel to CF line. Add note: "CUT 1 SELF."

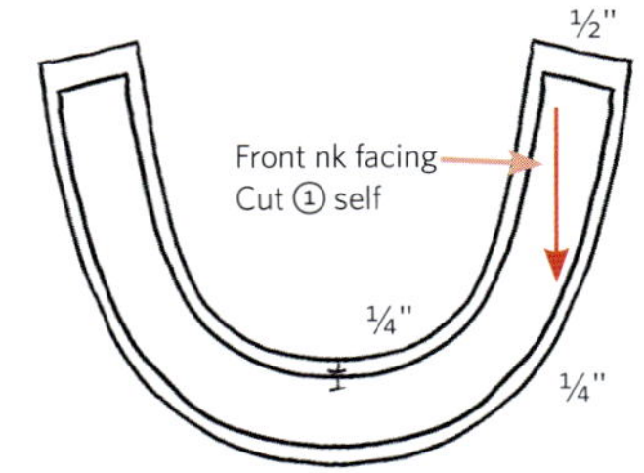


### TRACING THE BACK NECK FACING PATTERN

**1.** On a wide new sheet of paper, draw a vertical line down the middle of the page. This will represent your CB line. Fold paper in half along this line. Place on table with folded CB line on right-hand side.

**2.** Place draft's neck facing area on top, aligning draft's CF/CB line with the CB fold beneath. Weight down.

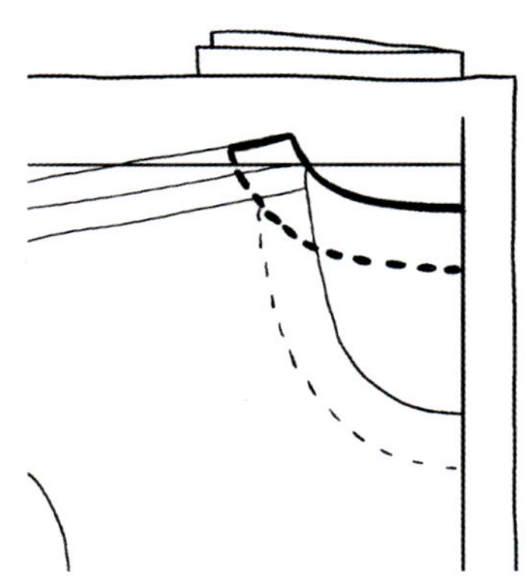

**3.** Using tracing wheel, trace along back neckline, extended shoulder seam, and back facing's outer edge. Remove draft paper and pencil in lines clearly.

**4.** Next, add SAs. I'd recommend:

- ¼" (6 mm) on neckline and outer edge
- ½" (1.3 cm) on shoulder seams

**5.** Pin the two paper layers together and cut out. Snip notch through both layers along back neck, ¼" (6 mm) from CB. Remove pins and unfold.

**6.** Place grainline parallel to CB line. Add note: "CUT 1 SELF."

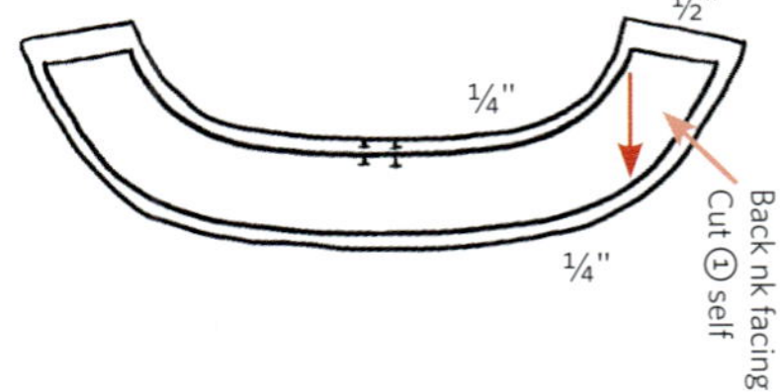

# Sewing

## HAND-SEWING STITCHES

- Running stitch
- Even backstitch
- Combination stitch
- Spaced backstitch
- Hemstitch

## FABRIC OPTIONS

This project is best sewn from light or midweight woven fabric without stretch. The photographed tops are sewn from double gauze and midweight linen, and the photographed dress is sewn from a midweight cotton gauze. If you'd like a drapier look, try fibers such as Tencel or silk. A thin chambray might be lovely, too. Pretty much any woven fabric is fair game, as long as it's lightweight enough for an easy top, and as long as it's something you'd like to wear against your skin. Feel free to experiment with repurposing old textiles—a soft old sheet might be a wonderful choice.

## OTHER MATERIALS

You're welcome to reinforce your neck facings with fusible or sew-in interfacing. I often have poor results with interfacings, so I tend to avoid interfacing as much as possible. On a project like this, it is possible to achieve tidy, attractive neck facings without interfacing. But if you like to add it, that's great, too.

## CUTTING THE FABRIC

See Cutting Fabric on page 85 for tips on cutting. You'll need to cut the following pieces and quantities:

- Front body × 1 self
- Back body × 1 self
- Front neck facing × 1 self, (optional) × 1 interfacing
- Back neck facing × 1 self, (optional) × 1 interfacing

## STAYSTITCHING

I'd highly recommend staystitching the necklines of your front and back panels before you start constructing your top. These temporary stitches will protect the cut neckline edges from being stretched and warped as you handle the project during sewing. The neckline is most vulnerable to this warping because it has significant bias-cut portions, which are stretchier than on-grain or cross-cut areas. It's also visually prominent when you're wearing the top (unlike the bias-cut underarm area, for example).

**1.** To staystitch, take two backstitches to anchor thread at one end of the front neckline, then make a line of large running stitches along the neckline, just inside the SA. For example, if you've included ¼" (6 mm) SA along the neck edge, place your staystitches slightly closer to the cut edge—perhaps $\frac{3}{16}$" (5 mm) from the edge.

**2.** When you reach the other end of the neckline, do not anchor thread off yet. Instead, lay fabric panel on top of its paper pattern piece and tug thread snug to cinch fabric slightly, ensuring that the fabric neckline edge is same length as (or even a little shorter than) the paper neckline edge. Take two backstitches to anchor off.

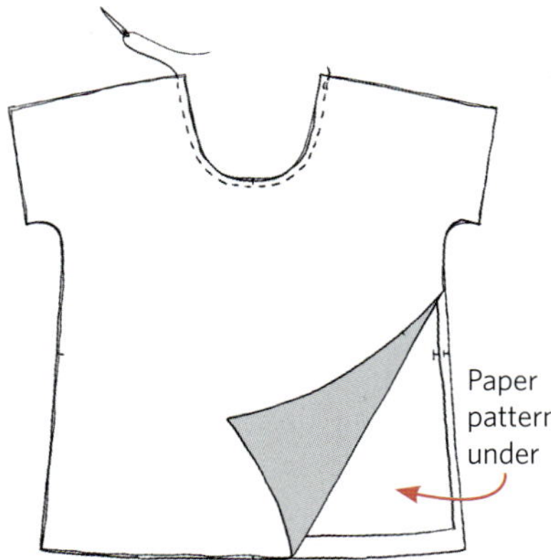


**3.** Repeat staystitching on back neckline.

## SEWING SHOULDER SEAMS

You'll sew the shoulders using the French seam technique, which offers an attractive self finish.

**1.** Align front and back panels along shoulder seams, with WST. Pin.

**2.** Use running stitch to sew along shoulders, ¼" (6 mm) from the raw edge. (This is half of the SA amount provided in the pattern.)

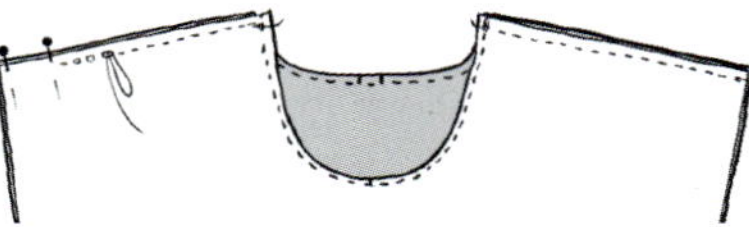

**3.** Trim away ⅛" (3 mm).

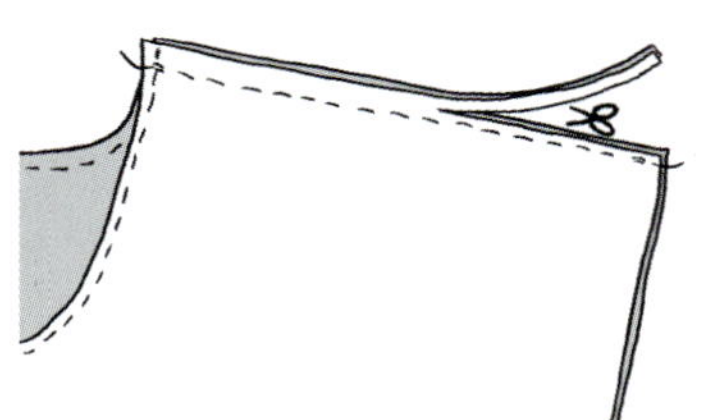

**4.** Press SAs open.

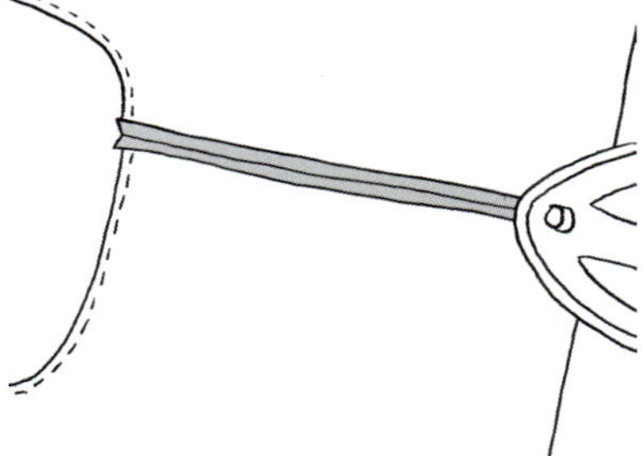

**5.** Turn panels WS out and press seams flat, so that seams are flush on fold. Place a few pins to prevent layers from shifting.

**6.** Use backstitch to sew along shoulders at ¼" (6 mm) from edge. (This is the other half of the pattern's SA amount.)

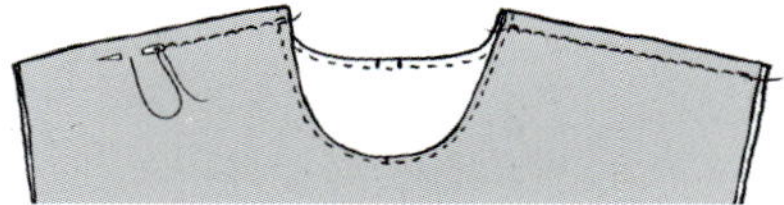

**7.** Press flat, then open to RS of garment and press SAs toward back panel.

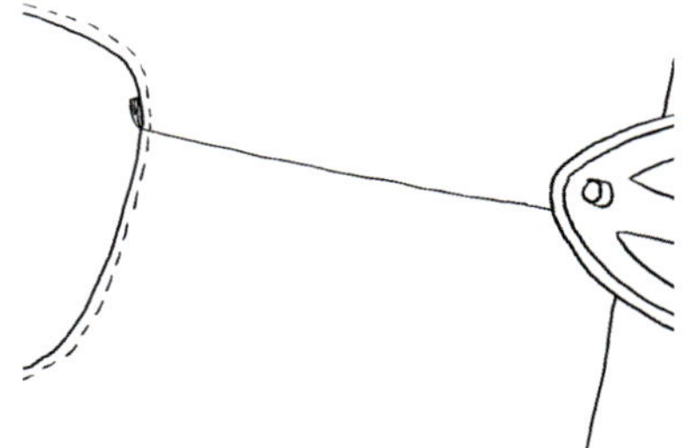

## FINISHING THE NECKLINE

**1.** At ironing board, lay front neck facing on top of its paper pattern piece, with RST. Use pattern's marked fold line as a guideline to prepress facing's outer edge inward by ¼" (6 mm). Repeat for back neck facing.

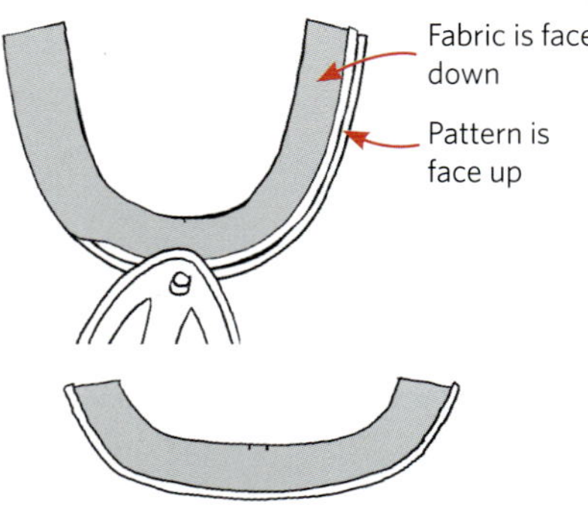


**2.** Unfold pressed facing edges for the moment—crease should still be visible. With RST, align front and back neck facings along shoulder edges. Pin.

**3.** Use running stitch to sew along shoulder edges, using pattern's ½" (1.3 cm) SA amount.

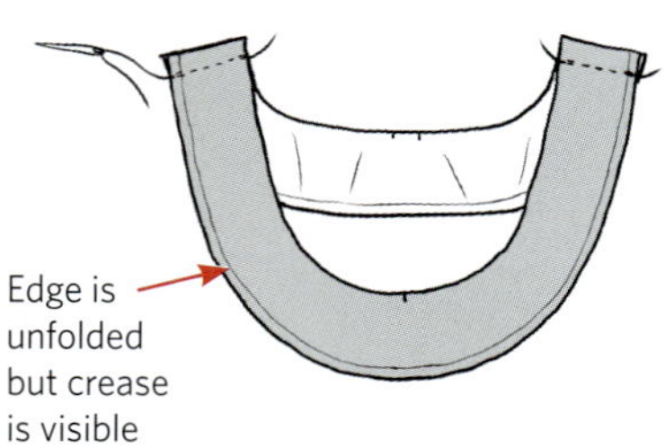


**4.** Press SAs open. Trim triangles at corners of SAs to reduce bulk, as shown.

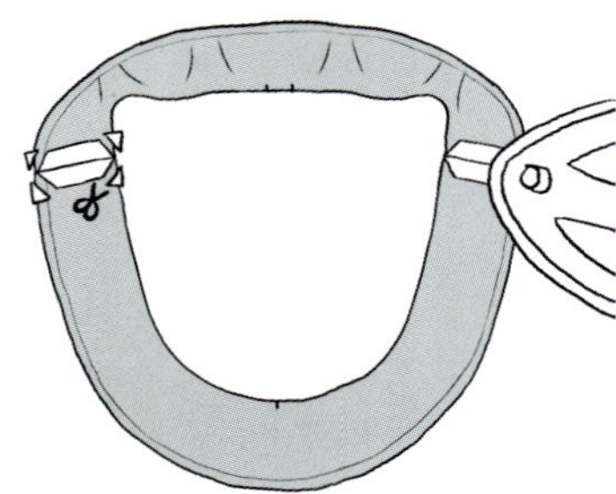

**5.** Lay front and back body panels (which are now joined at shoulder) flat on table, RS up. Lay facing flat on top of body, RS down. Align necklines, matching up shoulder seams and center notches, and pin.

**6.** Use combination stitch to join facing to body along neckline, using pattern's ¼" (6-mm) SA.

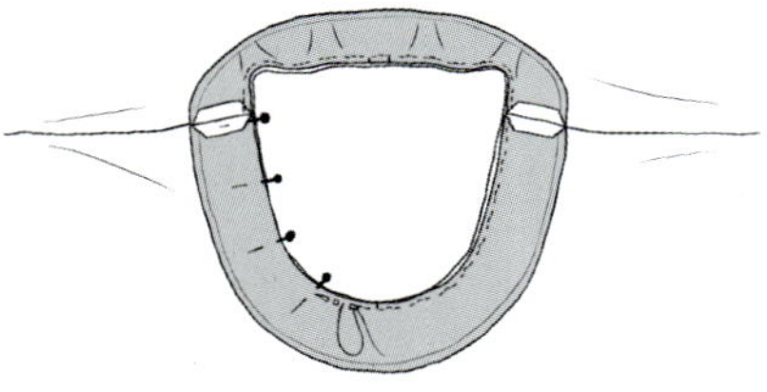

**7.** Press facing toward SA. Use spaced backstitch to understitch through all layers, as shown, to join facing to SA.

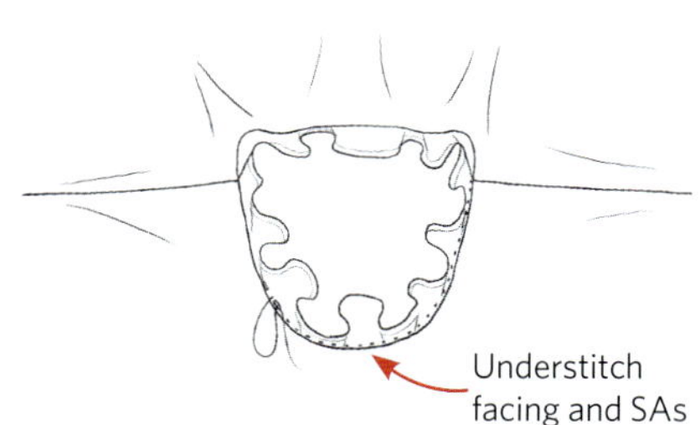


**8.** Flip facing to inside of garment and press neck opening flat. Refold facing's outer edge and press it again if needed. Carefully pin along folded outer edge of facing to prevent it from shifting against the garment's body.

**9.** Use hemstitch (or running stitch, or another stitch of your choice) to secure the outer perimeter of the facing to the garment. Remember the backside of your stitches will be visible on the outside of the garment, so select a stitch that will look appealing from the outside.

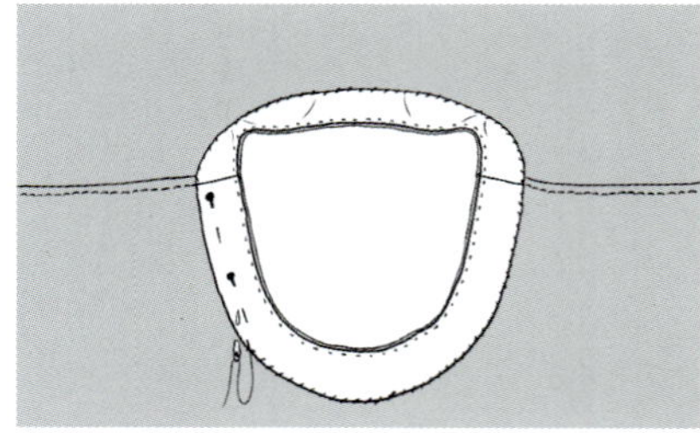

**10.** Press.

## SEWING THE SIDE SEAMS

You'll sew the side seams/sleeve inseams using the French seam technique, just as you did at the shoulders.

**1.** Align front and back panels along side seams/sleeve inseams, with WST. Pin.

**2.** Use running stitch to sew along side seam/sleeve inseam edges, ¼" (6 mm) from the raw edge. (This is half of the SA provided in the pattern.)

**3.** Trim away ⅛" (3 mm).

**4.** Press SAs open.

**5.** Turn panels WS out and press seams flat, so that seams are flush on fold. Place a few pins to prevent layers from shifting.

**6.** Use backstitch to sew along edges at ¼" (6 mm) from edge. (This is the other half of the pattern's SA amount.)

**7.** Press flat, then open to RS of garment and press SAs toward back panel.

## HEMMING

**1.** Turn garment inside out. Press sleeve opening edges ¼" (6 mm) inward.

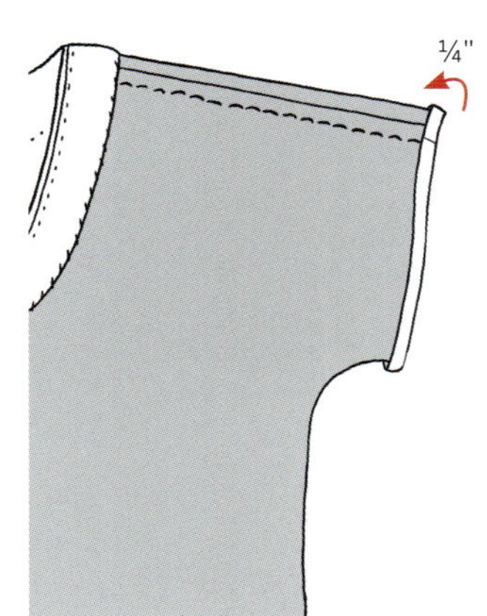


**2.** Press sleeve opening edges another ½" (1.3 cm) inward. Pin.

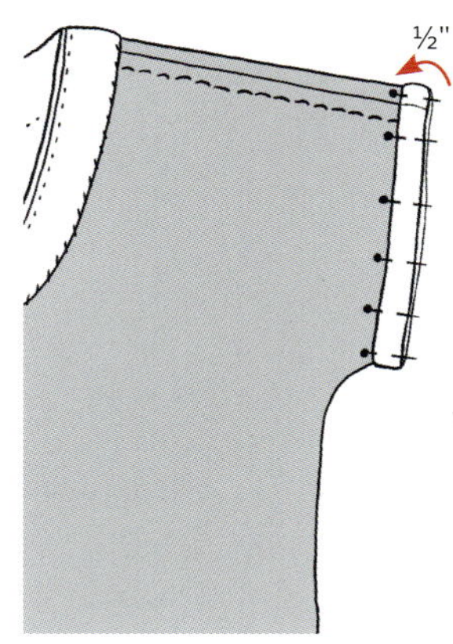


**3.** Use hemstitch to secure hem.

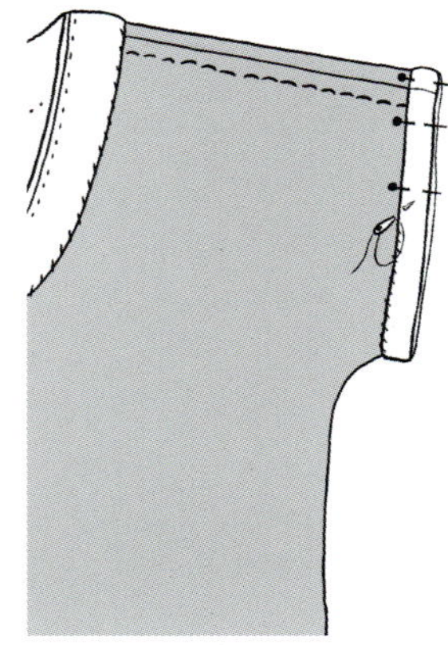

**4.** Press bottom edge of garment ¼" (6 mm) inward.

**5.** Press bottom edge another 1½" (3.8 cm) inward. Pin.

**6.** Use hemstitch to secure hem.

## STITCHING A LABEL

1. If you'd like to embroider a label for your woven top, determine its dimensions and then add ¼" (6 mm) of hem allowance all around. Mark this shape onto your chosen label fabric. Optionally, add fusible interfacing or another layer of fabric behind to stiffen and strengthen the label. If you're using another layer of fabric, you can baste or pin it to hold.

2. Use a pencil or other marking tool to draw desired design.

3. Use embroidery floss or other thick thread to create chainstitch lines tracing your design.

4. Cut along hem allowance lines to remove excess fabric, then press ¼" (6 mm) hem allowance under, all around the perimeter. Baste if desired.

5. Pin label to garment at desired location. Optionally, baste and check to ensure label is aligned as desired.

6. Secure label to garment using hemstitch, running stitch, or other stitch of your choice.

# Variations

This woven boxy top project is a great starting point for all sorts of patternmaking and sewing variations. You can play with using different stitches or construction techniques. You can add style lines and embroidery, as I've done in my first variation. Try different widths, lengths, neckline shapes, etc. Add pockets or a button placket or a gathered skirt—or all of these at once, as I've done in the dress variation. Experiment and see what styles you can create.

## Embroidered Yoke Top

This variation features a yoke with allover embroidery. The neck is finished with a self lining, and there is a button placket at center back.

The yoke was created using simple style lines that I added to my basic pattern. For visual interest and for efficiency in my fabric cutting layout, I added other style lines, too.

If you'd like to add allover embroidery to one or more panels of your top, you have two options: Embroider your design before cutting out the fabric panels or embroider after the top is constructed. I chose the former, because it meant that if the fabric shrank a bit from my stitches, the final garment would still fit as intended. However, feel free to embellish your garment after the fact—in an easy-fitting top like this one, it's still pretty likely to fit you, even if it shrinks a bit. Using an embroidery hoop should help you avoid some puckering.

For my design, I used tailor's chalk to mark a grid of lines onto my uncut yoke fabric. I marked this grid to be slightly larger than the yoke panel that I planned to cut out. Then, with embroidery floss, I stitched lines of long running stitches both horizontally and vertically, using my chalk marks as guides. I left my thread ends loose at the start and finish of each line. Once my embroidery work was done, I weighted the pattern pieces down and anchored the embroidery thread ends into the SAs before cutting each piece.

When sewing the yoke and other style line seams, I flat-felled the SAs. The first pass on these seams was running stitch, and then I felled the allowances with hemstitch.

## Dirndl Dress

The dirndl dress is a simple pattern-making variation on the basic boxy top. To create mine, I shortened the front and back bodice patterns. Then I drafted a skirt pattern that was basically two very wide rectangles, each with two times more width than the bodice's waistline measurement. For the neckline, I drafted a V shape instead of the round neck, and I added triple-turned hems at center front to create an overlapping button placket. I also made a rectangular patch pocket pattern, then slashed and spread the pattern 1½" (3.8 cm) to create extra space at the pocket opening to accommodate the volume of whatever the pocket will hold.

When sewing, I followed the basic directions, with a few additional steps:

- I finished the neckline using an inside bias binding (see page 152 for a how-to).
- The skirt side seams were finished using basically the same French seam techniques as for the shoulder and bodice side seams. The only difference was that in the second line of stitching, I used running stitch instead of backstitch. I chose to use running stitch because it's much faster on those long skirt seams, and because the skirt is so loose-fitting that its side seams are unlikely to come under much strain and therefore don't need as much strength.
- I gathered the skirt's top edge using two parallel lines of long basted running stitches. Then I joined the skirt to the bodice using backstitch. I finished the waist SA with bias-cut seam binding (see page 152 for a how-to) that I attached with running stitch and hemstitch.
- To create the patch pockets, I made a double-turned hem at the top edge using hemstitch. I finished the side and bottom raw edges with overcasting, then turned them under and pressed. The pockets were secured to the skirt using fell stitch.
- After the dress was otherwise complete, I stitched the buttonholes, attached the buttons, and made back waist ties using the spaghetti strap method detailed on page 200.

# *Tiffany Downs*

*(she/her)*, owner of vintage clothing shop Silver Thimble and Liberation Bakery
LOUISVILLE, KENTUCKY, USA

Tiffany Downs has always preferred hand sewing. As a child, she learned to sew by hand and then by machine, but she disliked the machine. "It was always frustrating for me," she remembers. "I felt like it slowed me down from the end result I wanted."

Eventually Tiffany moved on to other creative pursuits, and it wasn't until a decade ago that she felt the urge to sew again. She decided to try hand-stitching a piece of clothing this time. "I thought, 'Well, I've got needles, I have thread, so I'm just gonna make it by hand,'" Tiffany says. "And that was the beginning—I was hooked. I haven't stopped."

Today, Tiffany is the owner of a vintage clothing shop for which she hand-stitches some original pieces. She also gardens and runs a bakery. Regardless of her medium, Tiffany approaches her creative work as an artist.

***Immediacy of handwork.*** I love hand sewing because to me it can feel as expressive as drawing. It's just you, your hands, the needle, and fabric. The less space between an artist and their medium, the more heart they can put into their work.

***Just simple.*** I'm not someone who knows a million stitches. I was taught as a little girl and then picked up thread and just made things come together. And there are so many amazing people out there who are making incredible historical garments and are using a huge vocabulary of stitches from years past. But I'm not that person. I'll disappoint you with my stitch knowledge. It's mainly just running and hemming stitches for me. It's just simple.

***Take it everywhere.*** I sew in my studio, but then also everywhere. Sometimes I'm in the living room, watching mysteries. Sometimes I'm in the bedroom on the bed, listening to an audiobook. I take it everywhere.

***Sewing with chronic illness.*** I have an illness that damages my nervous system. I have neuropathy and arthritis in my hands. I don't know how long I'll be able to do what I love. But until the time comes when I can't, that's what I'm going to be doing. Each garment I make now is a big victory to me. It's a small way I can say I am not giving up.

I know the garments I make now will keep me happy for years to come. And whatever happens to my hands in the future, I will always find a way to make things. Creating is an essential part of who I am. Maybe in the future I'll start gluing clothes together or something. I'm pretty stubborn. Who knows? But I do know there's always, always a way.

***Wear your happiness.*** Happiness is beautiful. When you're proud of what you're wearing, when there's a beautiful story behind it, when there is love and patience put into it, then you're going to be happy and proud to wear it. You're going to be happy and look beautiful in it.

# LEGGINGS

What could be more satisfying than drafting and stitching up a pair of versatile custom-fit leggings? Made from four-way stretch fabric, leggings are quite forgiving in terms of fit. While sewing, you'll focus on stitches and techniques that have lots of stretch potential. Being able to hand-sew with knits opens up a whole new world of handsewn garment possibilities. So stitch up some nice stretchy leggings, and as you do, let yourself dream of all the other knit garments you might like to try.

# Patternmaking

To draft leggings, you'll take some measurements from your own body. Then, because you're drafting a very snug-fitting garment, you'll probably want to subtract out some negative wearing ease. In other words, the garment will be slightly smaller than your actual body so the fabric will stretch to lie smoothly against your skin. In order to figure out an appropriate amount of negative wearing ease, you'll need to assess the stretchiness of the fabric you're planning to use.

### MEASURING YOUR BODY

Before drafting take several measurements from your own body. While measuring wear very snug-fitting, thin clothes or just your underwear.

To begin, set up some landmarks for yourself by tying strips of elastic, ribbon, yarn, or scrap fabric around the following places:

- Natural waist (where your body creases when you tip to the side like a teapot)
- Hip (widest part of your rear)
- Thigh (widest part of your upper leg)
- Knee (just above your kneecap)
- Calf (not an important measurement for everyone, but it's helpful if you have fuller calves)
- Ankle (just above the anklebone, or wherever you'd like your leggings to end)

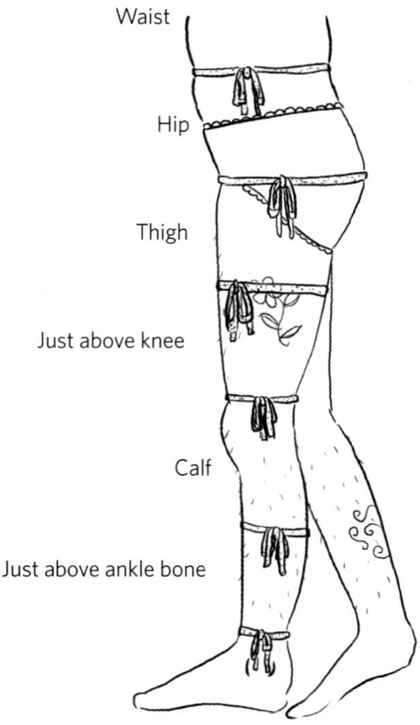

With landmarks in place, measure the following:

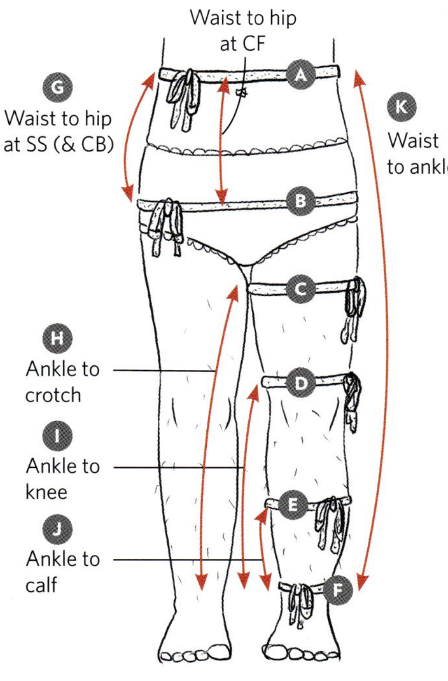


**A.** Waist circumference

**B.** Hip circumference

**C.** Thigh circumference (fullest point)

**D.** Knee circumference

**E.** Calf circumference

**F.** Ankle circumference

**G.** Waist to hip level at CF, side seam, and CB (these might all be the same measurement, or they might not)

**H.** Ankle to crotch along inseam

**I.** Ankle to knee along inseam

**J.** Ankle to calf along inseam

**K.** Outseam length (this is theoretical, measured from waist to ankle at level, but it may change during patternmaking)

**L.** Rise (measured from chair to waist at side seam)

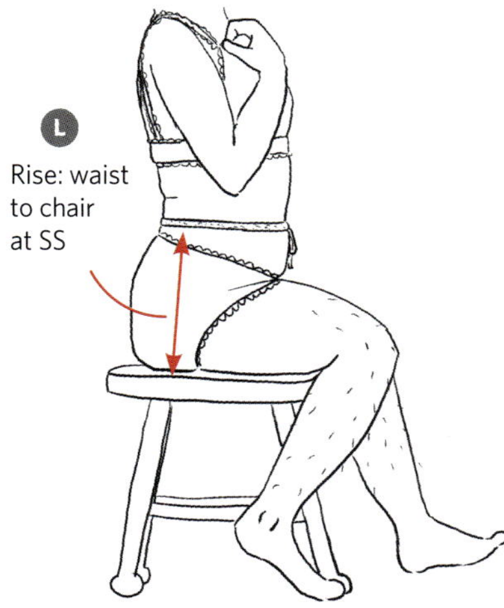


While you're wearing snug clothing, you may also find it helpful to take visual reference photos of your front, side, and back views, so that you can look back later and study how your body volume is distributed. This can help you make some informed decisions as you draft for your own body's shape.

## CALCULATING YOUR FABRIC'S STRETCH PERCENTAGE

In order to calculate negative wearing ease, you'll need to measure your particular fabric's stretch potential. (Read Fabric Options on page 127 before choosing a fabric—be sure you're using a fabric with four-way stretch!) With fabric in hand, here's how to find the stretch percentage.

**1.** Lay fabric on a smooth, flat surface, with grainline oriented vertically.

**2.** Measure a 10-centimeter horizontal span and mark with pins. (I prefer metric rather than imperial measurements for this, because metric numbers are easier for the calculations.)

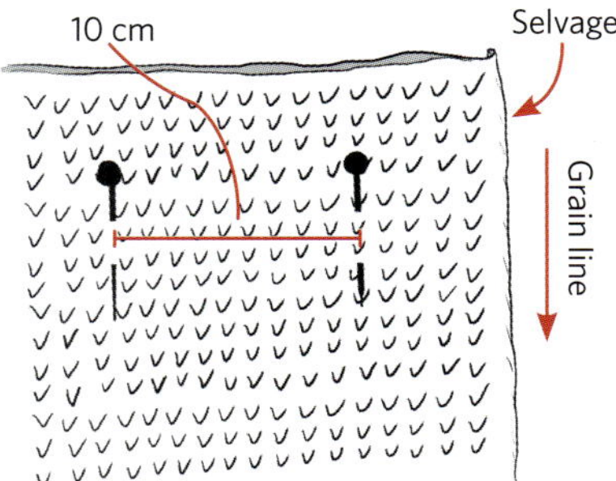


**3.** Fold fabric back along pin level. Lay a ruler flat with zero point held at first pin, then stretch fabric at second pin to see how far the fabric naturally stretches. This is a bit unscientific, because you want to stretch the fabric as far as it can easily pull without stretching so far that you're distorting its structure. Try to stretch to the amount of tension that you'd want the fabric to be under while you're wearing it—snug, but not too tight. Now note how far the second pin has reached on the ruler. (Again, I like to look at the metric measurement here.)

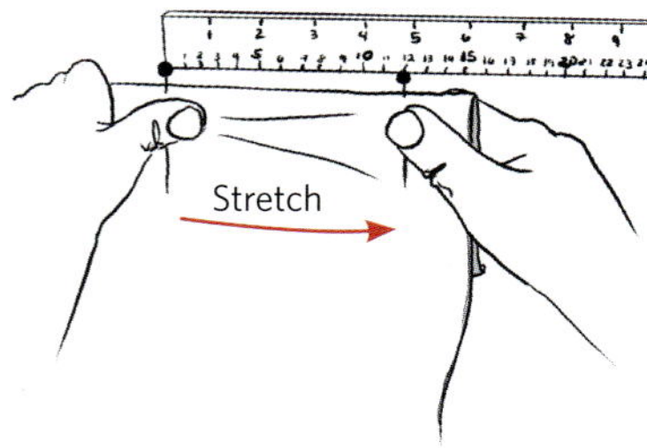


**4.** How many centimeters did the fabric stretch? Multiply this number by 10 to find your fabric's natural stretch percentage.

For example, if my fabric stretched to 13 cm, it stretched 3 cm (beyond its original 10 cm). I'd then multiply 3 cm by 10 to calculate a 30 percent stretch.

You've just calculated your fabric's natural stretch potential. Now you have a choice to make. When subtracting out the negative ease for your leggings:

- You can subtract the full amount of stretch potential your fabric has to offer. This will produce a snug pair of leggings.
- Or you can subtract a smaller stretch percentage than what your fabric is capable of. This will result in a slightly less tight pair of leggings. (I often like to use 10 percent as my stretch percentage, even if my fabric is capable of stretching more.)

I wouldn't recommend trying a larger stretch percentage than what your fabric is capable of, because that will result in an uncomfortably tight pair of leggings.

Once you've decided what stretch percentage you'll use, you're ready to calculate the final measurements.

## CALCULATING THE DIMENSIONS

You'll calculate your garment's dimensions with the stretch reduction in mind. You'll only need to do these reductions for the garment's widths—the vertical dimensions can remain unchanged from your body's actual measurements.

The first column represents your body's actual measurement; the next column will need to be calculated by finding the stretch percentage of the body measurement. (For example, if your body's waist circumference is 36" [92 cm] and you're using a 10 percent stretch reduction amount, you'd write 36" in the first blank and 3.6" [9.2 cm] in the second blank.) Then proceed with the calculations as written. Note that the hip circumference is the only measurement that will be divided by 4 rather than 2. The final column represents the numbers you'll use to draft.

- Stretch Percentage: ______

**Widths:**

- Waist circumference
  ______ – ______ = ______ ÷ 2 = ______
- Hip circumference
  ______ – ______ = ______ ÷ 4 = ______
- Thigh circumference
  ______ – ______ = ______ ÷ 2 = ______
- Knee circumference
  ______ – ______ = ______ ÷ 2 = ______
- Calf circumference
  ______ – ______ = ______ ÷ 2 = ______
- Ankle circumference
  ______ – ______ = ______ ÷ 2 = ______

**Lengths:**

- Waist to hip at front ______
- Waist to hip at side ______
- Waist to hip at back ______
- Ankle to crotch ______
- Ankle to knee ______
- Ankle to calf ______
- Outseam ______
- Rise height ______

You'll begin by drafting your shapes onto a large piece of paper. The draft will consist of a single leg shape, plus a rectangle for a waistband and a rectangle for an ankle band. Later, you'll trace off the final pattern pieces.

## SETTING UP THE LEG AREA

**1.** With a ruler, draft a long vertical line down the middle of the paper. This line will represent the leggings' outseam. Make it slightly longer than your expected outseam measurement.

**2.** Near the bottom of the outseam, square a long line in both directions to represent the ankle level.

**3.** Along the outseam, measure your ankle-to-calf length from the ankle level, and square out a long line to represent the calf level.

**4.** Along the outseam, measure your ankle-to-knee length from the ankle level, and square out a long line to represent the knee level.

**5.** Along the outseam, measure your ankle-to-crotch length from the ankle level, and square out a long line to represent the crotch level.

**6.** Now you'll start plotting widths along the leg. Find the number you wrote in the last column for the ankle circumference calculation. From the outseam, measure left along ankle level and plot this measurement with a tick mark. From the outseam, measure right along ankle level and plot this same measurement with a tick mark.

**7.** Repeat along the calf level, measuring the final calculation's amount to the right and left of the outseam and making tick marks.

**8.** Repeat along the knee level, measuring the final calculation's amount to the right and left of the outseam and making tick marks.

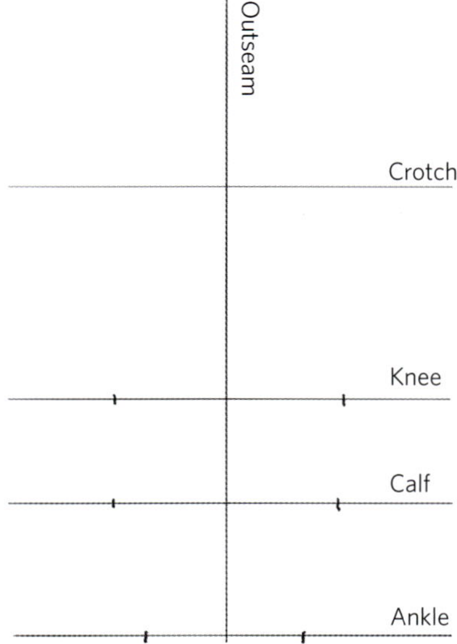


## REFINING THE HIP AREA

**1.** Find the number you wrote in the last column for the hip circumference calculation. (This should be the final number after you divided by 4.) We'll refer to this as your "quarter-hip measurement." From the outseam line, measure left and right along crotch level and mark your quarter-hip measurement with tick marks.

**2.** From each of the quarter-hip tick marks you just made, square long lines upward.

**3.** Until now, the draft has been symmetrical on each side of the outseam line—that is to say, the front and back sides of the body have been treated the same. Now you'll begin to differentiate, because in the hip area, the body is quite notably not symmetrical from front to back. Label the left line you just squared as the CB line and the right line you just squared as the CF line.

**4.** You'll begin drafting curved extensions on front and back at crotch level so that your body has a "saddle" in which to sit. The curved extension will be deeper on the back than the front, because most of a body's girth is toward the back (in the buttocks) at the crotch level. Begin by dividing your quarter-hip measurement by 3.

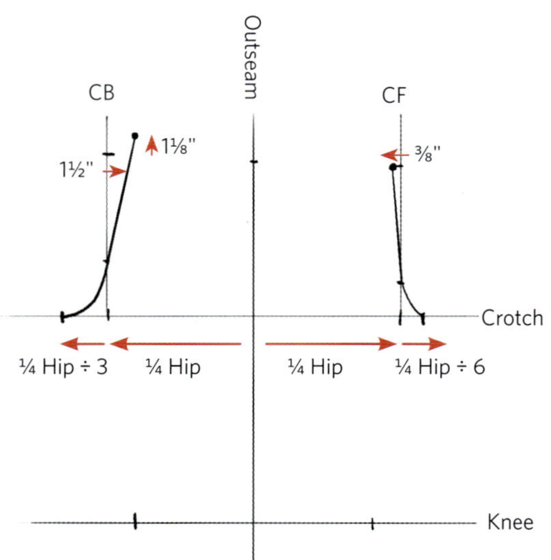


Use this number to measure to the left along the crotch line from CB. Draw a tick mark. This tick mark will represent the outermost point of your back crotch extension.

**5.** Divide your quarter-hip measurement by 6. Use this number to measure to the right along the crotch line from CF. Draw a tick mark. This tick mark will represent the outermost point of your front crotch extension.

**6.** Find your rise measurement on your list of vertical dimensions. Use this measurement to measure and make tick marks along the outseam, CB, and CF lines, measuring from the crotch line upward. These tick marks represent the approximate level of your waistline.

**7.** Next, you'll refine these waist placement marks to better capture the three-dimensional shaping of the waist in relation to the body. Find the waist tick mark along the CB line. Now measure inward (toward the outseam line) by 1½" (3.8 cm) and upward (toward the top of the paper) by 1⅛" (3 cm). Mark this new point clearly with a dot.

**8.** Find the waist tick mark along the CF line. Now measure inward (toward the outseam line) by ⅜" (1 cm). Mark this new point clearly with a dot.

**9.** Now you'll begin to build a CB rise curve. Estimate a point along the CB line that is approximately one-third of the way from the crotch line to the waist tick mark. Make a straight line connecting from this spot to the adjusted waist dot you marked in step 7.

**10.** Estimate a point along the CF line that is approximately one-quarter of the way from the crotch line to the waist tick mark. Make a straight line connecting from this spot to the adjusted waist dot you marked in step 8.

**11.** For each side (front and back), draft a smooth curve that feeds gracefully from your crotch line extension mark into the straight line. You can use curve tools to achieve these lines, but I prefer freehanding to sketch out suitable lines. For a general sense of the shapes you're aiming for, see the diagram on the left.

### REFINING THE WAIST AREA

**1.** Square a line from the top of the CB line, pointing in toward the outseam line. This new line should be at least 2" (5 cm). Square another line from the top of the CF line, pointing in toward the outseam line. This line should also be at least 2" (5 cm).

**2.** Freehand a gentle curve to connect these two squared lines. You'll likely be creating a very subtle backward S curve. This line may cross the waist tick mark you drew on the outseam line, or it may deviate from that point somewhat (which is fine). Your goal is simply to create a very gentle, smooth curve.

**3.** Before committing to this waistline, measure it carefully, walking or bending your ruler to get an accurate measurement. Compare this number with your body's anatomical waistline measurement (the final column of your waist circumference calculations).

- If your draft's waistline is the same as your calculated anatomical measurement, perfect! You can proceed to the next step.
- If your draft's waistline is slightly too long (within ½" [1.3 cm] of your anatomical measurement), you can probably leave it as is. The leggings' waistline will be stitched into a waistband anyway, and a slight length difference probably won't show.
- If your draft's waistline is significantly longer than your anatomical measurement (more than a ½" [1.3 cm] difference), you'll want to shave off some of the waistline. You can do this at CB, CF, or both, depending on what you think would best match your own body's distribution of volume. (You might want to refer to your front, side, and back photograph references here.) Know that where you remove, you will be deepening the "saddle" in which your body will sit in the leggings. So for example, if you think your body would benefit from a deeper saddle in back because you have full buttocks, then remove length all or mostly from the back. If you think your body is pretty balanced, consider splitting the difference between front and back. It's up to you. Once you've achieved an accurate waistline length, redraw your straight and curved lines.
- If your draft's waistline is shorter than your anatomical measurement, you'll want to add some length along the waistline. You can do this at CB, CF, or both, depending on what you think would best match your own body's distribution of volume. (You might want to refer to your front, side, and back photograph references here.) Once you've achieved an accurate waistline length, redraw your straight and curved lines accordingly.

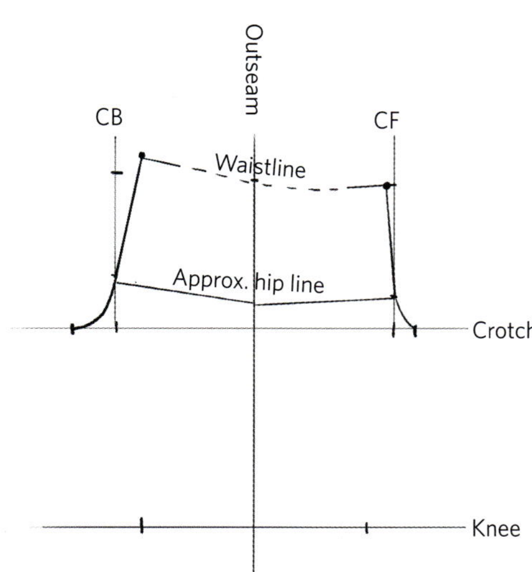


**4.** Now that the waistline is accurate, you'll want to check your hip measurement as well. Refer to your anatomical waist-to-hip measurements for front, side, and back, and mark them down along the CF, outseam, and CB lines. Then connect the marks with straight lines and measure the resulting line. Compare this measurement with the final column of your hip circumference calculations multiplied by two. In other words, compare it with your half-hip measurement (not your quarter-hip).

- If your draft's hipline is the same as your half-hip measurement, perfect! You can proceed to the next step.

- If your draft's hipline is slightly too long or short (within ½" [1.3 cm] of your anatomical measurement), you can probably leave it as is. A slight difference in stretchy fabric isn't likely to affect the fit much.
- If your draft's hipline is significantly longer or shorter than your half-hip measurement (more than a ½" [1.3 cm] difference), you may want to adjust the rise curves in that area to achieve a more accurate measurement. You can carve into the front and/or back rise seams if the draft's hipline is too long, or you can bump out the front and/or back rise seams if the draft's hipline is too short. As with the waistline, you'll need to decide where to remove or add based on a spatial understanding of your own body's shape. Photographic references of your front, side, and back views can help. Once you've achieved an accurate hipline measurement, make sure your finalized rise seams create smooth, continuous lines.

**5.** By now, you've probably drawn and redrawn this area of the pattern multiple times. Consider using a colored pencil or marker to highlight the finalized lines. This will make it easier to identify them later.

## REFINING THE LEG AREA

**1.** You've completed the hip area, but the leg portion needs to be finalized. To begin, draw straight lines to connect the dots between ankle, calf, knee, and crotch tick marks, as shown. This creates a provisional inseam that is probably somewhat angular.

**2.** To soften any angles that resulted, freehand smooth, gentle curves. You may be changing the leg's circumference measurements very slightly here, but the difference will be too subtle to be noticeable.

**3.** To improve the fit along the thigh area, you may wish to carve in by approximately ⅜" (1 cm) midway between the crotch and knee levels, and redraw the line there to create a smooth, gentle curve. If you're concerned about the thigh circumference, though, you can measure the draft's thigh circumference and compare it with your anatomical number. Adjust that area of the draft as needed, using smooth, gentle curved lines to blend.

**4.** To ensure clean hemming, you'll need right angles at the ankle-inseam intersections. To create these right angles, extend your inseam lines down straight for 1" (2.5 cm) or so. Slide your gridded ruler or a square tool along the inseam line until you find a line that intersects with the ankle level at approximately one-third of the distance toward the outseam. Draw this line. Then soften the angle by drawing a smooth, gentle curve.

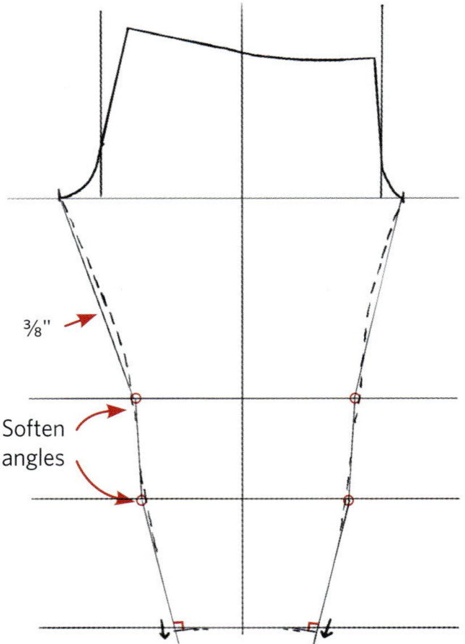

## DRAFTING THE ANKLE BAND AND WAISTBAND LINES

**1.** Decide how tall you'd like the ankle band to be. I like to make mine 1½" (3.8 cm) tall, but this is an individual design decision.

**2.** On your leg pattern draft, draw a line to shorten the leg by the band width amount. This new line should be parallel to the ankle line you just finished drafting. Make sure to follow the curve of the original ankle line as you draw a parallel one.

**3.** Cross out your original ankle line; the new one will be your stitch line on the leg pattern.

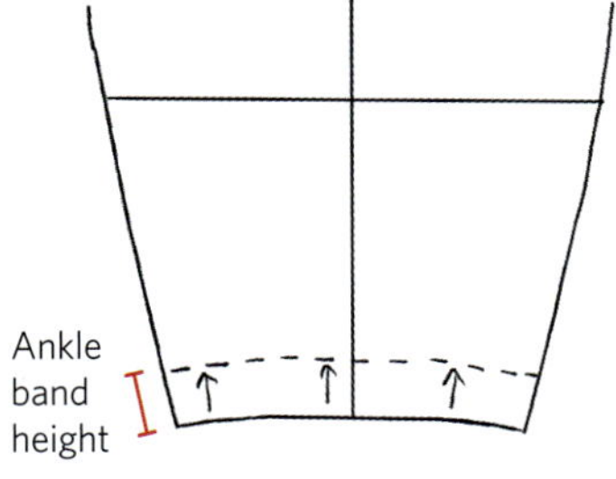


**4.** Decide how tall your waistband should be. I'd recommend making it ⅛" (3 mm) taller than the elastic you'll use. For example, if you're using ¾" (2 cm) elastic, make a waistband that is ⅞" (2.3 cm) tall.

**5.** On your leg pattern draft, draw a line to lower the waistline by the waistband width amount. This new line should be parallel to the pattern's waistline. Make sure to follow the curve of the waistline as you draw a parallel one.

**6.** Cross out your previous waistline; the new one will be your stitch line on the leg pattern.

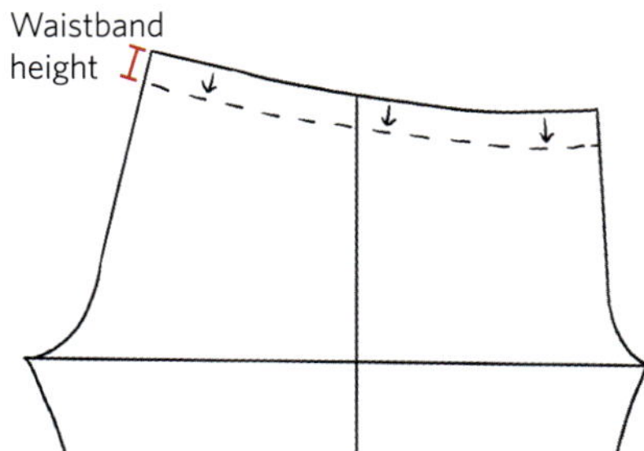


## TRACING THE LEG PATTERN

**1.** Place draft on top of a new large sheet of paper. Weight down.

**2.** Using tracing wheel, trace leg panel's entire perimeter of finalized lines: lowered waist, front and back rises, inseams, and raised ankle. Trace calf, knee, and crotch levels, too. Remove draft paper and pencil in lines clearly. Add notches along inseam edges at calf and knee levels. Also measure and mark notches at midpoint between knee and crotch levels on both inseams. (This distance will differ on back and front inseams, which is normal.) Add notch at outseam point along the ankle line. Measure and add notch halfway along waistline. Place single notch somewhere midway along front rise, and place double notch somewhere midway along back rise.

**3.** Next, add SAs. I'd recommend ½" (1.3 cm) on all edges.

**4.** Cut out. Snip notches.

**5.** Place grainline along outseam. Add note: "CUT 2 SELF."

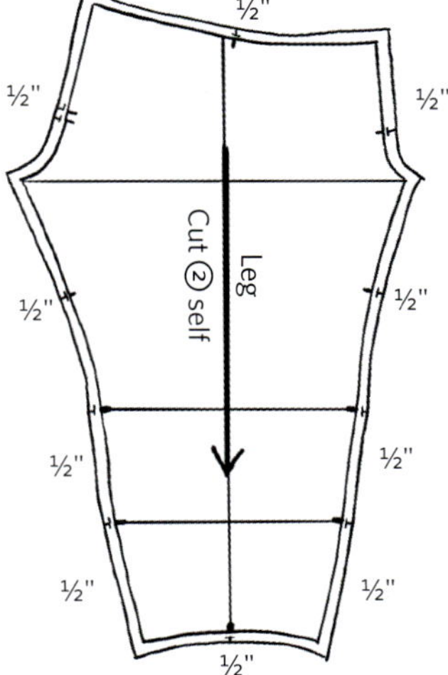

## DRAFTING THE ANKLE BAND PATTERN

**1.** Draft a rectangle. Its height should be twice as tall as your desired finished ankle band height. Its width should be equal to your reduced ankle circumference. (This should be the number in the third column of your ankle circumference calculations.)

**2.** Add notches at midpoints along top and bottom edges.

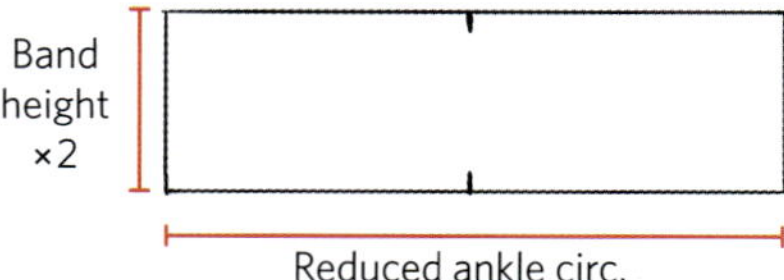


**3.** Next, add SAs. I'd recommend ½" (1.3 cm) on all edges.

**4.** Cut out. Snip notches.

**5.** Place vertical grainline. Add note: "CUT 2 SELF (OR RIB)."

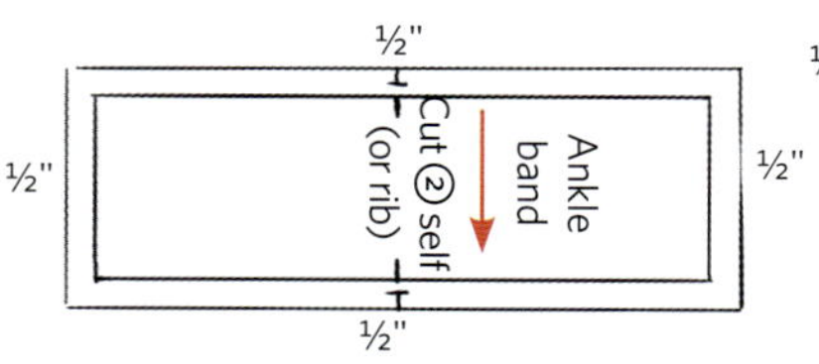


## DRAFTING THE WAISTBAND PATTERN

**1.** Draft a rectangle. Its height should be twice as tall as your desired finished waistband height. Its width should be equal to your reduced waist circumference. (This should be the number in the third column of your waist circumference calculations.)

**2.** Along top and bottom edges, add three notches to divide the rectangle into quarters.

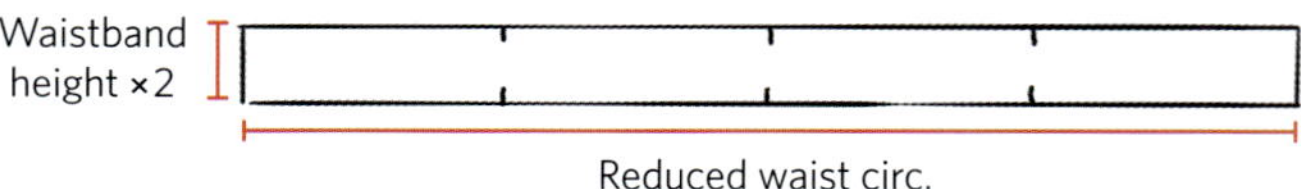


**3.** Next, add SAs. I'd recommend ½" (1.3 cm) on all edges.

**4.** Cut out. Snip notches.

**5.** Place vertical grainline. Add note: "CUT 1 SELF (OR RIB)."

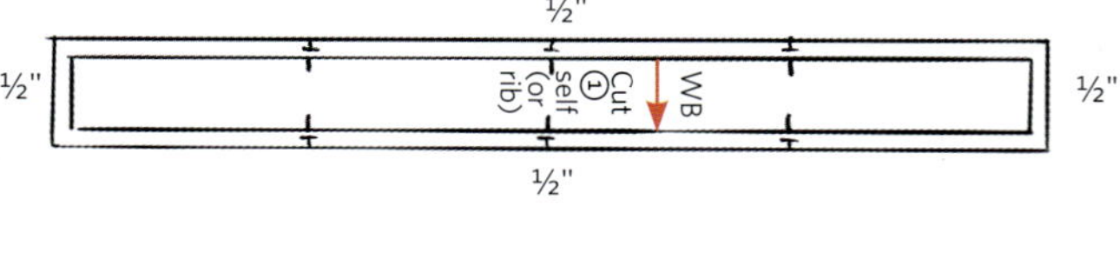

# Sewing

## HAND-SEWING STITCHES

- Backstitch
- Running stitch
- Combination stitch
- Whipstitch
- Overcasting (optional)

## FABRIC OPTIONS

These leggings are best sewn from midweight knit fabric. Importantly, the fabric will need to have four-way stretch—it will need to offer good stretch both horizontally and vertically—in order to produce a well-fitting, well-functioning pair of leggings. (Otherwise the leggings will be difficult to wear—for example, their waistline will ride down in back when you sit, and the ankles will pull up when your knees bend.) Horizontal stretch is typical in knit fabrics, but vertical stretch is generally achieved only through the inclusion of some spandex/elastane fiber content. I like using cotton-spandex blends for leggings, and usually it doesn't take much spandex to achieve reasonable vertical stretch. Something like 95 percent cotton and 5 percent spandex will work well. You can also try fabrics that feature bamboo, wool, or some other fiber instead of cotton.

Four-way stretch jersey is a perfect choice, but you can also find suitably stretchy ribs, waffle knits, scubas, or other knit fabrics. Again, the most important quality is that the fabric must have vertical as well as horizontal stretch.

If desired, you can use a separate rib or other contrasting fabric for the waistband and ankle bands. These areas do not need four-way stretch—they can simply stretch horizontally. (For the colorblocked leggings here, I used a 100% cotton baby rib that has little to no vertical stretch.) If you'd prefer to use your main "self" fabric for these areas, though, that's fine, too.

## OTHER MATERIALS NEEDED

You'll need elastic for the waistband. Something like ¾" (2 cm) or 1" (2.5 cm) is perfect for leggings, but feel free to use something slightly wider or narrower.

## CUTTING THE FABRIC

See Cutting Fabric on page 85 for tips on cutting. You'll need to cut the following pieces and quantities:

- Leg × 2 self
- Ankle band × 2 self (or rib)
- Waistband × 1 self (or rib)

### SEWING THE INSEAMS

For each leg panel:

**1.** Fold leg in half, RST, so that its inseam edges are aligned. Pin, using notches to help with alignment.

**2.** Use backstitch to sew along inseam edge with ½" (1.3 cm) SA amount.

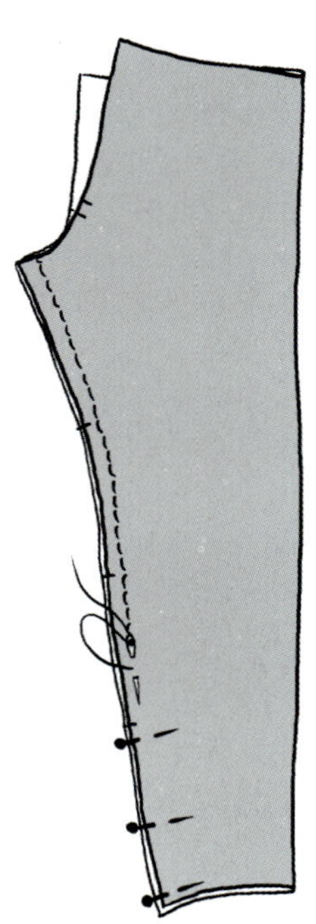

**3.** Optional: Use overcasting to finish the inseam edges together. (This step is optional because jersey yardage typically doesn't unravel much. However, the overcasting can be an attractive addition to your leggings' interior, if you have the interest, time, and patience to add it.)

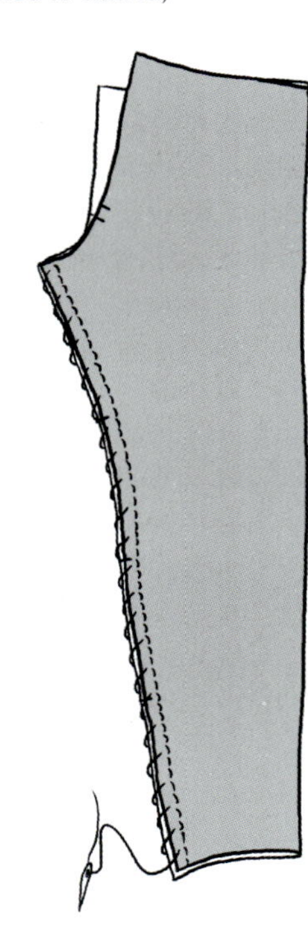

### JOINING THE LEGS

**1.** Turn one leg RS out, and slide that one inside the other leg (which is still WS out). Align and pin the rises, using notches to help with alignment. It's helpful to push the legs' SAs in opposite directions to balance their bulk.

**2.** Use backstitch to sew along rise edge, with ½" (1.3 cm) SA.

**3.** Optional: Use overcasting to finish the rise edges together.

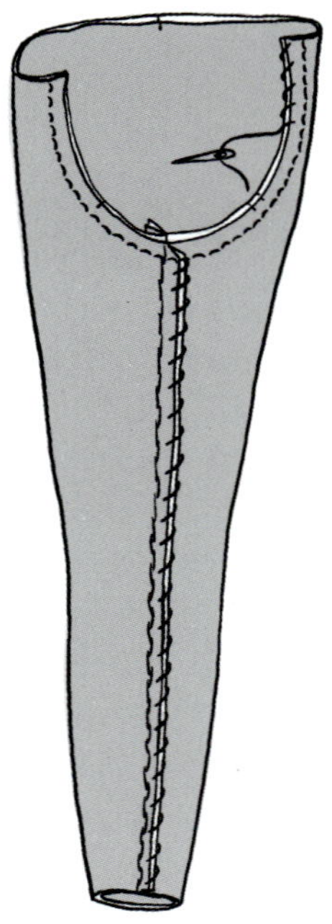

**4.** Turn leggings RS out.

## SEWING THE ANKLE BANDS

For each ankle band:

**1.** Fold ankle band piece in half to align its shorter edges, with RST. Pin.

**2.** Use backstitch, running stitch, or combination stitch to sew along the short edge, using pattern's SA amount. (Any of these stitches will work well here, so pick your favorite to use.)

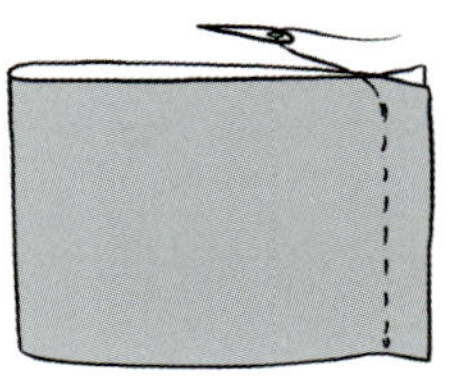

**3.** Snip triangles at edges of SAs, as shown, to reduce bulk.

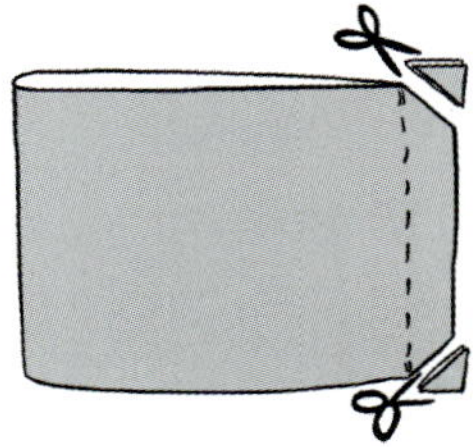

**4.** Press SAs open.

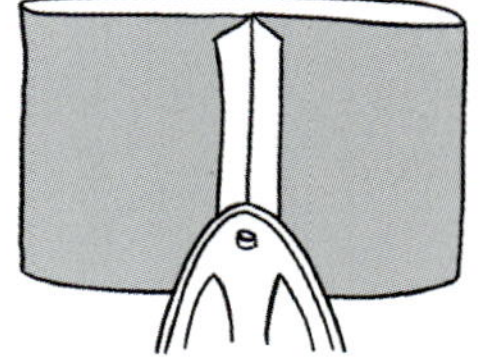

**5.** Fold band in half to align its longer edges, WST, and press.

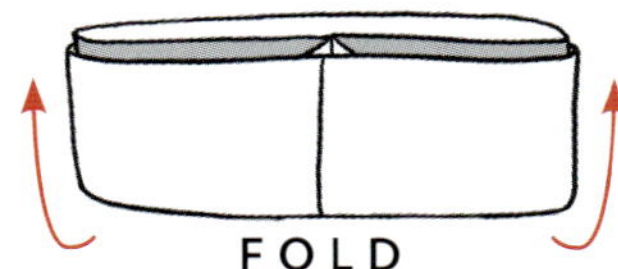


**6.** With legs turned RS out, place band over RS of one of the legs so that band and leg raw edges are aligned, as shown. Align band-joining seam with leg inseam. Align other notches. Pin.

**7.** Use backstitch through all layers to join band to leg at ½" (1.3 cm) from edge.

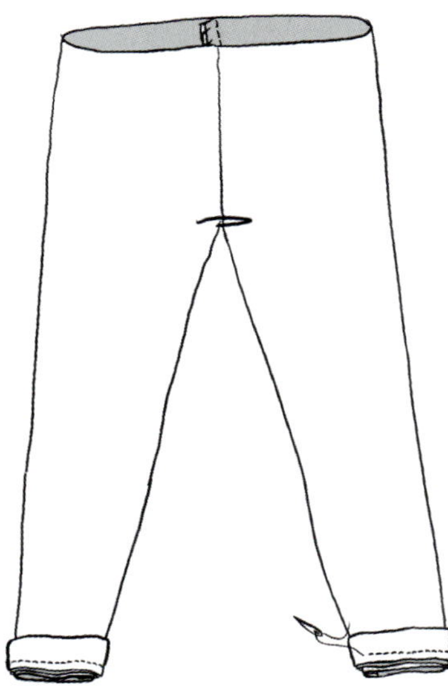

**8.** Optional: Use overcasting to finish the leg and ankle edges together.

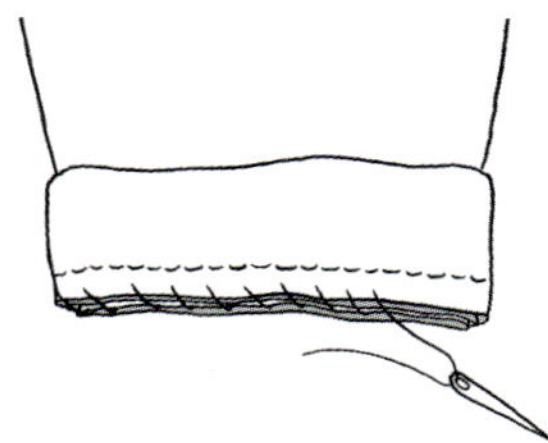

**9.** Press SAs up toward leg.

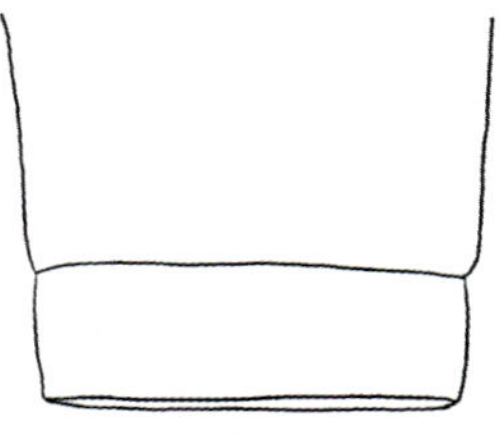

Press SA up

## SEWING THE WAISTBAND

**1.** Fold waistband piece in half to align its shorter edges, with RST. Pin.

**2.** Use longish running stitches to baste through both layers along the short edge, using ½" (1.3 cm) SAs. (You'll remove these stitches later.)

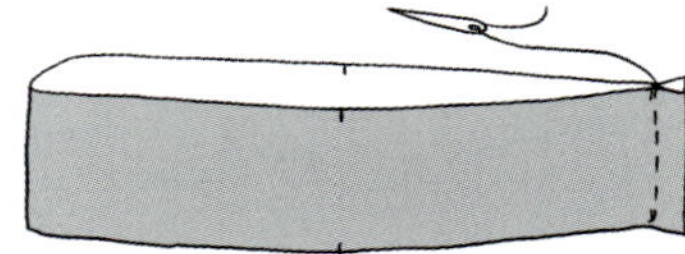

**3.** Snip triangles at edges of SAs, as shown, to reduce bulk.

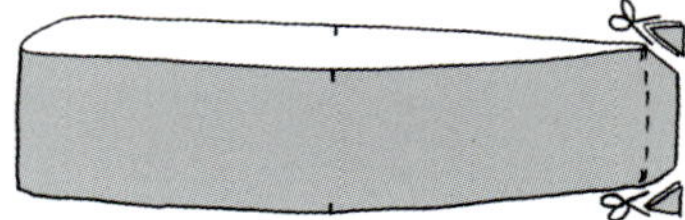

**4.** Press SAs open.

**5.** Fold waistband in half to align its longer edges, with WST, and press.

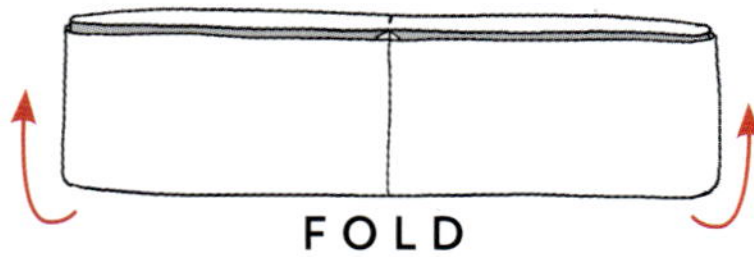


**6.** With joined legs turned RS out, place waistband over joined legs' waistline so that waistband and joined legs' raw edges are aligned, as shown below. Align waistband-joining seam with back rise seam or with an outseam, as you prefer. Align other notches and seams. Pin.

**7.** Use backstitch through all layers to join waistband, with ½" (1.3 cm) SA.

**8.** Optional: Use overcasting to finish the legging and waistband edges together.

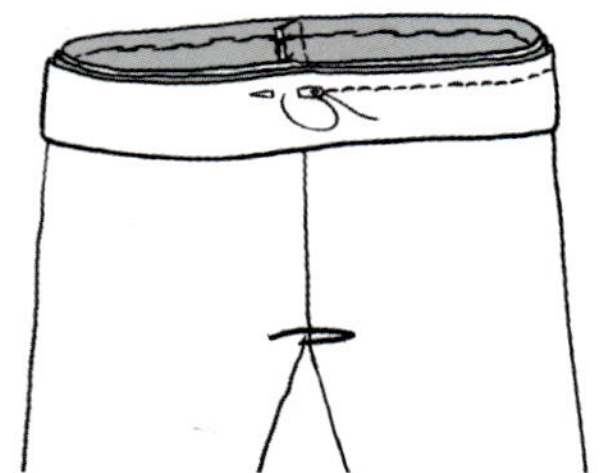

**9.** Press SAs down toward legs.

## ADDING ELASTIC

**1.** Remove loose running stitches that you basted on waistband's short joining edge.

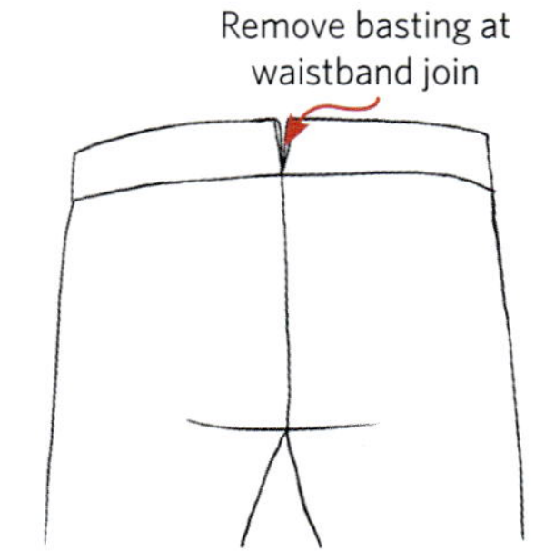


**2.** Fasten safety pin to one end of elastic. (No need to trim elastic to a specific length yet.) Use safety pin to thread elastic through the waistband.

**3.** Try on leggings and adjust elastic, pinning it to your desired length. Make sure elastic is not twisted.

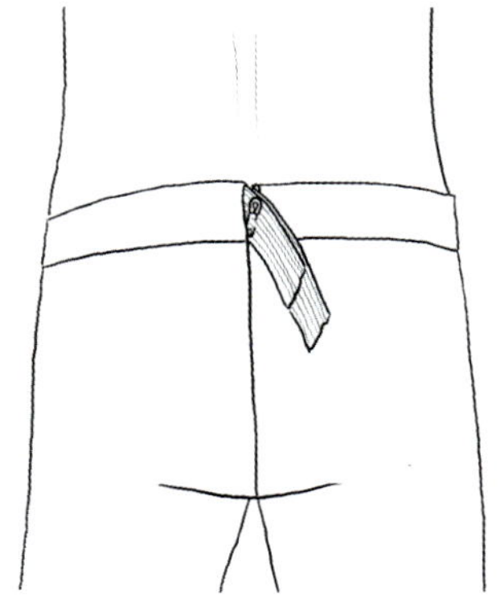

**4.** Trim elastic to desired length, leaving 1" (2.5 cm) overlap amount.

**5.** Pull elastic away from waistband enough that you can manipulate the ends easily. Garment will cinch along elastic to facilitate this.

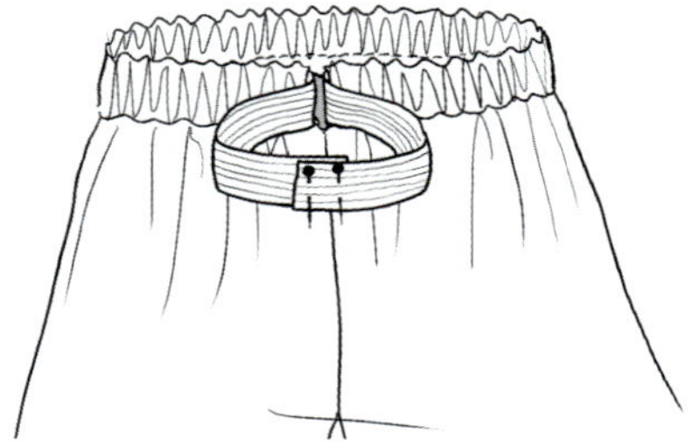

**6.** Double-check that elastic is not twisted. Overlap ends by 1" (2.5 cm), pin, and use small whipstitches around overlap rectangle's perimeter. This will secure elastic.

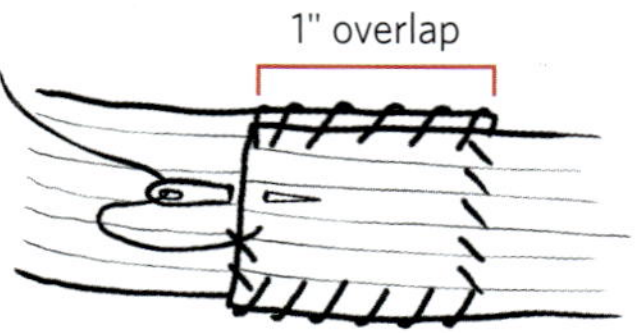


**7.** Stretch waist and manipulate fabric until all elastic disappears back into waistband.

**8.** Make sure waistband's opening edges are still tidily folded under, arrange the folds so that they are kissing, and use whipstitch to close the opening. Start whipstitching at the bottom of the inside waistband, stitch up to the top, then stitch over and down the outside of the waistband. Then push needle through to inside waistband and anchor off.

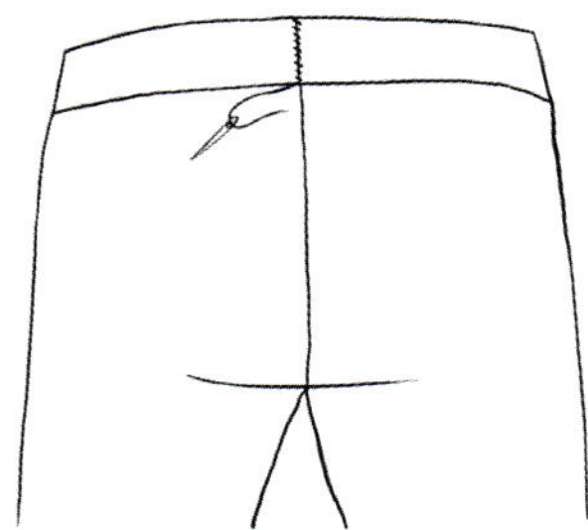

**9.** Optional: Place a few little embroidery stitches at the CB on the waistband. This will help you distinguish front from back when dressing. Alternatively, you can embroider a little label, as described on page 108 in the woven boxy top project.

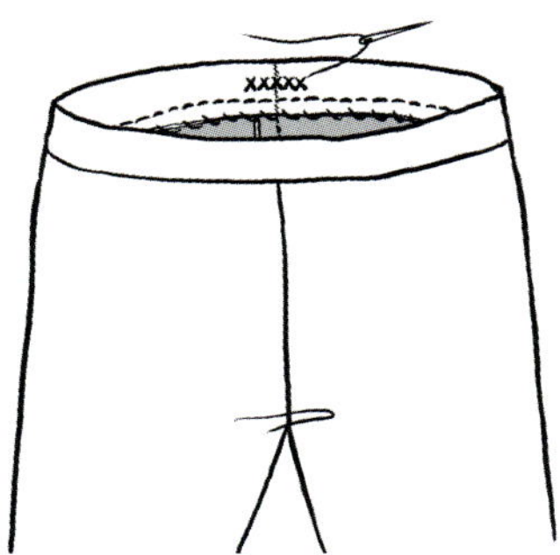

# Variations

The basic instructions make a pair of leggings that sit up at the natural waist-line and end at your anklebone, with ankle bands to cinch. However, you can make leggings that hit anywhere you'd like, with different finishes and with any other styling variations. You might even add a simple little pocket, or create some style lines on your pattern pieces and play with colorblocking, or whatever else you can dream up.

## Calf-Length Leggings with Hems

For this version, I followed the basic instructions, but with a couple of patternmaking tweaks:

- After drafting the basic leg pattern, I decided on the desired length and drew a new hemline at this level on the pattern, squaring the corners so that the inseam edges would join in a smooth line.
- I skipped drafting ankle bands and did not remove any additional length from the legs.
- Instead of adding SA along the ankle edges, I added hem allowance. This amount is somewhat of an aesthetic decision. I chose to add ¾" (2 cm).

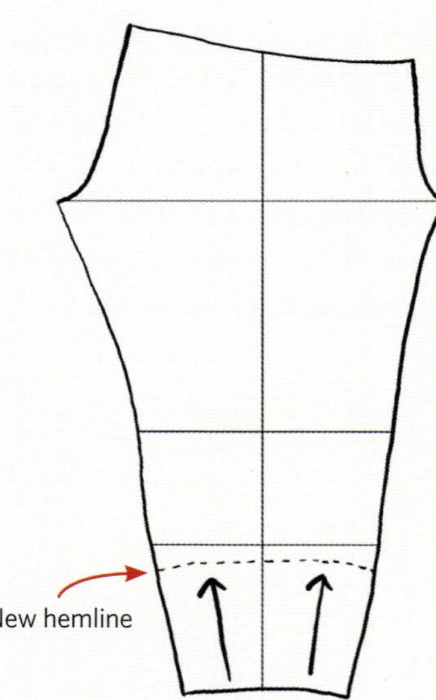

In sewing, I did the following:

- After joining the legs together, I used my iron to press and prepare double-turned hems (see page 182). With my ¾" (2 cm) hem allowance, I turned under ¼" (6 mm) first and then turned under the remaining ½" (1.3 cm).

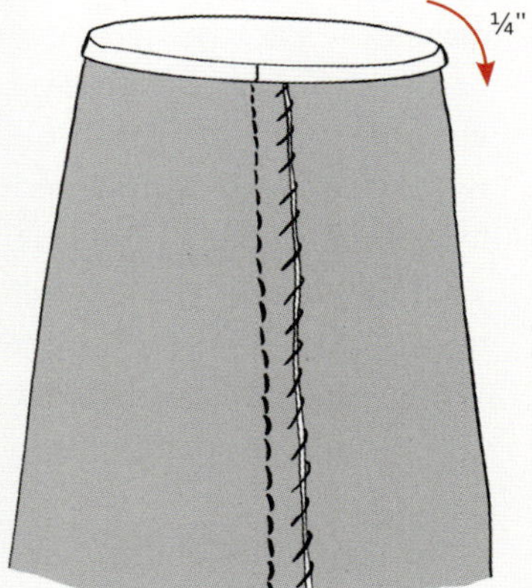


- I secured the hems with somewhat loose, medium-size whipstitches.

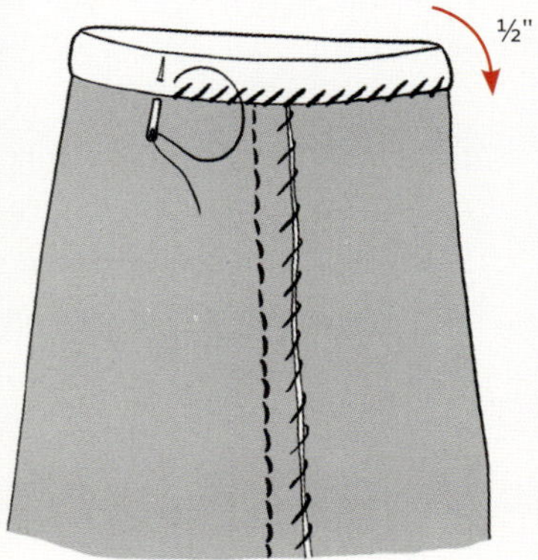

# *Mathew Gnagy*

*(he/him)*, founder of Modern Maker Schoolhouse, manager of Department of Historical Clothing and Dress for Colonial Williamsburg Foundation

WILLIAMSBURG, VIRGINIA, USA, AND CENTRAL SWEDEN

For Mathew Gnagy, hand sewing is a practice in connecting to humans from the past. "When I'm sitting there in silence, doing that work, I can almost feel myself in that lineage with those people," Mathew explains. "And it's really a wonderful, and an almost spiritual, experience."

Years ago, impressed by centuries-old Spanish tailors' manuals he was translating, Mathew decided to sew some of their garments. Hand sewing seemed most appropriate. As he grew to appreciate hand sewing's merits, he resolved to share it with others in a modern context, too. "And then I started experimenting," he recalls.

Today, Mathew is a prominent, prolific teacher. He manages the historical clothing department at Colonial Williamsburg. As a craftsman, he strives to use efficient, appropriate techniques. And he emphatically eschews perfectionism.

***Gingham beginnings.*** When I was about eight or nine years old, I stole a tablecloth that my older sister had. She really loved *The Wizard of Oz*, and she had this blue checked gingham fabric. And I stole it, cut out a little T-tunic, and hand-sewed it together. That was my first sewing. My sister was not pleased.

***Efficiency.*** When I'm creating something by hand, I'm thinking, "What's the most efficient process for this? Should I be sewing this seam first, or that?" Because sometimes it's really different in hand sewing.

Hand sewing and machine sewing can be more or less neck-and-neck in speed. When you're doing high-level work, they really are almost the same.

***Visible hand sewing.*** I don't personally believe in hand sewing that can "pass" as machine sewing, because I think that does hand sewing a huge disservice and makes machine sewing seem way cooler than it actually is. I never want hand sewing to be invisible, because then you can't inspire somebody else with what gets you going.

***Peeking inside.*** I love going into a museum and—as much as I can—peeking inside a garment that is anywhere from 100 to 400 years old. It's so exciting to see the things that people did. Some of them are quite strange.

***Against perfectionism.*** I make stitches that are the right size for the fabric and the longevity of the garment. But a lot of other people are taught to make stitches just as small and neat and tidy and perfect as you can make them. I find myself constantly pushing against this elitism and snobbery that has slipped into handwork because of couture sewing.

***No rules.*** Always, at all costs, avoid slipping into a "one-true-way" mentality. Anyone who says there is only one way to do it is stuck in that perfection world, and they're going to take you there with them. And it's incredibly limiting.

There should be no limits. People have been hand-sewing for thousands of years. There are no rules. There should be no rules. The whole world of hand sewing is your toolbox. Don't get stuck in one way. That's the best advice that I can give.

# GATHERED SKIRT

This classic skirt features on-seam pockets and a hand-picked zipper at center back. The patternmaking is fairly simple—it's basically modified rectangles—but you'll learn how to contour the waistline to suit your particular body, ensuring that the skirt's hem will hang parallel to the floor.

The hand sewing on this project includes lots of new skills: stroked gathers, on-seam pockets with French seams, a hand-picked zipper, bias-bound SAs, and more. So although the styling of the skirt is simple, this project will serve as a showcase for all sorts of beautiful techniques.

# Patternmaking

For this gathered skirt, you'll only need a handful of measurements, but there are still some cool three-dimensional contour concepts to think about as you're drafting. One could draft a very comparable skirt using nothing but rectangles (with the added benefit that you can make a project with minimal or zero fabric waste). If you'd like to approach the project that way, that's terrific! I'm going to show you, though, how to draft shapes with slightly more complexity to accommodate your own body's particular shape.

Specifically, a typical rectangle-built skirt will offer the same amount of garment length on the front as on the back. Depending on how high or low you wear the skirt, and depending on your body's distribution of volume, and depending on the way your spine and pelvis are tilted, this may cause the skirt to hike up in the front or in the back. Rounder tummies can result in a skirt hiking up in front, especially if you wear the skirt up high on your waist. (This phenomenon can be particularly exaggerated on pregnant bodies.) Oftentimes if you wear a skirt low on your frame, you may find the skirt hiking up in back because it must pass over the fullness of the buttocks.

None of this means anything is wrong with your body, or even with the pattern shapes. Your body is perfect just as it is! And there are plenty of good reasons one might like to stitch a skirt from rectangles. Furthermore,

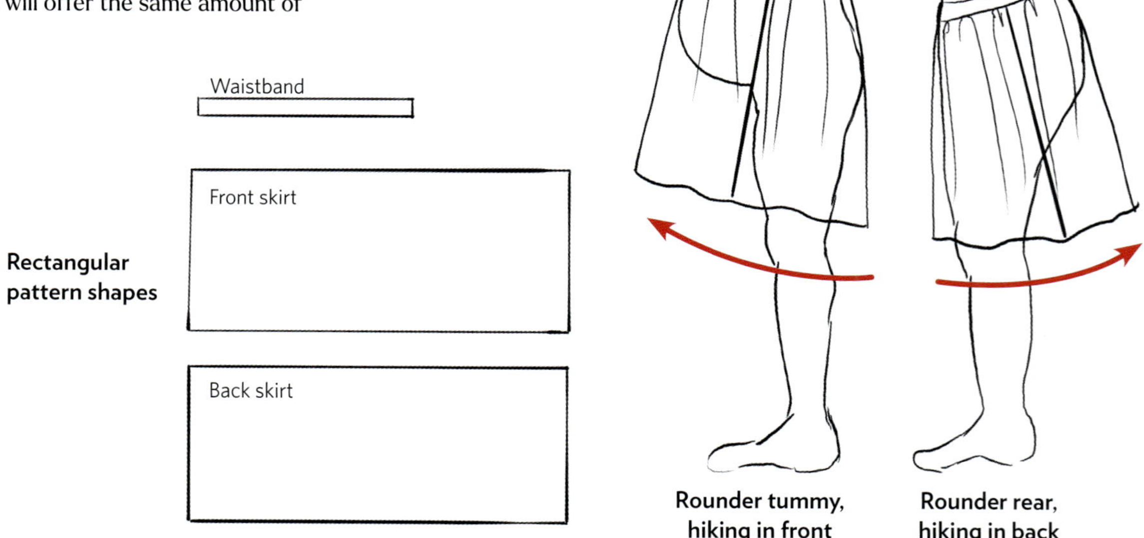


Rectangular pattern shapes

Rounder tummy, hiking in front

Rounder rear, hiking in back

in some cases, this hiking may be minimal or nonexistent. However, if you're curious how to draft a skirt using a method where the hem will fall evenly regardless of your body's individual distribution of volume, read on.

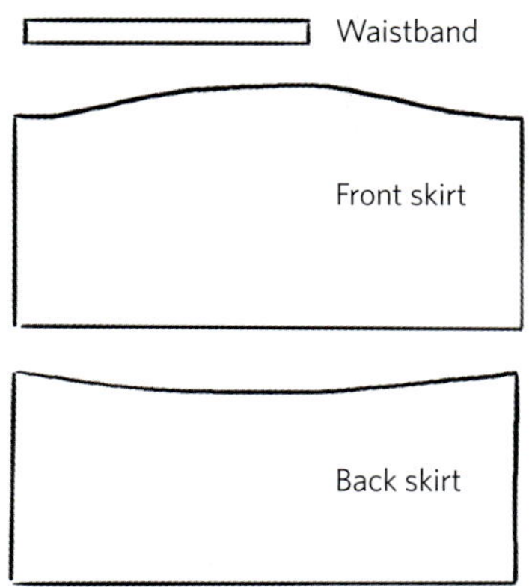


**Contoured waistline on patterns to accommodate body's distribution**

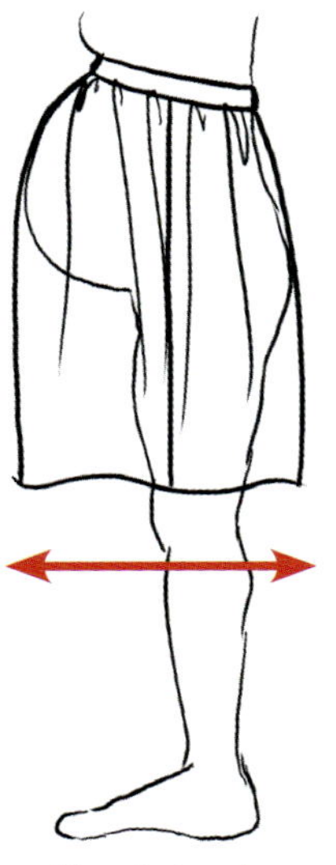

**Hem is level**

## MEASURING YOUR BODY

While measuring, wear very snug-fitting, thin clothes or just your underwear.

To begin, tie a strip of elastic, ribbon, yarn, or scrap fabric around your waist. In this case, "waist" means wherever you want the top of the skirt to sit—it need not be at your anatomical waistline. Do a wiggly little dance to make sure that the strip settles into a natural position on your body. Know that the strip may not be parallel to the floor when it is settled naturally. It may be higher in front than in back, or vice versa.

With this strip in place, proceed to take the following measurements:

- Waist circumference (measured along the strip you just tied, which should be at your desired waistband level; be sure to relax your belly as you measure this)
- Hip circumference
- Distance from waist strip to desired skirt length at center front
- Distance from waist strip to floor at center front
- Distance from waist strip to floor at side seam
- Distance from waist strip to floor at center back
- Desired pocket position (distance from waist strip to where you'd like the top of an imaginary pocket opening)

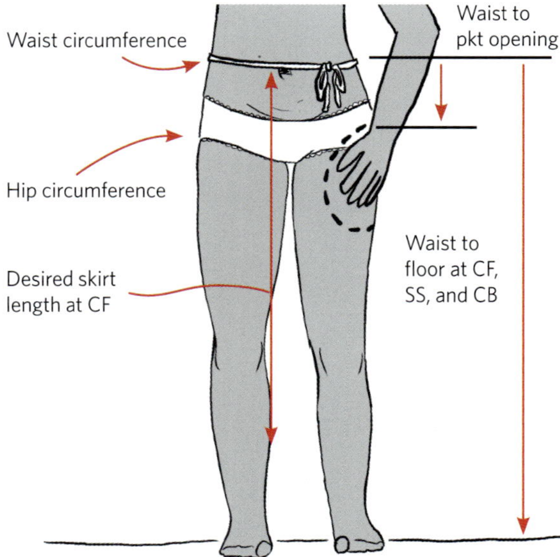

#### FINDING YOUR PREFERRED GATHERING RATIO

Your skirt's volume will be gathered into a woven waistband. The amount of gathering volume is up to you. You might like to use a 1.5-to-1 ratio, or a 2-to-1 ratio, or 3-to-1, or whatever suits your fancy. Your preference will probably vary depending on the fabric you're using (based on its weight, drape, etc.) and the particular proportion you'd like to achieve. Thicker fabrics generally will do best with lower gathering ratios, while thinner fabrics will look great with higher ratios.

To decide on a ratio for this project, you can "audition" ratio amounts with the fabric you're planning to use. Here's how:

**1.** Thread needle with a long length of thread. Spread out your intended fabric and place two pins to mark out an 18" (45.7 cm) section along the crossgrain cut edge (the cut edge perpendicular to the selvages). Now, without anchoring thread at start or end, make a line of large running stitches that are approximately ¼" (6 mm) long. This line of stitches should be ¼" (6 mm) from the raw edge.

**2.** Thread needle with another long length of thread. Without anchoring thread at start or end, make another line of large running stitches, this time ½" (1.3 cm) from the raw edge. These stitches should match the first line so that the needle enters and exits at the same placements, as shown.

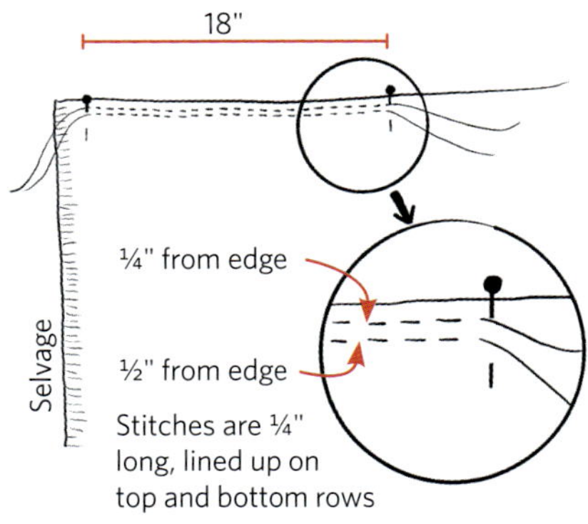


**3.** Lay fabric smoothly on a table. Now carefully pull threads to cinch fabric, trying to arrange gathers evenly. Cinch fabric until you have a gathering amount that looks pleasing to you.

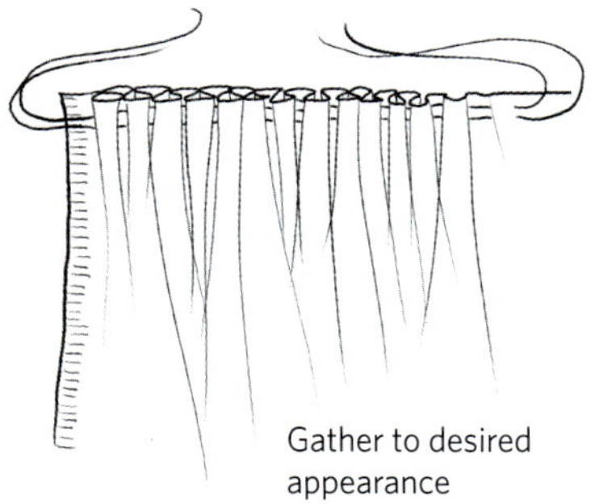


**4.** Arrange the edge of a piece of paper to slightly overlap the cinched raw edges and pin in place carefully to secure. Wind threads around end pins in figure-eight formation to hold temporarily.

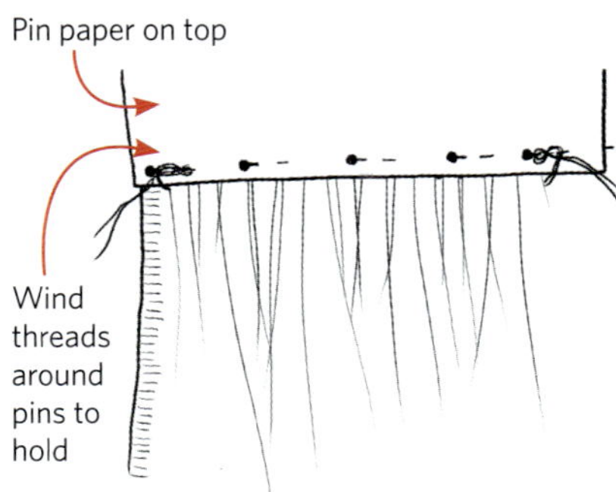


**5.** In front of a mirror, hold paper up at waist level on your body, with gathered area falling down naturally. Imagine that this is the amount of gathering your skirt will have. Do you like it? Do you wish there were more gathers? Or do you feel like it's too much, and the gathered area has become too stiff?

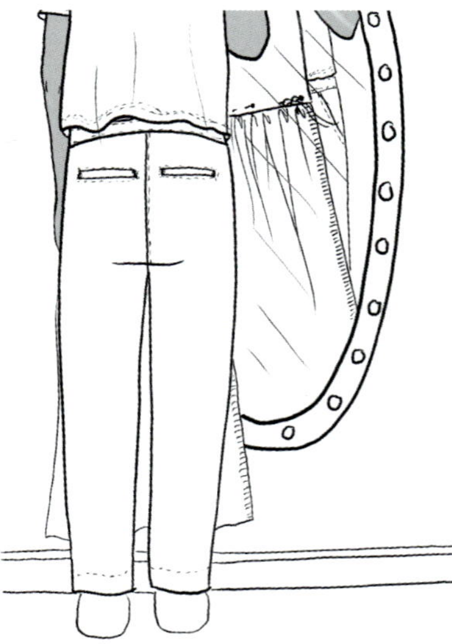

**6.** Back on the table, make any adjustments needed to your gathering amount. Cinch or loosen as desired and repin. Audition again at the mirror. Repeat until you're satisfied.

**7.** Once you're pleased with the gathering amount, measure the cinched area's length on the paper.

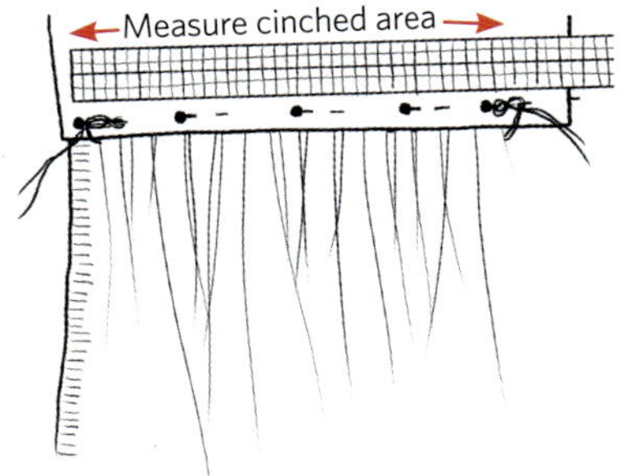


**8.** Divide 18" (45.7 cm) by the length of the cinched area on the paper to find your gathering ratio number. Jot this down for later use. For example, if you've cinched the fabric to an 8" (20.3 cm) area, you'll divide 18 by 8 to calculate a gathering ratio number of 2.25.

## CALCULATING THE DIMENSIONS

With body measurements and gathering ratio determined, you're ready to do a bit of math and then start drafting.

## SIDE AND BACK ADJUSTMENTS

First, you'll calculate the differences in length between front, side, and back.

Look at the measurements you took from waist strip to floor at CF, side seam, and CB. Let's call the CF measurement your "front distance," the side seam measurement your "side distance," and the CB measurement your "back distance."

- front distance − side distance = side adjustment
- front distance − back distance = back adjustment

Jot down those adjustment numbers for the moment.

## TOTAL SKIRT CIRCUMFERENCE

Next you'll calculate the width of fabric you want to gather into the waistband, using your waist measurement and gathering ratio number.

Find your waist circumference measurement. Add ¾" (2 cm) of wearing ease to that number. Then multiply by your gathering ratio number. This will be your total skirt circumference.

For example, if your waist is 35" (about 89 cm), you'd add ¾" (2 cm) of wearing ease to get 35¾" (about 91 cm). Then multiply by your gathering ratio—perhaps 2.25, to use our example—to get roughly 80½" (205 cm) total skirt circumference.

Compare this total skirt circumference with your hip circumference to be sure that your skirt circumference will be nice and roomy for your hips. You probably have plenty of room unless you've used a very scant gathering ratio. If it seems like you might not have much extra space for your hips, increase your skirt gathering ratio and recalculate the skirt circumference.

## PLOTTING THE FRONT

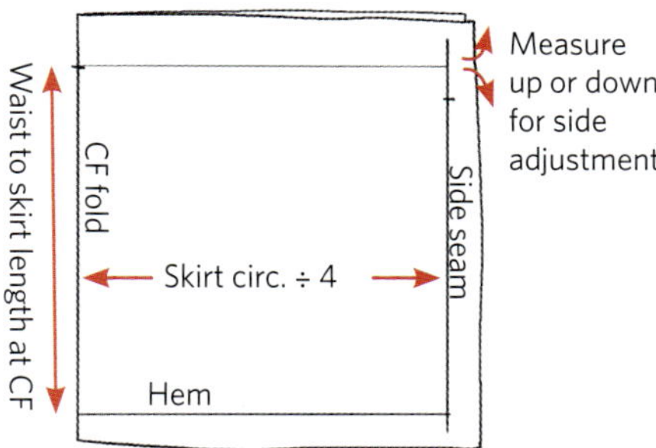


**1.** Find (or tape together) a very large sheet of paper. Fold in half down the middle, and lay on your table with fold on the left. This fold will represent your CF line.

**2.** Divide your total skirt circumference by four to find your quarter-skirt circumference. Draft a long line parallel to the CF fold, distanced by your quarter-skirt circumference amount from the fold. This line will represent your side seam.

3. Near the bottom of your paper, square a long line across. This will be your hem fold line.

4. Along the CF fold, measure up from your hem the amount of your distance from waist strip to desired skirt length at CF. Make a tick mark and square over to intersect with the side seam line.

5. Refer to your side adjustment number. If it was positive, measure down that amount from the waist-side seam intersection and make a tick mark. If it was negative, extend the side seam up a bit, then measure up that amount from the waist-side seam intersection and make a tick mark.

## PLOTTING THE BACK

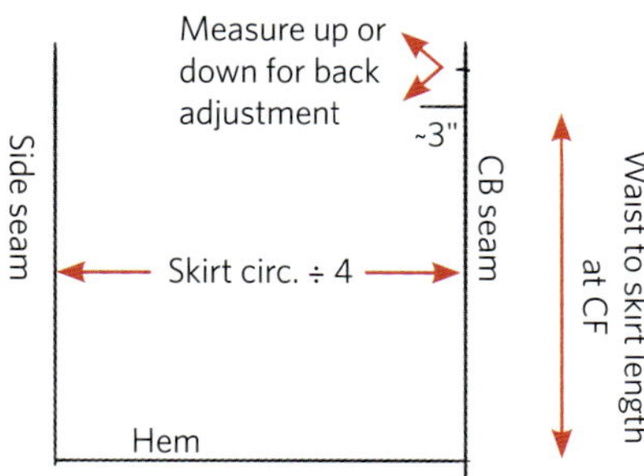


1. Find (or tape together) a large sheet of paper. Draw a long vertical line near the right-hand side. This line will represent your CB seam.

2. Next you'll draw a long line that is parallel to the CB line to represent your side seam. This line should be placed your quarter-skirt circumference away from the CB line.

3. Near the bottom of your paper, square a long line across. This will be your hem fold line.

4. Along the CB line, measure up from your hem the amount of your distance from waist strip to desired skirt length at CF. Make a tick mark. Then refer to your back adjustment number. If it was positive, measure down that amount from the tick mark and square 3-ish inches (7.6-ish cm) to the left. If it was negative, measure up that amount from the tick mark and square 3-ish inches (7.6-ish cm) to the left.

## DRAFTING THE WAISTLINE

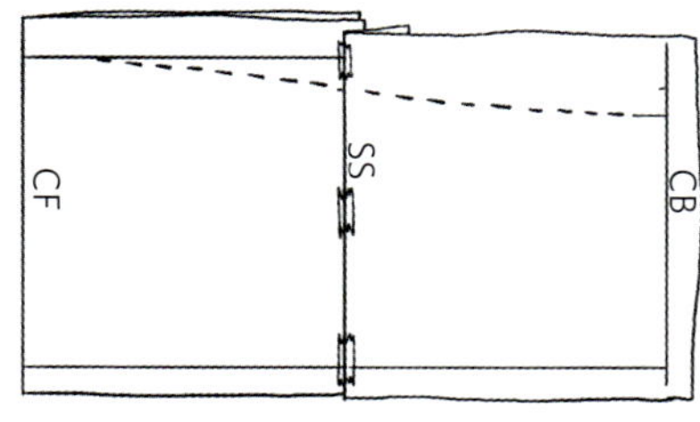


1. Fold paper under along back pattern's side seam line. Overlap back pattern with front so that side seam lines and hemlines are aligned. Pin or tape to hold temporarily.

2. Freehand a smooth line that connects the CF at waistline with the tick mark at the side seam and the squared line at CB. This line should preserve at least 3" (7.6 cm) of squared line at CF before gently curving toward the side seam tick mark. It should then proceed smoothly and continuously toward the CB, where it should preserve at least 3" (7.6 cm) of squared line at CB. See diagram as a guide.

## DRAFTING THE POCKET

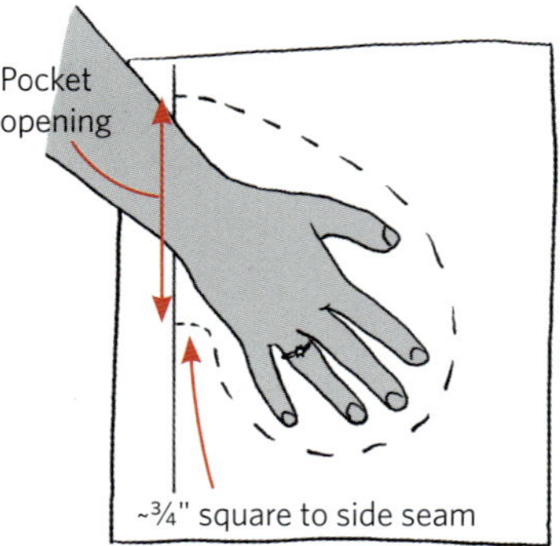


1. Draw a long vertical line on a fresh sheet of paper. Imagine that this line is the side seam of your skirt on your nondominant hand's side. Now "slip" your nondominant hand through an imaginary pocket opening in this side seam, and spread out your fingers once they are in the imaginary pocket.

2. With your nondominant hand's fingers spread wide, trace a smooth round shape around your hand, as shown. Leave a bit of extra space around your hand so that your pockets will be roomy.

**3.** Now slowly start slipping your hand out of the imaginary pocket. Imagine how your hand might be configured as it slides out—it wouldn't be comfortable to have to squeeze your fingers together, right? It's good to have a pocket opening with a bit of extra room so that your hand can stay relaxed as it slips in and out.

In my own clothes, I like to have pocket openings that are approximately 2" (5 cm) wider than half of my hand circumference (measured with fingers smooshed together but flat). The extra space provides the right amount of ease for my taste. You might prefer a different amount, though—when in doubt, measure a few of your own clothes to see what you like.

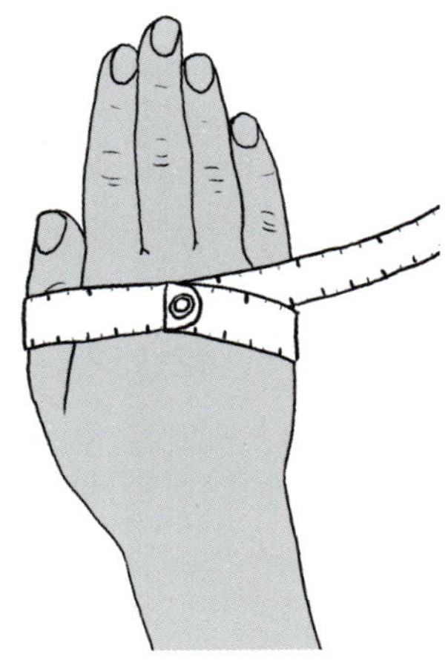

With this in mind, draw a couple of tick marks along the side seam line. These marks should represent where you'd like your pocket opening to begin and end. Square out from the lower tick mark for approximately ¾" (2 cm).

**4.** Connect the round pocket shape to the pocket opening marks, including the squared portion at the lower mark. This completes your pocket shape. Make any tweaks needed. Your goals are to ensure that your hand will slip comfortably through and sit comfortably inside, and that the edges of the pocket are smooth, gentle curves.

**5.** Measure your final pocket opening length and jot the number down.

**6.** Next, add SAs. I'd recommend ⅝" (1.6 cm) on all edges.

**7.** Cut out. Snip notches even with ends of pocket opening along side seam.

**8.** Place grainline parallel to side seam line. Add note: "CUT 4 SELF (OR POCKETING)."

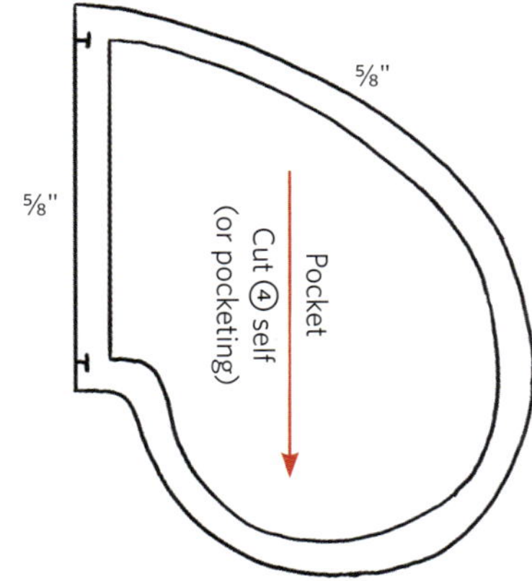


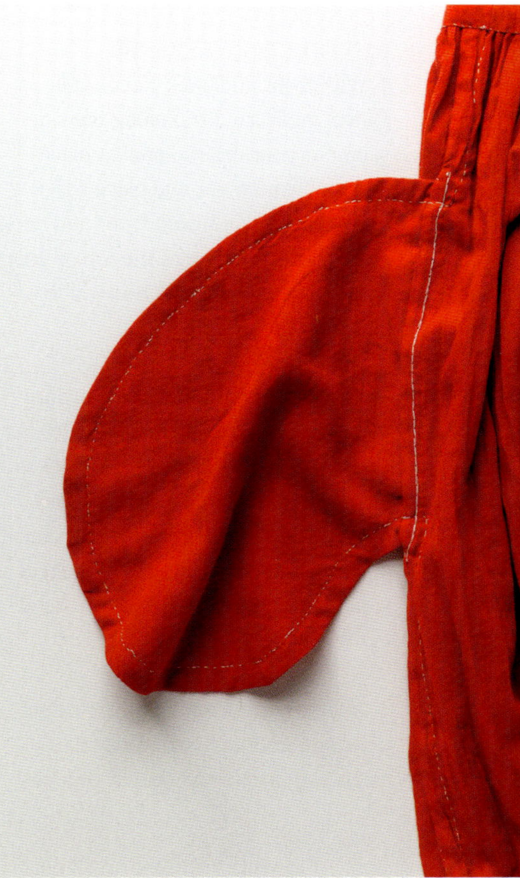

#### FINALIZING THE FRONT AND BACK PATTERNS

**1.** With front and back pieces still joined, measure down along the side seam for your desired pocket placement measurement and place a tick mark that touches both front and back pieces. This represents the top of your pocket opening and will be used to make notches.

**2.** From that first tick mark, measure down your pocket opening's length (as determined while drafting the pocket piece earlier), and place another tick mark that touches both front and back pieces. This represents the bottom of your pocket opening and will be used to make notches.

**3.** Somewhere between that bottom tick mark and the bottom hemline, add one more tick mark that touches both pieces. This tick mark will be used to make matching notches for your side seam.

**4.** Decide how tall you want your waistband to be. Something between ¾" (2 cm) and 1¾" (4.4 cm) would work best for a waistband height. If the waistband is much narrower, it might have trouble holding the bulk of a gathered skirt. If it is much wider, it might need to have a contoured shape in order to lie smoothly on your body.

**5.** Lower the skirt pattern's waistline by drawing a line that is parallel to the original but lowered by the amount of your waistband height. For example, if you're planning to have a 1" (2.5 cm) waistband, draw a parallel new waistline that is 1" (2.5 cm) below the original. Cross out or erase the original line.

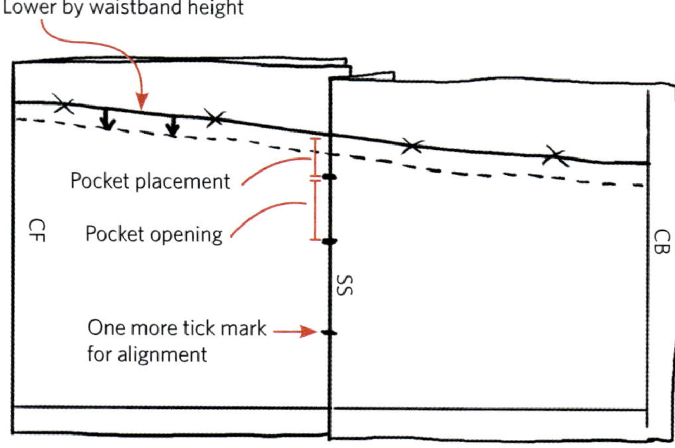


**6.** Remove pins or tape to separate front and back skirt patterns.

**7.** Measure front pattern's waistline and mark a notch halfway along it.

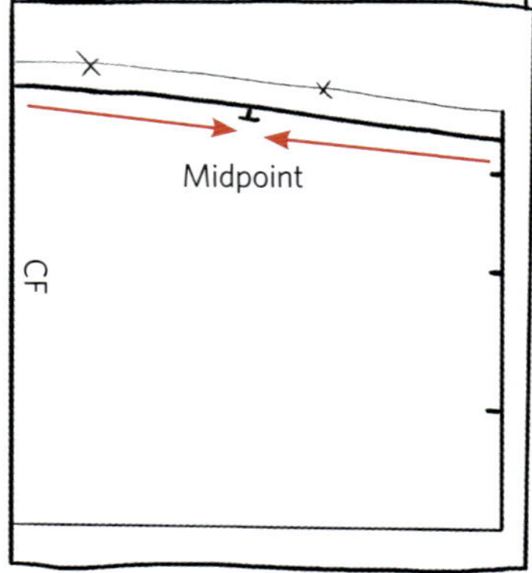


**8.** Measure back pattern's waistline and mark a notch halfway along it.

**9.** Next, add SAs. On both front and back skirts, I'd recommend the following:

- ⅝" (1.6 cm) SA on side seams
- ¾" (2 cm) on CB seam (and nothing on CF line, which is still folded)
- ⅜" (1 cm) SA on waistline
- 2" (5 cm) for hem allowance

**10.** Pin front skirt's two paper layers together and cut out. Snip notches. Remove pins and unfold. Snip notch along waist at CF. Place grainline parallel to CF. Add note: "CUT 1 SELF."

**11.** Cut out back skirt panel. Snip notches. Place grainline parallel to CB. Add note: "CUT 2 SELF."

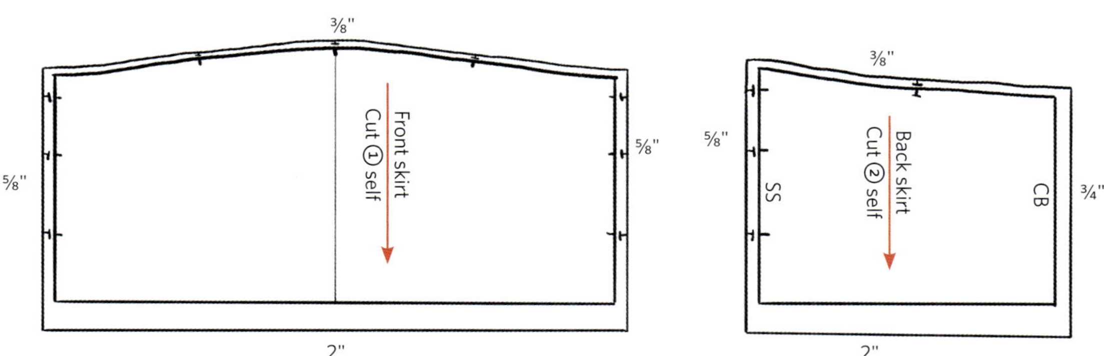


## DRAFTING THE WAISTBAND

**1.** On a new long sheet of paper, draw a long horizontal rectangle. Its width should be equal to your waist circumference with the ¾" (2 cm) of wearing ease added. The height should be equal to your desired waistband height.

**2.** Fold or measure this rectangle to divide its length into eighths, and mark notches at these points, as shown.

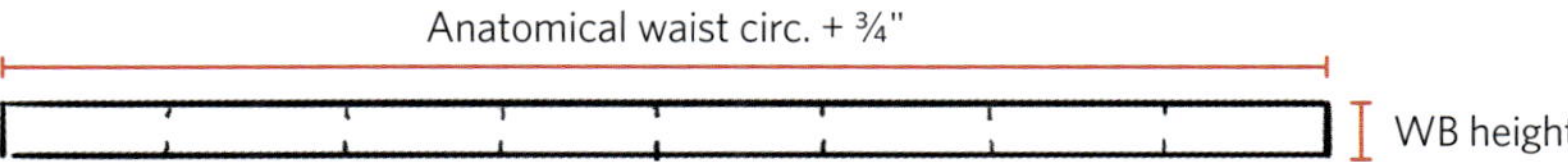


**3.** Next, add SAs. I'd recommend ⅜" (1 cm) on all edges.

**4.** Cut out. Snip notches.

**5.** Place grainline parallel to long edges. Add note: "CUT 2 SELF AND 1 INTERFACING."

Waistband
Cut ② self and ① interfacing
⅜"
⅜"
⅜"
⅜"

# Sewing

## HAND-SEWING STITCHES

- Running stitch
- Even backstitch
- Combination stitch
- Spaced backstitch
- Whipstitch and/or hemstitch
- Fell stitch

## FABRIC OPTIONS

This gathered skirt can be sewn from all sorts of woven fabrics. I like using a light- or medium-weight fabric, but you could try a heavier fabric, too, and simply include less volume in the skirt. I can imagine lovely versions being sewn in everything from voile to chambray, quilting cotton to corduroy. When in doubt, try "auditioning" the fabric using the instructions in the Finding Your Preferred Gathering Ratio section on page 142, and assess whether the fabric might stitch up into a skirt that you'd like to wear.

If you're using a heavier material for the skirt, you may wish to use a lighter fabric for your pocketing in order to reduce bulk. In this case, look for a fabric that is lightweight but densely woven.

## OTHER MATERIALS

You'll also need:

- Fusible or sew-in interfacing to stiffen the waistband (or, if you'd prefer, you can substitute a layer of canvas or some other stiff fabric)
- Zipper (should be at least as long as the distance from your waistband to widest hip level)
- Bias strips cut to at least 1½" (3.8 cm) wide, at least as long as twice the length of your skirt
- Optional: hook and eye

## CUTTING THE FABRIC

See Cutting Fabric on page 85 for tips on cutting. You'll need to cut the following pieces and quantities:

- Front skirt × 1 self
- Back skirt × 2 self
- Waistband × 2 self, × 1 interfacing
- Pocket bag × 4 self or pocketing

### ATTACHING THE POCKETS

You'll attach the on-seam pockets using a lovely, clean French seam finish.

**1.** Place a pocket bag piece along one of the skirt panels' side seams, WST, using notches to align. Pin. With running stitch, join using ¼" (6 mm) SA along the entire pocket bag opening edge.

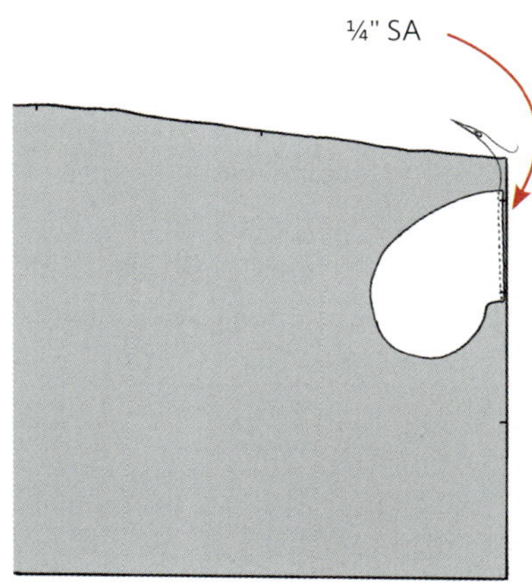


**2.** Trim stitched SAs by half.

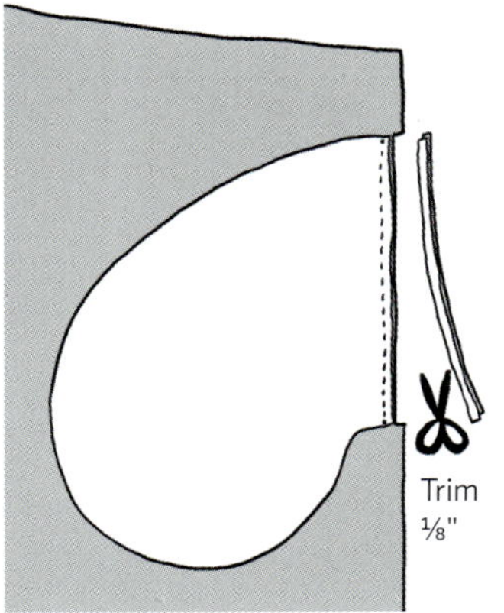


**3.** Press pocket bag crisply away from skirt panel.

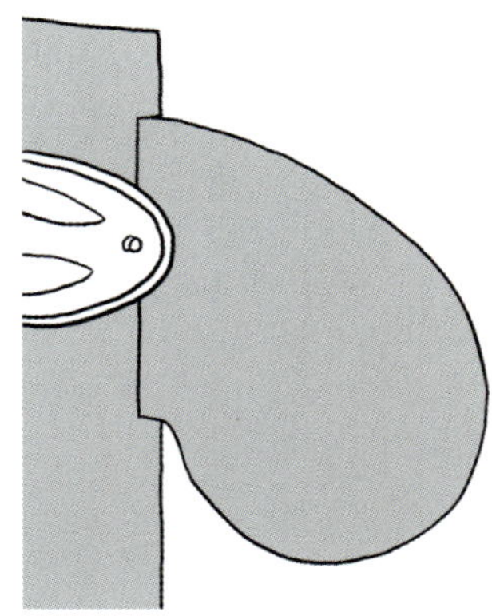

**4.** Fold and press pocket bag in toward skirt with RST.

**5.** With even backstitch, stitch along pocket's side seam edge using ¼" (6 mm) SA.

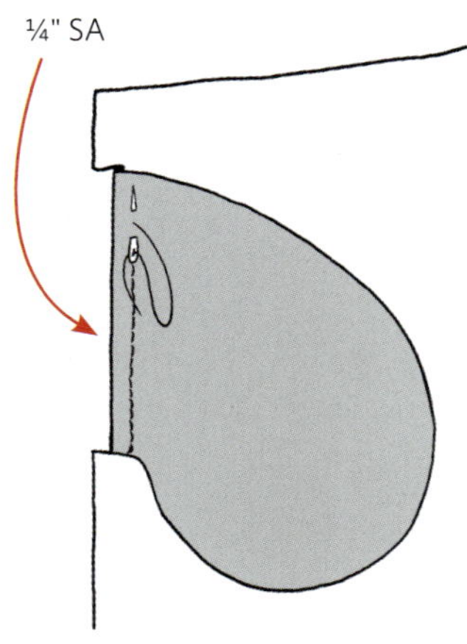


**6.** Press bag crisply away from skirt panel.

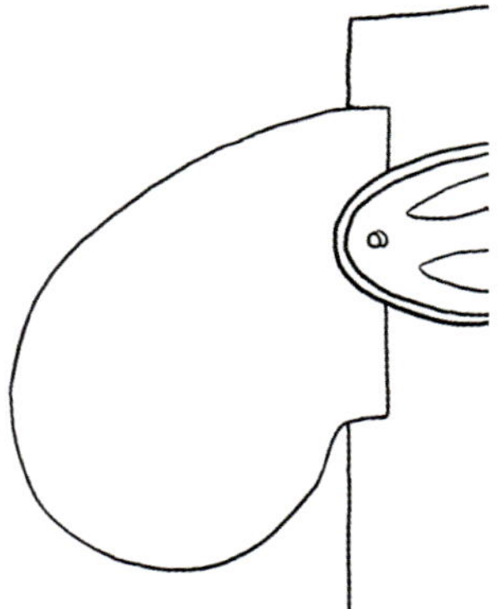

**7.** Repeat for other three pocket bag pieces, attaching one to each of the remaining skirt panel side seams.

## SEWING THE SIDE SEAMS

**1.** Place one of the back panels on top of the front panel, with WST and pocket bags aligned. Pin. With running stitch, join using ¼" (6 mm) SA. Stitch from the waist down to the pocket bag, pivoting and stitching along the pocket bag's rounded outline, then pivoting again at the bottom of the pocket opening, and finally stitching down to the bottom of the skirt.

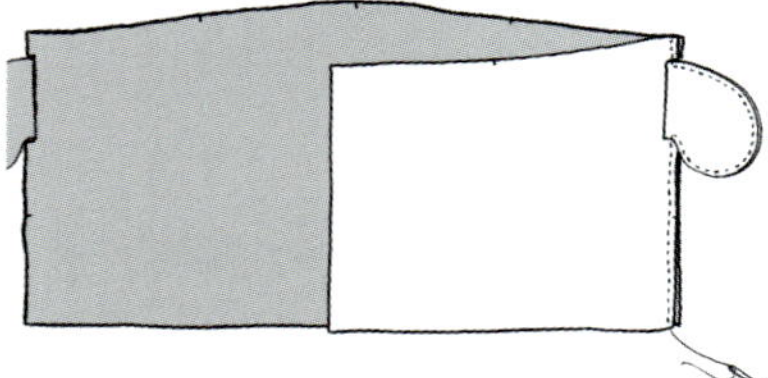

**2.** Snip into SAs at top and bottom of pocket opening, as shown. (Snip close to stitching without cutting the thread.)

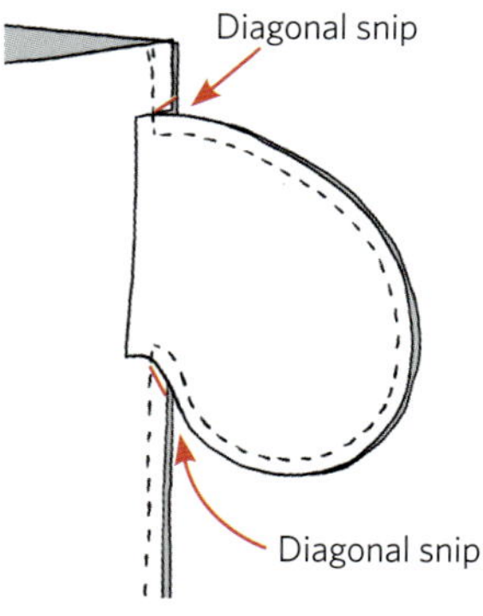


**3.** Open out the seam you just sewed and finger-press SAs open.

**4.** Fold and press the seam crisp and flat, with RST.

**5.** With even backstitch or combination stitch, stitch along same path (side seam, then pivot to stitch around pocket bag, then pivot to finish side seam). Use ⅜" (1 cm) SA.

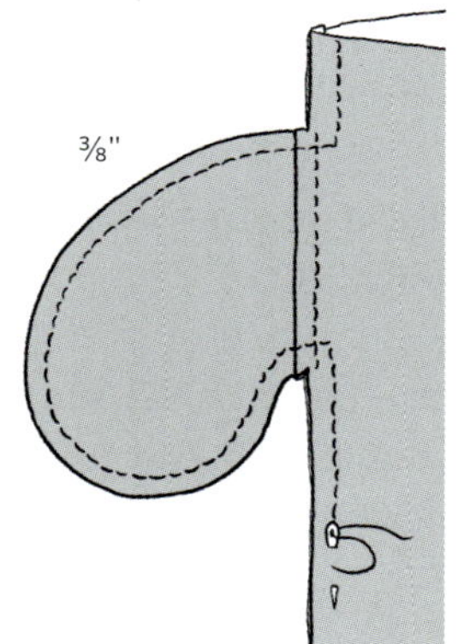


**6.** Open panels and, with RS facing up, press SA and pocket bag toward front of garment.

**7.** Repeat on other side seam.

## SEWING THE CB SEAM

**1.** With RST, align skirt's CB edges and pin.

**2.** Measure your zipper's length (measuring only the area that has teeth, not the extra lengths of tape at beginning and end). Now subtract your waistband height, and then add ⅝" (1.6 mm). Jot this number down—this is the amount of zipper that will be attached to your main skirt section.

For example, if you're beginning with a 10" (25.4 cm) zipper and you're planning a 1½" (3.8 cm) waistband, you'll calculate 10 – 1½ + ⅝ = 9⅛" (25.4 – 3.8 + 1.6 = 23.2 cm) of zipper that will be attached to your main skirt section.

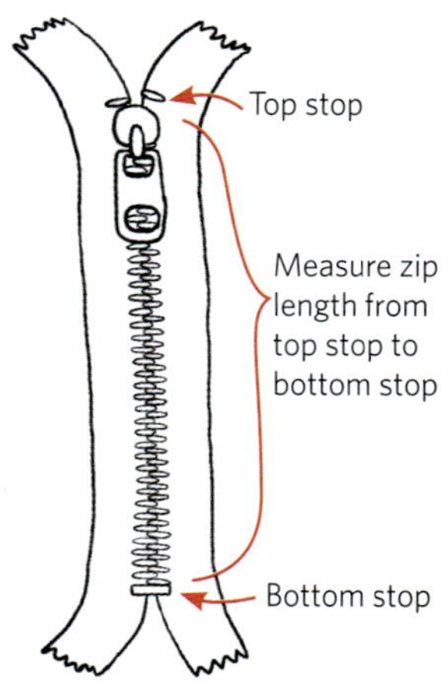


**3.** Measure down from waistline along CB edges by the amount you calculated and place a pin or chalk mark. This is where your zipper will end.

**4.** Baste from this point up to the waist edge, using large running stitches and a ¾" (2 cm) SA. Anchor thread ends loosely at start and finish.

**5.** Below the zipper point, make a line of permanent stitches, using either combination stitch or even backstitch, along the CB edges to the bottom hem edge. Use ¾" (2 cm) SA.

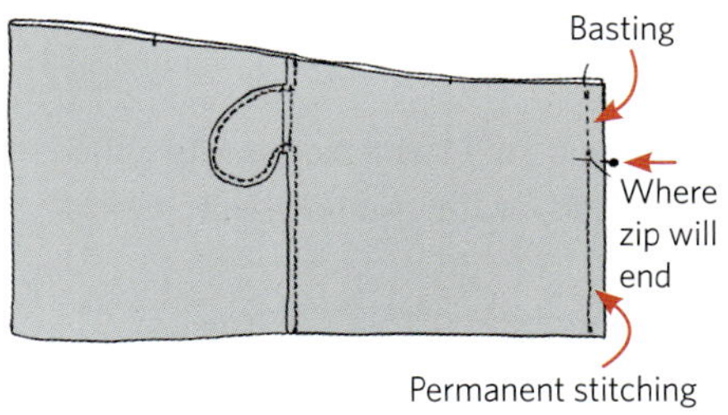


**6.** The entire CB seam has now been stitched, partly with basting and partly with permanent stitches. Press SAs open.

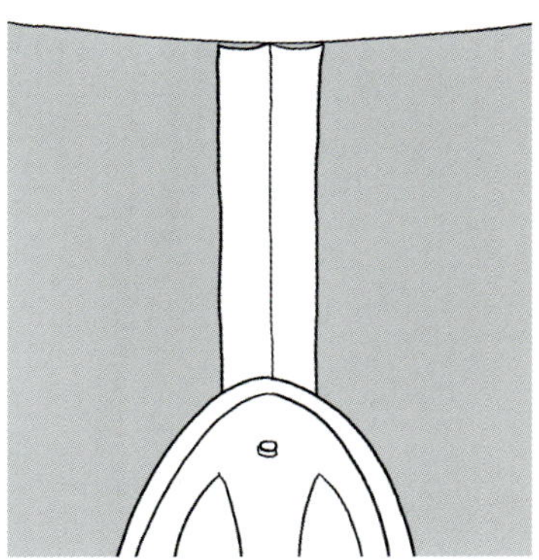

**7.** Lay skirt with WS facing up. Place zipper face down over CB basting so that it is centered on the seam. The zipper's bottom stopper should be located at the point where you switched from basting to permanent stitching. Part of the zipper will extend past the top of the waist edges. Pin zipper to back skirt panel, being very careful to keep zipper centered over seam, and then baste zipper tape onto the skirt, as shown. (Be careful to pin and baste only through back panel layers—don't include the front panel. You can slip a hardcover book in between the layers if that helps.) Once basting stitches are placed, remove pins.

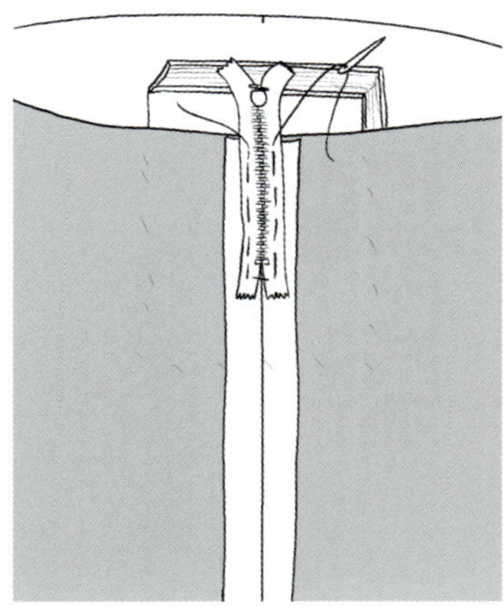

**8.** Flip skirt RS out. Using spaced backstitch, attach zipper by stitching through all basted layers. Stitch line should be approximately ⅜" (1 cm) away from seam. Start at waist on one side of zipper, then square across the zipper at the bottom (just underneath zipper stop), and stitch back up to waist on other side. Remove basting.

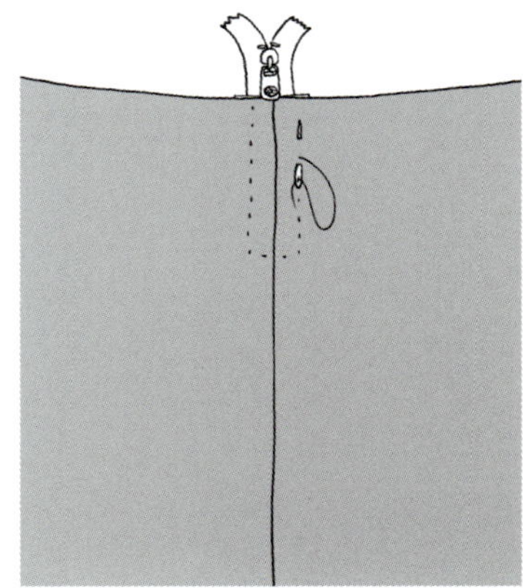

**9.** Trim CB SA so that it does not extend beyond long edges of zipper tape. For example, if SA is peeking out from beneath zipper tape by ¼" (6 mm), then trim ¼" (6 mm) along entire CB SA on both sides.

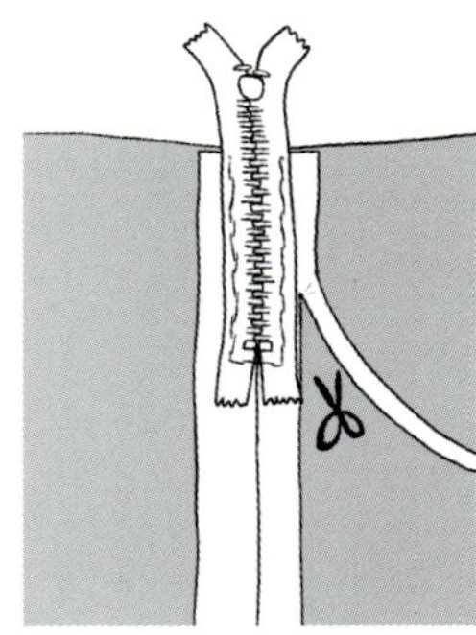

**10.** With RST, lay a bias strip face down along one edge of CB SA, aligning raw edges. Bias strip should be continuous along entire CB SA, including over zipper tape, from bottom hem up to raw waist edge. Pin and stitch through all layers, using running stitch and ⅜" (1 cm) SA amount.

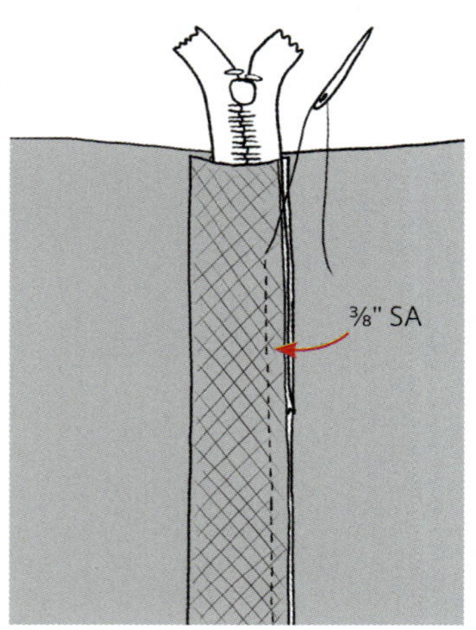


**11.** Press bias strip away from zipper. Press other edge of bias strip under by ¼" or ⅜" (6 mm or 1 cm).

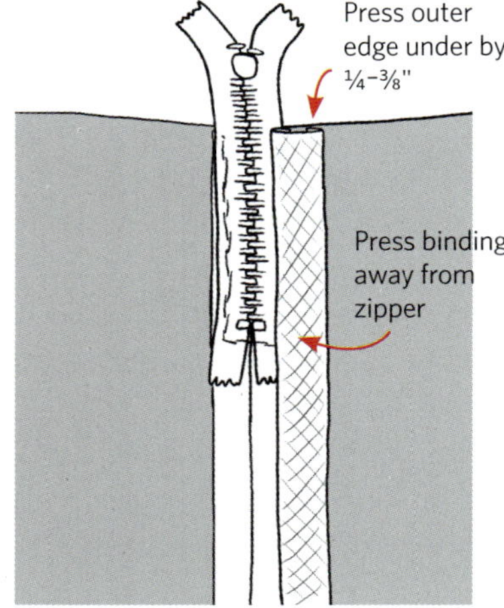


**12.** Fold bias strip underneath SA and pin. Whipstitch or hemstitch to secure folded bias edge to underside of SA.

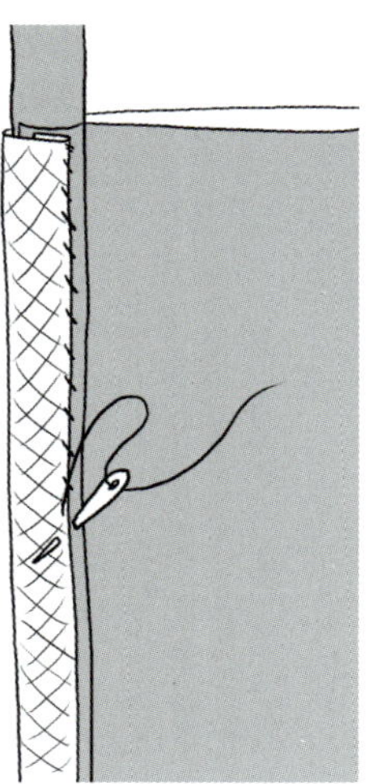

**13.** Repeat steps 10 through 12 for other CB SA edge.

## PREPARING THE GATHERS

**1.** With a long single length of thread, make a line of long, even running stitches (each stitch should be approximately ¼" [6 mm] long) along raw edge of front skirt's waist, ¼" [6 mm] from raw edge. With another long length of thread, make an identical line of running stitches that is ¼" [6 mm] below the first line. These two sets of stitches should be vertically aligned so that stitches are paired.

**2.** Repeat step 1 with separate lengths of thread for the two back skirt panels.

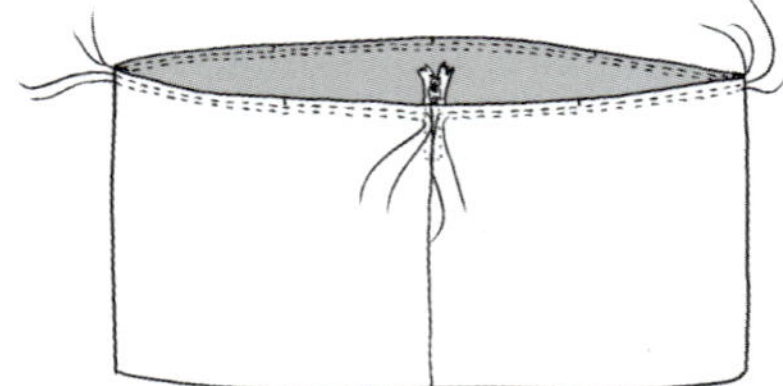

### ASSEMBLING THE WAISTBAND

**1.** First apply interfacing to the WS of one of your waistband pieces. If you're using fusible interfacing, press to apply. If using sew-in interfacing or a layer of stiff fabric, baste around the perimeter to secure.

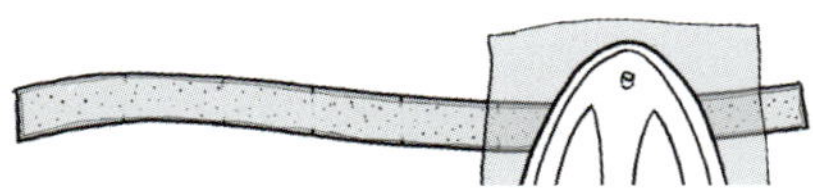

**2.** Pin waistband pieces together along one long edge, RST. Stitch seam using combination stitch and a ⅜" (1 cm) SA amount.

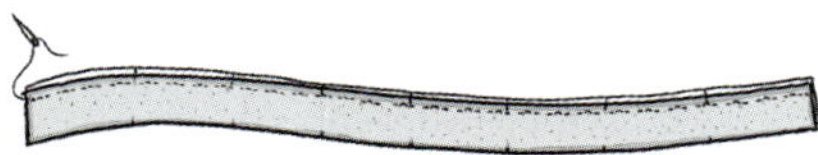

**3.** Press SAs open.

**4.** Press all four edges of joined waistband under by ⅜" (1 cm), as shown. Baste with long running stitches to hold.

### ATTACHING THE WAISTBAND

**1.** Unzip skirt and lay it on a large flat surface. Pull gathering thread pairs to start cinching skirt. Don't worry about cinching to exactly the right length yet—just cinch enough that the skirt will be manageably gathered for pinning to the waistband. Cinch threads on front and back panels.

**2.** Arrange skirt RS facing up. Pin waistband face up along skirt's waist edge, aligning notches, with waistband's edge overlapping skirt edge by ⅜" (1 cm). (In other words, waistband's edge should fall between the two lines of gathering stitches.) At CB, waistband ends should align with CB seam.

**3.** Cinch further if needed to match skirt waistline with length of waistband. Then wind thread ends around pins in figure-eight form to secure temporarily. Readjust gathers and pins if needed to achieve even distribution.

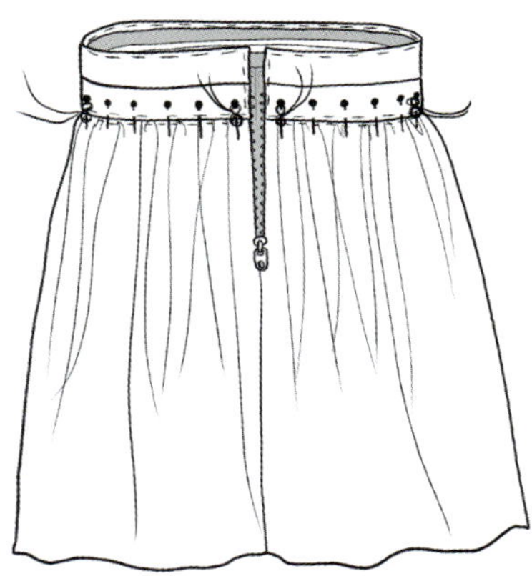

**4.** Now you'll use tidy fell stitches to secure the waistband edge onto the skirt. To fell, slip needle through each fold of gathered fabric, then up into waistband edge and out. Repeat for every fold, all the way along the waistband. This will be somewhat time consuming, but it's satisfying. Remove pins as you go to avoid unnecessary tangles.

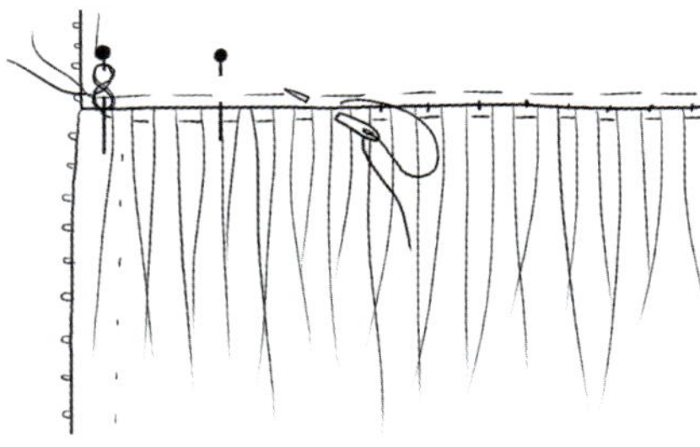

## Stroked Gathers

In order to achieve tidy stroked gathers, you can use your needle's tip to stroke along the valley of each gather, orienting it vertically. Stroke before each stitch, and you'll end up with gathers that are all parallel. You'll also ensure that your raw edges are safely hidden away inside your waistband.

5. Carefully pin waistband's short ends to zipper. Zipper teeth should be even with the folded edge of waistband.

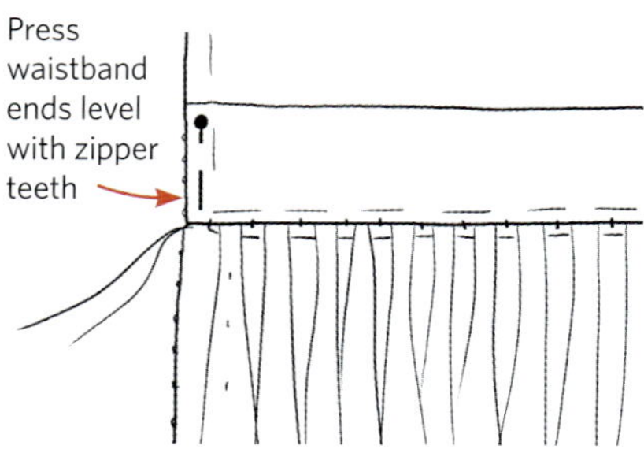


6. Turn skirt inside out. Fold waistband's other long edge down to inside of garment so that edge matches felling stitch line. This will close the waistband. Match notches and pin.

7. Using tidy fell stitches, whipstitches, or small running stitches, secure pinned long edge down to inside of garment. You don't need to be quite as careful to capture each gather this time, although if you have time and patience, it will make for a very neat finish. Remove pins along long edge as you go. Once done stitching, remove all gathering baste threads. (Don't remove pins on waistband's short ends yet.)

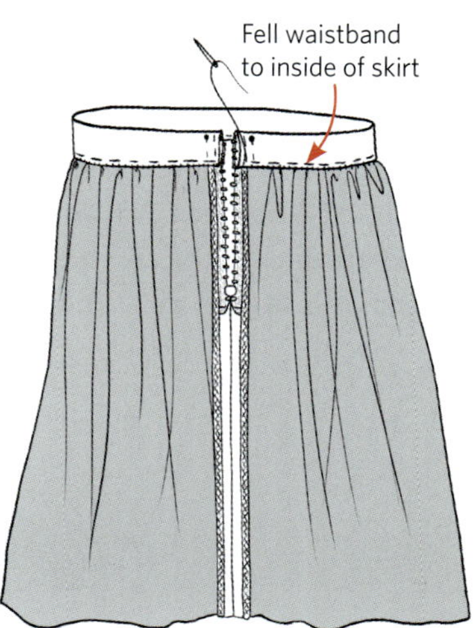


8. Turn skirt RS out again. Fold and tuck away any visible seam allowance corners and zipper tape ends. Using spaced backstitch, stitch through all layers to close up short ends of waistband and attach zipper tapes, which are sandwiched between waistband layers. Stitching should be about ¼" (6 mm) away from edge.

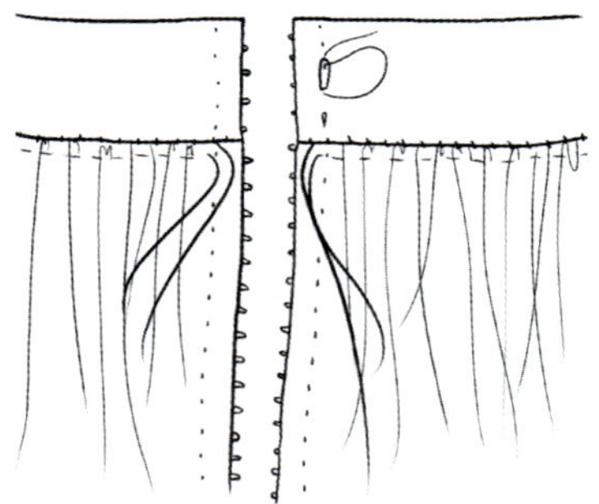

9. Optionally, use whipstitch to attach a hook and eye at the top of the waistband.

## HEMMING

**1.** Try on skirt. Place pins, chalk, or other markings to indicate your desired skirt length. (This may coincide with the original length you'd intended, or it may be a bit different.)

**2.** Press raw edge under ¼" (6 mm). Then fold and press again to achieve your desired skirt length. Place pins or baste to hold.

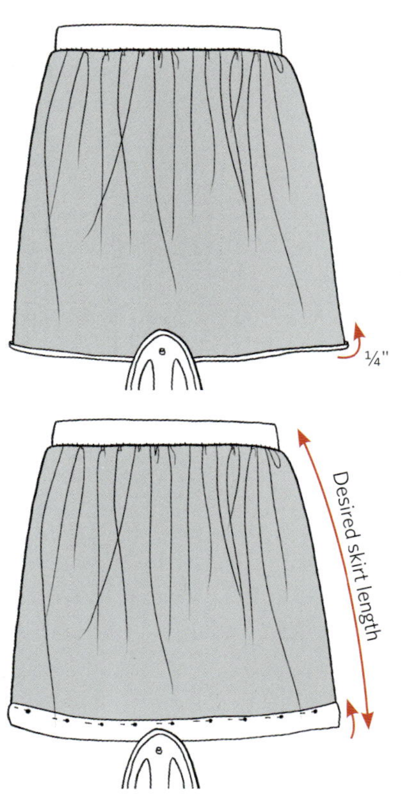


**3.** Use hemstitch (or whipstitch or small running stitches, if you'd prefer) to secure hem. Remove pins or basting.

# *Hetal Shrivastav*

*(she/her)*, founder and creative head of RaasLeela Textile
AHMEDABAD, GUJARAT, INDIA

As a fashion student, Hetal Shrivastav had no idea she would one day lead a company making exclusively hand-stitched clothes. Even when she decided to start her own brand, Hetal intended to create machine-sewn clothing. But finding a reliable, affordable tailor proved difficult. Then she had an idea.

"I thought, let's just skip the whole idea of having a machine-stitched product," Hetal explains. "One, we can provide employment to the artisans. And two, we can skip the whole problem with the tailors." Hetal hand-stitched the first collection herself, meanwhile hoping to persuade local artisans the idea was even possible.

Initially the artisans were skeptical, but they agreed to make a few garments. The clothing drew praise, and the artisans began to feel real pride in their creations. And things took off.

"All over the world, before the machine, everyone was doing it by hand. But here in India, people had forgotten the practice. They just knew embroidery," Hetal says. "So our task was to use embroidery stitches to stitch a garment." Twelve years later, RaasLeela continues to offer entirely handsewn clothes, stitched by an all-woman team.

***Loving the imperfection.*** Hand sewing has this very imperfect look. Some stitches are smaller, some are bigger. There might be one or two stitches that are missed if the seam is very thick. There are knots in between. We love this imperfection. While in machine sewing everything is so perfect, it looks a little dead compared to a hand-stitched product.

***Stitch equality.*** From the designer's point of view, I like running stitch most because all my artisans can do running stitch. There are some stitches that require a very specific skill set, and not everyone has that, so they might feel a little inferior. But running stitch is something everyone can do. Running stitch kind of connects them, so that they're all on the same level.

***Sewing together.*** All the artisans like to work in groups. They always talk while they work. They talk about their neighbors, their own generation, their mothers. Even if they're working from home, they gather at each other's places.

***Independent agency.*** We want to give the artisan the opportunity to think while they're making it. We don't want them to be like another sewing machine, just simply sitting in a corner and following instructions. We want them to get involved. While making something, they should like it. If someone likes red, they can choose to work only with red. And if somebody likes multicolor, they can use whatever color they want, wherever they want.

***Surprises.*** On each product, we put one surprise element. So if the whole shirt has running stitch all over it, on the sleeve you might find a small butterfly. And some other dress, they might put a flower with a pot. Just random. Now that is something that machines can't do. If you put embroidery into a machine, there can't be surprises. By hand, we can always do different things at any time.

# T-SHIRT

The modern T-shirt's typical construction is inextricably tied to the industrial machines used to make it, so hand-stitching a T-shirt is a task of reverse engineering. How do you construct a deeply conventional garment in a deeply unconventional way? It's a radical question, and there's truly no "right" answer. What follows is a method I've evolved over time, playfully applying some of the same stitches humans have practiced for millennia.

There are infinite great ways to hand-sew a T-shirt. I love that! Please stretch out into the spaciousness of this project: Make a good but improbable thing with fabric, thread, two hands, and a curious mind.

# Patternmaking

T-shirt fit is quite personal. Whether you like snug, loose, or somewhere in between, you can draft your T-shirt pattern to taste. You'll begin by taking some measurements from your actual body. But as you did for the woven boxy top, it will also be helpful to pull out a few knit tops (or tunics or dresses) that you like and study their measurements. They don't need to match the exact styling of the T-shirt you're planning to sew—they just need to have select elements that you like. Even if you don't own anything that fits you in the way you'd like, it can still be helpful to study the measurements of knit garments you own so that you can make educated guesses about the dimensions you'd prefer.

## MEASURING YOUR BODY

Measure and record the following:

- Body length (HPS to desired garment length)
- Bust level (from HPS)
- Waist level (from HPS)
- Bust circumference
- Waist circumference
- Hip circumference
- Shoulder width
- Neck width
- Front neck drop
- Armhole depth
- Bicep circumference
- Sleeve length (CB to LPS to desired sleeve length)
- Sleeve opening circumference (measured at desired sleeve length)

## MEASURING OTHER GARMENTS

Lay each garment flat on a table. Pinch at both underarm-side seam intersections and pull gently to smooth the area that is between your hands. Then smooth the rest of the torso by patting any wrinkles toward the edges until they are gone. The sleeves will not lie flat, but that's fine—you'll be focusing on the torso measurements first. Mark these down.

Once you've measured all torso-related points, readjust garment so that sleeve is flat and then take dimensions of sleeve- and armhole-related areas.

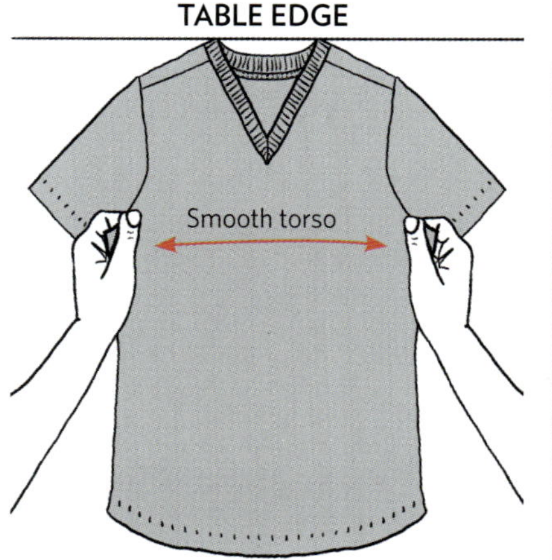


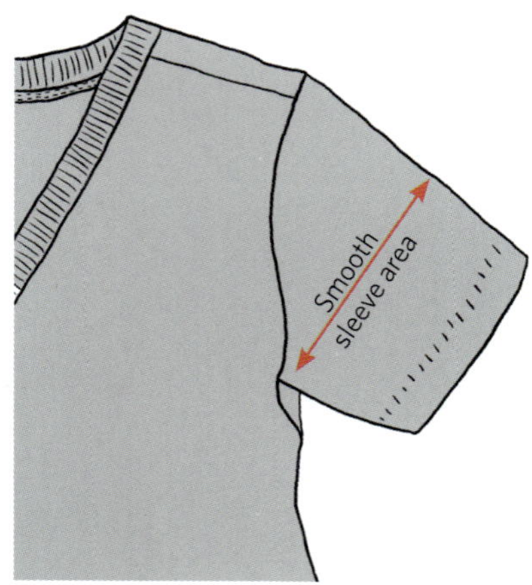

## DECIDING THE DIMENSIONS

For each measurement, study the numbers you've taken from your own body and from the clothes you wear, and decide what you'd like to use for your T-shirt draft.

In case you're still unsure what numbers to use, I'm including a few recommendations based on my own fit preferences. Feel free to disregard these if you've already determined what you prefer.

- Body length: For a basic T-shirt, I like to use the length from HPS to hip level.
- Bust circumference: I add 4" (10.2 cm) to the anatomical bust circumference.
- Waist circumference: I add at least 4" (10.2 cm) to the anatomical waist circumference.
- Hip circumference: I add 4" (10.2 cm) to the anatomical hip circumference.
- Shoulder width: I add 2" (5 cm) to the anatomical shoulder width.
- Neck width: I add 2" (5 cm) to the anatomical neck width.
- Front neck drop: I add ½" (1.3 cm) to the anatomical front neck drop.
- Armhole depth: I add ½" (1.3 cm) to the anatomical armhole depth.
- Sleeve length: I use 7½" (19 cm) beyond LPS, but it's very much a matter of personal preference.
- Sleeve opening circumference: For a short sleeve, I add 3" (7.6 cm) to my anatomical bicep circumference (but it depends a lot on sleeve length).

You're welcome to choose whichever measurement you'd like for the shoulder width measurement. However, the T-shirt construction techniques that I'll be sharing are probably best suited to drop-shoulder styles, in which the shoulder width is roughly 2" (5 cm) wider than your body's anatomical measurement. So if you'd like to follow my recommended sewing techniques, you may wish to use a wide-ish shoulder, too. That said, you can make it work with a more anatomical shoulder, so don't feel limited by this guideline if you'd rather go narrower.

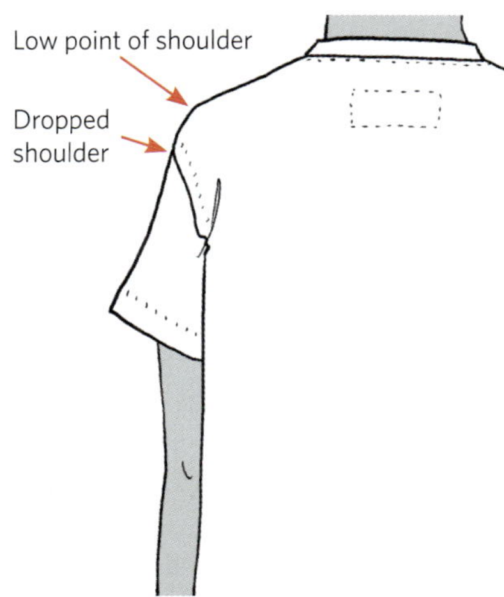


## MARKING LEVELS

As in previous projects, you'll be drafting only half of the T-shirt because the garment will be symmetrical. You'll initially draft the front and back body together.

1. Draw a long CF/CB vertical line down the right-hand side of a large sheet of paper.

2. Square a long line across the top. This will be the HPS level.

3. From HPS level, measure down desired body length and square long line across bottom. This will be the sweep level.

4. From HPS level, measure down armhole depth plus 1" (2.5 cm) and square across a long line. This will be the underarm level.

   The underarm level should be placed at 1" (2.5 cm) below the armhole depth amount to account for the 1" (2.5 cm) shoulder slope you'll be plotting in a later step.

5. From HPS level, measure down bust level from HPS and square across a long line. This will be the bust level.

6. From HPS level, measure down waist level from HPS and square across a long line. This will be the waist level.

7. Along CF/CB line, find midpoint between HPS and underarm levels, and

square across a long line. This will be the across-torso level.

Please note that the spacing may look different for you than in the example shown here, and that's okay—each person's body is different.

HPS
Across torso
Underarm
Bust
Waist
Sweep
CF/CB

### DRAFTING NECKLINE AND SHOULDER

1. From CF/CB line, measure along HPS and make tick mark at one-half of neck width amount.

2. From CF/CB line, measure along HPS and make tick mark at one-half of shoulder width amount.

3. From HPS level, measure along CF/CB line and make tick mark at front neck drop, then square across ½" (1.3 cm).

4. From HPS level, measure along CF/CB line for ½" (1.3 cm) and square across 2" (5 cm) for back neck drop.

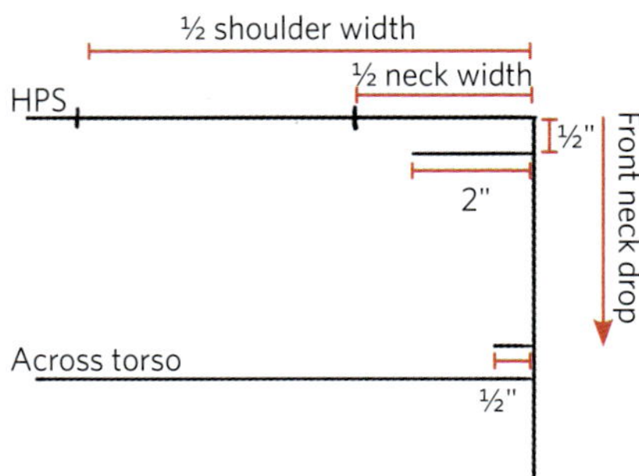


5. Draw a smooth front neck curve connecting short front neck drop line to neck width tick mark. Maintain about ½" (1.3 cm) that is squared to the CF/CB line before curving.

6. Draw a smooth back neck curve connecting the short back neck drop line to neck width tick mark. Maintain about 2" (5 cm) that is squared to the CF/CB line before curving.

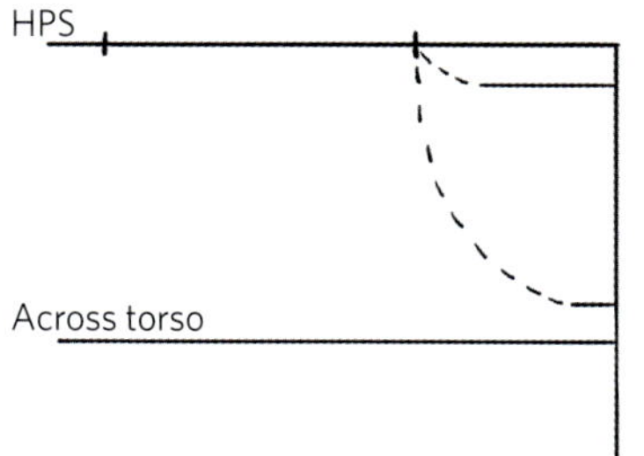


7. From shoulder width tick mark, measure down 1" (2.5 cm) for shoulder slope and place a point. This will be the low point of shoulder.

8. Draw a straight line that connects neck width tick mark to low point of shoulder. This line will be the shoulder fold. (The true shoulder seam will be drawn lower in a later step.)

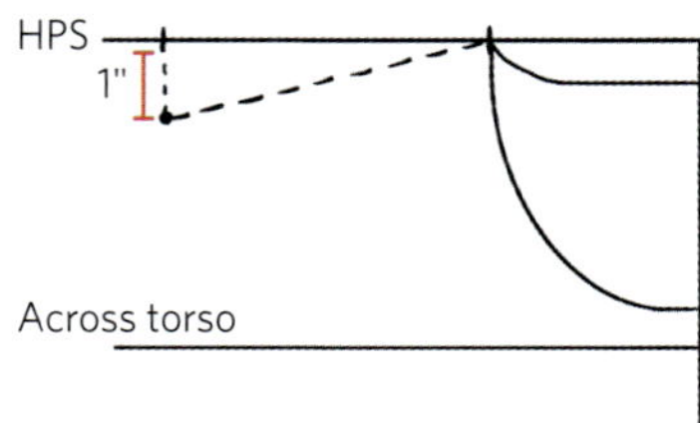


### DRAFTING SIDE SEAM AND HEM

1. From CF/CB line, measure along underarm level and make a tick mark at one-quarter of bust circumference amount. (Please note that you're marking this onto the underarm level, not the bust level, even though it's the bust measurement.)

2. From CF/CB line, measure along waist level and make a tick mark at one-quarter of waist circumference amount.

3. From CF/CB line, measure along sweep level and make a tick mark at one-quarter of hip circumference amount.

4. Next, draw your side seam by blending a smooth line to connect underarm, waist, and sweep tick marks. You may choose to draw a line that hits wider than your waist tick mark—I often draw a straight line to connect underarm and sweep tick marks, which

typically means the waist area receives more wearing ease than originally planned. This is your choice, though. If you want to maintain your intended fit, then try to draw a smoothly curved line that passes through all three tick marks. Regardless, make sure your line is smooth, without angular or wavering areas.

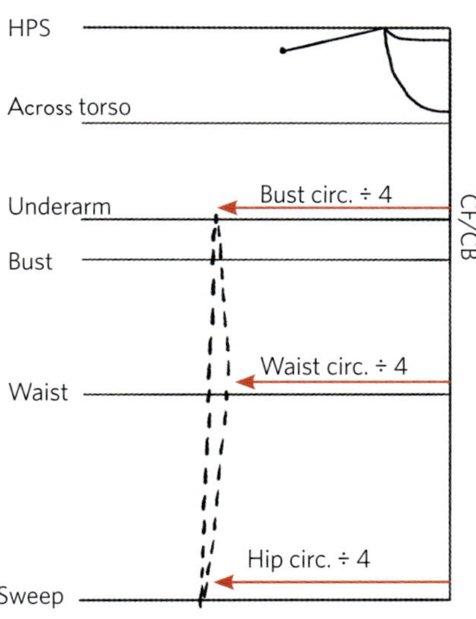


**5.** To ensure clean sewing, find a right angle between the bottom of the side seam and your sweep. Unless your side seam happens to be exactly parallel to the CF/CB line, you'll need to adjust the sweep line accordingly.

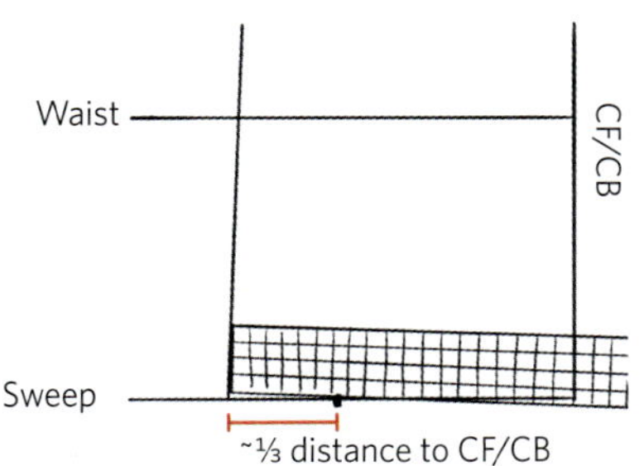


Slide your gridded ruler or a square tool along the side seam until you find a line that intersects with the sweep level at approximately one-third of the distance toward the CF/CB line. Draw this line. Then soften the angle by drawing a smooth, gentle curve.

You're welcome to draw a shirttail-style hemline if you'd prefer. However, note that you'll still benefit from at least ½" (1.3 cm) of right angle at the side seam before you curve downward. In this case, square ½" (1.3 cm) at the bottom of the side seam before beginning to draft the shirttail curve.

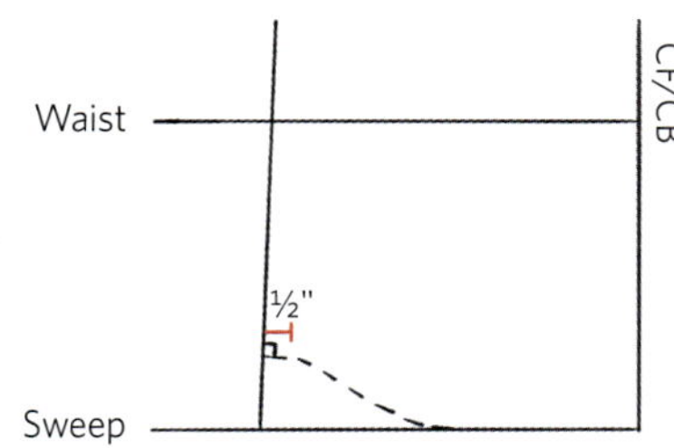


## DRAFTING ARMHOLES

You'll draw both front and back armholes onto the same draft (just like you did with the necklines).

**1.** From the underarm point (intersection of side seam and underarm level), measure in along underarm level by ½" (1.3 cm) and make a tick mark.

**2.** From the low point of shoulder, drop down a line that is parallel to CF/CB line and extends to the across-torso level.

**3.** Starting at this intersection with the across-torso level, freehand a smooth, continuous curve that connects to the underarm-level tick mark from step 1, as shown. Aim for a lazy J shape. Sketch this curve with light pencil passes, repeatedly, until you've found a line that curves gently and gracefully into the underarm. This curve completes your back armhole.

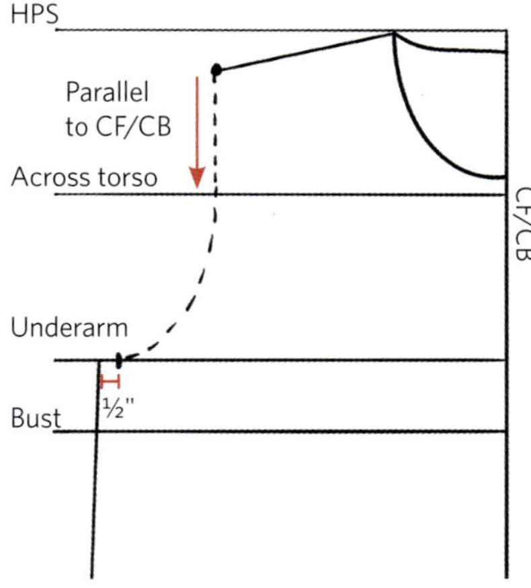


**4.** Now draft your front armhole. At the same intersection point with the across-torso level, measure ½" (1.3 cm) to the right and make a tick mark. Next, start at the low point of shoulder and begin sketching a line that connects through this tick mark and scoops down to the underarm-level tick mark from step 1. The curve should be very gradual as it descends through the across-torso level. Once past the across-torso level, your line should be more scooped than the back armhole curve.

The front armhole should be more strongly scooped to allow the arm a comfortable seat, or "saddle," in the shirt. Did you know that your arms actually hang from the front of your body, not the sides? Look in a mirror and raise your arms overhead. Notice that your armpits face forward, not to the sides. This is why armholes are most comfortable when they offer more "saddle" in the front.

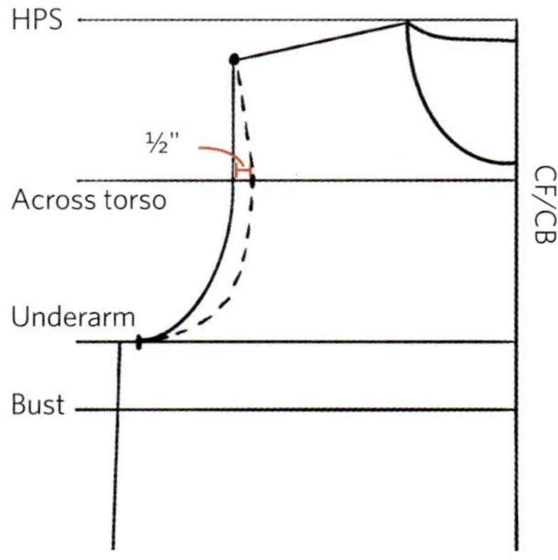


**5.** Measure front and back armhole curves and jot down measurements for later reference.

## FINALIZING TORSO DRAFT

**1.** If you were to stitch up a T-shirt based on these current shapes, you'd likely find that the shoulder seams did not sit at the true crest of your shoulders, so that the garment would be falling slightly backward on your body. In order to correct for this, you can convert the current shoulder line into a fold line, and draw a new shoulder seam that is slightly forward.

Draw a shoulder seam line that is parallel to the top fold line but ½" (1.3 cm) below it.

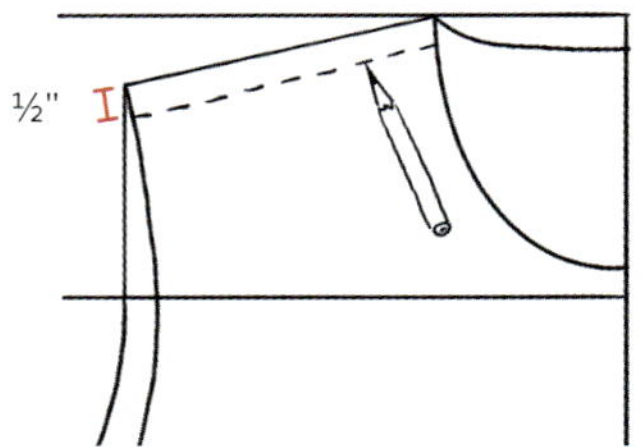


**2.** To "unfold" the top fold line, begin by folding paper backward along this line. Then use tracing wheel to trace along the upper section of front armhole, shoulder seam, and upper section of front neckline.

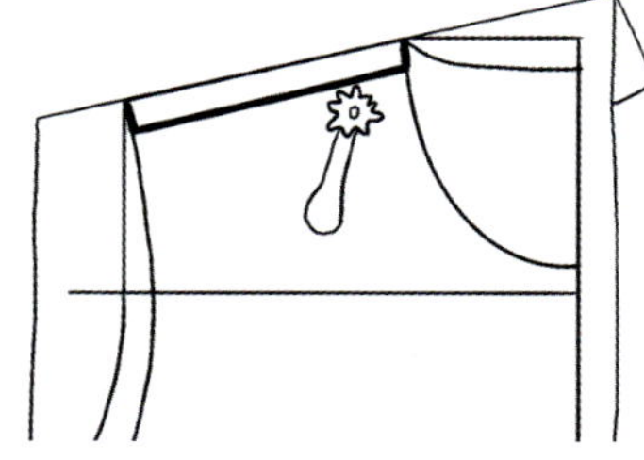

**3.** Unfold paper, and pencil in the lines you just traced. They'll form the upper edges of your back panel.

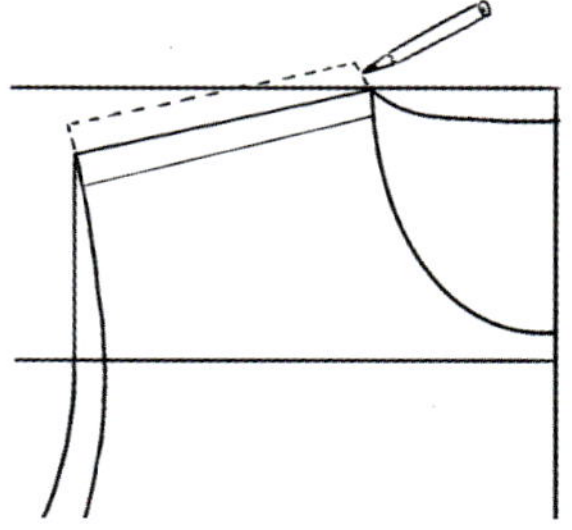

**4.** Next, you'll add matching notches on the armhole curves. These will help you to align edges accurately when stitching the sleeve into the armhole.

**A.** Measure up from the underarm point along the front armhole curve and place a notch mark at 3" (7.6 cm) from the underarm point.

**B.** Measure up along the back armhole curve and place a notch at 3" (7.6 cm) and another at 3½" (8.9 cm).

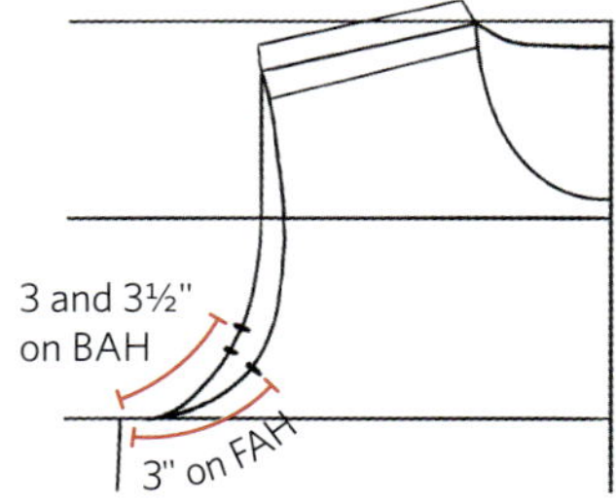


These armhole notch measurements are good clean numbers that I like to use, but please know that they're somewhat arbitrary—you're welcome to place the notches in slightly different positions if you'd prefer. Just note that you'll need to use the same numbers when plotting notches onto your sleeve cap later.

**5.** Decide how wide your finished neckband will be. I like a finished neckband height of approximately ½" (1.3 cm), but you're welcome to try something a little bit wider or narrower.

## Is Your Draft Loose- or Snug-Fitting?

My basic recommended side seam SA amounts are appropriate for a special seam technique I'll be sharing in the hand-sewing section. However, this seam technique works best for garments that aren't tight. So if you've drafted your T-shirt to be fairly snug, I'd recommend felling the SAs instead. In this case, you'll probably want your SA amounts to match, instead of differing between front and back, so follow italicized recommendations for front pattern and front inseam of sleeve pattern.

**6.** Redraw necklines, parallel to the original lines but your neckband's width in from the edge. Erase or mark out the old lines. Measure along new front and back neck curves and mark lengths onto your draft for later reference.

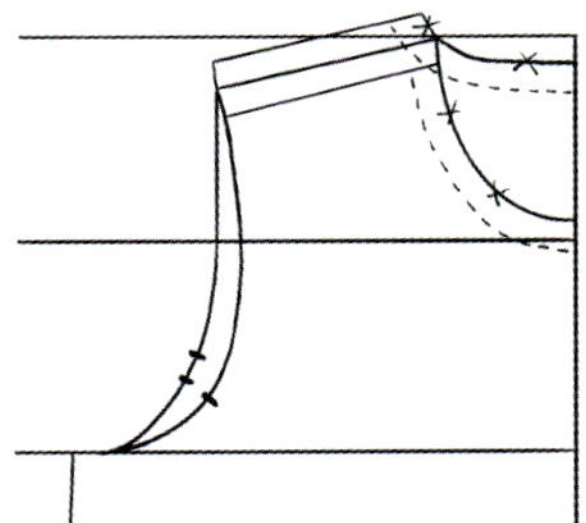

### TRACING FRONT TORSO PATTERN

**1.** On a new large, wide sheet of paper, draw a long vertical line down the middle. This will represent your CF line. Fold the paper in half along this line. Place on table with folded center front line on right-hand side.

**2.** Place torso draft on top, aligning draft's center front/center back line with the lower sheet's folded edge. Weight down.

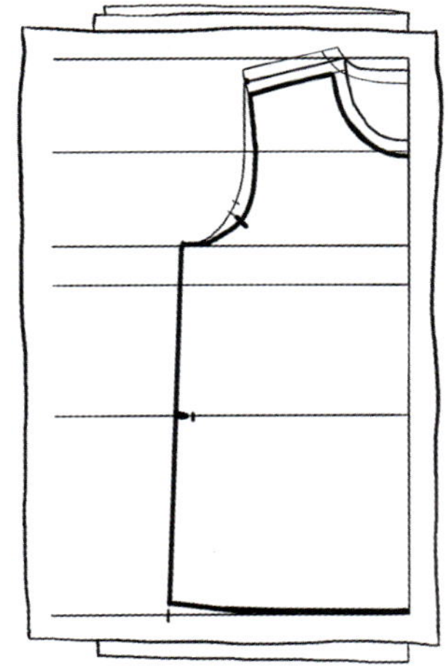

**3.** Using tracing wheel, trace along sweep, side seam, front armhole, forward shoulder seam (the lower line), and front neckline. Trace front armhole notch. Also trace a notch at waist level. Remove draft paper and pencil in lines clearly.

**4.** Next, add SAs. For the hand-sewing techniques I'll be sharing, I'd recommend:

- ¼" (6 mm) on neckline
- ¾" (2 cm) on shoulder seam and armhole
- ¼" (6 mm) on side seam (or ¾" [2 cm] if shirt is snug-fitting)
- 1" (2.5 cm) on sweep

**5.** Pin the two paper layers together and cut out. Snip notches. Remove pins and unfold. Then snip notch at CF neck edge.

**6.** Place grainline parallel to CF. Add note: "CUT 1 SELF."

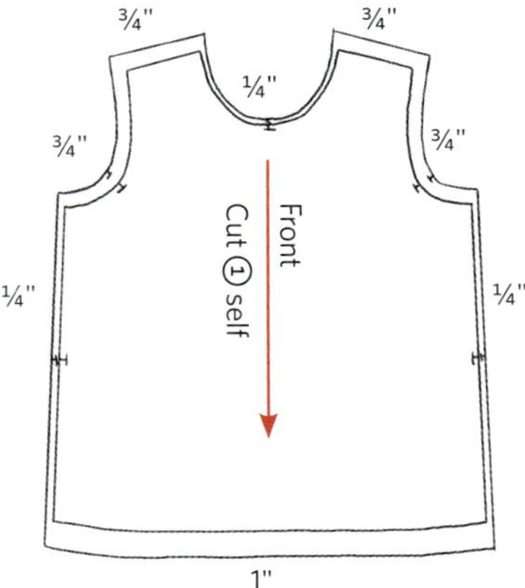

#### TRACING BACK TORSO PATTERN

**1.** On a new large, wide sheet of paper, draw a long vertical line down the middle. This will represent your CB line. Fold the paper in half along this line. Place on table with folded CB line on right-hand side.

**2.** Place torso draft on top, aligning draft's CF/CB line with the lower sheet's folded edge. Weight down.

**3.** Using tracing wheel, trace along sweep, side seam, back armhole, extended shoulder seam (the uppermost line), and back neckline. Trace back armhole notches. Also trace a notch at waist level. Remove draft paper and pencil in lines clearly.

**4.** Next, add SAs. For the hand-sewing techniques I'll be sharing, I'd recommend:

- ¼" (6 mm) on neckline
- ¾" (2 cm) on shoulder seam and armhole
- ¾" (2 cm) on side seam (should be different from front)
- 1" (2.5 cm) on sweep

**5.** Pin the two paper layers together and cut out. Snip waist and armhole notches. Also snip notch ¼" (6mm) from CB fold on neckline. Remove pins and unfold.

**6.** Place grainline parallel to CB. Add note: "CUT 1 SELF."

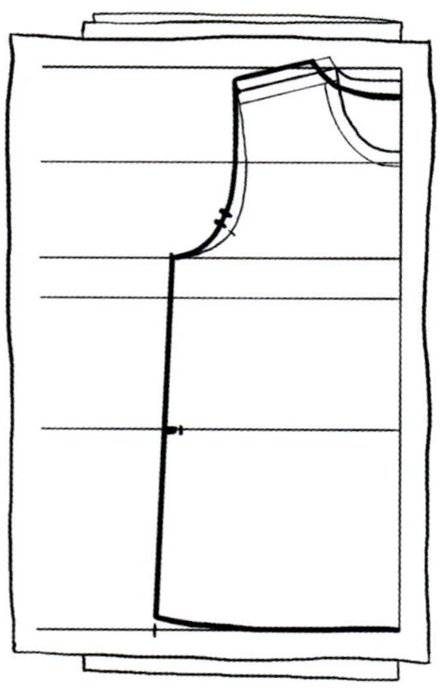

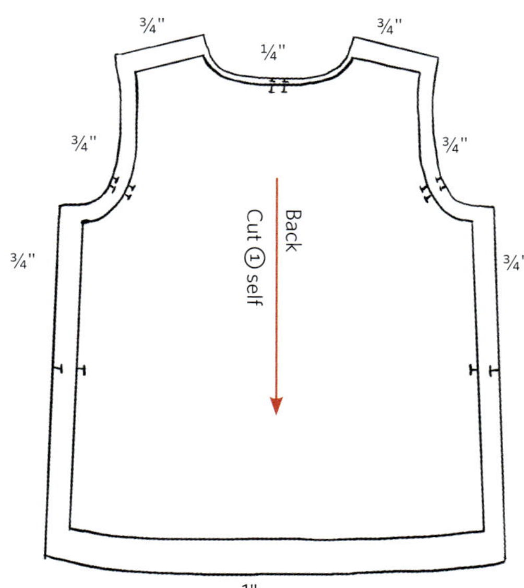

# Understanding Sleeve Drafting Theory

Drafting sleeves was one of the most bewildering tasks for me in my early patternmaking years. The lower part of a sleeve is fairly simple—it's basically a tube—but the sleeve cap (that curvy bell-shaped section at the top) felt very mysterious. After all, it has to fit around the front, side, back, and top of the ball of your arm, as well as around your underarm. And once it's joined to the garment, the cap's fit will affect the fit of the rest of the garment.

As I eventually learned, sleeve drafting is actually pretty simple once you get the hang of it. In the coming pages you'll learn more about the concepts that go into drafting a sleeve cap. Then you'll be ready to draft your own!

## Sleeve Cap Length

The first thing to know: A sleeve always needs to be drafted to fit into its armhole. Sometimes the sleeve cap edge is drafted to be somewhat longer than that armhole, such as on many woven garments, so that the sleeve cap has enough fabric to be eased around the ball of your arm. Other times, as in many knit garments such as our T-shirt here, the sleeve cap edge is drafted to be roughly equal to the armhole circumference.

Refer to the front armhole (FAH) and back armhole (BAH) measurements you marked down while drafting your torso pieces. Add these together to determine your total armhole circumference. Your sleeve cap length will need to be roughly equal to this number.

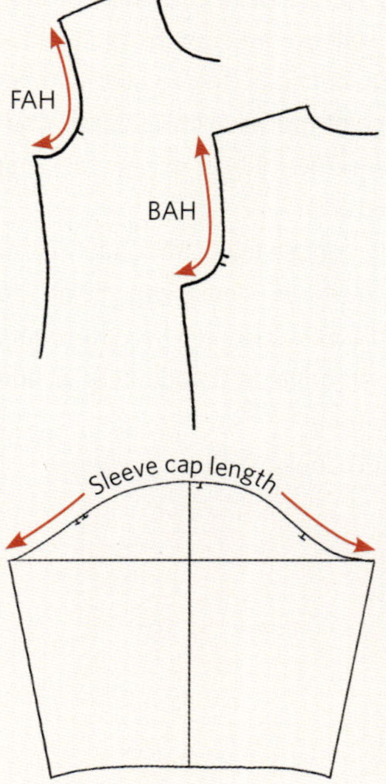


## Sleeve Pattern Length

When you originally determined your garment dimensions, you measured sleeve length from CB to your low point of shoulder (LPS) to your sleeve. That was a helpful way to measure when you were still deciding how wide your shoulder width should be. But now that you've committed to a shoulder width, you'll need to quickly calculate how long your actual sleeve pattern should be—the sleeve length from LPS.

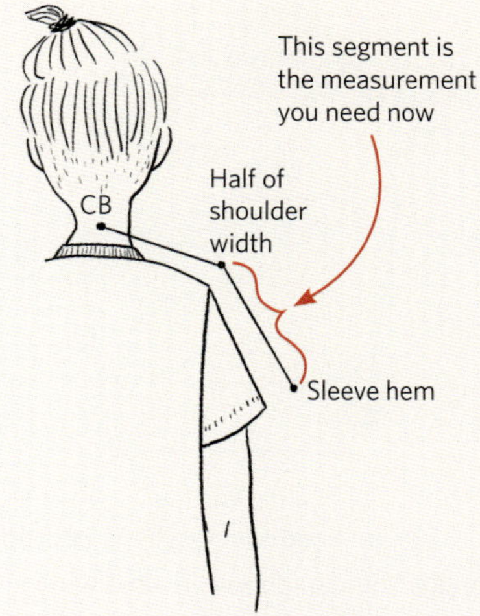


In order to calculate the sleeve pattern's length, you'll need to subtract half of the across-shoulder width from your earlier measurement.

- sleeve pattern length = desired length from center back – (shoulder width ÷ 2)

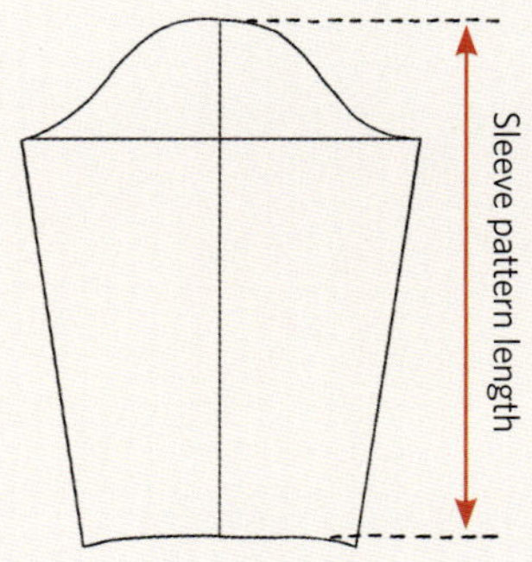

## Sleeve Cap Height

The sleeve cap is everything that happens above the underarm level: It's the curvy bell-shaped area at the top of the sleeve. That bell shape is designed to offer contour around your shoulder, allowing for a cleaner fit.

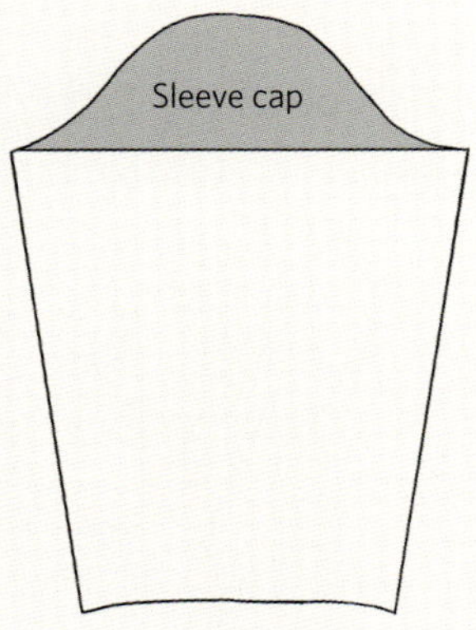


The cap height is a stylistic decision, really. You can choose from a wide range of numbers, but the one you choose will affect the way the sleeve looks on your body. It will also affect your range of motion when you wear the garment.

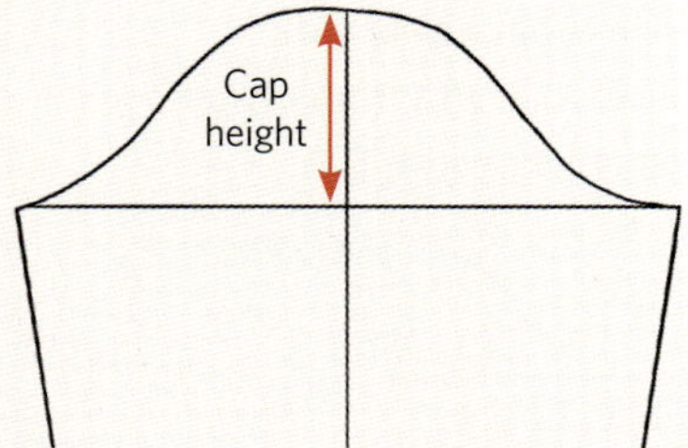


As a general rule, a shallower sleeve cap will produce a boxier-fitting sleeve, which will have lots of excess fabric at your underarm when arms are relaxed, but which will enable you to lift your arm easily without the body riding up, too.

T-shirts are, as the name indicates, more T shaped, with minimal cap height. This makes them a great option for athletics and comfortable movement, because they're built with lots of range of motion. However, they usually have some folds of excess fabric at the underarm.

By contrast, a traditional tailored suit has a tall sleeve cap, giving the jacket a clean look when the wearer is, say, standing at a podium or sitting in a meeting.

Let's look at a few examples.

### ZERO CAP HEIGHT

In this first example, we're looking at an extremely boxy top. The sleeve has a cap height of zero—no cap at all.

The woven boxy top on page 93 also has no sleeve cap height—it just looks a bit different because the sleeves are cut in one piece with the body, so you don't see armhole seams.

It looks cute lying flat on the table, and it's very easy to move in. When the wearer's arms are relaxed at their sides, there's a lot of excess fabric at the underarm. The sleeve "wings out" a lot at the outseam area, too.

None of this is inherently good or bad—these are just facts to know when deciding how much cap height you'd like for your own design.

### LOTS OF CAP HEIGHT

This next example is pretty much the exact opposite of the first. Here, the sleeve has a high cap.

This sleeve naturally rests with the sleeves down at the wearer's sides. Therefore it looks very clean when the arms are at ease, and there isn't much excess fabric. There is little or no winging at the outseam.

However, it's more difficult to lift the arms, as these sleeves are not optimized for movement. The garment may ride up if the wearer reaches overhead.

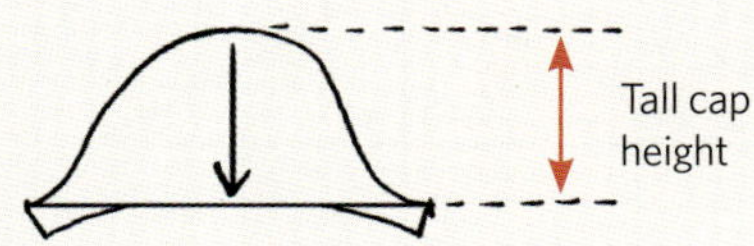


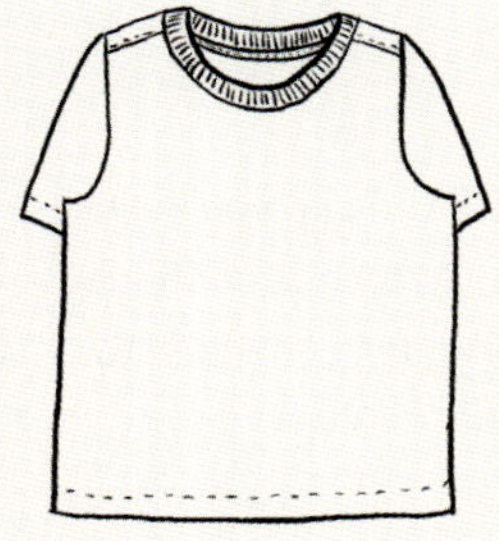

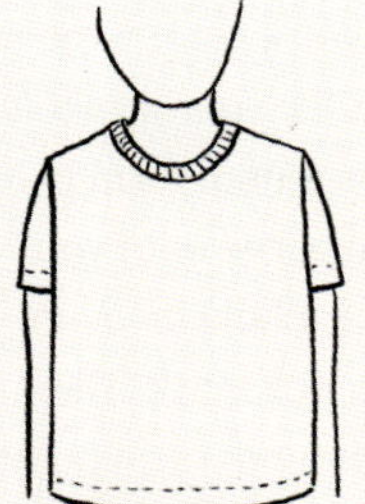

### MODERATE CAP HEIGHT

Finally, here is a sleeve that has a more moderate sleeve cap height. This one's height is roughly 20 percent of the total armhole measurement.

This sleeve rests at a diagonal when the garment is laid flat. There is some excess fabric at the underarm when the garment is worn, but not as much as with zero cap height. There is some outseam winging. The wearer can have arms up or down, and the shirt will hike only somewhat when arms are lifted.

This is the sleeve that I recommend drafting for your T-shirt. However, if you have a preference for some other cap height amount, feel free to use that instead.

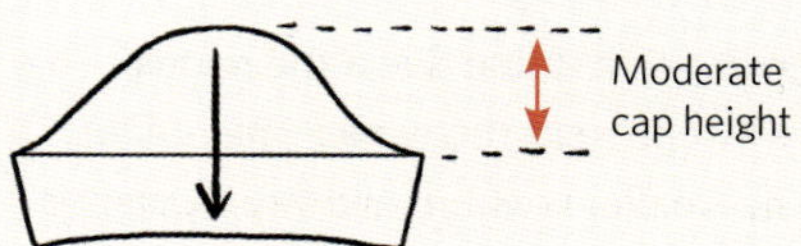

## Plotting the Basic Sleeve

**1.** On a large sheet of paper, draw a long vertical line down the middle. This will represent the center line of your sleeve. Somewhere midway along the vertical line, square a long line across. This represents the underarm level of your sleeve.

**2.** Calculate desired cap height. I'd recommend:

- sleeve cap height = total armhole ÷ 5

**3.** Measure up from the intersection point and place a tick mark. This represents the top of your sleeve.

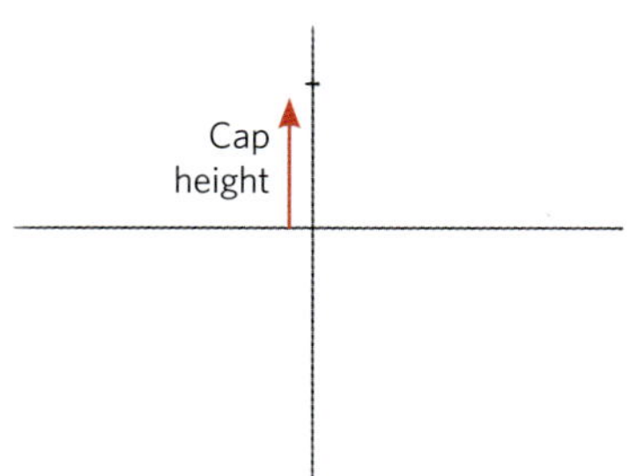


**4.** Divide total armhole measurement in half, then subtract ⅛" (3 mm). Find this number on your ruler. This is what you'll use to draw your next line.

Place the ruler's zero-inch end at the cap height mark, and swing the ruler until it intersects with the underarm line at the number you just measured. Trace along the ruler's edge to connect, as shown. Repeat for the other side. These lines will serve as provisional cap lines. You'll shape them next.

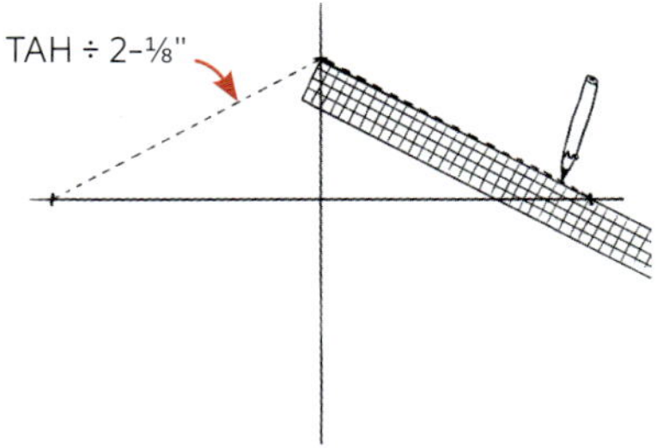


### DRAFTING THE SLEEVE CAP CURVE

The left half of your sleeve will represent the back half, and the right will represent the front. Because your arm hangs toward the front of your body, you'll need slightly different cap shaping on the back and front.

**1.** Divide provisional cap lines roughly into thirds. From left to right, label these intermediate points A, B, C, and D, as shown.

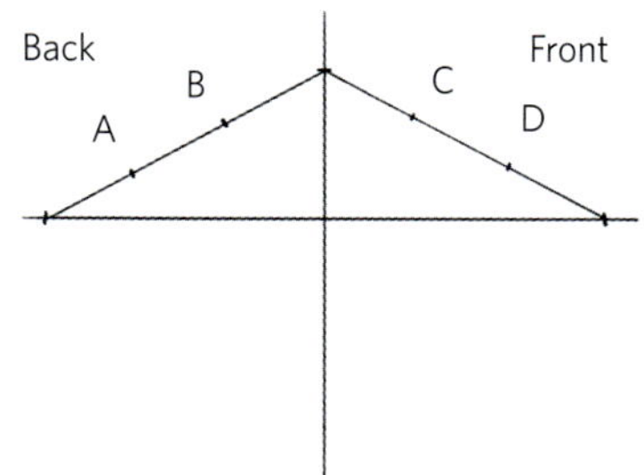


**2.** Between the back underarm point and A, sketch a curve that scoops in roughly ⅛" (3 mm), as shown.

**3.** At or near B, curve line up ½" (1.3 cm).

**4.** Line should pass through top tick mark of sleeve's center line.

**5.** At or near C, curve line up ⅜" (1 cm).

**6.** At or near D, line should pass through provisional straight line.

**7.** Between D and front underarm point, line should scoop in roughly ¼" (6 mm).

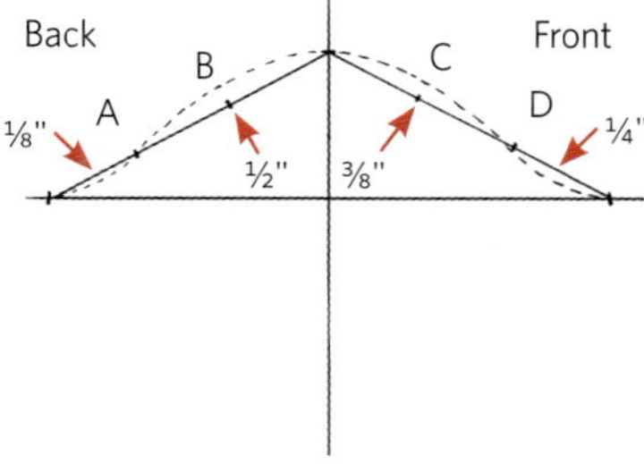


**8.** Assess the curved cap you've just sketched. It should form a continuous, smooth curve. Adjust as needed to achieve a gradual contour.

**9.** You've just drafted a nice sleeve cap shape. However, you'll want to check that it's a good fit for your armhole. Starting at the back underarm point, measure up along curve until you reach your back armhole measurement, and place a tick mark. Then, starting from front underarm point, measure up along curve until you reach the front armhole measurement, and place a tick mark. There is probably a gap between these two marks. This gap represents your sleeve cap ease.

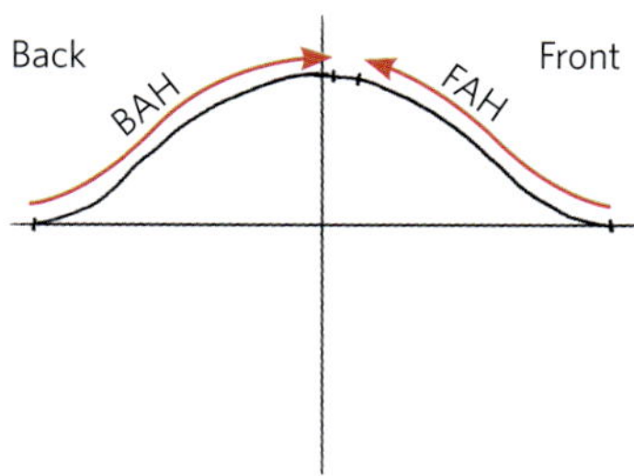


**10.** Measure the gap between tick marks.

- If the distance is ½" (1.3 cm) or less, you're in good shape—no adjustments needed! Find the midpoint between marks and place a notch. You'll align this notch with the shoulder seam when sewing.
- If the tick marks met at exactly the same point, that means your cap line and armhole are exactly the same measurement. In other words, you have no cap ease, and that's fine for this stretchy knit T-shirt. Place a notch at this meeting point.
- If the distance is greater than ½" (1.3 cm), consider lowering your sleeve cap slightly and/or bringing in the shape along the underarm line slightly (reducing equally on both sides) in order to shorten the curve. Then repeat steps 9 and 10 to be sure you've achieved a gap of ½" (1.3 cm) or less.
- If the tick marks crossed (so that there's an overlap), that means your cap line is shorter than your armhole. First, double-check your measurements. Remeasure the front and back armholes from your torso draft, and redraw the provisional cap lines. Then repeat steps 1–10. If your calculations are accurate, your curved sleeve cap should have some sleeve cap ease.
- After rechecking everything, if you still have negative cap ease, try increasing your cap height slightly and/or widening along the underarm line slightly (increasing equally on both sides). Then repeat steps 9 and 10 to be sure you've achieved a gap that measures somewhere between 0 and ½" (1.3 cm).

## DRAFTING THE HEMLINE AND INSEAMS

**1.** Refer to your calculated sleeve pattern length:

- sleeve pattern length = desired length from CB – (shoulder width ÷ 2)

Starting at the top of the sleeve cap, measure down along the center line and mark sleeve length with a tick mark. Then square across in both directions. This line represents the hem.

**2.** Now apply your desired sleeve opening measurement to this new line, placing half on each side of the center line.

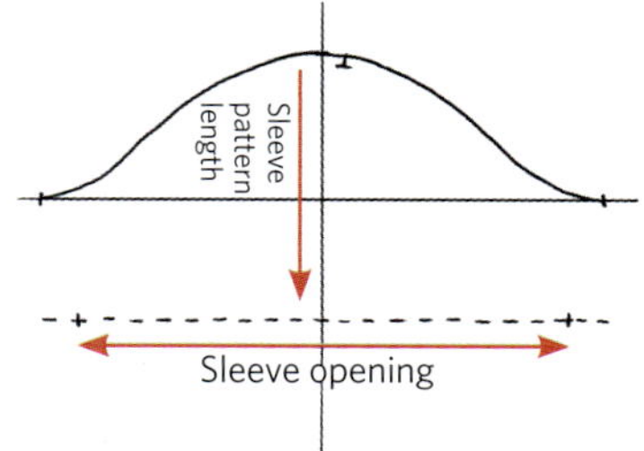


**3.** Draft inseams by connecting underarm and hem points with straight lines.

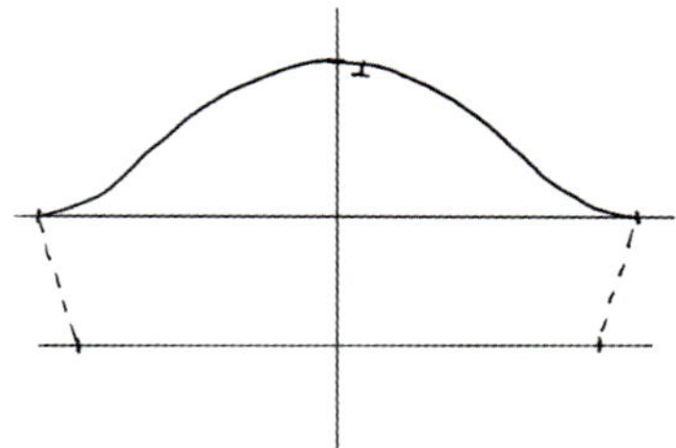

## FINALIZING THE SLEEVE PATTERN

**1.** Add matching notches to front and back portions of sleeve cap. Beginning at front underarm point, measure up 3" (7.6 cm) along curve and place notch. Beginning at back underarm point, measure up 3" (7.6 cm) and 3½" (8.9 cm) along curve and place notches.

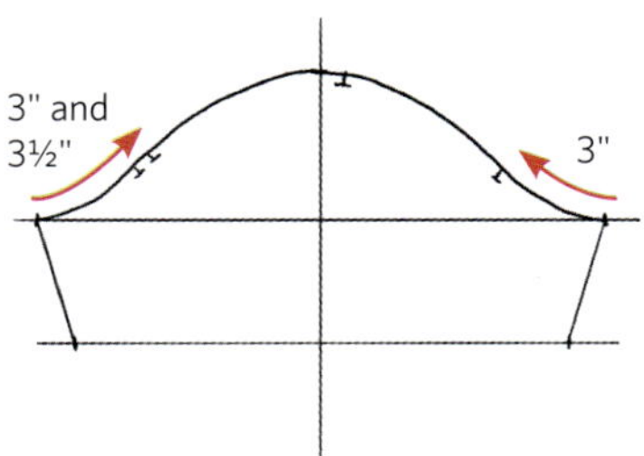

2. Next, add SAs. I recommend:

- ¾" (2 cm) on back inseam and sleeve cap
- ¼" (6 mm) on front inseam (or ¾" [2 cm] if shirt is snug-fitting)
- 1" (2.5 cm) on hem

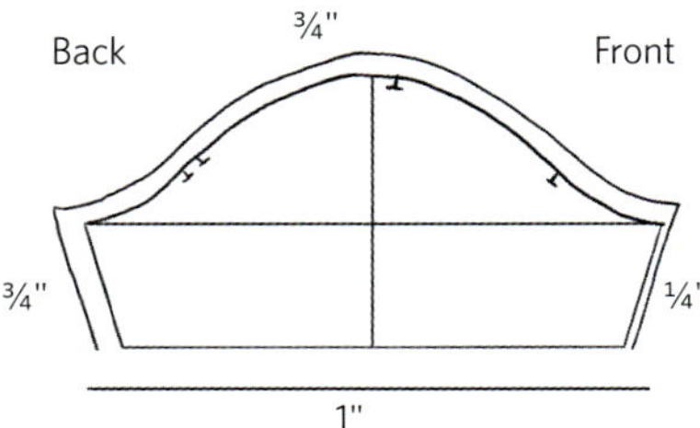


3. Fold paper along the hem's true fold line (not the hem allowance cut line you just drew), and trace inseam stitch and cut lines. This will ensure that your sleeve hem will fold up neatly for sewing, even though you probably don't have right angles at the inseam-hem intersections.

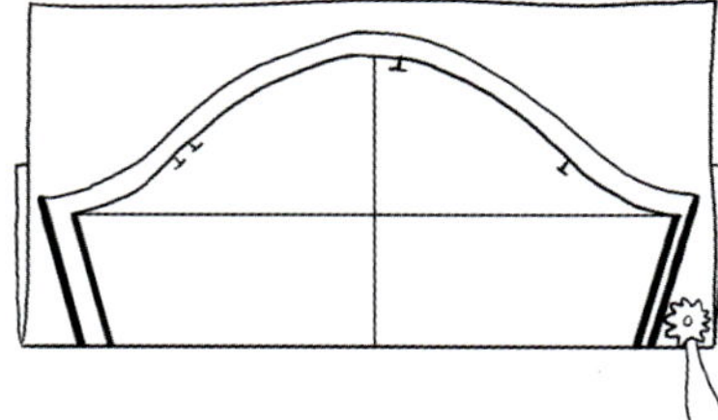

4. Unfold and pencil in traced lines.

5. Cut out. Snip notches.

6. Place grainline parallel to center line. Add note: "CUT 2 SELF."

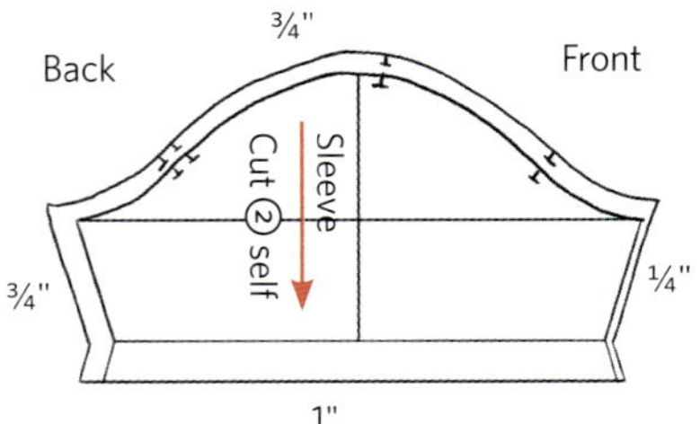

## DRAFTING THE NECKBAND

**1.** Refer to the finished neckband width you decided on while drafting the torso.

**2.** Calculate torso's total neckline circumference. To do so, refer to front and back neckline lengths marked on your torso draft. Add together, then multiply by two to find the total neck circumference.

**3.** The neckband should be somewhat shorter than the torso's neckline circumference in order to lie flat against your skin. In other words, it should stretch slightly when sewn in.

If you don't shorten your neckband somewhat, the neckband will stick up away from the skin, like a very tiny turtleneck.

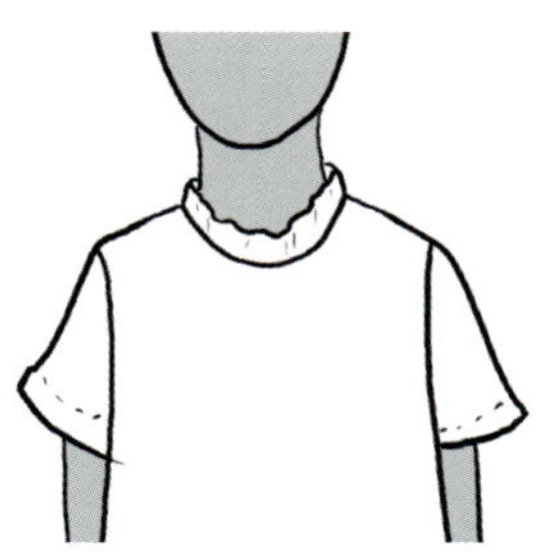

In order to achieve a flat neckband, I like to reduce by at least 15 percent:

- total neckline circumference × 0.85 = neckband length

A reduction of 15 percent is a general guideline, but if you're using a very stretchy knit, you might reduce by 20 percent or more.

**4.** On a long sheet of paper, draw a rectangle that is:

- As long as the reduced neckband length
- Twice as high as your desired neckband (the neckband will fold over, so you'll need double the height to achieve that finished measurement)

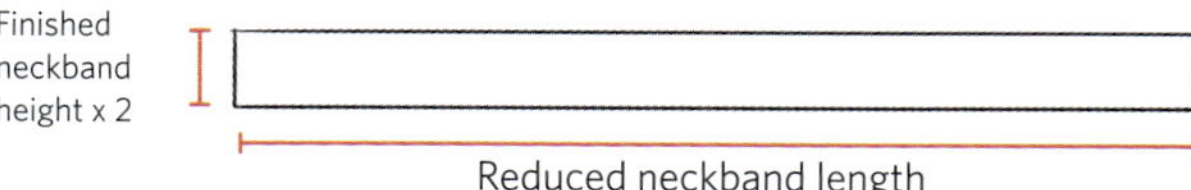


**5.** Divide neckband's length into quarters and place notches along top and bottom edges.

**6.** Next, add SAs. I'd recommend ¼" (6 mm) on all edges.

**7.** Cut out. Snip notches.

**8.** Place grainline parallel to short ends. Add note: "CUT 1 SELF (OR RIB)."

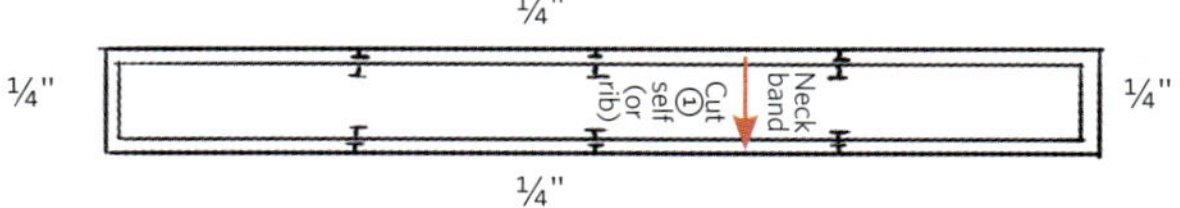


## DRAFTING THE CHEST POCKET (OPTIONAL)

I'd recommend waiting to draft the chest pocket until you've sewn your T-shirt, so that you can "audition" the pocket's size and position on your body. If you'd rather pattern the pocket now, though, see the instructions on page 182. You can hold the front body pattern up to yourself in lieu of the actual T-shirt.

# Sewing

## HAND-SEWING STITCHES

- Even backstitch
- Whipstitch
- Running stitch
- Overcasting
- Diagonal backstitch
- Herringbone stitch (optional)
- Bartack (optional)

## FABRIC OPTIONS

This T-shirt works well in medium-weight knit jersey. I like using cotton or other natural fibers, but you can use whatever you prefer. You're welcome to experiment with other fabric weights, too, and with other knit constructions. The T-shirt fabric doesn't need to have four-way stretch the way the leggings did, but it's fine if it does. However, make sure that your fabric has some horizontal stretch.

## CUTTING THE FABRIC

See Cutting Fabric on page 85 for tips on cutting. You'll need to cut the following pieces and quantities:

- Front × 1 self
- Back × 1 self
- Sleeve × 2 self
- Neckband × 1 self (or rib)
- Chest pocket × 1 self (optional, and I'd recommend waiting to cut until after sewing the shirt)
- Also cut a back neck binding strip of self (or rib) fabric along the stretchy cross-grain—it should be 1⅛" (2.9 cm) tall and slightly longer than the back neckline

## SEWING THE SHOULDER SEAMS

You'll flat-fell the shoulder seams for a strong, clean, attractive seam finish.

**1.** Place front panel on top of back panel, RST. Align along shoulder seams and pin.

**2.** Looking at the front panel as you stitch, sew shoulder seams using even backstitch and ¾" (2 cm) SA amount.

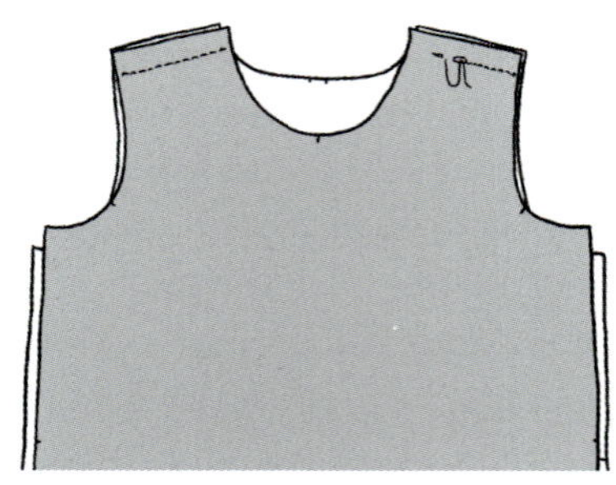

**3.** Press SAs toward back panel.

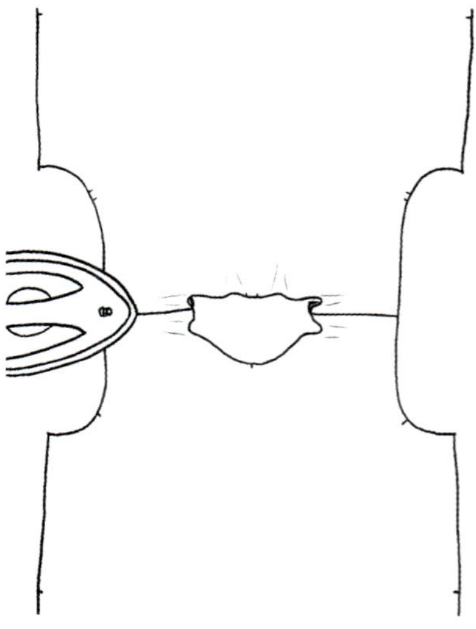

**4.** Next, prepare to fell SAs.

**A.** Trim half of the width of the back panel's shoulder SAs (but do not trim the front panel's SAs).

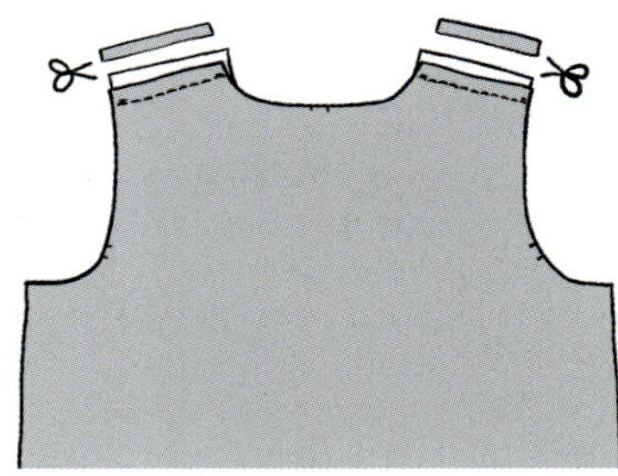

**B.** Fold front panel's SAs around and under back SAs, so that all raw edges are concealed. Pin and/or baste.

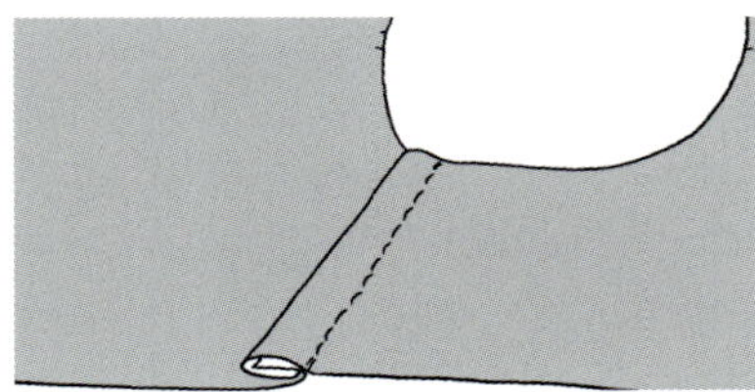

**C.** Use whipstitch to secure folded edges down.

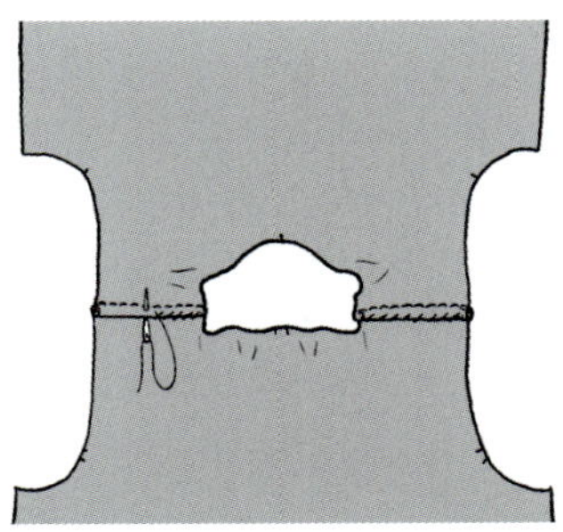

**5.** Press.

## JOINING THE NECKBAND

**1.** Fold neckband with RST so that the two short ends are aligned. Using running stitch or even backstitch, join with ¼" (6 mm) SA amount.

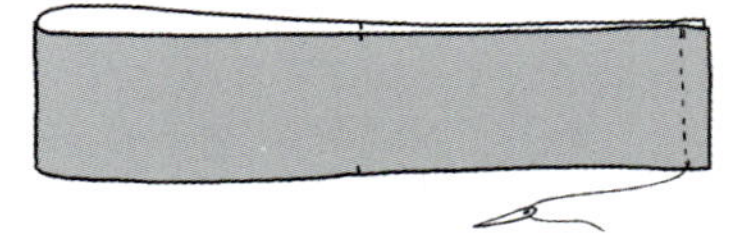

**2.** Snip corner triangles to reduce bulk. Be careful not to cut into your seam as you trim away these triangles.

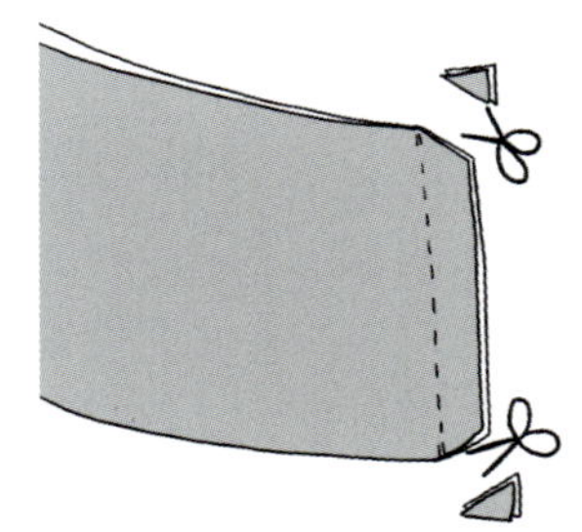

**3.** Press neckband SAs open.

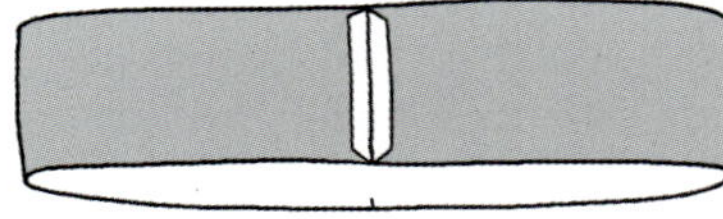

**4.** Fold neckband in half, WST, along the length of the neckband. Align raw edges. Press fold.

**5.** In a moment, you'll align the neckband join seam with one of the garment's shoulder seams. Pick one of the shoulder seams for this. Pinch at that shoulder seam, then pinch garment's raw neckline edges along each other all the way across the neckline to find the halfway point. Snip a little notch at this point.

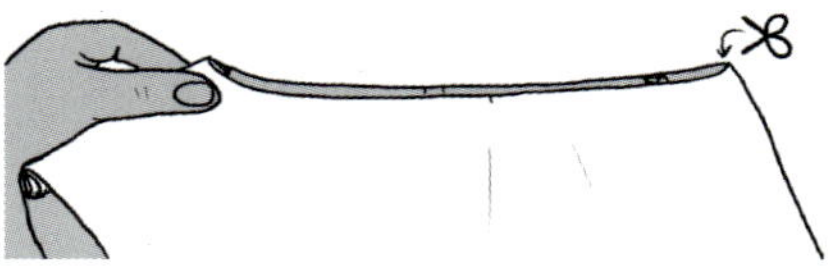

**6.** Align selected shoulder seam with new notch and pinch neckline edges along each other to find quarter-points. Snip notches at those two points, too.

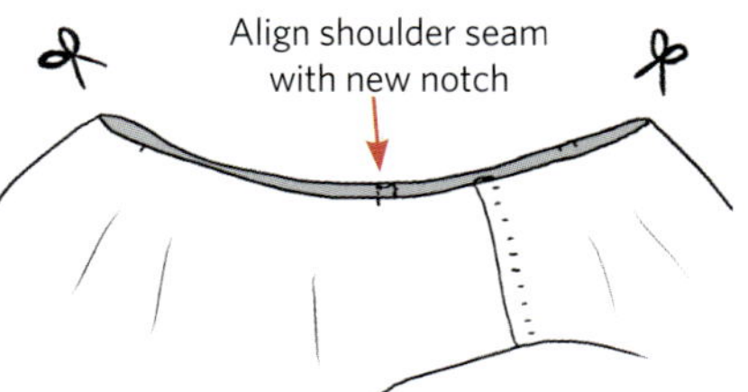


**7.** You've now designated four equidistant points (one shoulder seam and three new little notches) for neckband alignment. Facing garment RS, pin folded neckband's raw edges to garment neckline edges, using your four alignment points. Once you've placed the first four pins, fill in the gaps with more pins. You will need to stretch the neckband slightly to fit. Add enough pins that the raw edges seem securely aligned.

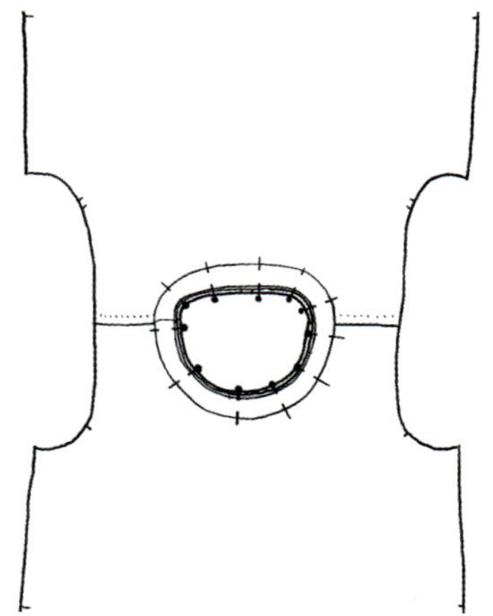

**8.** Stitch seam using even backstitch and ¼" (6 mm) SA.

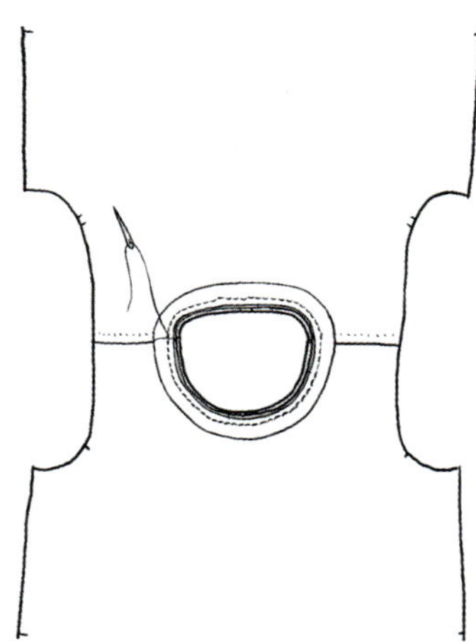

**9.** Overcast SAs along front neckline. (Start at one shoulder and stop at the other. Do not overcast back neck.)

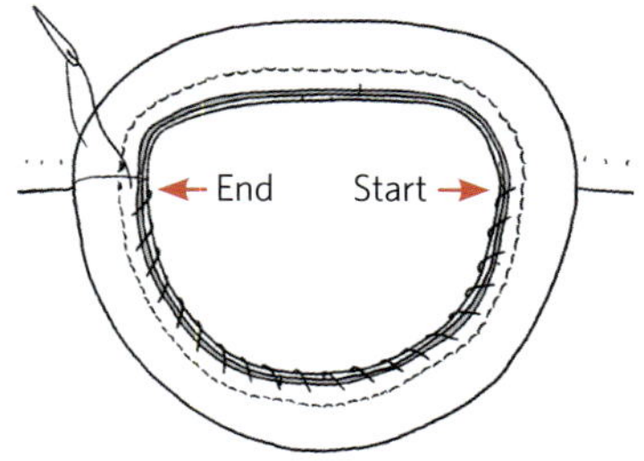


**10.** Working from RS, press neckband away from garment. (SAs will press toward garment.)

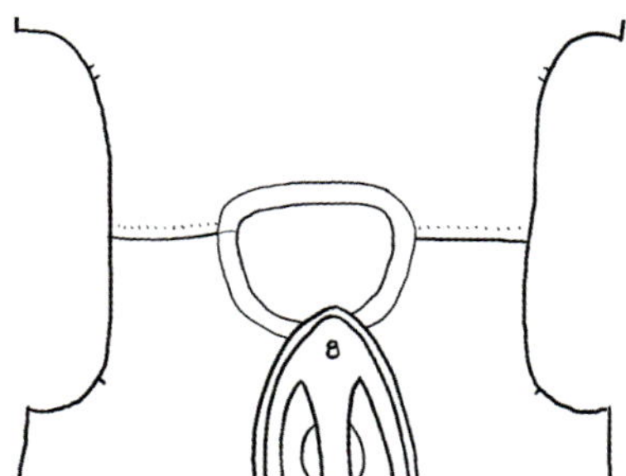

## BINDING THE BACK NECK SEAM

You'll apply an inside binding to cover the back neck SAs, giving the garment a clean look. This binding may also help to limit your back neck from stretching too wide.

**1.** Trim SAs on back neckline by half their width. Be careful not to cut into neckline stitching or front neck SAs.

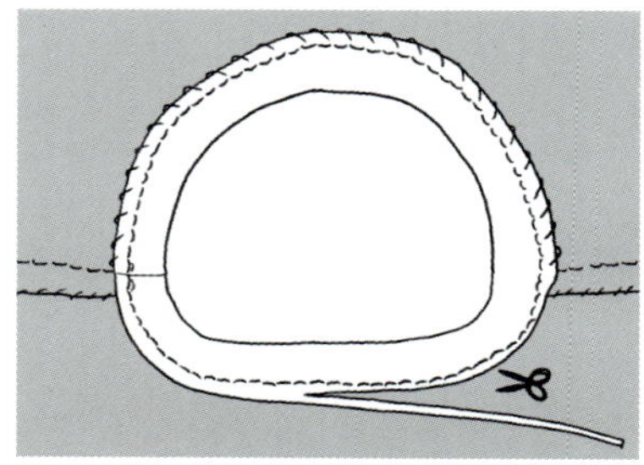

**2.** Place binding strip WS up. Fold top edge downward ¼" (6 mm) along the whole length. (If your fabric is resistant to this press, feel free to baste.)

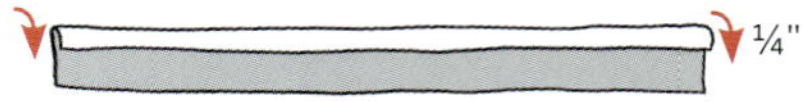


**3.** Press lower edge upward ¼" (6 mm) along the whole length. (Again, baste if needed.)

**4.** With binding strip's raw edges face down, center the strip on top of back neck stitch line. Start pinning at CB and pin outward to shoulder seams. Stitch line should be centered underneath binding as you pin. When you reach each shoulder seam, trim binding short enough to tuck under approximately ¼" (6 mm). Folded ends should land at shoulder seams. Replace pins with basting if desired.

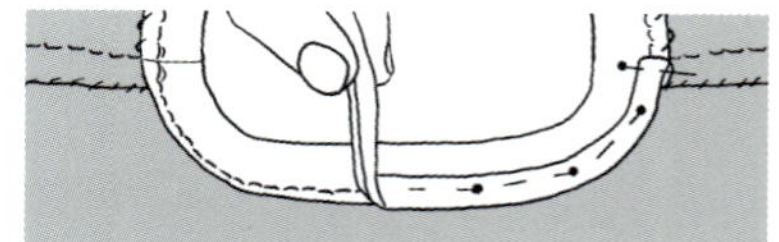

**5.** Whipstitch along entire perimeter of the binding. When stitching the upper edge, try to catch only one layer of the neckband so that stitches will not show on the outside. When stitching the lower edge, you will be attaching binding directly to the body, so these stitches will show on the outside. Plan whipstitch length and spacing so that it looks good to you on the outside. (There's no right or wrong here—it's a matter of personal taste.)

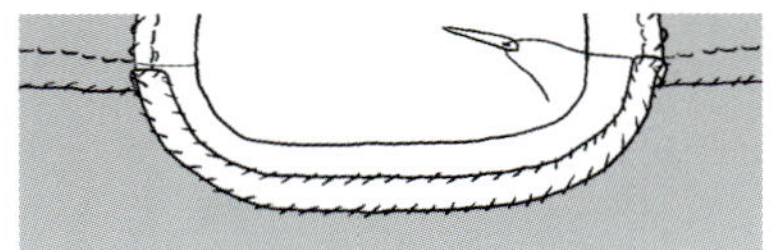

## JOINING THE SLEEVES

You'll sew the sleeves in flat, which means you'll attach them to the armholes before sewing side seams and sleeve inseams. Then you'll fell the SAs, like you did for the shoulder seams.

**1.** Pin sleeves to armholes, RST. Begin by aligning underarm points, single and double notches, and top notches at shoulder seams. Then fill in the gaps with more pins.

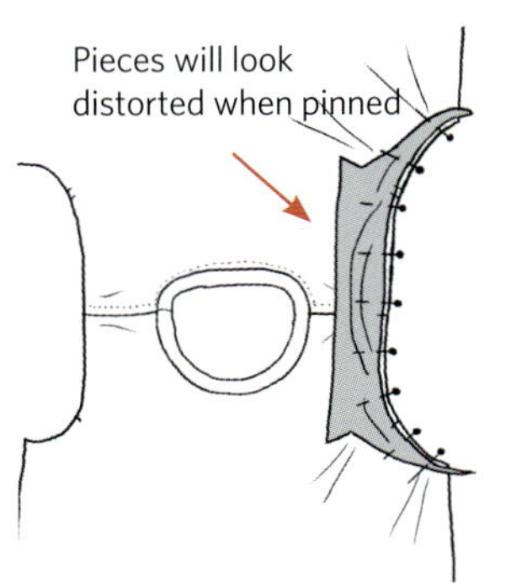


You may find that the edges seem unlikely to fit together before you place these pins. It's normal for the edges to appear that way when joining a sleeve cap to an armhole—after all, the cut edges are different lengths and shapes. But the stitch lines are close in length, so as long as you pin carefully now, the pieces should stitch together without puckers.

**2.** Stitch seams using even backstitch and ¾" (2 cm) SA.

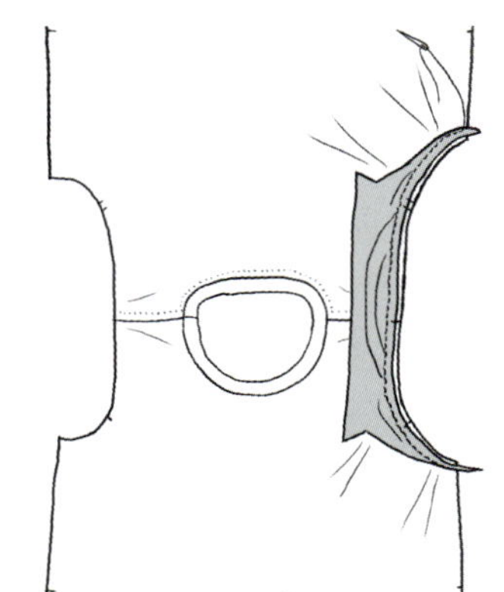

**3.** Press SAs toward body.

**4.** Next, fell SAs down onto the body.

**A.** Trim away half of body panels' SA width along armhole seams. Do not trim sleeves' SA. Also, do not trim allowance at shoulder seams, because that would require you to slice through your shoulder seam stitches. Instead, trim until you've almost reached the shoulder seam, and then snip off. Skip over the shoulder seam and continue trimming, leaving a little tab at the shoulder seam.

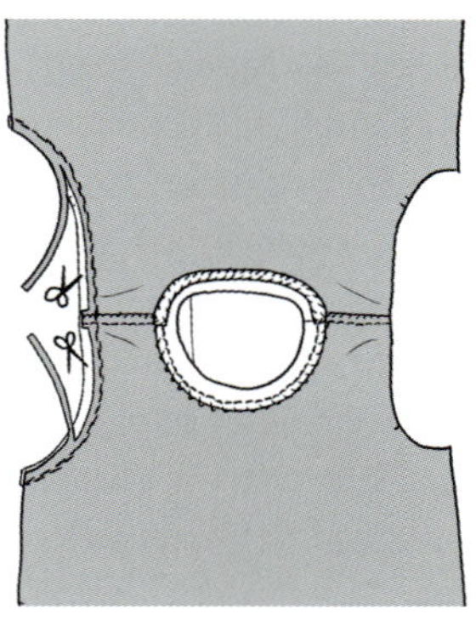

**B.** Fold sleeve SAs around and under body SAs, so that all raw edges are concealed. At shoulder seam area, snip tab in half by cutting between shoulder's backstitch and whipstitch lines. Then fold and smoosh each half toward its respective armhole so it can be hidden away inside the felled allowances. Pin liberally or baste.

**C.** Use whipstitch to secure folded edges down.

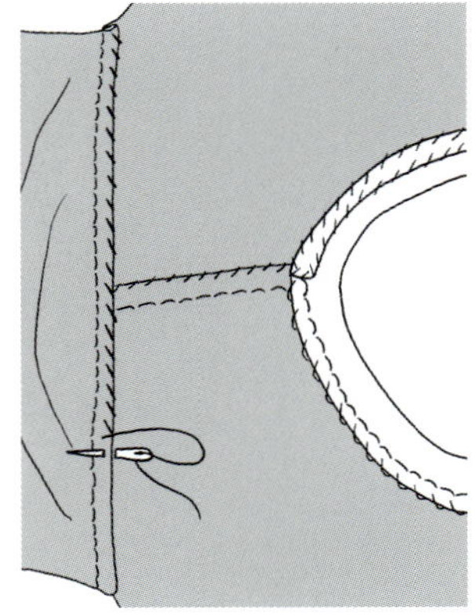

**5.** Press.

### STITCHING THE SIDE SEAMS AND SLEEVE INSEAMS

Because the sleeves are already joined, you can now sew the side seams and sleeve inseams in one continuous line of sewing. For this step, I love to use a modified version of the historical mantua-maker's seam technique, which allows you to secure down the SAs while constructing an actual seam. With one line of stitching, you'll accomplish everything (almost like the modern-day serger/overlock machine, except that this mantua-maker's seam binds the SAs with fabric instead of thread).

## Is Your Draft Loose- or Snug-Fitting?

In my experience, this modified mantua-maker's seam technique works better for garments that aren't tight. So if you've drafted your T-shirt to be fairly snug, I'd recommend felling the SAs instead, following the basic process used for the shoulder and armhole seams. In this case, you'll probably want your SA amounts to match, instead of differing as I recommended in the patternmaking section. If it's too late for that, you can follow steps 1 through 3 below, then stitch with even backstitch at ¾" (2 cm) from the back panel's raw edge, and then fold and fell the back SAs around to the front.

**1.** Optional but helpful: Flip your work to the WS and prepress up all hem allowances by 1" (2.5 cm). You could wait to do this later when hemming, but it's just a little bit easier now while the garment is still open flat.

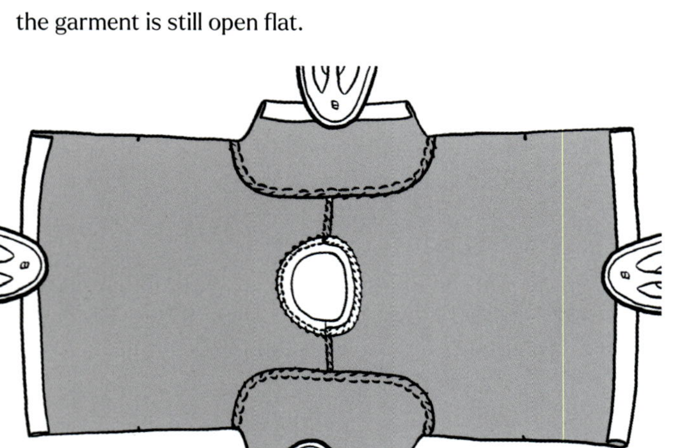

**2.** Fold garment down, RST, so that hems are aligned. Arrange so that front panel is facing up.

**3.** Recall that the front and back panels have different SA amounts—the front has ¼" (6 mm) and the back has ¾" (2 cm). Carefully align seams now so that the back SAs extend ½" (1.3 cm) past the front, and place pins. Make sure that notches, hems, and seams are aligned (but offset by that ½" [1.3 cm] margin). Pin.

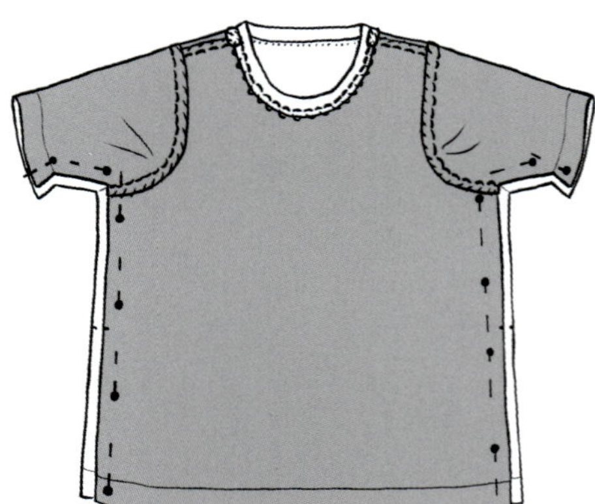

**4.** Fold back panel's allowances ¼" (6 mm) inward so that front and back SAs are kissing. Press or baste to hold.

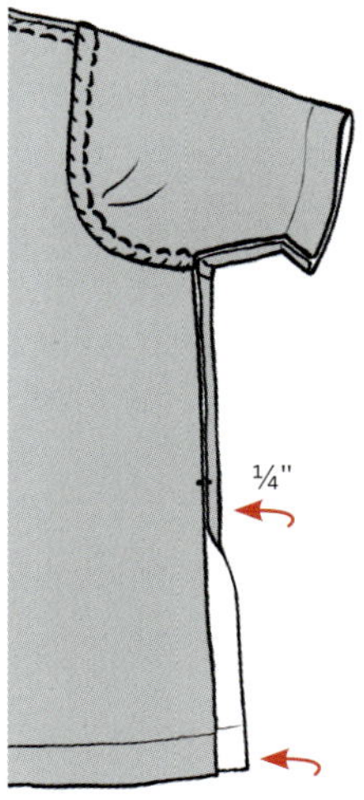


**5.** Next, fold back panel's allowances another ¼" (6 mm) inward so that they are enveloping front panel's allowances. Pin or baste to hold.

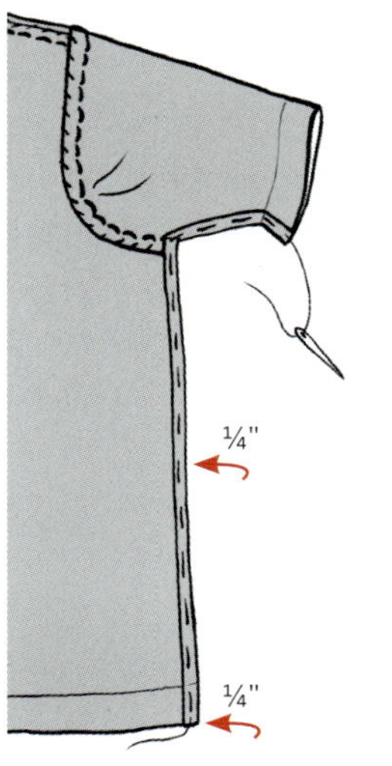


**6.** Use diagonal backstitch through all layers to secure down the folded allowances. Be sure every stitch is puncturing through all layers. Stitch side seam and inseam in one continuous line. (It will be thick to stitch through underarm intersection—just go slow and use a thimble.)

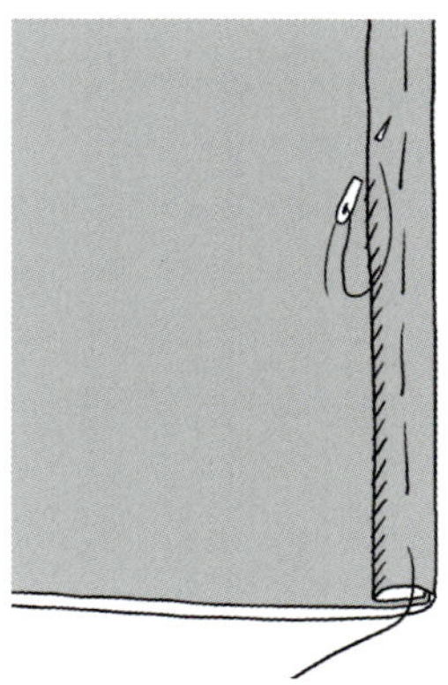

**7.** Press mantua-maker's seams flat, and then press SAs toward the back.

## HEMMING

For the hems, you can use any stretchy hemming stitch that you like. I like to use whipstitch or herringbone stitch, but feel free to deviate in favor of your own preferences and ideas.

I recommend trying a double-turned hem for the sleeve hem, as detailed below. Store-bought knit T-shirts use single-turned hems, but I've found that careful pressing enables an attractive double-folded hem. (The leggings variation on page 133 uses this technique, too.) On a double-turned knit hem, I like to use whipstitch.

For the bottom hem, if you have a strongly curved hem shape (such as a shirttail-type hemline), you'll probably find it easier to do a single-turned hem. In this case, I especially like herringbone stitch, because it neatly thread-binds the raw edge while providing lots of stretch and a neat look on the outside.

**1.** Press the sleeve's raw hem edge up by ¼" (6 mm). Then press it up another ¾" (2 cm) (the remainder of your HA) and pin.

**2.** Use whipstitch to secure sleeve hem down. Whipstitch is a good option because its zigzagging thread trajectory offers a lot of stretch potential.

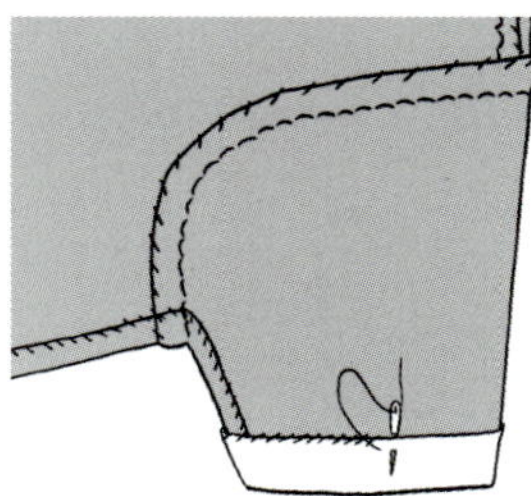

**3.** For the bottom hem, if it's strongly curved, I'd recommend a single-turned herringbone stitch hem. Fold the full 1" (2.5 cm) allowance upward and press, then pin. The raw edge will ruffle a bit as you fold and pin around the curve, but place lots of pins to distribute the ruffling fullness and it will work fine.

## Double-Turned Knit Hems

In woven clothing, double-turned hems (folded twice to enclose the raw edge) are standard practice. However, in ready-made knit clothing, the hems are almost always single-turned (folded just once), with the raw edge thread-bound.

For hand-sewing the T-shirt sleeve hems, I used a double-turned hem. This requires diligent pressing and/or basting to prepare, but it functions just as well as a single-turned hem.

For a more curved bottom hem, or when you'd prefer the minimized bulk of a single-turned hem, use a hemming stitch that offers some thread-binding to the raw edge, such as herringbone, catchstitch, or whipstitch.

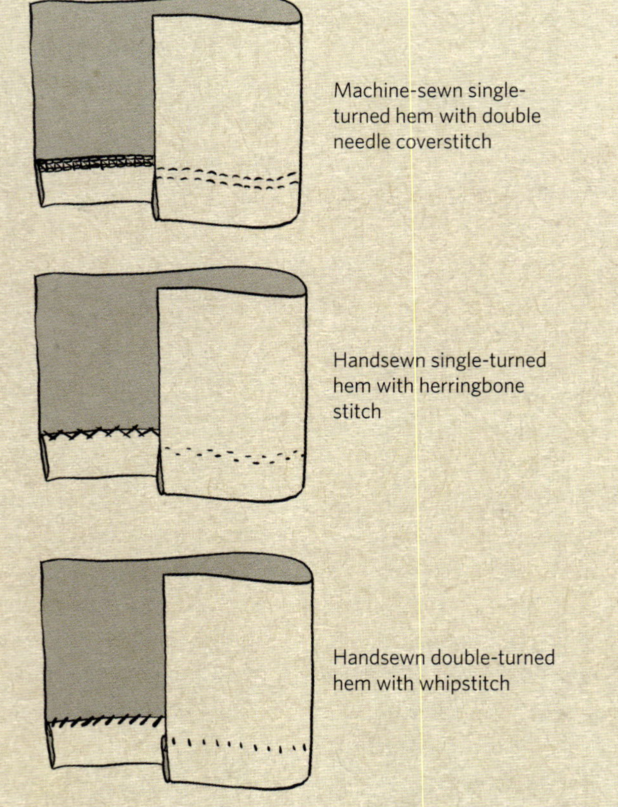

Machine-sewn single-turned hem with double needle coverstitch

Handsewn single-turned hem with herringbone stitch

Handsewn double-turned hem with whipstitch

**4.** Now secure the raw edge to the body using herringbone stitch. As you arrive at the ruffly bits, take a bit of the ruffle on your needle and pull needle through, then take a stitch as usual into the body. The ruffles will be minimized as you stitch them down.

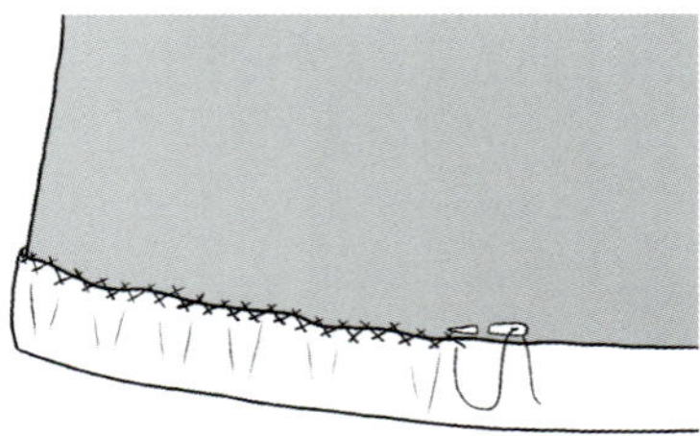

**5.** Press.

### ADDING A CHEST POCKET (OPTIONAL)

**1.** Devise a paper pattern.

- If you already own a shirt with a great chest pocket, feel free to copy its dimensions (don't include SAs yet) and cut out a paper version that you can hold up to your new shirt.
- If you don't own anything with a suitable pocket, try drawing a likely candidate on a piece of paper with your ruler and pencil, then cut out your educated guess. (Again, no SAs yet.)

2. Pull on your shirt, stand in front of a mirror, and hold up paper pocket. Adjust paper piece (by trimming away or taping on paper) as needed until you like the shape and size. Find a good placement, then place pins just beyond each corner.

3. Once you've finalized shape, size, and placement, place paper template over a new sheet of paper. Trace the shape and add SAs. I'd recommend:

- 1" (2.5 cm) on pocket opening
- ⅜" (1 cm) on all other edges

Place grainline down the center. Add note: "CUT 1 SELF."

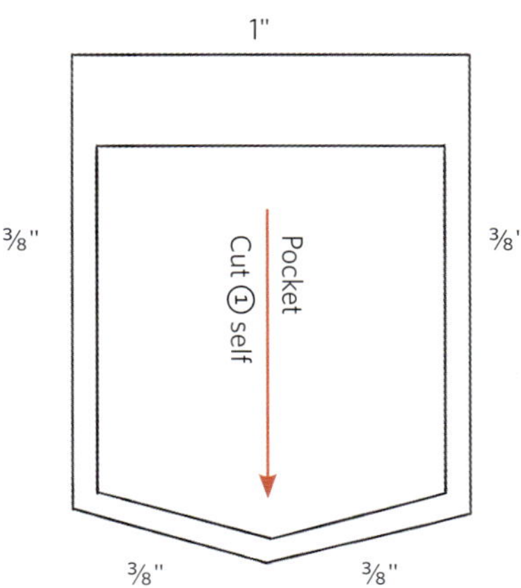


4. Cut pocket out of fabric.

5. Fold under all edges except top, and press. Baste if desired.

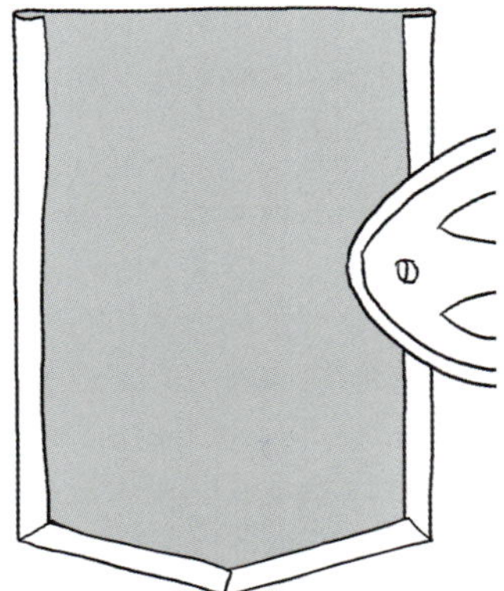

6. Fold down top hem. (I like to do it twice—the first fold is ¼" [6 mm] and the second fold is ¾" [2 cm].) Pin. Hem using your favorite hemming stitch. Stretchiness isn't quite as important here unless you're planning to use the pocket a lot. Still, I like to use whipstitch.

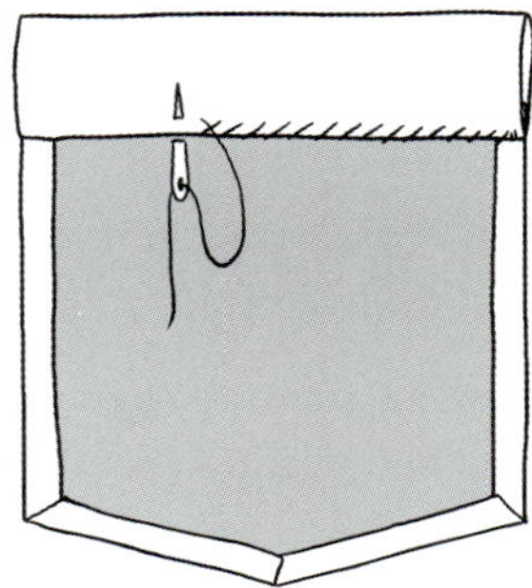

7. Pin or baste pocket onto shirt. Try on once more to be sure you like size and placement.

8. Use whipstitches, fell stitches, or another stitch to attach. If you plan to use this pocket a lot, you may wish to add bartacks or other reinforcement stitches at the top corners.

## STITCHING A LABEL

See instructions on page 108 in the woven boxy top project.

# Variations

To create the two versions shown here, I mainly made different choices about body lengths and widths. I drafted the basic, short-sleeved T-shirt during a pregnancy, so it features a roomy, swingy sweep, with plenty of vertical length to fall over a baby bump. The off-white shirt (at right) has a slightly slimmer shape, with longer sleeves and a more cropped body length. The blue shirt also features longer sleeves, with sleeve cuffs added using the same methods detailed for ankle bands in the leggings project.

Beyond these variations, you can create infinite other styles by making simple changes to your basic pattern. For example, you can:

- Lengthen the panels to make a tunic or dress pattern. Widen as needed to accommodate hips, range of motion, and style preferences. Add side slits if you'd like.
- Create multiple panels by drawing style lines, or straighten side seams and then adjust their angles to swing forward for visual interest.
- Add a Henley placket. Stitch up in a waffle knit or another cozy fabric.
- Create a neck facing instead of using a neckband.
- Omit sleeves in favor of sewing a tank top. Cut a quick test fit sample from cheap jersey and mark or trim armholes to desired shape. Then transfer new armhole shapes to pattern pieces and cut from your garment fabric.
- Use a narrower shoulder width (not a drop-shoulder style) and join sleeves by setting them "in the round" instead of flat. To do so, stitch side seams and sleeve inseams separately before joining sleeves into armholes. Then pin sleeves into their respective armholes, RST, matching notches and seams. Stitch with even backstitch. Then fell or overcast SAs.

# *Sofia Alba*

*(she/her)*, Waldorf school teacher, sashiko teacher, sewist

BUENOS AIRES, ARGENTINA

As a child, Sofia Alba asked her grandmother Alba, a prolific maker, to teach her to sew. Instead of sitting the young Sofia down at a machine, Alba insisted that Sofia learn to hand-stitch first. Sofia agreed, and thus her hand-sewing education began.

As a young teenager, Sofia again requested that her grandmother teach her to machine-sew, but Alba declined. Whether Alba hoped to steer Sofia toward handwork or she just didn't have the interest to teach machine skills, Sofia doesn't know. Regardless, by young adulthood, Sofia could do everything by hand.

Today, although Sofia owns a machine, she chooses to stitch exclusively by hand.

***Sewing for herself.*** The first time I made clothes for me was in a hand-sewing class. You know when something talks to your soul, as though you've been waiting for it to appear? I've been hand-sewing for so long. I've been making clothes for my kids. It's just one step more.

***A special dress.*** It's the most complicated garment I've made for myself. I really like it. And it's so fresh. It's so, so fresh. When I wear it, many people tell me, "Your dress is so nice." And I tell them, "I made it myself, and all by hand."

***Protective stitches.*** I made some sleeveless shirts for my smaller kid. When I put them on him, I really love the idea that he's being protected by my stitches. And I feel the same way when I wear clothes I made by myself.

***The long game.*** Maybe it takes me more than a year because I have a busy life. I might get one hour with my project, and sometimes it's just ironing some parts, and then it has to wait for the next month. And I'm really okay with that. It gives me great pleasure that I have something in my life that takes me a lot of time, a lot of work.

***Sewing everywhere.*** I always have a sewing basket I can put on my lap and sew. I have really long meetings on Thursdays. So Wednesday nights, I prepare my basket with the things I'm going to need. And I advance a lot in those meetings.

I wouldn't be able to do it with a sewing machine. I would have to wait to have that moment, sitting at the sewing machine. My kids couldn't be around. At home, I usually sit nearby while my kids are in the living room, and I can be hand-sewing.

***Starting over.*** Every time I start a new project, I get all the questions again, you know? I even ask myself, "Will I be able to do it?" That's why when I finish something, I feel so proud.

***Power in your hands.*** There's something about when people say, "It is not possible to hand-sew a whole garment," and it is possible. It feels very powerful when you've done it—like you can survive. You can make your own clothes.

# HOODIE

A cozy handsewn hoodie can be so comforting. With each stitch, you can invest care and love into the cloth. Snuggle into it on a hard day and notice how your strong stitches hold, maintaining a soft sanctuary for you.

This knit hoodie project offers a surprisingly simple patterndrafting method, but it yields a very attractive raglan-sleeve sweatshirt. As you sew, you'll use lots of techniques found in the T-shirt project, but you'll also construct a beautiful lined hood, complete with handsewn eyelets for the encased drawstring.

# Patternmaking

To pattern this hoodie, you'll take some dimensions from your body, add a bit of wearing ease, draft a basic garment shape, and start tracing off your pattern pieces. Then you can draft a custom hood based on your pattern's neckline and a couple of body measurements.

## MEASURING YOUR BODY

To draft your hoodie, you'll need these measurements:

- Body length (HPS to desired garment length)
- Waist level from HPS
- Front neck drop
- Neck width
- Largest torso circumference (depending on your body, it might be your bust, waist, or hip circumference)
- Shoulder width
- Armhole depth
- Head circumference
- Sleeve length (CB to LPS to desired sleeve length)—I like mine to reach to my first knuckles, but it's up to you
- Wrist circumference
- Hood depth (with hair in your usual style, measure from one pupil to the other, wrapping tape measure loosely around back of head)

- Hood height (measure from one HPS to the other, wrapping tape measure loosely over top of head; then divide this number in half)

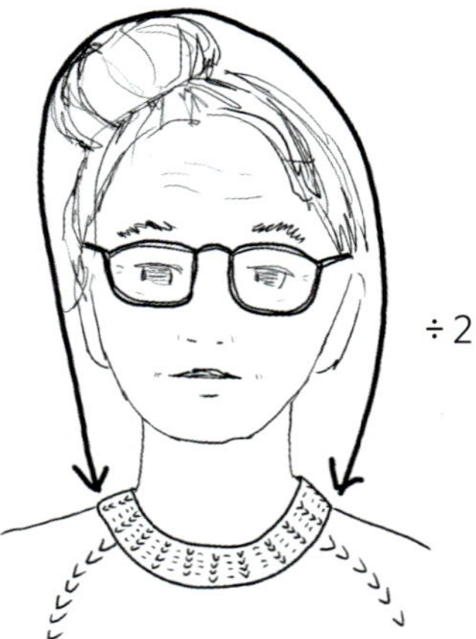


- Pocket placement from HPS (as desired)—I like the top of the pocket to sit approximately 2" (5 cm) above belly button
- Pocket opening length (as desired)—I like about 2" (5 cm) longer than my hand's width when measured with fingers squished together
- Pocket width (as desired)

## DECIDING THE DIMENSIONS

You'll want to add wearing ease to a few of your anatomical measurements. The amount of wearing ease you choose to include is up to you. Feel free to study ease amounts of similar garments you like, as you did in the woven boxy top and T-shirt projects. Or you can follow the amounts that I like to use:

- Front neck drop: I like to add 1" (2.5 cm) to the anatomical neck drop.
- Neck width: I like to add 2" (5 cm) to the anatomical neck width.
- Largest torso circumference (depending on your body, it might be your bust, waist, or hip circumference): I like to add 4 to 6" (10 to 15 cm) to the anatomical circumference.
- Underarm depth: I like to add 2" (5 cm) to the anatomical underarm depth.
- Wrist circumference: I like to add ½" (1.3 cm) to the anatomical wrist circumference.
- Hood height: I like to add 1" (2.5 cm) to the hood height.

## MARKING LEVELS

As with previous projects, you'll be drafting only half of the hoodie shape, because the garment will be symmetrical. You'll initially draft the front and back body and sleeve shapes all together, and then trace off the separate components.

**1.** Draw CF/CB vertical line down right-hand side of a large, wide sheet of paper.

**2.** Square a long line near the top. This will be the HPS level.

**3.** From HPS level, measure down desired body length and square long line across bottom. This will be the sweep.

**4.** From HPS level, measure down waist level and square across a long line. This will be the waist level.

**5.** From HPS level, measure down ⅝" (1.6 cm) and square across a line that is approximately 2" (5 cm) long. This will be the back neck level.

**6.** From HPS level, measure down front neck drop and square across a line that is approximately ½" (1.3 cm) long. This will be the front neck level.

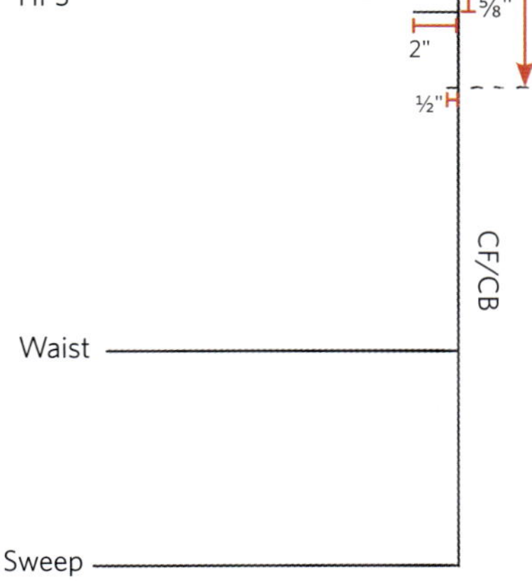


## MARKING WIDTHS

**1.** Refer to desired torso circumference with wearing ease included. Along sweep line, measure across one-quarter of desired torso width and then square up through and beyond waist level. This is your side seam.

**2.** Along HPS line, make tick mark at one-half of neck width amount.

**3.** Along HPS line, make tick mark at one-half of shoulder width amount.

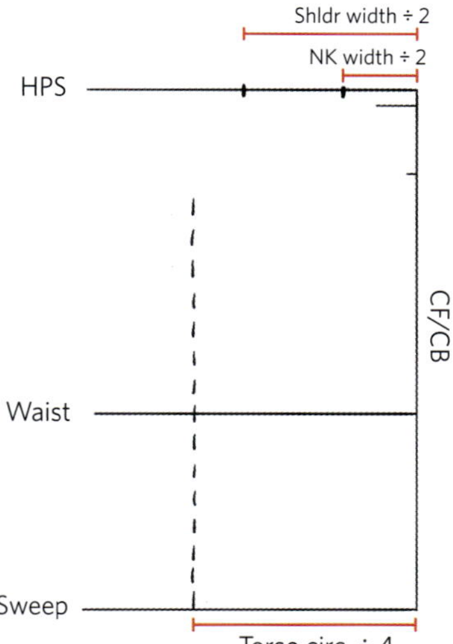


These instructions produce a true boxy torso—there's no tapering for waist shape and so on. If you'd prefer a more fitted shape, feel free to nip in the waist a bit or to differentiate between bust and hip widths. Just mark the measurements you'd like at each level, and then draw a smooth, curved line to blend between these measurements. (In this case, you'll probably want to measure and mark your bust level so that you know where to plot each circumference.)

### DRAFTING THE NECKLINE

**1.** Draw a smooth front neck curve connecting from short front neck drop line to neck width tick mark. Maintain about ½" (1.3 cm) that is squared to the CF/CB line before curving.

**2.** Draw a smooth back neck curve connecting from the short back neck drop line to neck width tick mark. Maintain about 2" (5 cm) that is squared to the CF/CB line before curving.

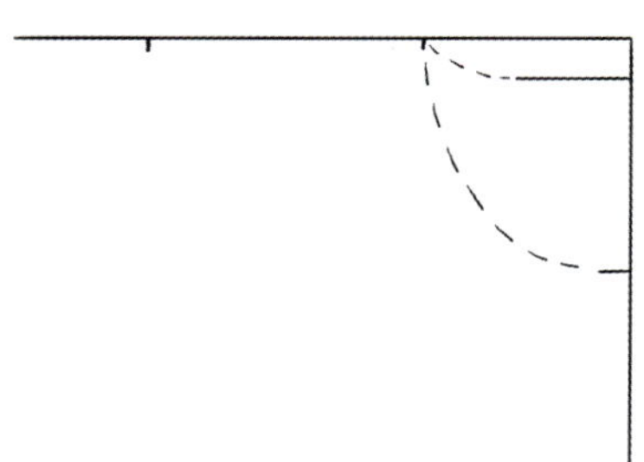

**3.** Measure each curve and jot down measurements. I like to mark them along the pattern pieces.

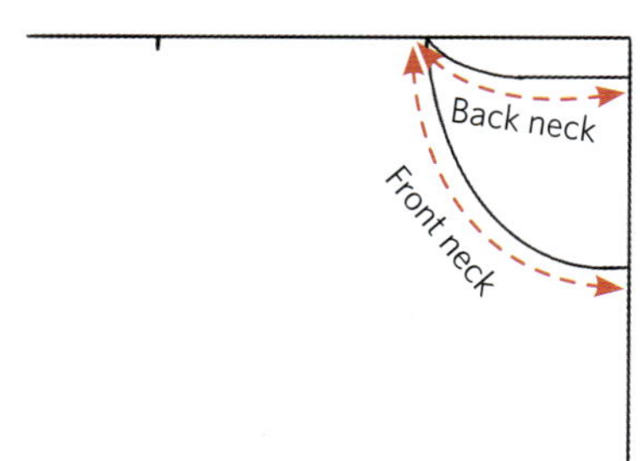


**4.** Add front and back neck curve measurements together, then multiply by two to determine current neck circumference measurement. Compare this with your head circumference. The draft's opening is probably somewhat smaller than your head, and that's okay as long as your fabric has enough stretch to accommodate your head as it fits through. If you think it's going to be too tight, widen the neck a bit and/or deepen the front neck drop, and redraw necklines. Remeasure and repeat as needed until neckline is big enough to accommodate your head.

### DRAFTING THE SLEEVE

**1.** At shoulder width tick mark, square down 1" (2.5 cm) and make a little tick mark. This is your LPS.

**2.** With a ruler, connect from HPS through LPS, and then continue the line far beyond. This will be your sleeve "outseam" line (though there will be no actual seam here).

**3.** Locate your desired-sleeve-length-from-CB measurement. Begin plotting this by measuring from CB to HPS, then pivoting ruler and continuing to measure along sleeve outseam until you reach desired sleeve length measurement. Make tick mark.

**4.** Beginning at sleeve length tick mark from previous step, square down a line that is half of your desired wrist circumference. Make a tick mark at its end.

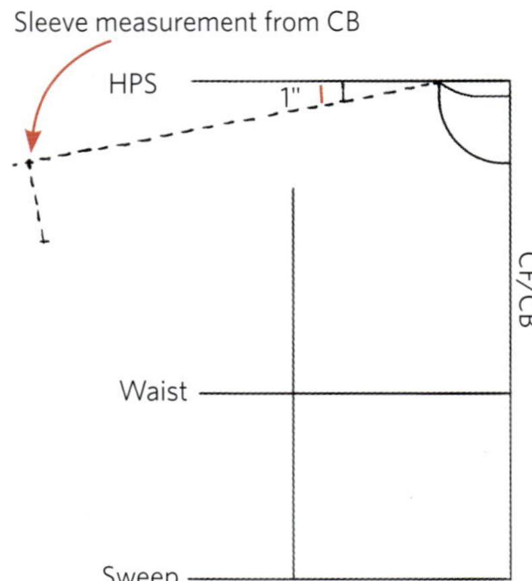


**5.** Lock zero point of ruler at LPS, and swing ruler's other end until your desired armhole depth hits the side seam line. Make a tick mark there for underarm.

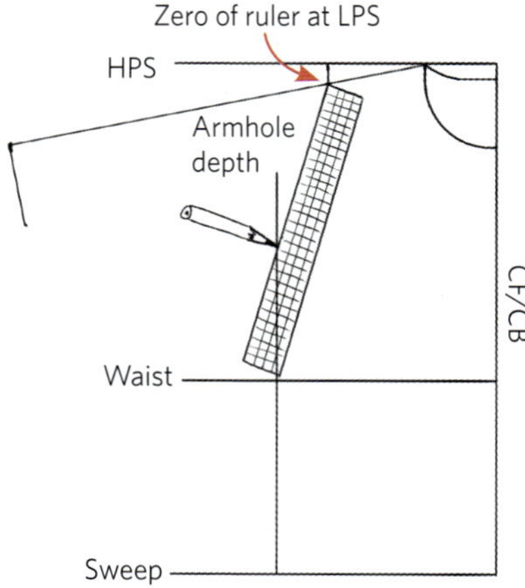

**6.** Connect underarm point to bottom of wrist. That's your sleeve inseam.

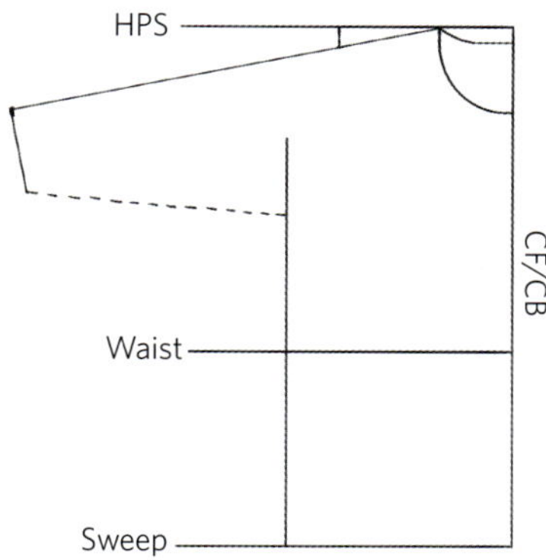


## FINALIZING THE TORSO DRAFT

**1.** Next, you'll draw the raglan seam lines for front and back. These lines should connect from the underarm point to wherever you'd like along the front and back necklines. (This is an aesthetic decision.) You can make straight lines or curved ones. And they can follow the same angle on front and back, or different ones. The only rule is that the lines will need to connect the underarm point to somewhere along each neckline.

**2.** Decide what height measurement you'd like to use for sleeve and bottom hem cuffs. (This is another aesthetic decision. I like to use 2" [5 cm] for both, but it's up to you.)

**3.** Raise bottom hem and sleeve hem by desired cuff height. Then mark out or erase the cuff section so you're not confused later.

**4.** Draw proposed pocket onto your draft. Refer to pocket dimension and placement measurements that you had planned and plot onto the draft accordingly. The dimensions, placement, and shape are mostly aesthetic decisions; do be sure, though, that your hand will fit through whatever pocket opening you devise. Also know that a straight line for the pocket opening will be easiest to hem. (Otherwise you'll probably need to create facings, which are easy enough but not included in these directions.)

**5.** Add notches along raglan lines. Randomly place single notch for front sleeve raglan line as shown and double notches for back sleeve.

**6.** Add notch on side seam at waistline level.

**7.** Add notch midway along sleeve inseam (roughly elbow level).

**8.** Add notch halfway across torso's bottom hem. Measure for accuracy.

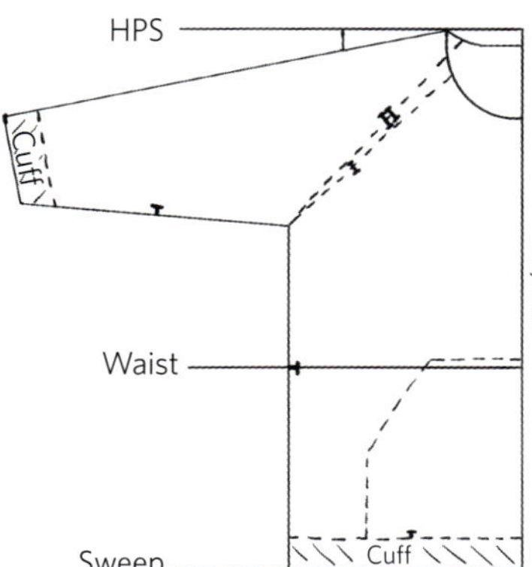


## TRACING THE FRONT TORSO PATTERN

**1.** On a new large, wide sheet of paper, draw a vertical line down the middle. This will represent your CF line. Fold the paper in half along this line. Place on table with folded CF line on right-hand side.

**2.** Place torso draft on top, aligning draft's CF/CB line with the folded line drawn in step 1. Weight down.

**3.** Using tracing wheel, trace along front neckline up to front raglan seam, then trace front raglan seam, side seam, and bottom hem (minus the cuff area). Also trace all notches except back raglan seam notches and sleeve notch. Trace pocket outline. Remove draft paper and pencil in all lines clearly.

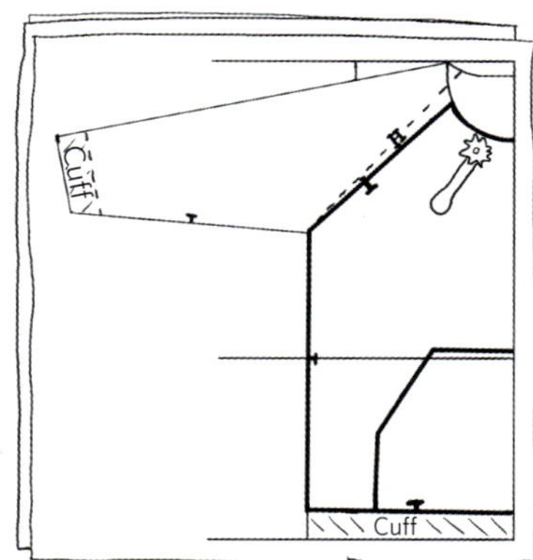


**4.** Next, add SAs. I'd recommend ⅜" (1 cm) on all edges.

**5.** Pin the two paper layers together and cut out. Snip notches. Remove pins and unfold. Snip notch at CF neck. Snip notch at CF hem. Mark drill holes for pocket placement.

**6.** Place grainline parallel to CF. Add note: "CUT 1 SELF."

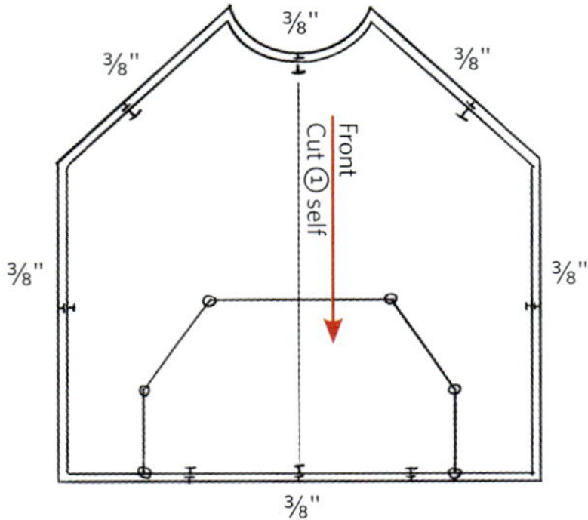


## TRACING THE BACK TORSO PATTERN

**1.** On a new large, wide sheet of paper, draw a vertical line down the middle. This will represent your CB line. Fold the paper in half along this line. Place on table with folded CB line on right-hand side.

**2.** Place torso draft on top, aligning draft's CF/CB line with the folded line drawn in step 1. Weight down.

**3.** Using tracing wheel, trace along back neckline up to back raglan seam, then trace back raglan seam, side seam, and bottom hem (minus the cuff area). Also trace all notches except front raglan seam notches and sleeve notch. Remove draft paper and pencil in all lines clearly.

**4.** Next, add SAs. I'd recommend ⅜" (1 cm) on all edges.

**5.** Pin the two paper layers together and cut out. Snip notches. Add notch along back neckline, ¼" (6 mm) from CB. Add notch along bottom hem, ¼" (6 mm) from CB. Remove pins and unfold.

**6.** Place grainline parallel to CB. Add note: "CUT 1 SELF."

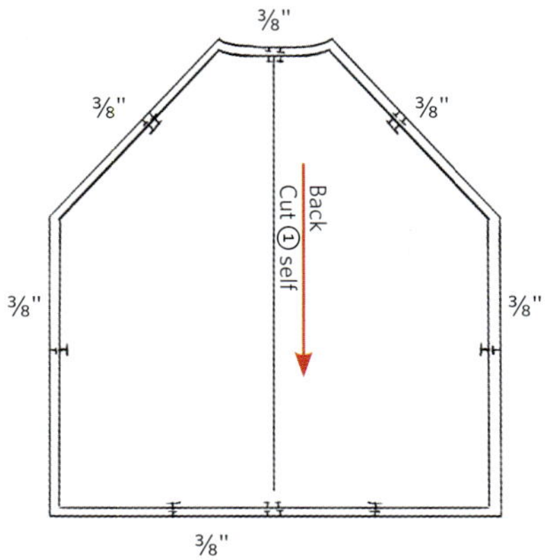


## TRACING THE SLEEVE PATTERN

**1.** On a new large sheet of paper, draw a long vertical line down the middle. This will represent your sleeve "out-seam" line. Fold the paper in half along this line. Place on table with fold on top.

**2.** Place torso draft on top, aligning draft's sleeve outseam line with the folded line drawn in step 1. Weight down.

**3.** Using tracing wheel, trace sleeve hem (minus the cuff area), inseam, front and back raglan seams, and front and back necklines up to raglan seams. Trace elbow notch and raglan sleeve notches.

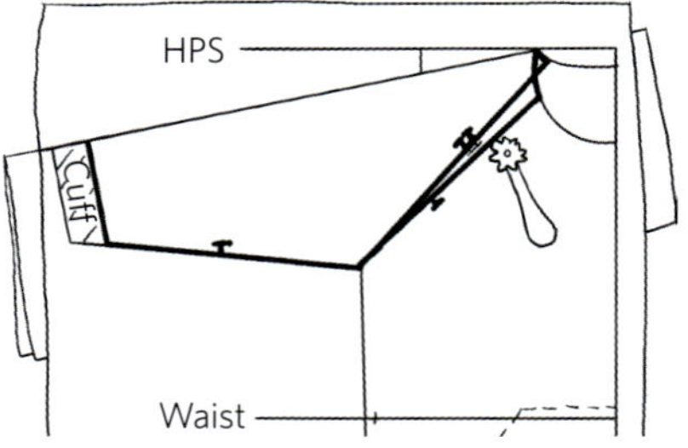


**4.** Remove draft paper, and pencil in front-related lines. Then open out folded paper and pencil in back-related lines on the other side of the fold. Also add notch along bottom hem at out-seam line.

**5.** To ensure clean sewing, you'll need a right angle between the bottom of the inseam and the sleeve hem. Extend inseam lines slightly. Slide gridded ruler or a square tool along the inseam until you find a line that intersects with the hem at approximately one-third of the distance toward the outseam line. Draw this line. Then soften the angle by drawing a smooth, gentle curve.

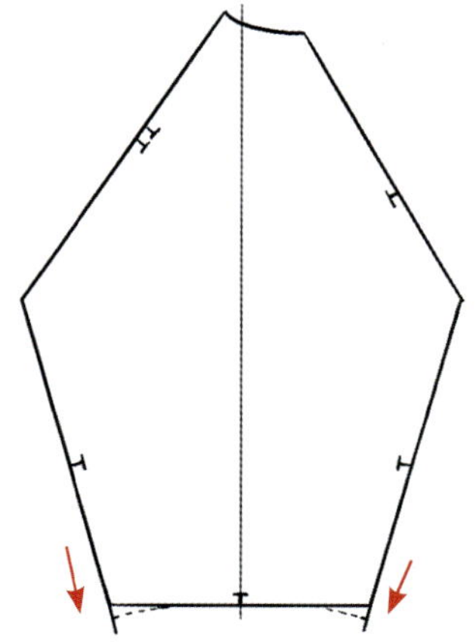

**6.** Next, add SAs. I'd recommend ⅜" (1 cm) on all edges.

**7.** Cut out. Snip notches.

**8.** Place grainline parallel to outseam line. Add note: "CUT 2 SELF."

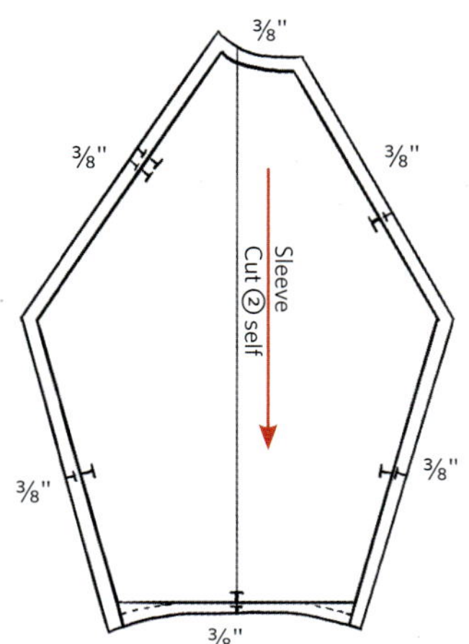


## DRAFTING THE BOTTOM CUFF

**1.** Calculate bottom hem cuff length by multiplying total torso circumference by 0.85 or 0.9. This reduction will help the bottom edge of the main body to cinch nicely into the cuff.

**2.** Draw rectangle that is length of previous calculation, and twice as tall as desired bottom cuff height.

**3.** Add notches to divide length into eighths.

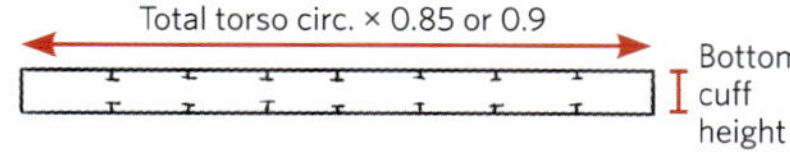


**4.** Next, add SAs. I'd recommend ⅜" (1 cm) on all edges.

**5.** Cut out. Snip notches.

**6.** Place grainline parallel to short ends. Add note: "CUT 1 SELF (OR RIB)."

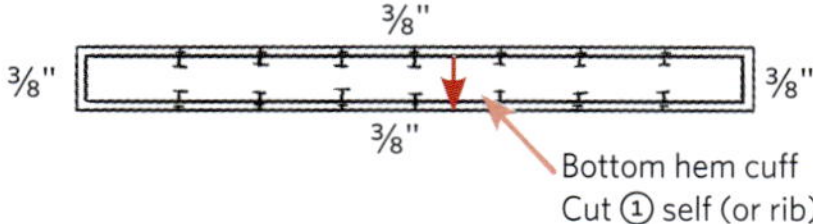


## DRAFTING THE SLEEVE CUFF

**1.** Draw rectangle that is length of desired wrist circumference, and twice as tall as desired sleeve cuff height.

**2.** Add notches to divide length in half.

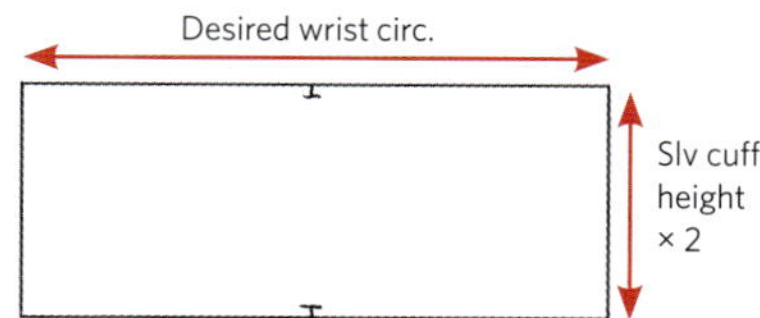


**3.** Next, add SAs. I'd recommend ⅜" (1 cm) on all edges.

**4.** Cut out. Snip notches.

**5.** Place grainline parallel to short ends. Add note: "CUT 2 SELF (OR RIB)."

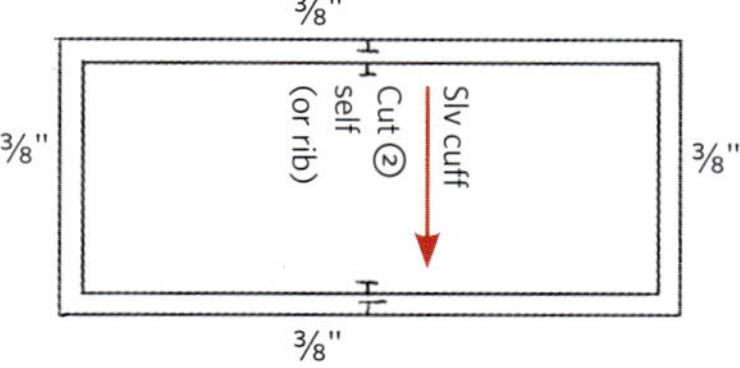


## TRACING THE POCKET PATTERN

**1.** On a new medium-size sheet of paper, draw a vertical line down the middle. Fold in half along this line. Place on table with folded line on right-hand side.

**2.** Place torso draft on top, aligning draft's CF/CB line with folded edge underneath. Pocket outline should be roughly centered over the folded paper.

**3.** Trace pocket outline. Remove draft and pencil in lines clearly.

**4.** Next, add SAs. I'd recommend:

- ⅜" (1 cm) on all edges except pocket opening edges
- 1" (2.5 cm) or other desired hem allowance amount for pocket opening edges

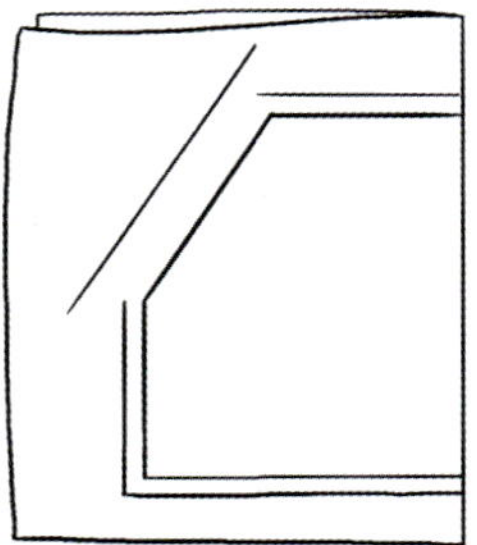

**5.** Temporarily unfold paper. Make new fold along pocket opening fold line (not the SA line), then use tracing wheel to trace pocket perimeter near opening.

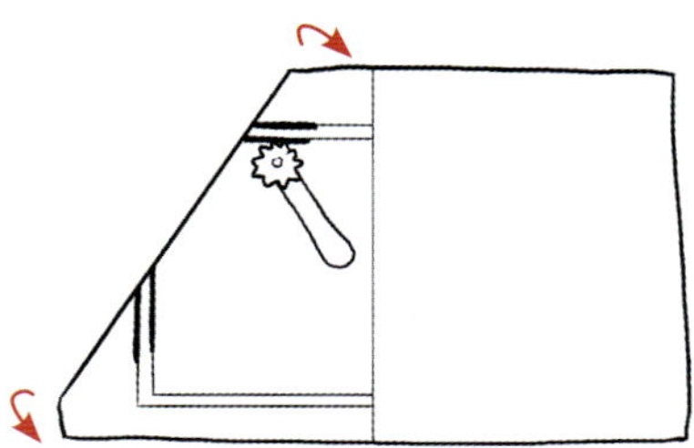

**6.** Unfold top layer of paper, and pencil in lines clearly. Use these as guides for angled SAs near pocket opening.

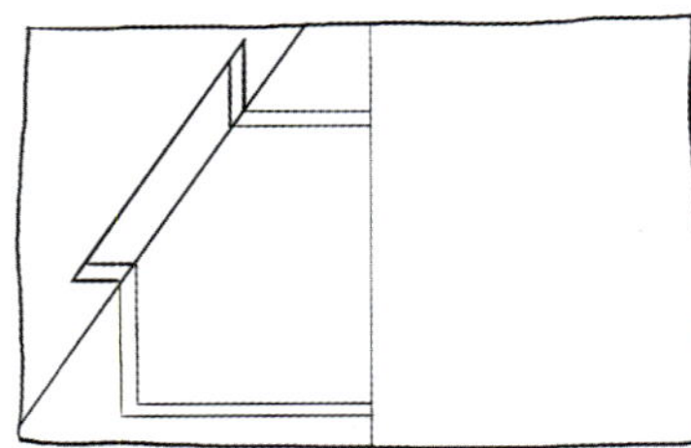

**7.** Refold paper along center line. Pin the two paper layers together and cut out. Remove pins and unfold.

**8.** Place grainline parallel to center fold line. Add note: "CUT 1 SELF."

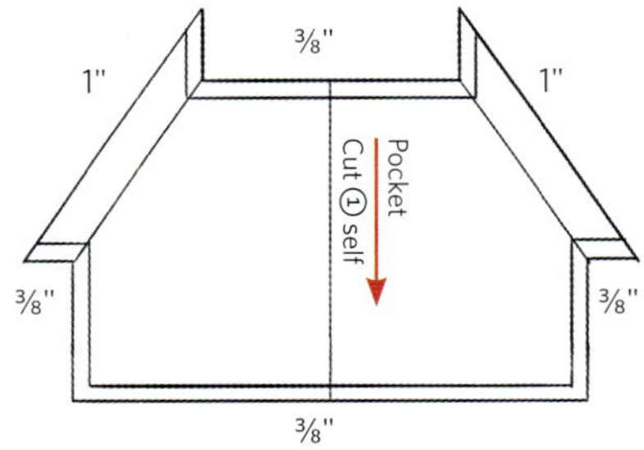


If you drafted curved pocket openings, you may need to finish openings with facings or binding instead of hems.

## DRAFTING THE HOOD

**1.** Locate hood depth and hood height measurements. In addition, measure front neck curve from CF to front raglan sleeve. Measure back neck curve from CB to back raglan sleeve. Finally, measure neckline stitch line along raglan sleeve.

**2.** Draw rectangle that is height of hood height and width of half of hood depth.

**3.** Estimate midpoint along top line and make tick mark.

**4.** Estimate point one-third of the way down along left-hand line and make tick mark.

**5.** Draw smooth curve to connect these tick marks.

**6.** Extend right-hand line downward 2" (5 cm) and square to the left for ½" (1.3 cm).

**7.** Measure up from bottom of left-hand line ⅝" (1.6 cm) and square to the right for 2" (5 cm).

**8.** Draw a gentle S curve to connect previous two squared lines, as shown, with S curve crossing horizontal line somewhere in the middle (does not need to be exact).

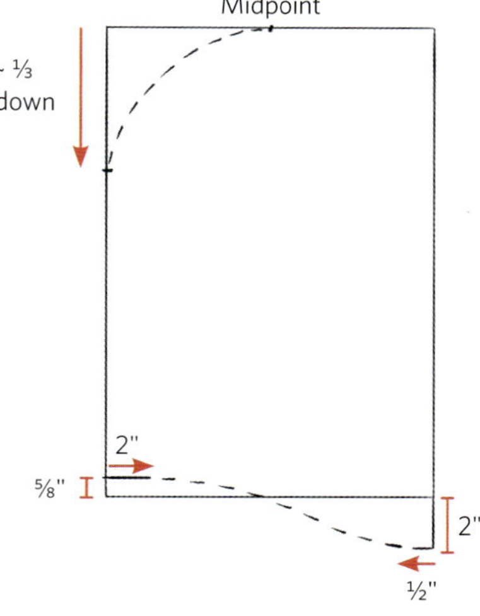


**9.** Starting on right-hand end, measure along S curve until you reach ¼" (6 mm) more than the front neckline amount from step 1. Place notch. Continue measuring along S curve for distance of raglan sleeve's neckline edge from step 1. Place notch. Continue measuring along S curve until you reach the back neckline amount from step 1 and place tick mark. (If you need to extend the line to reach your back neck measurement, do so.) Then square up 1" (2.5 cm).

The first notch is placed at ¼" (6 mm) beyond half front neckline length so that you can have a ½" (1.3 cm) overlap of the hood at CF. This will create a sturdier neckline when sewn.

**10.** Draw a gentle S curve (or a simple candy-cane-shaped curve if you needed to extend the line in step 9) to connect this squared-up line with the upper area of hood; you'll rejoin the left-hand vertical line perhaps one-third up along the left-hand vertical line.

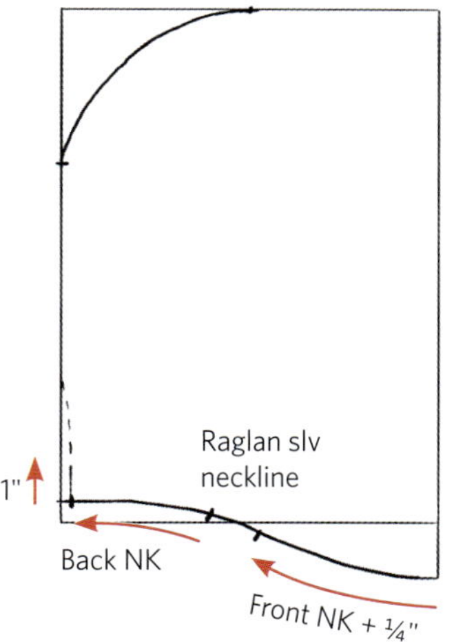


**11.** Draw intended hood casing stitch line for your hood's drawstring. I like mine 1" (2.5 cm) inward from hood opening edge, but it's up to you.

**12.** Draw desired position of drawstring eyelets or buttonholes. I like these centered in my 1" (2.5 cm) casing, and approximately 1" (2.5 cm) above the neckline seam.

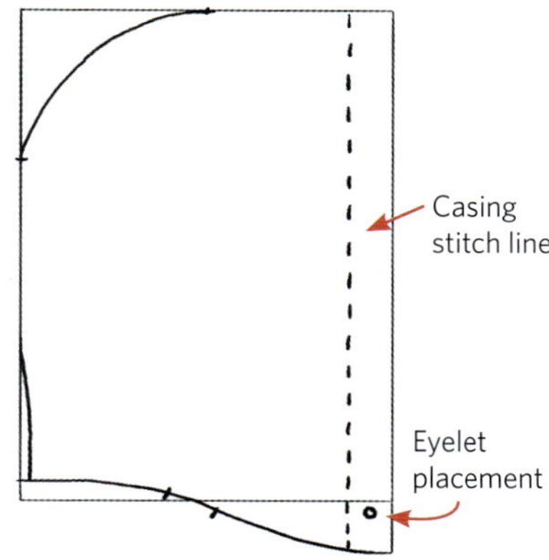


**13.** Next, add SAs. I'd recommend ⅜" (1 cm) along all edges.

**14.** Cut out. Snip neckline notches. Also snip notch somewhere along center back curve.

**15.** Place grainline parallel to CF edge. Add note: "CUT 4 SELF."

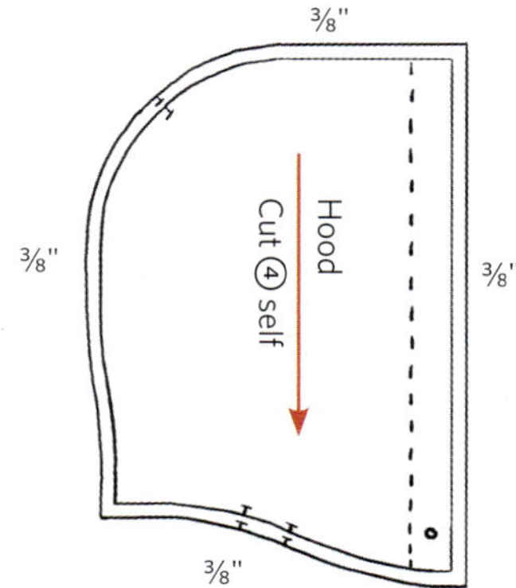

# Sewing

### HAND-SEWING STITCHES

- Herringbone stitch or catchstitch
- Overcasting
- Spaced backstitch
- Even backstitch
- Bartack
- Whipstitch
- Combination stitch
- Running stitch
- Basting
- Depending on techniques chosen, you may also need buttonhole stitch, hemstitch, fell stitch

### FABRIC OPTIONS

This hoodie works well in French terry, fleece, or other cozy knit fabrics. I like using cotton or other natural fibers, but you can use whatever you prefer. You're welcome to experiment with other knit constructions. However, you will want your fabric to have at least a bit of horizontal stretch.

You'll also likely want to use some rib fabric for the sleeve cuffs and bottom hem cuffs. If needed, you can use your self garment fabric instead, as long as it has some decent horizontal stretch.

### OTHER MATERIALS NEEDED

You will need approximately 1½ yards (1½ meters) of some sort of cord, twill tape, or other ribbon-like material for your hoodie's drawstring. If you would like to make your own, you can use a thinner fabric (knit or woven) and stitch your own spaghetti strap cord to use. You might also wish to make a 3" (7.6 cm) length of spaghetti strap cord (or other strip material) for a locker loop (the little loop on the back or inside of a garment that can be used to hang it on a hook).

For the drawstring casing openings, you can sew eyelets (if your drawstring is skinny) or buttonholes (if you want to use a thicker cord or if you enjoy sewing buttonholes). However, if you'd

## How to Sew a Spaghetti Strap

To make a strip of spaghetti strap, cut a long strip of 1" (2.5 cm)-wide fabric on the straight grain (parallel to selvages). The strip's length depends on how long you want your hoodie drawstring to be—for the pictured hoodie, I used a 45" (114.3 cm) length. Press all edges under by ¼" (6 mm). Fold in half so that WS are concealed, and use quick whipstitches to join folded edges, forming spaghetti strap.

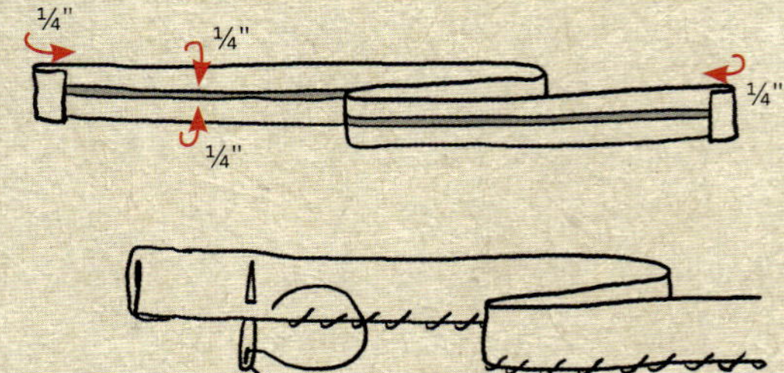

rather use hardware, you can install metal eyelets, in which case you'll need the materials and tools for them. (Instructions will not be given here for installing the hardware.)

For back neck binding, you may be able to use a strip of self garment fabric. However, if your main fabric is bulky, you may wish to use a small strip of thinner jersey fabric instead.

### CUTTING THE FABRIC

See Cutting Fabric on page 85 for tips on cutting. You'll need to cut the following pieces and quantities:

- Front torso × 1 self
- Back torso × 1 self
- Sleeve × 2 self
- Hood × 4 self
- Bottom hem cuff × 1 self (or rib)
- Sleeve cuff × 2 self (or rib)
- Pocket × 1 self
- 1 small strip of cross-cut self or thinner jersey for back neck binding—cut 1" (2.5 cm) by 12" (30.5 cm) to be safe, but you'll trim length later when sewing

Transfer pocket placement drill hole marks onto front panel using thread, pins, or a water-soluble marking tool. Transfer eyelet placements onto one mirrored pair of hood pieces. Remove pins or weights. Store fabric pieces safely until you're ready to sew.

### ASSEMBLING THE POCKET

**1.** First hem the pocket openings. To hem, begin by pressing openings under by 1" (2.5 cm) or whatever your pattern hem allowance is. Then use herringbone stitch, catchstitch, or other hemming stitch of choice to secure edges down.

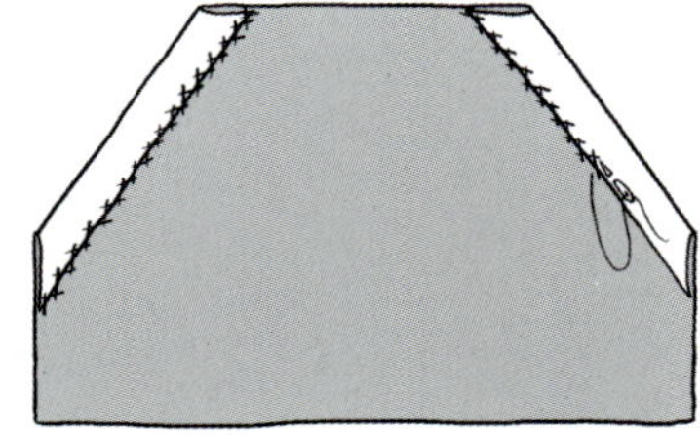

**2.** For top and side edges of pocket, use overcasting to thread-bind.

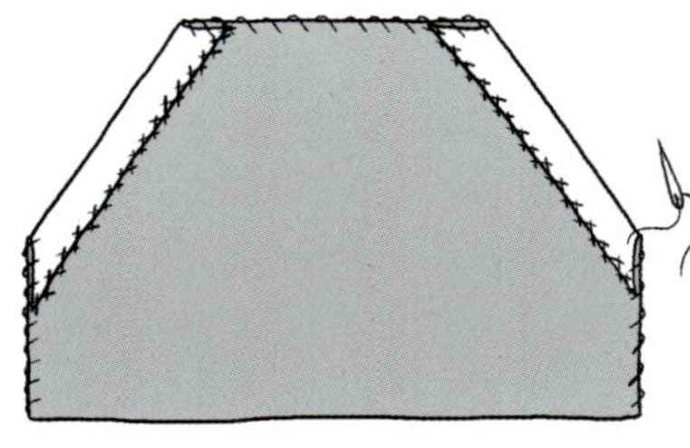

**3.** Press the overcast edges under by ⅜" (1 cm) and baste to hold.

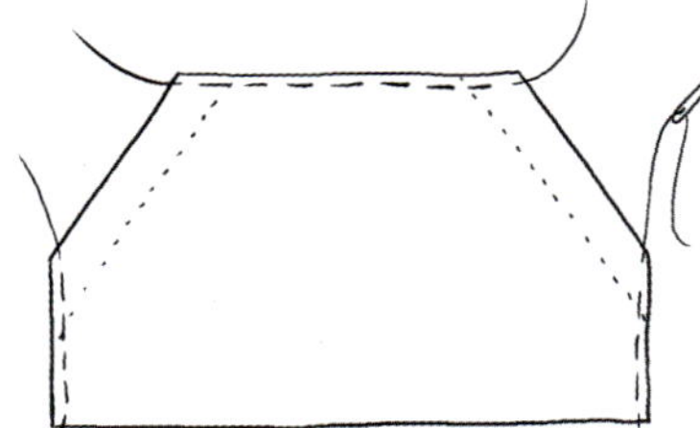

**4.** Place pocket carefully into position on front panel, using drill hole marks as a guide. Then pin and topstitch pocket to front panel, using spaced backstitch, even backstitch, or other stitch of choice. With separate length of thread, baste pocket's bottom edge to panel, using ¼" (6 mm) SA.

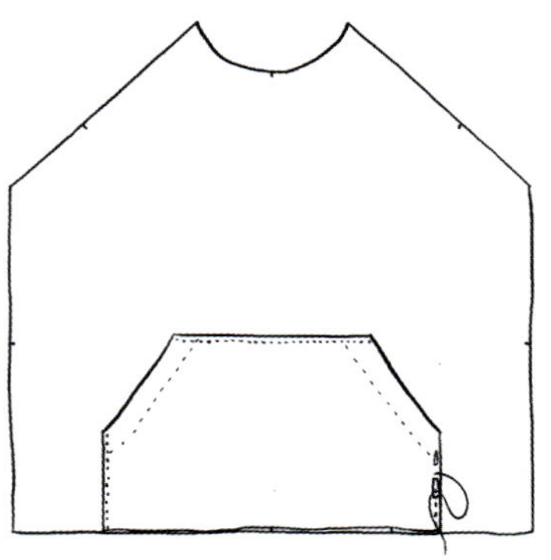

**5.** Make bartacks at edges of pocket openings, through all layers, to fortify openings.

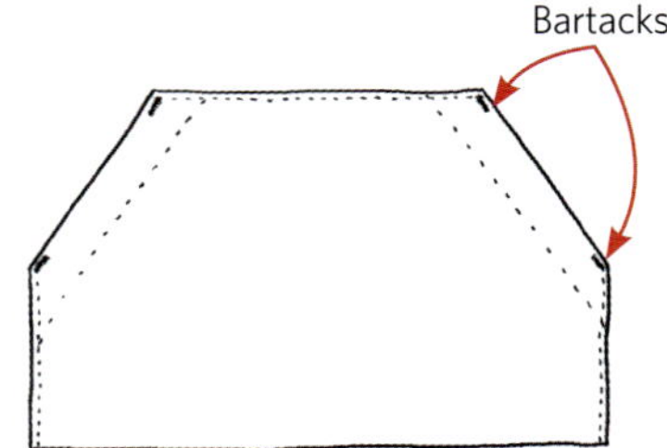

### ASSEMBLING THE HOOD

**1.** On a mirrored pair of hoodie pieces, find the eyelet or buttonhole markings you made. You'll create drawstring openings on these two individual pieces (through a single layer of fabric).

If making eyelets, puncture a large hole in each of the two hood pieces using an awl, knitting needle, or tiny sharp scissors. This hole should be large enough, or at least nearly large enough, to accommodate your intended drawstring. Now make tight, deep whipstitches repeatedly around the holes until a dense wreath of whipstitches have formed an eyelet. Your stitches will stretch the opening a little wider. You'll need to make sure the opening is wide enough to fit your drawstring through comfortably.

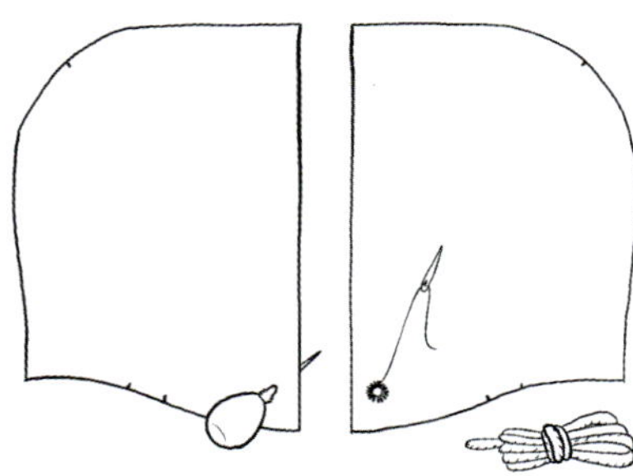

If making buttonholes, follow the instructions on page 76 to create.

If installing hardware eyelets, follow your kit's instructions to install.

**2.** Take the two hood pieces you just worked on, and with RST, pin them along their center seam. Stitch together along center seam using combination stitch or even backstitch, with ⅜" (1 cm) SA. You've now created your outer hood. Repeat these steps with the other pair of hood pieces to construct your hood lining.

**3.** Press SAs open.

**4.** Take both hoods and align with RST. Pin along front edge and stitch together using combination stitch or even backstitch, with ⅜" (1 cm) SA.

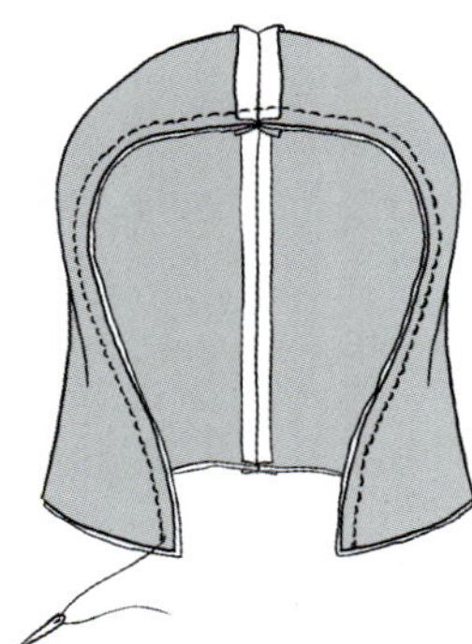

**5.** Press SAs open, then turn hood RS out and press front edge flat. Make sure seam is neatly pressed along the edge (instead of wavering between the hood's outside and lining).

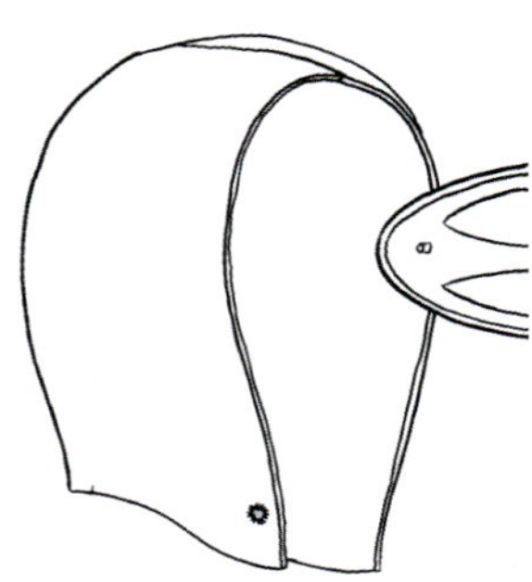

**6.** Place a line of edgestitches approximately ⅛" (3 mm) from front edge. You can use loose, small running stitches here, or spaced backstitch, or another stitch of your choice. If you hold your needle nearly perpendicular to the fabric, you can make a stabstitch-type line of running stitch, which will look more like tidy little dots of thread on both sides. If you're using a stitch that looks different on the front and back, be sure that you're working from the outside of the hood so that the "public side" of your stitches will show.

**7.** Baste raw bottom edges together to hold layers as one.

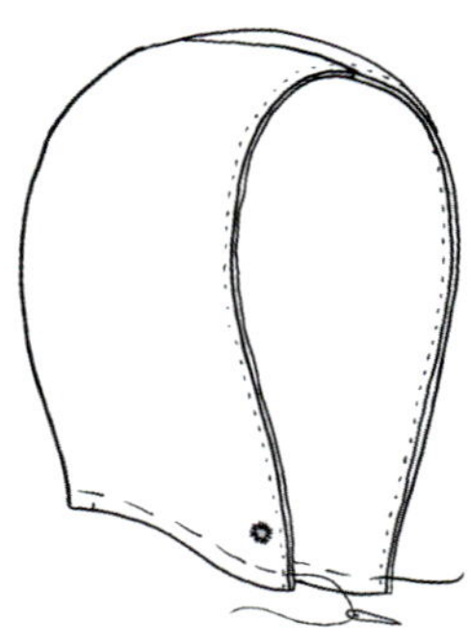

**8.** Mark and sew casing line through all layers, following the casing width from edge that you decided while patternmaking. For this line of stitches, I'd recommend using whichever stitch you used in step 6, and working from the outside of the hood again.

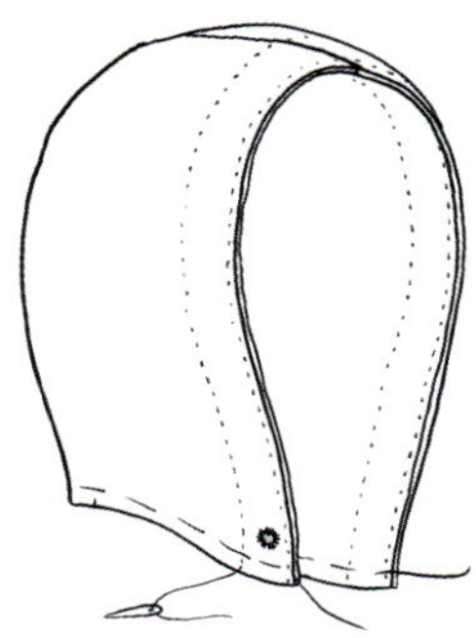

**9.** Overlap raw edges of hood by ½" (1.3 cm) and baste to hold. This overlap will later be stitched into the neckline.

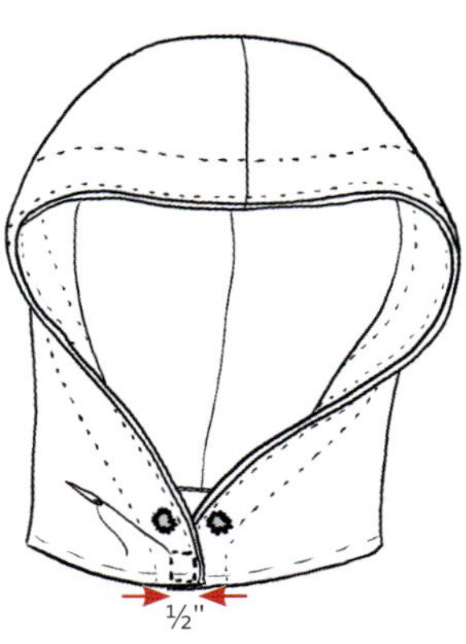


## SEWING RAGLAN SEAMS

**1.** With RST, align sleeves' front raglan seams with front torso's raglan seams. Align notches and pin. Stitch with backstitch or combination stitch, with ⅜" (1 cm) SA. (For visual clarity, diagram shows sewing facing sleeve panels. But for tidiest interior, sew facing the front torso panel.)

**2.** Use overcasting to finish raw edges together.

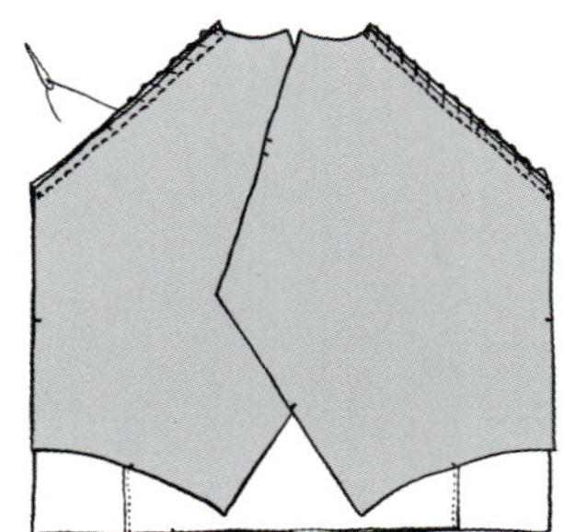

**3.** Press SAs toward sleeves.

**4.** Optional: Topstitch through all layers with even or spaced backstitch.

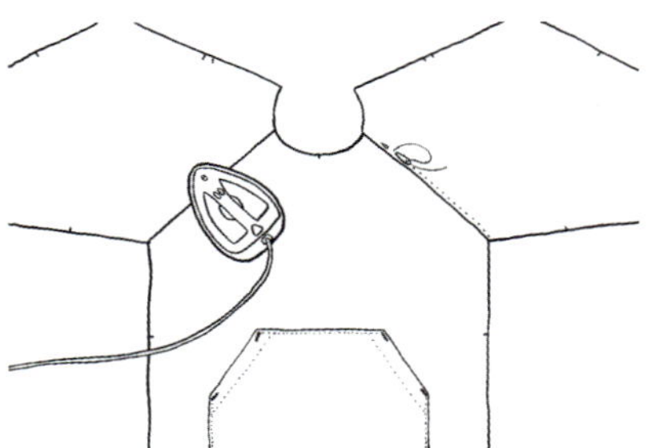

**5.** Repeat steps 1 through 4 to attach sleeves' back raglan seams to back torso.

## ATTACHING THE HOOD

**1.** Turn garment inside out. With hood RS out, slide it into garment and pin onto neckline, with RST. Be careful to match all notches. The hood's CF overlap should be centered over neckline's CF notch.

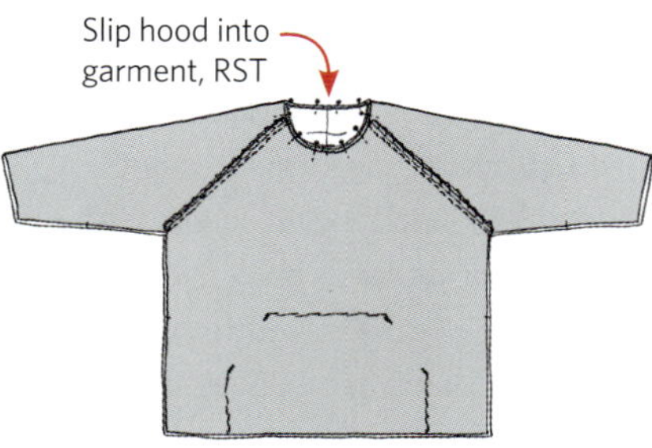


**2.** Facing the hood side (rather than the body of the garment), use loose, small even backstitches to attach through all layers, with ⅜" (1 cm) SA.

**3.** Use overcasting through all layers to finish raw edges. (You can skip overcasting the back torso's neckline, but all else should receive overcasting.)

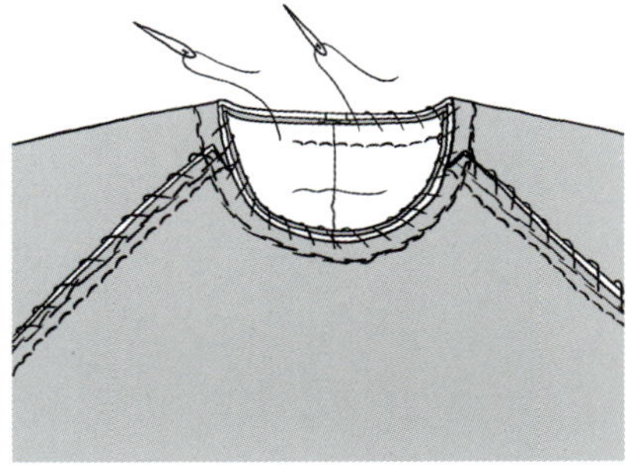

**4.** Pull hood up away from body, then press SAs toward body.

**5.** Next, take back neck binding strip that you previously cut to 1" (2.5 cm) wide by 12" (30.5 cm) long. Press long edges under by ¼" (6 mm).

¼"

¼"

**6.** Pin strip on top of back neck SAs, spanning between back raglan seams. Fold short edges under, and trim as needed so that the strip does not extend past back raglan seams. Strip should entirely cover back neck SAs. (Trim back neck SAs' width a bit if they're too wide to be covered easily.) If desired, baste and remove pins.

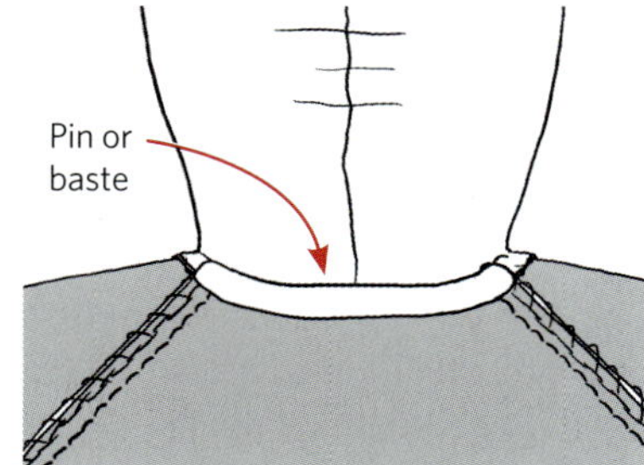


**7.** Use tidy whipstitches to stitch around perimeter of strip, securing it to hood and body, and covering back neck's SAs.

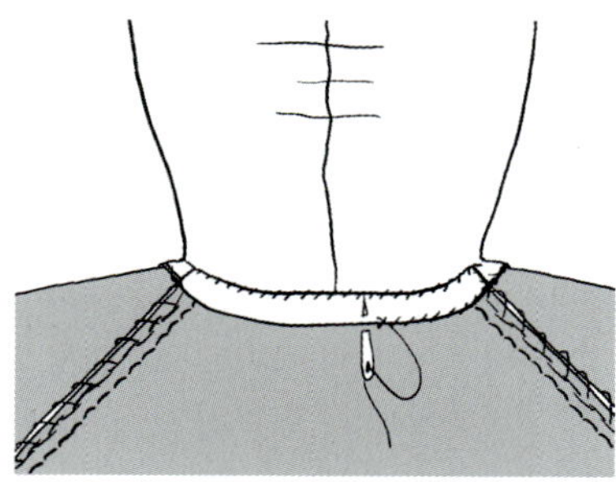

**8.** Slide hoodie cord through casing. Knot ends to prevent them from slipping inside.

## STITCHING THE SIDE SEAMS AND INSEAMS

**1.** With garment inside out, fold in half to align side seams and sleeve inseams. Pin, matching all seams and notches. Use combination stitch or even backstitch to sew, with ⅜" (1 cm) SAs.

**2.** Use overcasting through all layers to finish raw edges.

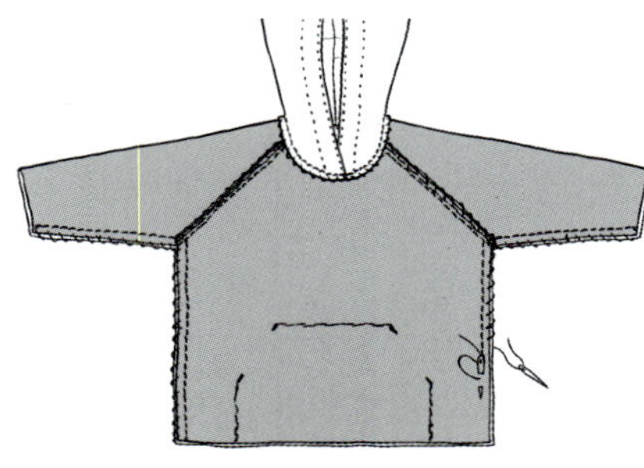

**3.** Press SAs toward back of garment.

## ATTACHING THE CUFFS

**1.** For each sleeve cuff and the bottom hem cuff, fold in half with RST and stitch short ends closed using running stitch, combination stitch, or backstitch. SA should be ⅜" (1 cm).

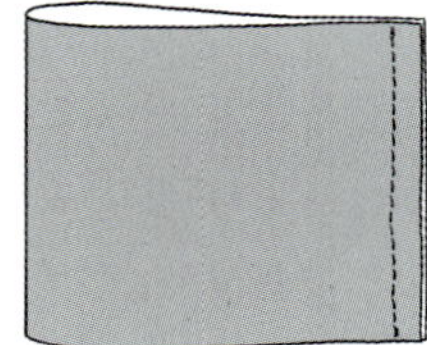

**2.** For each cuff, press SAs open. Snip triangles in SA corners, as shown, to reduce bulk.

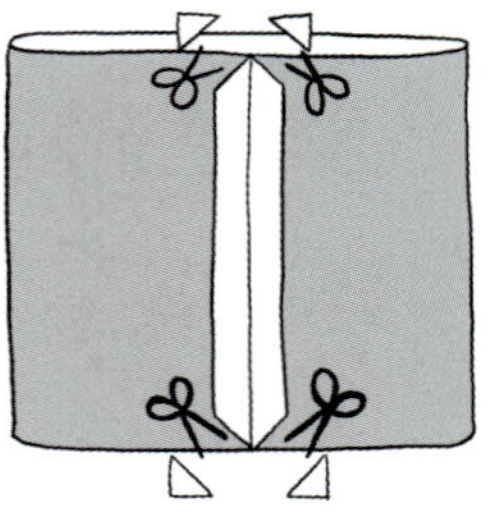

**3.** Fold cuffs in half lengthwise, WST, and press.

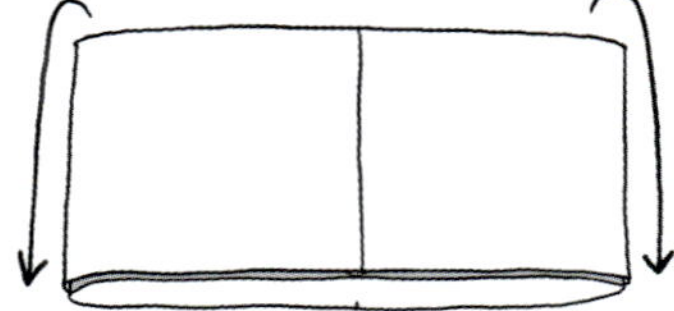

**4.** With garment RS out, pin each cuff onto outside of its respective garment edge, matching all seams and notches, and use loose even backstitches to attach.

**5.** Use overcasting through all layers to finish raw edges.

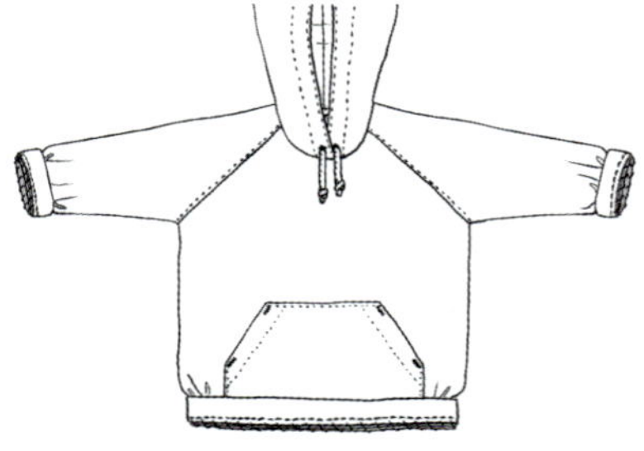

**6.** Press SAs away from cuffs toward body.

### SEWING A LOCKER LOOP (OPTIONAL)

**1.** Make a short piece of spaghetti strap, or use twill tape or other ribbon. Strip should be approximately 3" (7.6 cm) long.

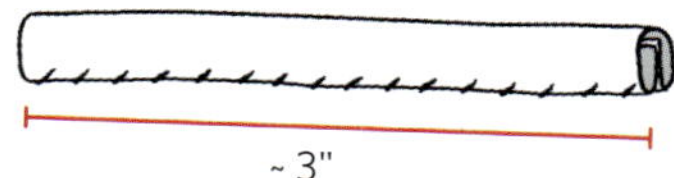


**2.** Fold short ends under and pin onto back neck binding strip. Ends should be approximately 1½" (3.8 cm) apart, centered over CB.

**3.** Use tiny whipstitches, hemstitches, or fell stitches to secure each end to the neck binding. Feel free to pick up some of the inner layers beneath the binding, too—this will make the locker loop stronger.

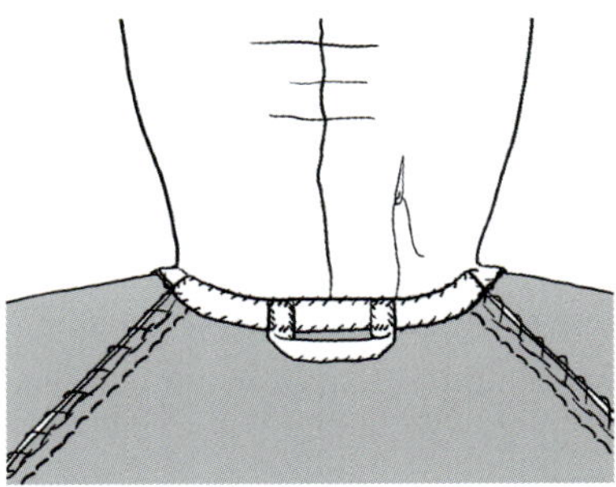

### STITCHING A LABEL (OPTIONAL)

See instructions on page 108 in the woven boxy top project.

# Variations

The little toddler hoodie was drafted using the same basic drafting instructions given in this project. I did choose to deviate for a few measurements such as wearing ease amounts and shoulder slope, because a toddler's body is so much smaller than an adult one. If you are drafting for a child, try examining several of the child's preexisting garments (much as described in the T-shirt project) and measuring key points to inform your choices. Otherwise, though, just use your best judgment and enjoy—children's clothes are especially rewarding to make.

# *Alexis Bailey*

*(she/her)*, pattern designer, sewist, owner of Wear We're Going
DALLAS, TEXAS, USA

Alexis Bailey has been sewing since she was a child. Like many, though, she didn't start hand-sewing clothing until adulthood. In 2019, while traveling in Europe, Alexis found herself missing sewing. Eventually, she says, "I started thinking about how easy it is to take knitting with you, and I thought, 'Why can't we do the same thing with sewing, and hand-sew our clothes?'"

Alexis began searching for others who might have thought of this. She stumbled upon Bernadette Banner's historical hand-sewing videos. Then she began hand-stitching modern garments. In 2020, Alexis opened an online shop offering garment hand-sewing kits. They were received with enthusiasm. Her business grew from there.

Eventually, Alexis began designing zero-waste sewing patterns under the name Fibr & Cloth Studio, which also offered hand-sewing supplies. Today, she continues to offer patterns, supplies, and kits under her rebranded business, Wear We're Going. In her own stitching practice, she says, roughly one in ten garments are sewn by hand these days. "I make hand sewing a priority when I want to slow down," she explains. "I hand-sew when I have a project that will take some time and has repetitive, simple seams."

***Relationship with hand sewing.*** Honestly, it's a love-hate relationship and an off-and-on dating adventure.

***Slow and fast.*** Hand sewing obviously takes more time than my industrial sewing machine, so sometimes projects I can finish quickly are my priority.

***Favorite tool.*** I love beeswax, and I love using it with linen thread, which is my favorite thread.

***Favorite stitches.*** The backstitch is my favorite hand stitch—it's very meditative. But I also fully enjoy felling everything. Felling is fun to me.

***No rules.*** I don't believe in rules when creating, so that probably describes my whole process. I do what works for me and add in the "rules" as I go. I couldn't really tell you if I hand-sew "wrong" or not, ya know?

***Patience and hand sewing.*** The pace of my life is moving differently, and hand sewing has taken a back seat. I want to get back into it and learn to be patient with myself in the process. The impatient part of me needs to make peace with the fact that it is hard to see the finished garment when you're just starting, whereas a machine-sewn garment comes together quickly.

***A grounding force.*** Hand sewing grounds me more than anything else, and perhaps that is why, having stepped away from it, I feel the need to get back to it more. The grounding process of needing to sit and focus on your work, your hands, amidst the chaos that is everyday life—that grounding is so satisfying.

***Advice to beginners.*** Be patient—make the time and play with different stitches until you're comfortable. Hand sewing is a language, and you will have your own dialect of it as you create your work. It won't look like anyone else's, and that's the beauty of it. Enjoy the process and trust your hands as you learn.

# UNDIES

Imagine having a handsewn secret: underwear! This sweet little project will take your handsewn wardrobe to the next level. Undies are small, so they stitch up fairly quickly. Sew a pair for the days when you want to feel special, or make a whole set and enjoy them every day.

You'll spend most of your stitching time creating the elastic casings for waist and leg openings. These casings, while time consuming, will ensure easy garment repair later on. With a few hours of thoughtful stitching now, you'll be able to wear your special underwear for years and years to come.

# Patternmaking

Take a few measurements from your body and then draft yourself a great custom-fit pattern. You may want to test the pattern with some cheap knit fabric before cutting into the good stuff—after all, underwear is a close-fitting garment, and everyone has their own preferences regarding style and coverage. After a quick test fit, you'll be ready to launch into some serious underwear-stitching.

## MEASURING YOUR BODY

To prepare for measuring, tie an elastic or other strip of material around your torso at your desired underwear waistband position. This is your waist elastic. Tie another at hip level. Now measure the following:

- Waist circumference (measured at waist elastic level)
- Hip circumference
- Vertical distance between waist and hip levels at center front
- Rise length (measured from waist elastic, while sitting on a flat chair)
- Crotch saddle length (measured from waist elastic at center front, down between legs, and up to waist elastic at center back)

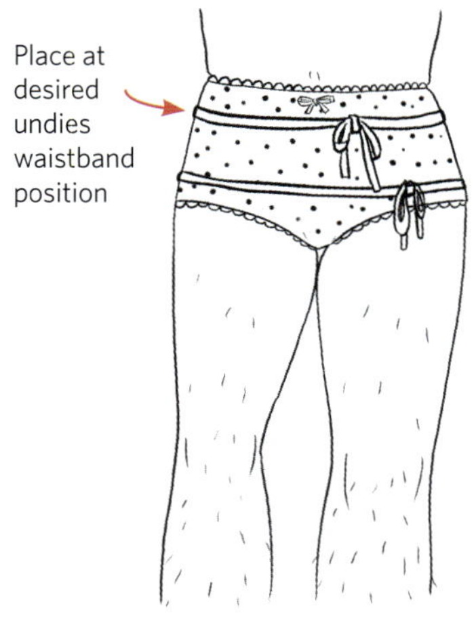


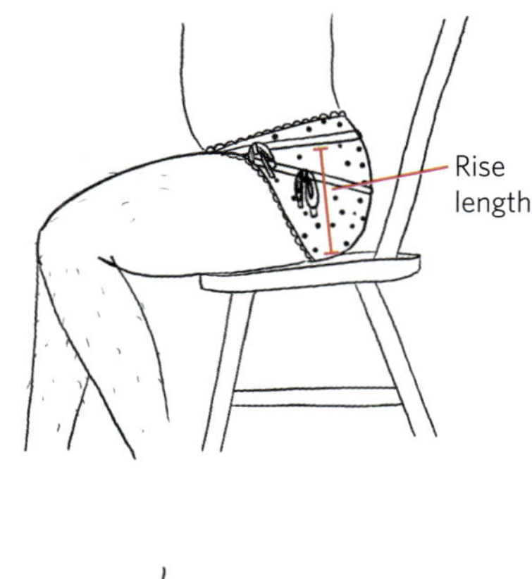


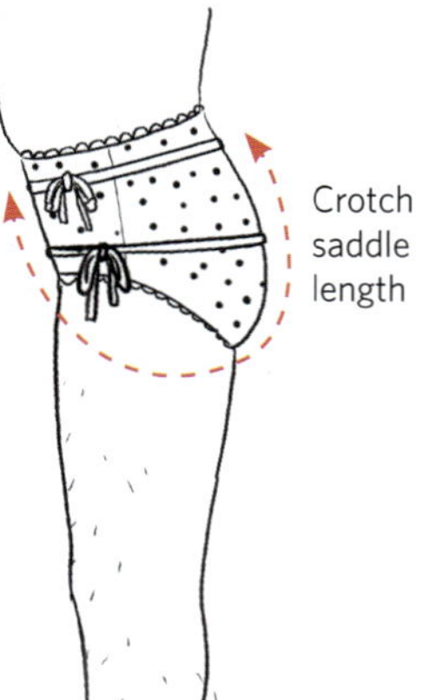

## MARKING LEVELS

As in previous projects, you'll draft only one half of the underwear, because the garment will be symmetrical. You'll initially draft the front, gusset, and back shapes all together, and then you'll trace off the separate components.

1. On a long sheet of paper, draw a vertical line down the right-hand side. This line will represent CF/CB.

2. Square a long line across the top. This will be the provisional front waist level.

3. From provisional front waist level, measure down crotch saddle length and square a long line across—this will be the provisional back waist level.

4. Along CF/CB line, find midpoint between provisional waist levels. Square across carefully at this midpoint.

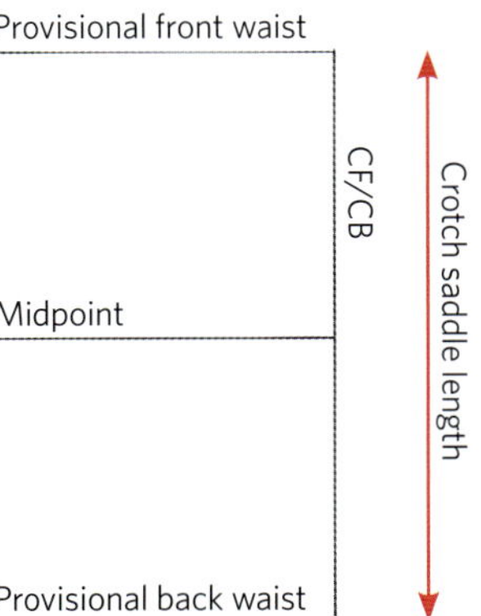


5. Fold paper in half along this new line. Orient folded paper so that front waist line is face up.

6. Measure down from front waist level using the waist-to-hip-level distance, and square across. This will be the hip level.

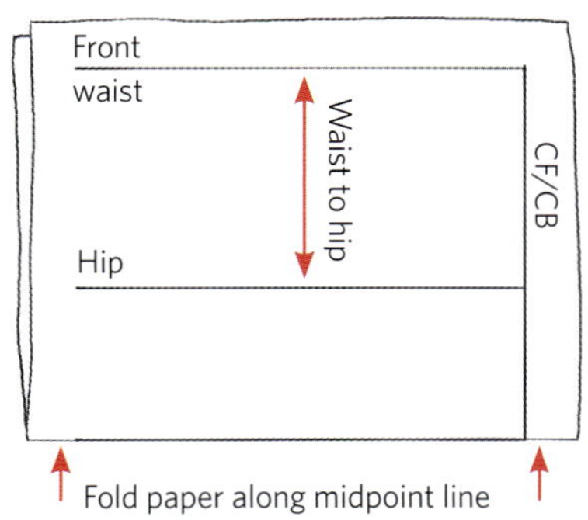


## DRAFTING THE SIDE SEAM

1. Divide waist circumference in four, then subtract 1" (2.5 cm) of negative ease. Measure out from CF/CB line along front waist level for the amount just calculated and place tick mark.

2. Divide hip circumference in four and then subtract 1" (2.5 cm) of negative ease. Measure out from CF/CB line along hip level for the amount just calculated and place tick mark.

3. Connect tick marks to form side seam. I'd recommend using a straight line. Alternatively, you can connect with a gentle curve, but you may find that this produces "hip wings." (You can assess when checking the fit later.)

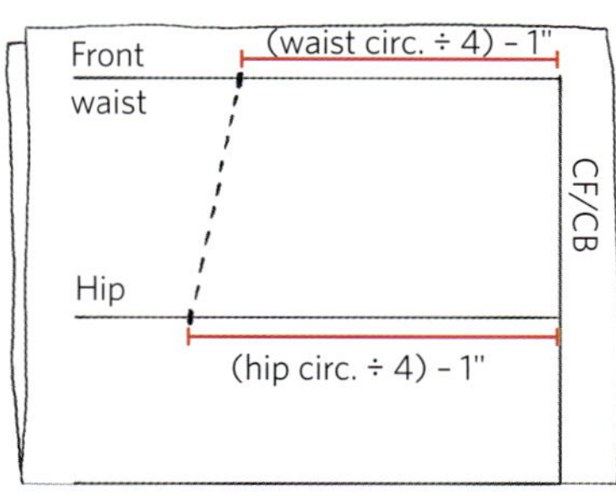


4. Use tracing wheel or pin to carefully trace side seam and hip lines so they transfer to folded paper underlayer.

5. Unfold paper, and pencil in traced lines onto back panel.

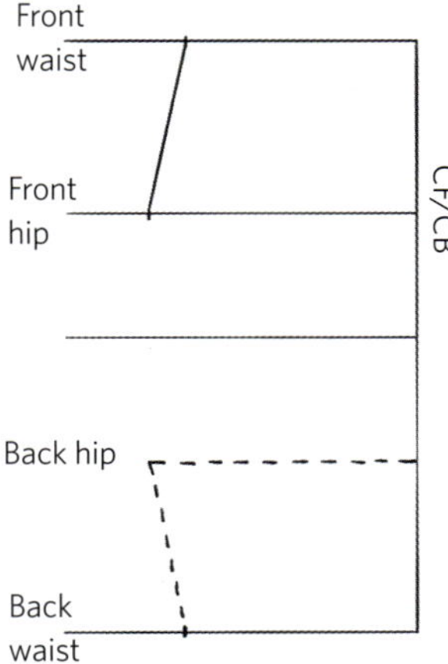


## SETTING UP THE GUSSET

1. Starting at front waist level, measure down along CF/CB line and mark rise height amount, then square across 1½" (3.8 cm). This will be the front joining seam for your crotch gusset.

**2.** Starting at front joining seam, measure down 5½" (14 cm) along CF/CB line and square across 2½" (6.4 cm). This will be the back joining seam for your crotch gusset.

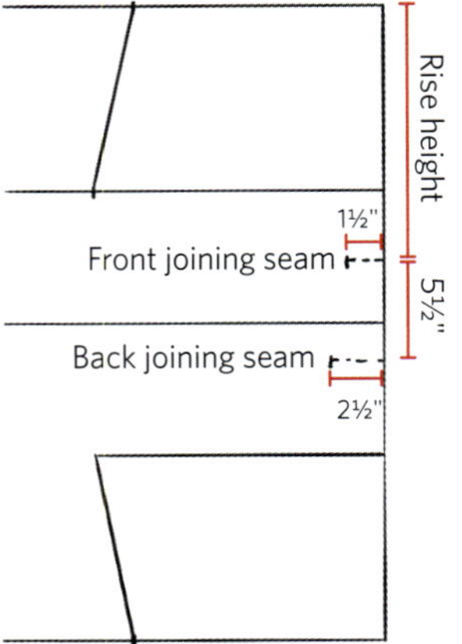


#### DRAFTING LEG OPENINGS AND GUSSET EDGE

**1.** Draw provisional leg openings by drafting straight lines that connect joining seams to hip points.

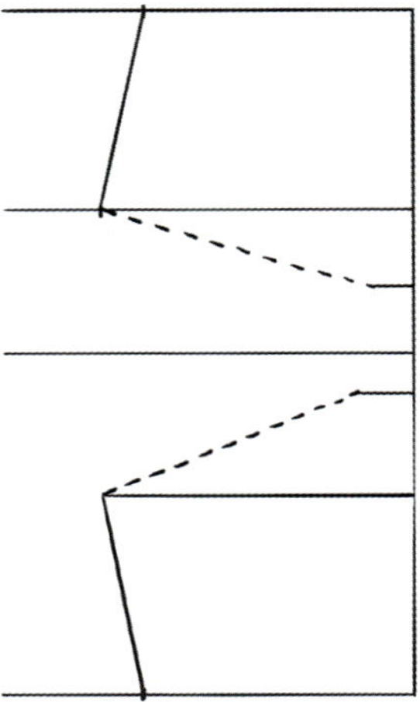

**2.** Sketch a gentle curve to bump front leg opening inward by approximately 1½" (3.8 cm). (You can assess this amount later when testing fit.)

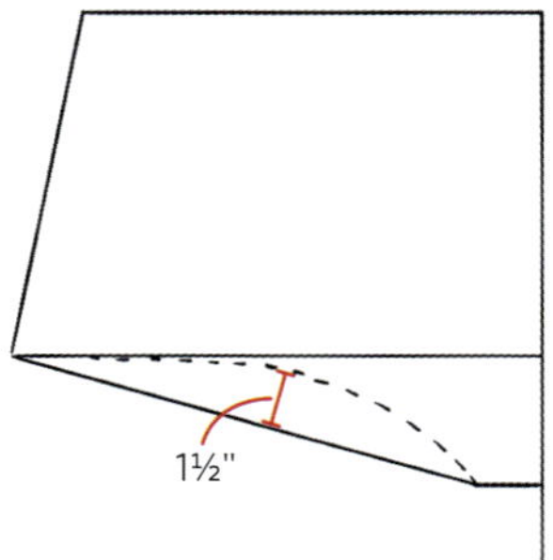


## Customizing the Crotch Gusset

Perhaps you're wondering about the arbitrary measurements given for the crotch gusset. These numbers are often useful across a wide range of body sizes and shapes, so they're a good starting place. However, if you'd prefer, you can measure a pair of underwear you already own and like to wear.

For the front joining seam measurement, measure the width along the crotch gusset's front joining seam. Divide by two, and use this number in place of 1½" (3.8 cm) in step 1.

For the back joining seam measurement, measure the width along the crotch gusset's back joining seam. Divide by two, and use this number in place of 2½" (6.4 cm) in step 2.

For the crotch gusset length, measure your underwear's crotch gusset length (distance between front and back joining seams). Use this in place of 5½" (14 cm) in step 2.

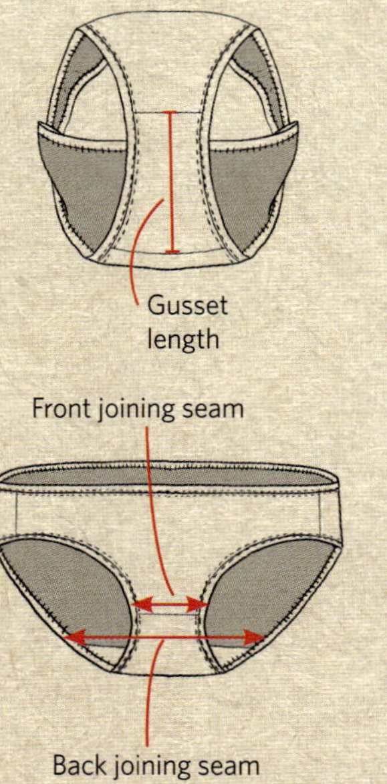

**3.** Next, consider the shape of the back leg opening. This will depend on your personal fit preferences.

- If you'd like ample coverage (which is my personal preference), sketch a gentle curve to bump the back leg opening outward. For now, bump it outward by approximately ⅝" (1.6 cm). You can assess this amount when testing the fit later.
- If you'd like somewhat less coverage, leave the back leg opening line straight.
- If you'd like scantier coverage, carve the back leg opening inward by the amount of your choice. For guidance, you can refer to dimensions of panties you already own and like to wear.

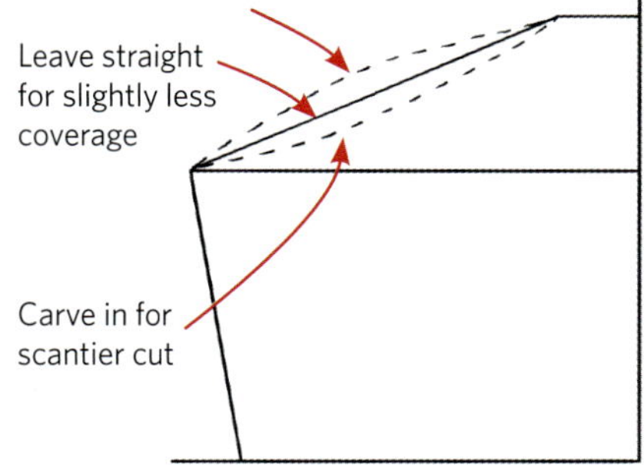


**4.** Once leg opening lines have been finalized, sketch a gentle curve for gusset edge, carefully transitioning between front and back leg opening lines. You can redraw leg openings a bit in order to blend smoothly with gusset area.

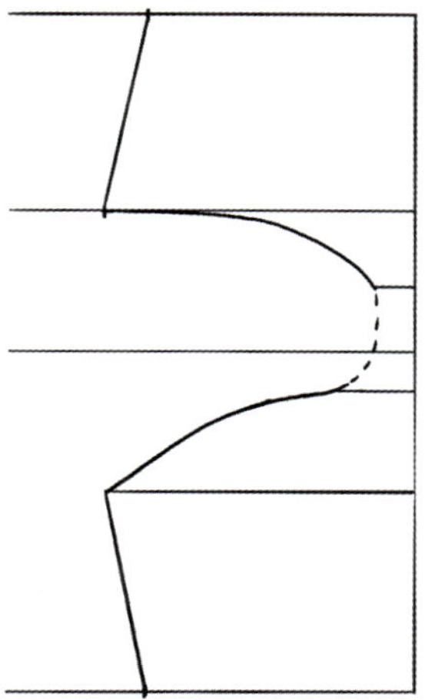

## REFINING THE WAISTLINE

**1.** To accommodate anatomical tilt of waist, lower front waist at CF line by ½" (1.3 cm), maintaining a right angle to CF line for at least 1" (2.5 cm). Then connect to side seam with gentle curve.

**2.** To accommodate anatomical tilt of waist, raise back waist at CB line by ½" (1.3 cm), maintaining a right angle to CB line for at least 1" (2.5 cm). Then connect to side seam with gentle curve.

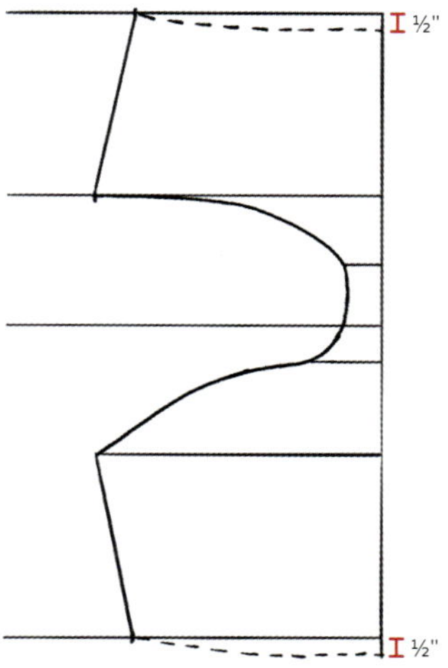


## TRUEING THE PATTERN PIECES

**1.** Cut along gusset's back joining seam to separate back panel. Fold paper under along the side seam.

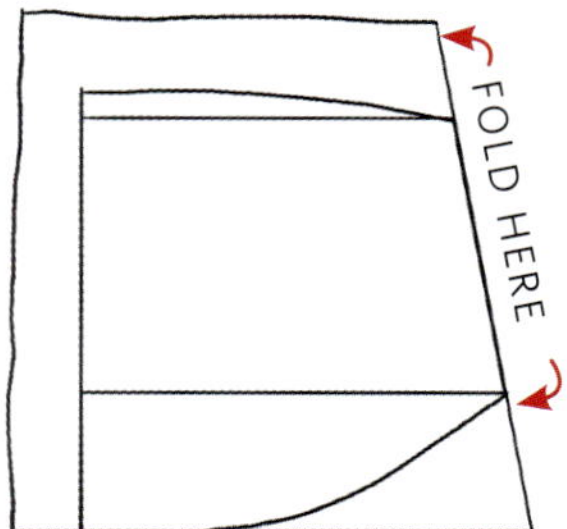

**2.** Place back panel, with folded side seam overlapping front panel, as if sewn together at side seams. Use weights or tape to secure temporarily.

**3.** Assess waistline transition between front and back panels. Adjust lines as needed to ensure a smooth transition. Erase or cross out old lines for clarity.

**4.** Assess leg opening transition between front and back panels. Adjust lines as needed to ensure a smooth transition. Erase or cross out old lines for clarity.

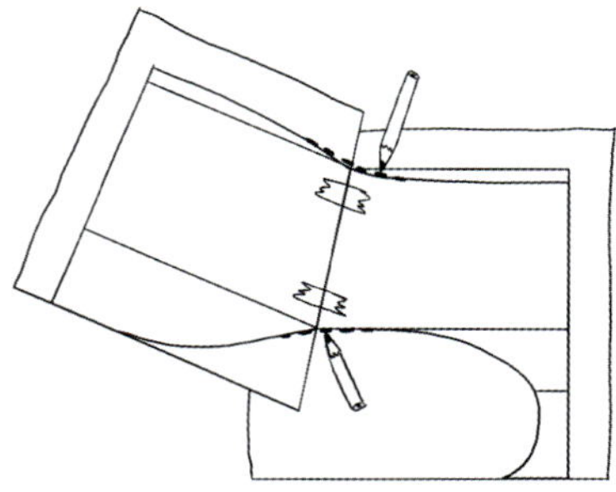

**5.** Remove weights or tape to separate again.

## TESTING THE FIT

Before you finalize your pattern pieces and invest several hours of careful stitching, I'd recommend using some cheap or repurposed old jersey (a big old T-shirt would work well for this) and basting together a quick fit test.

**1.** First, trace off a mirrored-out test front pattern:

- Slip a new folded sheet of paper underneath front draft, aligning fold with draft's CF line.
- Trace front waist, side seam, leg opening, and crotch's front joining seam.
- Remove draft and pencil in lines.
- Add ½" (1.3 cm) SAs on side seam and crotch joining seam edges. (Add no SA on waist or leg opening.)
- Pin paper layers and cut out. Remove pins. Unfold. Place grainline along center.

**2.** Repeat to trace off test back pattern.

**3.** Trace off test gusset pattern. For gusset, add ½" (1.3 cm) SAs on joining seam edges, but add no SA on leg opening edges.

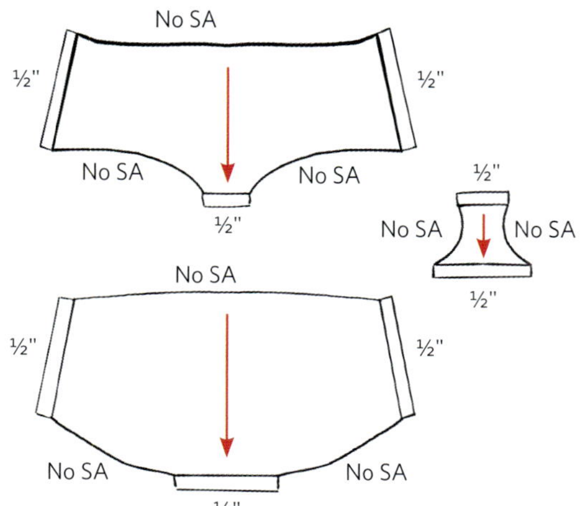


**4.** Cut one of each pattern piece out of test fabric.

**5.** Using running stitch, baste gusset to front panel, RST, with ½" (1.3 cm) SA.

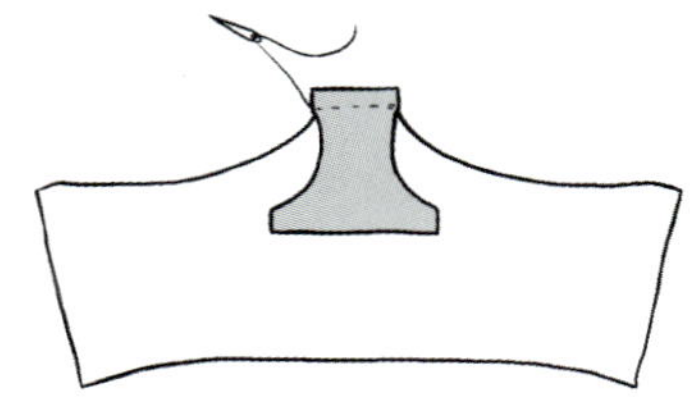

**6.** Using running stitch, baste gusset to back panel, RST, with ½" (1.3 cm) SA.

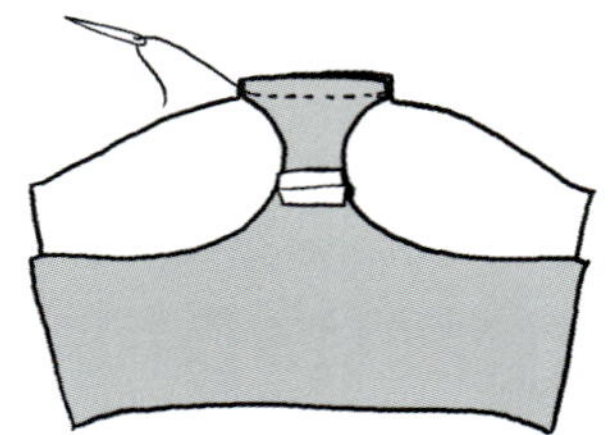

**7.** Using running stitch, baste side seams together, RST, with ½" (1.3 cm) SA.

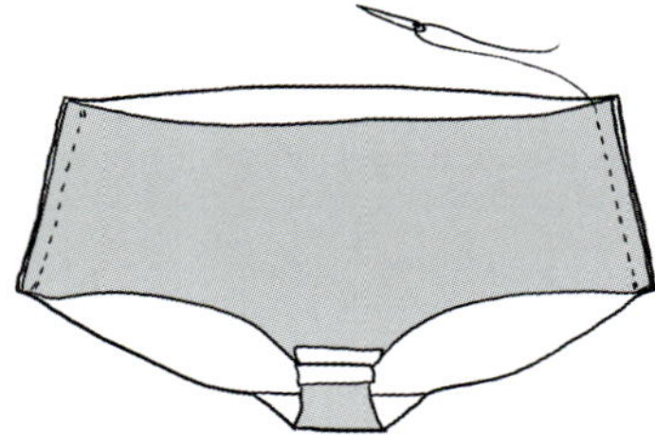

**8.** Slip underwear on and assess fit. Remember that the final version will have elastic cinching in the edges, so any rippling bits along the back leg opening will be snug against your skin. With that in mind, jot down notes as you ask yourself the following:

- Is the waist high or low enough for your taste? If not, how much would you like to adjust up or down?
- Is the waist circumference comfortable? How about the hip circumference? If not, how much more or less fabric do you think you'd need?
- Do you like the amount of coverage on front and back? If too much fabric, use a safety pin to pinch out the excess. If not enough, place a safety pin where you need more, and jot a note of how much more fabric you'd like in that area.
- Do you like the gusset width? If too much fabric, use a safety pin to pinch excess. If too little, jot a note of how much more is needed.
- Are the gusset seam placements okay? If you'd rather have them farther forward or back, what are the measurements you'd use?
- Are there any other adjustments you'd make? If so, what measurements would you use to adjust?
- Optionally, would you like to place any style lines? See page 221 for tips. You can draw these directly on your fit test with a marker.
- Optionally, take front, side, and back view photographs so you'll have a good visual reference as you're making any pattern adjustments.

**9.** Using your notes and optional photos, make all adjustments necessary on your pattern draft, then re-true to ensure smooth transitions at seamlines.

## ADJUSTING FOR ELASTIC CASINGS

The lines you've drafted and tested represent the underwear's dimensions including elastic casings. For the actual pattern pieces, you'll now need to remove the casing width from each relevant edge.

**1.** First, calculate the casing width you'll use. I'd recommend making your casing width approximately ¹⁄₁₆ to ⅛" (2 to 3 mm) wider than your elastic. So if your elastic is ¼" (6 mm) wide, I'd plan casings that are a scant ⅜" (1 cm) wide.

**2.** Once you've calculated the casing width, lower waistline by this amount on front and back panels. Line should be parallel to original waistline. Once complete, erase or cross out old lines.

**3.** Move leg openings inward by this amount on front and back panels and on gusset edge. Lines should be parallel to original leg opening lines. Once complete, erase or cross out old lines.

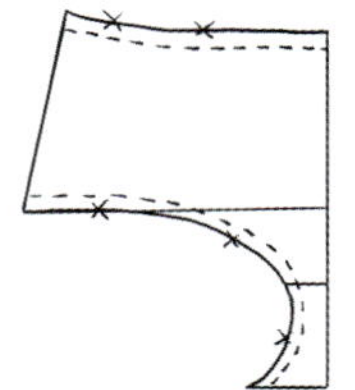

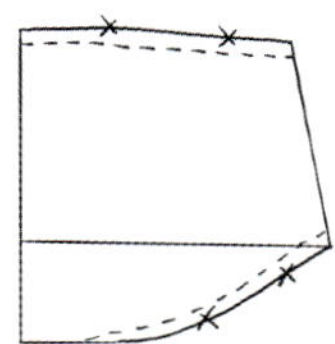

**4.** For each of the lines you've just adjusted (all waist and leg opening edges), measure line length and jot down measurement on pattern draft. You'll refer to these when drafting casings.

**5.** Mark notch points halfway along front and back waistlines.

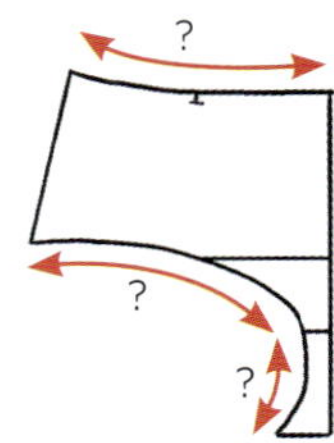


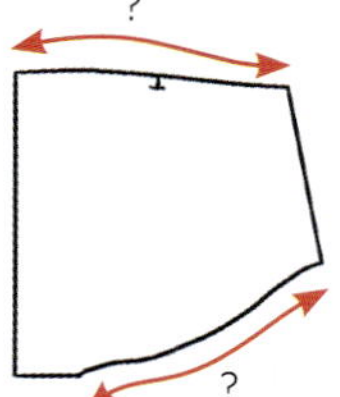

#### TRACING THE PATTERN PIECES

**1.** First, trace off a mirrored-out front pattern:

- Slip a new folded sheet of paper underneath front draft, aligning fold with draft's CF line.
- Trace front waist, side seam, leg opening, and crotch's front joining seam. Trace midpoint notch along waistline.
- Remove draft and pencil in lines.
- Add ⅜" (1 cm) SAs on all edges.
- Pin paper layers and cut out. Snip notch. Remove pins. Unfold. Snip a waistline notch at CF. Place grainline along center. Add note: "CUT 1 SELF."

**2.** Repeat to trace a back pattern.

**3.** Repeat to trace a gusset pattern, but you won't need to trace or snip any notches. Note for gusset pattern should be: "CUT 2 SELF."

#### DRAFTING THE WAIST ELASTIC CASING

**1.** Calculate waist casing length by totaling front and back waistline lengths marked on your draft. Then multiply by two. This will be the length of your waist casing.

**2.** Draw rectangle that is length of previous calculation and twice as tall as elastic height, plus ¼" (6 mm) for wiggle room. (So if using ¼" [6 mm] elastic, draft pattern height of ¾" [2 cm].)

**3.** Add notches to divide length into eighths.

**4.** Next, add SAs. I'd recommend ⅜" (1 cm) on all edges.

**5.** Cut out pattern and snip notches.

**6.** Place grainline parallel to short ends. Add note: "CUT 1 SELF."

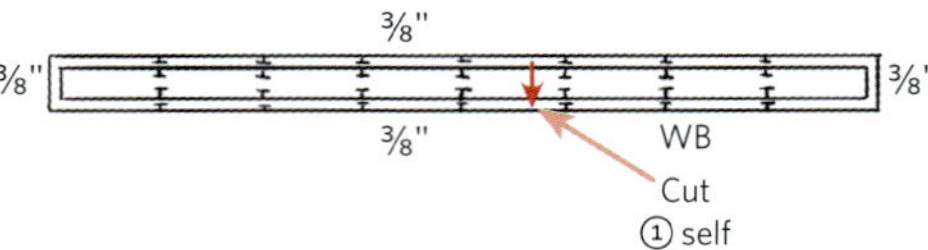


#### DRAFTING THE LEG ELASTIC CASING

**1.** Calculate leg casing length by totaling leg opening lengths along draft (front + gusset + back). This will be the length of each leg casing.

**2.** Draw rectangle that is the length you just calculated and same height as waist casing.

**3.** Add notches to divide length into quarters.

**4.** Next, add SAs. I'd recommend ⅜" (1 cm) on all edges.

**5.** Cut out pattern and snip notches.

**6.** Place grainline parallel to short ends. Add note: "CUT 2 SELF."

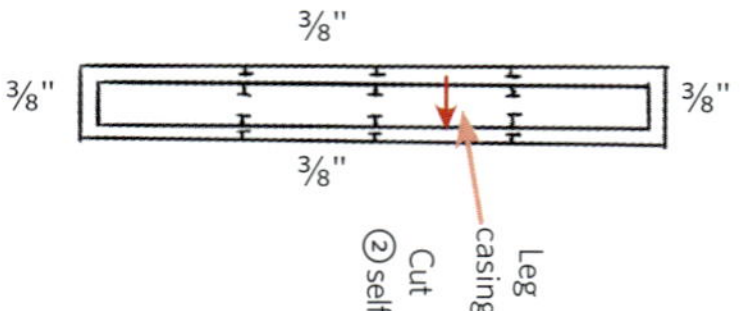

# Sewing

### HAND-SEWING STITCHES

- Even backstitch
- Whipstitch
- Basting
- Herringbone stitch or catchstitch

### FABRIC OPTIONS

A medium-weight stretchy jersey or other knit is best for this underwear project. I like using cotton or other natural fibers, but you can use whatever you prefer. You're welcome to experiment with other fabric weights, too, and with other knit constructions. However, you will want your fabric to have some horizontal stretch.

If desired, you can try colorblocking by using a different color for your elastic casings than you're using for the main body.

### OTHER MATERIALS NEEDED

You will need several yards (meters) of thin elastic for your waist and leg openings. This should be basic elastic, without special edgings or fold creases, because it will be hidden away inside casings. I like ¼" (6 mm) elastic, but something slightly narrower or wider would also work.

## Why Make Elastic Casings?

If you've ever machine-sewn underwear before, you're probably aware of the typical ways that elastic is applied. It's generally topstitched directly to or around the raw edge, which is a quick, effective method.

For handsewn undies, though, I quickly realized that it's pretty labor intensive (and honestly, pretty annoying) to topstitch skinny elastic onto jersey's curling raw edges using appropriately stretchy hand stitches. Even something relatively speedy, like whipstitch, is slow in the face of all those curling jersey edges. And while I'm open to labor-intensive, fussy handwork, it didn't seem worth it. Because, at least in my own experience, the elastic is one of the first areas that wears out on a typical pair of underwear. So after a few years, I'd likely have to painstakingly remove all of that elastic, iron the re-curling jersey edges, and then repeat the entire process.

Instead, I've come to prefer investing my time into attaching elastic casings. Yes, it takes a bit of time to set up, but it ensures that you can easily add, remove, and re-add elastic, now and in the future. The instructions that follow will guide you through my preferred elastic casing method.

That said, if you'd rather try a topstitching application method, that's great! All of us modern clothing hand sewists are just kind of making it up as we go along. Give it a try and see what you can come up with. Maybe you'll discover something amazing.

## CUTTING THE FABRIC

See Cutting Fabric on page 85 for tips on cutting. You'll need to cut the following pieces and quantities:

- Front × 1 self
- Back × 1 self
- Gusset × 2 self
- Waist casing × 1 self
- Leg casing × 2 self

## SEWING FIRST GUSSET SEAM

**1.** Arrange gusset pieces on top of each other, with RST.

**2.** Slip front panel in between gusset layers (front panel can be RS up or down—it doesn't matter), aligning front gusset joining seam. Pin.

**3.** Join with even backstitch and ⅜" (1 cm) SA.

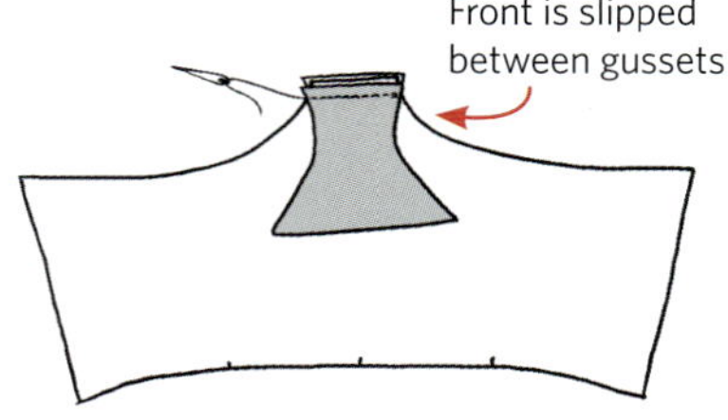


**4.** Snip triangles through all layers to reduce bulk.

**5.** Open out and press, with SAs toward gusset.

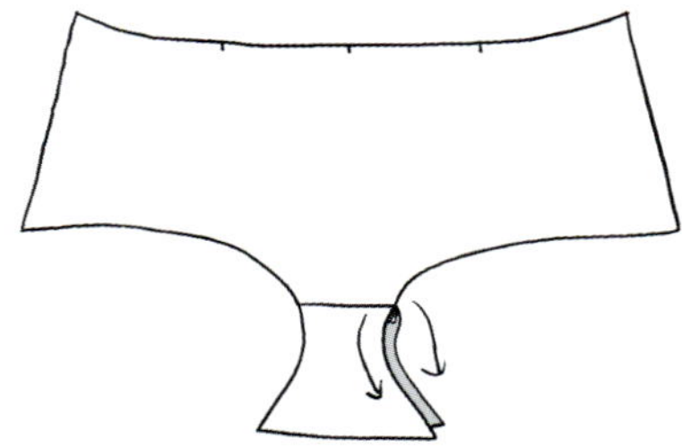

## SEWING THE SECOND GUSSET SEAM

**1.** Place undies with RS facing up. Place back panel, RS facing down, on top of project, aligning back panel's gusset join seam with gusset. Pin to top layer of gusset only.

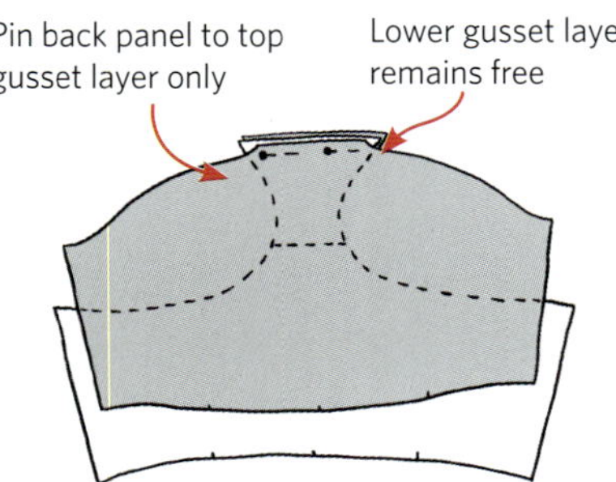


**2.** Bunch or roll up front and back panels so that they fit onto gussets.

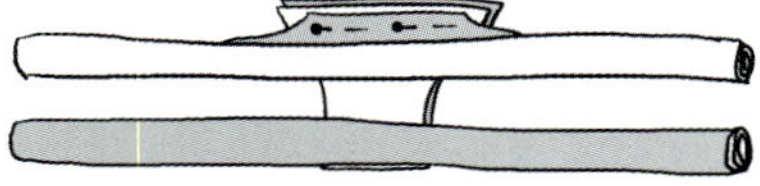

**3.** Pull lower layer of gusset around so that gussets are encircling everything, with wrong sides facing out. Align gusset layers' free ends with each other and redo pins to incorporate all three layers.

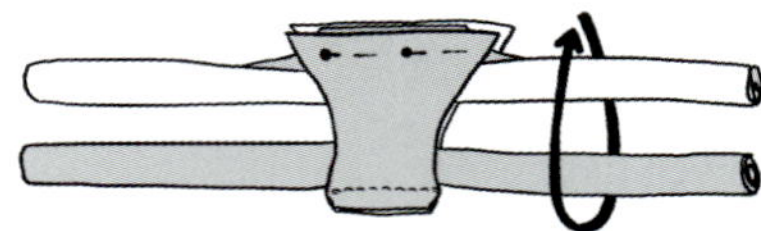

**4.** Use even backstitch to join with ⅜" (1 cm) SA.

**5.** Snip triangles through all layers to reduce bulk.

**6.** Pull rolled panels out and open everything. Press.

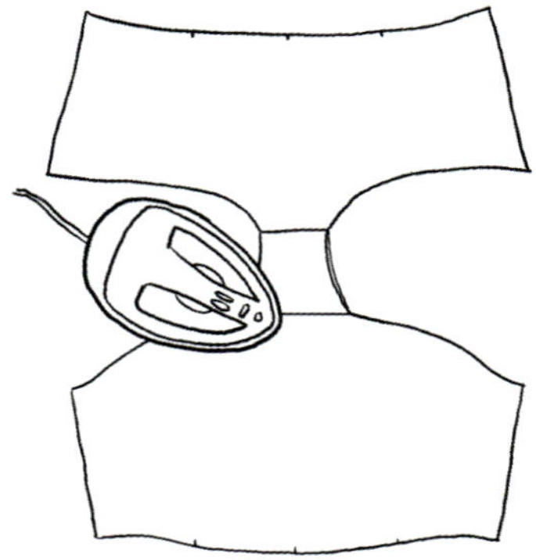

## SEWING THE SIDE SEAMS

**1.** With underwear's RST, pin side seams.

**2.** With front panel facing you, use even backstitch and ⅜" (1 cm) SAs to join.

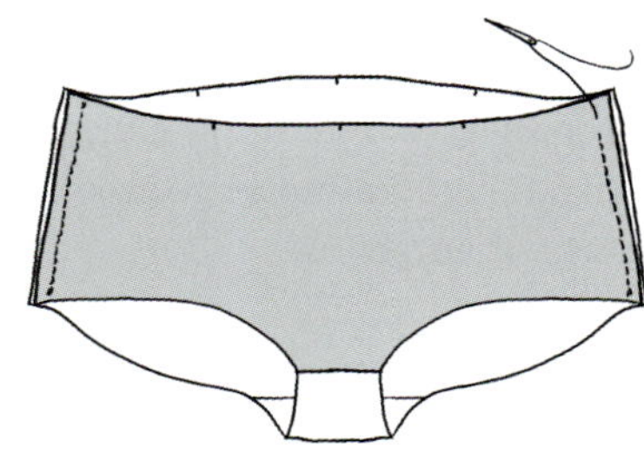

**3.** Press SAs toward back panel.

**4.** Use whipstitch to fell SAs onto back panel.

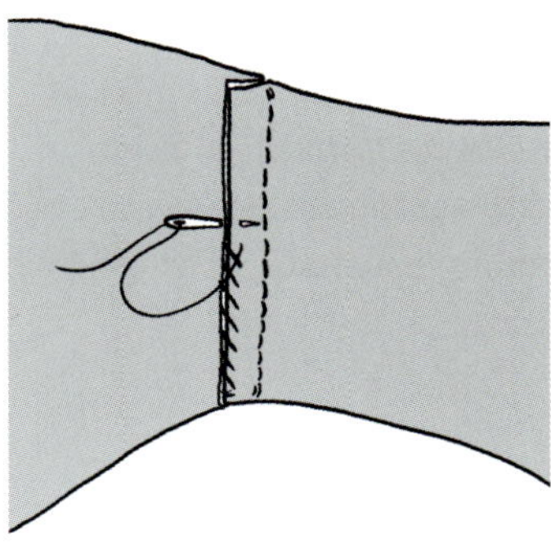

When felling seam allowances here, I don't recommend trimming and folding them as you might do on a woven garment or in another context. Folding edges would add an extra layer of bulk, and on these close-fitting undies' side seams, minimizing bulk is a priority to ensure comfort. Also, jersey's raw edges typically don't do much unraveling, so it's not strictly necessary to "clean-finish" them.

## ATTACHING THE ELASTIC CASINGS

**1.** Fold each casing piece in half, with RST, and baste short ends together with running stitches and ⅜" (1 cm) SA.

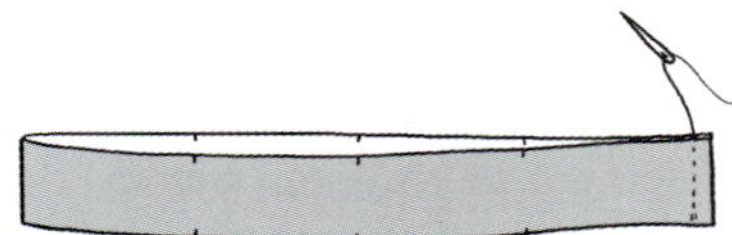

**2.** Press SAs open and clip triangles to reduce bulk.

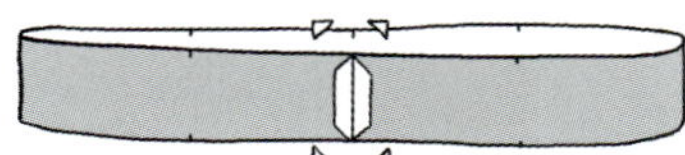

**3.** Fold each casing in half along its length, WST, and press.

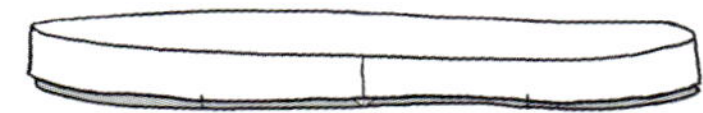

**4.** Align waist casing's join seam with a side seam or center back notch of garment, and pin through all layers to attach to outside of garment along waistline.

**5.** Use Hera marker or other marking tool to mark stitch line. (I like to mark in from the casing's fold, instead of its raw edges, to ensure that my casing's width will be very accurate.) Stitch line should be ⅜" (1 cm) from raw edges.

**6.** Use even backstitch through all layers to attach casing to garment. Don't leave a gap—you'll slip the elastic in later by removing casing's basting.

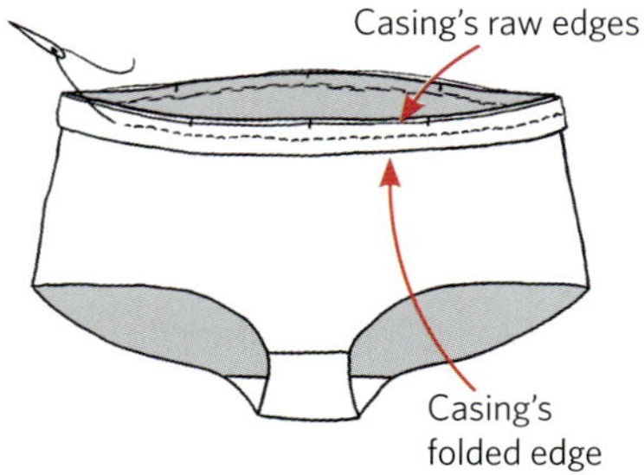


**7.** To attach leg casings, decide where to place the casing join seam. (I like to place mine somewhere on the back leg opening down near the gusset seam.) Then you'll need to create little notches along garment's leg opening by notching at intended joining seam point, then pinching edges carefully along each other to find halfway point on the other side and notching, and then finding midpoints.

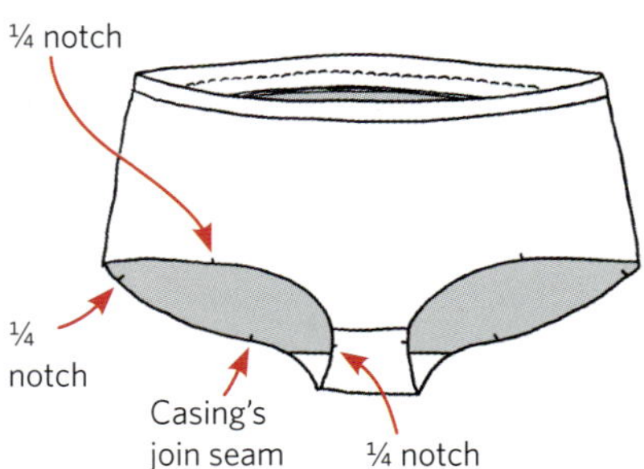

8. Once you have four equidistant notches snipped on each leg opening, complete steps 4 through 6.

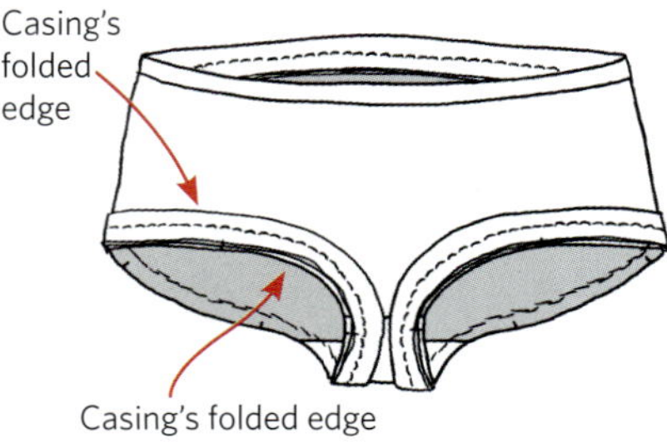


9. Press all casing joins so that SAs point toward garment.

## FELLING THE CASING SAs

Fell all casing SAs to garment using catchstitch, herringbone stitch, or another stretchy, thread-binding stitch of your choice.

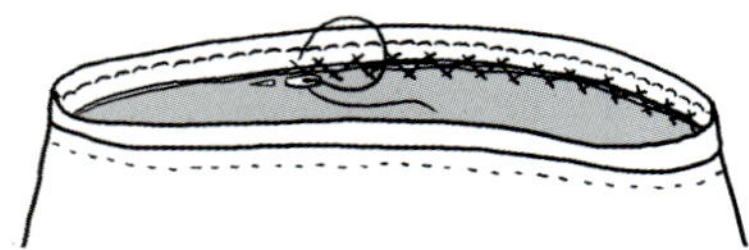

## INSERTING THE ELASTICS

1. For each casing, remove basting at casing join.

2. Use a safety pin to pull elastic through waist casing, but don't cut elastic yet.

3. Pull on underwear, pin elastic to desired length, and trim to ½" (1.3 cm) longer than that length.

4. Repeat steps 2 and 3 for one of the leg openings.

5. Measure elastic from step 4 and cut another elastic to the same length, then thread it through the other leg opening.

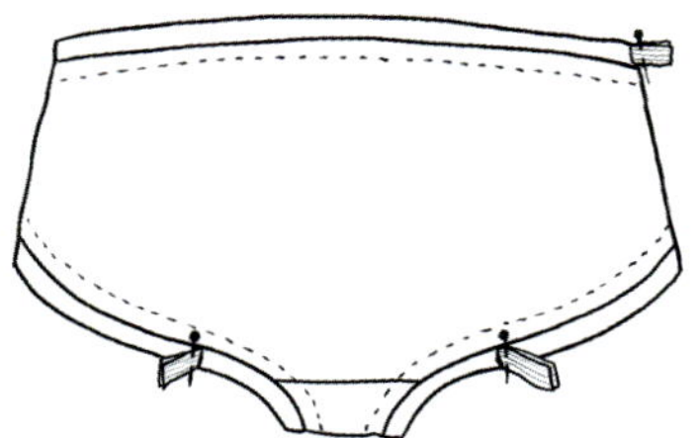

6. For each casing, make sure elastic is not twisted, then overlap ends by ½" (1.3 cm) and use tiny whipstitches around the overlap to secure. (I like to whipstitch around the entire perimeter of the overlap rectangle.)

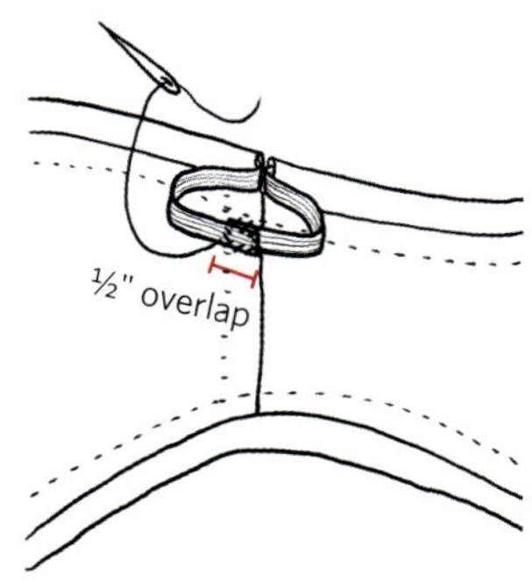


7. Stretch casing and manipulate fabric until all elastic is pulled back into waistband. Then make sure casing opening edges are still tidily folded under, arrange them so that they are kissing, and use tiny whipstitches to close the opening. Start whipstitching at the bottom of the inside casing, stitch up to the top, then stitch over and down the outside of the casing. Then push needle through to inside casing and anchor off.

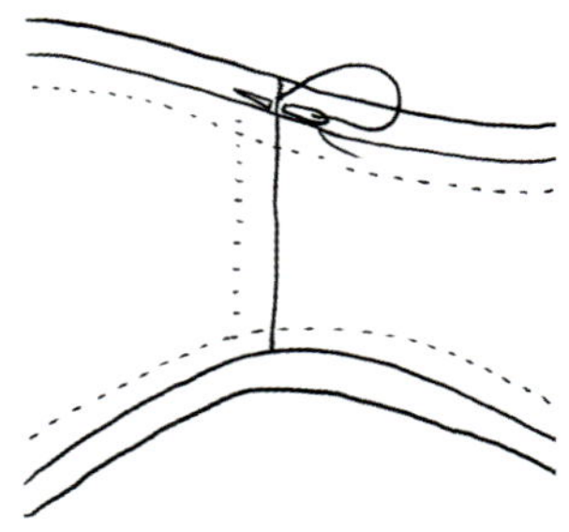

8. Place 3 or 4 little tacks (piles of backstitches) through all layers, roughly equidistant along each casing, to ensure that elastic won't twist while wearing.

# Variations

If you're stitching underwear with style lines, you can join style line seams as with side seams. That is, you'll sew them using even backstitch, then fell SAs down in your preferred direction. For felling, you can use whipstitch, herringbone stitch, catchstitch, or another stretchy, thread-binding stitch of your choice.

The photographed sample here shows another way to create style lines. Instead of drafting them during patternmaking, you can improvise the style lines directly on the fabric before cutting. Simply overlay scraps of fabric until you like their general arrangement. Trim as needed and fold edges under. Pin and/or baste, then cut out the entire front (and/or back) panel. To secure colorblocked joins, you can use whipstitch or fell stitch, working from the outside. On the underside, secure any raw edges using whipstitch, herringbone, etc.

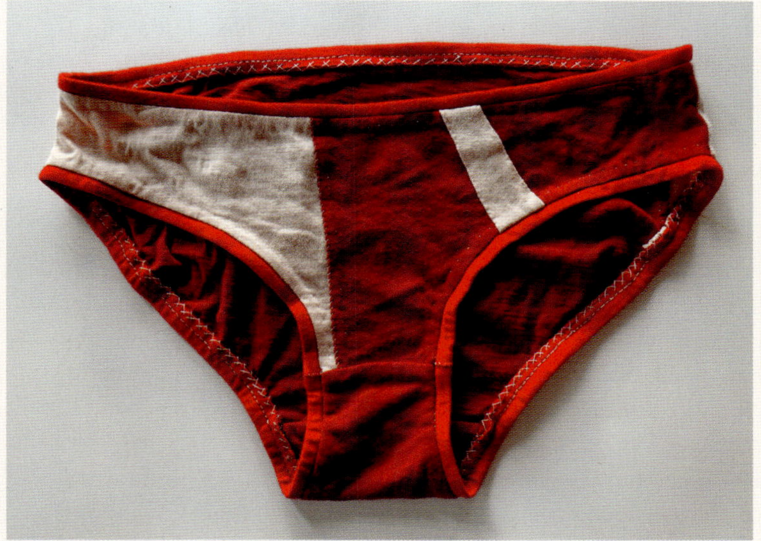

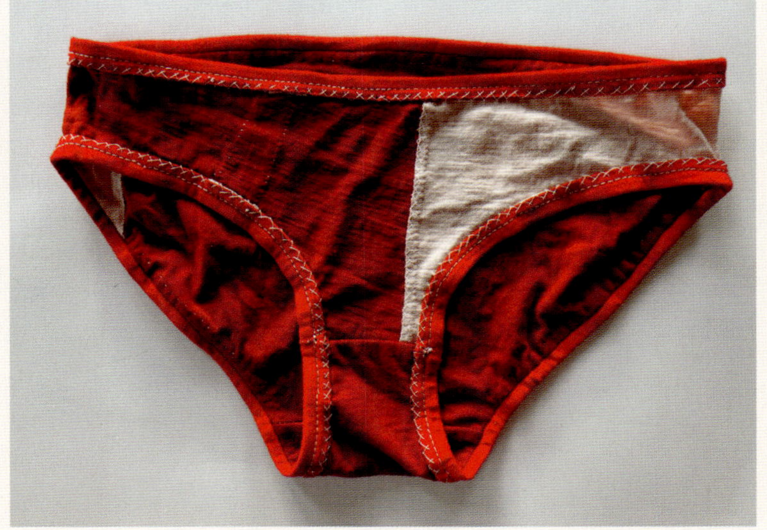

# Cal Patch

*(she/her)*, teacher, maker, crafty farmer
ACCORD, NEW YORK, USA

Cal Patch has been making things since childhood, but she never thought she'd hand-sew entire garments. Growing up, she embroidered and sewed simple projects, eventually attending fashion school. For years, Cal worked in the clothing industry. Then she began teaching patternmaking, sewing, and crochet. Throughout, sewing was a decidedly machine-based process for her.

"I've always been a machine sewer, and I still am," Cal explains, "but four or five years ago, I just fell head over heels, hard and fast. And now, if I could, I would hand-sew everything." She is drawn to the soothing slowness of hand sewing, and she appreciates that she can do it anywhere, including on her couch. "And I'm a big fan of my couch time," she laughs, "so my only issue is that it competes with my crochet now, which used to be what I mostly did on the couch. Now I have a lot more projects piled up on the couch next to me."

Cal describes herself as a slow worker, so she suspects she'll always rely on the machine for projects that need to be sewn quickly—especially for garments she makes to sell. But she estimates that she hand-sews at least one in three garments these days. "I'm doing all the handsewn ones that I can," Cal says.

***Favorite hand-sewing tool.*** The leather thimble that I made myself because I was overwhelmed trying to figure out what kind of thimble to buy. I was thimble-shopping online during the pandemic. I was about to rack up like $200 worth of thimbles in my shopping cart because they come in sizes and you want to try them on. And then a friend was like, "Couldn't you just make one?" About five minutes later, I had made one. That's still my favorite.

***The "just-right" stitch.*** My favorite stitch is the combination between running stitch and backstitch. I was calling it "combination stitch" at first, and then I started calling it "walking stitch" because it's almost as fast as running, but not quite. That's probably what I use the most. It's fast and strong. It's like "Goldilocks and the Three Bears"—it's the middle bear. You know, it's the "just-right" stitch.

***Slow fashion.*** A lot of people, when they learn to machine-sew, get excited and make tons of stuff that they don't actually wear. For me, that's never been an issue because I'm slow even by machine. But sewing by hand can help people be a little more thoughtful and reflective.

***Advice for newcomers.*** Mending is a good introductory place. If you have a seam that busts open on a garment, you could just stitch up that little seam. And you know, it almost doesn't matter how you stitch it up—just any putting the needle back and forth through the fabric is going to close up that hole. And then when you find out how fun and cool it is, there are so many great resources to learn more.

# WOVEN BUTTON-UP SHIRT

The button-up shirt is a staple in many people's wardrobes. Use whatever light- to midweight woven fabric suits your fancy, and start enjoying days lived in handsewn shirts. Despite the professional look of a button-up, you'll be pleased to find that the patternmaking and sewing is not difficult. There are lots of steps, but taken one at a time, each step is pretty simple. So settle in and enjoy the process. By the end of the project, you'll be marveling at the beautiful results that have emerged from your diligent, straightforward work.

- If your front and back lengths overlap each other, you'll need to double-check your measurements. Remeasure the front, back, and yoke armholes, and redraw the provisional cap lines. Then repeat steps 1 through 12. If your calculations are accurate, your curved sleeve cap should have some sleeve cap ease.

## FINALIZING THE SLEEVE DRAFT

**1.** Add matching notches to front and back sleeve caps. Beginning at front underarm point, measure up 3" (7.6 cm) and place a notch. Beginning at back underarm point, measure up 3" (7.6 cm) and 3½" (8.9 cm) and place notches.

**2.** Find the sleeve cap ease you marked between tick marks while checking sleeve cap length. Now mark the midpoint between these tick marks by placing a notch.

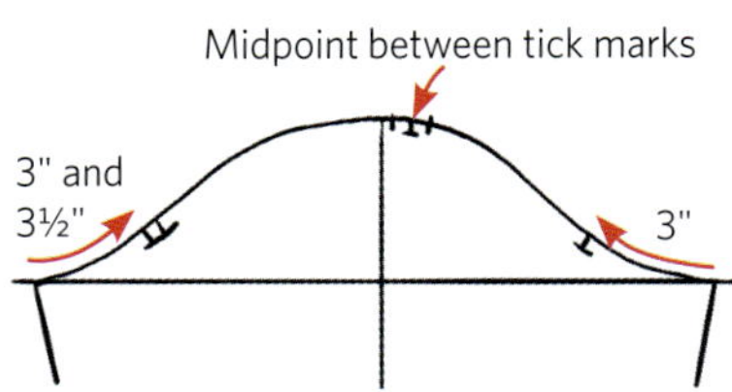


**3.** Next, add seam allowances. I'd recommend:

- ½" (1.3 cm) on wristline
- ¾" (2 cm) on sleeve cap and inseam edges

**4.** Cut out. Snip notches, including for pleats and at elbow level. Also snip notch at bottom of slit.

**5.** Place grainline parallel to center line. Add note: "CUT 2 SELF."

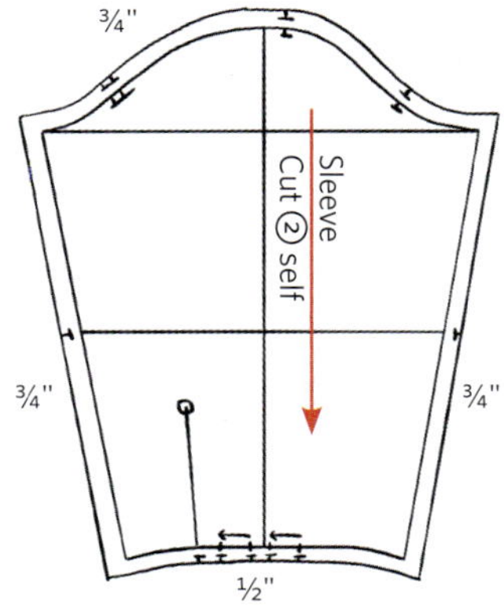


## DRAFTING THE SLEEVE PLACKET PATTERN

**1.** Measure placket slit line on sleeve pattern.

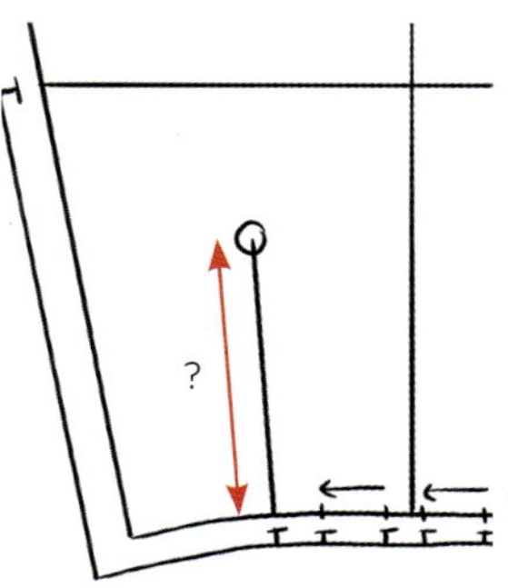


**2.** On a fresh sheet of paper, draw a vertical line for the length of your sleeve's slit line. Make tick marks to indicate top and bottom. Circle top tick mark—this will be a drill hole when cutting and marking fabric pieces.

**3.** Square across in both directions from bottom tick mark.

**4.** Draw two parallel lines flanking the slit line, ¼" (6 mm) away to each side. Connect tops of all three lines. The rectangular shape you've now drafted represents the stitch line you'll follow in order to begin attaching the placket piece to your sleeve.

**5.** Draw a parallel line that is ⅜" (1 cm) to the left of this rectangle. Draw another parallel line that is ⅜" (1 cm) beyond the first. These lines represent the fabric you'll fold to create a ⅜" (1 cm) binding around your placket underlayer.

6. Draw a tall parallel line that is ¾" (2 cm) to the right of your rectangle from step 4. Draw another tall parallel line that is ¾" (2 cm) beyond the first. These lines represent the fabric you'll fold to create a ¾" (2 cm) binding around your placket overlayer.

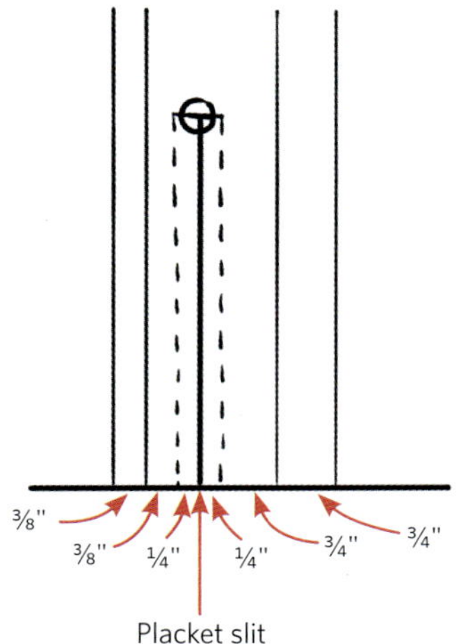


7. Now you'll add levels along the top edge. First, square a line across that is ½" (1.3 cm) higher than your rectangle from step 4.

8. Next, draw a line ¼" (6 mm) above the previous one, extending across the ¾" (2 cm)-wide section on the right.

9. Draw a pointy cap for this rightmost section, as shown. The exact angle is up to you. This shape will form the top of your placket overlayer, so the angle will be a small aesthetic element.

10. Next, add SAs:

- ¼" (6 mm) on left and right edges
- ½" (1.3 cm) on lower edge
- ¼" (6 mm) on pointy cap
- ¼" (6 mm) on short left-hand side of placket "tower"

Do not add SA to the remainder of top edge—the rest of the top edge already has ½" (1.3 cm) allowance from step 7.

11. Place a notch at the bottom of your rectangle's middle line. When cutting and marking fabric pieces, you'll use the drill hole and this notch to align pieces for sewing.

12. Cut out. Snip notch.

13. Place grainline parallel to slit line. Add note: "CUT 2 SELF (OPT.: CUT 2 INTERFACING)."

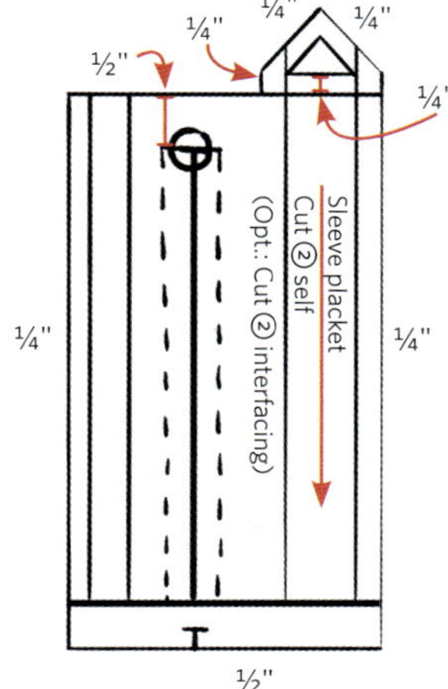


## DRAFTING THE SLEEVE CUFF PATTERN

1. First, calculate your sleeve cuff length. Refer to your hand circumference measurement, then add ⅝" (1.6 cm) to accommodate the sleeve placket's overhang length. This total will be your cuff length.

2. On a new sheet of paper, draw a rectangle. Its length should be as calculated above. Rectangle's height should be twice as tall as cuff height you decided while drafting your sleeve pattern.

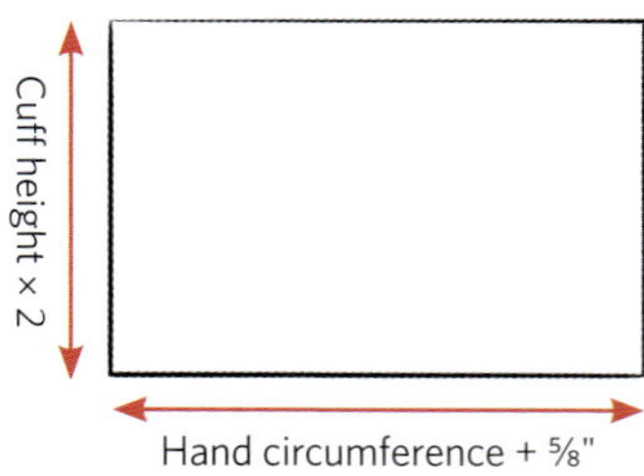


3. Next, add SAs. I'd recommend ½" (1.3 cm) on all edges.

4. Cut out. Place grainline parallel to long sides. Add note: "CUT 2 SELF. CUT 2 INTERFACING."

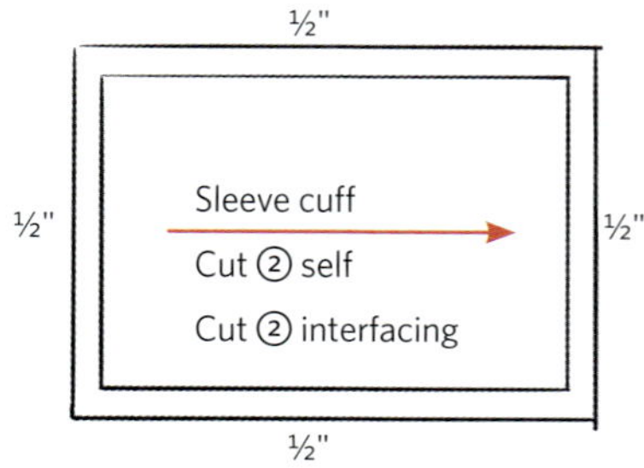

### DRAFTING THE COLLAR STAND

**1.** Refer to front neckline. (You measured this from lowered shoulder seam to CF.) Add half of placket width to this amount to calculate true front neckline length.

**2.** Refer to back neckline. (You measured this from extended shoulder seam to CB.) This will be the back neckline length.

**3.** On a fresh sheet of paper, draw a vertical line near left-hand side. This will represent the center back (CB) line of your collar stand and collar.

**4.** Square a horizontal line along the middle of your paper. This line will establish a grid for you to build your collar pieces. We'll call this line the "horizontal guideline."

**5.** From CB line, measure to the right along horizontal guideline and mark a notch at back neckline length amount. This notch will align with the shoulder seam when sewing.

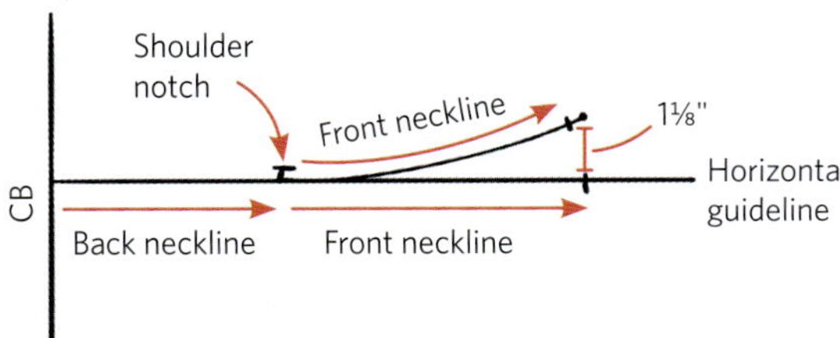


**6.** From this shoulder notch, measure to the right along horizontal guideline and make a tick mark at front neckline length amount. Now measure up from this tick mark 1⅛" (3 cm) and make a dot.

**7.** Connect shoulder notch to dot with a smooth, gradual, continuous curve.

**8.** From shoulder notch, measure along curve until you reach your front neckline length amount and place tick mark. This will be the end of your collar stand, where it aligns with your CF placket edge. You've now drafted the lower edge of your collar stand.

**9.** Square up ¼" (6 mm) from end-of-collar-stand tick mark, making your line perpendicular to the curve's contour in that spot.

**10.** Using gridded ruler, draw a line that is parallel to lower edge of collar stand but 1⅛" (3 cm) above it. This establishes your collar stand's upper edge.

**11.** Find where you squared up ¼" (6 mm) from end of lower curved line, and sketch a little rounded curve that connects into the upper curved line, as shown.

**12.** Measure half-placket-width amount (½" [1.3 cm] for me) in along lower curved line, and square up. Where squared line intersects with upper curved line, make a notch. This will be where your collar end aligns with collar stand at CF. Your collar stand draft is now complete.

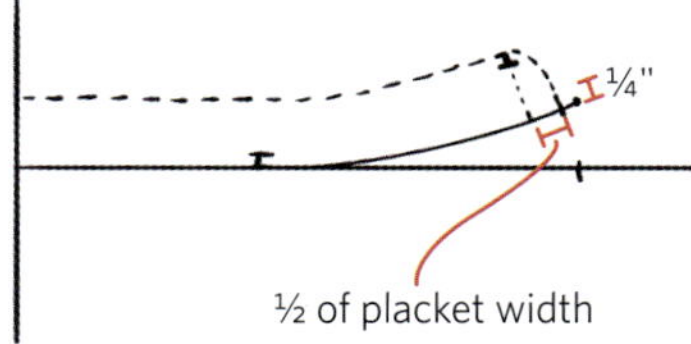


If you'd like your shirt to have only a stand collar, without an additional piece, you can stop drafting right here! Your collar draft is done.

## DRAFTING THE COLLAR

You'll draft the collar on top of the collar stand draft. Therefore, to avoid confusion, I'd recommend using a different pencil color for the following steps.

**1.** Beginning at the CB/upper curve intersection, trace along upper line for roughly one-third of its length. Then pause your line.

**2.** From collar stand's CF notch on upper edge, measure up ½" inch (1.3 cm) and make a dot.

**3.** Connect from paused line through dot with a smooth, gradual, continuous curve. This will be the upper edge of your collar, although the line's exact length isn't yet finalized.

**4.** Measure collar stand's upper edge from CB to CF notch—this is the length that your collar and collar stand should be joined. Write it down. From CB, measure along collar's upper edge line (from step 3) and make a tick mark at the measurement you just wrote down. This tick mark represents the endpoint of your collar's upper edge.

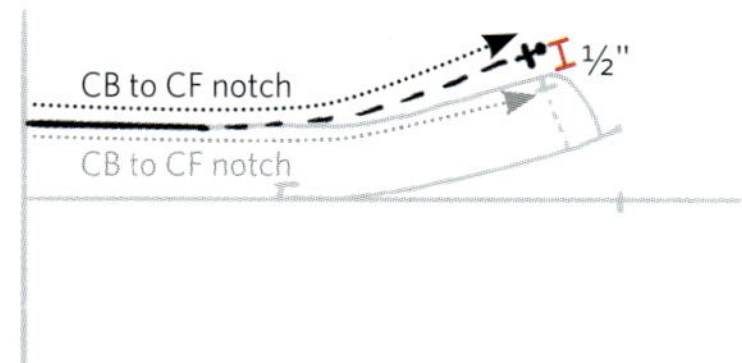


**5.** Find intersection of CB line and collar's upper line. Now measure down 1⅞" (4.8 cm) and square a 2" (5 cm)-long line to the right from center back. Then pause your line.

**6.** The rest of the collar draft is up to you—it's a matter of design. Consider how long you want your collar points to be, and the angle at which you'll want them to relate to CF. My collar points are 2⅞" (7.3 cm) long, but that's simply a design choice. Also, my collar points are pointed, but you can round them or make any other shape you'd enjoy.

**7.** If you'd like to "audition" your collar shape before stitching it up in fabric, you can trace this shape onto a fresh folded piece of paper, with fold aligned at draft's CB line, then cut out. Wrap around your neck as though wearing the shirt. Make note of any adjustments you'd like to make to the collar's shape or dimensions, then apply to the draft.

**8.** From CB line, measure along upper edge of collar stand draft for 4" (10.2 cm) and place notch. From CB line, measure along upper edge of collar draft for 4" (10.2 cm) and place another notch. These notches will align with each other when sewing.

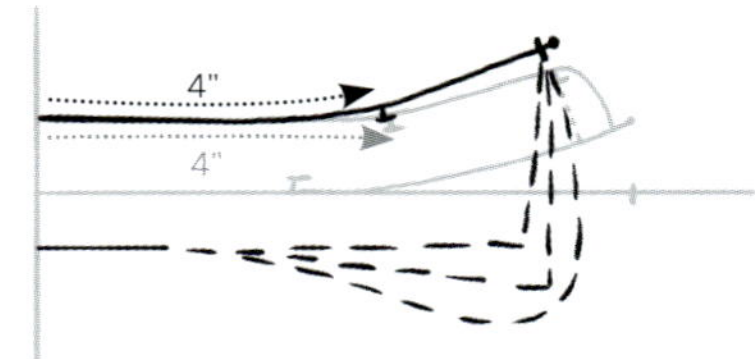


## TRACING THE COLLAR STAND PATTERN

**1.** Lay draft over a fresh sheet of folded paper, with fold aligned underneath draft's center back line. Trace around collar stand shape. Be sure to capture both notches along upper edge, as well as the notch on the lower edge. Remove draft. Pencil in lines clearly.

**2.** Next, add SAs. I'd recommend ¼" (6 mm) on all edges.

**3.** With paper still folded, add notches to upper and lower edges, ¼" (6 mm) from CB fold.

**4.** Pin layers. Cut out. Snip notches. Remove pins.

**5.** Place grainline perpendicular to CB line. Add note: "CUT 2 SELF. CUT 1 INTERFACING."

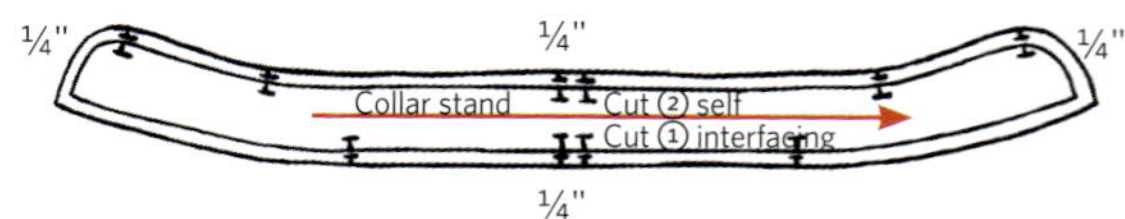

## TRACING THE UNDERCOLLAR PATTERN

**1.** Lay draft over a fresh sheet of folded paper, with fold aligned underneath draft's CB line. Trace around collar shape. Be sure to capture notch along upper edge. Remove draft. Pencil in lines.

**2.** Add a notch somewhere in the middle along the lower edge.

**3.** Next, add SAs. I'd recommend ¼" (6 mm) SAs on all edges.

**4.** Add notches to upper and lower edges, ¼" (6 mm) to each side of CB fold.

**5.** Pin layers. Cut out. Snip notches. Remove pins.

**6.** Place grainline perpendicular to CB line. Add note: "CUT 1 SELF."

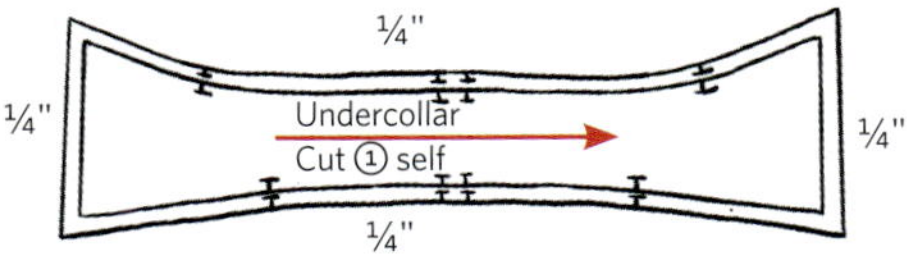


## TRACING THE OVERCOLLAR PATTERN

The pattern you just traced will serve as the lower layer of your collar. The collar will consist of two fabric layers, plus an interfacing layer. In order for their joining seam to roll naturally to the WS of the collar (thus neatening the final sewn appearance), you'll want to slightly bump out the outer edges of the overcollar pattern. Here's how:

**1.** Lay undercollar pattern over a fresh sheet of folded paper, with fold aligned underneath pattern's CB back line. Trace around collar's stitch line. Be sure to capture all notches. Remove draft.

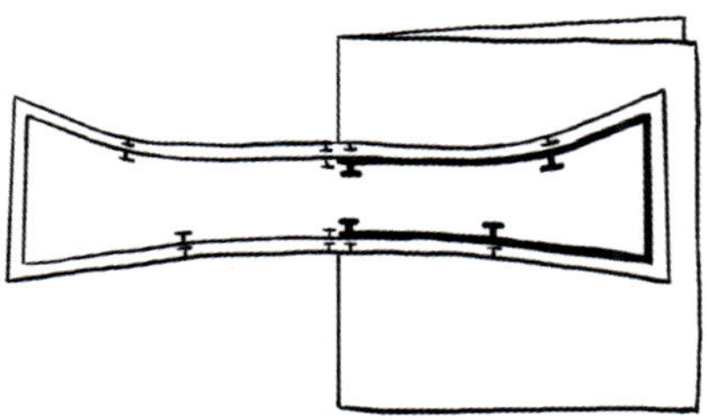

**2.** Pencil in lines.

**3.** Draft a parallel line that is ⅛" (3 mm) below lower edge of collar. Begin drafting parallel line that is ⅛" (3 mm) outside pointed area of collar but then blends to zero at top right corner of collar pattern, as shown. These lines will replace the lower and side lines, so you can erase or cross out the originals to avoid confusion.

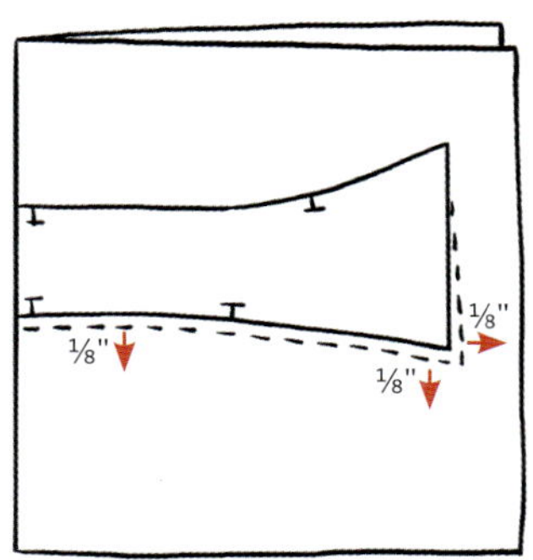


**4.** Next, add SAs. I'd recommend ¼" (6 mm) on all edges of overcollar outline you've just created.

**5.** Pin layers. Cut out. Snip notches. Remove pins.

**6.** Place grainline perpendicular to CB line. Add note: "CUT 1 SELF. CUT 1 INTERFACING."

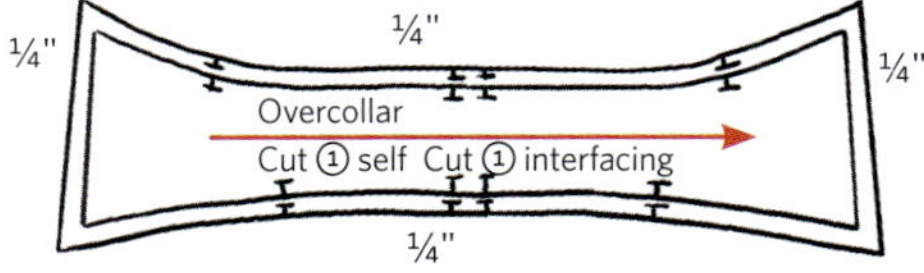

# Sewing

### HAND-SEWING STITCHES

- Basting
- Running stitch
- Whipstitch
- Hemstitch
- Even backstitch
- Combination stitch
- Spaced backstitch
- Buttonhole stitch
- Overcasting
- Bartack
- Depending on techniques chosen, you may also need fell stitch

### FABRIC OPTIONS

This button-up shirt can be sewn in any light- to midweight woven fabric. Depending on fiber and weave, you can create dramatically different looks. Try a dense cotton flannel for a cozy shirt. A drapey Tencel chambray might produce a chic top, while a crisp shirting would look more professional and a slubby silk could be party-ready. Some of my favorite fiber options are cotton, linen, hemp, and Tencel; you might also consider wool or silk. A plain weave is perfect; twill is lovely; satin weave or waffle weave would be delicious; a jacquard weave might offer a wonderful texture. Try solids, plaids, stripes, prints, tie-dye—whatever tickles your interest! You can't go wrong.

### OTHER MATERIALS NEEDED

You will need interfacing for the sleeve cuffs and collar pieces, and perhaps for the sleeve plackets and CF plackets as well. I prefer sew-in woven interfacing over the fusible variety, but feel free to use whatever you like. If you're feeling experimental, you can forgo store-bought interfacing and instead use cotton canvas or some other thick, dense, structured fabric from your stash.

You will also need a set of buttons for your CF placket and sleeve plackets. The size and quantity are up to you. The buttons should fit nicely onto your placket width—I usually prefer my buttons' diameter to be no more than half as wide as the placket.

### CUTTING THE FABRIC

See Cutting Fabric on page 85 for tips on cutting. You'll need to cut the following pieces and quantities:

- Front torso × 2 self
- Back torso × 1 self
- Back yoke × 2 self
- Sleeve × 2 self
- Sleeve cuff × 2 self, × 2 interfacing
- Sleeve placket × 2 self, (optional) × 2 interfacing
- Collar stand × 2 self, × 1 interfacing
- Undercollar × 1 self
- Overcollar × 1 self, × 1 interfacing
- Optional: CF placket × 2 interfacing (see notes below)
- Optional: chest pocket × 1 or × 2 self (save some self fabric for later—you'll devise the pattern and cut and sew these after the shirt is complete so that you can audition the dimensions and placement on the finished garment)

- Optional: scraps of self fabric for 1 or 2 locker loops (each locker loop needs roughly 1⅛" [3 cm] by 4" [10.2 cm] of self fabric)

Transfer sleeve placket slit drill hole marks onto sleeves and sleeve plackets.

If you'd like to add interfacing to the CF placket, measure the length of your front torso pattern's CF placket, including seam and hem allowance. Also make note of your finished placket width (in my case, 1" [2.5 cm]). Cut two strips of interfacing to these dimensions (placket length by placket width).

### STAYSTITCHING

It's a good idea to staystitch the necklines and armholes of your torso and yoke pieces to prevent their bias-cut raw edges from getting stretched out during handling. See page 104 in the woven boxy top project for details on how to staystitch. I'd recommend creating secure lines of running stitch within the SAs of the following:

- Front torso pieces: necklines, armholes
- Back torso piece: armholes
- Back yoke pieces: necklines

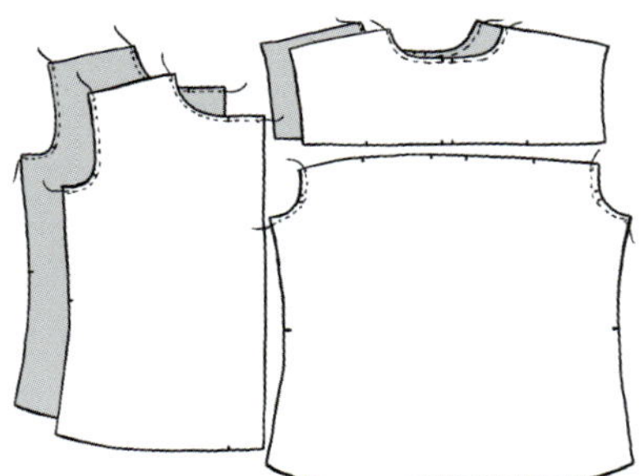

### APPLYING INTERFACINGS

You'll want to apply your interfacings before beginning to construct the shirt. If using fusible interfacing, apply using your iron. If using sew-in interfacing, apply by basting through all layers around the interfacing pieces' perimeters.

- Sleeve cuffs: interface WS of one-half of each cuff piece
- Sleeve plackets: interface WS of each placket piece, then re-mark drill holes
- Collar stand: interface WS of one of the stand pieces
- Overcollar: interface WS
- CF plackets: interface WS of front edges

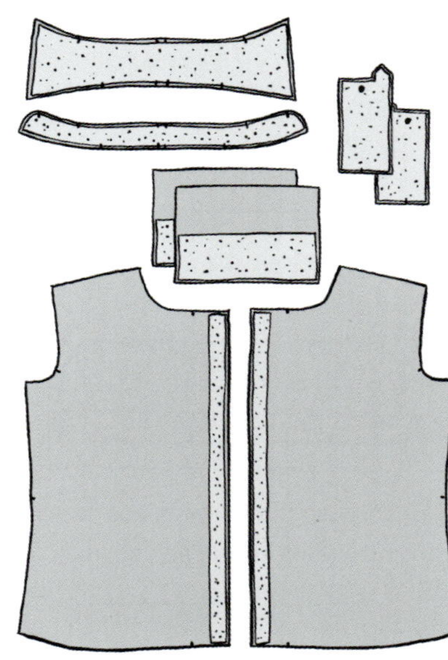

### SEWING LOCKER LOOP(S)

You have the option to sew a locker loop or two for this shirt. One can be sewn to the inside at the center back neck where the collar stand attaches to the shirt. The other can be stitched to the outside at the back torso's box pleat. For each, you'll need to cut a rectangle of roughly 1⅛" (3 cm) by 4" (10.2 cm) from your self fabric. Then follow the directions here.

1. Press long edges under by ¼" (6 mm).

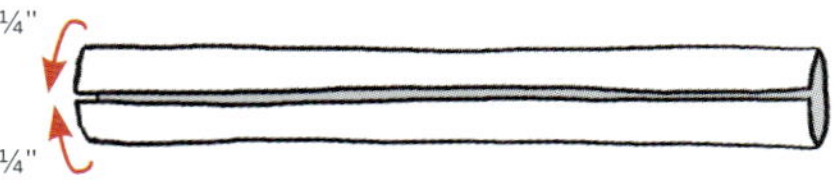


2. Fold in half, WST, so that WS are concealed. Pin.

3. Use whipstitch or another stitch of choice to join folded edges.

4. Optional: Whipstitch along other long edge for a balanced aesthetic.

### SEWING CENTER FRONT PLACKETS

**1.** On each front torso piece, fold placket's width under (to WS) and press. (For example, if your pattern features a 1" [2.5 cm] placket, fold 1" [2.5 cm] under.)

**2.** Repeat, folding under your placket's width again. Press. Pin or baste.

**3.** Use hemstitch or other stitch of choice to secure edge down. When selecting a stitch, consider how both sides of the stitch will look on the finished garment. For example, if you're facing the inside of the garment while sewing, consider that the backside of your stitches will be facing out when you wear the shirt.

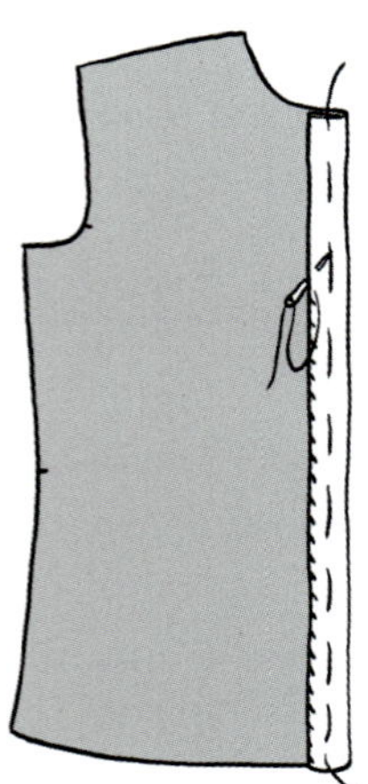

**4.** Optional: Use same stitch to edgestitch on or near outer folded edge of plackets for a balanced aesthetic. If you used sew-in interfacing to reinforce the plackets, this will also help secure the interfacing's other edge.

### CONSTRUCTING THE SLEEVE CUFFS

**1.** For each cuff piece, fold under and baste the ½" (1.3 cm) SA on the long interfaced edge.

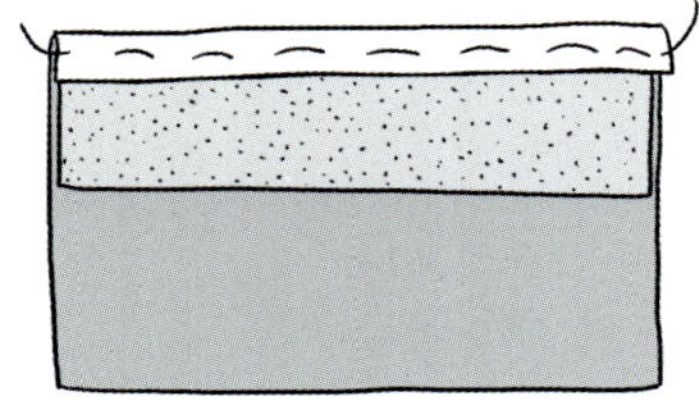

**2.** Fold cuff pieces backward (so that RSs are facing) and pin or baste short ends.

**3.** Using ½" (1.3 cm) SAs, stitch through all layers to close short ends. You can use small running stitches, even backstitch, or combination stitch.

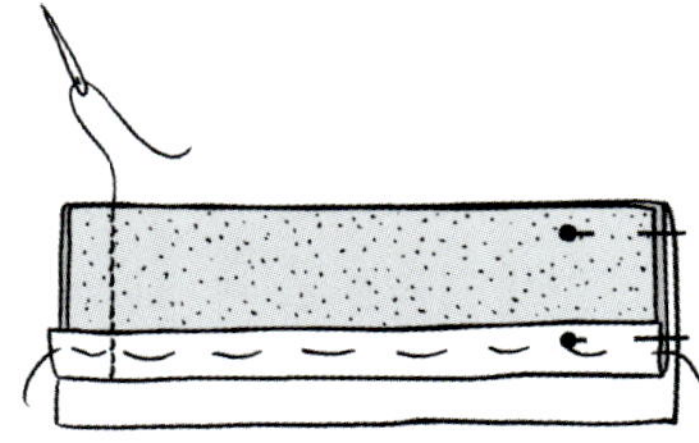

**4.** Snip corner triangles to reduce bulk.

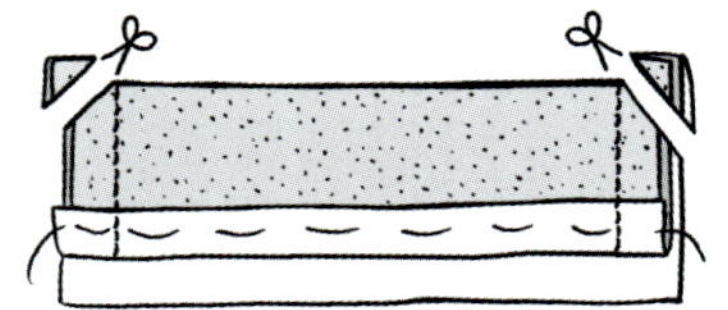

**5.** Turn, push out corners, and press. Do not remove long edge's basting.

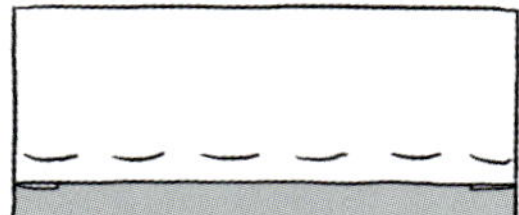

### CONSTRUCTING THE COLLAR

**1.** With RST, pin overcollar and undercollar pieces together, aligning outer and side edges. Skip the edge that will be seamed to the collar stand. To align the outer and side edges, you'll need to do a bit of easing and stretching as you pin, because the overcollar's edges are slightly longer than the undercollar's.

**2.** Using ¼" (6-mm) SA, seam together the side and outer edges using small even backstitches or small running stitches.

**3.** Snip corner triangles and clip curved areas to reduce bulk.

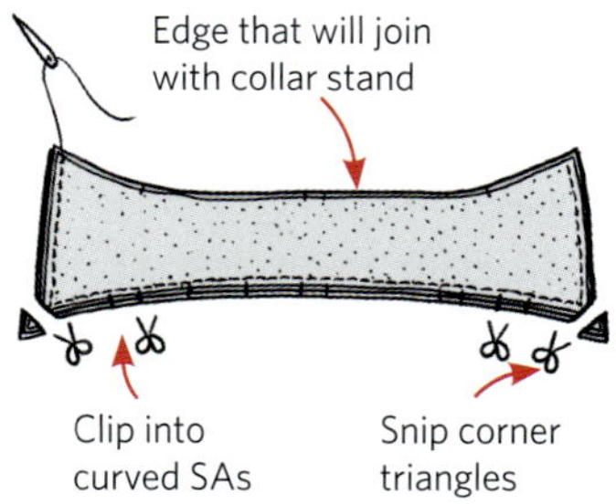


**4.** Finger-press SAs open, then turn. Push corners out carefully. Align the remaining raw edges and pin. Baste layers together.

**5.** Press seamed edges with iron. Notice that the seam will roll slightly to the undercollar side—this is intentional and will hide the seam when you're wearing the shirt.

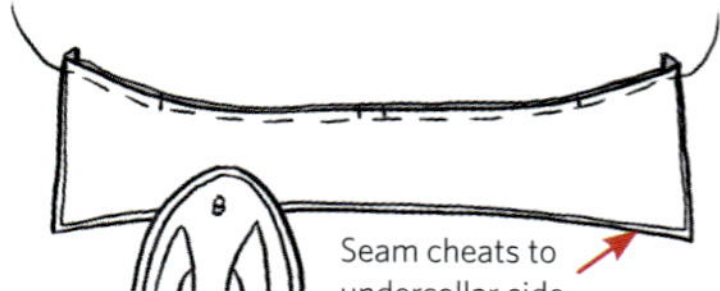

**6.** Facing the overcollar, topstitch edges using attractive stitch of choice—you might consider stabstitch-type running stitches, whipstitch, or spaced backstitch. Do not remove basting.

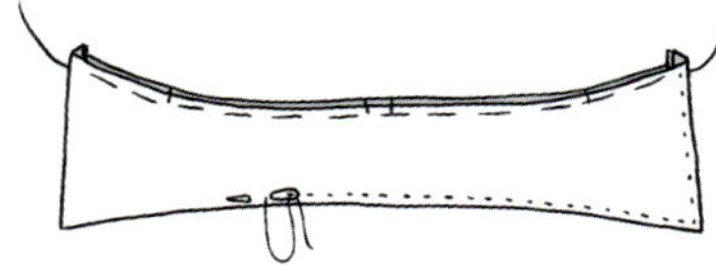

## JOINING THE COLLAR TO THE STAND

**1.** Fold under and baste SA on the lower edge of interfaced collar stand piece.

**2.** Place collar stand pieces RST. Slip collar between them, with overcollar side facing the uninterfaced collar stand piece. Align all notches. Note that the collar's ends should align with the stand's outermost notches. Pin.

**3.** Using ¼" (6 mm) SA, stitch along entire outer edge of collar stand through all layers, using small running stitches, even backstitch, or combination stitch.

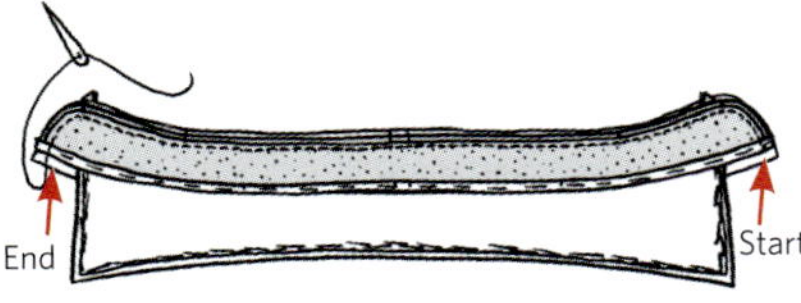


**4.** Clip to reduce bulk, finger-press SAs, and turn RS out. Press with iron.

**5.** Facing the overcollar, topstitch upper and side edges of collar stand. Use attractive stitch of choice—you might consider stabstitch-type running stitch, whipstitch, or spaced backstitch. Ideally, the stitches will look tidy on both sides of the collar stand, so I like to use stabstitch-type running stitches here that are inserted at a 45-degree angle to the fabric's surface so they look like tiny dots on both sides of the work.

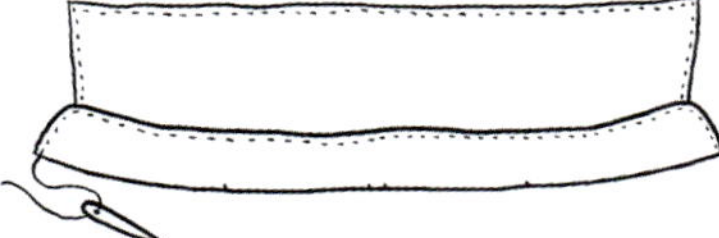

## SEWING THE SLEEVE PLACKETS

**1.** Mark stitch line onto WS of each placket piece. First, draw a straight line to connect notch and drill hole. This line represents the slit you'll cut later.

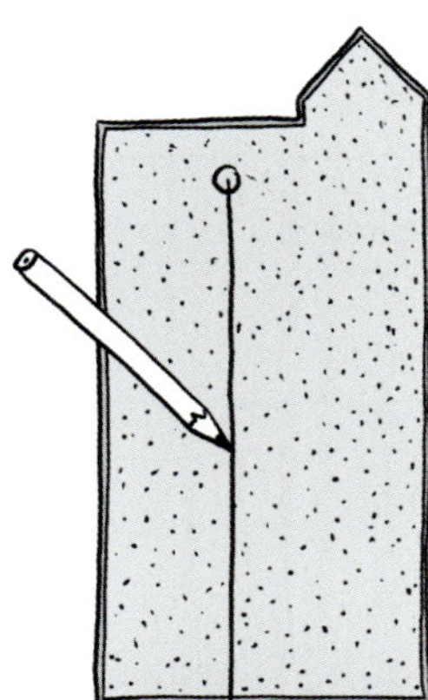

**2.** Draw lines ¼" (6 mm) to each side of the first line. Connect all three lines across the top, forming a boxy upside-down U shape. These outer lines will be your stitch lines.

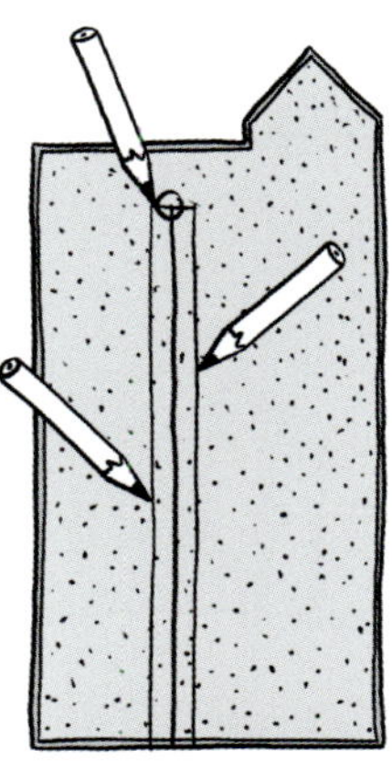

**3.** Place each placket face down onto the WS of each sleeve piece. (Both plackets and sleeves should have RSs facing down.) The plackets' towerlike sides should be oriented toward the sleeves' center lines. If this is not possible with all RSs facing down, then you probably have the wrong plackets on the wrong sleeves—switch them to the other sleeves, and you should be all set.

**4.** Align plackets' marked drill holes and slit notches with drill holes and notches on sleeves. Pin.

**5.** Stitch around each placket's marked stitch line box using tiny running stitches. Stitches should be especially small going around the corners.

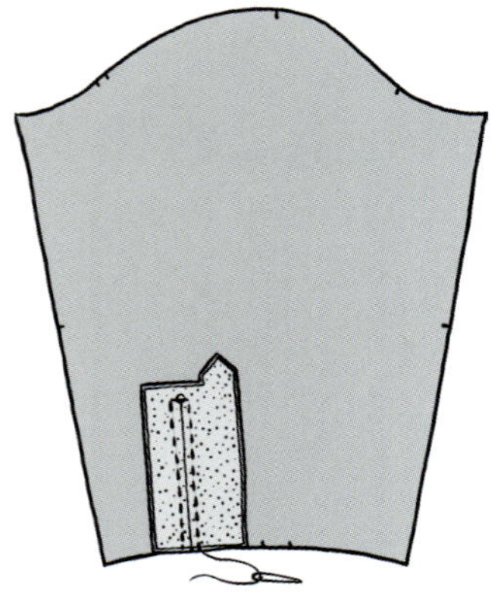

**6.** Cut up the center line, stopping approximately ⅜" (1 cm) before your top stitch line. Then cut two forking lines that reach almost to the corners of your stitch line, forming a Y-shaped cut.

**7.** Make a ¼" (6 mm) horizontal snip where tower connects to the rest of the placket.

**8.** Fold and press ¼" (6 mm) on sides of placket, as well as short side of tower and angled top of tower. (Do not fold top edge of main placket yet.)

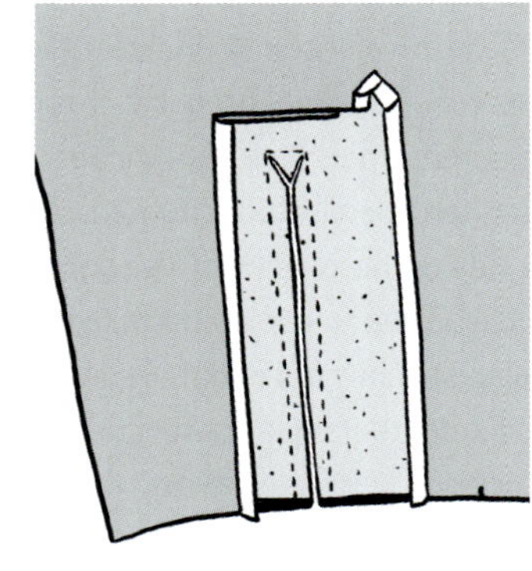

**9.** Press loose placket sides, one by one, toward slit's SAs.

**10.** Turn through and flip to RS of sleeves.

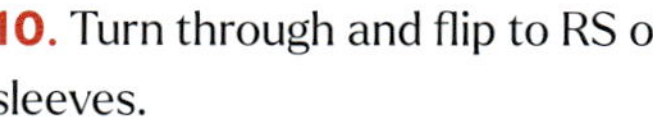

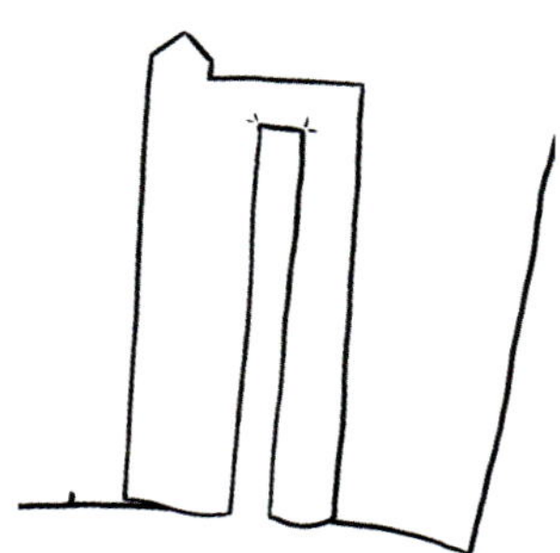

**11.** On non-tower side, align folded edge so that it just barely covers stitch line. Press, pin, and then stitch down with whipstitch or even backstitch.

**12.** On tower side, align folded edge so that it just barely covers stitch line. Press and pin. Stitch down, using the topstitching option of your choice (tidy running stitches, spaced backstitch, etc.). Your line of stitching should begin at the sleeve cuff edge, work up toward and round the pointed top of the tower, and stop at the slit end level.

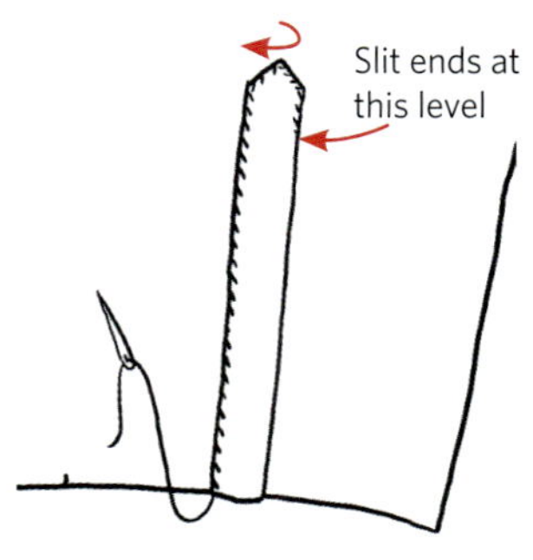

**13.** Stitch a horizontal line just past the top of slit area, through all layers, to hide away all remaining raw edges. You can use the stitch of your choice here. Optionally, you can also stitch a boxed X shape for added reinforcement and style.

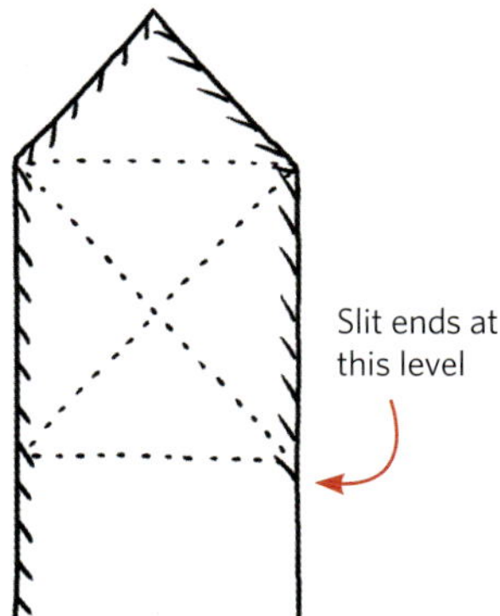


**14.** Press.

## BASTING THE BACK PLEAT

**1.** Fold back torso panel in half, WST, and align pleat notches. Baste a line perpendicular to top edge, beginning at pleat notches and sewing down approximately 2" (5 cm).

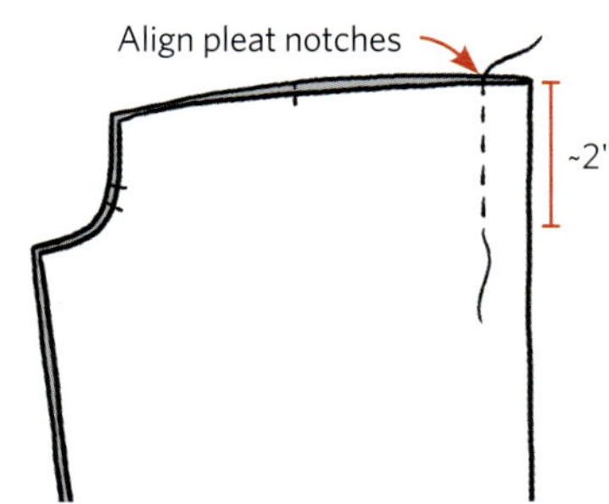


**2.** Open and press, arranging pleated fabric to form a centered box pleat.

**3.** Baste through all layers to secure pleat.

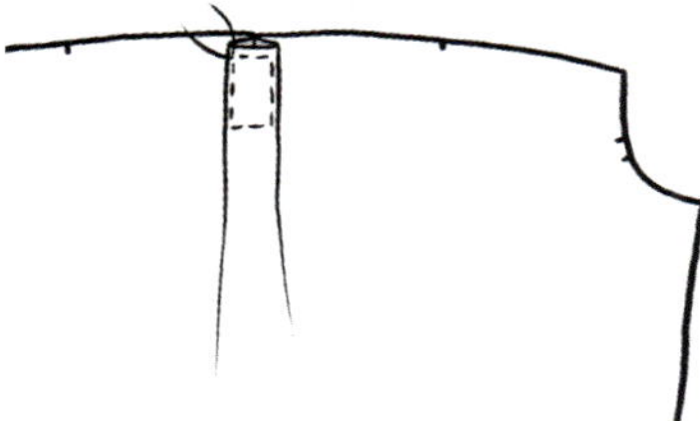

**4.** Optional: Pin and then baste locker loop over box pleat, with locker loop ends aligned with SAs (or even dangling beyond them, if you want a shorter locker loop). Exact length and arrangement of locker loop is up to your design eye. Baste thoroughly to avoid shifting.

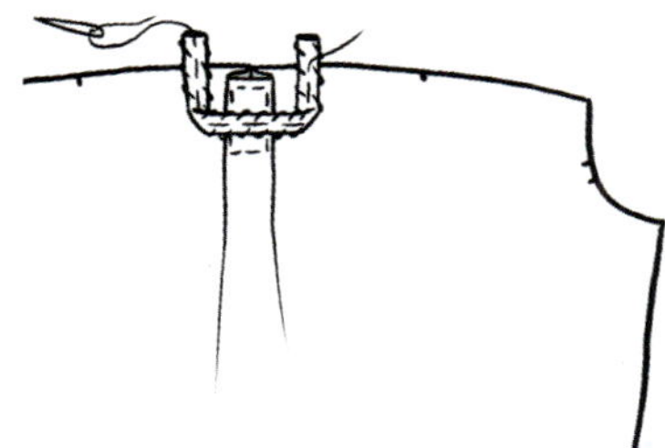

## JOINING THE YOKE TO THE BACK

**1.** Arrange yoke pieces on top of each other, with RST.

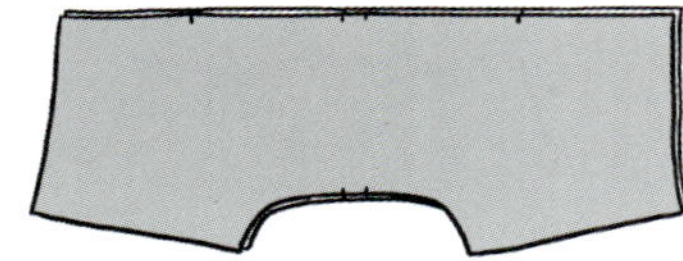

**2.** Slip back panel between yoke layers (back panel can be RS up or down—it doesn't matter), aligning all notches along yoke seam. Pin.

**3.** With ½" (1.3 cm) SA, stitch through all layers to join, using stitch of choice (combination stitch, even backstitch, or tiny running stitches).

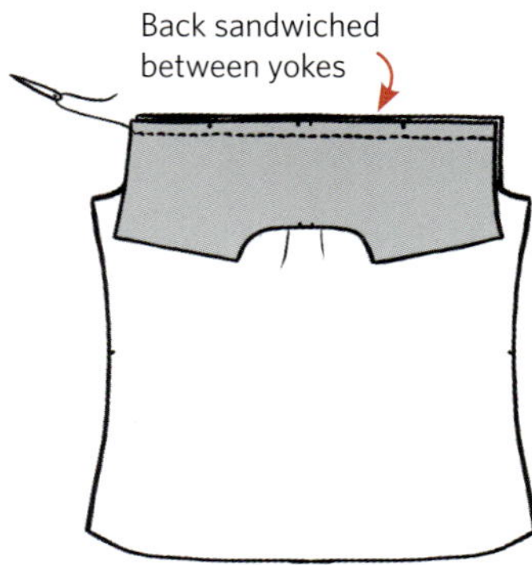


**4.** Clip corner triangles to reduce bulk.

**5.** Open out and press. (For cleanest results, press on garment's RS first, then WS.) Remove pleat and locker loop basting.

**6.** Facing RS of garment, topstitch using stitch of choice (even backstitch, spaced backstitch, and running stitch are good options).

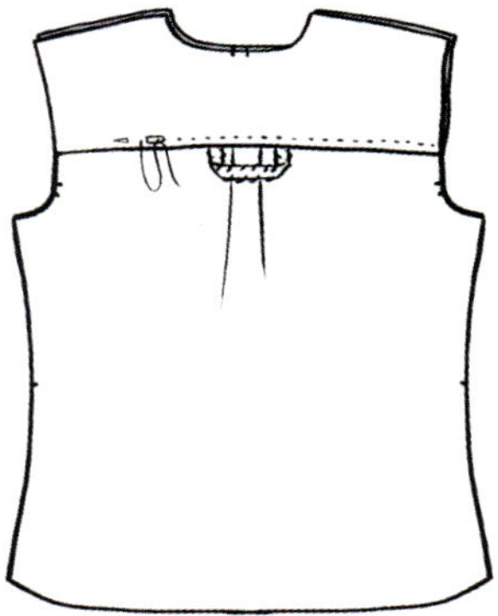

### SEWING THE SHOULDER SEAMS

**1.** Place back body on table with RS facing up. Arrange front torso pieces on top, with RSs facing down toward back. Align shoulder seams and pin fronts to top layer of back yoke along shoulders.

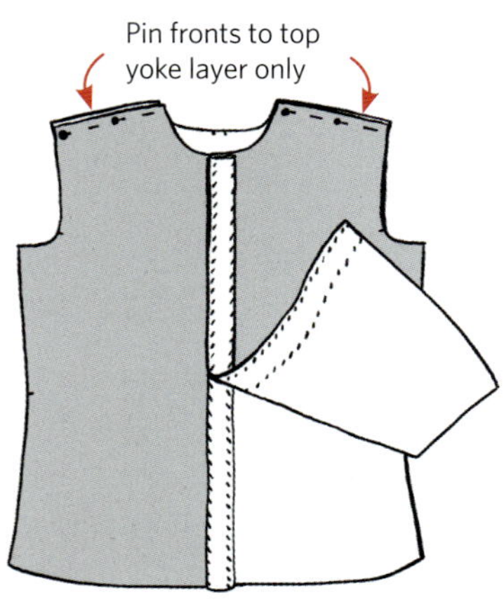


**2.** Roll body pieces up tightly, leaving lower layer of back yoke unrolled. Pull lower layer of back yoke down as shown.

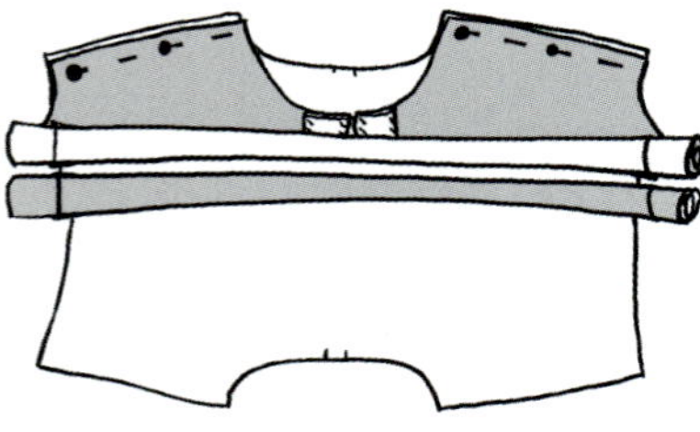

**3.** Pull lower layer of back yoke up and around on top of rolled parts, so that its shoulder edges align with the pinned shoulders. Repin to secure all layers together.

**4.** Sew shoulder seams using even backstitch or combination stitch, with ½" (1.3 cm) SAs.

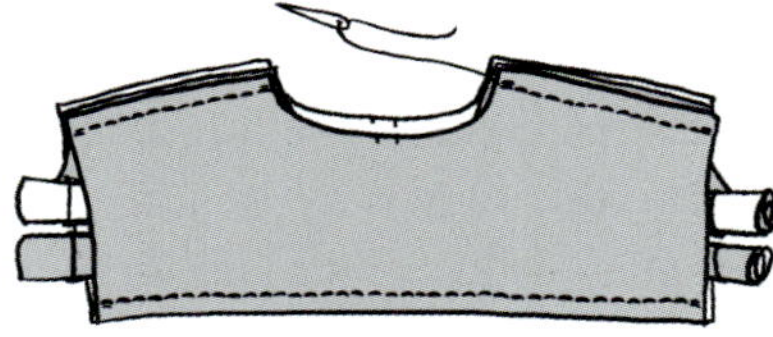

**5.** Clip corner triangles to reduce bulk.

**6.** Turn through (exciting!) and notice that all SAs are now concealed inside the back yoke's layers, leaving a clean appearance. Press crisply.

**7.** Facing RS of garment, topstitch using stitch of choice (even backstitch, spaced backstitch, and running stitch are good options).

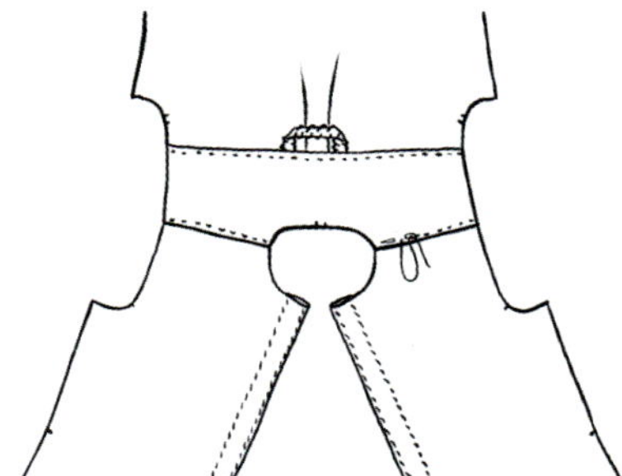

### ATTACHING THE COLLAR

**1.** Optional: Pin and then baste locker loop onto inner garment neckline at center back, with locker loop ends aligned with SAs (or even dangling beyond them, if you want a shorter locker loop). Exact length and arrangement of locker loop is up to your design eye. Baste thoroughly to avoid shifting.

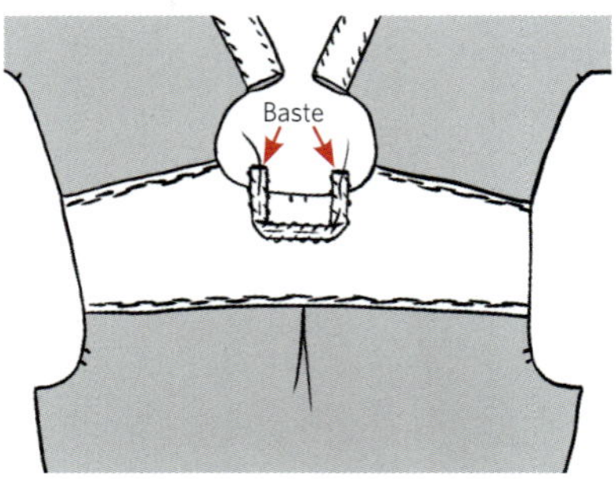


**2.** Locate unbasted edge of collar stand. Pin this edge, RS down, onto WS of garment's neckline. Align all notches and edges.

**3.** With ¼" (6 mm) SAs, sew together through all layers (except basted collar stand layer) to join. Use combination stitch, even backstitch, or tiny running stitches.

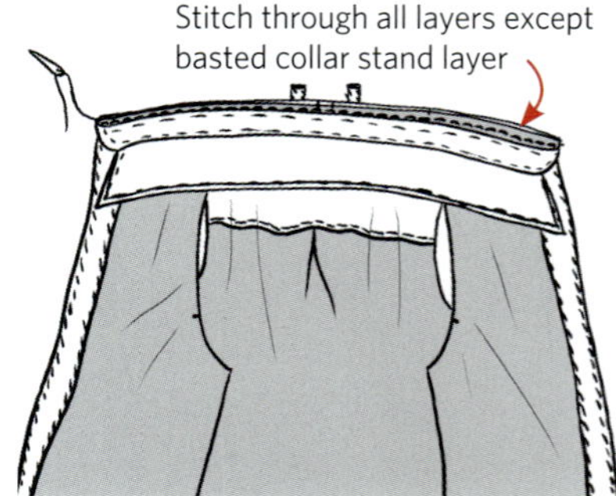

**4.** Press collar stand up away from garment.

**5.** Pull basted edge down over SAs and align basted edge so that it just barely covers stitch line. Pin. The SAs should now be entirely concealed.

**6.** Secure edge down using whipstitch, fell stitch, or hemstitch. Remove basting.

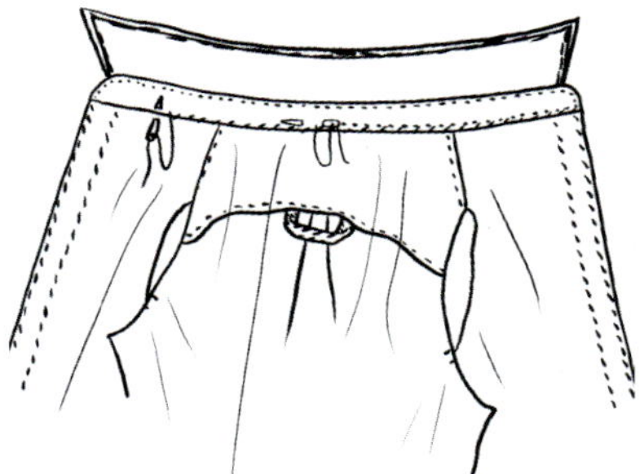

**7.** Optional: Topstitch seam using stitch of choice (even backstitch, spaced backstitch, and stabstitch-type running stitch are all good options).

**8.** Press.

## ATTACHING THE SLEEVES

**1.** Pin each sleeve to armhole, RST, matching notches (front, back, and shoulder seam). If single and double notches don't match up, you're probably pinning the sleeves into the wrong armholes, so switch sleeves. Carefully distribute cap ease by using lots of pins.

**2.** Facing the sleeve, use neat, smallish even backstitches to sew seam, with ¾" (2 cm) SAs.

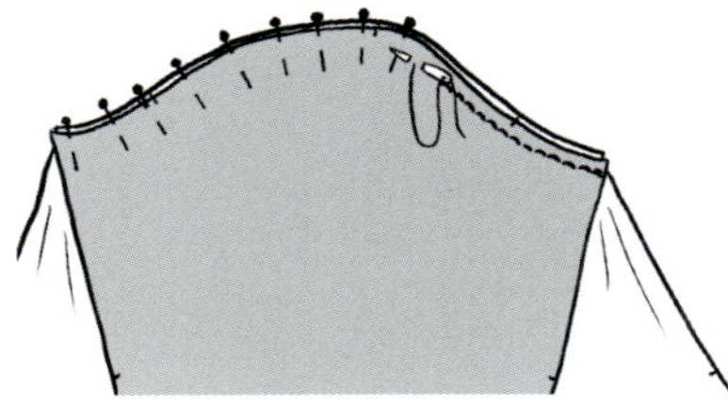

**3.** Trim half of armhole's SA (don't trim sleeve SA), leaving little tabs at shoulder and yoke seams so that you avoid slicing through those seams' stitch lines.

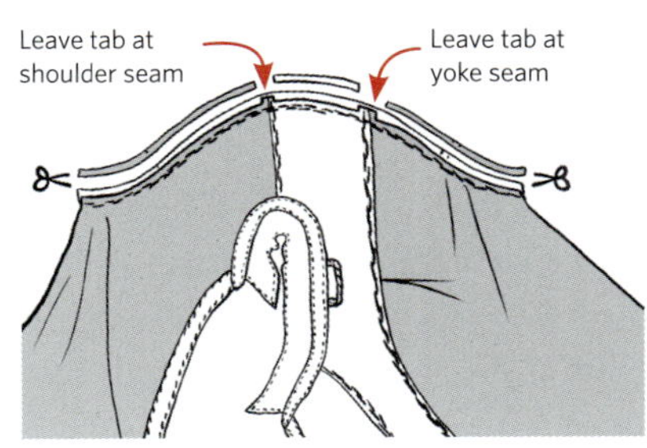


**4.** Fold and press under sleeve SA so that it completely encases the trimmed armhole SA. Smoosh down the seam tabs you cut, concealing them as well. Pin and/or baste.

**5.** Fell down this folded SA onto the garment, using stitch of choice (hemstitch, whipstitch, and fell stitch are all good options). Press.

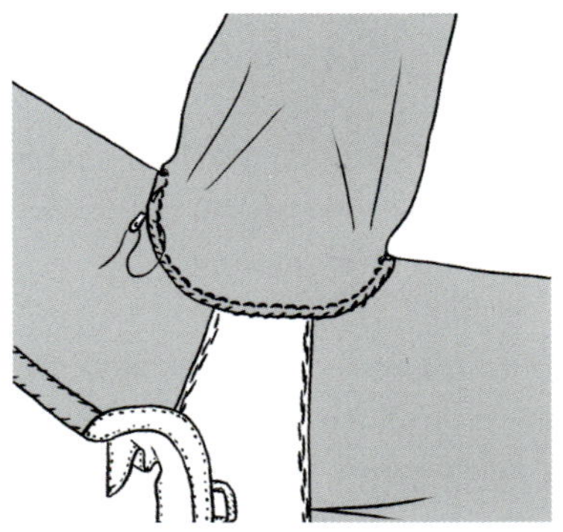

## SEWING SIDE SEAMS AND SLEEVE INSEAMS

**1.** Fold garment, RST, so that side seams and sleeve inseams are aligned. Pin, matching all notches and edges. Be particularly careful to align underarm points, so that they intersect cleanly when sewn.

**2.** Facing the front torso, stitch seam using even backstitch, combination stitch, or tiny running stitches. SAs should be ¾" (2 cm).

**3.** As you did for the armholes, you'll now fell the SAs. Press SAs toward back. Trim half of SA's under layer, leaving a little tab at underarm seam so that you avoid slicing through that seam's stitch lines. To reduce bulk, cut tab in half by cutting between structural seam stitch line and felling stitch line. Don't slice through any stitches; just cut the fabric in two.

**4.** Fold and press under top SA layer so that it completely encases the trimmed lower allowance. Smoosh down the seam tabs that you cut, concealing them as well. Pin and/or baste.

**5.** Fell down this folded SA onto the garment, using stitch of choice (hemstitch, whipstitch, and fell stitch are all good options).

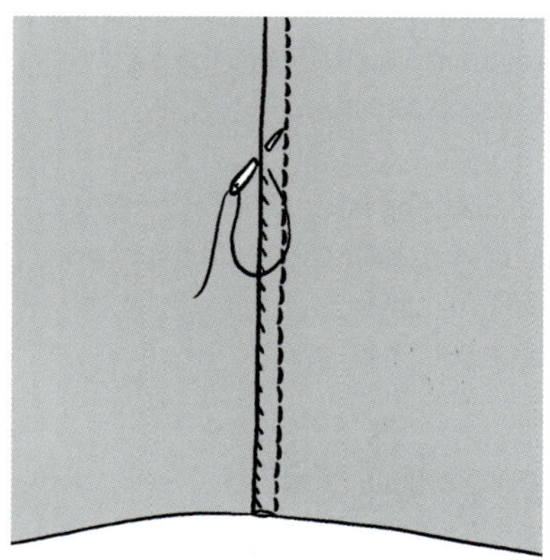

**6.** Press.

### ATTACHING THE CUFFS

**1.** With sleeves RS out, use pleat notches as guides to fold each pleat toward the placket. Baste carefully through all layers to secure pleats.

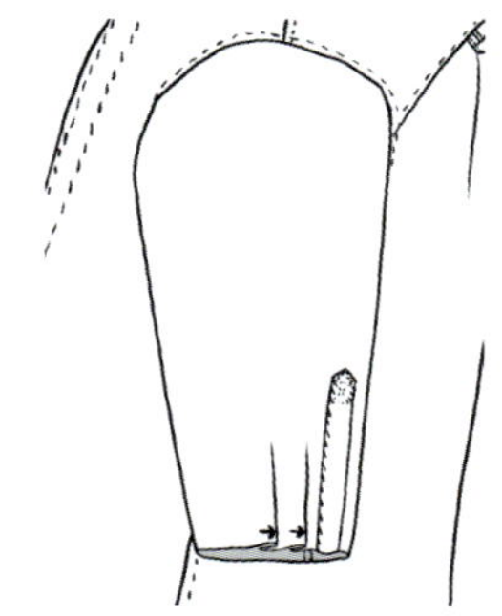

**2.** Locate unbasted edge of each cuff. Pin this edge, RS down, onto WS of sleeve edge.

**3.** Using ½" (1.3 cm) SA, sew together through all layers (except basted cuff layer) to join, using combination stitch, even backstitch, or tiny running stitches.

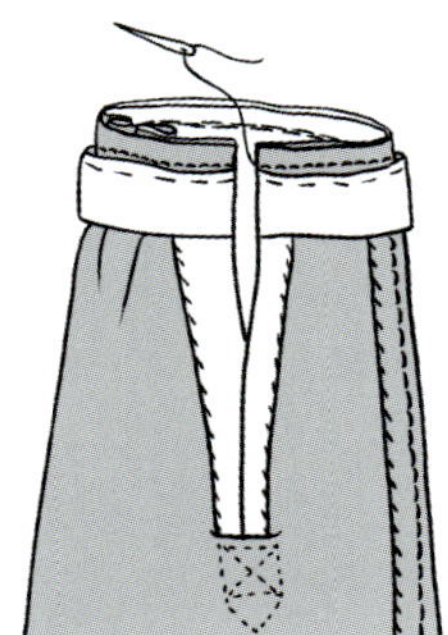

**4.** Press cuffs out away from garment. Pull basted edge down over SAs, and align basted edge so that it just barely covers stitch line. Pin. The SAs should now be entirely concealed.

**5.** Secure edge down using whipstitch, fell stitch, or hemstitch. Remove basting.

**6.** Topstitch around entire cuff's perimeter, using stitch of choice (even backstitch, spaced backstitch, and stabstitch-type running stitch are all good options). Press.

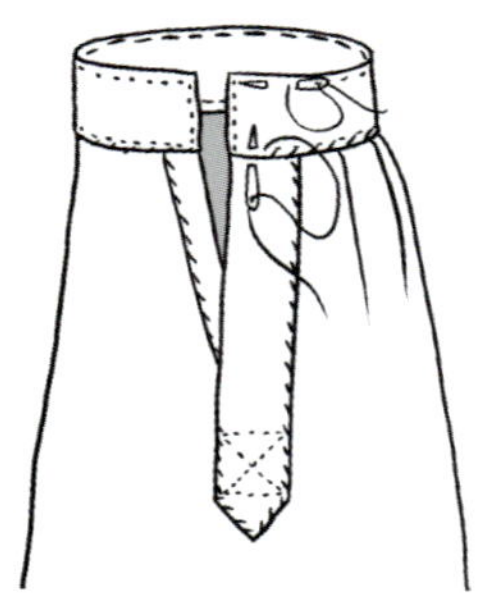

### HEMMING

**1.** Turn and press bottom hem under by ¼" (6 mm). Then press under by another ¼" (6 mm).

**2.** Pin and/or baste.

**3.** Secure edge down using whipstitch, fell stitch, hemstitch, or other hemming option of choice.

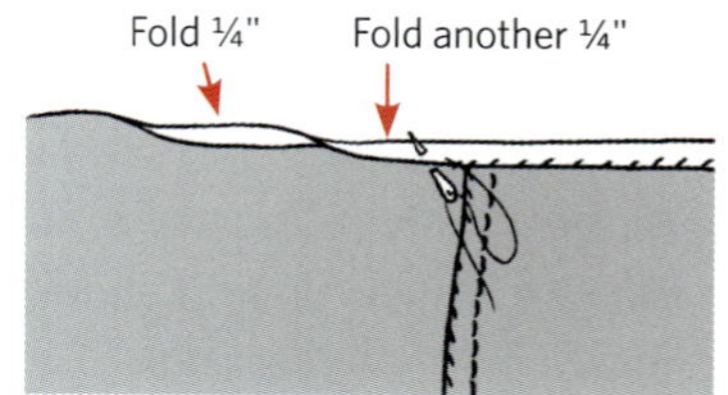


**4.** Press.

### MARKING AND SEWING BUTTONHOLES

**1.** First, stitch up one or more test buttonholes. To do so:

**A.** Take a scrap of self fabric and fold twice to create a three-layer mock-up placket. Baste fold down to hold.

**B.** Mark a slit that is the same length as your button's diameter. Baste a little box around this slit to hold all layers together.

**C.** Use a chisel or small, very sharp scissors to carefully cut slit.

**D.** Cut a length of the thread you plan to use for your buttonholes. (This need not match the thread you used for garment construction—I usually use something thicker and stronger.)

**E.** Use buttonhole stitches to bind edges of slit. I like to fan my stitches around the ends, but you can create whatever style buttonhole you'd prefer. Spacing of stitches is at your discretion—experiment here and see what you like.

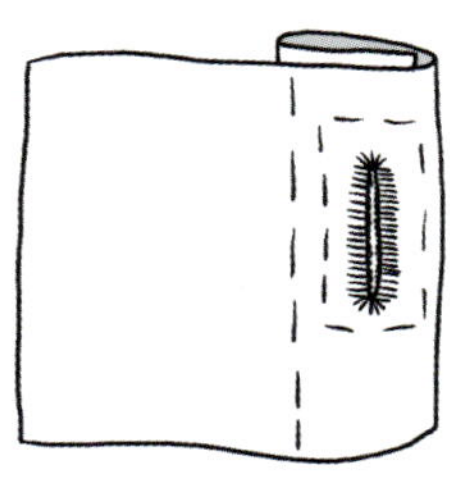

**F.** Test size of buttonhole to make sure button will fit through appropriately.

**G.** Repeat above steps as needed until you feel confident sewing buttonholes with this fabric, thread, and needle.

**2.** Mark buttonhole onto collar stand. The buttonhole should be the length you determined in previous step. To find its placement, determine CF (half of your placket width distance in from the edge), then move toward the edge by ⅛" (3 mm). The slit should run roughly parallel to the neckline seam. (For example, if my placket is 1" [2.5 cm] wide, I'd divide that number in half and then subtract ⅛" [3 mm] to determine that the buttonhole should begin ⅜" [1 cm] from the edge.)

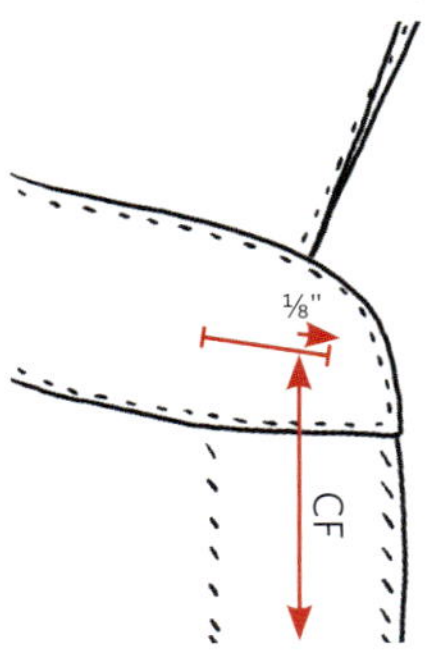


**3.** Pin garment closed, starting a little below the collar area and working down, and aligning plackets on top of each other. Try on garment. Mark where bust's widest point is. This level is an important placement for a buttonhole, so that you won't get gaping. Unpin and remove garment and lay flat again.

**4.** Use physical buttons to "audition" quantity and spacing of placket buttons. Be sure to place a button at the bust level you marked, and another at the collar stand where you marked the first buttonhole. Add more buttons to test how many more you'd like to include. Once you've determined where the other buttons should go, mark all buttonholes. A ruler will help you achieve even spacing. Be sure to mark a buttonhole on each sleeve cuff, too—I like to center the buttonhole along the cuff's height, and then for placement from the cuff's short end, I use a distance that is ⅛" (3 mm) shorter than my button's diameter. (For example, if my button is ½" [1.3 cm] in diameter, I place the end of the buttonhole ⅜" [1 cm] from the cuff's short end.)

5. Baste through all layers around perimeter of each buttonhole placement. The basted box should be at least ¼" (6 mm) away from slit on all sides.

6. Use chisel or small, sharp scissors to cut each buttonhole slit.

7. Stitch all buttonholes. Remove all basting.

## ATTACHING THE BUTTONS

1. Pin garment closed again, this time all the way from collar stand to bottom hem. Align plackets on top of each other as you go. Pin sleeve cuffs closed, too.

2. Use pencil to push through each buttonhole and mark a button placement on the lower placket. Button placements should be centered in each buttonhole except the collar stand button—that one should be half your placket's width in from the edge (directly over CF). For sleeve cuffs, try on shirt and pin cuffs closed to the dimension that you like. Then push pencil through buttonholes to mark cuff button placements.

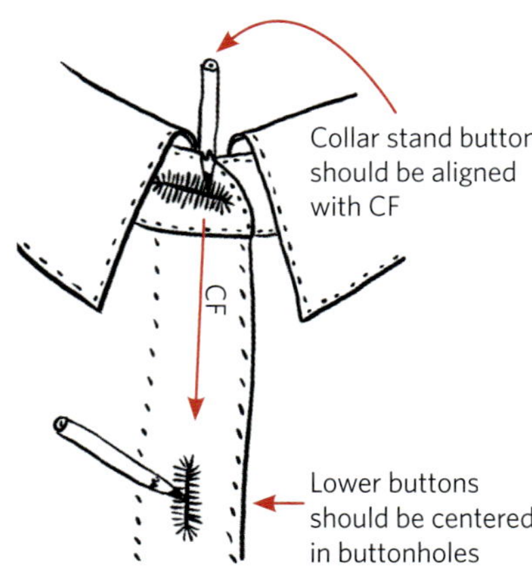


3. Remove pins and eyeball pencil markings. Adjust as needed to make uniform and tidy.

4. For each button:

A. Thread needle, then double thread, knotting ends together. Trim tails to approximately ⅛" (3 mm).

B. Take tiny stitch on RS of garment, exactly at point where button should attach. Take one more in the same place to securely anchor.

C. Stitch up and down through button and all layers, leaving a bit of space between button and garment. (This space will allow for the thickness of the buttonhole placket.) Repeat, stitching up and down several times and always leaving that same space.

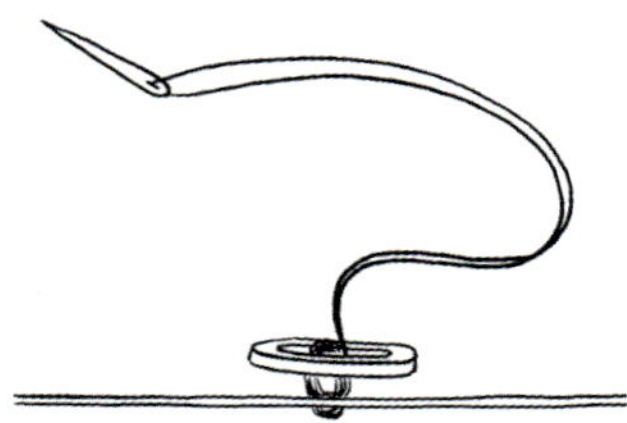

D. Bring needle between button and garment, and wrap thread three to five times around the stitches you've taken, creating a thread shank for your button.

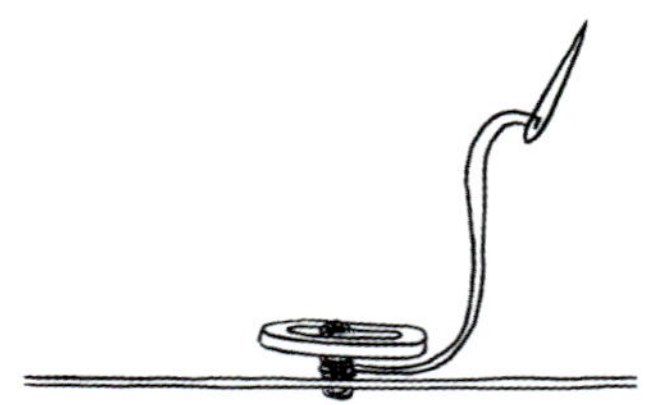

E. Sink needle to WS of garment and take two tiny stitches in place to anchor. Then burrow thread between layers of button placket, emerging at least ⅝" (1.6 cm) away. Snip thread flush with fabric.

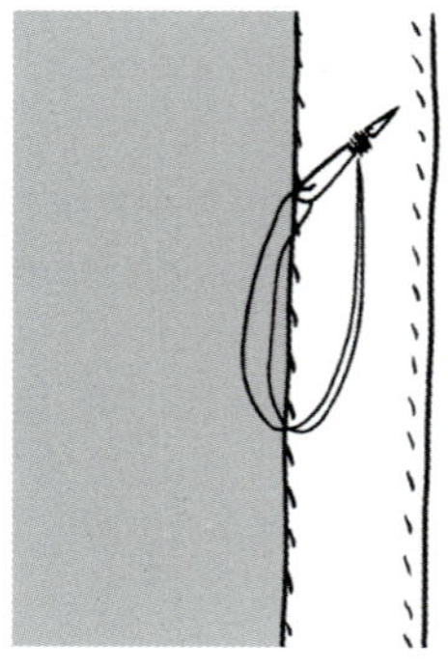

### AUDITIONING AND SEWING CHEST POCKET(S)

**1.** On a piece of scrap paper, draft a rectangle or other pocket shape to a size and proportion that you think you might like for your pocket(s). Don't add seam or hem allowances. Cut out.

**2.** Wearing the shirt, stand in front of a mirror and hold the mock-up paper pocket in the position where you think you might like your pocket to be. Place a couple of pins to hold. Stand back and assess.

**3.** Once you've determined a good placement, insert pins carefully into garment at top corner points, then remove paper without removing placement pins. Take off shirt and lay it flat on table.

**4.** Make any adjustments needed to pattern shape and size. Use a ruler to check placement pins in relation to center front edge, and adjust if needed or desired. (You may wish to square them in relation to the edge.) If you will be adding symmetrical pockets to both sides, measure and place two more pins in equivalent points on the other side.

**5.** Trace pocket pattern onto fresh sheet of paper.

**6.** Next, add SAs. I'd recommend:

- 1" (2.5 cm) on top edge
- ⅜" (1 cm) on all other edges

**7.** Place grainline perpendicular to top edge. Add note: "CUT 1 [OR 2] SELF."

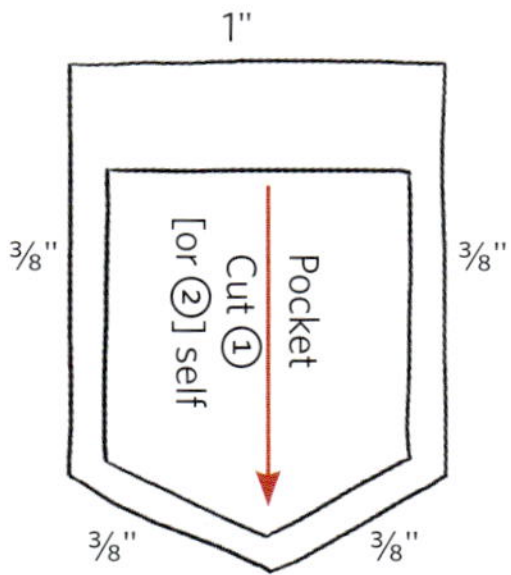


**8.** Cut pocket(s) out of self fabric.

**9.** Thread-bind side and bottom edges using overcasting stitch. Then fold under by ⅜" (1 cm) and press.

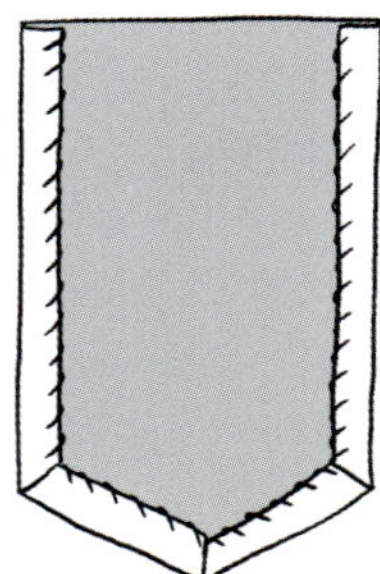

**10.** Fold under and press top edge by ¼" (6 mm), then fold and press again by ¾" (2 cm). Pin.

**11.** Use stitch of choice to hem top edge. (Whipstitch, fell stitch, hemstitch, and tiny running stitch are all good options. If you sew facing the RS of the pocket, you could also try even or spaced backstitch.)

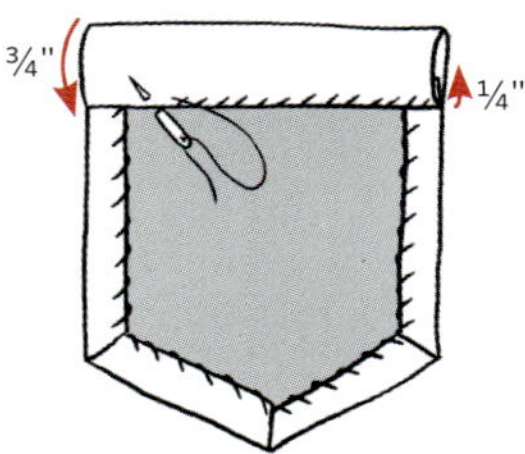


**12.** Pin pocket in place. Try on shirt again to double-confirm placement.

**13.** Once satisfied, stitch through all layers to attach pocket to shirt using stitch of choice. (Whipstitch, fell stitch, hemstitch, running stitch, even or spaced backstitch, or blanket stitch are all good options.)

**14.** Sew little bartacks in top corners through all layers. Bartacks can be horizontal or vertical.

### STITCHING A LABEL (OPTIONAL)

See instructions on page 108 in the woven boxy top project.

# *KZ Stevens*

*(she/her)*, slow stitcher, teacher, patternmaker, bag maker, CAD designer
BENNINGTON, VERMONT, USA

For KZ Stevens, hand sewing is an essential part of life. Originally an avid knitter, she began to do a lot of mending. "Hand sewing, for me, started from mending, and from the idea to hand-sew precious little pieces of fabric onto something that I wanted to last longer," KZ recalls. "I think I thought of garment sewing as too big to do."

When KZ learned to machine-sew, she appreciated being able to sew clothes she liked to wear. She was never excited about machine sewing itself, though. When KZ eventually discovered garment hand sewing, she took to the idea right away—its emphasis on process over product was a good fit.

Now, KZ estimates that almost everything she wears each day is either entirely or mostly handsewn. And nearly every day, she says, she is stitching. "There aren't many days I go without hand-sewing something," KZ explains. "I can't really go a day without it, because for me it's my meditative practice."

***Favorite tools.*** Definitely my little pincushion with my favorite needles in it. My favorite needles are old needles, which seem to be stronger. And I like short needles when I hand-sew clothing.

***Favorite stitch.*** The one I use the most is running stitch, and that's mostly for my bag work. But when I'm doing garments, hemstitch is ultimately my favorite, because I love the way it looks on both sides of the garment. Honestly, I don't really use many other stitches. I think I use four total.

***Tactile sewing.*** I still haven't learned to use a thimble. The only time I use a thimble is for either mending or quilting. But any clothing I've sewn so far is always linen or cotton, so I don't find I need it. People ask me, "Do you use a thimble?" I don't. For me—it's like if you're gardening or doing the dishes—I need to feel that tactileness; it informs my brain.

***Advice to newcomers.*** Just start and see how it makes you feel, running the needle and thread through the fabric. Don't get so caught up with your tools or fabric or the "right way." Really just get the feeling of it. Because once you get that, you'll understand—you can go backward and you can figure out what kind of fabric you like, what kind of thread, what kind of needle. It doesn't have to be one way. Just make something. Wear it. And if it starts to wear, then you'll notice where it's starting to wear, and then you might learn something else.

***It looks like my hand.*** Even with the running stitch, I think people assume there's one way. And I say, "Look at my stitches close up. You might think they look exact. You're just assuming that. But actually look close up. It looks like my hand." And that's exactly what it should look like. It's not done on the machine.

# JEAN JACKET

I've always felt invincible in a good jean jacket. And a custom-fit, hand-stitched version is extra cool. By drafting a pattern based on your own measurements and your own fit preferences, you can be sure the finished product will feel good to wear. This is an involved project, both in patternmaking and certainly in sewing. It'll take some determination. Denim is thick, so use a good thimble and take plenty of breaks. But have faith—all of those little stitches make the jacket absolutely beautiful to behold. It's a lot of work, but it's worth it.

# Patternmaking

First, you'll measure some basic dimensions on your body. Then you'll add room for wearing/stylistic ease and draft the torso and sleeve shapes. Next, you'll apply style lines to create the classic jean jacket seaming. Once those are set, you'll draft some smaller pieces: pockets, pocket flaps, collar, cuffs, facings, and so forth. There are lots of pieces, but the actual patternmaking is relatively straightforward. Just take one step at a time, and before you know it, you'll be ready to cut into some denim and sew, sew, sew!

## MEASURING YOUR BODY

To draft your jean jacket, you'll need these measurements:

- Body length (HPS to desired garment length)—hip level can be nice, but it's up to you
- Bust level (from HPS)
- Waist level (from HPS)
- Bust span (distance from nipple to nipple)
- Front neck drop
- Neck width
- Bust circumference
- Waist circumference
- Hip circumference
- Shoulder width
- Armhole depth
- Sleeve length (CB to LPS to desired sleeve length)—mine hits halfway down my hand, but it's up to you
- Hand circumference (with thumb and fingers smooshed in flat and tight)

## DECIDING THE DIMENSIONS

You'll want to add wearing ease to a few of your anatomical measurements. The amount of wearing ease you choose to include is up to you. Feel free to study ease amounts of similar garments you like, as you did in the woven boxy top project. Or you can follow the amounts that I like to use:

- Front neck drop: I like to add ½" (1.3 cm) to the anatomical neck drop.
- Neck width: I like to add 1" (2.5 cm) to the anatomical neck width.
- Bust and hip circumferences: I like to add 6" (15.2 cm) to the anatomical circumferences.
- Shoulder width: I like to add 1½" (3.8 cm) to the anatomical shoulder width.
- Armhole depth: I like to add 1½" (3.8 cm) to the anatomical armhole depth.
- Hand circumference: I like to add 2" (5 cm) to the anatomical circumference to calculate my desired sleeve opening measurement.

## MARKING TORSO LEVELS

As in previous projects, you'll be drafting only half of the jacket torso shape, because the garment will be symmetrical. You'll initially draft the front and back body together, then add style lines, and finally trace off the separate components.

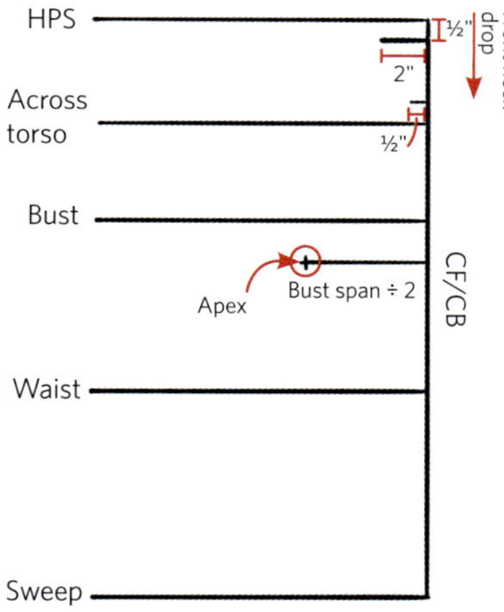


**1.** Draw CF/CB vertical line down right-hand side of a large sheet of paper.

**2.** Square a long line across the top. This will be the HPS level.

**3.** From HPS level, measure down desired body length and square long line across bottom. This will be the sweep.

**4.** Refer to your bust span measurement and divide it in half. Then, from HPS level, measure down HPS-to-bust distance and square across a line that is your half-bust-span length. Make a tick mark. This point represents your anatomical bust apex point. Circle it for later reference. Erase the rest of the line, so as to avoid later confusion with the bust-level line you'll draw at the base of your armholes.

**5.** From HPS level, measure down armhole depth plus 1" (2.5 cm). Square across a long line. This will be the bust level.

The extra 1" (2.5 cm) added here is meant to accommodate the 1" (2.5 cm) shoulder slope you'll draft.

**6.** Measure distance between HPS level and bust level. Find midpoint and square across a long line. This will be the across-torso level.

**7.** From HPS level, measure down HPS-to-waist distance and square across a long line. This will be the waist level.

**8.** From HPS level, measure down ½" (1.3 cm) and square across a line that is approximately 2" (5 cm) long. This will be the back neck level.

**9.** From HPS level, measure down front neck drop and square across a line that is approximately ½" (1.3 cm) long. This will be the front neck level.

## DRAFTING THE NECKLINE AND SHOULDER

**1.** From CF/CB line, measure along HPS and make tick mark at one-half of neck width amount.

**2.** From CF/CB line, measure along HPS and make tick mark at one-half of shoulder width amount.

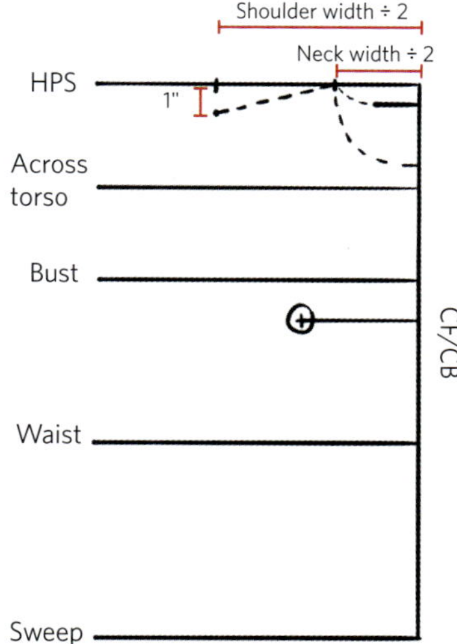


**3.** Draw a smooth front neck curve connecting from short front neck drop line to neck width tick mark. Maintain about ½" (1.3 cm) that is squared to the CF/CB line before curving.

**4.** Draw a smooth back neck curve connecting from the short back neck drop line to neck width tick mark. Maintain about 2" (5 cm) that is squared to the CF/CB line before curving.

**5.** Measure each curve and jot down measurements. I like to mark them along the pattern pieces.

**6.** From shoulder width tick mark, measure down 1" (2.5 cm) for shoulder slope and place a point. This will be the low point of shoulder.

**7.** Draw a straight line that connects neck width tick mark and low point of shoulder. This line will be the shoulder fold. (The true shoulder seam will be drawn lower in a later step.)

## DRAFTING THE SIDE SEAM

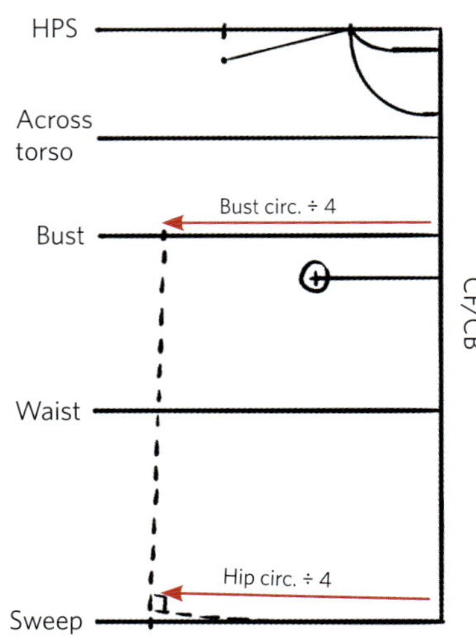


**1.** From CF/CB line, measure along bust level and make tick mark at one-quarter of bust circumference amount.

**2.** From CF/CB line, measure along sweep and make tick mark at one-quarter of hip circumference amount.

**3.** Next, draw your side seam by connecting the bust and hip tick marks with a straight line.

A note: Drafting a straight line between bust and hip works fine if your waist is smaller than bust and hip. But if your waist or abdomen is actually larger, you'll probably want to draft a slightly different line shape here. From CF/CB line, measure along waist and make tick mark at one-quarter of waist circumference amount. Then draft a smoothly curving side seam line that passes through bust, waist, and hip tick marks. This curved side seam line should now provide the perfect space and shape.

**4.** To ensure clean sewing, you'll need a right angle between the bottom of the side seam and your sweep. Unless you used the same measurement for bust and hip widths (so that the side seam is exactly parallel to the CF/CB line), you'll need to adjust the sweep line accordingly. Slide your gridded ruler or a square tool along the side seam until you find a line that intersects with the sweep level at approximately one-third of the distance toward the CF/CB line. Draw this line. Then soften the angle by drawing a smooth, gentle curve.

**5.** Decide how wide you want the bottom band to be. (I like 1½" [3.8 cm].) Use this width to measure up from the adjusted sweep line and draft a parallel line. This new line will be the bottom edge of your body panels. Measure it and mark the measurement on the draft for later reference.

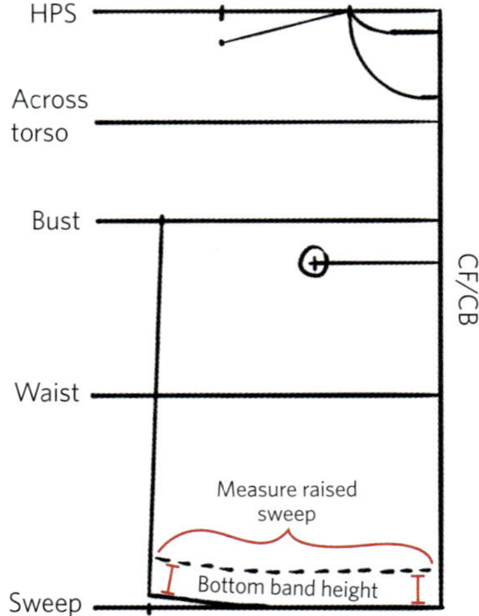


## DRAFTING THE ARMHOLE

**1.** From the underarm point (intersection of side seam and bust level), measure in along bust level by ½" (1.3 cm) and make a tick mark.

**2.** From the low point of shoulder, drop down a line that is parallel to CF/CB line and extends to the across-torso level.

**3.** Starting at this intersection with the across-torso level, freehand a smooth, continuous curve that connects down to the bust-level tick mark from step 1, as shown. Sketch this curve with light pencil strokes, repeatedly, until you've found a line that curves gently and gracefully into the underarm. This curve completes your back armhole.

**4.** Now draft your front armhole. At the same intersection point with the across-torso level, measure ½" (1.3 cm) to the right and make a tick mark. Next, start at the low point of shoulder and begin sketching a line that passes through your tick mark and scoops down to the bust-level tick mark from step 1. The curve should be very gradual as it descends through the across-torso level. Once past the across-torso level, your line should be more scooped than the back armhole curve.

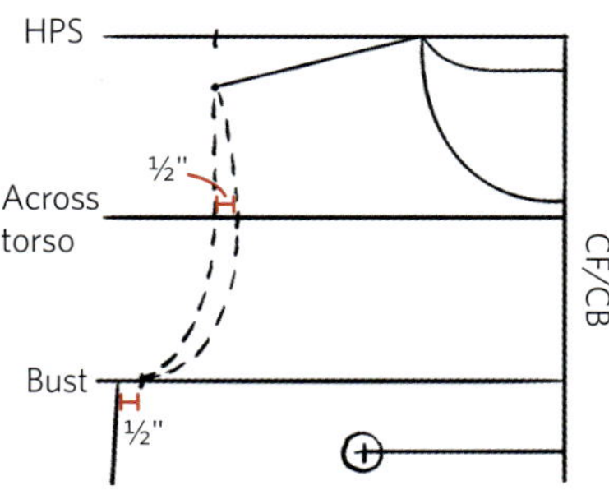


## DRAFTING THE FORWARD SHOULDER SEAM

For this style, you'll draft the shoulder seam to fall 1½" (3.8 cm) forward of the top fold line.

**1.** Draw a line that is parallel to the top fold line but 1½" (3.8 cm) below it. This new line will be your shoulder seam.

**2.** To "unfold" the top fold line, begin by folding paper backward along this line. Then use tracing wheel to trace along the upper section of front armhole, shoulder seam, and upper section of front neckline.

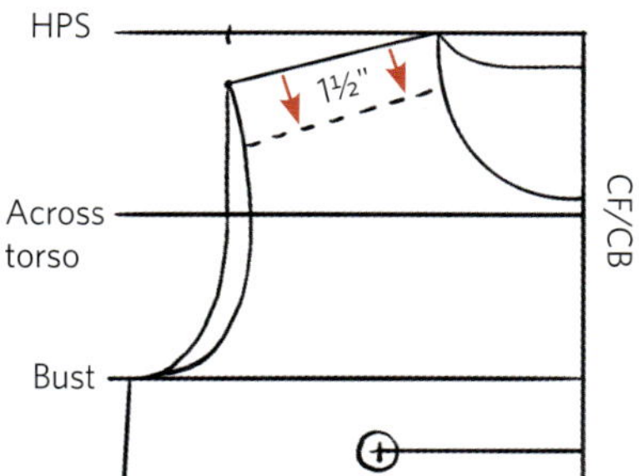


**3.** Unfold paper, and pencil in the lines just traced. They'll form the upper edges of your back yoke.

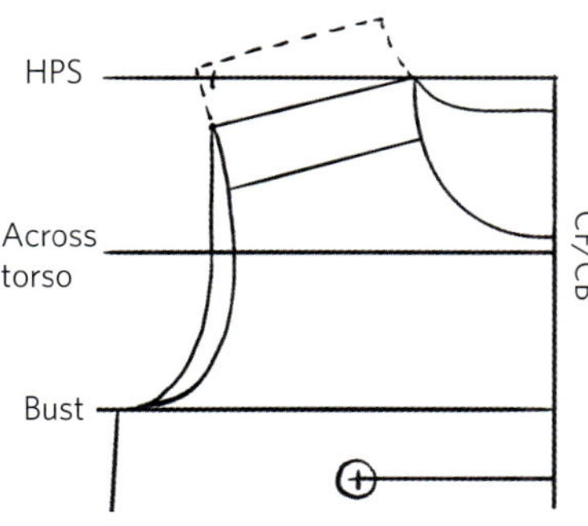


## DRAFTING STYLE LINES

You'll be adding lots of style lines to the torso draft in order to create those classic jean jacket seams and other styling details. If you're in a hurry, you can draft the front and back style lines onto the same draft you've been using (but make sure to designate a special pen color for the front vs. back style lines). However, all of those lines might get confusing, so I'd recommend tracing a fresh copy of your draft to use for your front torso lines, and another copy of the draft to use for your back torso lines. Remember to trace the front neckline, front armhole, and lowered shoulder seam when tracing the front torso draft. And remember to draft the back neckline, back armhole, and extended shoulder seam when tracing the back torso draft. For both front and back, you can omit the bottom band portion and simply trace the upper sweep line.

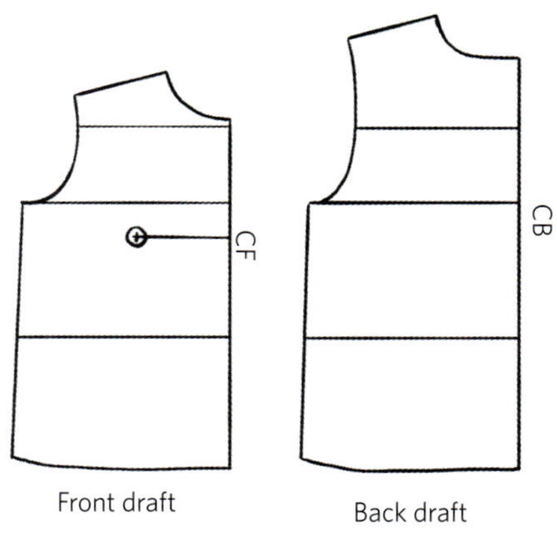

#### STYLE LINES FOR THE BACK TORSO DRAFT

**1.** The across-torso level will now become the style line for your back yoke.

**2.** The lower portion of your back torso will consist of a wide center panel flanked by two narrower side back panels. To divide the torso draft for this paneling, you can place the seamline wherever you'd like. I like to place mine by measuring my back yoke seam line and marking a point that is three-quarters of the way out from the CB line toward the armhole. Then I square down to the upper sweep line. This new line represents a style line dividing the CB panel from the side back panel.

**3.** Optionally, you can add a bit of tapering at the hem (if you built several inches of extra dimension into your draft's sweep width). Starting at the style line–sweep intersection point, measure a small amount (½" [1.3 cm], perhaps, or something similar) to the left and make a tick mark. Now connect this tick mark up to the style line–yoke seam intersection with a straight line. This new line is what you'll use to cut out your side back panel. The triangle formed by these lines is kind of like dart takeup—it's the amount of fabric that you're pinching out by moving your side back panel's line over. You can gray out the triangle, as it will no longer really exist.

**4.** Measure back armhole and jot down this length for later reference. Then place notches: Beginning at underarm point, measure up along armhole curve for 3½" (8.9 cm) and 4" (10.2 cm) and draw notches.

**5.** Measure back neckline and jot down this length for later reference.

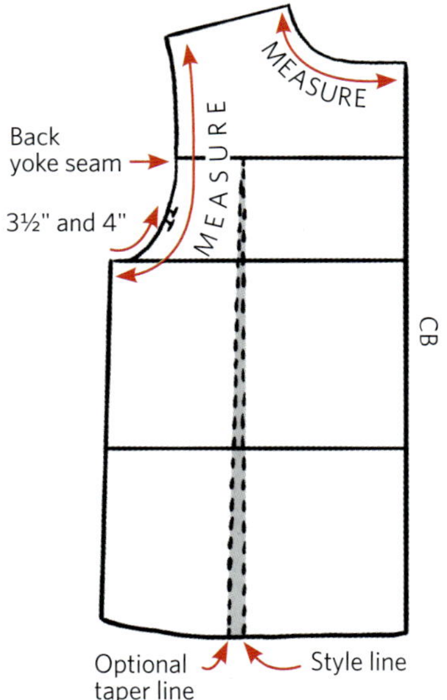


#### STYLE LINES FOR THE FRONT TORSO DRAFT

This is a more involved set of lines, but they're mostly arbitrary design decisions. So if you enjoy diving into the creative side of things, this next part will probably be especially fun for you.

**1.** First, you'll want to draft a line for your front yoke. I'd recommend drafting it to be somewhat lower than the across-torso level. The exact placement is up to you; if you're uncertain, try standing in front of a mirror and adhering a strip of skinny tape to yourself where you think you might like this line. Remember that this line will also create the tops of your pocket flaps. So imagine where you'd like the tops of your chest pockets to hit. Once you've found a level you like, measure how far down from HPS the tape is located on your body. (Then leave the tape on—you may wish to develop more tape lines over the next few steps.)

**2.** Transfer that measurement to your front torso draft by measuring down from the HPS level along the CF line and then squaring over to the armhole. This line will be your front yoke. Don't worry if it hits close to your armhole level, or even below it. As long as you like the placement on your own body, that's perfect. This is truly a design decision.

**3.** Next, you'll draft your chest pockets. You'll draft a basic shape for the pockets themselves, and then draft a slightly wider shape for the pocket flaps. I like to have the pocket flaps extend beyond the edges of the pocket by at least ¼" (6 mm) on each side, but this is also a design decision. Note that both the pockets and the pocket flaps and will begin at the yoke seam and extend downward from there. The sizes, shapes, and positioning are up to you. (I like to center my pocket over my bust point.) Again, you might find it helpful to "audition" the size, shape, and position of these elements using tape on yourself in front of a mirror. Once you have something you like, transfer those measurements/lines to your draft. Draw in your intended button placement for the pocket.

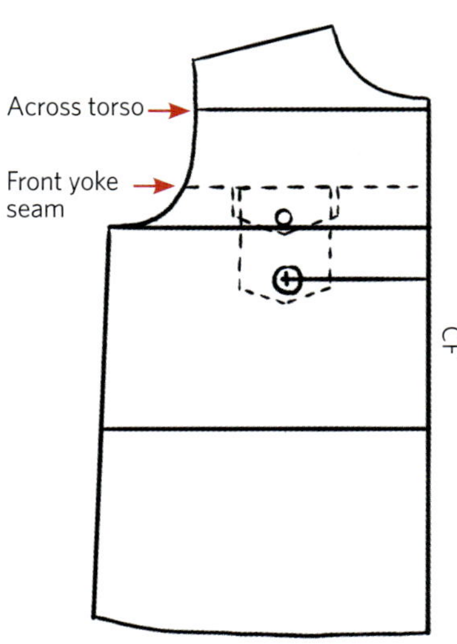


**4.** Measure inward from the pocket's outline by ½" (1.3 cm) on each side and draw short parallel lines. Also draw a line parallel to the yoke seam that is ½" (1.3 cm) below the yoke seam and that connects your short parallel lines. The bracketlike shape you've just drawn will serve as the pocket opening's outline.

**5.** The pocket opening will be finished using a little facing, so draft lines that are parallel to the pocket opening outline but ¾" (2 cm) outside of it. These lines (shown in gray) will serve as the outer edges of the facing.

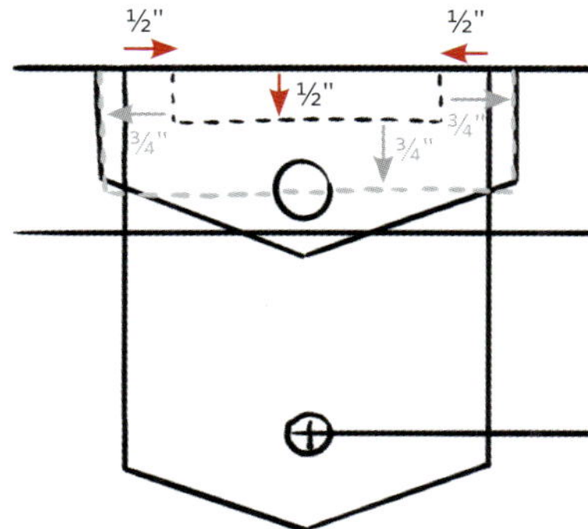


**6.** Jean jackets typically have two vertical style lines on each front panel. These lines extend down from the front yoke, passing through or under the pocket, and narrow toward each other as they reach the bottom band. As with the other front style lines, the placement and spacing of these lines is up to you. Feel free to experiment with tape at the mirror again. I like to space them in relation to the pocket. To do so, find the midpoint of the pocket flap's top edge, and square a line from there down to the sweep line. Then find two points along the yoke line that are equidistant from this pocket center line and make tick marks. Find two points along the sweep line that are equidistant from the pocket center line and make tick marks. Connect the dots to draft your style lines. An important note: To avoid extremely bulky seams (not fun to sew!), I'd recommend that your chest pocket opening's ends extend at least ½" (1.3 cm) beyond each vertical style seam, or else I'd suggest that the pocket opening's ends stay between the vertical style seams. If you need to redraw the style lines or pocket elements in order to accommodate this, do so now and erase the old lines.

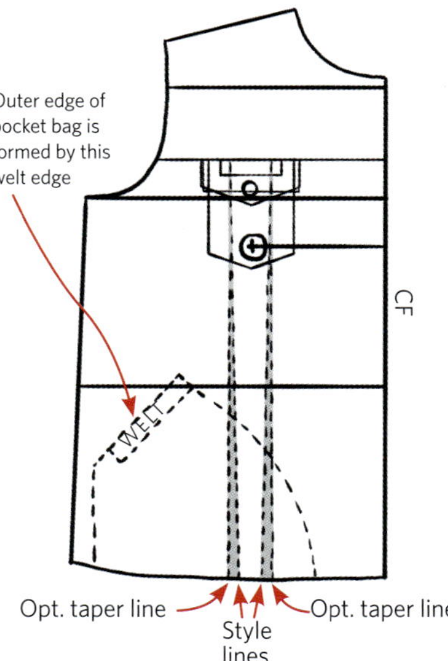

**7.** Optionally, as with the back draft, you can add a bit of tapering at the hem (if you built several inches of extra dimension into your draft's sweep width). Starting at the intersection of the outer vertical style line and the sweep, measure a small amount (½" [1.3 cm], perhaps, or something similar) to the left and make a tick mark. Now connect this tick mark up to the style line–yoke seam intersection with a straight line. This new line is what you'll use to cut out your side front panel. Repeat, if desired, to taper second style line.

**8.** Draft a welt pocket rectangle if you plan to include welt pockets. This welt can be angled and positioned wherever you like. Feel free to audition this with tape as well. It should be long enough to accommodate your hand comfortably. (For a welt pocket length, I like to add 1½" [3.8 cm] to half of my anatomical hand circumference. But feel free to use whatever dimension you like.) The width of the welt is to taste. (I like somewhere between ½" [1.3 cm] and 1" [2.5 cm].) For position, you might like the top of the welt to hit near your waist level, but again, this is up to you.

**9.** Once the welt rectangle is drafted, draw a shape for the rest of the pocket bag. (This bag will live inside of your jacket, and its outline won't be visible from the outside.) You can follow a shape like the one in the illustration or use a different shape. Just make sure there's enough room for your hand and anything you might wish to store in the pocket. The bottom of the pocket bag will hit at the lower edge of your torso draft. The outer side line of the pocket bag is formed by the outer edge of the welt rectangle.

**10.** Decide how wide you want your CF overlap to be. (For example, I like a 1¼" [3.2 cm] overlap.) Now divide that width in half, and draw parallel lines that are that half-distance to each side of CF line. (The distance between these new lines should equal your desired overlap width.)

**11.** The front panels' CF edges will be finished by folding under to create facings. Draft a dotted line to represent the facing's outline. You'll see a line of stitches outlining this facing shape on the outside of the garment when it is sewn. The shape is up to you, but typically this line is parallel to the CF line. As it approaches the neckline, it curves outward and then parallels the curve of the front neck all the way to the shoulder seam. See the illustration as a guide. The facing width is up to you, but I like my facing to be at least 1½" (3.8 cm) wide. This way it accommodates the entire length of buttonholes for my ⅝" (1.6 cm) buttons.

**12.** Draw in button placements along the CF line. You can use however many buttons you'd like; oftentimes five or six buttons are used, but that's up to you. Placement is also at your discretion. It's helpful to know what size buttons you're planning to use. If you'd like some guidelines, here are a few:

Measure the diameter of your intended buttons. I'd recommend placing the first button's center at least one diameter's amount lower than the front neck drop edge. For example, if your buttons are ⅝" (1.6 cm) in diameter, place the first button's center point at least ⅝" (1.6 cm) below the front neck drop.

It's nice to place another button at the level of your bust point so that you won't experience any straining or gaping.

Once you've plotted your top and bust-level buttons, measure the distance between them and decide

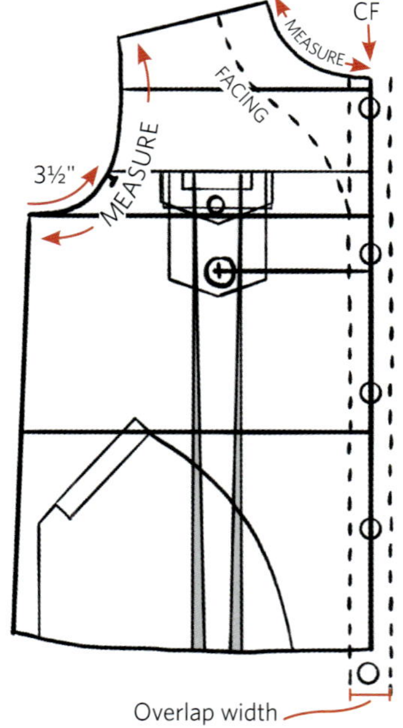

whether you'd like to add zero, one, or two buttons between them. Divide the distance evenly to plot the button(s).

Based on these first buttons, you now have a spacing standard for the rest of your button placket.

You'll also want to center a button on your bottom band, so draw this in where it would land on your draft. Consider respacing the rest of the buttons if the distribution looks off.

**13.** Measure front armhole and jot down this length for later reference. Then place notch: Beginning at underarm point, measure up along armhole curve for 3½" (8.9 cm) and draw a notch.

**14.** Measure front neckline from shoulder to CF (not to overlap edge) and jot down this length for later reference.

## TRACING THE BACK YOKE PATTERN

**1.** On a new wide sheet of paper, draw a vertical line down the middle of the page. This will represent your yoke's CB line. Fold the paper in half along this line. Place on table with folded CB line on right-hand side.

**2.** Place back torso draft's yoke on top, aligning draft's CB line with the CB fold. Weight down.

**3.** Using tracing wheel, trace along yoke seam, back armhole, extended shoulder seam, and back neck. Trace a notch where vertical style line intersects with yoke. Remove draft paper, and pencil in lines and notch clearly.

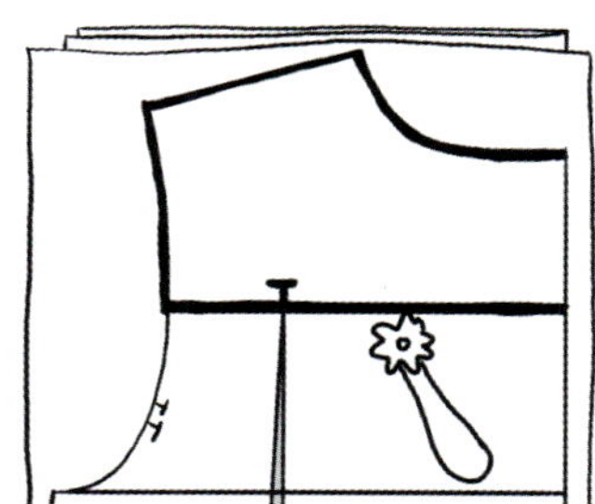

**4.** Measure the partial back armhole and jot down this length for later reference.

**5.** Next, add SAs. I'd recommend:

- ½" (1.3 cm) on neckline
- ¾" (2 cm) on all other edges

**6.** Pin the two paper layers together and cut out. Snip style line notch. Also snip notches ¼" (6 mm) from CB edge on neck and yoke. Remove pins and unfold.

**7.** Place grainline perpendicular to CB. Add note: "CUT 1 SELF."

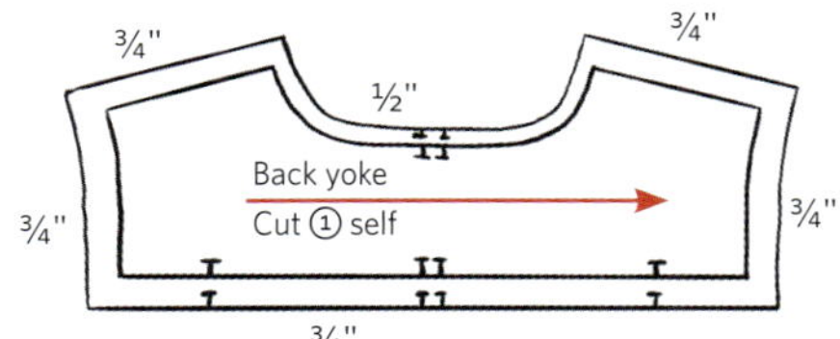


## TRACING THE CENTER BACK TORSO PATTERN

**1.** On a new large, wide sheet of paper, draw a long vertical line down the middle. This will represent your CB line. Fold the paper in half along this line. Place on table with folded CB line on right-hand side.

**2.** Place back torso draft on top, aligning draft's CB line with the folded edge of paper underneath. Weight down.

**3.** Using tracing wheel, trace along sweep, right-hand style line, and yoke seamline. Trace a notch at waist level. Remove draft paper and pencil in lines clearly.

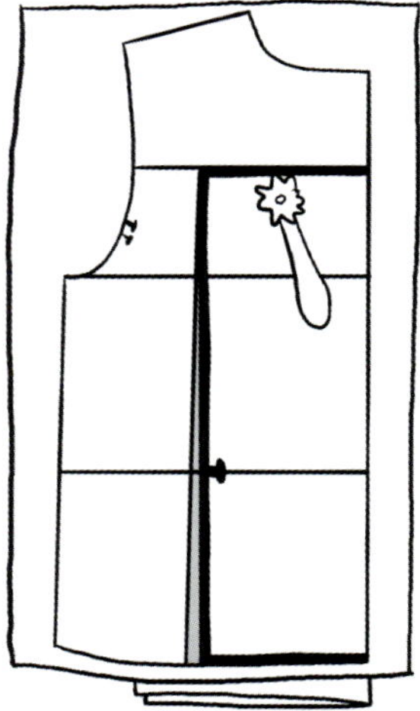

**4.** Next, add SAs. I'd recommend:

- ½" (1.3 cm) on sweep
- ¾" (2 cm) on all other edges

**5.** Pin the two paper layers together and cut out. Snip notch at waist level. Also snip notches ¼" (6 mm) from CB edge on yoke and sweep. Remove pins and unfold.

**6.** Place grainline parallel to CB. Add note: "CUT 1 SELF."

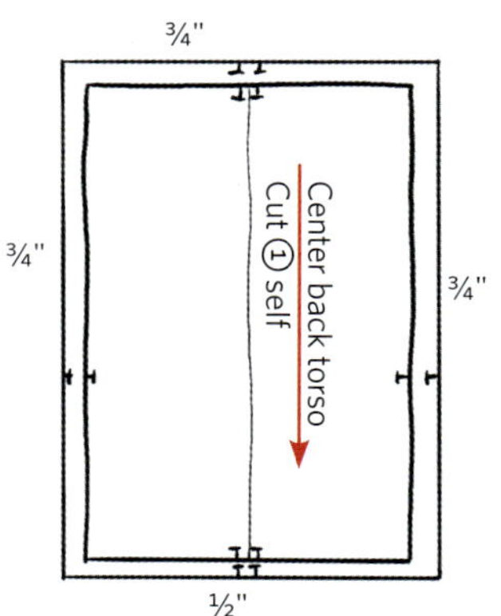


## TRACING THE SIDE BACK TORSO PATTERN

**1.** Take a new sheet of paper and lay the back torso draft on top, centering the side panel area over the paper. Weight down.

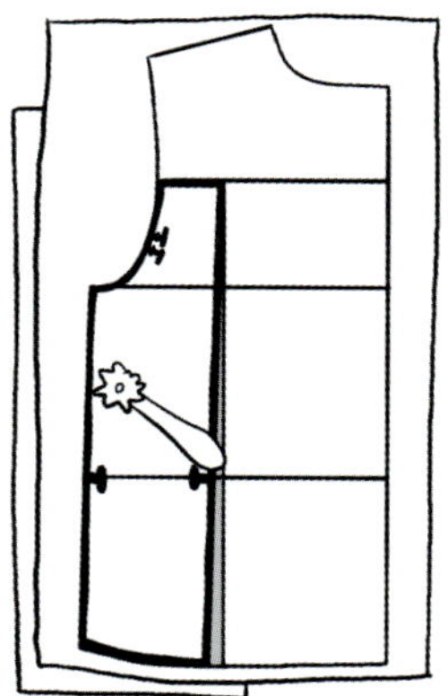

**2.** Using tracing wheel, trace along yoke, left-hand style line, sweep, side seam, and underarm lines. Trace underarm notches. Also trace notches at waist level on side seam and style line. Remove draft paper and pencil in lines clearly.

**3.** Next, add SAs. I'd recommend:

- ½" (1.3 cm) on sweep
- ¾" (2 cm) on all other edges

**4.** Cut out. Snip notches.

**5.** Place grainline perpendicular to yoke seam. Alternatively, depending how tapered your shape is, you might prefer to center the grainline along this pattern's vertical length. Add note: "CUT 2 SELF."

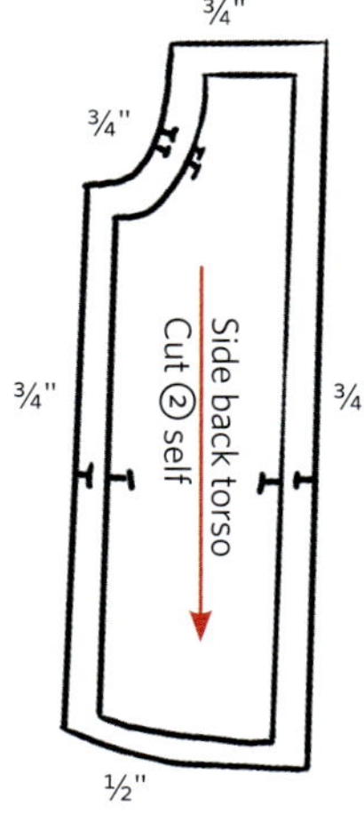


## TRACING THE FRONT YOKE PATTERN

**1.** On a new wide sheet of paper, draw a vertical line somewhere near the middle. This line will represent the fold line at the outer edge of your button placket. Fold under along this edge and orient paper on table so that the fold is on the right-hand side. Lay the front torso draft on top, with the draft's button placket edge aligned on top of the new paper's fold. Weight down.

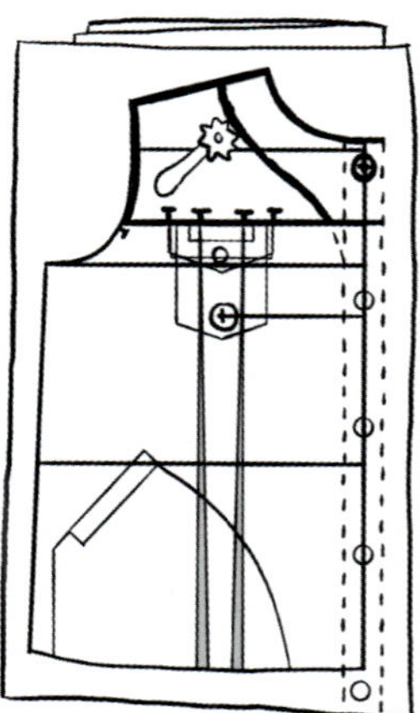

**2.** Using tracing wheel, trace along front armhole, shoulder seam, front neck, and yoke seam. Trace armhole notch if it lands within yoke area. Also trace notches where the pocket flap intersects with the yoke seam, and where the vertical style lines intersect with the yoke seam. In addition, trace the facing's dotted line. Trace button placement points along CF line. Remove draft paper and pencil in lines clearly. Make sure facing's dotted line has imprinted through to the lower layer of paper, and then unfold it. Pencil in the facing extension, too.

**3.** Next, add SAs. I'd recommend:

- ¾" (2 cm) on armhole and shoulder seam
- ½" (1.3 cm) on neckline and yoke seam
- ⅜" (1 cm) on facing edge

**4.** Cut out. Snip notches. Also snip notch along neckline at CF. Snip notches on neck and yoke seam edges at placket edge fold line.

**5.** Place grainline parallel to CF. Add note: "CUT 2 SELF."

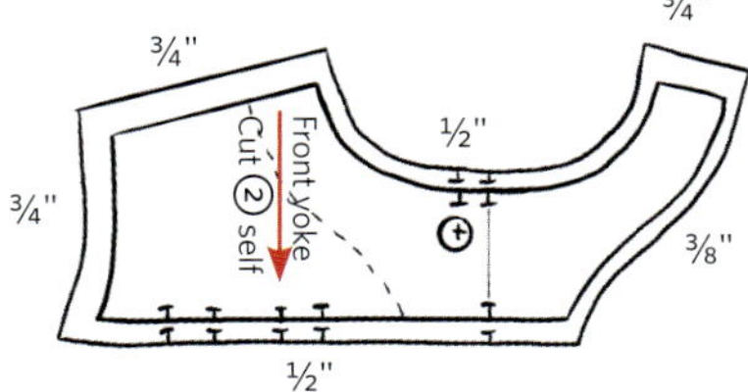


## TRACING THE CENTER FRONT TORSO PATTERN

**1.** On a new sheet of paper, draw a long vertical line. This line will represent the fold line at the outer edge of your button placket. Fold under along this edge and orient paper on table so that the fold is on the right-hand side. Lay the front torso draft on top, with the draft's button placket edge aligned on top of the new paper's fold. Weight down.

**2.** Using tracing wheel, trace along sweep, rightmost vertical style line, and yoke seam. Trace notch at waist level on vertical style line. Also trace the facing line. Trace button placement points along CF line. Trace any part of chest pocket outline that is located on the CF torso panel. Remove draft paper and pencil in lines clearly. Make sure facing's dotted line has imprinted through to the lower layer of paper, and then unfold it. Pencil in the facing extension, too. Circle any lower corners of chest pocket that are located on this panel—they will become placement drill holes when cutting and marking fabric.

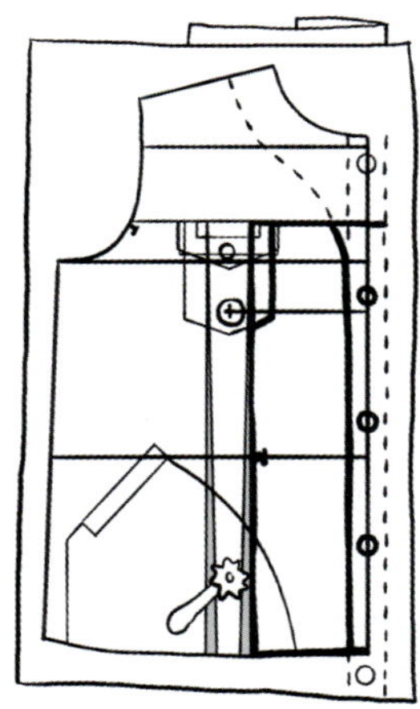

**3.** Next, add SAs. I'd recommend:

- ½" (1.3 cm) on sweep
- ¾" (2 cm) on vertical style line
- ½" (1.3 cm) on yoke seam
- ⅜" (1 cm) on facing edge

**4.** Cut out. Snip notches. Also snip notches on yoke seam and sweep edges at placket edge fold line.

**5.** Place grainline parallel to CF. Add note: "CUT 2 SELF."

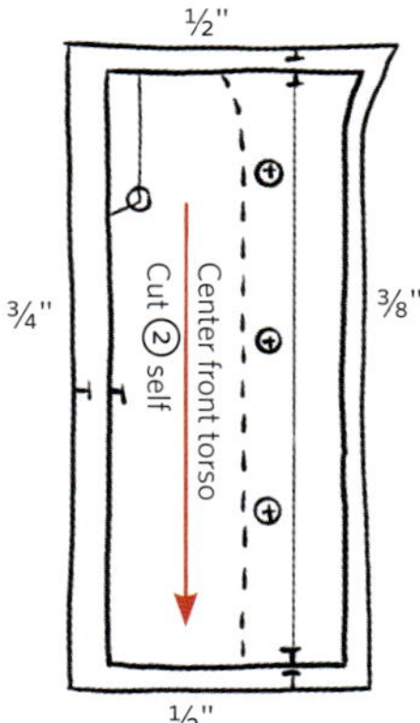

## TRACING THE MID-FRONT TORSO PATTERN

**1.** Place front torso draft on top of a new sheet of paper. Center the mid-front torso panel over the paper. Weight down.

**2.** Using tracing wheel, trace along yoke seam, vertical style lines that border the mid-front torso panel, and sweep. Trace notches at waist level on vertical style lines. Also trace the bust point. Trace any part of chest pocket outline that is located on the mid-front torso panel. Remove draft paper and pencil in lines clearly. Add another notch point at the midpoint of the yoke seam edge. (This notch will help you center the pocket elements.) Circle any lower corner of the chest pocket that is located on this panel—it will be a drill hole.

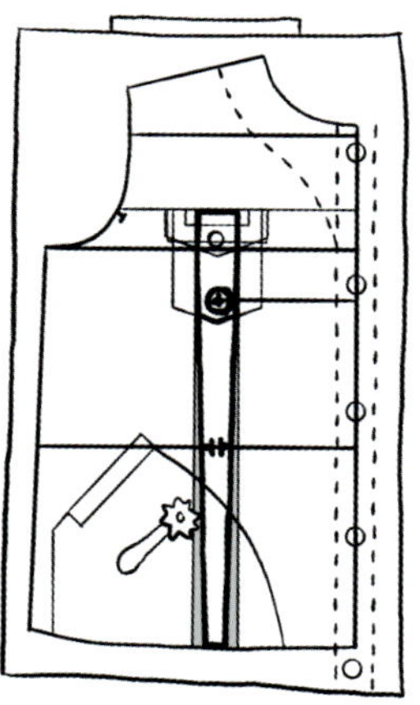

**3.** Next, add SAs. I'd recommend:

- ½" (1.3 cm) on sweep and yoke seam
- ¾" (2 cm) on both vertical style lines

**4.** Cut out. Snip notches.

**5.** Place grainline down the center of the panel. Add note: "CUT 2 SELF."

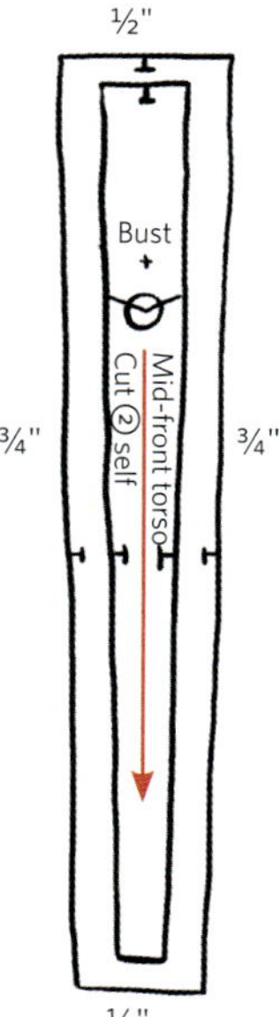


## TRACING THE SIDE FRONT TORSO PATTERN

**1.** Place front torso draft on top of a new sheet of paper. Center the side front torso panel over the paper. Weight down.

**2.** Using tracing wheel, trace along side seam, armhole, yoke seam, left-most vertical style line, and sweep. Trace notches at waist level on side seam and on vertical style line. Also trace the welt rectangle and armhole notch, if applicable. Trace any part of chest pocket outline that is located on the side front torso panel. Remove draft paper and pencil in lines clearly. Circle corners of welt rectangle—they will be drill holes. Also circle any lower corners of chest pocket that are located on this panel—they will also be drill holes.

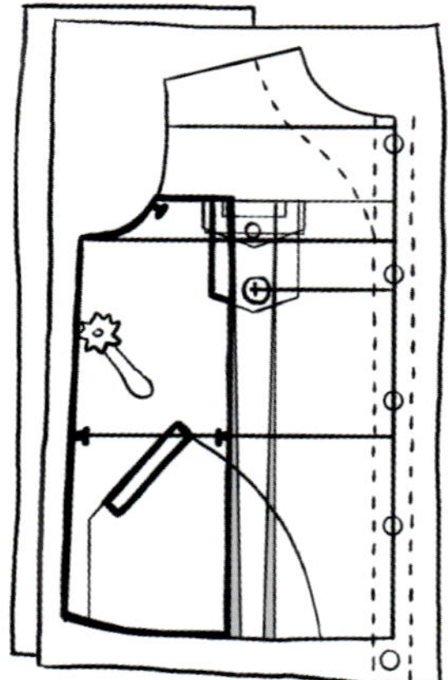

**3.** Next, add SAs. I'd recommend:

- ½" (1.3 cm) on sweep and yoke seam
- ¾" (2 cm) on all other edges

**4.** Cut out. Snip notches.

5. Place grainline perpendicular to yoke seam, or down the center of the panel, as you prefer. Add note: "CUT 2 SELF."

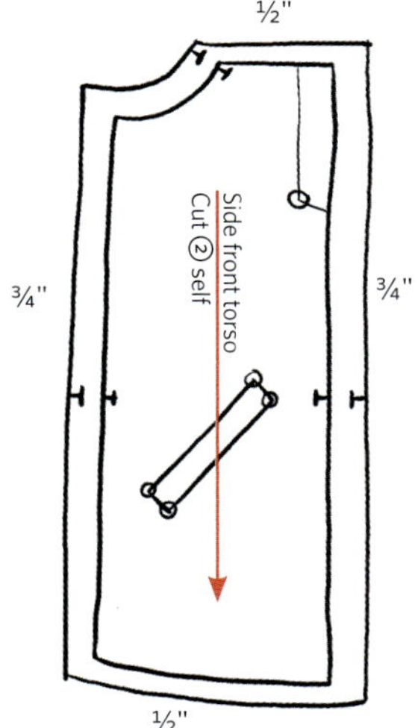


## TRACING THE CHEST POCKET PATTERN

1. Place front torso draft on top of a new sheet of paper. Center the chest pocket over the paper. Weight down.

2. Using tracing wheel, trace along chest pocket outline. Remove draft paper and pencil in lines clearly. Add a notch at the midpoint along the pocket's top edge.

3. Next, add SAs. I'd recommend ½" (1.3 cm) on all edges.

4. Cut out. Snip notch.

5. Place grainline down the center. Add note: "CUT 2 SELF."

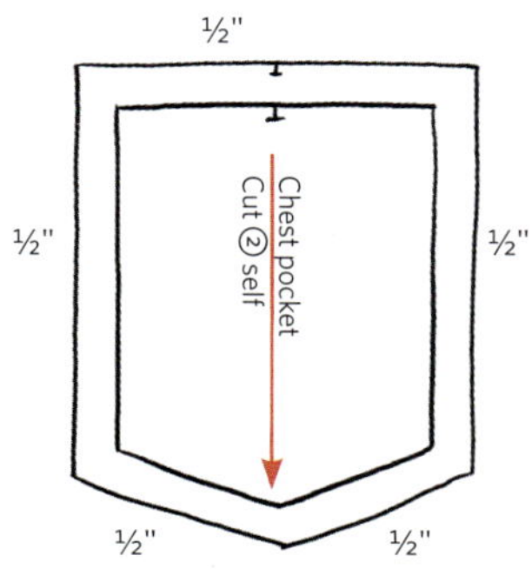


## TRACING THE CHEST POCKET FLAP PATTERN

1. Place front torso draft on top of a new sheet of paper. Center the chest pocket flap over the paper. Weight down.

2. Using tracing wheel, trace along chest pocket flap outline. Remove draft paper and pencil in lines clearly. Add a notch at the midpoint along the pocket flap's top edge.

3. Next, add SAs. I'd recommend ½" (1.3 cm) on all edges.

4. Cut out. Snip notch.

5. Place grainline down the center. Add note: "CUT 4 SELF."

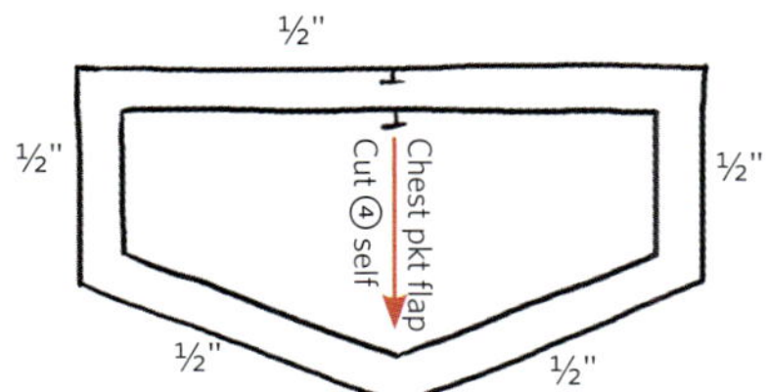


## TRACING THE CHEST POCKET FACING PATTERN

1. Place front torso draft on top of a new sheet of paper. Center the chest pocket over the paper. Weight down.

2. Using tracing wheel, trace along outline of the chest pocket opening's facing. Remove draft paper and pencil in lines clearly. Add a notch at the midpoint along the top edge.

3. Next, add SAs. I'd recommend:

- ½" (1.3 cm) on short top edges (the bits that will be stitched into the yoke seam)
- ¼" (6 mm) on opening edges (the squarish U shape)
- no added SA on the other edges of the facing

4. Cut out. Snip notch.

5. Place grainline down the center. Add note: "CUT 2 SELF."

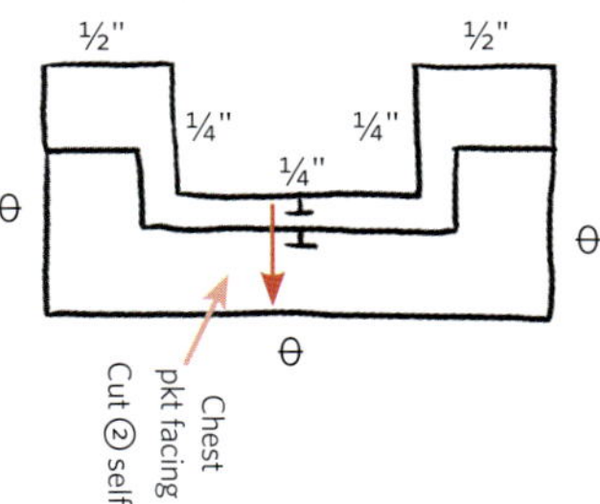

### TRACING THE WELT POCKET PATTERNS

**1.** Place front torso draft on top of a new sheet of paper. Center the welt pocket bag outline over the paper. Weight down.

**2.** Using tracing wheel, trace along welt pocket bag outline. Also trace welt's rectangular outline. Remove draft paper and pencil in lines clearly.

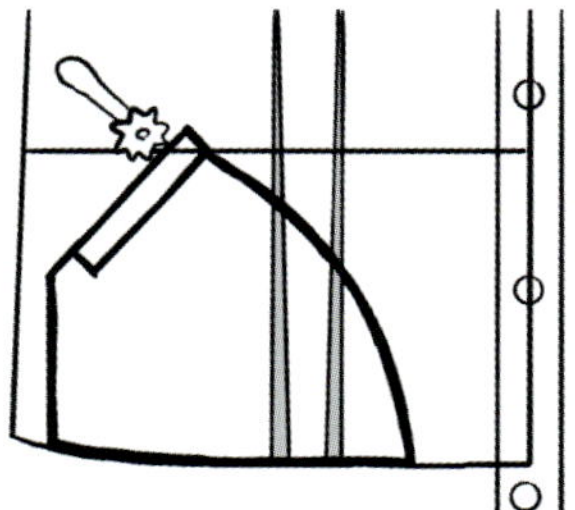

**3.** Next, add SAs. I'd recommend ½" (1.3 cm) on all edges.

**4.** Cut out.

**5.** Place grainline down the center. Add note: "CUT 2 SELF." This pattern piece is your pocket bag backing.

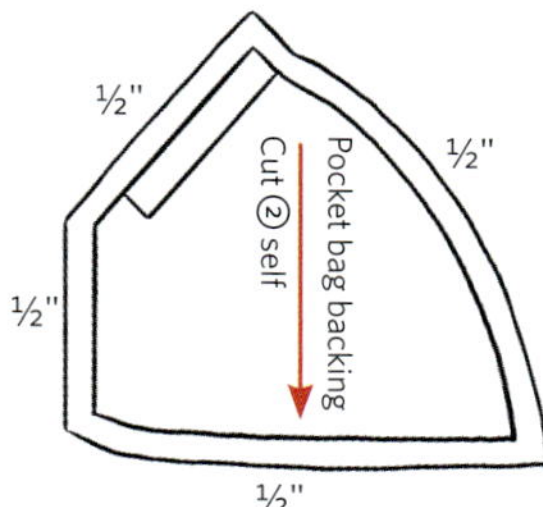


**6.** Trace off a new copy of this pocket pattern, including SAs and the welt's rectangular shape. You'll now modify this new copy of the pattern to include extra dimension for folding the welt itself, and this modified pattern piece will be used to cut the pocket bag fronts.

**A.** Draw a pair of cross-marks, 2" (5 cm) apart, somewhere along right-hand long edge of welt rectangle.

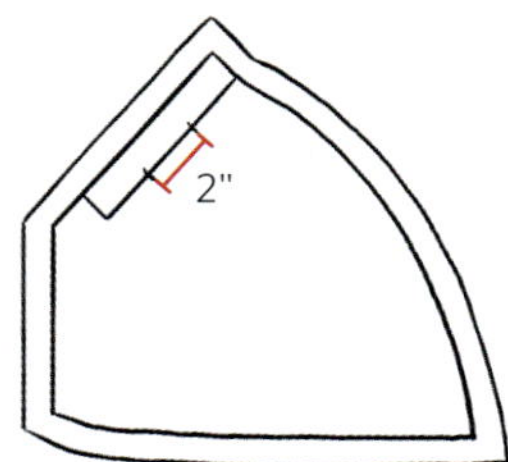


**B.** Use ruler to extend this long edge's line until it reaches the edges of the pattern shape. Then cut along this line and separate.

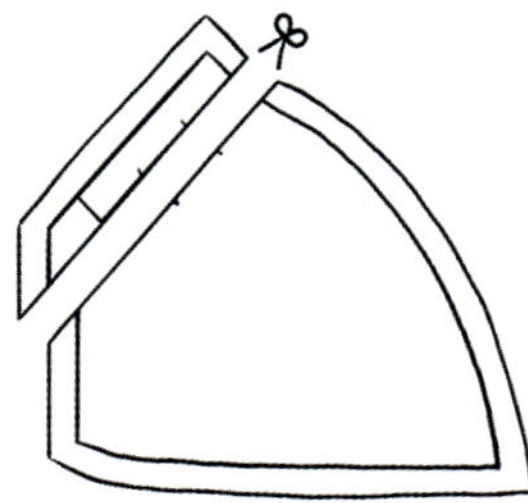

**C.** Take a new bit of paper and draw a pair of long parallel lines that are spaced apart by twice as much as your intended welt height. (For example, if your welt rectangle is ¾" [2 cm] tall, these lines should be spaced 1½" [3.8 cm] apart.) Somewhere along these long lines, square cross-lines that are 2" (5 cm) apart.

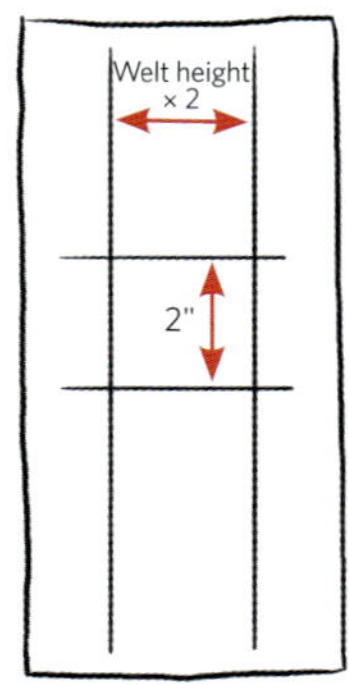


**D.** Slip this new paper underneath the cut pattern pieces, and align cut edges with the long parallel lines. Slide along these lines until cross-lines are aligned with cross-marks. Tape to secure.

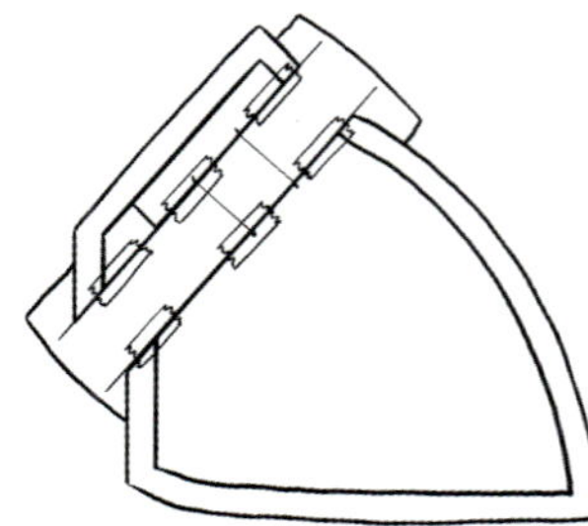

**E.** Fold under on the left-hand line of this gap, then unfold. You've just created a crease on this left-hand line.

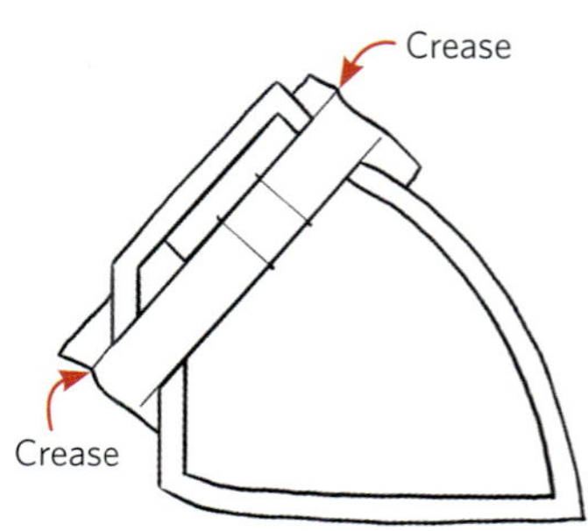

**F.** Pull creased line across to align with right-hand line of the gap, and smooth down to fold cleanly. You've just created a pleat of sorts, which mimics how the fabric will be folded to create the welt. Pin to hold.

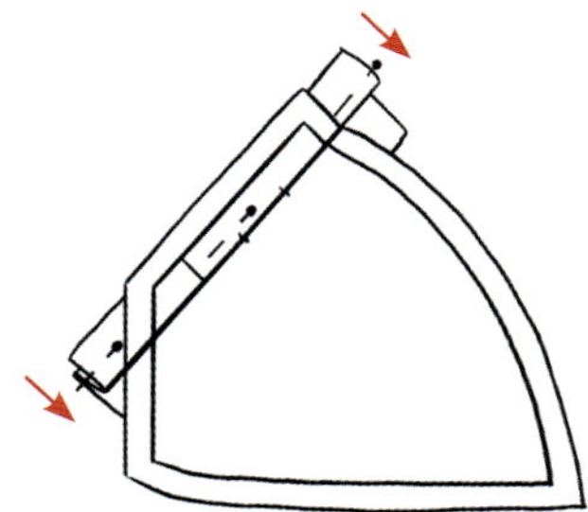

**G.** Your pattern probably has SAs because you copied it from the pocket bag backing pattern. If not, add ½" (1.3 cm) SAs now. Then trim away extra paper, slicing through all layers of the pleated paper as you cut.

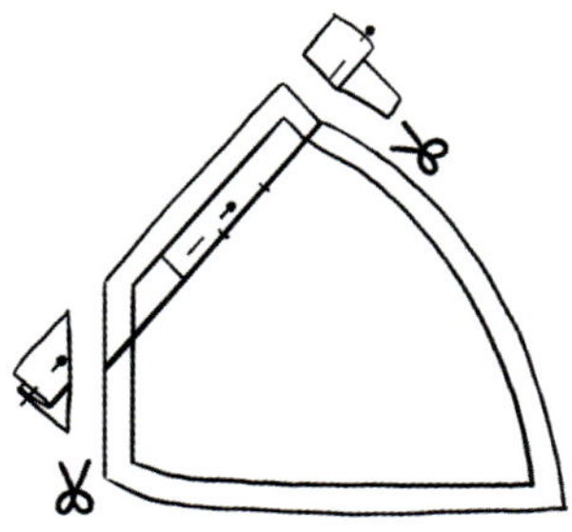

**H.** Remove pins. Snip notches in pattern edges as shown: at ends of first crease you made, and where crease touched edges at line it was folded to. Circle corners of welt rectangle—they will be drill holes when cutting and marking fabric.

**I.** Place grainline parallel to pleat folds. Add note: "CUT 2 SELF."

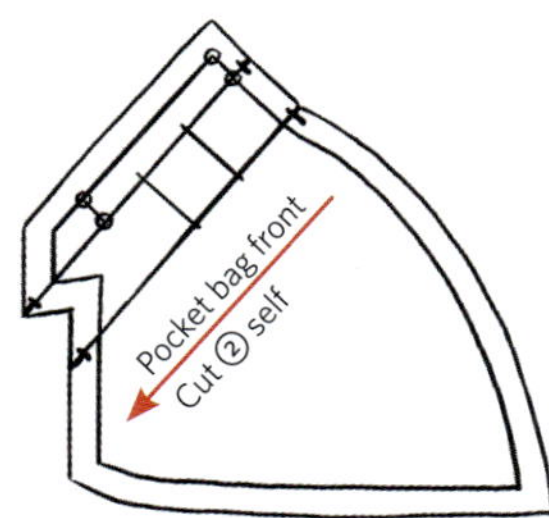


## PLOTTING THE BASIC SLEEVE

**1.** On a large sheet of paper, draw a long vertical line down the middle. This will represent the center line of your sleeve. Make a tick mark near the top.

**2.** Calculate sleeve length:

- Sleeve pattern length = desired sleeve length from CB – (shoulder width ÷ 2) – cuff height

I like using a 1½" (3.8 cm) cuff height, but it's your choice as designer.

**3.** From top tick mark, measure down along center line and make another tick mark at sleeve length amount. Square out in both directions to create provisional wristline.

**4.** Calculate total armhole (TAH) circumference by totaling the front and back armhole measurements from your original front-and-back-torso draft. Jot your TAH number down.

**5.** Calculate sleeve cap height:

- Sleeve cap height = TAH ÷ 3.5

Please note: You can use any sleeve cap height you'd like. (See discussion of cap heights on page 170 in the T-shirt project.) For the button-up shirt, I recommended a slightly shallower cap height (TAH ÷ 4), to give the shirt a nice, roomy sleeve. For this jean jacket, I'm recommending a slightly taller cap (TAH ÷ 3.5) to achieve a cleaner look while still offering a roomy, easy-fitting sleeve. But if you'd prefer a different amount, that's great, too!

**6.** From top tick mark, measure down along center line and make a tick mark at sleeve cap height amount. Square out in both directions to create a bicep line.

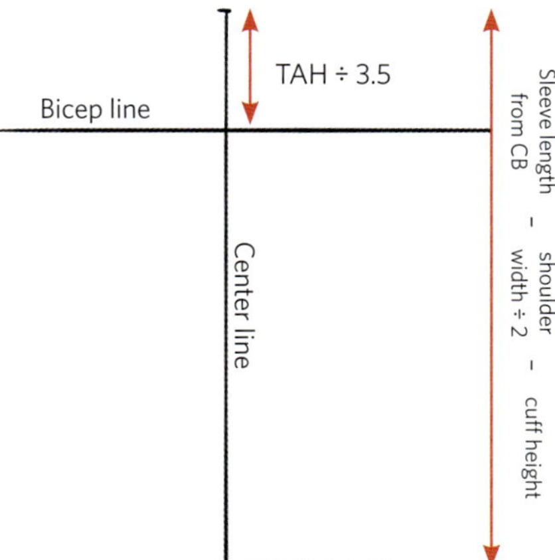

**7.** Calculate provisional cap line lengths using the TAH from step 4:

- Provisional line length = TAH ÷ 2

**8.** Plot provisional line lengths onto draft by placing zero point of ruler at top tick mark of center line and swinging ruler until provisional line length intersects with bicep line. Place a tick mark at intersection point. Repeat on other side of center line.

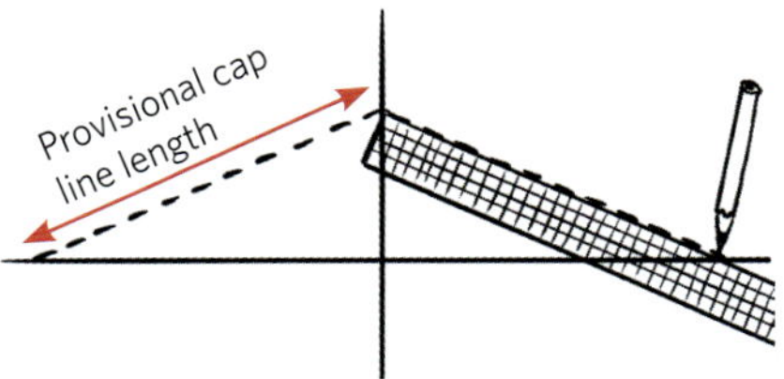


## DRAFTING THE SLEEVE WRISTLINE AND INSEAMS

**1.** Calculate wristline circumference by adding ⅜" (1 cm) to your sleeve opening measurement (see page 260 for my recommended ease amount beyond your basic hand circumference measurement). This extra ⅜" (1 cm) added to your sleeve opening measurement will be absorbed into a shaped sleeve seam, as though it were taken up by a dart.

**2.** Plot half of wristline circumference on each side of the center line using tick marks.

**3.** Draw sleeve inseam lines by connecting bicep and wrist tick marks with straight lines on each side of center line.

**4.** To ensure clean sewing, you'll need a right angle between the wristline and sleeve inseam. Slide your gridded ruler or a square tool along the inseam until you find a line that intersects with the wristline at approximately one-third of the distance toward the center line. Draw this line. Then soften the angle by drawing a smooth, gentle curve.

**5.** Find an approximate elbow level by finding midpoint between bicep level and wrist level and squaring across in both directions.

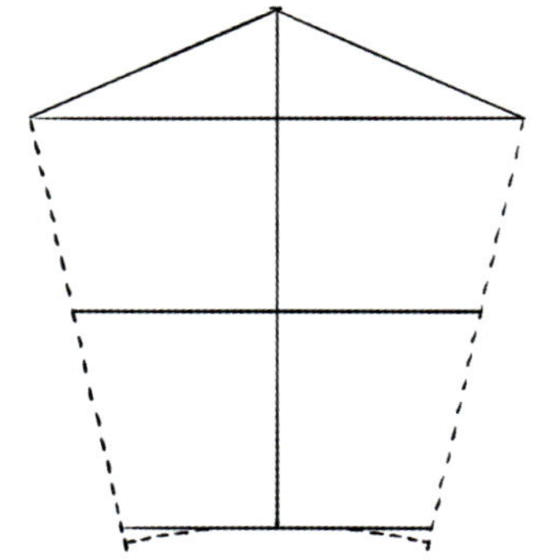

## DRAFTING THE SLEEVE CAP SHAPE

The left half of your sleeve will represent the back half, and the right will represent the front.

**1.** Divide provisional cap lines roughly into quarters. From left to right, label these intermediate points A, B, C, D, E, and F, as shown.

**2.** Between the back underarm point and A, sketch a curve that scoops in roughly ¼" (6 mm), as shown.

**3.** At or near B, curve line up ⅜" (1 cm).

**4.** At or near C, curve line up ¾" (2 cm).

**5.** Line should pass through top tick mark of sleeve's center line.

**6.** At or near D, curve line up ⅝" (1.6 cm).

**7.** At or near E, line should pass through provisional straight line.

**8.** At or near F, line should scoop in ⅜ or ½" (1 or 1.3 cm).

**9.** Assess the entire curved line you've just sketched, and smooth as needed to achieve a continuous, gently curving line.

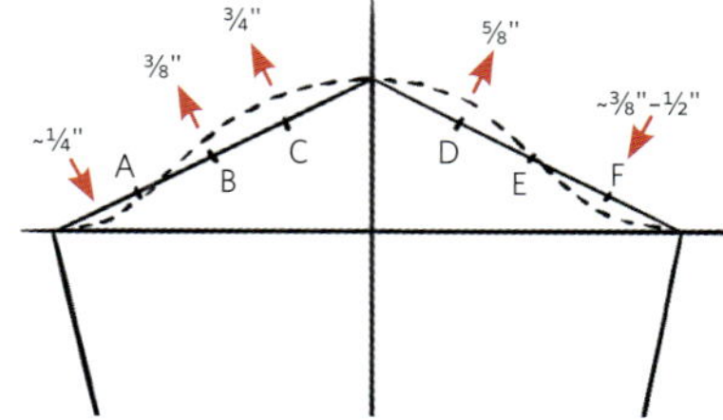


**10.** Refer to front armhole length from front-and-back-torso draft (be sure you're only measuring up to the forward shoulder seam line). Now you'll plot this length along your sleeve's front sleeve cap. Beginning at front underarm point, measure up along cap curve for the measurement of your front armhole. Place a tick mark.

**11.** Refer to back armhole length from front-and-back-torso draft (be sure you're measuring the back armhole to include the area that folds down to the forward shoulder seam line). You'll now plot it along your sleeve's back sleeve cap. Beginning at back underarm point, measure up along cap curve for the measurement of your back armhole. Place a tick mark. There should be a gap between the front and back tick marks. This gap represents your sleeve cap ease.

**12.** Measure the distance between tick marks.

- If the distance is 1" (2.5 cm) or less, you're in good shape—no adjustments needed!
- If the distance is greater than 1" (2.5 cm), consider lowering your sleeve cap slightly and/or bringing in the shape along your bicep line slightly (reducing equally on both sides) in order to shorten the curve. Then repeat steps 1 through 12 to be sure you've achieved a gap of 1" (2.5 cm) or less.
- If your front and back armhole measurements overlapped each other, you'll need to double-check your measurements. Remeasure the front and back armholes from your front-and-back-torso draft, and redraw the provisional cap lines. Then repeat steps 1 through 12. If your calculations are accurate, your curved sleeve cap should have some sleeve cap ease.

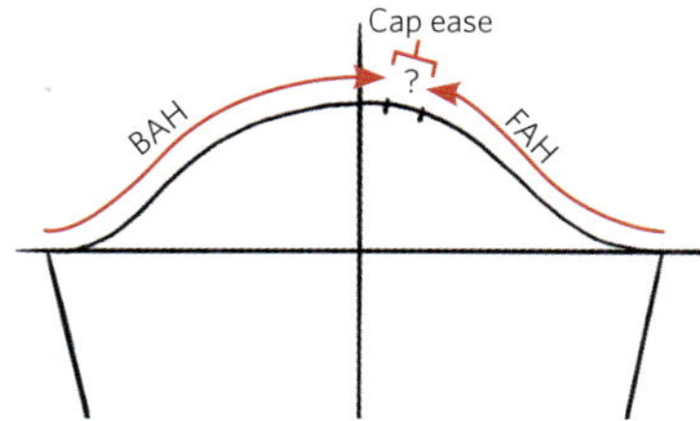


## FINALIZING THE SLEEVE DRAFT

**1.** Add matching notches to front and back portions of sleeve cap. Beginning at front underarm point, measure up 3½" (8.9 cm) and place a notch. Beginning at back underarm point, measure up 3½" (8.9 cm) and 4" (10.2 cm) and place notches.

**2.** Find the sleeve cap ease you marked between tick marks while checking sleeve cap length. Now mark the midpoint between these tick marks by placing a notch.

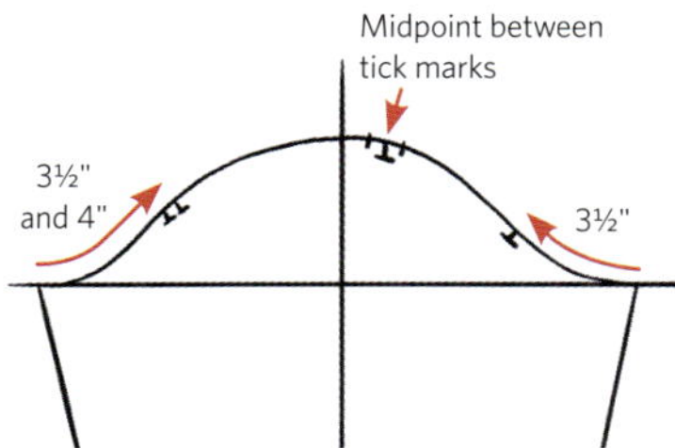


**3.** You'll place a vertical style line partway along the back half of the sleeve. This line will intersect with the yoke seam when the sleeve is set into the jacket. In order to achieve good alignment, measure along the back torso draft's armhole between underarm point and back yoke seam. Now use this measurement to plot a notch on your sleeve cap line by measuring up along sleeve cap curve, starting from back underarm point. This notch will be used to align with the yoke seam.

**4.** To find the lowest point of the vertical style line on your sleeve, find a point along the wristline that is approximately one-third of the distance from sleeve's center line to the back inseam. Make a tick mark.

**5.** Use a straight line to connect yoke notch with wrist tick mark. This is your basic style line to create a two-piece sleeve.

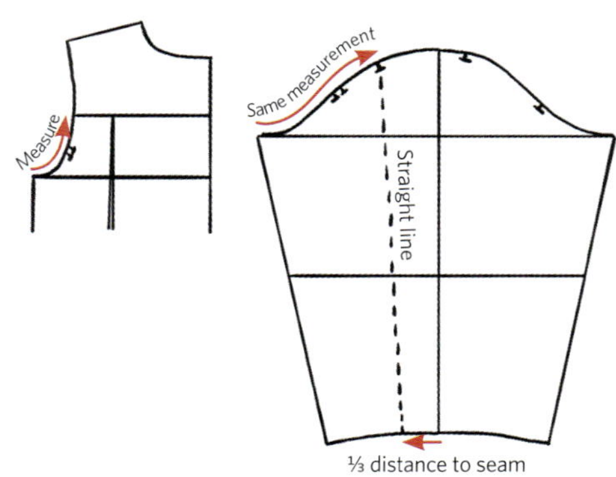

**6.** Refine the two-piece sleeve's style line by adding a bit of shaping. To do so, start at the wrist-style line intersection and measure ⅜" (1 cm) to the right along the wrist. Make a tick mark. Connect this new tick mark up to the elbow-style line intersection point. You've essentially created a "dart" with the dart point at elbow level and the dart legs extending to the wristline. When tracing off your pieces, this dart's shaping will be absorbed into the two pieces' seam shaping.

**7.** Decide how tall you want your sleeve vent to be. (I like to use 4" [10.2 cm] for the sleeve vent, but you can use a different number if you'd like.) Add ½" (1.3 cm) for construction purposes, and use this new number to measure up from wristline along style line and make a tick mark through both dart legs. This tick mark will be used to create matching points in the final patterns.

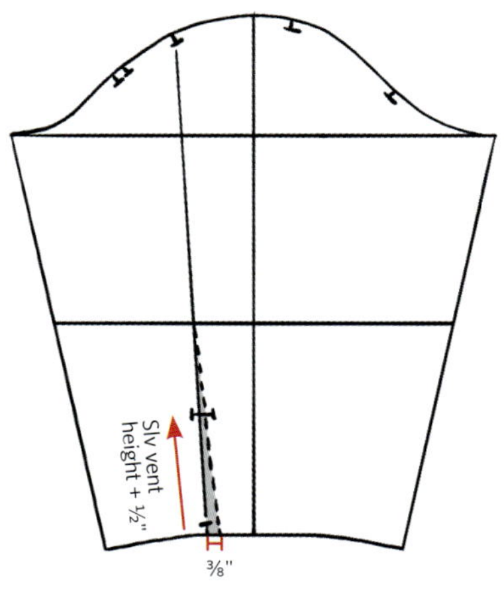


## TRACING THE FRONT SLEEVE PATTERN

**1.** Place sleeve draft on top of a new sheet of paper. Center the front sleeve panel over the paper. Weight down.

**2.** Using tracing wheel, trace along outline of the front sleeve, including sleeve cap, front inseam line, wrist, right-hand dart leg, and the rest of the vertical style line. Be sure to trace sleeve cap notches. Trace a notch at sleeve vent tick mark along style line. Also trace notches at elbow level along style line and inseam line. Trace center line. Remove draft paper and pencil in lines clearly. Circle notch at sleeve vent tick mark—this will be a drill hole to mark onto fabric after cutting.

**3.** Next, add SAs. I'd recommend:

- ½" (1.3 cm) on inseam and wristline
- ¾" (2 cm) on all other edges

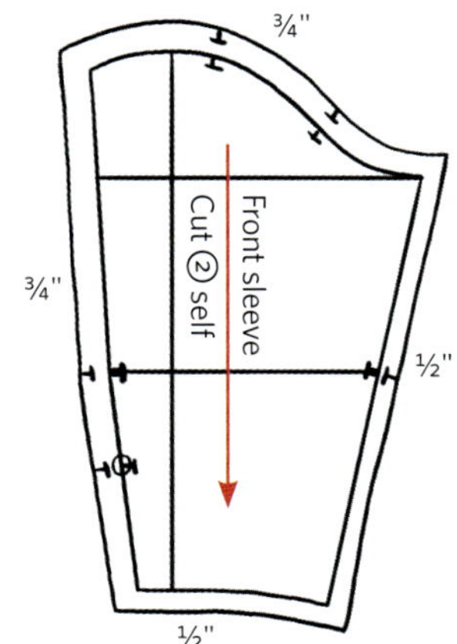


**4.** Cut out. Snip notches. Also snip a notch along wristline SA where style line intersects, as shown.

**5.** Place grainline parallel to center line. Add note: "CUT 2 SELF."

## TRACING THE BACK SLEEVE PATTERN

**1.** Place sleeve draft on top of a new sheet of paper. Center the back sleeve panel over the paper. Weight down.

**2.** Using tracing wheel, trace along outline of the back sleeve, including sleeve cap, vertical style line with left-hand dart leg, wrist, and back inseam line. Be sure to trace sleeve cap notches. Trace sleeve vent tick mark along style line. Also trace notches at elbow level along style line and inseam line. Remove draft paper and pencil in lines clearly. Circle notch at sleeve vent tick mark—this will be a drill hole to mark onto fabric after cutting.

**3.** Next, add SAs. I'd recommend:

- ½" (1.3 cm) on inseam and wristline
- ¾" (2 cm) on sleeve cap and vertical style line, EXCEPT
- 1⅛" (3 cm) along sleeve vent portion of style line edge, as shown

**4.** Cut out. Snip notches. Also snip a notch along wristline SA where style line intersects, as shown.

**5.** Center a vertical grainline down the sleeve panel. Add note: "CUT 2 SELF."

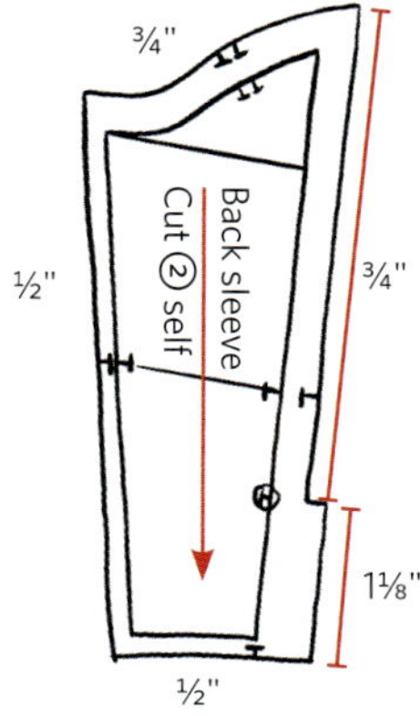


## DRAFTING THE SLEEVE CUFF PATTERN

**1.** On a new sheet of paper, draft a rectangle. Its height should be twice as high as your finished cuff height. (Refer to the measurement you opted for while drafting your sleeve pattern.) The rectangle's length should be your sleeve opening circumference plus ⅜" (1 cm). The ⅜" (1 cm) extra is to accommodate the underlap of your sleeve vent.

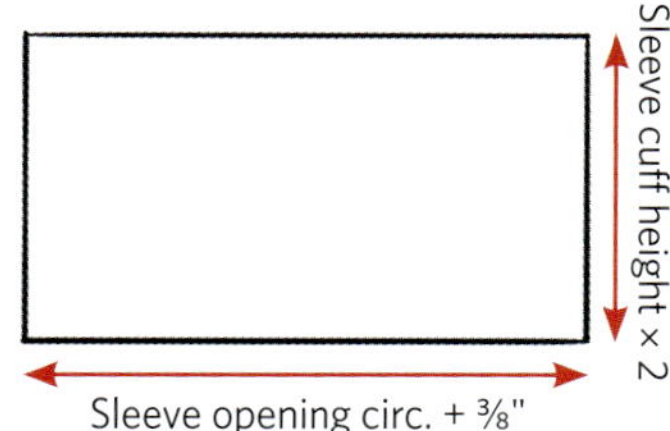


**2.** Next, add SAs. I'd recommend ½" (1.3 cm) on all edges.

**3.** Cut out. Place grainline parallel to long edges. Add note: "CUT 2 SELF."

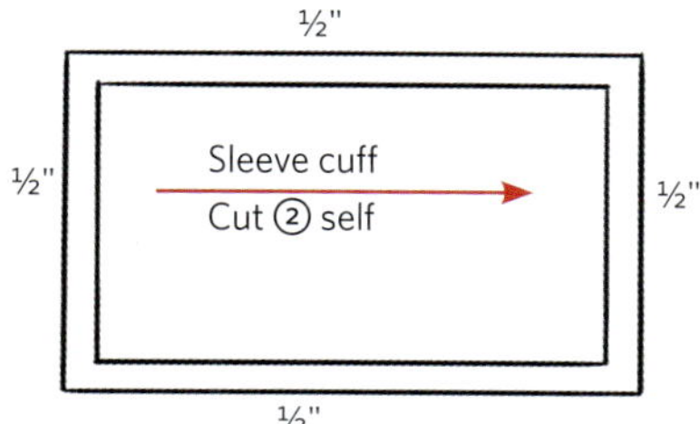


## DRAFTING THE BOTTOM BAND PATTERN

**1.** On a very long horizontal sheet of paper, square a vertical line down the middle. This line represents your center back. Fold paper along this line. Place on table with fold on left-hand side.

**2.** From center back line, square a long horizontal line to the right. This represents the folded edge of your bottom band.

**3.** Refer to the bottom band height you opted for while drafting your torso pattern. (I used 1½" [3.8 cm], but you may have decided to use a different height.) Draw parallel lines above and below your fold line that are each as far from the fold line as your desired band height.

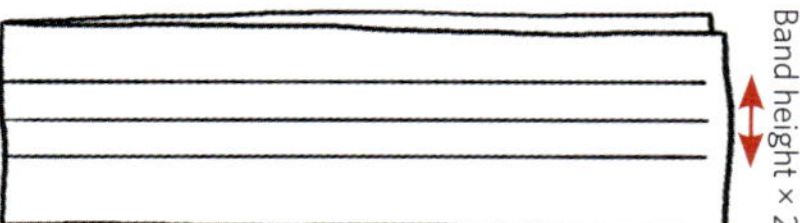


**4.** Refer to your back torso draft and measure the back sweep length (subtracting out any amount you may have tapered by creating "dart" takeup along the vertical style line). Now measure from CB line along horizontal lines and square a line at that back sweep measurement. This line will form notches that align with your side seams.

**5.** Refer to your front torso draft and measure the sweep length (subtracting out any amount you may have tapered by creating "dart" takeup along the vertical style lines). Now, from bottom band draft's side seam notches, measure that front sweep amount toward the right and square another line. This represents CF.

**6.** Refer to your center front placket width. Divide it in half and add this much length beyond your center front line. For example, if you're using a 1¼" (3.2 cm) placket width, add ⅝" (1.6 cm) beyond your CF line. Square a line here. This represents the end of your band.

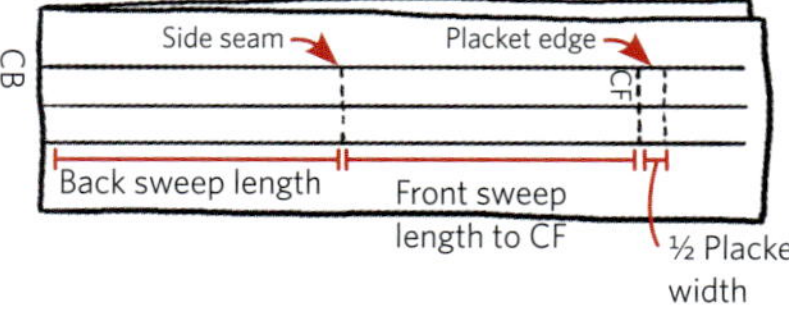

**7.** Next, add SAs. I'd recommend ½" (1.3 cm) on all edges.

**8.** Pin to hold layers. Cut out. Snip notches at side seam placements. Also snip notches ¼" (6 mm) from CB fold on top and bottom edges. Remove pins.

**9.** Place grainline parallel to horizontal fold line. Add note: "CUT 1 SELF."

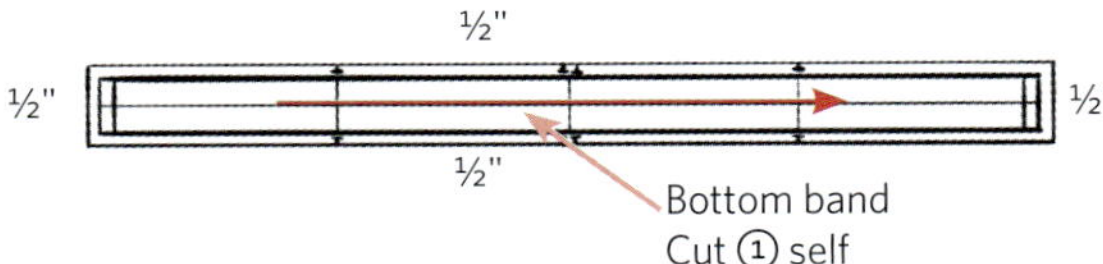

## DRAFTING THE COLLAR

This jean jacket draft will feature a standard convertible collar. Whereas the button-up shirt project had a collar and separate collar stand, this jacket will have a one-piece collar that rises up the neck and then folds down.

**1.** On front torso draft, refer to front neckline measurement (from shoulder to CF, but not including the added placket overlap).

**2.** On back torso draft, refer to back neckline from shoulder to CB.

**3.** On a long horizontal sheet of paper, draw a vertical line down the middle. This will represent the CB line of your collar. Fold paper along line. Place on table with fold on left-hand side.

**4.** Square a horizontal line to the right along your paper. This line will establish a grid for you to build your collar piece. We'll call this line the "horizontal guideline."

**5.** Add front and back neckline measurements. From CB line, measure to the right along horizontal guideline and make a tick mark at measurement you've just calculated. Square a line up.

**6.** Measure up from this tick mark ⅜" (1 cm) and make a dot.

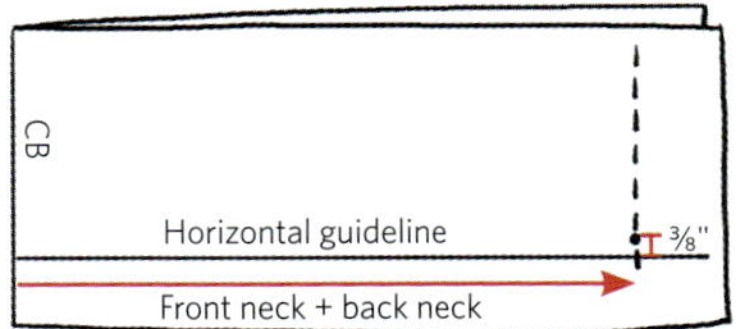


**7.** Eyeball a point that is approximately two-thirds of the way along horizontal guideline from CB line to dot. Place tick mark. Then connect from tick mark to dot with a smooth, gradual, continuous curve.

**8.** From horizontal guideline, measure up along CB line for your desired collar height, and then square a long line across.

When deciding on your desired collar height, remember that this collar won't have a separate stand piece, so it will rise up the neck and then fold down. For my jacket, I used a 3¼" (8.3 cm) collar height. This produced a collar that, when worn, folds to about a 2" (5 cm) collar height at CB.

**9.** From horizontal guideline, measure up along CB line ¼" (6 mm) and square over at least 1" (2.5 cm).

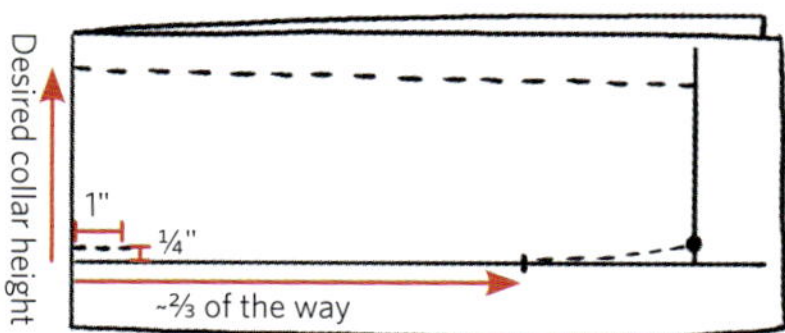


**10.** Draft a smooth, gradual, continuous curve to connect from this point to the horizontal guideline, as shown.

**11.** Measure up from this new curve for your desired collar height, and draft a parallel curve. These are the lines you'll use for your actual collar pattern.

**12.** Along the lower curve, measure from CB toward the right for your back neckline amount and place a notch. This notch will be aligned with your shoulder seam when sewing.

**13.** Measure from shoulder seam notch toward CF for your front neckline amount. This may hit at the dot, or it may hit slightly before the dot. If it's before, make a tick mark. This will be your CF point.

**14.** Finally, draft the collar point to whatever shape and dimensions you'd like.

For my collar, I extended the upper line straight for ½" (1.3 cm) and then connected it to my CF point with a straight line. It's a design decision, though, and totally up to you.

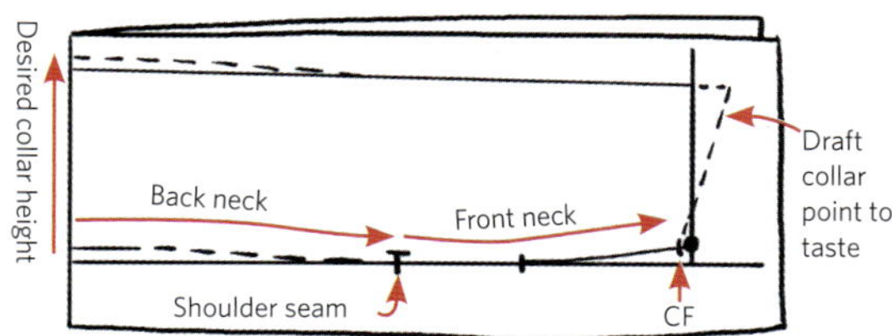


**15.** Next, add SAs. I'd recommend ½" (1.3 cm) on all edges (except CB fold).

**16.** Pin to hold folded layers. Cut out. Snip notches. Also snip notches ¼" (6 mm) from CB fold on top and bottom edges. Remove pins.

**17.** Place grainline perpendicular to CB line. Add note: "CUT 2 SELF."

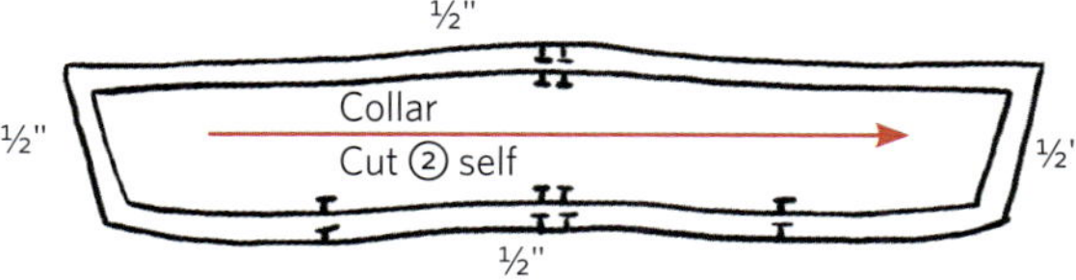

# Sewing

### HAND-SEWING STITCHES

- Running stitch
- Basting
- Even backstitch
- Combination stitch
- Hemstitch
- Whipstitch
- Fell stitch
- Spaced backstitch
- Overcasting
- Bartack
- Buttonhole stitch
- Optional: blanket stitch

### FABRIC OPTIONS

For this jean jacket project, denim is a classic choice. I like using a soft, slightly drapey 100 percent cotton twill-weave denim. Use new denim or repurpose old jeans like I did. (When repurposing, I had to add a CB seam. I felled it as for the side seams.) You're also welcome to use other woven fabrics of similar weight. You might try corduroy, midweight canvas, or even washable home-decor fabric. You can also opt for denim with some spandex built in.

### OTHER MATERIALS NEEDED

You will need a set of jeans-type metal buttons (called jean tack buttons in the clothing industry) for your CF placket and sleeve cuffs. The size and quantity are up to you—I used nine total (five along the placket, as well as pairs for the chest pockets and sleeve cuffs), but you might wish for more. Jean tack buttons have a shank button piece and a stud that hammers into the back. You can try other buttons instead and simply make a strong thread shank for them as you sew them in. However, I'd recommend jean tack buttons, both for their professional look and for the quick, satisfying fun of hammering them in.

You'll probably want to use two different types of thread for this project. For the basic construction seams you can use a medium-weight all-purpose thread, as long as it's strong and in good condition. But for the topstitching, you'll probably want to use a thicker, showier thread specifically intended for topstitching. For my jacket, I used a blue all-purpose thread for the basic seams and a gold topstitching thread for the visible stitches.

Optionally, you might wish to use interfacing for the sleeve cuffs, bottom band, and collar pieces, as well as a few other areas. I prefer sew-in woven interfacing over the fusible variety, but feel free to use whatever you like. If you're feeling experimental, you can forgo store-bought interfacing and instead use cotton canvas or some other thick, dense, structured fabric from your stash. That said, I skipped all forms of interfacing for my jacket, and it has held up beautifully without.

Denim comes in various thicknesses, but most are thick enough that you'll want to avoid stitching through too many layers at once. I'm recommending techniques here that should be doable on most appropriate-weight fabrics, but there are places where you'll still be pushing a needle through quite a bit of thickness. At the front yoke seams, I'm recommending that you use bias binding to finish the raw edges with minimal bulk. Use this technique anywhere else you'd like, too. Cut 2" (5 cm)-wide strips of bias binding from a lighter-weight woven fabric of your choosing. I'd recommend getting at least half a yard (half a meter) of this fabric and prepping a lot of strips ahead of time. If you have a rotary cutter and mat, you can cut quickly. If you don't, then a gridded ruler, marking tool, and pair of shears will work fine, too.

### CUTTING THE FABRIC

See Cutting Fabric on page 85 for tips on cutting. You'll need to cut the following pieces and quantities:

- Back yoke × 1 self
- Center back torso × 1 self
- Side back torso × 2 self
- Front yoke × 2 self
- Center front torso × 2 self
- Mid-front torso × 2 self
- Side front torso × 2 self
- Chest pocket × 2 self
- Chest pocket flap × 4 self
- Chest pocket facing × 2 self, (optional) × 2 interfacing
- Welt pocket bag backing × 2 self
- Welt pocket bag front × 2 self
- Front sleeve × 2 self
- Back sleeve × 2 self
- Sleeve cuff × 2 self, (optional) × 2 interfacing
- Bottom band × 1 self, (optional) × 1 interfacing
- Collar × 2 self, (optional) × 1 interfacing

Transfer marks for welt rectangle corners onto WS of side front torso pieces. Transfer marks for welt rectangle corners onto WS of pocket bag front pieces. Also transfer drill holes at top of sleeve vents to WS of sleeve pieces. Transfer chest pocket placement drill holes onto WS of center front torsos, mid-front torsos, and side front torsos.

### STAYSTITCHING

It's a good idea to staystitch the necklines and armholes of your torso and yoke pieces to prevent their bias-cut raw edges from getting stretched out during handling. See page 104 for details on how to staystitch. I'd recommend creating secure lines of running stitch within the SAs of the following:

- On the front torso pieces, staystitch the necklines and armholes.
- On the back torso pieces, staystitch the necklines and armholes.

### APPLYING INTERFACINGS (OPTIONAL)

If you decide to use interfacing, you'll want to apply it before beginning to construct the jacket. If using fusible interfacing, apply using your iron. If using sew-in interfacing, apply by basting through all layers around the interfacing pieces' perimeters.

- Sleeve cuffs: interface WS of both pieces
- Bottom band: interface WS of the piece

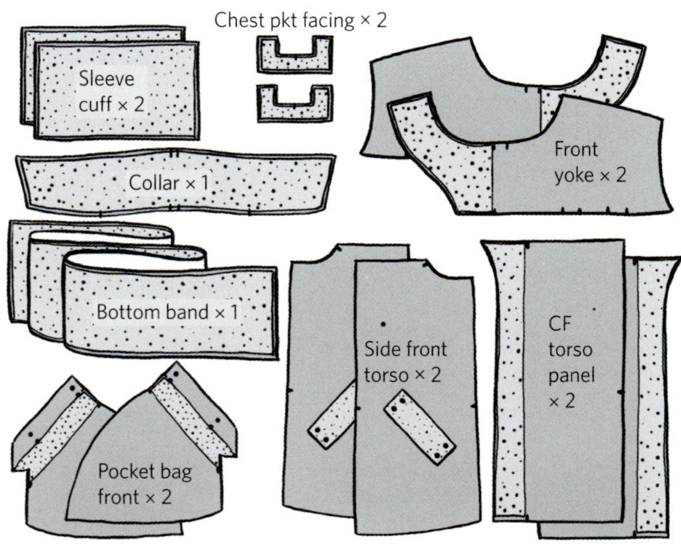

- Collar: interface WS of one piece
- Chest pocket facing: interface WS of both pieces
- Welt placement on side front panels: interface WS of both side front panels; for each, cut a rectangle of interfacing that is ¾" (2 cm) larger than welt in both length and height, then center it over welt placement area (see diagram as guide)
- Welt pocket bag fronts: interface WS of welt strip ("pleated" area) on both pieces (see diagram as guide)
- Front yoke panels: interface WS of center front facing area on both pieces (see diagram as guide)
- CF torso panels: interface WS of center front facing area on both pieces (see diagram as guide)

## ASSEMBLING THE BACK BODY

**1.** Place side back torso panels on top of CB torso panel, aligning them along the vertical style lines, RST. Pin, matching notches.

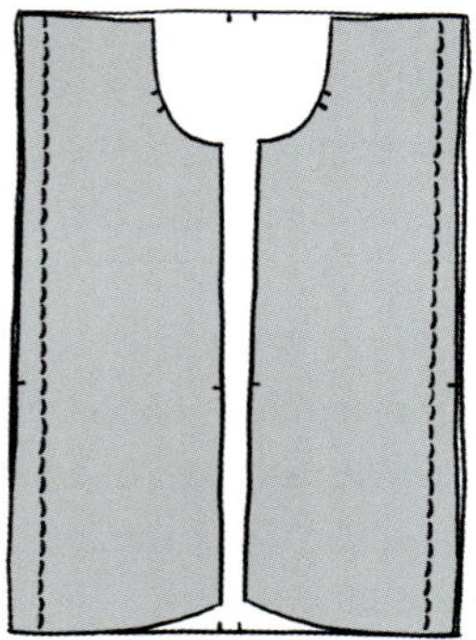

**2.** Looking at the side back torso panels as you stitch, sew both seams using even backstitch and regular thread. Use ¾" (2 cm) SA.

A note: If you'd rather use combination stitch for speed's sake on this jacket, you can substitute it for the even backstitched seams. If you have the time, though, and if you care about having a "pretty" jacket interior, you might like to use even backstitch instead. Note that the stitches don't have to be incredibly small—⅛" (3 mm) or a little longer will be perfectly sufficient. Remember that you'll be adding more lines of stitching (by felling and topstitching your seams), so these seams will be multiply reinforced.

**3.** Press SAs toward CB.

**4.** Next, prepare to fell SAs. Trim half of the width of the CB torso panel's SAs (but do not trim the side back torso panels' SAs). Then fold side backs' SAs around and under CB torso's SAs, so that all raw edges are concealed. Pin.

**5.** With topstitching thread, use hemstitch, whipstitch, fell stitch, or other stitch of choice to secure folded edges down. Press. The lower back body is now fully assembled.

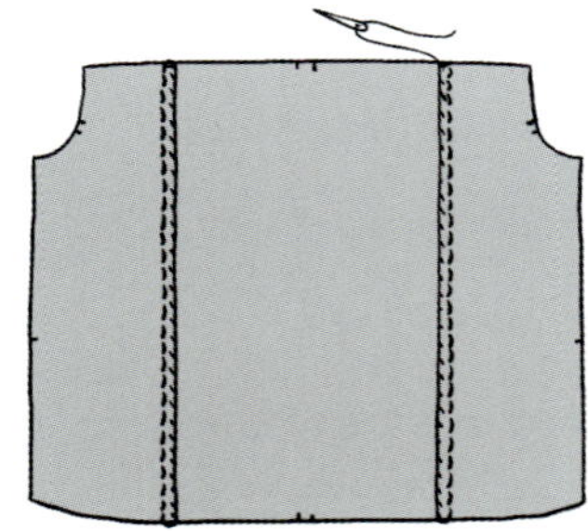

**6.** Align back yoke on top of lower back body, RST. Pin, matching notches and seam intersections.

**7.** Looking at the lower back body as you stitch, sew yoke seam using even backstitch and regular thread. Use ¾" (2 cm) SA.

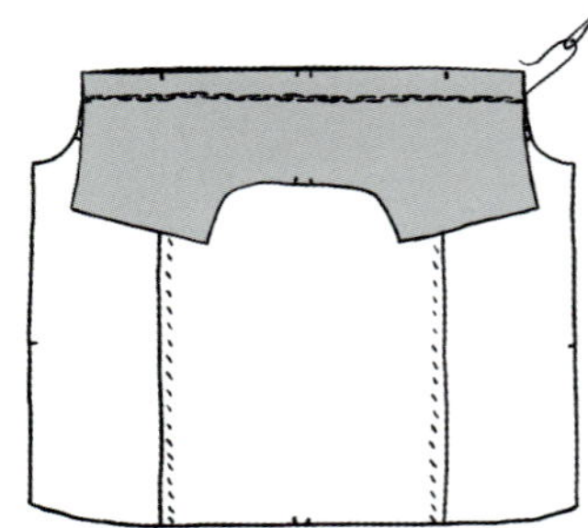

**8.** Press SAs toward yoke.

**9.** Prepare to fell SA. Trim half of the width of back yoke's SAs, then fold lower back body's SA around and under back yoke's SA so that all raw edges are concealed. Pin.

If you're finding it difficult to fold the areas of SA that are already thick from other flat-felled seams, you can actually "press" them by hitting them with a mallet (or hammer, very gently). You'd be surprised how much a couple of whacks can help compress thick SAs.

**10.** With topstitching thread, use hemstitch, whipstitch, fell stitch, or other stitch of choice to secure folded edge down. Press. The entire back torso is now fully assembled.

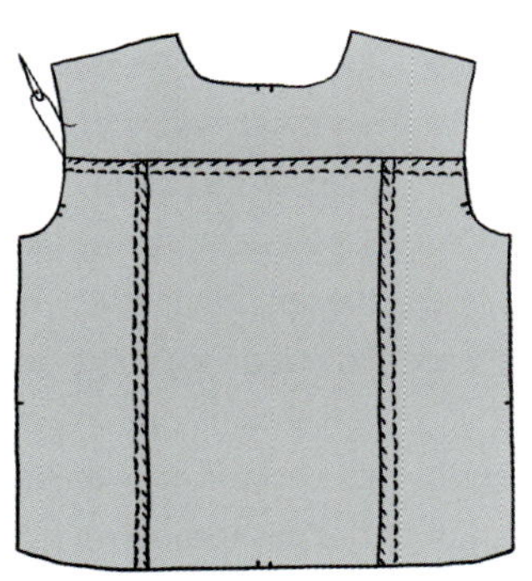

**11.** Consider adding another line of topstitching to each of the three seams you've just completed. You'll work this topstitching from the RS. If you choose to add topstitching, I'd recommend spaced backstitch or another stitch that looks similar to the stitches that felled your SAs. It's up to you, though!

You can also skip this line of stitching—it's largely for looks. Yes, it adds extra strength, but the flat-felled seams are already very strong. If you do choose to add topstitching, I'd recommend spacing it about halfway between the actual seam and the felling stitches.

### ASSEMBLING THE LOWER FRONT TORSO PANELS

**1.** Place mid-front torso panels on top of side front torso panels, aligning them along the vertical style lines, RST. Pin, matching notches.

**2.** Looking at the mid-front torso panels as you stitch, sew both seams using even backstitch and regular thread. Use ¾" (2 cm) SA.

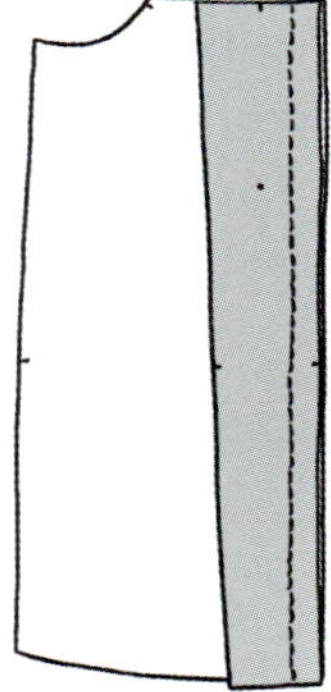

**3.** Press SAs toward side front panels.

**4.** Prepare to fell SAs. Trim half of the width of the side front panel's SAs (but do not trim the mid-front torso panels' SAs). Then fold mid-fronts' SAs around and under side fronts' SAs so that all raw edges are concealed. Pin.

**5.** With topstitching thread, use hemstitch, whipstitch, fell stitch, or other stitch of choice to secure folded edges down. Press.

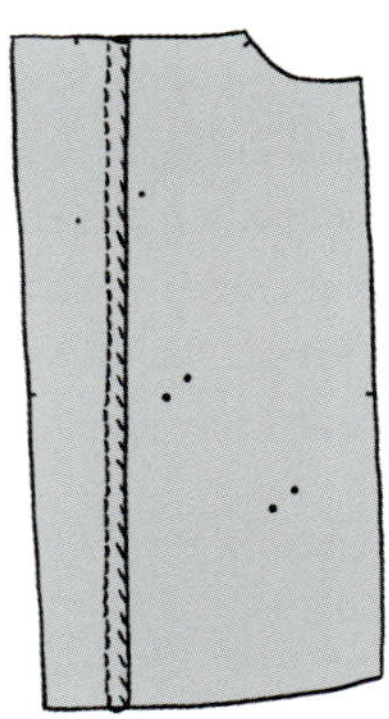

**6.** Place mid-front torso panels' other long edges on top of CF torso panels, aligning them along the vertical style lines, RST. Pin, matching notches.

**7.** Looking at the mid-front torso panels as you stitch, sew both seams using even backstitch and regular thread. Use ¾" (2 cm) SA.

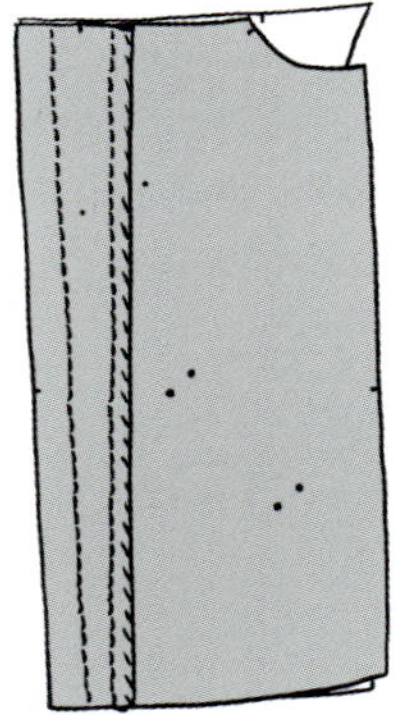

**8.** Press SAs toward CF panels.

**9.** Prepare to fell SAs. Trim half of the width of CF panels' SAs, then fold mid-fronts' SAs around and under CF panels' SAs so that all raw edges are concealed. Pin.

**10.** With topstitching thread, use hemstitch, whipstitch, fell stitch, or other stitch of choice to secure folded edge down. Press. The lower front torso panels are now joined.

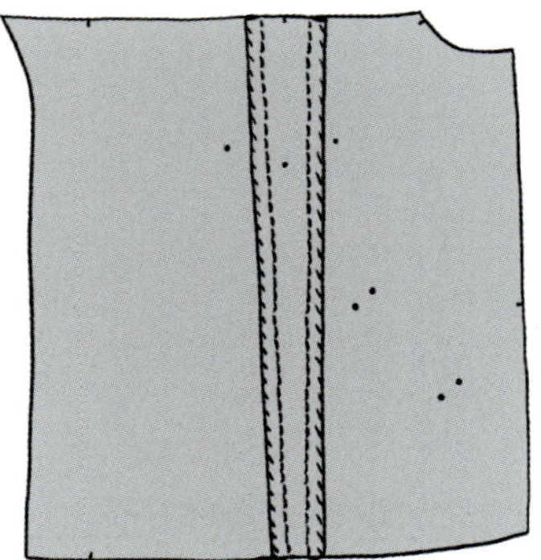

**11.** Consider adding another line of topstitching to each of the seams you've just completed. You'll work this topstitching from the RS. I'd recommend spaced backstitch or another stitch that looks similar to the stitches that felled your SAs. You can also skip this topstitching.

## PREPARING THE CHEST POCKET FLAPS

**1.** Align each pair of chest pocket flaps with RST. Pin. Using regular thread and combination stitch or small running stitches, sew around lower edges of flaps. Use ½" (1.3 cm) SA.

**2.** Snip corner triangles to reduce bulk. Then turn flaps RS out and press crisply.

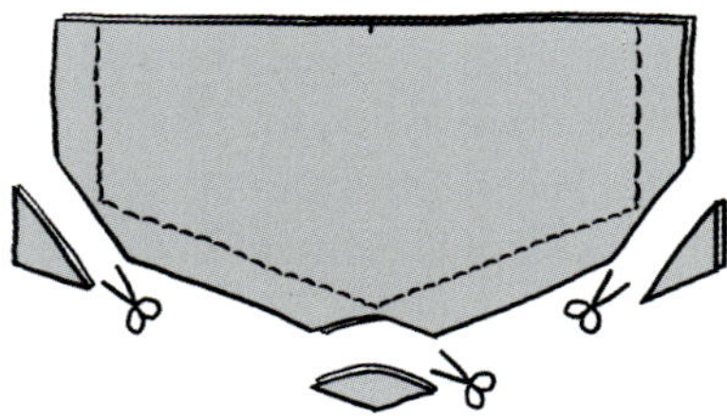

**3.** With topstitching thread, use stitch of choice (spaced backstitch, running stitch, whipstitch, blanket stitch, etc.) to add one or two lines of topstitching along the seamed edges.

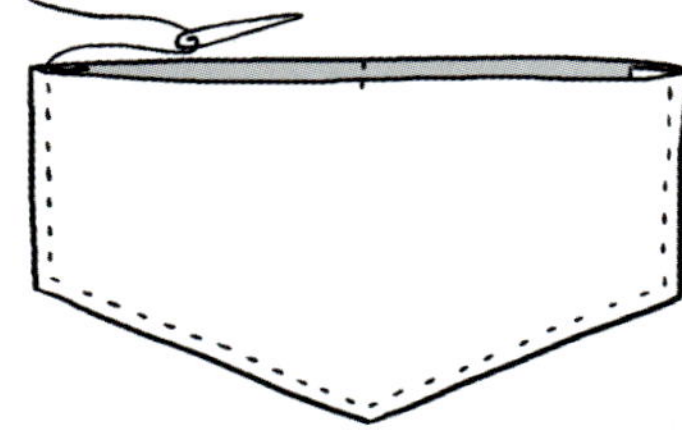

## FINISHING THE CHEST POCKET OPENING

**1.** Place chest pocket facings on top of lower front torso panels, RST. Use mid-front torso panel's center notch to guide placement, then pin. Using regular thread and combination stitch or small running stitches, sew around pocket opening shape. Use ¼" (6 mm) SA.

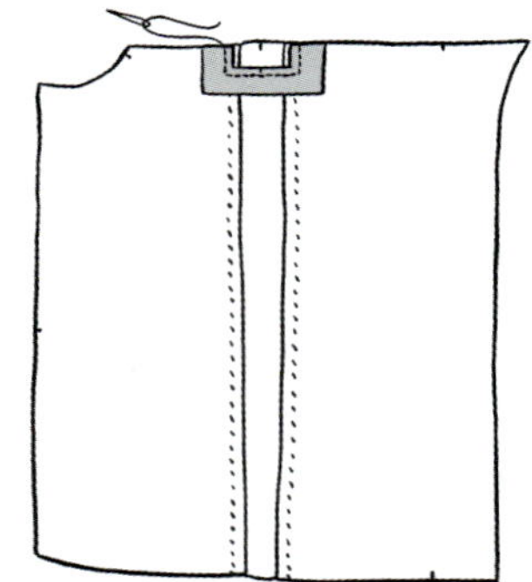

**2.** Trim torso fabric to match outline of facing's SA, as shown. Do not cut through already sewn seams if you encounter any. Instead, cut up close to stitching, but leave a narrow tab of fabric and leave stitching intact. You'll tuck these tabs out of sight shortly.

**3.** Snip slits into corners of opening shape. Cut to but not through stitch line.

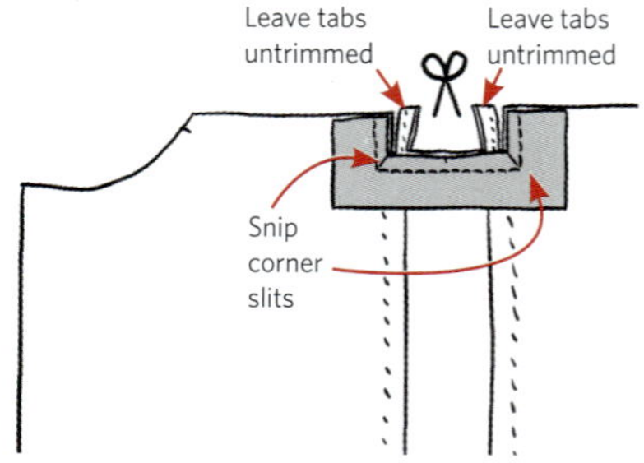

**4.** Turn facings to WS of jacket and press crisply. Tuck tabs in between facing and jacket, held close along seam. Pin facings onto torso panels.

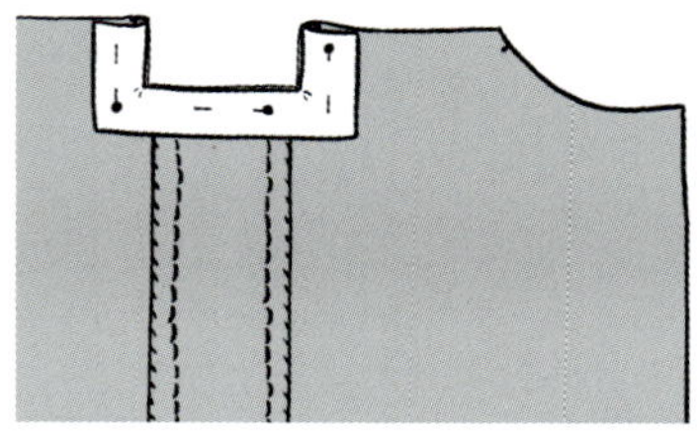

**5.** With topstitching thread, use stitch of choice (spaced backstitch, running stitch, etc.) to add one or two lines of topstitching along the seamed edges.

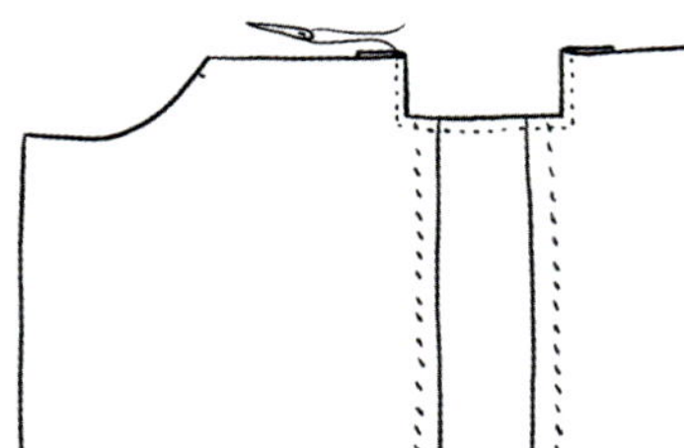

**6.** With regular thread, use overcasting stitch or blanket stitch to thread-bind raw outer edges of facing.

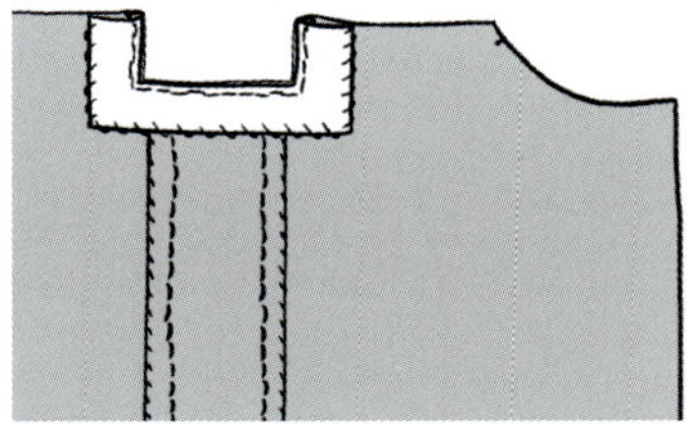

## APPLYING THE CHEST POCKET BAG

**1.** Optional: With regular thread, use overcasting stitch or blanket stitch to thread-bind side and lower edges of chest pocket. (This is optional because these edges will be tucked inside the pocket and will receive very little wear over time.)

**2.** Fold pockets' side and lower SAs (½" [1.3 cm]) toward RS and press. Baste to hold.

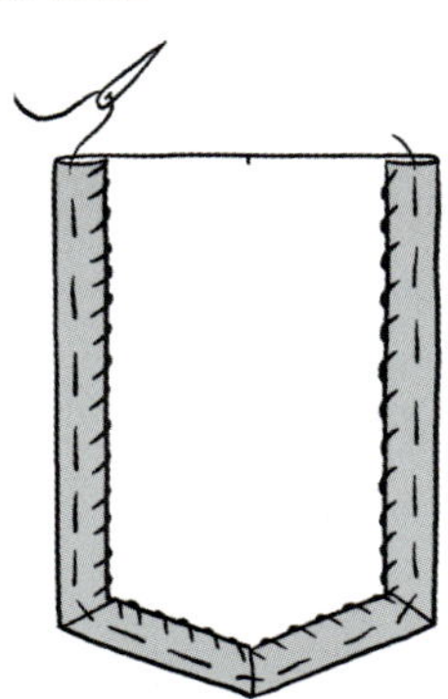

**3.** Position pocket bags in place on WS of front torso panels. Pocket bags' RSs should be facing front torso panels' WS. Center pockets behind pocket openings. Use drill holes as guides for pockets' lower corners. Pin. With topstitching thread and stitch of choice (hemstitch, whipstitch, or fell stitch are good options), secure pocket bags' edges through all layers onto front torso panels.

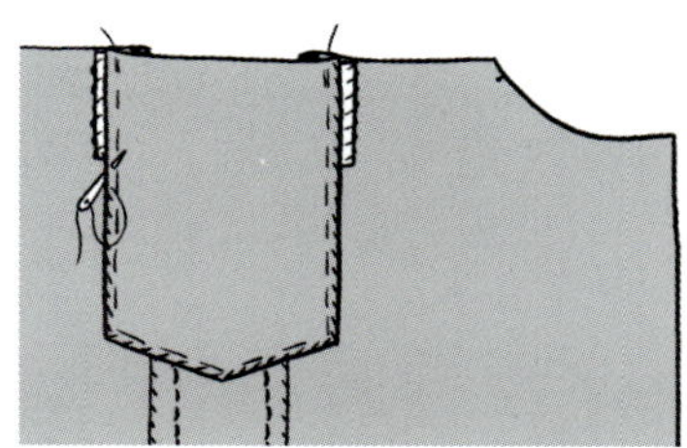

**4.** Optional: With topstitching thread, and facing the RS of the garment, use stitch of choice (spaced backstitch, running stitch, etc.) to add a second line of stitching along pocket bag edges.

**5.** On RS of garment, center pocket flaps on top of chest pockets and baste within SAs to hold.

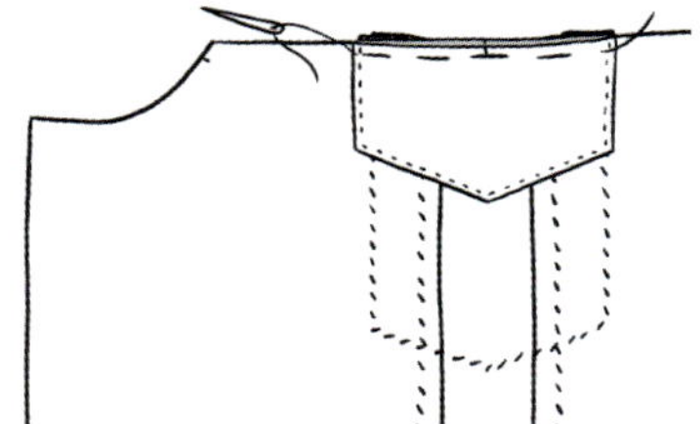

## STITCHING THE WELT POCKETS

**1.** Place welt pocket bag fronts on top of torso fronts with RST. Align pockets' and torsos' welt rectangle markings exactly on top of each other (use a pin to check for precision). Pin in place.

**2.** Use a ruler to draw in long edges of rectangle. Then use regular thread and tiny even backstitches to sew along each line. Stitch precisely, especially at the ends of the lines.

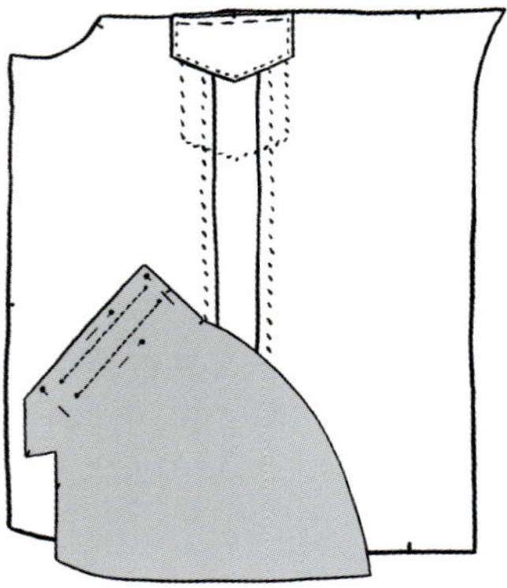

**3.** Cut a slit between the stitch lines, parallel to them and starting and ending approximately ¾" (2 cm) from the ends of the stitch lines. Then make careful diagonal cuts toward each end of stitch line. Diagonal cuts should nearly reach stitching, but not quite.

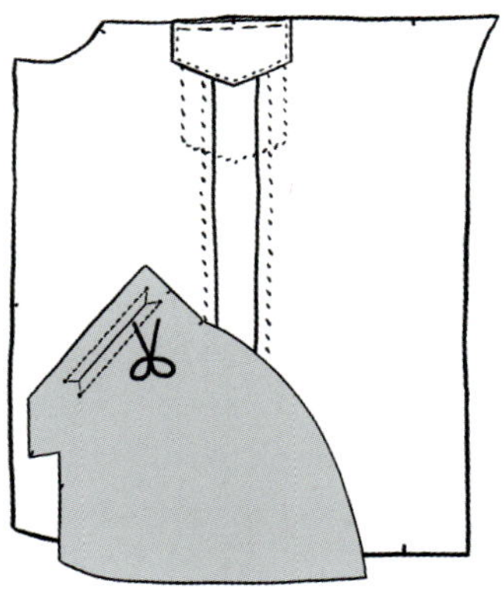

**4.** Using this slit, stuff pocket bag through to backside of torso and press rectangular shape crisply. You'll create a sort of window through the garment.

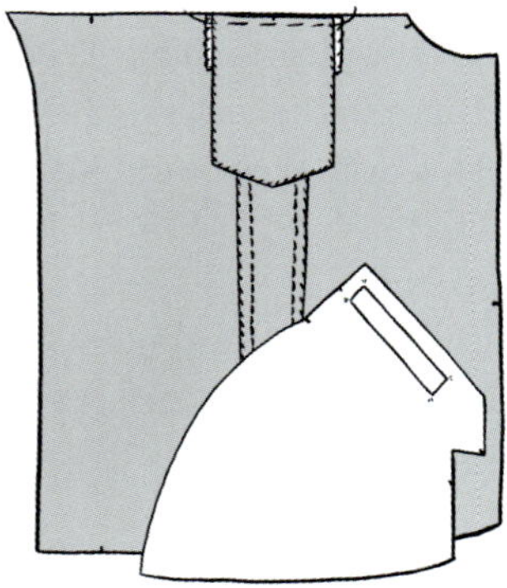

**5.** Create welt by folding up and then pleating fabric as shown. Match notches. Fold carefully, measure if needed, and then press. Pin through all layers to hold, then replace pins with basting.

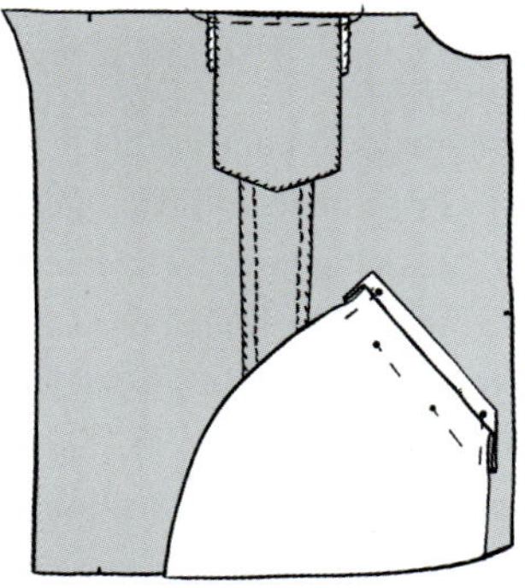

**6.** Working from RS of garment, use topstitching thread and topstitch of choice (even backstitch, tiny running stitches, etc.) through all layers to edgestitch around welt.

**7.** Use topstitching thread to stitch bartacks, fell stitch, or other stitching along short ends to reinforce.

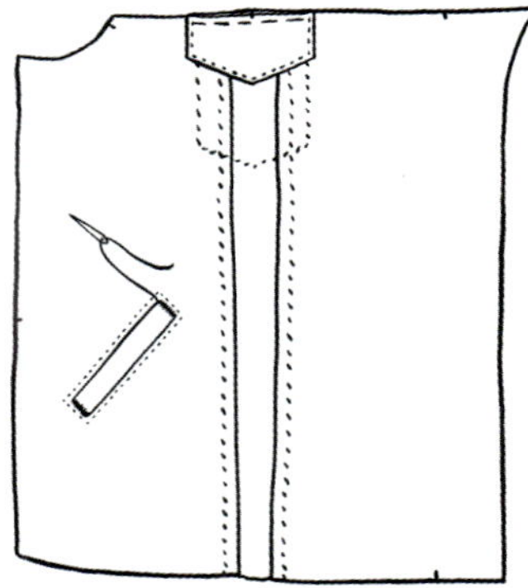

**8.** Pin pocket bag backings together with pocket bag fronts, RST, aligning all edges. Use regular thread and even backstitch (or combination stitch) to join pocket fronts and backings along their perimeter (except lower edge, which will be encased in the bottom band). Use ½" (1.3 cm) SA.

**9.** Use topstitching thread and overcasting or blanket stitch to thread-bind raw edges together. Alternatively, you can use thin bias binding to bind raw edges together.

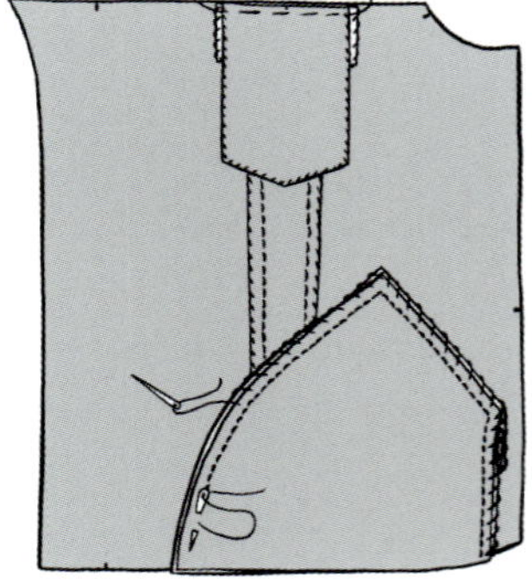

**10.** Baste bottoms of pockets to body, stitching through all layers.

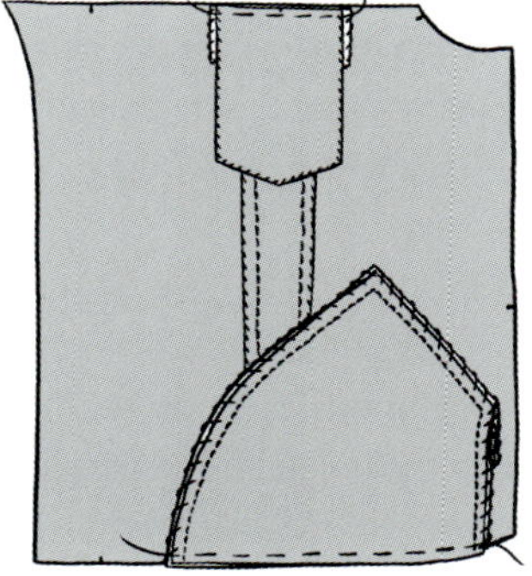

## JOINING THE FRONT YOKES

**1.** Align front yokes on top of lower front torsos, RST. Pin, matching notches and seam intersections.

**2.** Looking at the lower front torso as you stitch, sew yoke seams using even backstitch and regular thread. Use ½" (1.3 cm) SA.

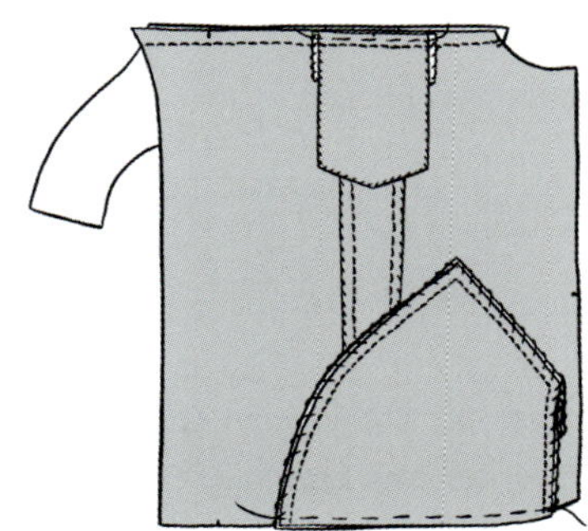

**3.** Press SAs toward yoke.

**4.** Next, finish yoke seams' raw edges using bias binding technique detailed on page 152 of gathered skirt project.

**5.** Facing RS and using topstitching thread, use spaced backstitch through all layers to secure SAs down. Stitching's spacing from seam should mimic flat-felled seams' spacing.

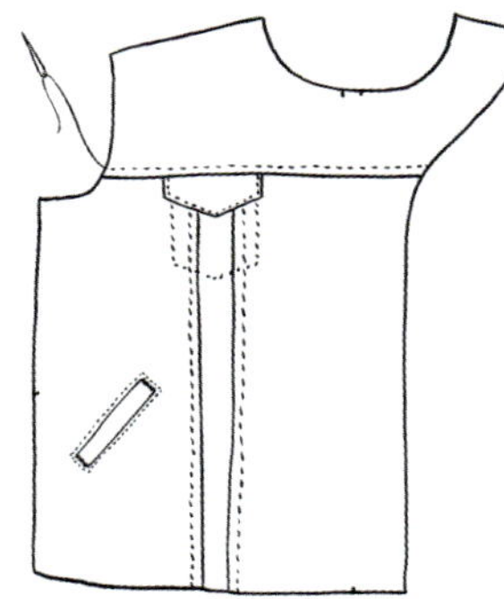

**6.** Consider adding a second line of topstitching to the yoke seams. For this line of stitching, as in step 5, I'd recommend spaced backstitch.

## STITCHING THE FRONT FACINGS

**1.** On CF edges, press under ⅜" (1 cm) SAs and baste to hold.

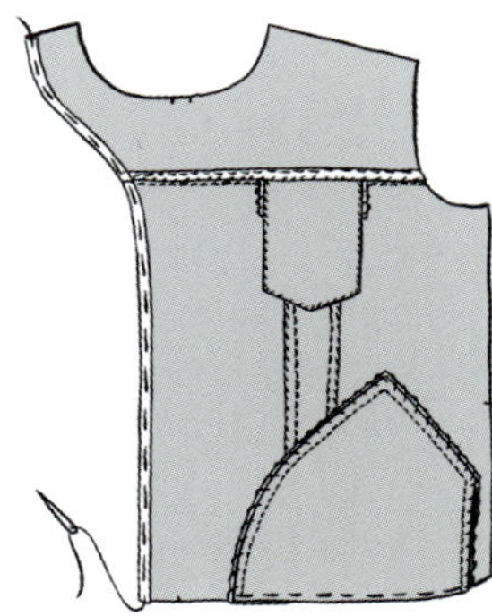

**2.** Fold facing backward (RST) at neck area, using placket fold notch as a guide for folding. Using regular thread and small even backstitches, stitch in from fold to CF, with ½" (1.3 cm) SA. This will be a very short line of stitching. (So if, for example, your pattern features a 1¼" [3.2 cm] placket width, you'll stitch in for half of that amount—⅝" [1.6 cm]—to reach CF.) Then anchor off.

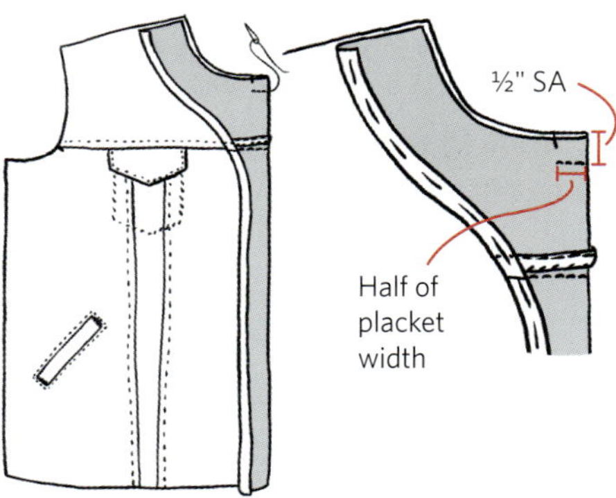


**3.** Snip in from raw edge of neckline to where your stitching ended, cutting to within a few threads of your stitches. Also snip triangle at fold to reduce bulk.

**4.** Turn placket RS out. Push out corner carefully. Allow remainder of front neck SA to remain upright. Now, guided by sewn top edge and placket fold notch at bottom edge, carefully press placket fold. Use a ruler as you go to ensure accurate fold placement. Pin. Optionally, baste and remove pins.

**5.** Using topstitching thread and your stitch of choice (hemstitch, whipstitch, fell stitch, etc.), secure facing's folded edges down to garment.

**6.** Baste facing and garment layers together along neckline and shoulder.

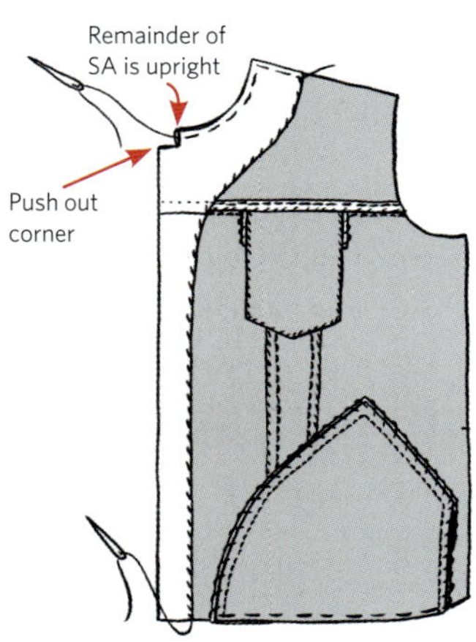


## SEWING THE SHOULDER SEAMS

**1.** Align front and back torso panels at shoulder seams, with RST. Pin.

**2.** Looking at front panels as you sew, stitch shoulder seams with regular thread and even backstitch. Use ¾" (2 cm) SA.

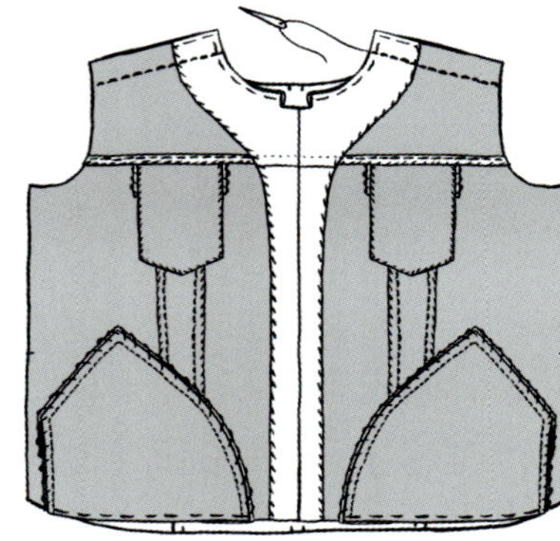

**3.** Press SAs toward the back body.

**4.** Prepare to fell SA. Trim half of the width of back shoulders' SAs, then fold front shoulders' SAs around and under back's SAs so that all raw edges are concealed. Pin.

**5.** With topstitching thread, use hemstitch, whipstitch, fell stitch, or other stitch of choice to secure folded edges down. Press.

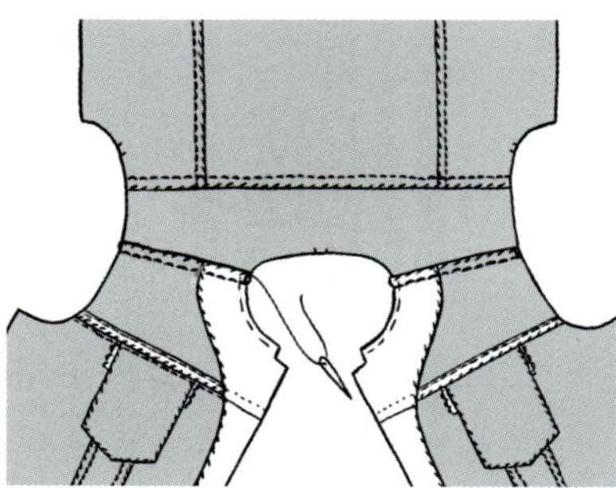

**6.** Consider adding another line of topstitching to the shoulder seams. You'll work this topstitching from the RS. I'd recommend spaced backstitch or another stitch that looks similar to the stitches that felled your SAs.

## CONSTRUCTING THE COLLAR

**1.** Fold under and baste SAs on the lower edge of one collar piece (this should be the uninterfaced piece, if you're using interfacing).

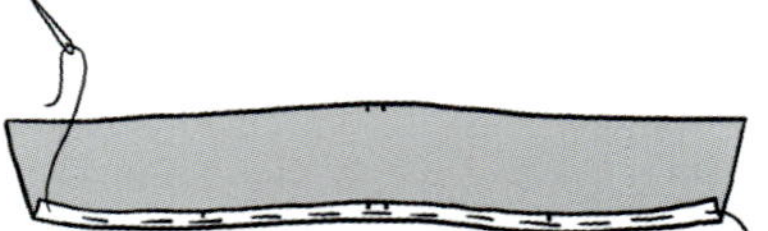

**2.** With RST, pin collar pieces together. Seam together the side and outer edges through all layers with ½" (1.3 cm) SA, using regular thread and small even backstitches or small running stitches.

**3.** Snip corner triangles and clip curved areas to reduce bulk.

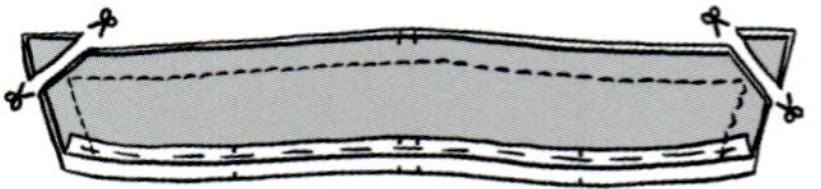

**4.** Finger-press SAs open, then turn. Push corners out carefully. Press seamed edges with iron.

### ATTACHING THE COLLAR

**1.** Locate unbasted edge of collar. Pin this edge, RS down, onto WS of garment's neckline. Align all notches and edges.

**2.** Sew together through all layers to join, with regular thread and using combination stitch, even backstitch, or tiny running stitches. Use ½" (1.3 cm) SA.

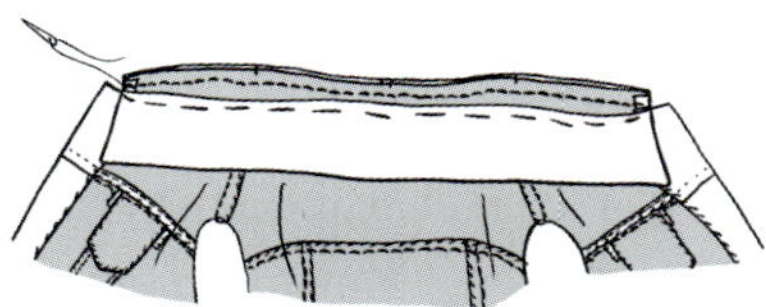

**3.** Press collar up away from garment.

**4.** Pull basted edge down over SAs and align basted edge so that it just barely covers stitch line. Pin. The SAs should now be entirely concealed.

**5.** With regular thread, secure edge down using whipstitch, fell stitch, or hemstitch. Remove basting.

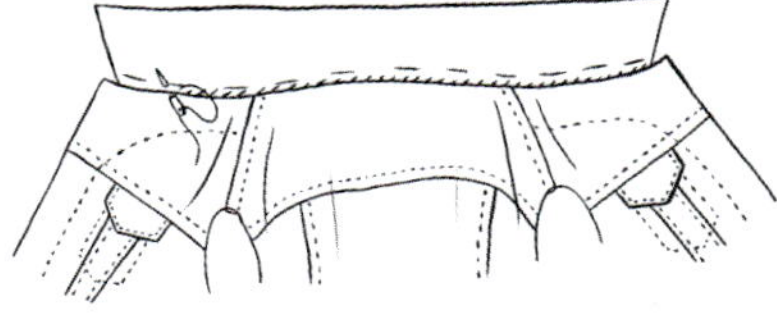

**6.** With topstitching thread, and facing WS of garment, sew around entire collar's perimeter using topstitch of choice (even backstitch, spaced backstitch, running stitch, etc.). Press.

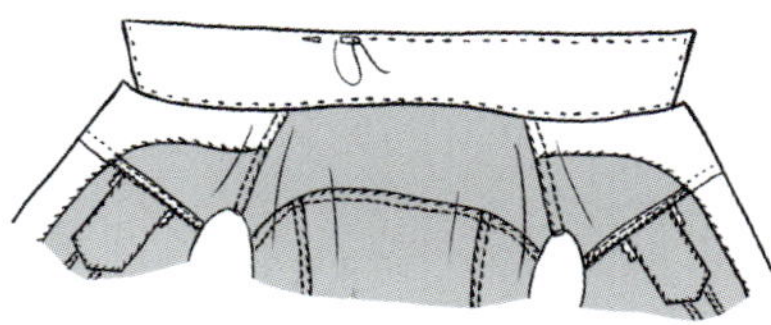

### SEWING THE SIDE SEAMS

**1.** Fold garment, RST, so that side seams are aligned. Pin, matching all notches and edges.

**2.** Facing the back torso, use regular thread to stitch seam using even backstitch or combination stitch. Use ¾" (2 cm) SA.

**3.** Press SAs toward front panels.

**4.** Prepare to fell SAs. Trim half of the width of fronts' SAs, then fold back's SAs around and under fronts' SAs so that all raw edges are concealed. Pin.

**5.** With topstitching thread, use hemstitch, whipstitch, fell stitch, or other stitch of choice to secure folded edges down. Press.

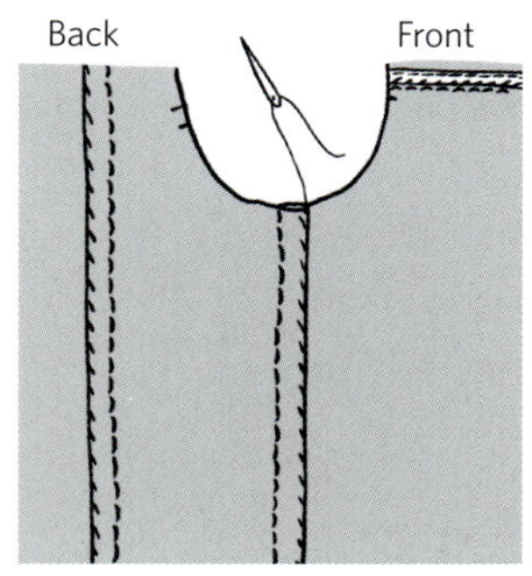


**6.** Consider adding another line of topstitching to the side seams. You'll work this topstitching from the RS. I'd recommend spaced backstitch or another stitch that looks similar to the stitches that felled your SAs.

### CONSTRUCTING THE SLEEVES

**1.** Align front and back sleeve pieces along vertical style seams, RST, matching notches. Note that the sleeve vent portion of the back sleeve will overhang the front sleeve's SA. (If your pattern follows my recommended SA amounts, the back sleeve will overhang the front by ⅜" [1 cm] along the sleeve vent.)

**2.** Facing the back sleeve, use regular thread to stitch seam, using even backstitch or combination stitch. Stitch only from sleeve cap to sleeve vent drill hole, then anchor off. Do not stitch along sleeve vent portion.

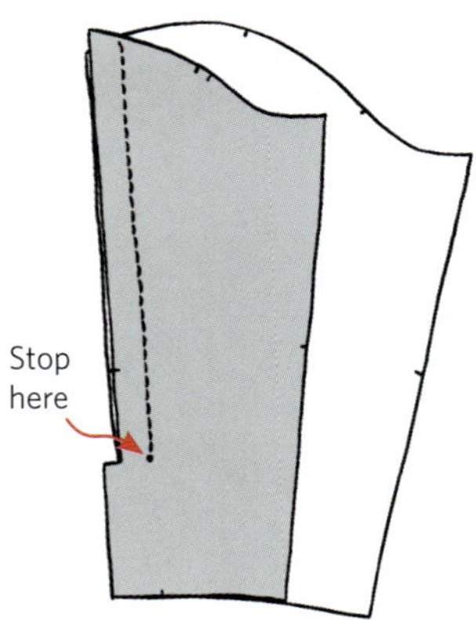


**3.** At level of sleeve vent notch, carefully cut a slit from SAs' raw edges to stitch line. Leave only a few threads of space between slit and stitching.

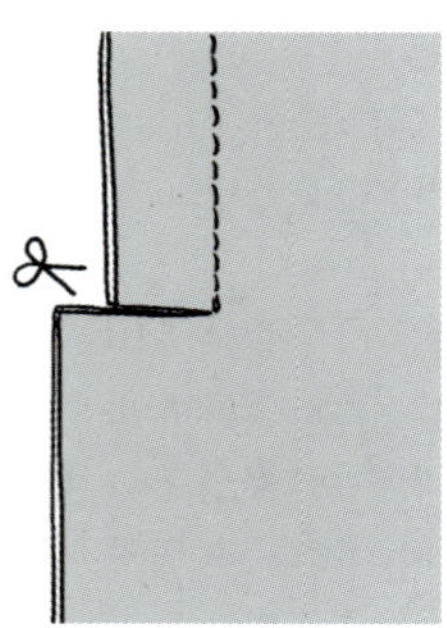

**4.** Press non-vent SAs toward front sleeve.

**5.** Prepare to fell SA. Trim half of the width of front's SA, then fold back's SA around and under front's SA so that all raw edges are concealed. Pin.

**6.** With topstitching thread, use hemstitch, whipstitch, fell stitch, or other stitch of choice to secure folded edges down. Press.

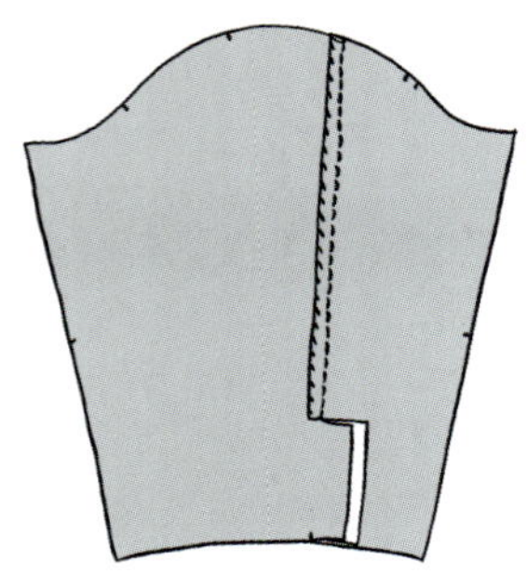

**7.** Consider adding another line of topstitching. You'll work this topstitching from the RS. I'd recommend spaced backstitch or another stitch that looks similar to the stitches that felled your SA.

**8.** Press a double-turned hem on each edge of the sleeve vent. (If your pattern follows my recommended SA amounts, you'll turn each edge under by ⅜" [1 cm], then ⅜" [1 cm] again.) Pin to hold.

**9.** With topstitching thread, use hemstitch, whipstitch, fell stitch, or other stitch of choice to secure folded edges down. Press.

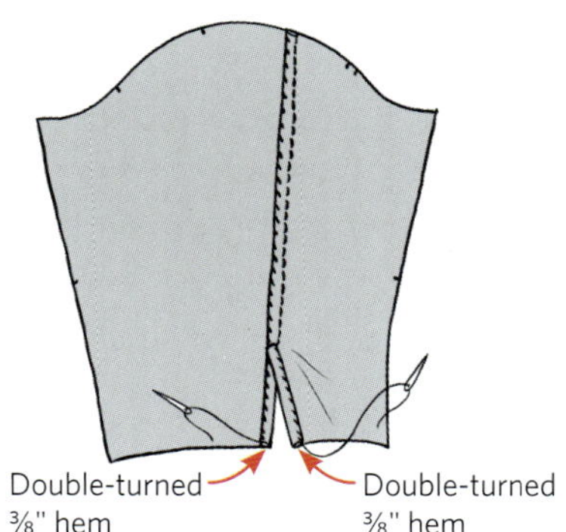


**10.** Consider adding another line of topstitching to front sleeve's vent hem. You'll work this topstitching from the RS. I'd recommend spaced backstitch or another stitch that looks similar to the stitches that secured down your hem. You can also add another line of topstitching to the back sleeve's vent hem if you'd like, although this will be the underlap of the vent and won't show quite as much.

**11.** Position vent edges with back sleeve's vent underlap centered under front sleeve's vent hem. Pin. Measure ½" (1.3 cm) down from vent's SA slit point, and use topstitching thread to stitch a tidy bartack through all layers.

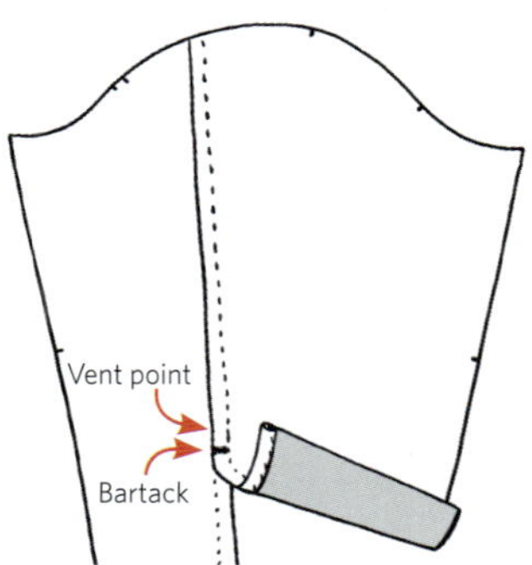


**12.** Fold sleeve with RST, aligning inseam edges. Pin, matching notches. With regular thread and even backstitch or combination stitch, sew inseams. Use ½" (1.3 cm) SA.

**13.** Use topstitching thread and overcasting or blanket stitch to thread-bind inseams' raw edges together. Alternatively, you can use thin woven bias binding to finish the inseams' raw edges together.

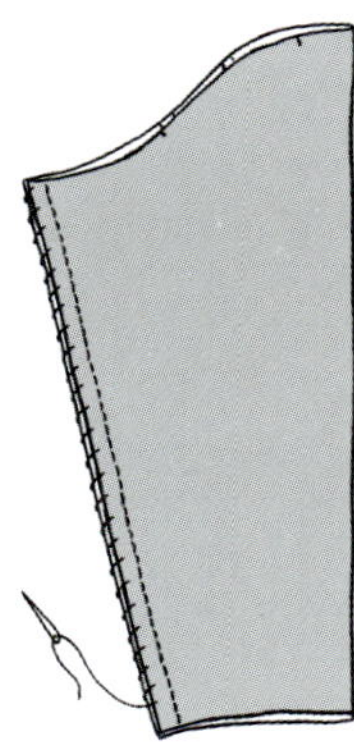

**14.** Press SAs toward back.

### CONSTRUCTING THE SLEEVE CUFFS

**1.** For each cuff piece, fold under and baste the ½" (1.3 cm) SA on one of the long edges.

**2.** Fold cuff pieces backward (so that RSs are facing) and pin short edges.

**3.** Using regular thread, stitch to join all layers, including basted SAs, as shown. You can use small running stitches, even backstitch, or combination stitch. Use ½" (1.3 cm) SA.

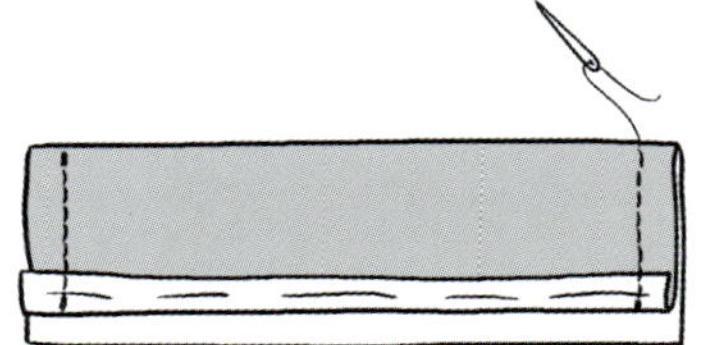

**4.** Snip corner triangles to reduce bulk.

**5.** Turn, push out corners, and press. Do not remove basting.

### ATTACHING THE SLEEVE CUFFS

**1.** Locate unbasted edge of each cuff. Pin this edge, RS down, onto WS of sleeve edge.

**2.** Using regular thread and ½" (1.3 cm) SA, sew together through all layers to join. You can use combination stitch, even backstitch, or tiny running stitches.

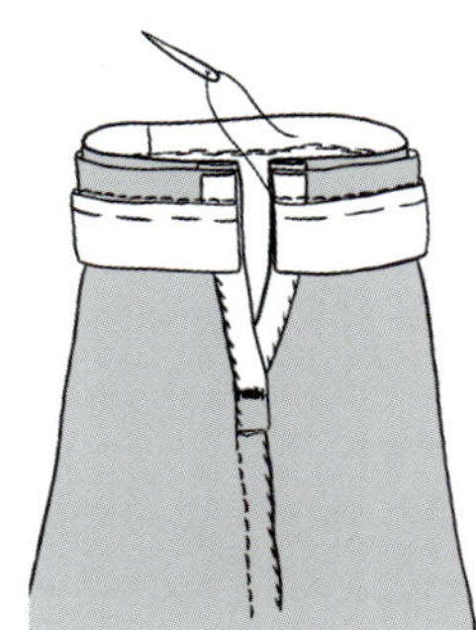

**3.** Press cuffs out away from garment.

**4.** Pull basted edge down over SAs and align basted edge so that it just barely covers stitch line. Pin. The SAs should now be entirely concealed.

**5.** With regular thread, secure edge down using whipstitch, fell stitch, or hemstitch. Remove basting.

**6.** With topstitching thread, sew around entire cuff's perimeter, using stitch of choice (even backstitch, spaced backstitch, running stitch, etc.). Press.

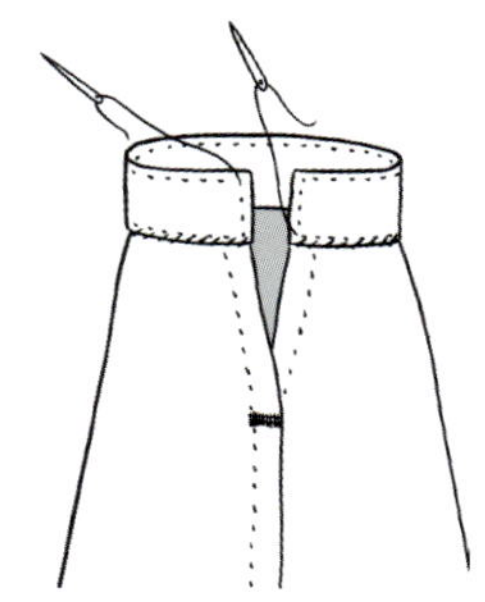

### SETTING IN THE SLEEVES

**1.** Arrange garment face up on table in front of you. Place sleeves next to their respective armholes. (Single notches at mid-underarm should be facing up; double notches at mid-underarm should be facing down.)

**2.** Open jacket, and working from inside of jacket, pin each sleeve into its respective armhole, RST, matching notches and seamlines. Place pins carefully through each "milestone" matching point: Inseams should match side seams; mid-underarm notches should match; sleeve's vertical seam should match back yoke seam; sleeve's notch near top of cap should match shoulder seam. Once these important points are pinned, add more pins to distribute and align edges all the way around. Carefully distribute cap ease by using lots of pins. At first, the sleeve cap edge will seem too long for the armhole. Pin generously and it'll fit.

**3.** Facing the sleeve, use regular thread and neat, smallish even backstitches to seam sleeve into armhole. Use ¾" (2 cm) SA. Remove pins as you go for easier sewing.

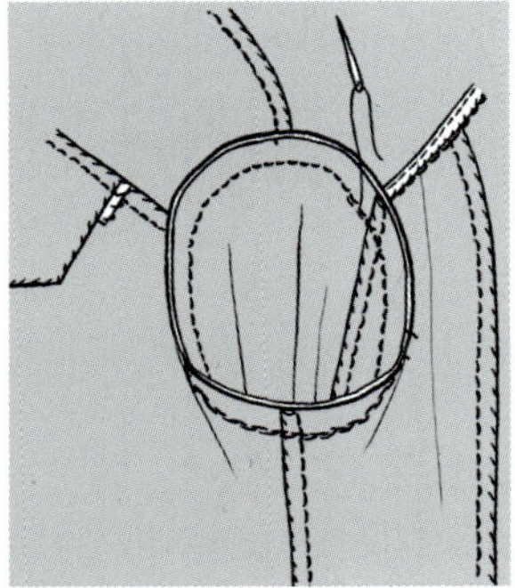

**4.** Press SAs away from sleeve.

**5.** To finish armhole SAs, you have options. You can:

- Use topstitching thread and overcasting or blanket stitch to thread-bind raw edges together. Press.
- Use thin bias binding to finish raw edges together. Press.
- Fell SA onto body. Trim half of width of body's SA (only the lower layer of your SA), leaving little tabs at shoulder, yoke, and side seams so you avoid slicing through those seams' stitch lines. Then fold sleeve's SA around and under body's so that all raw edges are concealed. (Smoosh and conceal tabs as you fold.) Pin and/or baste. Then, with topstitching thread, use hemstitch, whipstitch, fell stitch, or other stitch to secure folded edges down. Press.

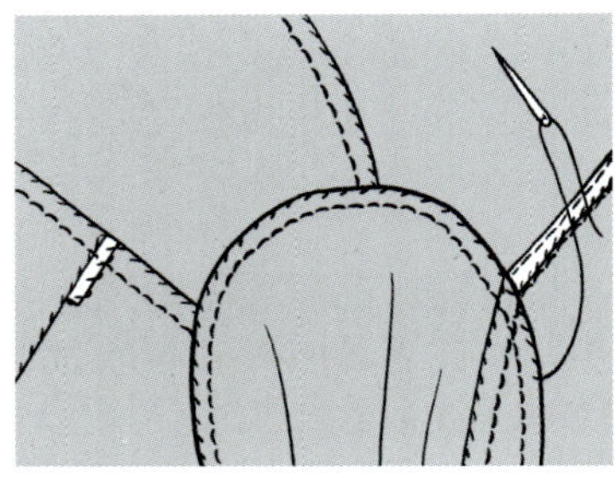

**6.** Consider adding one or two lines of topstitching through all layers (body and SA) to match jacket's other topstitched seams. You'll work this topstitching from the RS.

## CONSTRUCTING THE BOTTOM BAND

**1.** Fold under and baste the ½" (1.3 cm) SA on one of the long edges.

**2.** Fold band backward (so that RSs are facing) and pin short edges.

**3.** Using regular thread, stitch to join all layers, including basted SAs, as shown. You can use small running stitches, even backstitch, or combination stitch. Use ½" (1.3 cm) SA.

**4.** Snip corner triangles to reduce bulk.

**5.** Turn, push out corners, and press. Do not remove basting.

## ATTACHING THE BOTTOM BAND

**1.** Locate unbasted edge of band. Pin this edge, RS down, onto WS of jacket's bottom edge.

**2.** Using regular thread and ½" (1.3 cm) SA, sew together through all layers to join. You can use combination stitch, even backstitch, or tiny running stitches.

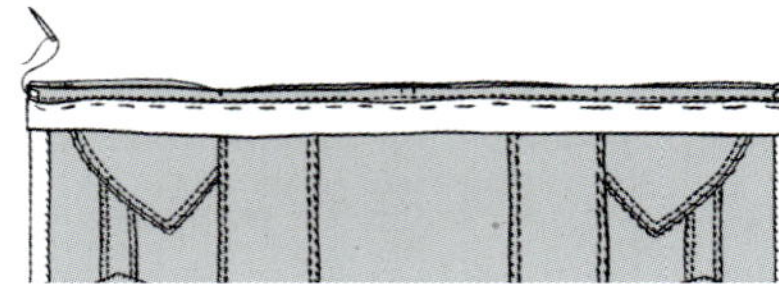

**3.** Press band out away from garment.

**4.** Pull basted edge down over SA and align basted edge so that it just barely covers stitch line. Pin. The SA should now be entirely concealed.

**5.** With regular thread, secure edge down using whipstitch, fell stitch, or hemstitch. Remove basting.

**6.** With topstitching thread, sew around entire band's perimeter, using stitch of choice (even backstitch, spaced backstitch, running stitch, etc.). Press.

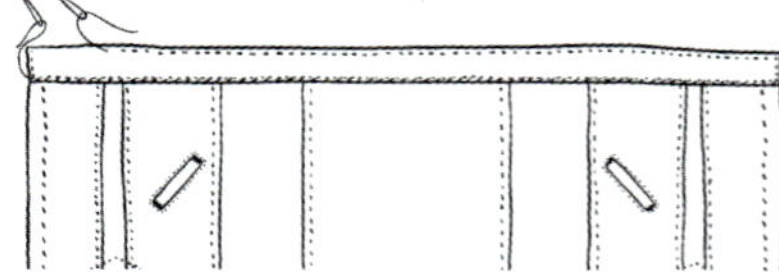

## MARKING AND SEWING THE BUTTONHOLES

**1.** First, stitch up one or more test buttonholes. To do so:

**A.** Take a scrap of self fabric and fold in half to create a two-layer mock-up placket. Baste fold down to hold.

**B.** Mark a slit that is the same length as your button's diameter. Baste a little box around this slit to hold all layers together.

**C.** Use a chisel or small, very sharp scissors to carefully cut slit.

**D.** Thread needle with single strand (not doubled) of topstitching thread.

**E.** Use buttonhole stitches to bind edges of slit. I like to fan my stitches around one end (the one nearer to the placket's folded edge) and create a boxy bartack at the other end, but you can create whatever style buttonhole you'd prefer. Spacing of stitches is at your discretion—experiment here and see what you like.

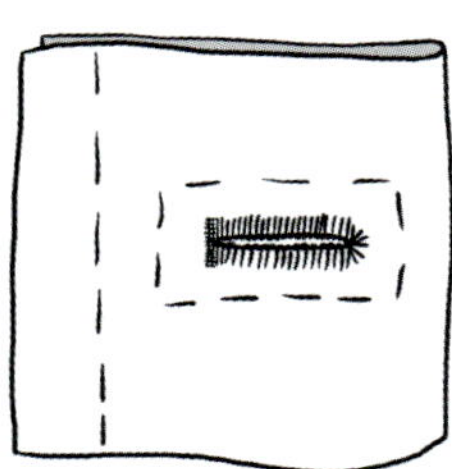

**F.** Test size of buttonhole to make sure button will fit through appropriately.

**G.** Repeat above steps as needed until you feel confident sewing buttonholes with this fabric, thread, and needle.

**2.** Mark buttonholes onto jacket. First, use pattern as guide to mark button placement points. Then extend buttonhole ⅛" (3 mm) toward placket. This creates space for the button's shank and three-dimensionality. Now measure from this endpoint into the garment for the buttonhole length that you've determined from your test buttonholes. Mark carefully. Repeat for all buttonholes, including on sleeve cuffs.

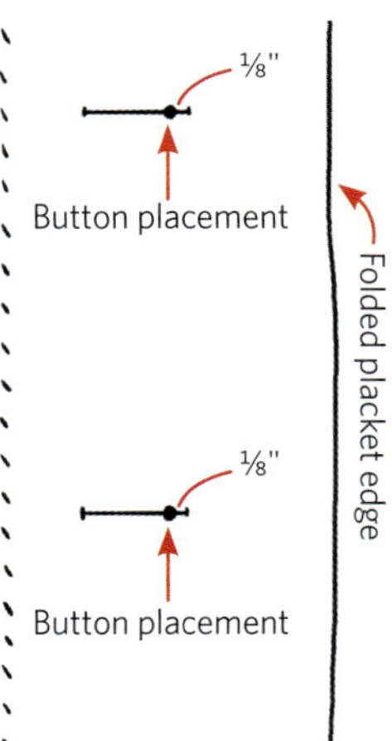


**3.** Baste through all layers around perimeter of each buttonhole placement. The basted box should be at least ¼" (6 mm) away from slit on all sides.

**4.** Use chisel or small, sharp scissors to cut each buttonhole slit.

**5.** Stitch all buttonholes. Remove all basting.

## ATTACHING THE BUTTONS

**1.** Use pattern as guide to mark button placement points. For sleeve cuffs, try on jacket and pin cuffs closed to the dimension that you like. Then push pencil through buttonholes to mark cuff button placements.

**2.** For each jean tack button, follow buttons' installation directions. In general, you'll likely be doing something like the following:

**A.** Press an awl (or very pointy knitting needle, or sharp, thick nail) through the button placement point to create a hole.

**B.** Push stud piece through hole from behind. Stud's pointy end should be facing up.

**C.** Place shank button piece on top of stud, centering it over stud's pointy end. Hold carefully together and flip to the garment's underside.

**D.** While still holding button onto stud, place project on wood block or other firm, sturdy surface. Use a mallet (or hammer, very gently) to tap the stud into the base of the button's shank. Tap until stud is pushed deep into button shank. When complete, stud should be flat against button shank, and the button should not be able to rotate.

# *Sarah E. Woodyard*

*(she/her)*, founder of Sewn Company,
educator, scholar, trained mantua-maker and milliner
WILLIAMSBURG, VIRGINIA, USA

As a small child, Sarah asked to "help" her grandmother with some hand quilting, so she was given a scrap and taught to make running stitches. That was the beginning of a lifelong relationship with hand sewing. Now, she reflects, "It is one of my life's greatest loves."

In the decades since that earliest lesson, Sarah has built a career in hand sewing—first apprenticing in Colonial Williamsburg's millinery shop, and now teaching hand sewing full time. She still has that scrap of her earliest childhood stitches.

"I love the process of hand sewing," she shares. "I love the drape of the clothing when I sew it by hand, and I love that I can take it anywhere. I also am interested in recreating historical garments to learn more about the anonymous makers and keep their skills alive."

Asked how hand sewing fits into the bigger picture of her life, Sarah responds: "I feel like it *is* my life. My life goes around it."

***Training and insight.*** I really started hand-sewing garments during my internship at the millinery shop in Colonial Williamsburg in the summer of 2006. I learned how to hand-stitch eighteenth-century English garments. In the evenings, I hand-stitched modern clothes using the techniques I learned during my internship.

I went on to do a seven-year hand-sewing apprenticeship in eighteenth-century English dressmaking that taught me how fast you can stitch by hand. That full-time experience showed me how stitchers from the past knew what they were doing, clothing lasted, and the work is aesthetically pleasing. So why not apply the same methods to my modern wardrobe?

***Favorite hand-sewing stitch.*** Felling. I find it extremely versatile.

***When and where.*** I hand-sew mostly during the day—there is nothing better than natural light. My favorite place to hand-sew is on my back porch, but I also hand-sew a lot in a wingback chair in my office. That said, I've hand-stitched in a living history museum, in my bed, in a car, at the dentist, at night with an OttLite, at the dining room table, during work trainings, at virtual and in-person sewing circles, on a plane, on a train . . .

***The liminal space.*** The most challenging part of hand sewing for me is the liminal space between thinking of a project and actually sitting down to create it.

***Learning more.*** I typically learn by studying garments pre-1840s that were originally handsewn and then just experimenting to make a historical recreation. Or being creatively inspired to take those skills and apply them to modern designs.

***Flow state.*** I am always chasing a "flow state," where everything melts away and your mind and body are in sync and you feel content and energized. Hand sewing does that for me.

***Newcomer advice.*** It is a practice—just do it every day for at least 15 minutes. It will look messy at first, but eventually the muscle memory will come, and it will just click one day. Keep practicing.

# JEANS

For thousands of years before the sewing machine, all clothes were sewn by hand—including thick, sturdy pants. Why not try your hand at a pair of jeans? First, you'll develop a pattern by tracing a preexisting pair you already love. Then you can follow my instructions to hand-sew jeans that will look pretty convincingly machine sewn—an amusing challenge. If that's not your game, though—if you'd rather prioritize ergonomic, efficient, comfortable stitches than machine look-alikes—feel free to construct your jeans in whatever way works best for you. No matter what, this project will be a huge accomplishment.

# Patternmaking

For this jeans project, you'll try your hand at taking a rub-off. Rather than drafting shapes based on measurements from your body, you'll create your patterns by tracing shapes from jeans you already own (or have access to) and love. This is a different approach to patternmaking, but it's no less empowering than patterndrafting. In fact, once you feel confident tracing patterns from preexisting clothes, you can suddenly make patterns for so many new types of clothing! Combined with a few pattern modification skills, you'll be able to pattern pretty much anything.

There are lots of ways to trace off the shapes of a preexisting garment. I'll show you my favorite method, but know that you're welcome to opt for other ways.

## What If I Can't Find a Well-Fitting Pair of Jeans?

Perhaps you don't have access to a pair of jeans that fit you well. Yes, you can try to borrow a pair from someone else, or buy a cheap pair from the thrift store. But there are some body sizes and shapes that are extremely underserved in the ready-to-wear market. And perhaps that's true for you. In that case, you have a few options.

If you have jeans that are functional but don't fit well, you can trace off their basic pattern, then make whatever modifications you feel they need. You can widen or taper as you see fit. You can lengthen or shorten. Make whatever changes you'd like. You'll probably want to baste together a test fit sample (which I'd recommend doing for every project anyway, but it would be especially helpful here).

If you don't have access to jeans that are even moderately functional for you, then I'd recommend looking into some of the amazing indie patterns that exist these days. (Muna and Broad is a great resource for plus-size bodies, for example, and they currently have a policy that if their size range is too small for a customer, they'll grade their patterns up to that customer's size for no additional cost.)

Or if you'd prefer to draft your own jeans pattern from scratch, then I'd recommend picking up a book on pants patterndrafting. Unfortunately that's a larger topic than this chapter can hold, and it's outside my area of expertise. But there are some great books out there to help you on your custom pants-patternmaking journey.

## SETTING UP

You'll need to prepare the jeans with some helpful markings. First, pick a side (wearer's right or wearer's left) that you'll trace. If you're not sure which to choose, I'd recommend tracing the wearer's right side, as that side often includes a coin pocket, so you'll be able to capture that detail as well.

In order to facilitate careful, accurate tracing, you'll want to thread-trace the center lines on the side you chose:

**1.** Match leg's inseam and outseam at hemline. Place a pin through both layers.

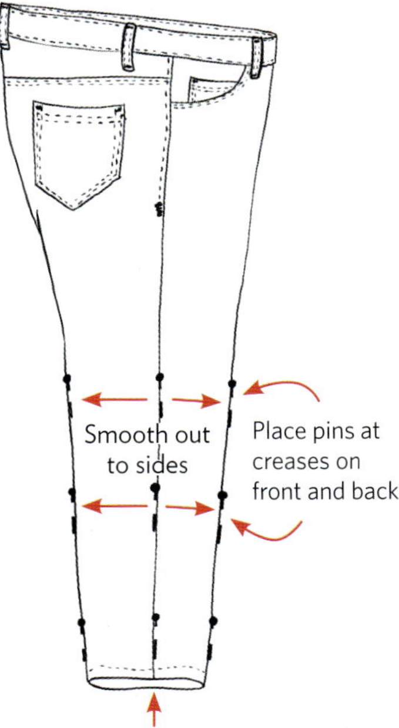


**2.** Smooth upward along jean, matching inseam and outseam as you smooth and placing pins through both. Continue until you've reached roughly knee level.

**3.** Smooth outward along pinned area to find accurate folds at the creases of front and back leg panels. Place pins.

**4.** Remove pins along inseam and outseam, but keep pins along center lines. Now smooth jeans flat with front panel facing up.

**5.** Using a yardstick or other long straightedge, place more pins to continue center line upward to waistband seam.

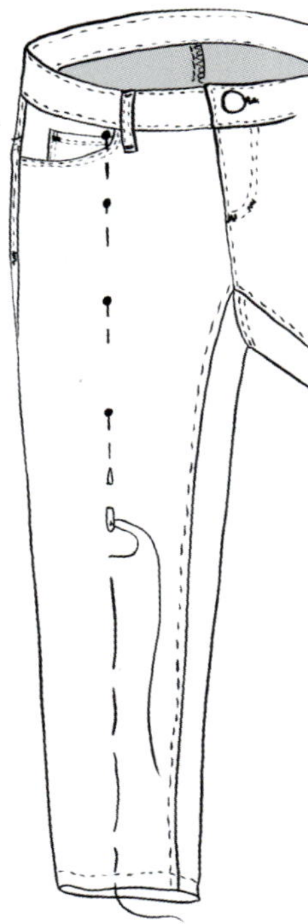

**6.** Replace all pins with very long, quick basting stitches through front layer only.

**7.** Repeat steps 4 through 6 on back of leg, but extend center line only as far as yoke seam (not waistband seam).

**8.** It will also be helpful to place level markers along your leg inseam and outseam.

- Knee level: Fold hem upward to be level with the crotch intersection. The fold represents your pattern's knee level. Place thread tacks or pins at this level on inseam and outseam.
- Hip level: Feel for the point where the bottom of the pocket bag meets the outseam. Place thread tack or pin.

To prepare for tracing, clear your worktable or floor (you can work on dense carpet, but not high-pile carpet). You'll need plenty of space to lay out your pattern paper, tools, and jeans. Next, lay down a thin, soft old blanket or large towel. (If you're using a carpeted floor, you can skip the blanket or towel.)

I'd recommend using a workaday table for rub-offs rather than your formal dinner table or another precious surface. You'll be pushing pins through until they hit the work surface, and you won't want to scratch up a nice tabletop. A good option might be a densely carpeted floor, which can handle the pinpricks but still allow you to trace accurate lines onto your paper.

Now set a large, long sheet of paper on top. The paper should be big enough for you to spread out one side of your jeans, with generous margins around all sides.

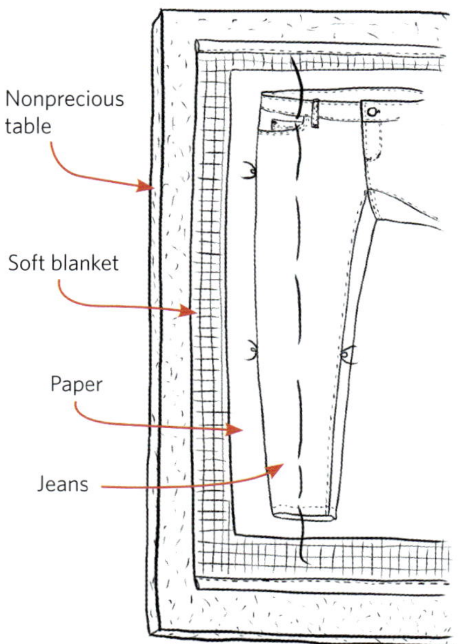


## TRACING THE FRONT PANEL

Typically, the front panel is somewhat narrower than the back, so you can lay the pants flat and smooth out the entire front panel easily.

If your front panel is wider than the back, you'll need to follow the process described for the back panel.

**1.** Lay jeans flat, front facing up, centered on top of paper (which is on top of blanket or towel). Be sure that the entire front leg panel is smooth and flat, including the crotch rise area. Place a few weighted objects to hold in place.

**2.** Use a pin to prick through all layers along waistband-joining seam, from CF to outseam. Pinpricks should puncture through paper each time.

**3.** Pinprick down along outseam, all the way to the bottom hem. Add extra pinpricks at hip and knee levels (the levels you marked with thread or pins).

**4.** Use pencil to trace along bottom hem.

**5.** Pinprick up along inseam, all the way to crotch intersection. Add extra pinpricks at knee level.

**6.** Pinprick up along crotch rise seam. Stop when you reach waistband join seam.

**7.** Now capture smaller details:

- Pinprick along front pocket opening.
- Pinprick along coin pocket shape, if applicable. Include the section that is hidden inside the front pocket.
- Pinprick along pocket facing—that's the denim panel to which the coin pocket is sewn. Again, include the section hidden inside the pocket.
- Using your fingertips to feel the shape, pinprick along entire front pocket bag's outline.

**8.** Pinprick in a few places along center line.

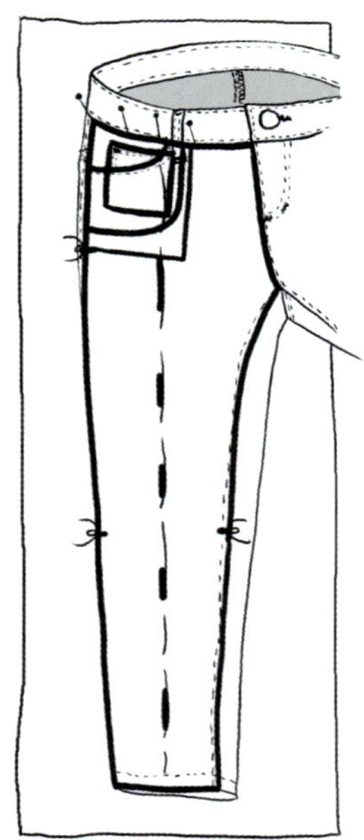

**9.** Leaving jeans as undisturbed as possible, carefully peek at paper underneath to make sure all pinpricks transferred properly.

**10.** Once you've verified that all has been traced, remove weights and jeans. Sketch in all pinpricked lines and points. (You'll neaten everything later.)

## TRACING THE BACK PANEL

The back panel is almost always wider than the front, which means you'll have to adjust the pants midway to ensure an accurate, complete tracing.

**1.** Using a yardstick or other long straightedge, draw a long line along center of a new sheet of paper. This line should be at least as long as jeans. Place paper on top of blanket or towel.

**2.** Smooth out back panel so that the outer half—everything between the thread-traced center line and the outseam—is flat.

**3.** Lay jeans flat on top of paper, back panel facing up, with thread-traced center line on top of paper's drawn line. Place weights along center line, checking with pin as you go to be sure that each section of the center line is accurately positioned over drawn line. Then weight down the rest of the outer half's area.

**4.** Use a pin to prick through all layers along yoke seam, from thread-marked center line to outseam. Pinpricks should puncture through paper each time.

**5.** Pinprick down along outseam, all the way to the bottom hem. Add extra pinpricks at hip and knee levels (the levels you marked with thread or pins).

**6.** Use pencil to trace along bottom hem until you reach thread-marked center line.

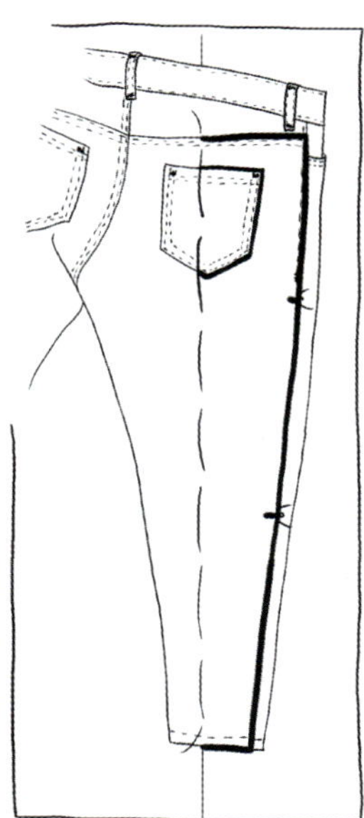

**7.** Pinprick along back pocket's outline on this side of center line. Peek at paper to make sure all pinpricks transferred properly. Then remove weights and lift away jeans.

**8.** Next, shift jeans so that the inner half of the back panel, including the crotch rise area, is flat.

**9.** Keeping jeans in this configuration, lay them flat on top of paper again, with thread-traced center line on top of paper's drawn line. Use a pin to check placement as you go. Jeans hem should line up neatly with previous tracing. Use a pin to verify that the center line–yoke seam intersection point is aligned with previous tracing. Once all is accurately placed, weight down.

**10.** Starting at thread-marked center line along bottom hem, use pencil to trace remainder of bottom hem.

**11.** Pinprick up along inseam, all the way to the crotch rise intersection. Add extra pinpricks at knee level.

**12.** Pinprick along crotch rise seam, then back yoke seam until you reach the center line again.

**13.** Pinprick along back pocket's outline on this side of center line.

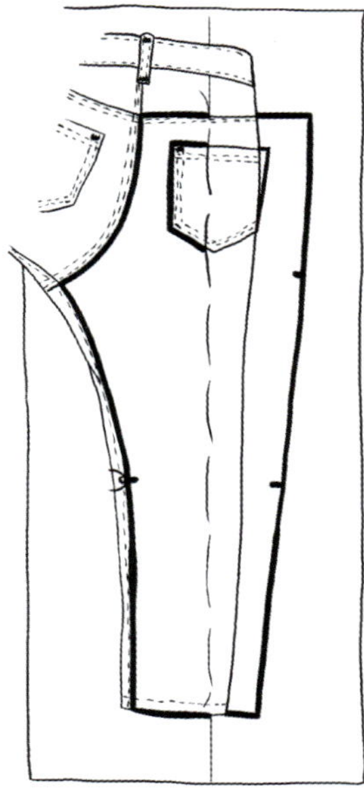

**14.** Leaving jeans as undisturbed as possible, carefully peek at paper underneath to make sure all pinpricks transferred properly.

**15.** Once you've verified that all has been traced, remove weights and jeans. Sketch in all pinpricked lines and points. (You'll neaten everything later.)

### TRACING THE BACK YOKE

Now you'll trace the back yoke on the same half of your jeans that you've been tracing (either wearer's right or wearer's left).

**1.** Place back yoke section of jeans over a new sheet of paper that is laid on the blanket or towel. Smooth yoke area flat, then weight down.

**2.** Pinprick along perimeter of back yoke: back crotch rise seam, waistband seam, outseam, and the seam that joins to the lower leg.

**3.** Try to eyeball the grainline of your yoke's fabric and pinprick a grainline.

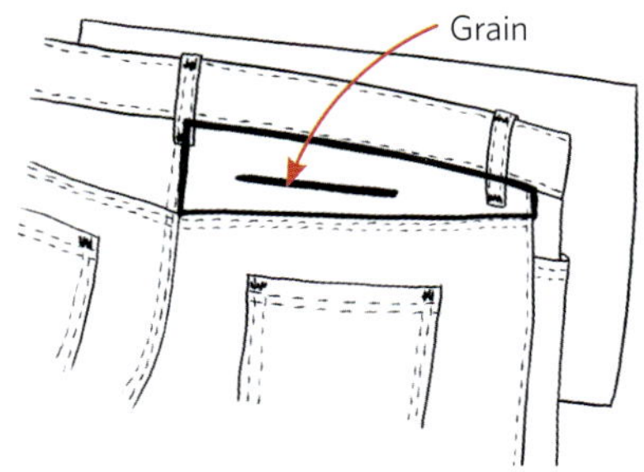


**4.** Peek at paper to ensure lines have transferred. Then remove jeans. Lightly pencil in lines.

### TRACING THE WAISTBAND

Some waistbands are composed of front and back panels, seamed together at the side seams. Others are composed of one long strip, with no side seams. Still others might have a center back seam. I like to give my waistbands side seams so that the jeans are more easily alterable later for changing bodies or different wearers.

If your jeans don't already have this, you'll want to thread-trace a little imaginary side seam onto your waistband so that you know where to divide your waistband sections. Use a ruler to extend the outseam line up into the waistband, and thread-trace this line.

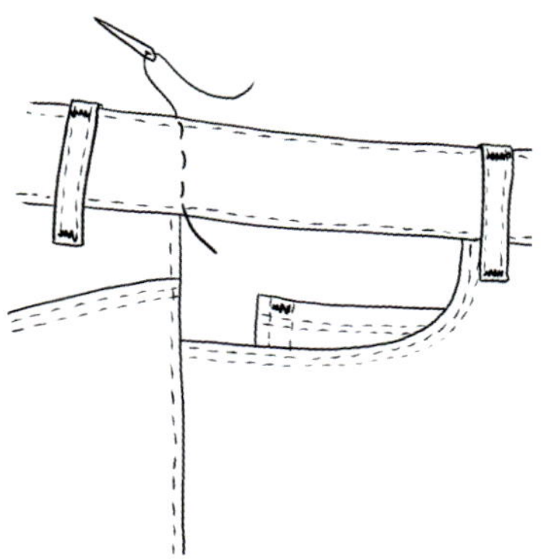

**1.** Place front waistband section of jeans over a new sheet of paper that is laid on the blanket or towel. Smooth front waistband area flat, then weight down. (Or pin it, since weights may be too large for the waistband.)

**2.** Pinprick along perimeter of front waistband: top edge, thread-marked side seam, waistband join seam, and finally the CF line or edge. (Depending on which half of the jeans you're tracing, you may also have some waistband underlap; don't trace that right now. Trace only as far as the CF line. You'll add underlap later when drafting your fly shield.) Pinprick along the fabric's grainline, too.

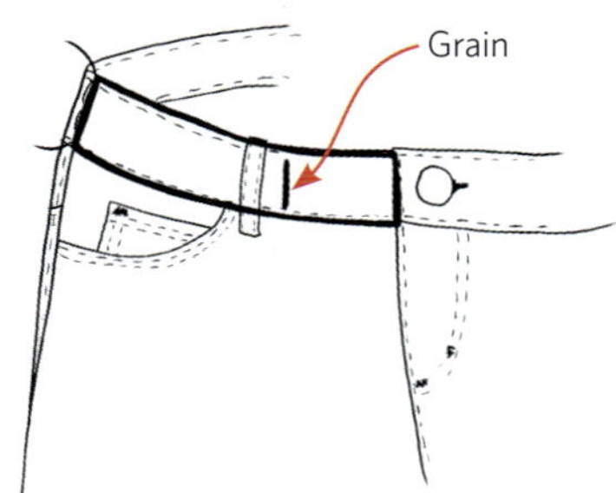


**3.** Peek at paper to ensure lines have transferred. Then remove jeans. Lightly pencil in lines.

**4.** Fold a long sheet of paper in half. Lay it on the blanket or towel. Place back waistband section of jeans over the paper, aligning waistband's CB with paper's fold. Smooth back waistband area flat, then weight or pin down.

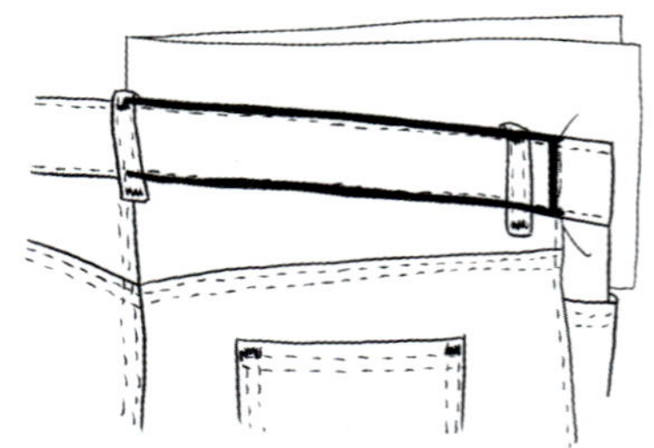

5. Pinprick along perimeter of half of the back waistband: top edge, thread-marked side seam, and waistband join seam. (CB line has already been marked with the paper's fold.)

6. Peek to ensure lines have transferred to paper. Then remove jeans. Lightly pencil in lines.

### TRUEING THE DRAFTS

Now that your basic panels' shapes have been traced, you'll want to clean up the lines and measure everything to ensure that it will all fit together. This process is often called trueing your pattern.

First, tidy up any lines that currently look a bit wavery. You can use a straightedge ruler or eyeball things, depending on what you think the lines need.

Next, measure every edge that will need to be joined to a different piece. Walk your ruler carefully along curved areas, and feel free to measure a couple of times to be sure you're getting accurate numbers. A little bit of fussiness now will be rewarded later with easier sewing and a better fit.

Specifically, measure and jot down the following:

- Front leg: waist edge (ignore the pocket line[s] for now), outseam, inseam
- Back leg: yoke edge, outseam, inseam
- Back yoke: waist edge, outseam, leg edge
- Front waistband: side seam, lower edge
- Back waistband: side seam, lower edge

Now compare the measurements of edges that will need to be joined:

- Front leg's waist edge and front waistband's lower edge
- Front leg's outseam and (back leg's outseam + back yoke's outseam)
- Front leg's inseam and back leg's inseam
- Back leg's yoke edge and back yoke's leg edge
- Back yoke's waist edge and back waistband's lower edge
- Front waistband's side seam and back waistband's side seam

For each of these joins, if there is a real discrepancy (see note below), you can troubleshoot in a couple of ways.

- Measure that seamline along the actual jeans, and compare that number with your drafts. Now adjust one or both lines, as needed, to reflect the actual jeans' dimensions. You might need to extend or shorten the top or bottom of the line, or you might need to reshape the line itself. If you're uncertain, you can lay the jeans on top of your draft and try to use them as a guide.
- Think about how well the jeans do or don't fit you in that area, and reason accordingly. For example, if your yoke's lower edge is ⅜" (1 cm) longer than the back leg's upper edge, consider how well the pants fit you in the hip area. Are they snug there? Then perhaps you'd like to extend the back leg's upper edge by ⅜" (1 cm) to match the yoke edge and improve the fit. Or if the jeans are loose through the hip, you might remove length from the yoke edge. If you're uncertain, you could also split the difference: Extend the back leg edge by 3⁄16" (5 mm) and shorten the yoke edge by 3⁄16" (5 mm).

Note: How much difference is a "real discrepancy" here? For most seams, I'd say that within ⅛" (3 mm) is fine, and you can leave it alone if you're not in the mood to sweat the details. But if it's more than a ⅛" (3 mm) difference, you'll probably want to correct it. For the outseams, you can probably get away with ¼" (6 mm) of difference. And for the inseams, it's actually common for the back leg inseam to be shorter than the front leg inseam by up to ½" (1.3 cm), so that the fabric hugs your body more closely as you wear it. Again, though, more than a ½" (1.3 cm) difference should probably be dealt with.

Once you've adjusted lengths to match, hold pattern draft lines against each other at all intersection points. (You can do this by folding under the paper that's beyond one of the lines, or by holding both sheets up to a bright window so that you can see both lines against each other.) Adjust lines as needed so that they continue smoothly across the intersection points.

Finally, measure up from hem to knee level on front and back (on both inseams and outseams) and adjust if needed to ensure that your knee-level notches will line up. Then measure along outseams from knee to hip notch level, and ensure that those notches will align, too.

## ADJUSTING FIT AND STYLING

Your basic pattern shapes are drafted and verified. The hard work is done! Now you have the opportunity to make any adjustments you'd like. If you love everything about the original jeans, then skip this step. But if there are ways you'd like to tinker with the fit or style details, here's your chance.

Here are a few examples of elements you might consider:

- Is the waist/hip area a smidge too small or large? If so, then you can adjust these areas on your pattern drafts. Remember you'll need to adjust multiple pattern pieces to make this change. Specifically, you'll probably be adjusting the front and back waistbands' side seams, the front leg draft's outseam, the back yoke's outseam, and the back leg draft's outseam. Then double-check the seams against each other to ensure the lengths still match and the angles join properly.
- Would you prefer a different leg shape? If the original jeans had a slim leg but you'd prefer something straighter or even flared, decide how many inches or centimeters you'll need to add to the original pattern to achieve your desired look. Then divide that number by four and add that quarter amount to each end of your front and back leg openings. Draw long, smooth lines connecting these points to the knee level, or perhaps up closer to the crotch/hip level. Then double-check the seams against each other for length and smooth intersections.
- Would you like to add style lines to your jeans? Go for it! Draft them on wherever you'd like, and then remember to add matching notches to facilitate accurate sewing.
- Would you like a shorter or longer leg? Reduce or extend it however much you'd like. Make sure you're happy with the new leg opening at this length, and if not, adjust accordingly.
- Do you like the depth of the original jeans' pocket bags? If not, here's your chance to deepen them (or make them shallower, if that's your preference). You can also make them wider.
- Feel free to change the size, shape, and position of the back pockets, too.

## FINALIZING THE DRAFTS

With pattern shapes determined, it's nearly time to trace off each pattern piece. First, you'll make a few quick additions.

**1.** On front draft, measure front waistline and mark a notch at midpoint.

**2.** On back draft, measure yoke seam edge and mark double notches at midpoint.

**3.** On back yoke draft, measure back waistline edge and mark a notch at midpoint.

**4.** On back yoke draft, measure lower edge that joins to leg, and mark double notches at midpoint.

**5.** On front waistband, measure lower edge and mark a notch at midpoint.

**6.** On (still folded) back waistband, measure lower edge and mark a notch at midpoint.

**7.** For front pocket bags, you'll need to ensure that the inner edge (the one closest to CF) is a straight line down. So if needed, use a ruler to straighten this edge's line. The pocket bag's bottom edge can be curved, but your sewing will be mildly easier with a straight line, so feel free to straighten the bottom line as well.

**8.** Extend front pocket opening line beyond outseam by ⅜" (1 cm) and blend down to hip notch. This added bit of dimension will create a very subtle "bubble" of fabric along your pocket opening, allowing space for your hand to fit more comfortably inside the pocket.

**9.** Make sure front pocket facing's curved outline is neat and clear.

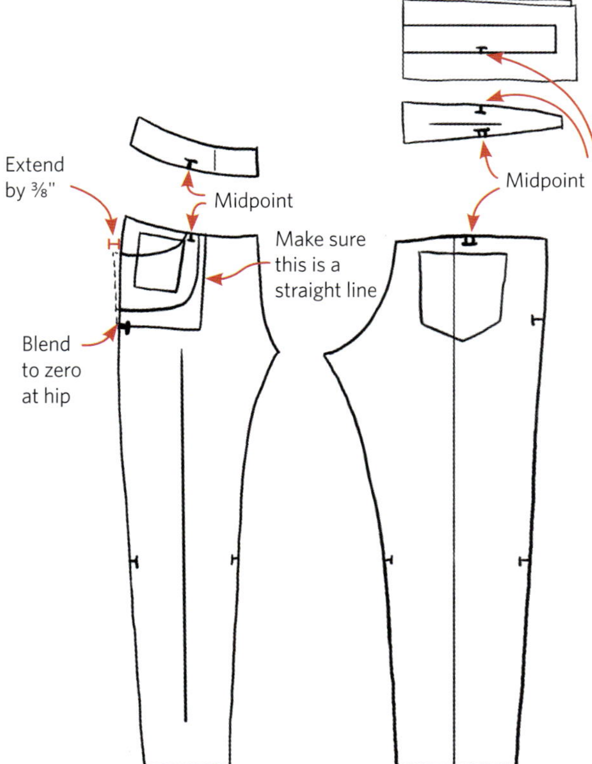


**10.** Next, you'll draft a few lines for the zipper fly area.

**A.** On preexisting jeans, measure length of zipper from top edge of waistband down to zipper stop. (Jeans' zipper stop usually looks like a solid metal box clamped around the bottom of the zipper.) Now subtract your new jeans draft's waistband height from that number to calculate how much zipper to plot along your draft's front rise.

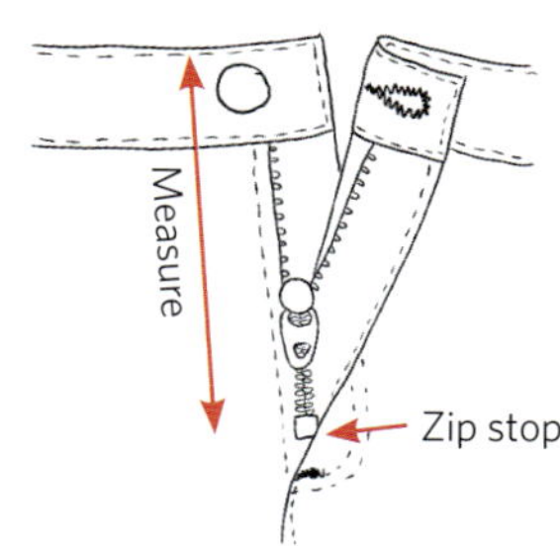


**B.** On front leg draft, use the number you calculated in part A to plot a light tick mark down from waist edge along front rise.

**C.** Measure ⅜" (1 cm) below tick mark and draw a notch. This is where your fly area will end and the rest of your front rise seam will begin.

**D.** Draft a line that is parallel to the rise edge but 1⅝" (4.1 cm) away, beginning at waist edge. Line should be straight for most of the length of the zipper area and then curve to meet notch level. This new line represents the edge of your fly shield.

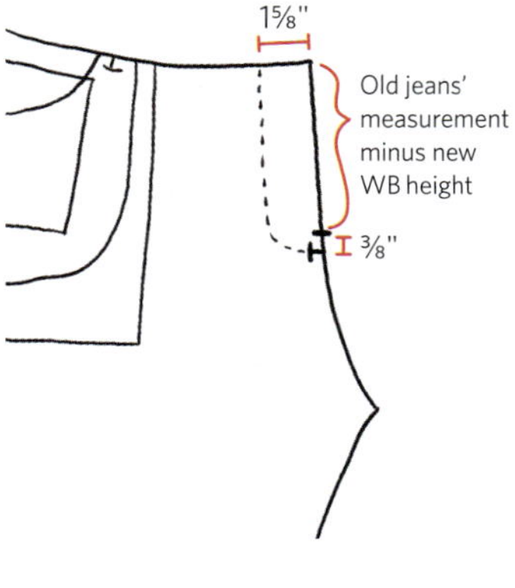

**11.** On the back leg draft, somewhere along the middle of the back rise line, plot double notches.

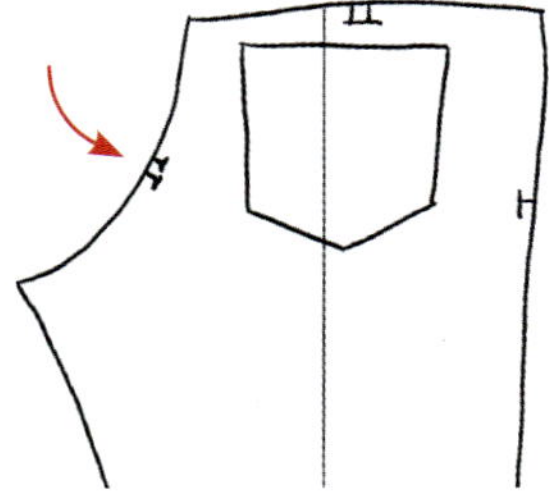

## TRACING THE FRONT LEG

**1.** Take a new large sheet of paper and lay the front leg draft on top. Weight down.

**2.** Using tracing wheel, trace along front rise, inseam, bottom hem, outseam up until pocket opening, pocket opening, and waistline. (Don't include the pocket cutout area, but make sure to trace the extended pocket opening line to include that "bubble" space.) Trace knee-level notches on inseam and outseam, and hip-level notch on outseam. Also trace front rise notch and mid-waistline notch (if it lands in this area). Trace center line. Remove draft paper and pencil in lines clearly.

**3.** Next, add SAs. I'd recommend:

- ½" (1.3 cm) on waist
- ½" (1.3 cm) on pocket opening edge
- ½" (1.3 cm) on outseam
- 1" (2.5 cm) on bottom hem
- ¾" (2 cm) on inseam
- ¾" (2 cm) on front rise

**4.** Cut out. Snip notches.

**5.** Place grainline along traced center line—this should be perpendicular to the center of the bottom hem. Add note: "CUT 2 SELF."

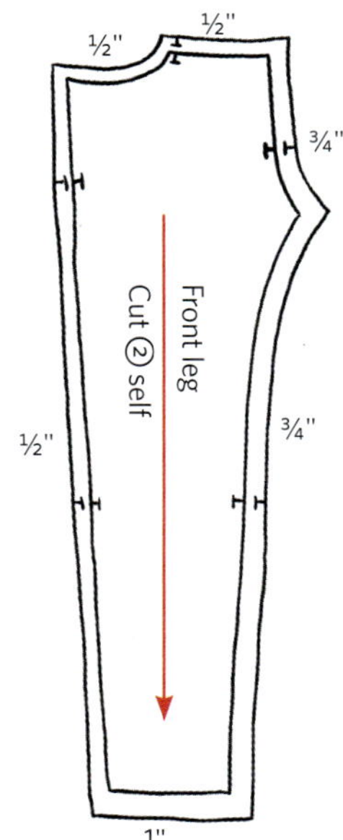


## TRACING THE BACK LEG

**1.** Take a large new sheet of paper and lay the back leg draft on top. Weight down.

**2.** Using tracing wheel, trace along back rise, yoke seam edge, outseam, bottom hem, and inseam. Trace knee-level notches on inseam and outseam, and hip-level notch on outseam. Also trace double notches at top edge midpoint and double notches along back rise. Trace center line. Trace drill holes at corner points of back pockets. Remove draft paper and pencil in lines clearly.

**3.** Next, add SAs. I'd recommend:

- ¾" (2 cm) on waist
- ½" (1.3 cm) on outseam
- 1" (2.5 cm) on bottom hem
- ¾" (2 cm) on inseam
- ¾" (2 cm) on back rise

**4.** Cut out. Snip notches.

**5.** Place grainline along traced center line—this should be perpendicular to the center of the bottom hem. Add note: "CUT 2 SELF."

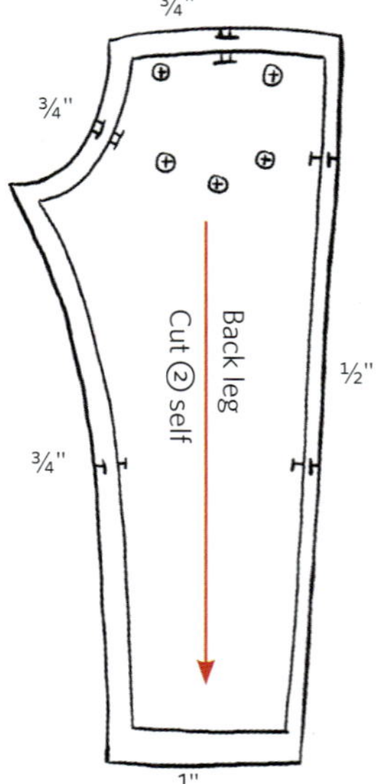

### TRACING THE BACK YOKE

**1.** Take back yoke draft. If it's kind of messy after trueing and any other adjustments, feel free to trace off a clean copy for your pattern. Otherwise, you can use this paper as your actual pattern.

**2.** Make sure you have a notch at midpoint of top edge, and double notches at midpoint of lower edge. Also verify that you have a clean grainline drawn in.

**3.** Next, add SAs. I'd recommend:

- ½" (1.3 cm) on top edge
- ½" (1.3 cm) on outseam
- ¾" (2 cm) on lower edge
- ¾" (2 cm) on back rise

**4.** Cut out. Snip notches.

**5.** Add note: "CUT 2 SELF."

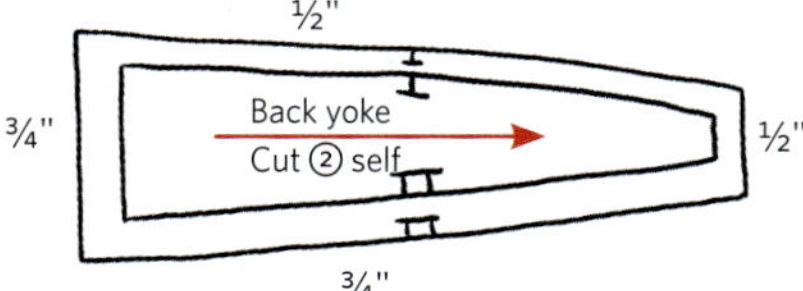


### TRACING THE FRONT WAISTBAND PIECES

**1.** Take front waistband draft and two new sheets of paper. You'll be tracing two different versions: one for wearer's right and another for wearer's left.

**2.** The wearer's left (WL) copy can be traced as is. (But do make sure your tracing ends up being an actual WL piece, with CF edge on the left-hand side of the draft and side seam on the right-hand side. Otherwise, flip the tracing to achieve this orientation.) Be sure to trace notch at midpoint along lower edge, and trace grainline.

**3.** The wearer's right (WR) version will begin by tracing the draft as is (but mirror it, so that CF edge is on right-hand side and side seam is on left-hand side). Trace notch along lower edge, and trace grainline.

**4.** Next, you'll add an underlap extension to WR front waistband. Extend upper and lower edges of waistband beyond CF line by 1⅞" (4.8 cm). Connect with a straight line that should be parallel to CF line. This will be the new edge of the WR waistband piece, allowing the extra length for a fly shield to underlap the jeans' fly area.

**5.** Next, add SAs to WL and WR front waistband pieces. I'd recommend ½" (1.3 cm) on all edges.

**6.** Cut out. Snip notches.

**7.** Add notes to each: "CUT 2 SELF."

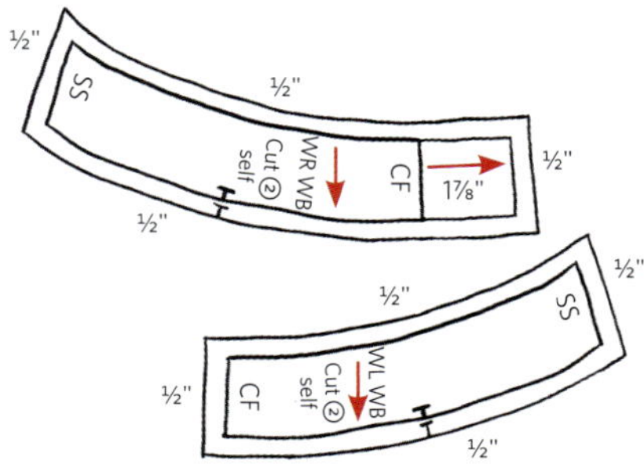


### TRACING THE BACK WAISTBAND

**1.** Take back waistband draft, which should still be folded. If it's kind of messy after trueing and any other adjustments, feel free to trace off a clean copy for your pattern, but make sure it's traced against a folded sheet of paper. If your draft is clean enough, you can skip tracing and just use this paper as your actual pattern.

**2.** Make sure you have a notch at midpoint of lower edge.

**3.** Place a grainline perpendicular to CB fold.

**4.** Next, add SAs. I'd recommend ½" (1.3 cm) on all edges.

**5.** Pin through all layers to prevent shifting. Then cut out and snip notches.

6. Remove pins and unfold. Add double notches straddled across CB on upper and lower edges.

7. Extend grainline across CB line. Add note: "CUT 2 SELF."

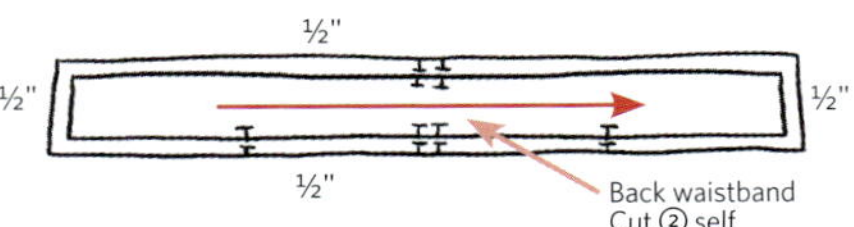


## TRACING THE FRONT POCKET

1. Take a new sheet of paper and fold in half. This fold will represent the fold line of your pocket piece, which will create the pocket edge closest to CF.

2. Lay the front leg draft on top, with pocket area centered over folded paper. Paper's fold should be directly beneath draft's pocket line closest to CF. Weight down.

3. Using tracing wheel, trace along waistline, original (nonextended) outseam, and bottom pocket edge. Also trace curved pocket opening and extended outseam. (You're tracing both versions right now.) Remove draft paper and lightly pencil in all lines.

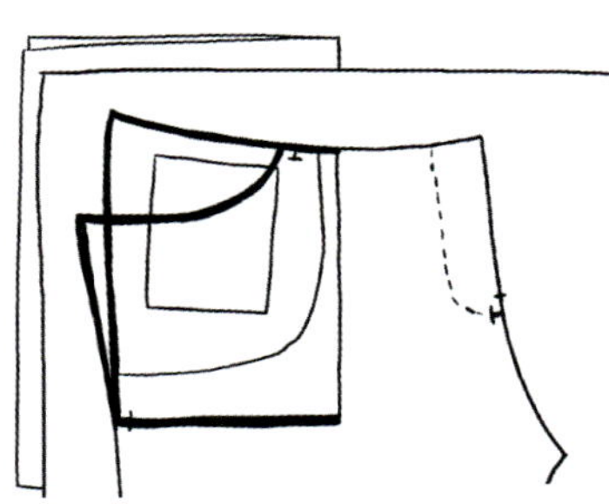

4. With paper still folded, check to see if all tracings imprinted on lower layer, too. If not, trace through.

5. Unfold paper. Pencil in lines like this:

On one side of the fold, pencil in bottom line, extended outseam, curved pocket opening, and waistline.

On the other side of the fold, pencil in bottom line, original outseam, and waistline. Add notches where curved pocket opening intersects with waist and outseam.

Add notches at both ends of center fold.

6. Next, add SAs. I'd recommend ½" (1.3 cm) on all edges.

7. Cut out. Snip notches.

8. Place grainline parallel to center fold. Add note: "CUT 2 POCKETING."

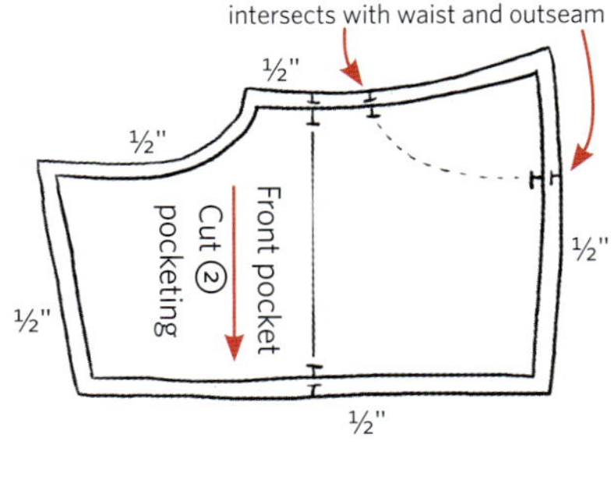


## TRACING THE FRONT POCKET FACING

1. Take a new sheet of paper and lay the front leg draft on top, with front pocket facing area centered over sheet. Weight down.

2. Using tracing wheel, trace around front pocket facing's outline: waistline, original outseam, and curved facing line. Also trace drill holes at corners of coin pocket. Trace a grainline that is parallel to CF. Remove draft paper and pencil in lines clearly.

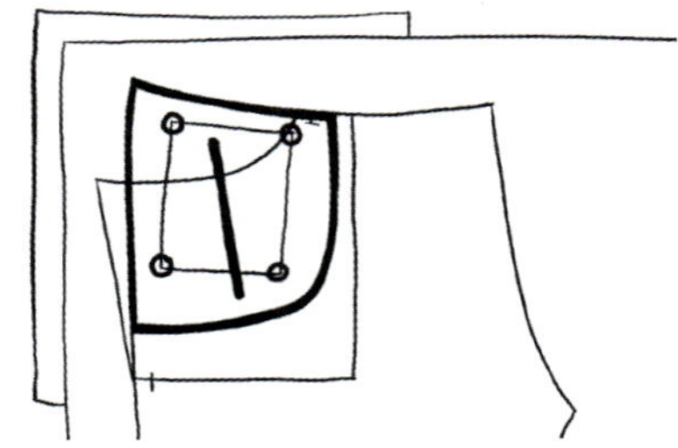

3. Next, add SAs. I'd recommend:

- ½" (1.3 cm) on waist edge
- ½" (1.3 cm) on outseam edge
- No SA along curved line

4. Cut out.

5. Add note: "CUT 2 SELF."

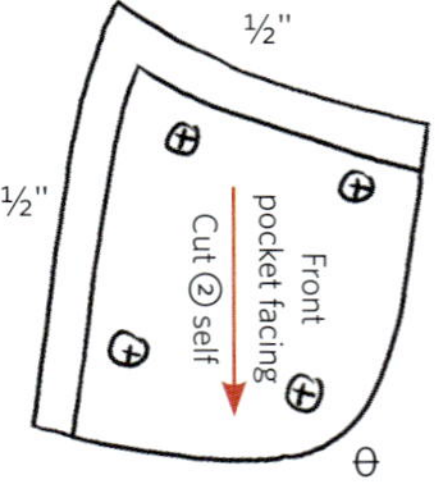

### TRACING THE COIN POCKET

**1.** Take a new sheet of paper and lay the front leg draft on top, with coin pocket area centered over sheet. Weight down.

**2.** Using tracing wheel, trace around coin pocket's outline, including section that will be hidden inside front pocket. Remove draft paper and pencil in lines clearly.

**3.** Next, add SAs. I'd recommend:

- ¾" (2 cm) on top edge
- ½" (1.3 cm) on all other edges

**4.** Cut out.

**5.** Place grainline perpendicular to top edge. Add note: "CUT 1 SELF."

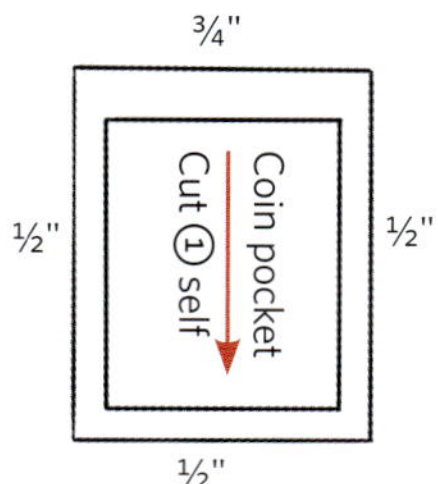


### TRACING THE BACK POCKET

**1.** Take a new sheet of paper and lay the back leg draft on top, with back pocket area centered over sheet. Weight down.

**2.** Using tracing wheel, trace around back pocket's outline. Trace a grainline that is perpendicular to top edge. Remove draft paper and pencil in lines clearly.

**3.** Next, add SAs. I'd recommend:

- ¾" (2 cm) on top edge
- ½" (1.3 cm) on side and bottom edges

**4.** Cut out.

**5.** Add note: "CUT 2 SELF."

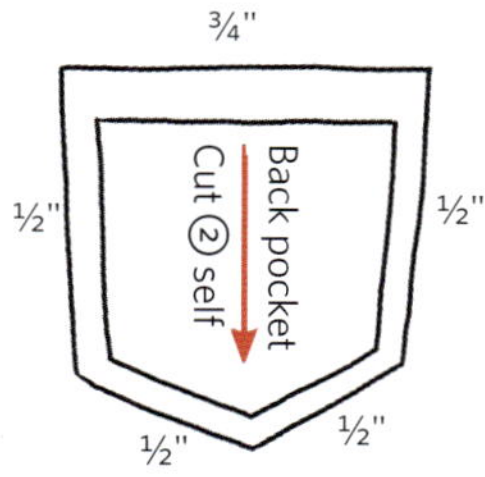


### TRACING THE ZIPPER FLY FACING

**1.** Take a new sheet of paper and lay the front leg draft on top, with zipper fly area centered over sheet. Weight down.

**2.** Using tracing wheel, trace around zipper fly shield's outline: waistline, curved line, CF line from notch up to waist. Remove draft paper and pencil in lines clearly.

**3.** Next, add SAs. I'd recommend:

- ½" (1.3 cm) on top edge
- ⅜" (1 cm) on CF edge
- No SA on curved edge

**4.** Cut out.

**5.** Place grainline parallel to CF. Add note: "CUT 1 SELF."

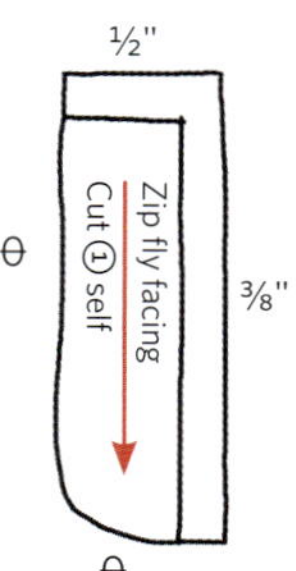


### DRAFTING THE ZIPPER FLY SHIELD

You'll draft this pattern piece based on measurements from the fly area of your front leg draft.

**1.** Take a new sheet of paper and fold in half vertically.

**2.** Draw a line parallel to fold but 1½" (3.8 cm) away.

**3.** Square a line to connect fold to parallel line near the top.

**4.** On front leg draft, measure from waistline down to notch where fly facing line intersects with front rise. On shield draft, measure down from top line along fold by this amount and plot a tick mark.

**5.** Add ¾" (2 cm) to amount plotted in previous step. Now take this larger number and measure down from top line along parallel line by this amount. Plot another tick mark.

**6.** Connect lower tick marks with a straight line.

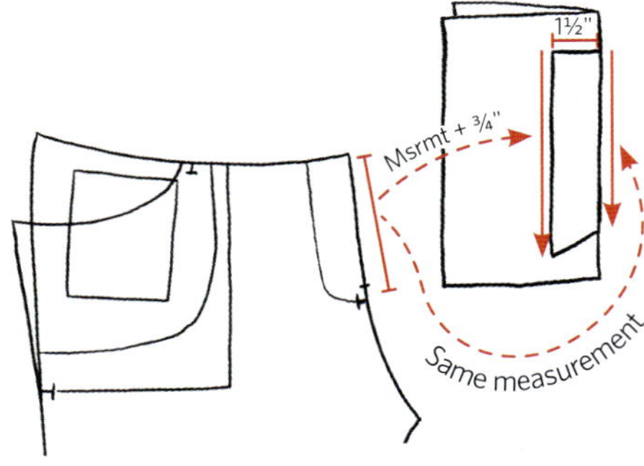


**7.** Next, add SAs. I'd recommend:

- ½" (1.3 cm) on top edge
- ½" (1.3 cm) on side edges
- ¼" (6 mm) on bottom edge

**8.** Pin layers together to prevent shifting. Cut out. Remove pins.

**9.** Unfold pattern piece.

**10.** Place grainline parallel to center crease. Add note: "CUT 1 SELF."

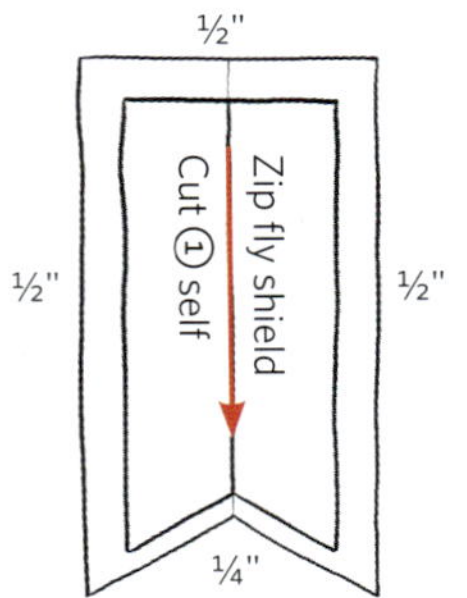

# Sewing

## HAND-SEWING STITCHES

- Tailor's tack
- Basting
- Whipstitch
- Even backstitch
- Overcasting
- Running stitch
- Herringbone stitch
- Blanket stitch
- Hemstitch
- Bartack
- Combination stitch
- Buttonhole stitch

## FABRIC OPTIONS

For these jeans, it will be important to select a denim that is similar to the fabric your preexisting jeans (the ones you traced) are made from. You should try to find fabric that is similar in weight and stretch, at the very least—otherwise your jeans are likely to fit very differently. For example, if your preexisting pair has 5% spandex content, they probably have a decent amount of stretch, and that may be one of the reasons you're able to fit into them, or at least one of the reasons you like the way they conform to your body. So if you took that pattern and then cut a new pair of jeans from 100% cotton (with no stretch), the new pair would likely be much too snug, or might not even accommodate your body at all. If possible, go to a store and select your fabric in person, bringing the original jeans along for comparison. If that's not possible, see if you can order a few decent-size swatches of different denim options online before buying yardage. Compare your swatches with your jeans: Tug on the fabrics side to side and up and down. Pinch in the middle and observe the way the fabric drapes down from your fingers. Compare the softness, if that's important to you. Take time and care in selecting just the right denim. You'll be glad later that you spent the time to get it right.

You'll also need a small amount (½ yard [½ meter] or so) of thinner woven fabric for the front pocket bags. A quilting cotton is fine here and can be a fun choice because it comes in so many nice prints. You can use any lightweight woven fabric that is somewhat densely woven. (Avoid thicker fabrics because their bulk will show through on your jeans, and avoid loosely woven fabrics because they may not be sturdy enough to hold objects in your pockets.)

## OTHER MATERIALS NEEDED

You will need a single button for the waistband of your jeans. You can use a jeans-type metal button (called a jean tack button) or some other button of your choosing. If it doesn't include a built-in shank, you can create a shank using strong thread.

You will need a metal jeans zipper that is at least as long as your preexisting jeans' zipper.

You'll need to use two different types of thread for this project:

- A medium-weight, all-purpose thread that matches the color of your denim's RS
- A thicker, showier thread specifically intended for topstitching

Optionally, you might wish to use interfacing for the waistband, zipper fly pieces, and maybe one or two other areas. I prefer sew-in woven interfacing over the fusible variety, but feel free to use whatever you prefer. If you're feeling experimental, you can forgo store-bought interfacing and instead use cotton canvas or some other thick, dense, structured fabric from your stash. That said, I skipped all forms of interfacing for my jeans, and they've held up beautifully without. So my instructions will not show interfacing.

### CUTTING THE FABRIC

See Cutting Fabric on page 85 for tips on cutting. You'll need to cut the following pieces and quantities:

- Front leg × 2 self
- Back leg × 2 self
- Back yoke × 2 self
- Wearer's right front waistband × 2 self, (optional) × 1 interfacing
- Wearer's left front waistband × 2 self, (optional) × 1 interfacing
- Back waistband × 2 self, (optional) × 1 interfacing
- Front pocket facing × 2 self
- Front pocket bag × 2 pocketing
- Back pocket × 2 self
- Coin pocket × 1 self
- Zipper fly shield × 1 self, (optional) × 1 interfacing
- Zipper fly facing × 1 self, (optional) × 1 interfacing
- Belt loop × 5 self (dimensions should be 1⅜" by 3½" [3.5 cm by 8.9 cm])
- Buttonhole reinforcement square × 1 self (you'll determine dimensions when sewing)
- Button reinforcement square × 1 self (dimensions should be 1½" [3.8 cm] square)

Transfer drill hole marks for pocket placements using tailor's tacks or other marking method.

### APPLYING INTERFACINGS

If you're using interfacing, you'll want to apply interfacing pieces before beginning to construct the jeans. If using fusible interfacing, apply using your iron. If using sew-in interfacing, apply by basting through all layers around the interfacing pieces' perimeters.

- Waistband sections: interface WS of one piece each (one WR front, one WL front, one back)
- Zipper fly shield: interface WS
- Zipper fly facing: interface WS

### ASSEMBLING THE BELT LOOPS

1. Fold down upper long edge approximately 3⁄16" (0.5 cm) to WS and press or baste.

2. Fold up lower long edge ⅜" (1 cm) and press or baste.

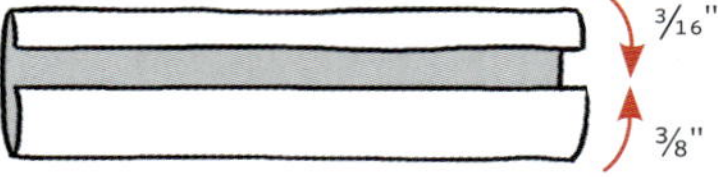


3. Fold up lower edge ⅜" (1 cm) again, so that it almost meets the upper fold but not quite (it should be offset by about 1⁄16" [2 mm]). Pin to hold.

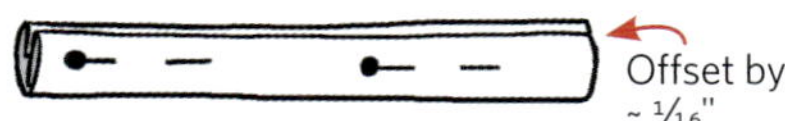


4. Whipstitch latest fold down, using camouflaging thread. Stitches should secure folded edge down onto layer beneath it but needn't puncture all the way through to the other side.

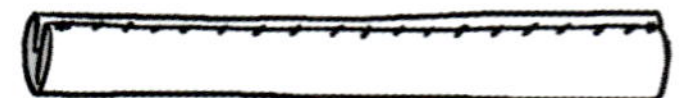

5. Flip over so that you're facing the front of the loop. Using topstitching thread, sew lines of even backstitch close to each long edge. I like to use a spacing of ⅛" (3 mm) from the edge, but it's an aesthetic decision.

6. Repeat all steps for remaining belt loops.

## PREPARING THE BACK POCKETS

**1.** Turn under and press top edge ¼" (6 mm) toward WS. Baste.

**2.** Turn under and press side and bottom edges ½" (1.3 cm) toward WS. Baste.

**3.** Optional: Use camouflaging thread to overcast side and bottom raw edges.

**4.** Turn and press top hem by ½" (1.3 cm). Baste to hold, smooshing in any overhanging bits at the corners.

**5.** Using camouflaging thread, make tiny whipstitches to secure sides and bottom of top hem, as shown.

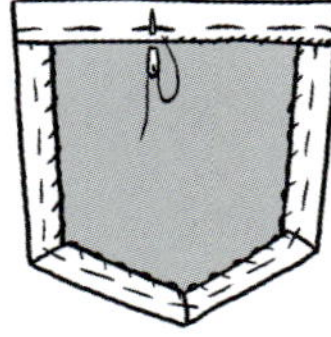

**6.** Turn pocket over to face front. Mark your top hem's topstitching line at ⅜" (1 cm) from edge, using a ruler and marking tool. Then stitch, using topstitching thread and even backstitch.

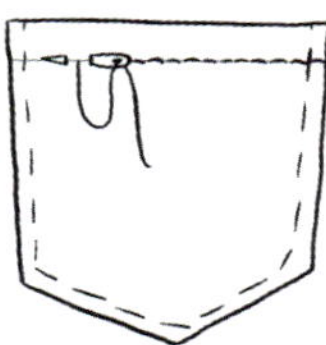

## PREPARING THE COIN POCKET

**1.** Turn and press side and bottom edges ½" (1.3 cm) toward WS. Baste to hold.

**2.** Optional: Use camouflaging thread to overcast side and bottom raw edges.

**3.** Turn and press double-turned top hem. Turn ¼" (6 mm) first, and then turn again ½" (1.3 cm). Baste to hold, smooshing in any overhanging bits at the corners.

**4.** Using camouflaging thread, make tiny whipstitches to secure sides and bottom of top hem, as shown.

**5.** Turn pocket over to face front. Mark your top hem's topstitching line at ⅜" (1 cm) from edge, using a ruler and marking tool. Then stitch, using topstitching thread and even backstitch.

## APPLYING THE BACK POCKETS

**1.** Working on a flat surface, place back pockets on top of back leg pieces, aligning corners with tailor's tacks. Pin. Then replace pins with basting.

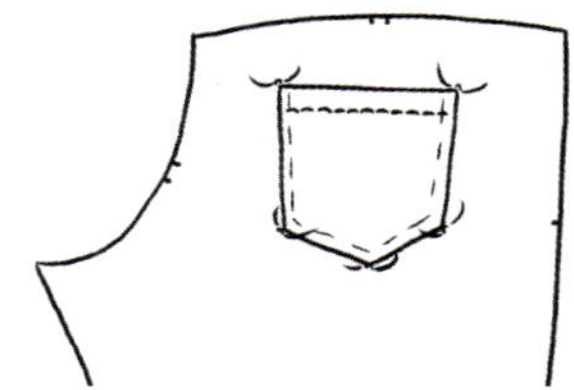

**2.** Using camouflaging thread and tiny whipstitches or fell stitches, secure side and bottom edges of pockets onto legs.

**3.** Remove basting.

**4.** With topstitching thread, make a line of even backstitch along side and bottom edges of pockets. Line should be approximately ⅛" (3 mm) away from edge.

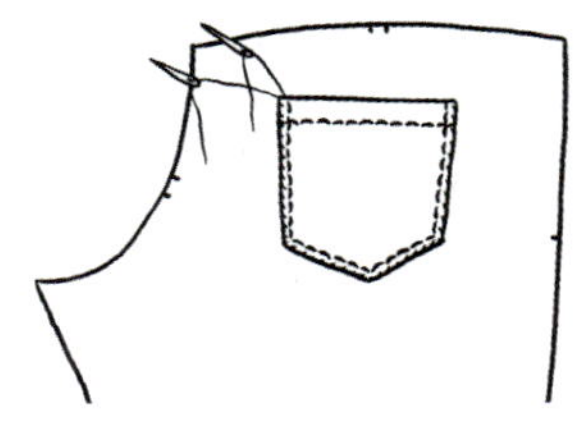

**5.** Optional: Make a second line of even backstitched topstitches along side and bottom edges, ⅛" or ¼" (3 mm or 6 mm) away from the first line.

## APPLYING THE COIN POCKET

**1.** Working on a flat surface, place coin pocket on top of wearer's right front pocket facing, aligning corners with tailor's tacks. Pin. Then replace pins with basting.

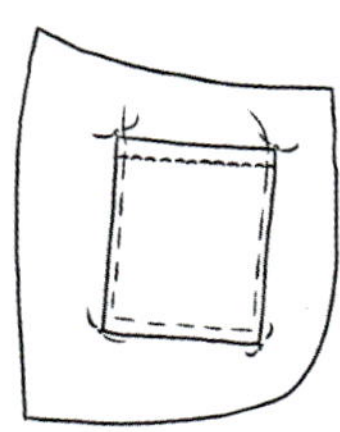

**2.** Using camouflaging thread and tiny whipstitches or fell stitches, secure side and bottom edges of pocket onto facing.

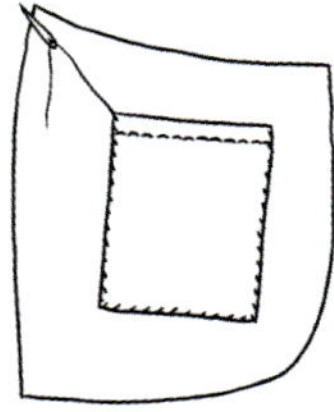

**3.** Remove basting.

**4.** With topstitching thread, make a line of even backstitch along side and bottom edges of pocket. Line should be approximately ⅛" (3 mm) away from edge.

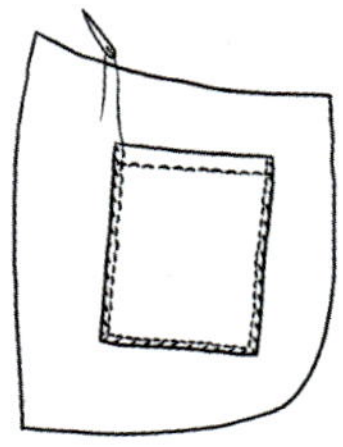

**5.** Optional: Make a second line of even backstitched topstitches along side and bottom edges, ⅛" or ¼" (3 mm or 6 mm) away from the first line.

## APPLYING THE FRONT POCKET FACINGS

**1.** Working on a flat surface, place front pocket facings on top of their respective pocket bags, aligning facings with pocket bags' notches. Pin.

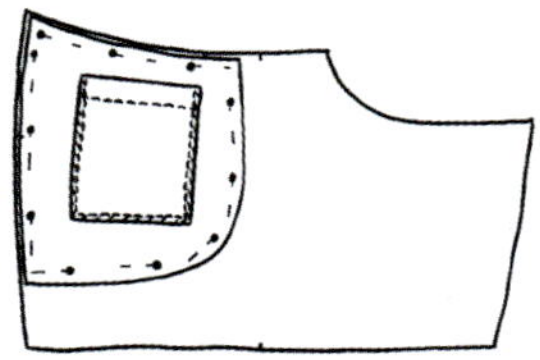

**2.** Using camouflaging thread and smallish running stitches, baste facings to pocket bags along outseam and waist edges. Stitch within SAs.

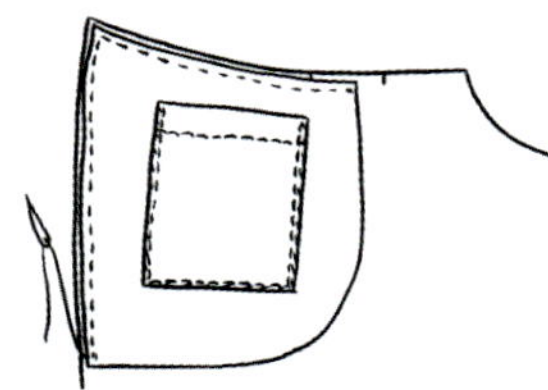

**3.** With camouflaging thread or topstitching thread (whichever you prefer), use herringbone stitch to secure facings' curved edges to pocket bags, thus thread-binding raw edges.

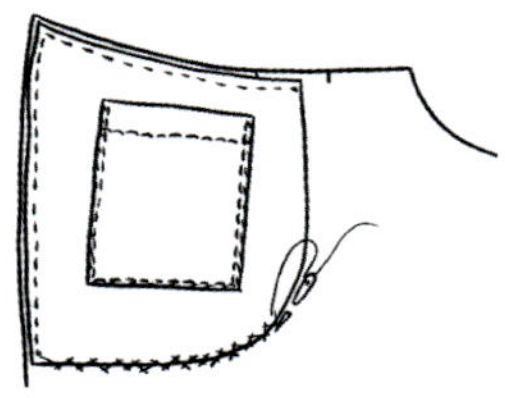

**4.** Press to "set" stitching.

## ATTACHING THE POCKET BAGS

**1.** With RST, place pocket bag on top of front leg, aligning curved pocket opening. Pin.

**2.** Use camouflaging thread and tiny running stitches to sew joining seam. Press.

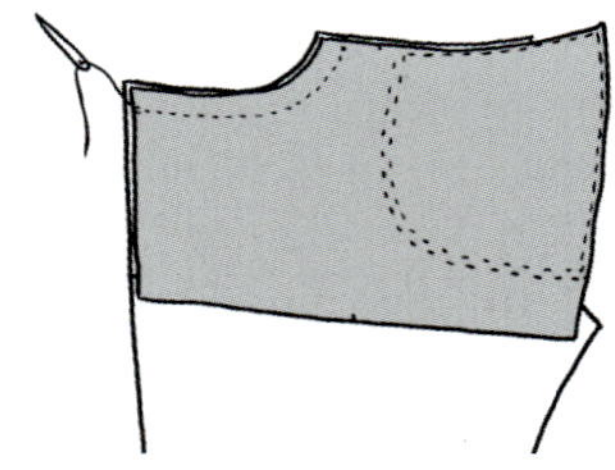

**3.** Trim SA to ⅜" (1 cm), clip into curved areas, then turn and press. As you press, shift the seam to the WS so that the pocketing is slightly to the underside by about 1⁄16" (2 mm).

**4.** Optional: Baste pocketing edge.

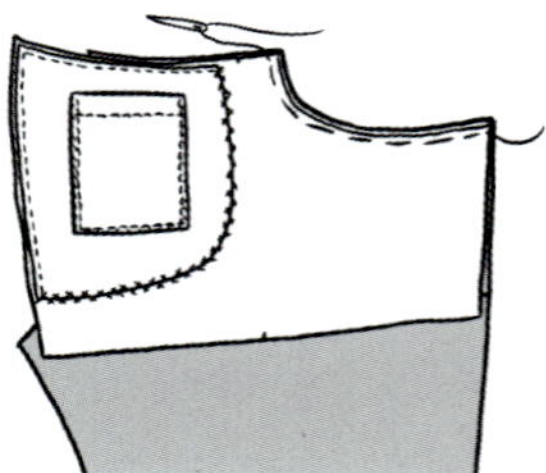

**5.** Flip work to face RS of front leg. Using topstitching thread and even backstitch, sew two parallel lines of even backstitch. Lines can be ⅛" and ¼" (3 mm and 6 mm) from edge, or to taste.

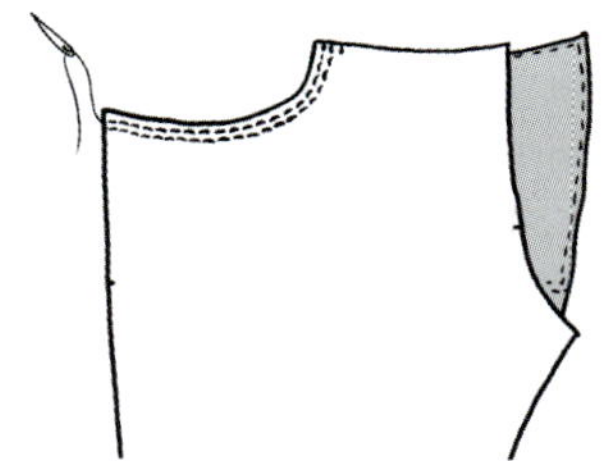

**6.** Remove basting.

**7.** Next, you'll begin creating a French seam to close the bottom of the pocket bag. Fold pocket bag in half backward, so that WST.

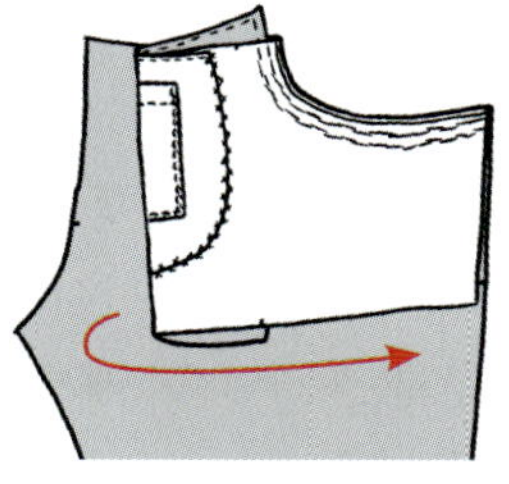

**8.** Align bottom edges, then pin. Sew with camouflaging thread and tiny running stitches, using ¼" (6 mm) SA. Press.

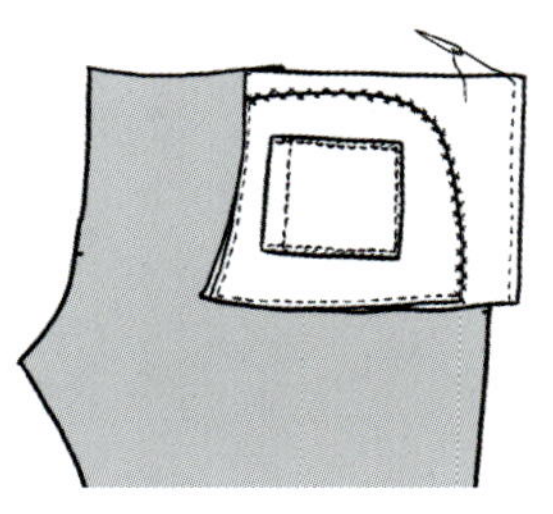

**9.** Trim SA to ⅛" (3 mm). Snip triangle at folded corner to reduce bulk.

**10.** Turn pocket so that RSs are together. Press. With camouflaging thread and even backstitch, sew bottom of pocket again, using ¼" (6 mm) SA. Press. You've completed the French seam.

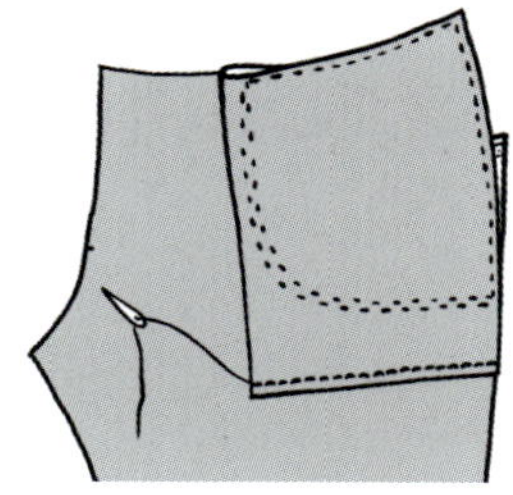

**11.** Pocket bag's center notch along the top edge will create the upper corner of pocket's folded edge. Press fold accordingly.

**12.** Flip to RS of front leg. Lay flat on table. Make sure pocket bag is lying totally smooth and flat underneath. Then align notches along waist edge and place pins through all layers to join pocket, pocket facing, and leg.

**13.** Nudge leg's outseam inward to align with pocket bag's outseam. (This will create a little bubble along the pocket opening, which is intentional. It offers ease for your hand to slip in and out.) Pin through all layers to hold.

**14.** Using camouflaging thread and running stitches, sew through all layers along pinned areas of waist and outseam. Stitches should be within SAs. These stitches won't show when you wear the jeans—they're meant to hold the layers together until you're ready construct the outseams.

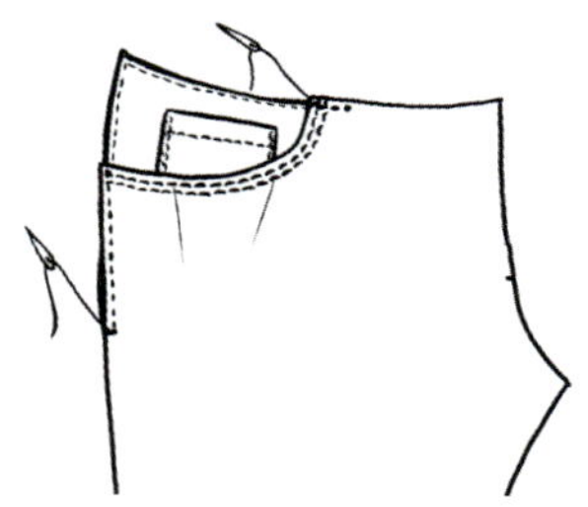

## ATTACHING THE BACK YOKES

**1.** Pin yokes to back legs, RST, matching notches and aligning edges.

**2.** With camouflaging thread and even backstitches, sew pieces together. Use ¾" (2 cm) SA.

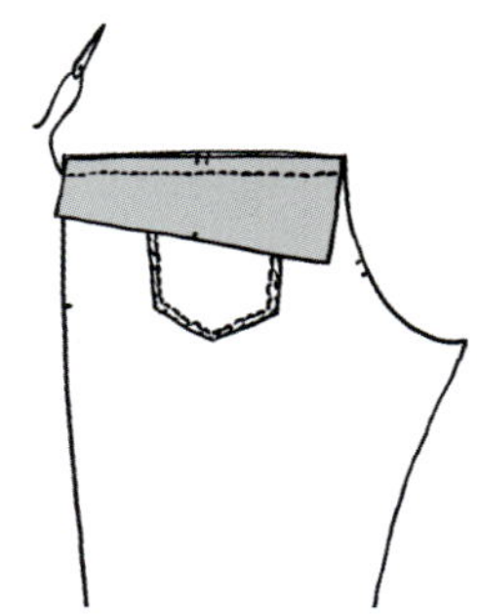

**3.** Press SAs down toward legs.

4. Prepare to fell SAs. Trim half of the width of leg pieces' SAs, then fold yokes' SAs around and under legs' SAs so that all raw edges are concealed. Pin. Then replace pins with basting that is very close to folded edge.

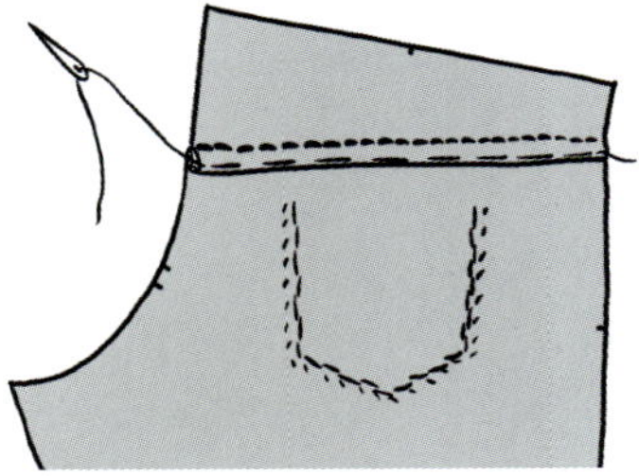

5. With topstitching thread, and facing the RS, make two lines of even backstitch to fell SAs down. Lines should be approximately ⅛" (3mm) and ¼" (6 mm) away from seam. Remove basting. Press.

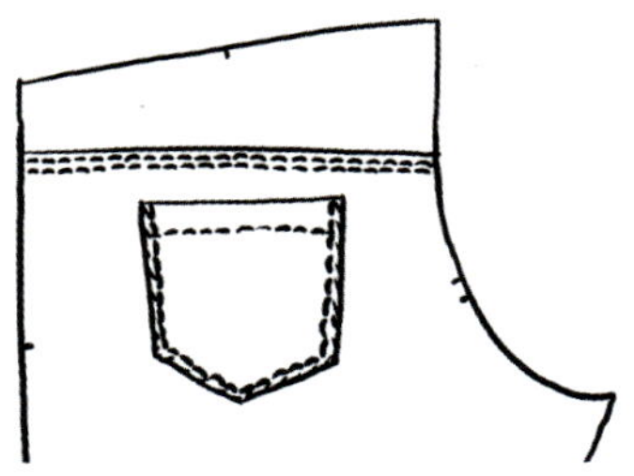

## STITCHING THE BACK RISE SEAM

1. With RST, line up back rise seams. Align edges and notches, taking extra care to align yoke seams perfectly with each other. I'd recommend looking at the wearer's right leg as you pin.

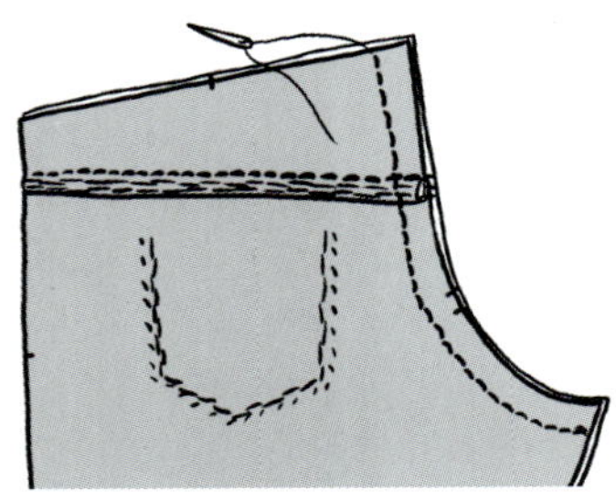

2. With waxed camouflaging thread and small even backstitches, and looking at the wearer's right leg, sew pieces together. Use ¾" (2 cm) SA. Pull thread snug after each stitch. Then press to "set" stitches.

A note: As a general rule, I recommend waxing thread before stitching any major construction seams on any project. In this case especially—on the back rise of a pair of jeans, which is sure to receive some strain—it's good to enhance the thread's strength by melting some wax into the fibers.

3. Turn to the RS of your work and press SAs toward wearer's left. Optionally, use a hammer or mallet to gently flatten the yoke seams along back rise edges. This can help to facilitate easier, tidier sewing.

4. Prepare to fell SAs. Trim half of the width of wearer's left SA. While trimming, be careful not to slice through yoke seam. Instead, trim up to within a few threads of the seam on each side, leaving a little tab where the yoke seam is.

5. Slice tab in half so that stitching is still intact. Now fold wearer's right SA around and under wearer's left SA. Pin as you go, smooshing half of tab upward and the other half downward as you pin, so that everything is concealed. Pinning will be a little tricky going around the sharpest curve of the crotch, but focus on one small section at a time, one pin at a time, and you'll succeed.

6. Once pins are in place, replace them with basting that is very close to folded edge. Along the yoke seam intersections, you may wish to add a few felling stitches with camouflaging thread to hold this bulky area down securely.

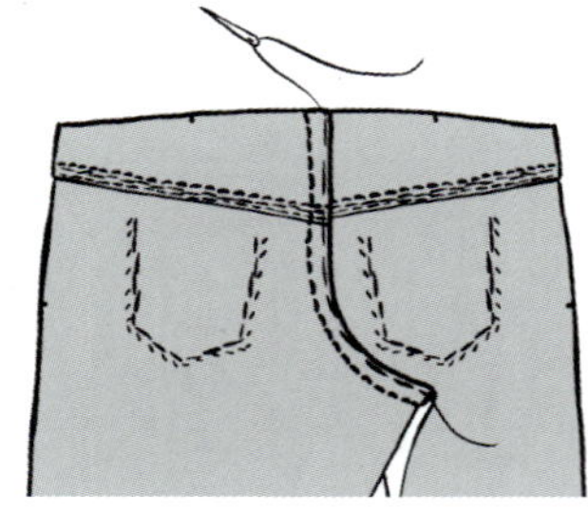

7. With topstitching thread, and facing the RS, make two lines of even backstitch to fell SAs down. Lines should be approximately ⅛" (3mm) and ¼" (6 mm) away from seam. Remove basting. Press.

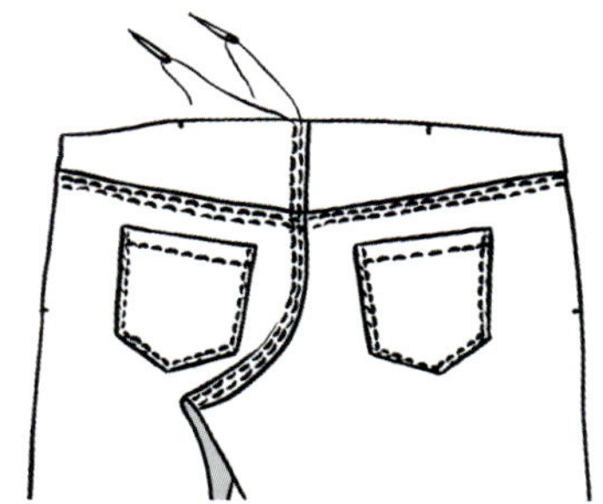

## PREPARING THE ZIPPER FLY

1. Fold zipper fly shield in half with RST. With camouflaging thread and biggish even backstitches, sew bottom edge. Use ¼" (6 mm) SA.

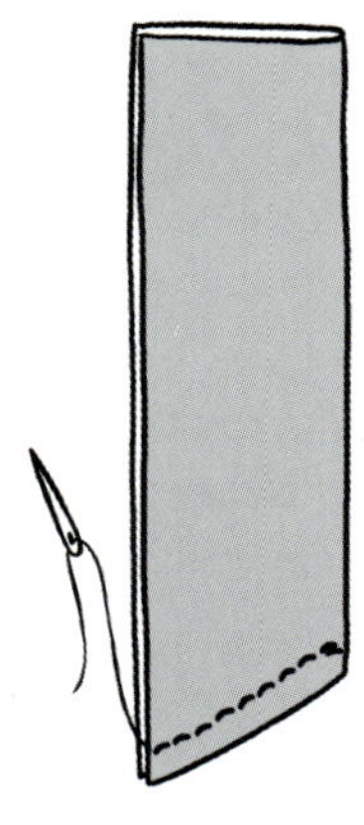

2. Clip triangle to reduce bulk, then turn fly shield RS out and press.

3. Using topstitching thread and overcasting or blanket stitch, thread-bind curved raw edge of fly facing and long raw edge of fly shield. Press to set stitching.

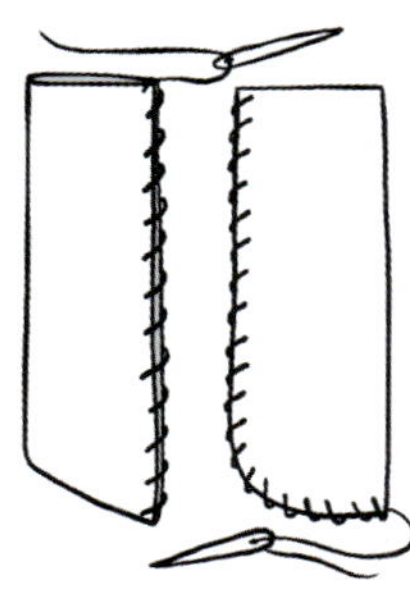

4. With RST, line up front rise edges from zipper stop notches down to crotch point. Pin. With camouflaging thread and small even backstitches, and looking at the wearer's right leg, sew pieces together. Use ¾" (2 cm) SA. Pull thread snug after each stitch. Then press to "set" stitches.

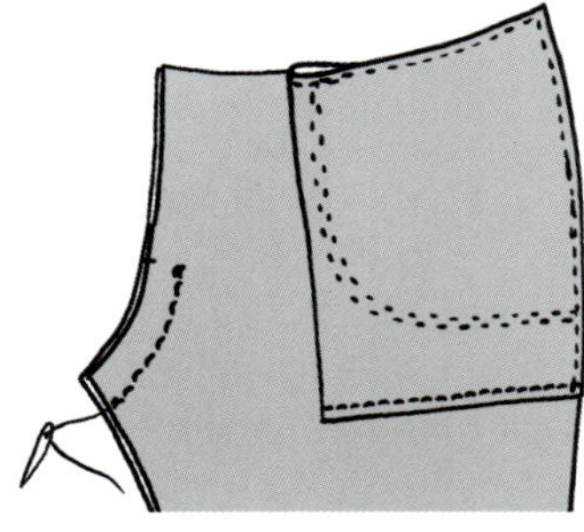

5. Snip from SA edge to notch. Now you'll finish the SAs below this point. Turn to the RS of your work and press SAs toward wearer's left.

6. Prepare to fell SAs. Trim half of the width of wearer's left SA. Then fold wearer's right SA around and under wearer's left SA. Pin, then replace with basting very close to folded edge.

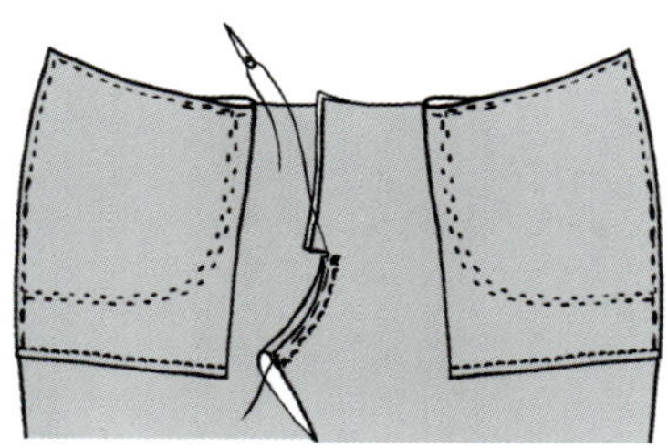

7. With topstitching thread, and facing the RS, make two lines of even backstitch to fell SAs down. Lines should be approximately ⅛" (3mm) and ¼" (6 mm) away from seam. Remove basting. Press.

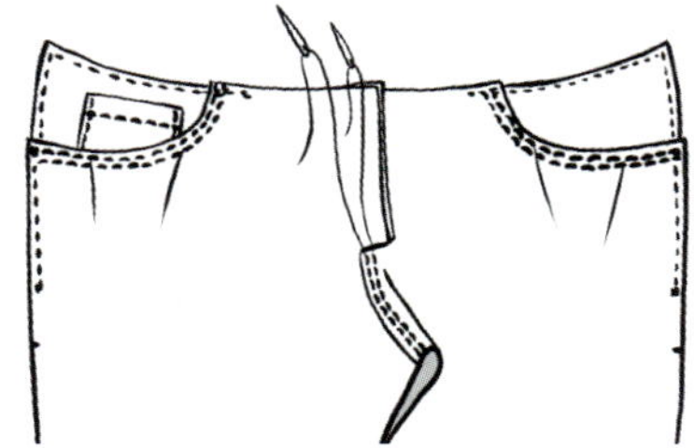

8. On wearer's left front leg, fold on CF line. Press and baste.

9. On wearer's right front leg, make a fold that is parallel to CF but ⅜" (1 cm) closer to raw edge. Press and baste. This will set up the wearer's right underlap, which is where your zipper will be hidden.

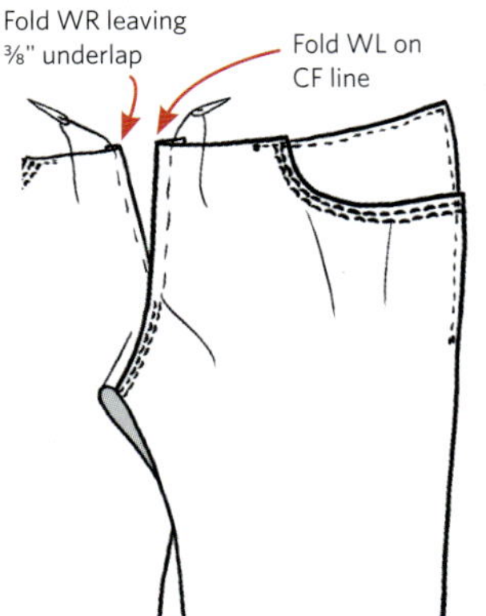


10. On fly facing, turn long straight edge under by ⅜" (1 cm). Press and baste.

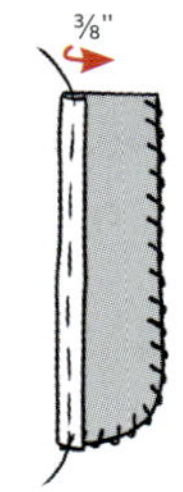


## CONSTRUCTING THE ZIPPER FLY

1. Looking at WS of front legs, place fly facing, RS up, onto wearer's left leg. Align it with pants' waist edge and CF folded edge, but then nudge fly facing 1⁄16" (2 mm) away from CF folded edge, so that it won't be visible from the outside. Pin.

2. Using camouflaging thread and careful hemstitches, secure folded facing to pant leg along CF. Stitches should only reach through the pant leg's SA—they shouldn't show through to the outside of the pants.

3. Flip to the RS. Using topstitching thread and even backstitch, topstitch along wearer's left CF edge, approximately ⅛" (3 mm) in from the fold. Stitches should pass through all layers for this step, including facing layer. You can make this line look continuous with the inner stitch line from your previous flat-felling.

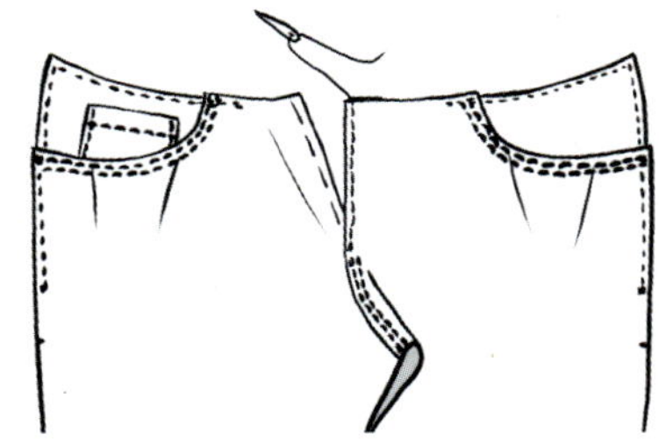

4. Slip zipper underneath wearer's right edge (the underlap side). Zipper teeth should be spaced ⅛" (3 mm) away from the edge. The zipper stop should be positioned about ⅜" (1 cm) above notch point. Pin, then use camouflaging thread to hemstitch fold onto zipper tape.

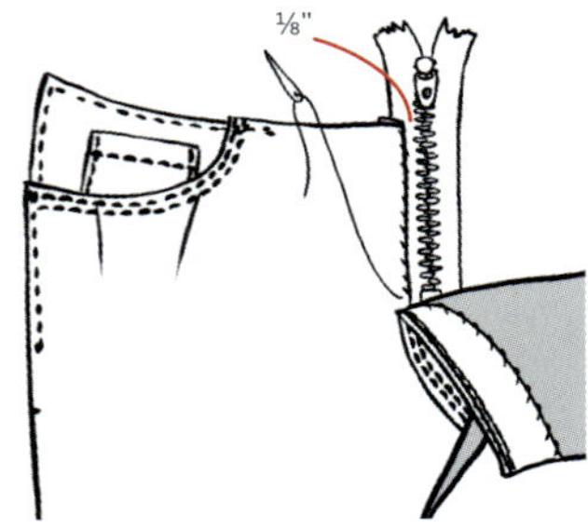


5. Slip fly shield behind wearer's right, aligned with the CF notch so that distance from folded edge to shield edge is 1½" (3.8 cm). Pin, then use topstitching thread and even backstitch through all layers to join.

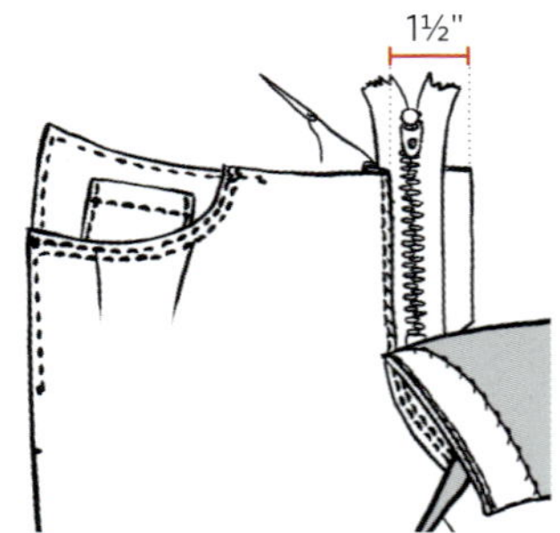


6. Optional: Flip to underside and, with topstitching thread, use overcasting or whipstitch to thread-bind zipper tape's edge with fly edge.

**7.** Lay legs flat on the table, facing up. Next, you'll pin the other edge of the zipper tape onto your jeans.

**A.** Slip ruler or a strip of cardboard between fly shield and zip. This will prevent pins from reaching fly shield.

**B.** "Close" the pants so that wearer's left leg overlaps wearer's right by ⅜" (1 cm) along CF area. It's important to be precise here.

**C.** Place pins so that the loose edge of the zipper tape is secured to layers above it.

**D.** Flip work to the WS. Holding fly shield out of the way, pinch and repin so that pins are holding only the zipper tape and fly facing. (Pins should no longer include pants' outer layer.)

**8.** With topstitching thread, use running stitch or even backstitch to sew along edge of zipper tape, securing it to the fly facing.

**9.** With topstitching thread, use even backstitch to sew along middle of zipper tape, again securing it to the fly facing.

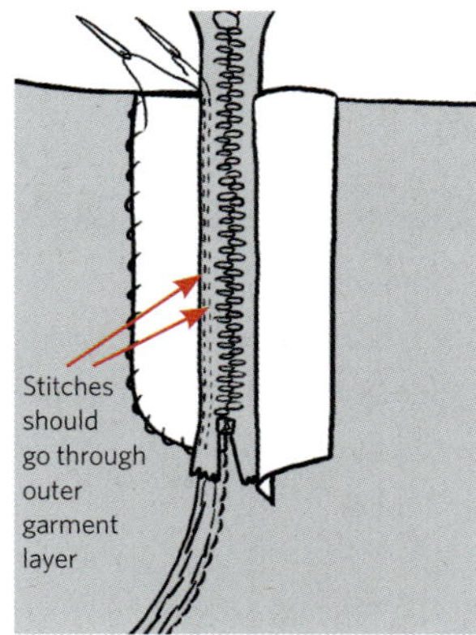


**10.** Flip work to RS. Smooth to flatten. Use pattern as guide to mark fly topstitching line(s). Bottom of curved stitching should be about ⅛" or ¼" (3 mm or 6 mm) above notch point. Slip ruler inside and pin only through fly facing and outer pant layer. Using topstitching thread and even backstitch, sew along marked line(s). You can stitch through zipper tape but not fly shield—hold the shield out of the way.

If you'd like to make topstitching extra tidy, trace off a fresh copy of the fly facing pattern but don't include SA. Then pin in place on RS of project and you can stitch along paper's edge.

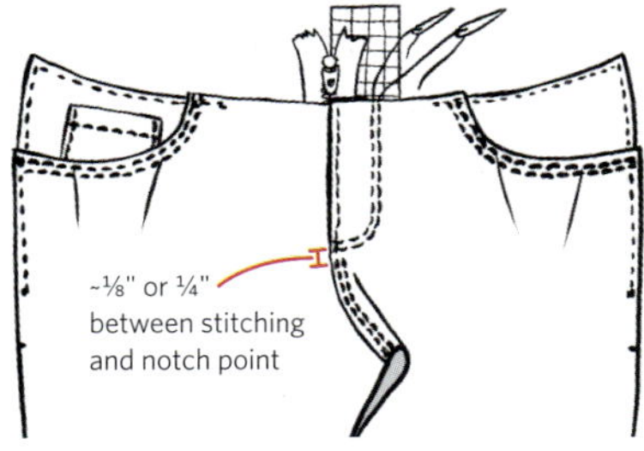


**11.** Remove all basting.

**12.** Using camouflaging thread and tiny, strong whipstitches or fell stitches, secure CF edge from curved topstitching's CF intersection point down to notch point. This will close any gap.

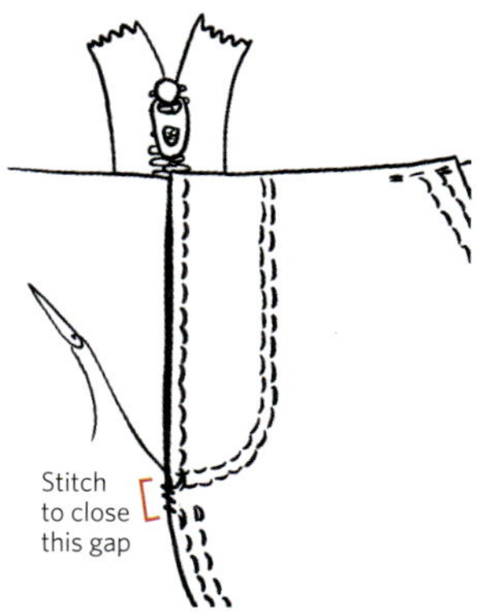


**13.** Stitch bartack (through all layers) at curved topstitching's CF intersection point. Also stitch a bartack (through all layers) somewhere along curviest point of curved topstitching.

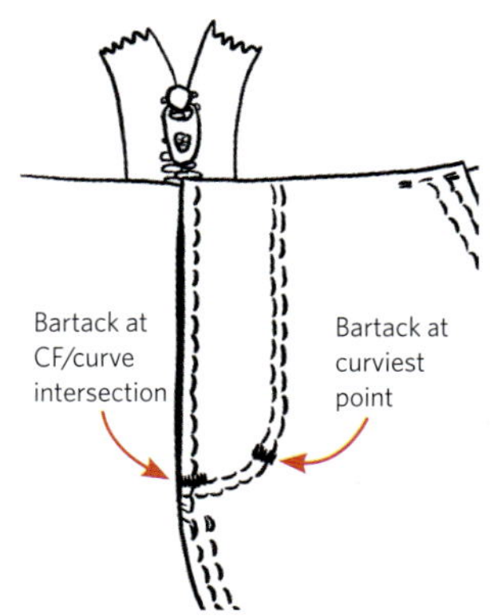


**14.** If needed, trim away excess zipper tape beyond waist SA.

## SEWING THE INSEAMS

1. With RST, align front and back panels along inseams, matching notches and seam intersections. Facing back panel, pin together. Front and back edges may be slightly different lengths—it's common for the back to be slightly shorter than the front between knee and crotch. If so, find the midpoints of front and back and pin together, then find more midpoints and pin those, and so on.

2. Using camouflaging thread and even backstitch, sew along both legs' inseams with one continuous line of stitching. Use ¾" (2 cm) SA.

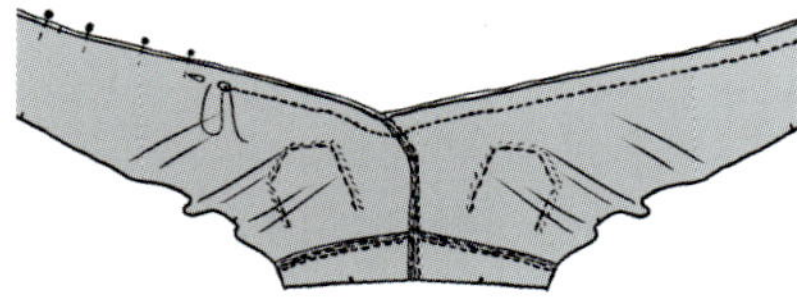

3. Flip to outside of garment and press SAs toward front panel.

4. Flip to inside of garment again and prepare to fell SAs. Trim half of the width of front panel SA. While trimming, be careful not to slice through front rise seam. Instead, trim up to within a few threads of the seam on each side, leaving a little tab where the seam is.

5. Slice tab in half so that stitching is still intact. Now fold back panel's SA around and under front panel's SA. Pin as you go, smooshing half of tab to the left and the other half to the right as you pin so that everything is concealed.

6. Once pins are in place, replace them with basting that is very close to folded edge.

7. Optional: With camouflaging thread, and facing the inside of the garment, hemstitch down.

8. With topstitching thread, and facing the outside, make a line of even backstitch close to seam, through all layers. Line should be approximately ¼" (6 mm) away from seam. Remove basting. Press.

## SEWING THE OUTSEAMS

1. With RST, align front and back panels along outseams, matching notches. Facing front panel, pin together.

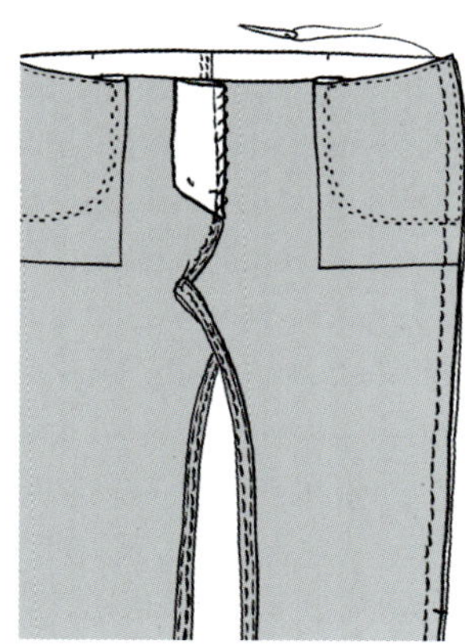

2. Using camouflaging thread and even backstitch, sew along each leg's outseam. Use ½" (1.3 cm) SA.

Helpful hint: A sewing bird or "third hand" arrangement may help here! See page 49 for tips.

3. Press flat. Then flip to outside of garment and press SAs toward back.

4. Flip to inside of garment. With topstitching thread, use blanket stitch or overcasting to thread-bind raw edges together.

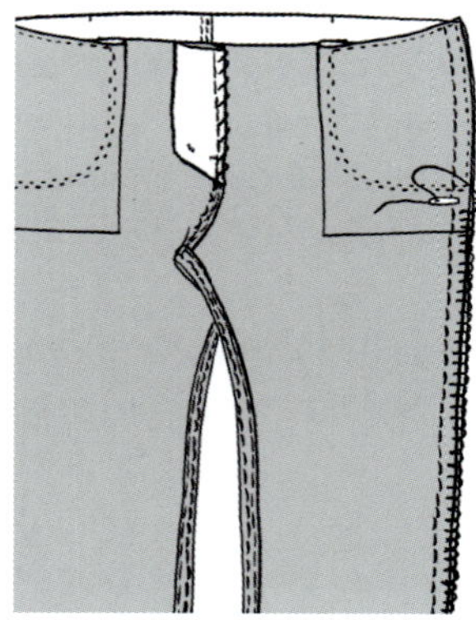

5. Flip to outside of garment. With topstitching thread, sew even backstitch through all layers along outseams, ⅛" (3 mm) to the back of the seams, from waist edge to bottom of front pocket.

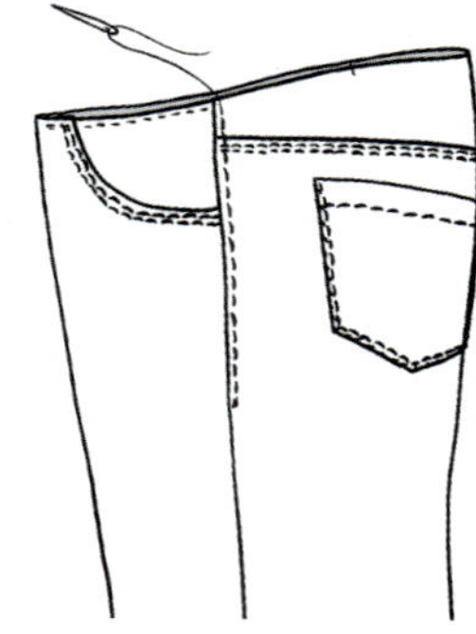

## STITCHING BARTACKS

Using topstitching thread, sew tidy bartacks in the following locations:

- At lowest point of outseam topstitching
- At top corners of back pockets
- At lowest parts of zipper topstitching, if you haven't completed those yet

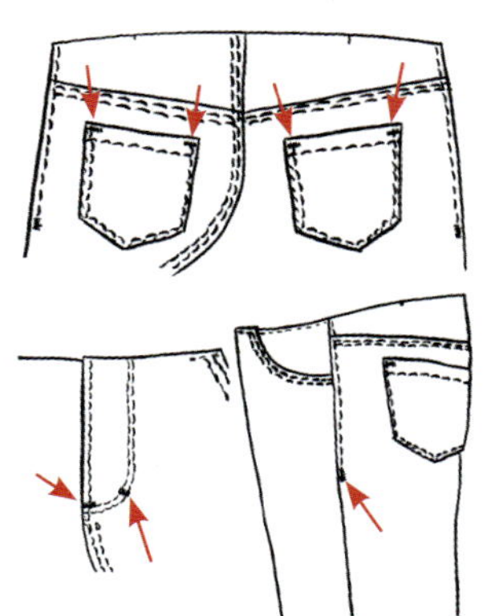

## CONSTRUCTING THE WAISTBAND

**1.** Pin front waistband panels to back waistband panel, RST, along their little side seams.

**2.** With camouflaging thread and even backstitch, sew seams. Use ½" (1.3 cm) SA.

**3.** Press seams flat. Then snip triangles to reduce bulk, and press SAs open.

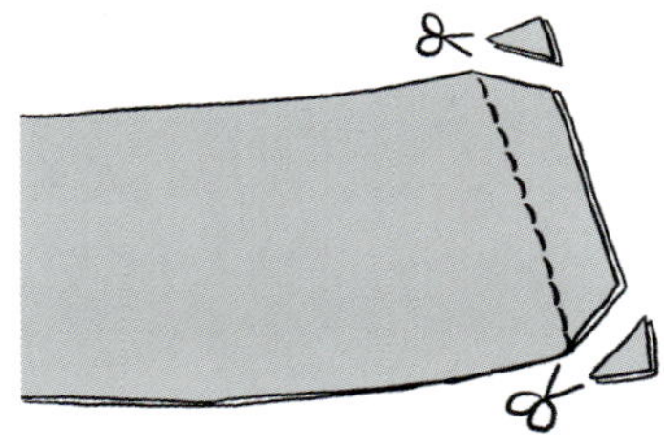

**4.** With RST, align top edges of outer waistband and inner waistband. Pin.

**5.** Seam together top edges using camouflaging thread and combination stitch. Use ½" (1.3 cm) SA.

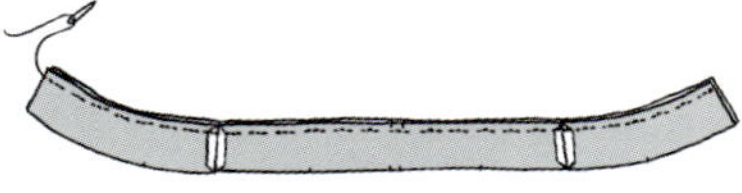

**6.** Press flat, then press SAs open. Then turn RSs out and press flat.

## ATTACHING THE WAISTBAND

**1.** Align outer waistband's lower edge with pants' waist edge, with RST. Remember how your right and left waistbands are two different lengths? Be sure you're aligning the longer front waistband with the fly underlap edge so that everything fits together. Pin together using lots of pins. I like to start by pinning at CB and then working around to the fronts, aligning notches and seam intersections along the way.

**2.** Using camouflaging thread and combination stitch, join layers. (You don't need to push your needle through all of the layers here if you don't want to—you can just join the waistband to the outermost layer of the jeans for now.) Use ½" (1.3 cm) SA.

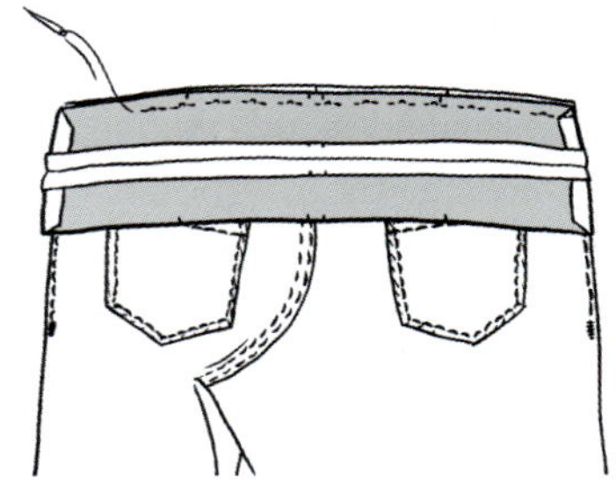

**3.** Fold under and press ½" (1.3 cm) SA along inner waistband's long edge. Baste to hold.

**4.** Now fold in the ½" (1.3 cm) SA at the ends of the waistband so that they are flush with the zipper fly ends. Baste to hold.

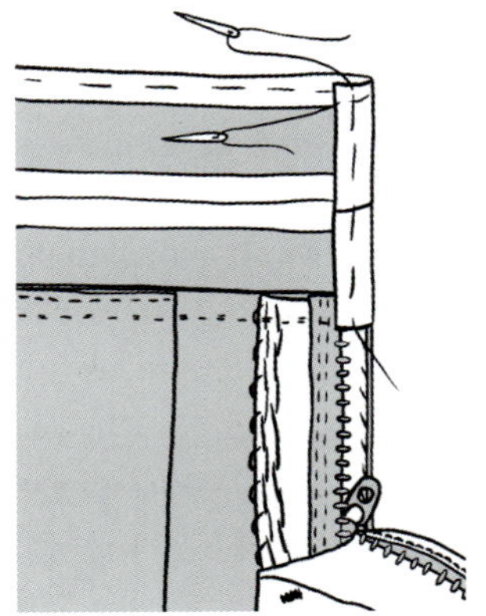

**5.** Turn waistband RS out and baste along top (folded) edge to hold it flat.

**6.** Facing outside of garment, press waistband away from the legs.

**7.** Aligning all notches and intersections, pin inner waistband's long end down to inside of jeans.

**8.** Using camouflaging thread, secure end down to garment, using tiny stitches in your stitch of choice—whipstitch, hemstitch, or fell stitch. Stitches don't need to pass through all layers.

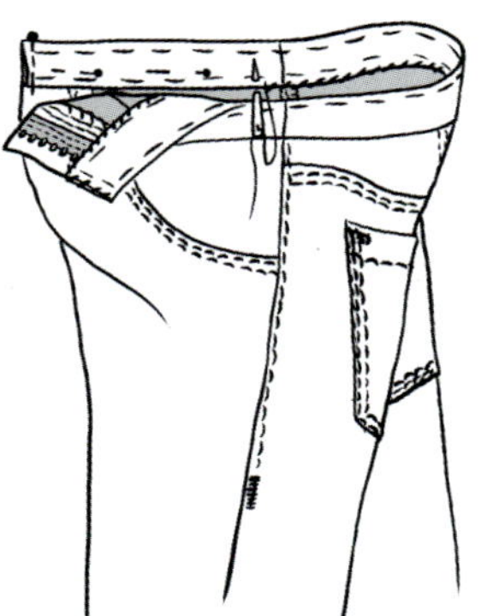

**9.** Facing outside of garment, topstitch through all layers at ⅛" (3 mm) from edge of entire waistband's perimeter, using topstitching thread and even backstitch.

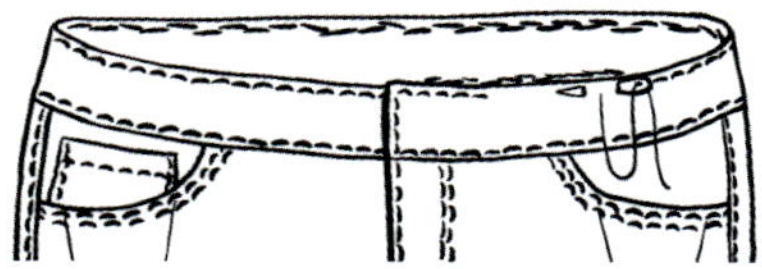

## SEWING THE BOTTOM HEMS

**1.** Fold the bottom edges under twice by ½" (1.3 cm). Baste.

**2.** Turn to RS of garment. Using a clear gridded ruler, mark topstitch line that is ⅜" (3 mm) away from edge.

**3.** Using topstitching thread and tidy even backstitches, sew through all layers to secure hems down.

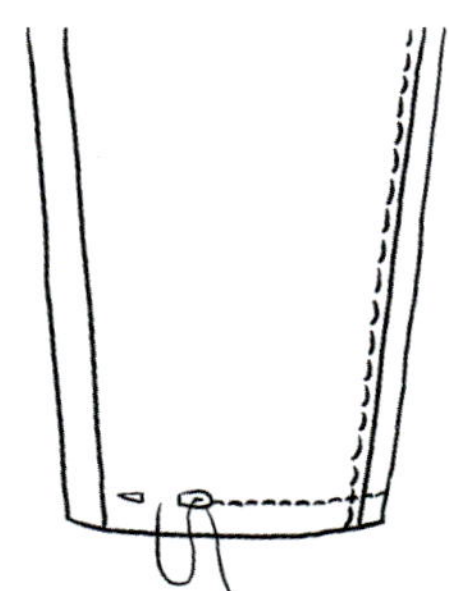

## MARKING AND SEWING THE BUTTONHOLE

**1.** First, stitch up one or more test buttonholes. To do so:

**A.** Take a scrap of self fabric and fold in thirds to create a three-layer mock-up to practice for your waistband. Baste folds down to hold.

**B.** Mark a slit that is the same length as your button's diameter. This slit should run parallel to the grain. Baste a little box around this slit to hold all layers together.

**C.** Use a chisel or small, very sharp scissors to carefully cut slit. Optionally, cut a tiny hole at one end of the slit to create the keyhole part of your buttonhole.

**D.** With camouflaging thread, overcast raw edges of slit and hole so that layers are thread-bound together.

**E.** With topstitching thread, use buttonhole stitches to bind edges of slit. Fan stitches around one end (the one nearer to the end of the waistband—this is where your optional keyhole would go) and create a boxy bartack at the other end. Spacing of stitches is at your discretion—experiment here and see what you like.

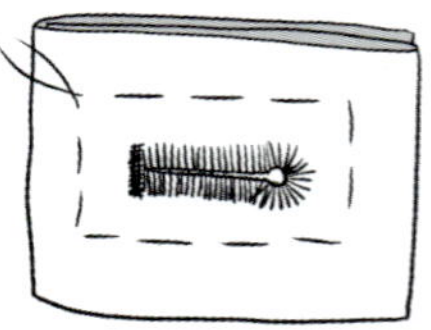

F. Test size of buttonhole to make sure button will fit through appropriately.

G. Repeat above steps as needed until you feel confident sewing buttonholes with this fabric, thread, and needle.

2. Mark buttonhole slit onto waistband. Slit should begin ⅛" (3 mm) toward CF from where the button should be centered. Length should be same as successful practice buttonhole.

3. Measure buttonhole sample's dimensions, including stitches. Now add ⅝" (1.6 cm) in all four directions to determine dimensions of buttonhole reinforcement rectangle. Cut from self fabric. Longer dimension should be along grainline.

4. Press ¼" (6 mm) under along all edges and baste.

5. Place rectangle on WS of waistband, centered over buttonhole slit area. Pin. Secure down with topstitching thread and whipstitch. (Whipstitches should not reach through to front.)

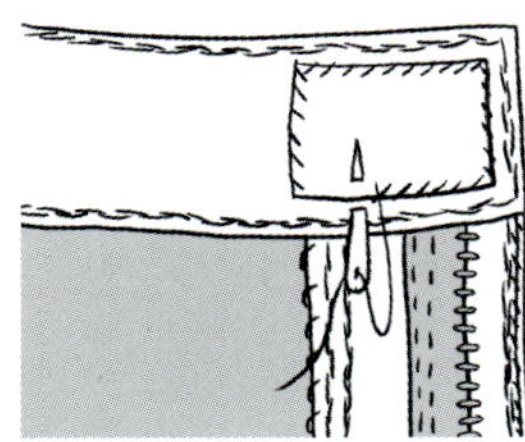

6. Return to RS of garment. Baste through all layers around perimeter of buttonhole. The basted box should be at least ¼" (6 mm) away from slit on all sides.

7. Proceed to cut and sew buttonhole as you practiced. Remove basting.

### ATTACHING THE BUTTON

1. Zip fly closed. Center and align waistband, and then stick pencil point through end of buttonhole that is closest to CF. Unzip and re-mark ⅛" (3 mm) closer to CF.

2. Cut 1½" (3.8 cm) square of self fabric.

3. Press ¼" (6 mm) under along all edges and baste.

4. Unzip fly. Place square on WS of waistband, centered under button placement. Pin. Secure down with topstitching thread and whipstitch. (Whipstitches should not reach through to front.)

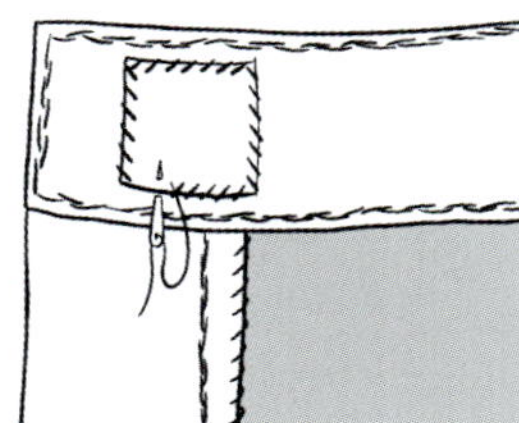

5. Return to RS of garment. If using a jean tack button, install now. If using a sew-on button, securely anchor a doubled strand of topstitching thread at button placement point, then attach button with multiple strong stitches through all layers. If button does not include a shank, leave a space between button and fabric as you sew, then wrap thread several times around thread shank to strengthen and secure. Sink needle to backside of waistband, anchor thread to secure, then burrow between layers and snip.

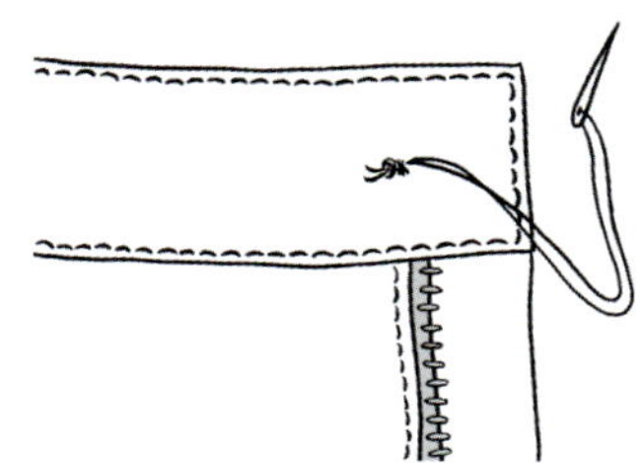

### ATTACHING THE BELT LOOPS

1. Optional: Using camouflaging thread and blanket stitch, quickly thread-bind the raw ends of all belt loops. (I opted not to do this step, but if it feels tidier to you, feel free to do this.)

2. For each belt loop, fold strip ½" (1.3 cm) under at one end.

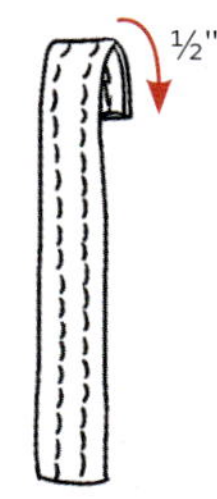


3. Place folded ends of belt loops along top of waistband at desired placements. (You can follow your original jeans as a guide or opt for different spacing as you prefer.) Clip or pin or baste to hold in place.

**4.** Using topstitching thread and tiny, dense whipstitches, secure folded ends of belt loops onto waistband.

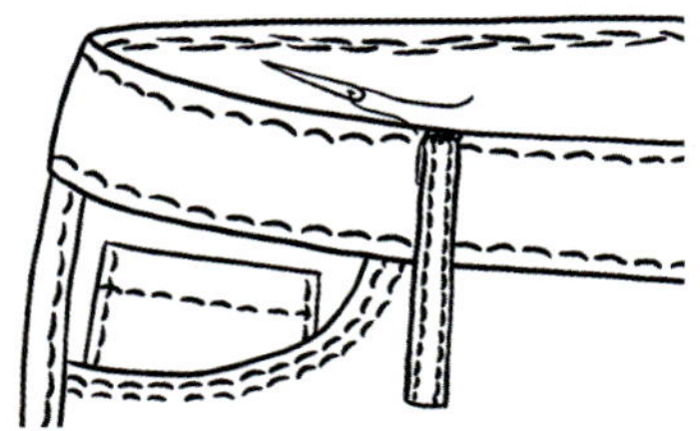

**5.** Tuck under bottom ends of belt loops by ½" (1.3 cm) and whipstitch those ends onto pants, too.

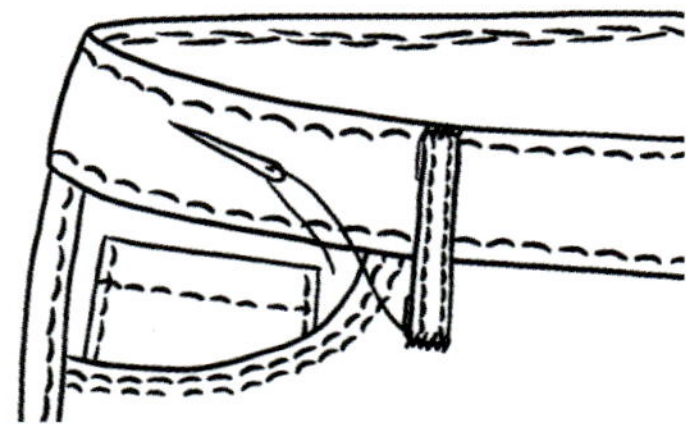

**6.** Optional: Once belt loops are attached, you can reach underneath them and tack down unsecured ends using camouflaging thread and thread-binding stitch of choice (blanket stitch, whipstitch, etc.). However, I skipped this step, and most ready-to-wear jeans don't have ends secured down, either.

## STITCHING A LABEL (OPTIONAL)

To make your jeans feel even more complete, you can add some sort of label at the back waistband. This label would traditionally be leather, but my vegan self enjoys finding alternative materials—canvas, linen, or even another shade of denim, for example. This is a tiny but prominent spot on your garment, so feel free to make it personally significant. Perhaps a bit of an old camping tent? Or a scrap of upholstery fabric from your old couch? When selecting material for the label, you'll probably want to find something that is dense, stiff, and thick.

**1.** Cut a rectangle of paper to audition your label's intended size and placement. Wearing jeans, pin the rectangle onto waistband and check in mirror or photograph to verify dimensions and location.

**2.** Once you've solidified your plan, mark rectangle onto label material. If you'll be turning under the cut edges, add SA. (I like ¼" [6 mm] along each edge, but it depends on your material.)

**3.** Optionally, embroider or otherwise embellish within the rectangle.

**4.** Cut rectangle out. If applicable, press raw edges under and baste.

**5.** Lay label flat onto jeans in desired position. Pin or clip. (Slipping a hardcover book inside jeans will make pinning easier.)

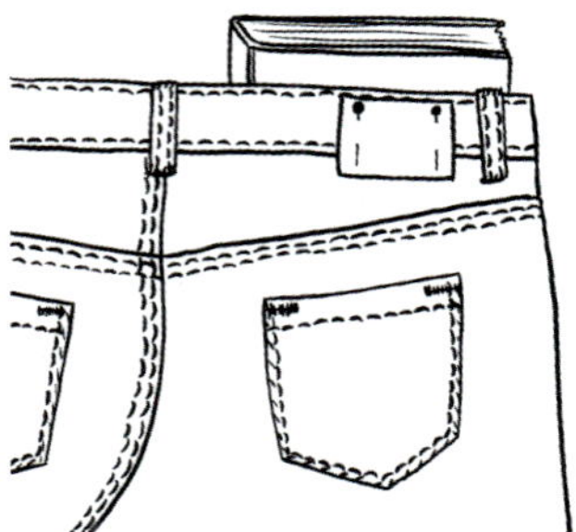

**6.** Try on jeans one more time to be sure you like placement.

**7.** Using topstitching thread, secure label down with whatever stitch you prefer. (I used even backstitch.)

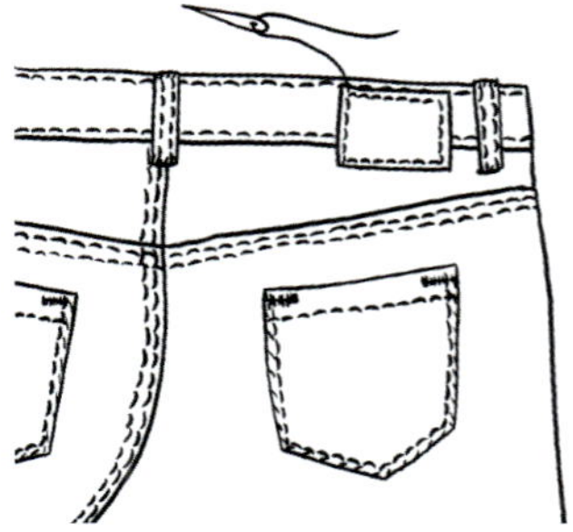

# *Natalie Chanin*

*(she/her)*, designer, artist, writer, founder of design label Alabama Chanin
SHOALS COMMUNITY, FLORENCE, ALABAMA, USA

For as long as Natalie Chanin can remember, she has been hand-sewing. It must have been her grandmothers who taught her, she says. Avid makers, they sewed whatever their families and homes needed. "It was just a part of everyday life," Natalie explains. "And consequently, just as if by osmosis, it was part of my life."

Having grown up in this "culture of making," Natalie suspects she always knew clothing could be sewn by hand just as well as by machine. And she always preferred sewing by hand. So when she was first starting her clothing label, Alabama Chanin, and she didn't have a machine, she simply hand-stitched the clothes instead.

"If I'm sewing, I get great satisfaction out of the stitch-by-stitch process, rather than taking the machine out and threading it," Natalie shares. "And I don't know—machines don't love me very much, so I just feel more connection to making when I'm doing it by hand."

Today, Alabama Chanin offers both hand- and machine-stitched designs. Natalie also heads The School of Making and Project Threadways. With all of her responsibilities, Natalie's sewing is mostly limited to repairs and small projects she feels called to do. She looks forward to a day when she'll have more time to sew and create for herself. Meanwhile, she is grateful for the work she's doing.

***Build a rhythm.*** When I sew, it's like some people feel about knitting—it's this very meditative action. I really enjoy things that aren't complicated, where you can build a rhythm and just get into that rhythm. I find the straight or running stitch a very easy, methodical space that you can get into. I feel the same about herringbone.

***Favorite hand-sewing tool.*** Because of the hand sewing that we do, which includes layers of cutting, I love a great pair of scissors.

***Skipping basting.*** I'm not very big on basting. I'm slightly lazy in that department. It's only when I really, really have to. If I'm working on something that needs to stay together when I'm traveling, I'll baste it together rather than using pins, because the pins can fall out. But I generally don't have a problem skipping basting. It generally works out okay for me.

***Fluid back and forth.*** At Alabama Chanin, we are very fluid back and forth between machine-made and handmade, and we definitely have some products that use both. Sometimes it's about the design aesthetic, and sometimes it's about the function. Sometimes it's about the fabric, and sometimes it's about the price.

***The hardest thing.*** Finding the time to sit down and sew these days seems to be the hardest thing. Time to get into it and time to do the work.

***Newcomer advice.*** Just take your time, settle in. Don't be afraid to try new things. And find yourself a group of people who share your vision for the work. Because we learn a lot through collaboration with others.

# Resources

## TOOLS AND TRIMS

You'll likely find most tools and supplies in your local shops. If you have trouble locating anything, though, here are a few places where I love to purchase specialized patternmaking and hand-sewing tools.

**Steinlauf & Stoller**
steinlaufandstoller.com

**WAWAK Sewing Supplies**
wawak.com

**Wear We're Going**
wearweregoing.co

**Bias Bespoke Supply Co.**
biasbespoke.com

# Further Reading

## PATTERNMAKING BOOKS

*Metric Pattern Cutting for Children's Wear and Babywear* by Winifred Aldrich

*Metric Pattern Cutting for Menswear* by Winifred Aldrich

*Metric Pattern Cutting for Women's Wear* by Winifred Aldrich

*Patternmaking Made Easy* by Connie Amaden-Crawford

*Patternmaking for Fashion Design* by Helen Joseph-Armstrong

*How to Draft Basic Patterns* by Ernestine Kopp, Vittorina Rolfo, Beatrice Zelin, and Lee Gross

*Design-It-Yourself Clothes: Patternmaking Simplified* by Cal Patch

## HAND-SEWING BOOKS

*Make, Sew and Mend: Traditional Techniques to Sustainably Maintain and Refashion Your Clothes* by Bernadette Banner

*Alabama Studio Sewing + Design: A Guide to Hand-Sewing an Alabama Chanin Wardrobe* by Natalie Chanin

*The Geometry of Hand-Sewing* by Natalie Chanin

*The Mary Frances Sewing Book, or Adventures Among the Thimble People* by Jane Eayre Fryer

*The Modern Maker Vol. 3: Hand Sewing Stitches for Garment Construction* by Mathew Gnagy

*The Workman's Guide to Tailoring Stitches and Techniques* by Fritz and Kathleen Kannik

*The Lady's Guide to Plain Sewing, Books 1 and 2,* by Kathleen Kannik

*Hand Sewing Clothing: A Guide* by Louisa Owen Sonstroem

*Handsewn: The Essential Techniques for Tailoring and Embellishment* by Margaret Rowan

*Couture Sewing Techniques* by Claire B. Shaeffer

## FITTING BOOKS

*Fitting Your Figure* by *Threads* magazine

*Smart Fitting Solutions: Foolproof Techniques to Fit Any Figure* by Kenneth D. King

*The Complete Photo Guide to Perfect Fitting* by Sarah Veblen

# Featured Makers

**Sofia Alba**
@sofiaalba.puntadas

**Alexis Bailey**
*wearweregoing.co*
@wearweregoing

**Natalie Chanin**
*alabamachanin.com/about-the-school-of-making*
@theschoolofmaking

**Tiffany Downs**
*silverthimble.co*
@silverthimbleco

**Mathew Gnagy**
*themodernmaker.co*
@mgnagydesign

**Cal Patch**
*calpatch.com*
@hodgepodgefarm

**Hetal Shrivastav**
*raasleela.co.in*
@raasleelatextile

**Louisa Owen Sonstroem**
*louisamerry.com*
@louisaowensonstroem

**KZ Stevens**
*kzstevens.com*
@kzstevens

**Sarah E. Woodyard**
*sewncompany.com*
@sewnstories
@sewncompany (YouTube)

# ACKNOWLEDGMENTS

I am so grateful for all the ways that love is intertwined with this book.

Writing it has been an exercise in realizing just how much I owe to my people, and just how interconnected and interdependent we really are. Every word was written thanks to my husband and to my mother, who took loving care of my little baby while I tried to string focused thoughts together. I owe every sentence to one or the other of them. Deep thanks, too, to my father, for inspiring me to write books, and for modeling quiet, patient endurance. I am grateful for my maternal great-grandmother, Louisa ("Dunky"), whose practice of hand-sewing clothing lives on in our family's stories and now in my hands. I've loved the journey of trying to learn what she already knew.

I have absolutely savored working with a team of knowledgeable, kind people at Storey. And by the time this book goes to print, there will doubtless be several dozen more people whose names belong on this page. But here's a start.

Deborah Balmuth has been a warm, encouraging "midwife" to this book, and I am grateful to have worked with such a master of book publishing. Diana Rupp's insightful ideas, support, and sense of humor were critical during the writing and editing phases. Carleen Madigan shepherded the book (and me) through the final edits with compassion, clarity, and wonderfully good humor.

Alethea Morrison created the wonderful visual design for this book, and she masterminded two incredibly fun, action-packed photo shoot days. She also held my hand through the illustrations, stitch snippets, and countless other details.

So much gratitude goes also to Melinda DeMauro and Mars Vilaubi for infusing so much beauty and thoughtfulness into the book's photography.

Erin Dawson undertook the massive project of building the book file, and she and Jennie Smith updated it with what must have been a million little edits. Emily Spiegelman painstakingly reviewed all of the (many, many) proofreader corrections. To all of them—I can't thank you enough.

Forever a supporter of those lucky enough to be her friends, Lori Guillard generously offered up her gorgeous home and gardens to the photo shoot. And to my beautiful friends and family who modeled for this book—Sasha Bajjo, Lori Guillard, Derri Owen, Paula Scharpf, Andy Zhao, and sweet little Teddy—thank you for filling these pages with your lovely, dear faces. I am so grateful to have you in my life and now, too, in this book.

# Glossary

***Back neck drop.*** The depth of a back neckline, measured from high point of shoulder.

***Band.*** An edge finish—it is a separate rectangle of fabric sewn onto the edge it is finishing.

***Bartack.*** A dense rectangle of stitches placed to reinforce an area of potential strain.

***Bias.*** A diagonal orientation of the fabric, in which it is cut at a diagonal to the direction in which it was woven or knit.

***Binding.*** An edge finish—it is a long strip of fabric sewn onto an edge. It can be sewn onto the inside or outside, or it can be folded around the edge so that it is visible on both sides.

***Bust.*** In patternmaking, the bust is the widest level of the chest area (usually at nipple level).

***Button shank.*** A spacing element between a button and the fabric to which it is attached. This element may be integral to the button itself, or it may be a thread shank created while attaching.

***Center back (CB).*** An important reference line on the body, oriented vertically down the center of the back. This line serves as the vertical axis when drafting back panels.

***Center front (CF).*** An important reference line on the body, oriented vertically down the center of the front. This line serves as the vertical axis when drafting front panels.

***Collar stand.*** A strip of fabric, usually roughly crescent moon–shaped, that is stitched to the neckline on its lower edge and to a separate collar piece on its upper edge. The collar folds over and down to cover the collar stand.

***Combo.*** An industry term for a garment's contrasting fabric. Combo is secondary to the main "self" fabric.

***Cross-grain.*** The fabric's orientation at a right angle to the direction in which it was produced. This line corresponds to a woven fabric's weft threads, or to a knit fabric's rows of yarn. It is generally perpendicular to the selvages.

***Drill hole.*** A garment industry term for a point on a pattern that needs to be marked onto fabric before sewing. Drill holes typically denote placement of pockets and other elements.

***Ease (noun).*** Additional volume added to a garment to enable functional movement or enhance style.

***Ease (verb).*** To carefully cinch a longer edge into a shorter one when sewing, so that there are no puckers or pleats.

***Edgestitching.*** A parallel line of stitching placed very close to a folded edge, usually roughly 1⁄16" (2 mm) away.

***Eyelet.*** A small round hole finished with a dense wreath of stitches.

***Facing.*** An edge finish—it is a separate piece of fabric, cut to match the shape of the edge it is finishing and sewn on.

***Finish.*** A method of securing a garment's raw fabric edges, whether by concealing or otherwise controlling them.

***Fly facing.*** A piece of fabric that finishes the fly opening's upper placket edge. This facing's shape is what determines the J-shaped topstitching visible on the outside of jeans' fly openings.

***Fly shield.*** A double-layered backing for a fly zipper.

***Forward shoulder seam.*** A shoulder seam that is intentionally placed somewhat forward of high-point-of-shoulder level on a pattern draft so that it will hit at a more anatomically suitable placement on the body.

***Front neck drop.*** The depth of a front neckline, measured from high point of shoulder.

***Gathers.*** Tidily scrunched (also called "shirred") fabric.

***Grainline.*** A line on a pattern piece that shows how to align the pattern with the fabric's weave or knit structure.

***Hem allowance (HA).*** A margin of extra fabric along an opening, usually along a lower edge. When sewing, the hem allowance is folded and stitched to secure, making a clean-looking finish.

***High point of shoulder (HPS).*** The intersection between neck and shoulder. This is usually where your flesh creases if you shrug a shoulder and tip your neck to that side.

***Hip.*** In patternmaking, the hip is the widest level of the lower torso (usually the fullest part of the buttocks).

***Interfacing.*** A stiffening, strengthening material that can be ironed or sewn to the WS of a garment's fabric. It is generally used on relatively small areas that need stiffening (cuffs, plackets, collars, etc.).

***Low point of shoulder (LPS).*** The shoulder tip; the point where shoulder and arm intersect. This is usually where your flesh creases if you raise your arm.

***Notch.*** A small perpendicular snip along the edge of a pattern. Notches are used to help align panels when sewing.

***Overcollar.*** The top layer of a collar that is visible when the garment is worn.

***Placket.*** An opening or slit in a garment, such as a center front button placket or a sleeve placket.

***Raw edge.*** A cut, unsecured fabric edge. Raw edges tend to be prone to fraying or unraveling.

***Right side (RS).*** The outer side of fabric on a garment.

***Seam allowance (SA).*** The margins along the edges of a pattern, used to stitch panels together so as to preserve the garment's desired finished dimensions.

***Self.*** An industry term for a garment's main fabric.

***Selvage.*** The long edge of yardage, typically a dense, self-finished woven edge or a glued and cut knit edge.

***Shoulder slope.*** The angle of a shoulder seam in relation to the horizontal axis.

***Sleeve cap.*** The bell-shaped area at the top of a sleeve. This area cups around the ball of the shoulder.

***Sleeve opening.*** A garment industry term for the bottom edge of a sleeve.

***Squaring a line.*** Drafting a 90-degree angle to a preexisting line.

***Straight grain.*** The orientation of a fabric's structure, which shows, and was created by, the direction in which the fabric was produced. Straight grain can be determined by examining a woven fabric's warp threads or a knit fabric's columns of loops. The straight grain is generally parallel to the selvages.

***Style line.*** A seam added to a pattern for design purposes. It generally doesn't have a major role in fitting.

***Sweep.*** A garment industry term for the bottom edge of a garment.

***Tick mark.*** A little perpendicular cross-mark along a line. This helps to denote an intersection point.

***Topstitching.*** A line of stitching meant to be seen on the outside of the garment. In hand sewing, topstitching is typically performed from the outside of the garment.

***Undercollar.*** The lower layer of a collar, not typically seen unless the collar is "popped."

***Understitching.*** A line of stitching that marries seam allowances to an interior element such as a facing or lining so that the seam rolls slightly to the inside of the garment.

***Waist.*** In patternmaking, the waist is the narrowest level of the mid-torso (usually where your flesh creases if you tip to one side). This is located near the bottom of the ribcage.

***Wrong side (WS).*** The inner side of fabric on a garment.

***Zip/zipper fly.*** The zippered crotch opening on a pair of pants.

## Abbreviations

There are a few abbreviations you'll see a lot throughout this book. Here's a quick key:

- CB: Center back
- CF: Center front
- HPS: High point of shoulder
- LPS: Low point of shoulder
- RS: Right side
- WS: Wrong side
- RST: Right sides together
- WST: Wrong sides together
- SA: Seam allowance
- WR: Wearer's right
- WL: Wearer's left

# Index

Page numbers in *italics* indicate photos or illustrations.

## G



## H



## I



## J

## K



## L

## N

# T

## U

## V

## W

## Z